Ethiopia & Djibouti

Northern
Ethiopia
p63

Djibouti
p306

Western
Ethiopia
p202

Addis Ababa
p30

Eastern
Ethiopia
p177

Southern
Ethiopia
p133

Sep 2017

Jean-Bernard Carillet, Anthony Ha

Contents

SURMI VILLAGE, KIBISH P175

BET MARYAM CHURCH P73

DIETMAR TEMPS, COLOGNE / GETTY IMAGES ©

ETHIOPIA / GETTY IMAGES ©

Contents

Welcome to Ethiopia & Djibouti

Ethiopia is like nowhere else on the planet – a beautiful country blessed with a peerless history, fabulous wildlife and some of Africa's most soulful peoples.

Nature's Bounty

Ethiopia is one of Africa's most beautiful countries and its landscapes are epic in both scale and beauty. Here is a place where you can trek more than 3000m above sea level or visit the lowest place on the African continent, the Danakil Depression. In between are lush highlands and stirring deserts, vertiginous canyons, sweeping savannah, vast lakes and high plateaus. Lying at the convergence of three tectonic plates, Djibouti offers a unique geological landscape including the vast salt lake of Lac Assal and the bizarre lunarscape of Lac Abbé.

Historical Wonders

The only African country to have escaped European colonialism, Ethiopia has retained much of its cultural identity and its story is one of Africa's most fascinating. It all begins with Lucy, one of our most celebrated ancient ancestors, moves effortlessly into the realm of ancient Aksum and then takes on power and passion as Christianity takes centre stage. And unlike so many other places in Africa, the ancients here left behind some extraordinary monuments to faith and power which serve as focal points for so many wonderful journeys. In neighbouring Djibouti, you'll have the chance to marvel at exceptionally well-preserved rock engravings hidden in the mountains.

Outdoor Adventures

Welcome to Africa's most underrated wildlife destination. The Ethiopian wolf is the ultimate prize – the sighting of a lifetime. There are gelada monkeys across the high northern plateau as well as other primates, while watching the extravagantly horned and sure-footed walia ibex cling to a rocky precipice is one of the great sights in nature. The birdwatching, too, ranks among the best in Africa. In Djibouti, there's superb hiking in the Goda Mountains, awesome whale-shark spotting in the Gulf of Tadjoura, as well as stunning diving amid coral-encrusted wrecks off Djibouti City.

Peoples with Proud Traditions

When it comes to human cultures, Ethiopia has an embarrassment of riches. There are the Surmi, Afar, Mursi, Karo, Hamer, Nuer and Anuak, whose ancient customs and traditions have remained almost entirely intact. A highlight of any trip here is witnessing one of the many festivals that are an integral part of the traditional culture, from age-old ceremonies marking rites of passage to Christian celebrations of singular passion, the impact upon those who witness such events can provide travel memories to last a lifetime.

Why I Love Ethiopia

By Anthony Ham, Writer

In a lifetime of travel in Africa, I've never been anywhere quite like Ethiopia. It has all the essential elements that call me back here time after time – wildlife you just don't find elsewhere, epic landscapes of rare beauty, an endlessly fascinating historical tale that provides depth and context to any journey through the country. But there is something else at large in Ethiopia; a spiritual dimension that infuses every aspect of travel here and brings ancient stories and landscapes to life in a way that I've never encountered anywhere else on the continent.

For more about our writers, see p352

Above: Mursi woman wearing a clay lip-plate (p169)

Ethiopia & Djibouti

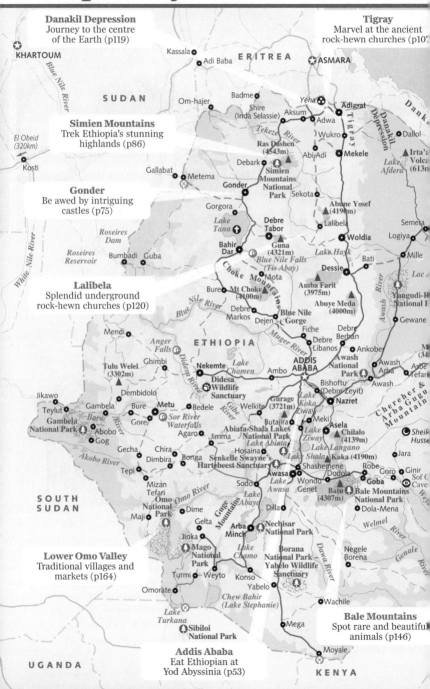

Danakil Depression
Journey to the centre
of the Earth (p119)

Tigray
Marvel at the ancient
rock-hewn churches (p10?)

Simien Mountains
Trek Ethiopia's stunning
highlands (p86)

Gonder
Be awed by intriguing
castles (p75)

Lalibela
Splendid underground
rock-hewn churches (p120)

Lower Omo Valley
Traditional villages and
markets (p164)

Bale Mountains
Spot rare and beautiful
animals (p146)

Addis Ababa
Eat Ethiopian at
Yod Abyssinia (p53)

KHARTOUM

ASMARA

ERITREA

SUDAN

Kassala
Adi Baba
Om-hajer
Badme
Shire (Inda Selassie)
Yeha
Adigrat
Aksum
Adwa
Wukro
Dallol
Tigray
Tekeze River
Ras Dashen (4543m)
Abi Adi
Mekele
Lake Afdera
Irta'a Volca (613m)
Debark
Simien Mountains National Park
Sekota
Abune Yosef (419?m)
Lalibela
Semera
Gallabat
Metema
Gonder
Logiya
Gorgora
Lake Tana
Debre Tabor
Woldia
Mille
El Obeid (320km)
Kosti
Guna (4321m)
Lake Hayk
Bati
Lac
Bahir Dar
Blue Nile Falls (Tis Abay)
Dessie
Roseires Dam
Roseires Reservoir
Bumbadi
Guba
Mota
Amba Farit (3975m)
Yangudi-R National F
Choke Mountains
Bure
Mt Choke (4100m)
Abuye Meda (4000m)
Gewane
White Nile River
Debre Markos
Dejen
Blue Nile Gorge
Fiche
Debre Berhan
Blue Nile River
Muger River
Debre Libanos
Ankober
Mendi
Anger Falls
ETHIOPIA
Awash National Park
M (34
Tulu Welel (3302m)
Ghimbi
Nekemte
Lake Chomen
Ambo
ADDIS ABABA
Awash Arba
Asbe Tefari
Jikawo
Dembidolo
Didessa Wildlife Sanctuary
Bishoftu (Debre Zeyit)
Awash
Cherecher & Arba Gugu Mountain
Teylut
Gambela
Bure
Metu
Bedele
Welkite
Gurage (3721m)
Nazret
Gambela National Park
Gore
Sor River Waterfalls
Agaro
Jimma
Lake Koka
Meki
Asela
Chilalo (4139m)
Sheik Huss
Abobo
Gog
Gecha
Chira
Dimbira
Bonga
Abiata-Shala Lakes National Park
Lake Abiata
Lake Ziway
Lake Langano
Kaka (4190m)
Jara
Tepi
Senkelle Swayne's Hartebeest Sanctuary
Awasa
Shashemene
Dodola
Robe
Goro
Ginir
Sof C Cave
Mizan Tefari
Sodo
Lake Awasa
Wondo
Genet
Dilla
Batu (4307m)
Bale Mountains National Park
Goba
SOUTH SUDAN
Omo National Park
Dime
Maji
Gelta
Guge Mountains
Lake Abaya
Dola-Mena
Welmel River
Jinka
Arba Minch
Nechisar National Park
Negele Borena
Mago National Park
Lake Chamo
Borana National Park Yabelo Wildlife Sanctuary
Genale River
Turmi
Weyto
Konso
Yabelo
Dawa River
Omorate
Chew Bahir (Lake Stephanie)
Wachile
Lake Turkana
Mega
Sibiloi National Park
Moyale

UGANDA

KENYA

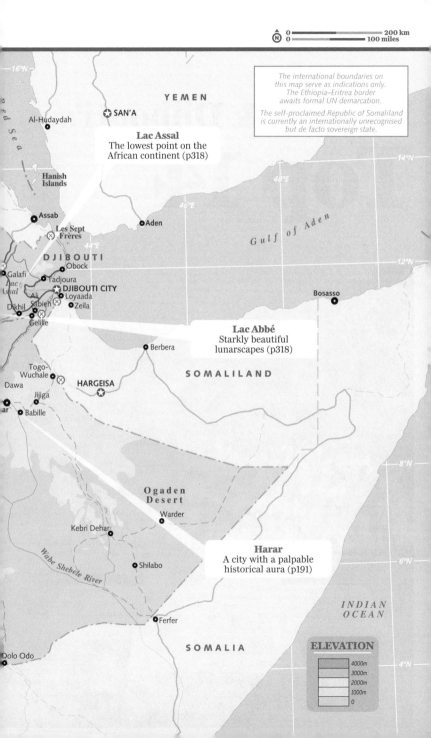

0   200 km
0   100 miles

YEMEN

⊛ SAN'A

Al-Hudaydah ●

Lac Assal
The lowest point on the
African continent (p318)

Red Sea

Hanish
Islands

● Assab

⊗ Les Sept
Frères

● Aden

Gulf of Aden

DJIBOUTI

● Obock

● Galafi

Tadjoura ●

Lac
Assal

⊛ DJIBOUTI CITY

Ali ● Loyaada
Sabieh ● Zeila

Dikhil ●

⊗ Gelille

Bosasso ●

● Berbera

Lac Abbé
Starkly beautiful
lunarscapes (p318)

Togo-
Wuchale ●
⊗

Dawa

⊛ HARGEISA

SOMALILAND

Jijiga ●

ar

● Babille

Ogaden
Desert

● Warder

Kebri Dehar ●

Wabe Shebele River

● Shilabo

Harar
A city with a palpable
historical aura (p191)

INDIAN
OCEAN

● Ferfer

SOMALIA

Oolo Odo ●

ELEVATION

4000m
3000m
2000m
1000m
0

Ethiopia & Djibouti's
Top 14

Lalibela

1 Nothing prepares you for the first time you see the rock-hewn churches of Lalibela (p120) and walk among them for real. Carved entirely out of rock, the still-functioning churches are large, artistically refined and mostly in excellent states of preservation. This is Orthodox Christianity at its most raw and powerful, with the extraordinary architecture adorned with wonderful paintings and enlivened with the soft chants of white-robed priests and pilgrims.

Simien Mountains

2 With deep canyons and bizarrely jagged mountains sculpting scenery so awesome that if you saw it in a painting you might question whether it was real, the Simien Mountains (p86) are one of the most beautiful ranges in Africa. They offer important protection for some of Ethiopia's endemic wildlife, and sitting amid a troop of tame gelada monkeys is an experience you'll never forget. This is terrific trekking territory, but is also easily accessible by car.
Below: Gelada monkey (p273)

Harar

3 By far the most intriguing city in Ethiopia, Harar (p191) is a joy to explore. Getting lost in its crooked alleyways is just as fascinating as visiting the many museums, markets and traditional homes packed inside the old city walls. And then there are the hyenas. Two families feed them by hand, and let you do it too, but these large carnivores wander through the city and you may just bump into one while walking about at night in one of Ethiopia's most unusual encounters.
Above: Shoa Gate market (p192)

Lac Abbé (Djibouti)

4 There is nothing on earth quite like the large, spikelike calcareous chimneys of Lac Abbé. Hot springs dot the landscape, and fumaroles can also be found. These surreal-looking formations are a geological work of art, the result of millennia of volcanic activity and wind erosion. Experiencing this eerie landscape at dawn or at sunset is truly exhilarating.

Gonder

5 Gonder (p75) preserves a treasure trove of history. The walls of the Royal Enclosure contain a half-dozen medieval palaces and a host of legends; you can easily imagine the grand feasts they held here as you walk among them. Further out are peaceful and atmospheric sites, including Fasiladas' Bath, the Kuskuam complex and Debre Berhan Selassie Church, saved from the marauding Sudanese Dervishes by a swarm of bees.
Below right: Painted ceiling of the Debre Berhan Selassie Church (p77)

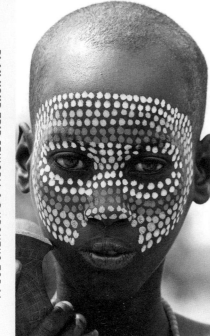

HECTOR CONESA / SHUTTERSTOCK ©

Lower Omo Valley Ethnic Groups

6 The Lower Omo Valley (p164) is a remarkable cultural crossroads. From the Mursi people with their lip plates to the Banna with their calabash hats or the body painting Karo, tradition runs deep here. While the commonly held notion that the more than a dozen ethnic groups residing here live completely outside modern society is wrong, walking through the markets and villages or attending one of the many ceremonies really can feel like stepping back in time.

Above: Young Daasanach man (p168)

Rock-Hewn Churches of Tigray

7 Hidden away like lost treasures in this arid landscape, the ancient rock-hewn churches of Tigray (p107) are the stirring mountain counterpoints to Lalibela's more famous city-bound churches. Partially carved and partially constructed, most sit on remote cliffsides requiring long walks (and sometimes steep climbs) and the sense of discovery upon arrival is a big part of their appeal. But they also delight for their artistic and historic merits alone.

Timkat

8 Timkat, the feast of Epiphany, celebrates the baptism of Christ with a three-day festival starting on 19 January. Join the procession behind regalia-draped priests as the church *tabots* (replicas of the Ark of the Covenant) are taken to a nearby body of water on the afternoon of the eve of Timkat. Next morning, the *tabots* are paraded back to the church accompanied by much singing and dancing. It's easily Ethiopia's most colourful festival and Gonder (p81) is the best place to experience it.

Above right: Timkat procession in Addis Ababa (p43)

Bale Mountains

9 The Ethiopian wolf is the rarest canid in the world, but on the 4000m-high Sanetti Plateau in the Bale Mountains (p147) you are almost guaranteed to see them. And when you're not watching wolves hunt giant molerats, your eyes will be drawn to the fairy-tale forests draped in 'old man's beard' and the sheer drop of the Harenna Escarpment. Though the mountains are prime trekking territory, there's no need to step out of your car to enjoy them since you can drive right through on the highest all-weather road in Africa.

Right: Ethiopian wolf (p149)

NATURESMOMENTSUK / SHUTTERSTOCK ©

LEN DEELEY UNDERWATER PHOTOGRAPHER / GETTY IMAGES ©

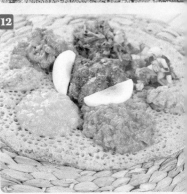

Whale-Shark Spotting

10 Don't know what a *Rhincodon typus* is? It's time to get an education in Djibouti. Expect your flippers to be blown off by an interaction with one of Mother Nature's most impressive creatures – the whale shark. Several individuals move through the Gulf of Tadjoura annually between November and January, and are a guaranteed wildlife experience.

Lac Assal (Djibouti)

11 Djibouti's version of the Dead Sea, Lac Assal, at 155m below sea level, ranks as the world's third-lowest point. Like most of Djibouti's lakes, which are saline and host incredible crystal formations, Lac Assal's shore is carpeted with spheres of halite and angular gypsum. For visitors, nothing beats a walk on the salt crust or a dip into the briny waters of the lake. It's encircled with volcanic mountains, which adds to the appeal.

Food

12 Culinary delights in Ethiopia? Oh yes. Eating Ethiopian-style is a wonderful experience, from the sense of community around a shared table to the diverse flavours that make it one of the most varied culinary scenes on the continent. Given that Ethiopian cooking is also known only to a select few beyond the country's borders, there's also a wonderful sense of discovery as you sit down to your first *shiro*, *doro wat* or *tibs*. Among the many candidates for a memorable meal, try Yod Abyssinia (p53) in Addis.

Danakil Depression

13 The actively volcanic Danakil Depression (p119) features a permanent lava lake and a vast field of yellow and orange sulphuric rocks. Just as interesting are the hearty Afar people who eke out a living from the baking, cracked plains. Though there are regular tours into its depths, travel here is not easy (and only possible as part of an organised tour) due to the lack of roads and services, and the soaring temperatures. The Danakil Depression may feel inhospitable, but the sense of exploration is very, very real.

Below: Dallol (p119)

Addis Ababa

14 Addis Ababa (p30) is evolving at a fast pace. The noisy, bustling capital of Ethiopia is blessed with an agreeable climate, with cloudless blue skies for about eight months of the year. It offers plenty of cultural highlights, including the Ethnological Museum and the National Museum. Addis is also famed for its buzzing restaurant scene and nightlife, with lots of eateries, bars, galleries and clubs. Dive in!

Bottom: Lion of Judah monument (p37)

13

14

Need to Know

For more information, see Survival Guide (p279 & p325)

Currency

Ethiopian Birr (ETB)
Djibouti franc (DFr)

Money

ATMs in major towns. Credit cards accepted in some top-end hotels (especially in Addis), but in very few restaurants or even midrange hotels. Bring US dollars in cash.

Language

Amharic, Tigrinya, Oromo, Somali, Sidama, Afar, Gurage, Welaita, Hadiya

Visas

Most nationalities can obtain one-month visas (US$50) on arrival at Addis Ababa's Bole International Airport. If arriving by land, obtain your visa in advance.

Mobile Phones

All mobile phones are operated by Ethio Telecom (www.ethionet.et). Whether you're using your home phone on a roaming plan or a locally bought phone and SIM card, expect connection problems, although the situation is improving.

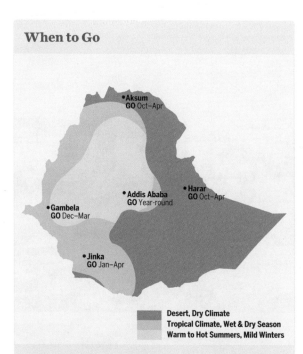

When to Go

- **Aksum** GO Oct–Apr
- **Harar** GO Oct–Apr
- **Addis Ababa** GO Year-round
- **Gambela** GO Dec–Mar
- **Jinka** GO Jan–Apr

Desert, Dry Climate
Tropical Climate, Wet & Dry Season
Warm to Hot Summers, Mild Winters

High Season
(Jan–Mar)

➡ Expect sunny skies and warm days.

➡ Good for wildlife watching and Ethiopia's most colourful festivals, including Timkat and Leddet.

➡ Book accommodation through an agent at festival time.

Shoulder Season (Oct–Dec)

➡ The country is green, skies are sunny, trekking is great and there are fewer visitors.

➡ Wildlflowers bloom in October and birds arrive en masse in November.

➡ December is excellent for the Danakil Depression.

Low Season
(Apr–Sep)

➡ Rainy season in southern Ethiopia; scorching hot temperatures in the lowlands.

➡ Overcast conditions; seeing wildlife is a challenge.

➡ Elsewhere it's uncomfortable rather than impossible to get around

Useful Websites

Lonely Planet (www.lonely planet.com/ethiopia) Destination information, hotel bookings, traveller forum and more.

Ethiopia: Land of Origins (www.ethiopia.travel) Improving government-run tourism website with good high-level information and inspiration.

Selamta (www.selamta.net) Travel information.

Ethiopian Treasures (www. ethiopiantreasures.co.uk) Categorised information on history and culture.

Ethiomedia (www.ethiopmedia. com) Range of sites covering news about Ethiopia.

Important Numbers

You need to drop the first zero from the number when calling Ethiopia from abroad.

Ethiopia's country code	🖉251
International access code	🖉00
Police	🖉991

Exchange Rates

Australia	A$1	Birr16.82
Canada	C$1	Birr16.82
Eurozone	€1	Birr23.99
Japan	¥100	Birr19.95
New Zealand	NZ$1	Birr16.08
UK	UK£1	Birr28.16
USA	US$1	Birr22.56

For current exchange rates see www.xe.com.

Daily Costs

Budget
less than US$50

➡ Basic double with private facilities: US$15–25

➡ Travel between cities by bus: US$8–17

➡ Local-style meals are tasty and cheap: from US$6–10

Midrange
US$50–100

➡ Double room in a comfortable hotel: US$25–75

➡ Occasional internal flight: US$115–250

➡ Dinner with alcohol at a midrange restaurant: US$10

Top End
more than US$100

➡ Accommodation in a full-board resort or an upmarket hotel room: from US$75

➡ Private 4WD with driver: US$180

➡ Fine dining at an upmarket restaurant: US$15 and up

Opening Hours

Banks 8.30–11am and 1.30–3.30pm Monday to Friday, 8.30–11am Saturday

Cafes 6am–9pm or 10pm

Government offices 8.30–11am and 1.30–3.30pm Monday to Friday, 8.30–11am Saturday

Internet cafes 8am–8pm Monday to Saturday, limited hours Sunday

Post offices 8.30–11am and 1.30–3.30pm Monday to Friday, 8.30–11am Saturday

Restaurants 7am–10pm; upmarket restaurants in Addis and other big towns generally open noon–3pm and 6–10pm daily

Shops 8am–1pm and 2–5.30pm Monday to Saturday

Arriving in Ethiopia

Bole International Airport (Addis Ababa; p61) Minibuses run to Piazza, Mexico Sq and Meskal Sq from 6am to 8pm (US$0.50). A taxi (US$30 to US$40) takes 20 to 30 minutes. Prices for foreigners are much higher than they are for locals and are normally quoted in US dollars (though they accept Birr). Airport shuttle is offered free by many hotels.

Bus Stations There is no public transport from either the long- or short-distance bus stations. Minibuses/taxis to the city centre cost US$0.50/30

Getting Around

Ethiopia is a huge place and – due to the terrain, the distances and the condition of the roads – it can take a long time to get anywhere.

Air Internal flights are huge time savers. The national carrier has an extensive network and solid safety record. It's usually cheaper to book your flight once in Ethiopia.

Bus Opt for the newer companies, which offer better service and more comfortable buses.

Car Though expensive, we recommend a 4WD with a driver. Having your own car allows you to stop wherever you want and saves time. The driver can also act as a guide-cum-interpreter. Also, some national parks can only be entered with a 4WD. Shop around and hire through a reputable agency.

For much more on **getting around**, see p293

PLAN YOUR TRIP NEED TO KNOW

If You Like...

Wildlife Watching

The region is a nature lover's dream. Ethiopia and Djibouti offer superb wildlife-viewing opportunities. A variety of charismatic species, some of which are found nowhere else in the world, can easily be approached under the supervision of a knowledgeable guide.

Bale Mountains National Park You're almost guaranteed to see Ethiopian wolves here. (p147)

Simien Mountains National Park Get up close and personal with gelada monkeys, walia ibex, and a possibility of seeing the Ethiopian wolf. (p86)

Harar Join the feeding frenzy – you'll never get this close to hyenas again! (p191)

Gambela National Park Migrating herds of antelope a million strong, but hard going to get there. (p220)

Bay of Ghoubbet This large bay is one of the most dependable locations in the world for close encounters with whale sharks. (p310)

Decan This small wildlife refuge near Djibouti City shelters various species, including cheetahs that have been rescued from illegal caging for trafficking purposes. (p315)

Birdwatching

Ethiopia is a major bird-watching destination and you never have to venture too far to get some shiny feathers in front of your binoculars. Twitchers also benefit from a relatively well-organised network of guides and tours.

Gibe Sheleko National Park All the classic highland species can be spotted in this park. (p218)

Bale Mountains National Park Offers easy access to both highland and lowland habitats and their associated species, including nine Ethiopian endemics. (p147)

Rift Valley Lakes The string of large lakes, from Ziway to Chamo, are surprisingly diverse, leading to a great variety of possible encounters over many days. (p138)

Yabelo Wildlife Sanctuary The locally endemic Ethiopian bush crow and white-tailed swallow are the major drawcards here. (p155)

Kafa Biosphere Reserve More than 300 species inhabit some of the west's densest forests. (p214)

Awash National Park More than 460 bird species have been recorded in this important way station for migratory species. (p181)

Omo National Park Newly accessible birding hotspot with some 312 species. (p175)

Gambela National Park Some of the birds here are seen nowhere else in Ethiopia, but getting here is a challenge. (p220)

History & Culture

Ethiopia offers a wealth of attractions for culture buffs, from centuries-old rock-hewn churches to atmospheric, historical towns and grand castles.

Ethnological Museum One of the best if its kind in Africa, this museum in Addis Ababa gives a great insight into the many different Ethiopian peoples and their rich cultures. (p32)

Harar The labyrinthine, walled old city is a pleasure to explore, and close encounters with wild hyenas add to its magic. (p191)

Aksum The cradle of Ethiopia's storied ancient history and the heartbeat of the country's Christian faith. (p93)

Lalibela Subterranean churches, gorgeously carved into the rock, rarely fail to wow visitors. (p121)

Gonder The various ruined castles in and around the city are exceptionally evocative. (p75)

Rock-hewn Churches of Tigray The story of Ethiopian Christianity's power and passion is told here in the most unlikely of places. (p109)

The Stelae Fields & Rock Engravings Around Dilla Mysterious stelae signposts to the past in the country's south. (p153)

Abourma It's quite a hike to get here, but you'll be rewarded with eye-catching rock engravings. (p322)

Festivals

Visitors are often overwhelmed by the sense of devotion that emanates from the incredibly colourful festivals held throughout the region. Some are so impressive that it's worth timing your trip around them.

Meskel One of Ethiopia's most colourful festivals, Meskel (best experienced in Addis) is famous for its cross-topped bonfires and elaborately dressed clergy. (p43)

Great Ethiopian Run Join thousands of joggers in Africa's biggest running race in Addis Ababa. (p43)

Jumping of the Bulls This coming-of-age ceremony is usually a highlight of visitors' time in Ethiopia for anyone lucky enough to see one. (p172)

Timkat Ethiopia's most important holiday celebrates Jesus' baptism with a lot of splashing of water and parading of replica Arks of the Covenant. Gonder, Addis and Aksum are fine places to join the celebrations. (p81)

Leddet During Leddet (Christmas) the faithful attend all-night church services, often moving from one church to another. Priests don their full regalia. Addis is the epicentre for this one. (p42)

Top: Stelae field, Aksum (p98), Ethiopia
Bottom: Waga totems, Konso (p162), Ethiopia

Trekking & Hiking

For an unforgettable taste of Ethiopia, lace up your boots and head into the landscape that covers the geological highs and lows.

Simien Mountains National Park This popular park holds some of the most stunning mountain scenery in Africa and trekking is easily organised. (p86)

Bale Mountains The combination of wildlife, scenery and facilities makes this a fantastic wilderness destination. (p149)

Menagesha National Forest Follow the trails through this wildlife-filled forest. (p217)

Lalibela & Tigray The community trekking programs in these areas offer both lovely scenery and a chance to get to know the locals. (p126)

Menz-Guassa Community Conservation Area This seldom-visited spot protects one of the most pristine high-alpine habitats in Ethiopia. (p132)

Goda Mountains What the little-known Goda Mountains lack in size is more than made up for in diversity, with walks of various lengths. (p319)

Dramatic Scenery

The Horn of Africa is brimming with natural wonders, from geological oddities to majestic mountains.

Danakil Depression Unique in the world, the sub-sea-level volcanic landscape here is eerily beautiful. (p119)

Simien Mountains National Park Huge cliffs, oddly formed mountains and unusual Afro-alpine habitat create one of the most stunning spots in Africa. (p86)

Bale Mountains National Park The Saneti Plateau is a barren, high-altitude landscape with top-notch vistas. (p147)

Abiata-Shala Lakes National Park Great crater lakes, hot springs and flamingos aplenty. (p139)

Lac Abbé Spikelike calcareous chimneys make for apocalyptic landscapes. (p318)

Lac Assal The great salt lake and black volcanic terrain of Lac Assal are extremely photogenic. (p318)

Traditional Cultures

An anthropologist's dream, Ethiopia is home to numerous ethnic groups, each with their own language and customs. The 200 dialects spoken in Ethiopia give an indication of the country's incredible diversity.

Kibish and southwest Omo Valley Meet the fierce Surmi people, who are known for their white body paintings. (p175)

Itang Mingle with the ritually scarred Nuer and Anuak peoples around Gambela. (p215)

Lower Omo Valley This awesome region is home to 16 ethnic groups, many of which have not strayed far from their ancient cultures. (p164)

Konso Villages The fortresslike villages here, built of stone and sticks, and the terraced fields are World Heritage listed. (p163)

Danakil Depression The Afar residing in this scorching hot desert still walk their camel caravans to the highlands to sell salt. (p119)

Dorze The woven houses are just one of the many fascinating things about this proud culture. (p161)

Offbeat Travel

Kibish Venture to the forgotten side of the Omo Valley and arrange a village stay to experience some of the most traditional cultures of Ethiopia. (p175)

Awra Amba Witness a small Utopia in the making. (p74)

Asaita When you reach this remote town in the Danakil Desert, your first impression may well be: 'Have I reached another planet?' (p186)

Abi Adi This is the rock-hewn churches of Tigray's least visited cluster, and all the better for it. (p112)

Sof Omar Cave Follow the Web River straight through a limestone ridge. (p151)

Creature Comforts

If you've had enough of trekking and bumping around in a 4WD, enjoy these wonderful places.

Limalimo Lodge Stunning contemporary perch built using local materials and with fabulous views. (p92)

Bale Mountain Lodge Finally, a world-class, scenically sited lodge worthy of this wonderful park. (p152)

Gheralta Lodge An unexpected splash of style and comfort in a remote region. (p115)

Korkor Lodge Marvellous views from shady vine-covered terraces and supremely comfortable rooms. (p115)

Negash Resort Wake up to the sing-song of birds in this great-value lodge. (p214)

Hôtel Village Vacances Les Sables Blancs A quiet retreat with a stellar beachfront setting. Fabulous for families and couples. (p321)

Month by Month

January

The most vibrant and busy time to visit, with Ethiopia's most colourful festivals and usually cool and dry weather. January is also an ideal month to visit Djibouti.

✯ Leddet (Christmas)

Leddet (6 to 7 January) is a dramatic throwback to a time when Christmas still had real meaning. The faithful attend all-night services, often moving from one church to another. Aksum and Lalibela are among the best places to experience Leddet, as is Addis Ababa.

✯ Timkat (Epiphany, celebrating Christ's baptism)

This three-day festival is the most colourful of the year. Join the thousands of white-robed faithful in Gonder as they sing and dance behind a solemn procession of regalia-draped priests. Other good places to be for Timkat are Addis Ababa and Aksum.

February

The heart of the dry season is the easiest time to travel around Ethiopia and it's a good time for trekking, wildlife-watching and diving. In Djibouti it's still the high season, with mild daytime temperatures and blue skies – great for multiday treks in the Goda Mountains or across Les Allols or Lac Assal.

◉ Antelope Migration

Herds of migrating white-eared kob and Nile lechwe over a million strong move through Gambela National Park – magic if you can make it into this, one of Africa's more challenging parks to access.

🏃 Trekking

The Simien Mountains are at their best – now is your chance to scale up Ras Dashen, Ethiopia's highest peak, and snap pictures of gelada monkeys.

March

The end of the high season. Days are warm and dry, and there's excellent wildlife watching around waterholes in the national parks. March is generally a great time to visit Djibouti – fewer tourists, cheaper airfares and bearable temperatures.

✯ Bull-Jumping Ceremony

In the Lower Omo Valley, witness a young man run across the backs of cattle to be initiated into the responsibilities of manhood, while, in a show of solidarity and stoic allegiance, women volunteer to be whipped with slender canes. Between late January and early April.

April

A transition month. Increasing temperatures in the Ethiopian lowlands are mitigated by heavy showers.

✯ Good Friday

From Thursday evening before Good Friday, the faithful fast until the Easter service, which ends at 3am on Easter Sunday. Held in March or April.

🎊 Fasika (Orthodox Easter)

Fasika marks the end of a vegetarian fast of 55 days. Stay up on the night of Easter Saturday in Lalibela to see hundreds of white-robed pilgrims crowd the courtyards of the churches and pray under the moonlight.

May

Pessimists decry the beginning of the rainy season, but the region is green and lush. Avoid the Lower Omo Valley as many roads are impassable.

August

The big annual rains continue to batter Ethiopia. Getting around is difficult. The hot season sends lowland temperatures in the two countries up to 45°C. Avoid visiting now.

September

The rains usually continue well into September; when they stop and you can see the horizon, Ethiopia is lush. By late September, rains may have subsided.

🎊 Kiddus Yohannes (New Year's Day)

At Ethiopian New Year (11 September), new clothes are traditionally bought for the occasion, particularly for children, and relatives and friends are visited.

🎊 Meskel (Finding of the True Cross)

Starting on 27 September, this two-day festival is the most colourful after Timkat. Bonfires are built, topped by a cross to which flowers, most commonly the Meskel daisy, are tied. Priests don their full regalia. Addis Ababa, Gonder and Aksum are good places to be.

October

Mid-October is a great time to visit Ethiopia – the countryside glows green. In Djibouti, October is transition month.

🎊 Irecha

On the first Sunday following Meskel, the Oromo people celebrate Irecha on the shores of Lake Hora. Devotees gather around ancient fig trees to smear perfume, butter and *katickala* (a distilled drink) on the trunks and share ceremonial meals of roasted meat, coffee and alcohol.

November

A great time to visit; expect plenty of wildlife in the national parks, and migratory birds begin arriving in great numbers.

🏃 Great Ethiopian Run

This 10km race takes over Addis Ababa on the last or second-to-last Sunday of November and attracts over 20,000 runners. Whether running or watching, it's a fun time and it's a great chance to see some of East Africa's elite athletes in action.

🎊 Festival of Maryam Zion

This vibrant festival is held only in Aksum. In the days leading up to the event on 30 November, thousands of pilgrims head towards Aksum. Celebrations start in front of the Northern Stelae Field, where the monarchs of the Orthodox church line the steps.

December

The weather is mostly dry throughout the region and it's a fine time for wildlife watching. Temperatures are also at their best – warm but not stifling. This is a great time to explore the Danakil Depression.

🎊 Kulubi Gabriel

Although not on the official religious holiday list, large numbers of Ethiopians make a pilgrimage to the venerated Kulubi Gabriel church, near Dire Dawa in the east (28 December).

🏃 Trekking

This is an ideal month for trekking in the Bale or Simien Mountains. It's dry and the skies are clear – perfect for capturing scenic landscapes.

🏃 Birdwatching

Calling all birders! Some 200 species of Palaearctic migrants from Europe and Asia join the already abundant African resident and intra-African migrant populations.

🏃 Whale-shark Spotting

Whale sharks migrate annually from their usual feeding grounds to the warm waters of the Gulf of Tadjoura to mate and give birth. They can be observed from November to January.

Itineraries

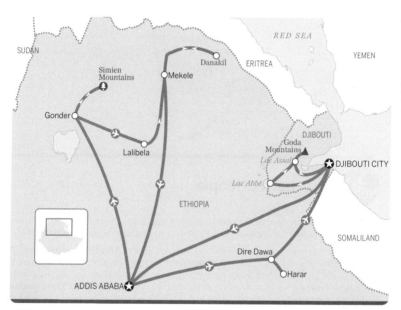

 2 WEEKS **Ethiopia & Djibouti's Grand Tour**

If you only have two weeks but want to see the best that Ethiopia has to offer, this is the itinerary for you, with a good mix of historical sites and towns, fabulous landscapes and wildlife, with some high-altitude trekking thrown in.

Spend a full day in **Addis Ababa**, long enough to sample its museums and fine restaurants, then fly to **Gonder**, one of the country's most monument-rich historic towns. Then it's on to **Simien Mountains National Park** for Ethiopia's best trekking and fine wildlife-watching. It's another short flight to **Lalibela**, then plan on a minimum of two days exploring the rock-hewn church masterpieces for which Lalibela is known. Then head north to **Mekele**, en route to a couple of nights in the **Danakil Depression**. Fly from Mekele back to Addis, where you may have to stay overnight, then fly east to **Dire Dawa** and stay long enough to catch onward transport to **Harar**, one of Ethiopia's most intriguing cities. With a few days still up your sleeve, return to Dire Dawa for a flight to **Djibouti City** and a three-day tour of **Lac Abbé**, **Lac Assal** and the **Goda Mountains**. Finish with a flight back to Addis.

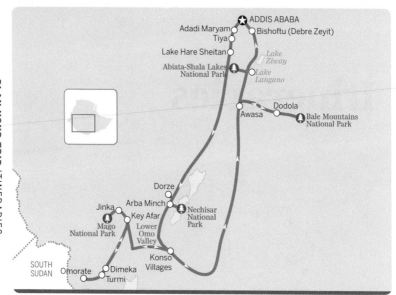

3 WEEKS Southern Ethiopia

While most visitors come to Ethiopia because of what's on offer in the north, it's just as rewarding to point your compass south with its fine landscapes and rich cultures.

You could start with the impressive rock-hewn church of **Adadi Maryam**. Then head south to World Heritage–listed **Tiya**, one of southern Ethiopia's most important stelae fields. Little is known about their significance; some of them are engraved with enigmatic symbols, which adds to the sense of mystery. Next stop: **Lake Hare Sheitan**, some 50km south of Tiya. It's a circular crater lake filled with deep-green waters – very photogenic.

Southwestern Ethiopia's largest city, **Arba Minch** is a good base if you want to explore the nearby **Nechisar National Park**, where you'll have a good chance to spot gargantuan crocodiles, zebras, Swayne's hartebeest and the odd Abyssinian lion. From Arba Minch you can also detour up the mountains to see the woven houses and traditional lifestyle in a **Dorze** village and then continue south and visit the amazing, fortresslike **Konso** villages, at the gateway to the cultural riches of the **Lower Omo Valley**.

In Omo, visits to ethnic villages such as those of the Mursi above **Mago National Park**, the Karo northwest of **Turmi** and the Daasanach along the mighty Omo River at **Omorate** will transport you to another world; as will the important markets in **Jinka**, **Dimeka** and **Key Afar**. If you're lucky, a Jumping of the Bulls ceremony will be happening during your visit.

Slip east before turning north for a night lakeside in modern and orderly **Awasa**. Then it's time for some remote trekking amid Ethiopian wolves and superb scenery in **Bale Mountains National Park** and around **Dodola**.

See the hot springs and flamingo flocks in **Abiata-Shala Lakes National Park** before unwinding in a lakeside resort and doing a bit or birdwatching at **Lake Langano**. Stop at **Lake Ziway** to see hippos, birdlife and island monasteries. You could spend another night on a lake at **Debre Zeyit** before returning to the chaos of Addis Ababa.

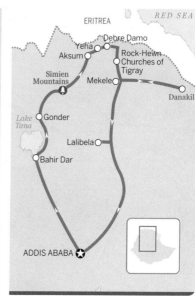

2 WEEKS The Wild West

A journey out into the lush, green west is one for trail blazers, with splendid mountain and lowland scenery, a taste of the south's fascinating cultural mix, and some coffee explorations en route.

Leaving Addis it's a short and easy drive to **Mt Wenchi** where a crater lake and a beautiful day walk awaits. Next head past golden fields to bustling **Jimma** and its museums. Stop off overnight in **Kafa Biosphere Reserve** for a day trek and a visit to the coffee museum, whereafter a long day's driving south will take you deep into Surma country and the village of **Kibish**. After a few days, venture into the wilds of **Omo National Park** in search of wildlife and wild landscapes, then up to the **Bebeka Coffee Plantation**. Drive along misty mountain ridges and through dense forests before descending into the steamy lowlands to fascinating **Gambela**, home of the Nuer and Anuak peoples. From Gambela you have two options – complete the loop by heading back to Addis via **Nekemte** and **Ambo**, which makes for a scenic mountain ride, or flying back to Addis from Gambela.

2 WEEKS Historical Circuit

The historical sights along this loop north of Addis Ababa are monumental in both scale and detail.

After a few days revelling in the chaos of **Addis Ababa**, head north to palm-fringed **Bahir Dar** for a day. Spend the next day at **Lake Tana** exploring some of the lake's centuries-old island monasteries. Next wander the extensive ruins of 17th-century castles in **Gonder**. Looming 100km north, the **Simien Mountains** are one of Ethiopia's most stunning national parks.

Push on to **Aksum** where pre-Christian tombs underlie splendid 1800-year-old stelae (obelisks). After two days, venture to the 3000-year-old ruins of Ethiopia's first capital, **Yeha**, and to the cliff-top monastery of **Debre Damo**. Then head south and search out Tigray's precarious and stunning **rock-hewn churches**. A short hop to the south is **Mekele**, which is the obvious launching pad for the desolate expanses of the **Danakil**. Back in Mekele, drive south to **Lalibela**. Its astounding rock-hewn churches and myriad tunnels have poignantly frozen 12th- and 13th-century Ethiopia in stone. After three or so days here, it's back to Addis Ababa.

Top: Surmi with body painting (p169), Ethiopia.

Bottom: View of the 'Bridge of God' (p156) between lakes Chamo and Abaya, Nechisar National Park, Ethiopia.

Regions at a Glance

Ready for the trip of your lifetime? Wherever you travel around Ethiopia and Djibouti, fantastic experiences, incredible landscapes and friendly encounters are practically guaranteed. Be swept up by the kinetic energy of Addis Ababa. Be awed by stunning mountainscapes and splendid monuments in Northern Ethiopia. Meet traditional ethnic groups in Southern and Western Ethiopia, then head to Eastern Ethiopia for a change of scene. Be sure to add Djibouti to your itinerary – this small country packs a punch.

Addis Ababa

Museums
Food
Nightlife

Museums

From your great-great- (repeat endlessly) aunt Lucy in the National Museum to the cultural insights of the Ethnological Museum, Addis is home to a collection of museums with few peers in sub-Saharan Africa.

Dine Out

Arriving in Addis Ababa is like stepping into one giant food feast. Old-fashioned cafes brew up what some say is the best coffee in the world. But it's the opportunity to dip your fingers into some delicious Ethiopian dishes that stands out.

Bar Hopping

Ethiopia is nothing if not exotic so why not try a night out with a difference? A *tej bet,* a bar serving *tej* (honey wine), is a good place to begin. Catch some live music at an *azmari bet* (bar).

p30

Northern Ethiopia

History
Landscapes
Trekking

Legendary Monuments

Lake Tana, Gonder, Aksum, Yeha and Lalibela are legendary among historians, while even lesser known sites, such as Debre Libanos, Gorgora and Mekele, offer plenty of ancient intrigue.

Stunning Scenery

Staring down a massive cavern in the Simien Mountains, up one of the soaring pinnacles of Tigray, or out across the volcanic creations in the Danakil Depression will live long in the memory.

Awesome Treks

There are high-alpine landscapes in the Simien Mountains and little-known Menz-Guassa Community Conservation Area, and treks through farms and villages around Lalibela and Tigray.

p63

Southern Ethiopia

Culture
Trekking
Lakes

Traditional Cultures

The Omo Valley isn't just the most fascinating cultural melange in Ethiopia, it could just be tops for the entire continent. Most of its multitude of ethnic groups haven't strayed noticeably far from their past.

Trekking

Most trekkers consider the Bale Mountains the best due to better facilities and near-guaranteed sightings of Ethiopian wolves. Lephis, Dorze, Konso and the Omo Valley also offer good trekking.

Natural Wonders

The Rift Valley runs the length of this region and along its path are various lakes; home to crocodiles (Chamo), hippos (Awasa), flamingos (Abiata and Chitu) and luxury resorts.

p133

Eastern Ethiopia

History
Exploration
Wildlife

Historic Harar

Eastern Ethiopia wouldn't be historical if not for World Heritage–listed Harar. Its old walled city centre, full of cobblestone alleys and symbolically designed stone homes, is captivating.

Intrepid Travel

Relatively few travellers venture east, and those who do rarely get off the Addis–Harar Hwy. This leaves places like Asaita and the caves and villages around Harar and Dire Dawa to the truly intrepid.

Wildlife

There's a good chance of meeting the elephants of Babille Elephant Sanctuary. A game drive in Awash National Park will take you past oryx and gazelle. And, of course, don't forget the urban hyenas of Harar.

p177

Western Ethiopia

Cultures
Adventure
Wildlife

Traditional Cultures

The ethnic Nuer and Anuak people are around Gambela, and the Gurage people are near Jimma. For the ultimate adventure, journey to the land of the Surmi people in southwest Omo.

Final Frontier

Even a country as little known as Ethiopia has to have its last frontier and that title goes to the west. With so few tourists venturing here, any journey is a guaranteed trailblazing adventure.

Wild Migration

Ethiopia lacks the stellar reputation of Kenya when it comes to big animals, but Gambela National Park is witness to a migration of white-eared kob and Nile lechwe up to a million strong, and the birdlife is out of this world.

p202

Djibouti

Outdoors
Geological Wonders
Ecotourism

Diving & Hiking

There's superb diving in the Gulf of Tadjoura and top snorkelling off Plage des Sables Blancs. From November to January you can swim alongside gigantic whale sharks near the Bay of Ghoubbet. The Goda Mountains offer great hiking options.

Epic Scenery

Djibouti offers unparalleled scenery. You might think you're walking on the moon at Lac Abbé or approaching Dante's *Inferno* at Lac Assal.

Staying in Nature

Explore the Goda Mountains and Forêt du Day, staying in traditional huts, spending your days hiking, enjoying mountain vistas and learning about traditional Afar culture.

p306

On the Road

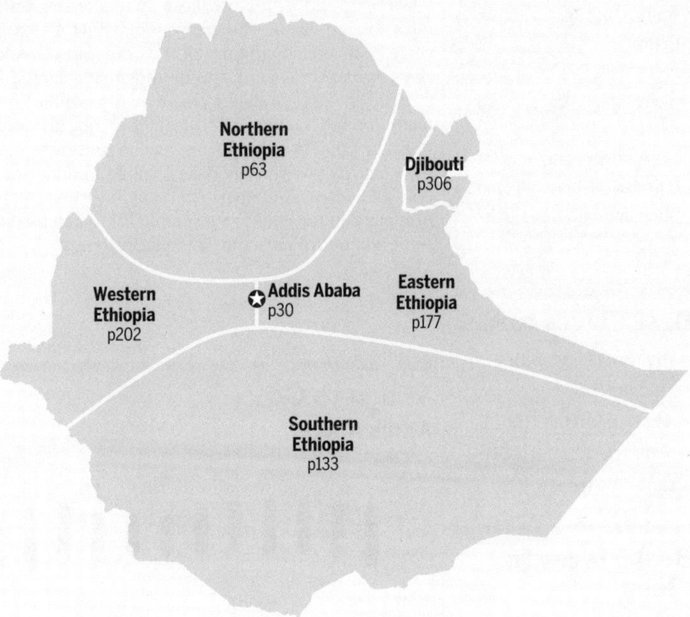

Northern
Ethiopia
p63

Djibouti
p306

Western
Ethiopia
p202

⭐ Addis Ababa
p30

Eastern
Ethiopia
p177

Southern
Ethiopia
p133

Addis Ababa

POP 4.5 MILLION / ELEV 2300M

Best Places to Eat

➡ Yod Abyssinia (p53)

➡ Kategna (p51)

➡ Itegue Taitu Hotel (p52)

➡ Sana'a Restaurant (p51)

➡ Lime Tree (p51)

Best Places to Sleep

➡ Sheraton Hotel (p49)

➡ Caravan Hotel (p45)

➡ Arequ Guest House (p45)

➡ La Source Guest House (p45)

➡ Addissinia Hotel (p49)

Why Go?

Since its establishment in the 19th century, Addis Ababa (አዲስ አበባ) has always seemed like a magical portal, a gateway to another world. For the rural masses of Ethiopia it was, and is, a city whose streets are paved in gold; for a foreign visitor, the gateway of Addis Ababa is at the verge of an ancient and mystical world. And yet, Addis – Africa's fourth-largest city and its diplomatic capital – is also a traffic-choked, sprawling city of no discernible beauty that many foreign visitors try to transit as quickly as possible. But take note: by skipping out on the contradictions of this complex city you run the risk of failing to understand Ethiopia altogether. And apart from anything else, Addis is the best place in the country to sample Ethiopian food, and has some wonderful museums and places to stay.

When to Go
Addis Ababa

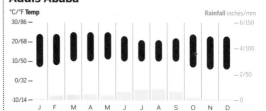

Jan The festivals of Leddet and Timkat add colour and pomp to any visit to Addis.

Sep Light a bonfire during the Meskel festival on 27 September.

Nov Bring your running shoes for the Great Ethiopian Run held in late November.

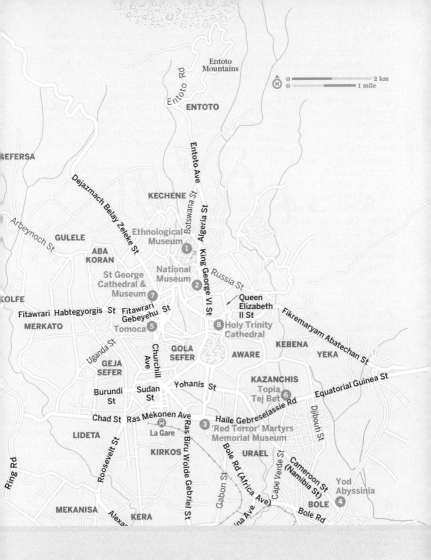

Addis Ababa Highlights

1 Ethnological Museum (p32) Delving into this excellent treasure trove.

2 National Museum (p33) See Lucy, one of our oldest ancestors.

3 'Red Terror' Martyrs Memorial Museum (p32) Staring in silent contemplation at this moving memorial.

4 Yod Abyssinia (p53) Tickling your tongue with your first *injera* and *wat*.

5 Tomoca (p54) Seeing what all the fuss is about at this time-worn coffee den.

6 Topia Tej Bet (p55) Taking an initiation in the delights of *tej* (honey wine)

before heading out to sample the city's nightlife.

7 St George Cathedral & Museum (p36) Visiting this fascinating religious museum.

8 Holy Trinity Cathedral (p37) Mingling with pilgrims at the final resting place of Emperor Haile Selassie.

History

Unlike Addis Ababa's numerous predecessors as capital, the locations of which were chosen according to the political, economic and strategic demands of the day's rulers, Addis Ababa was chosen for its beauty, hot springs and agreeable climate.

Emperor Menelik's previous capital, Entoto, was in the mountains just north of present-day Addis Ababa and held strategic importance as it was easily defended. However, it was unattractive and sterile, leading Taitu, the consort of Menelik II, to request a house be built for her in the beautiful foothills below, in an area she named Addis Ababa (New Flower). In the following decade, after Menelik's power increased and his need for defence waned, he moved his court down to Taitu and Addis Ababa.

A lack of firewood for the rapidly growing population threatened Addis' future in 1896 and Menelik even started construction of a new capital, Addis Alem (New World), 50km to the west. In the end, it was the suggestion of a foreigner (thought to be French) to introduce the rapidly growing eucalyptus tree that saved Addis Ababa's fuel needs.

Sights

Addis has some fantastic museums and churches scattered across the city, and it's these that are the city's main attractions.

Most sights are scattered throughout the city centre and Piazza, though there is a concentration of major museums and other sights in the vicinity of Arat Kilo and Siddist Kilo, which sit east of Piazza and north of the city centre.

★ 'Red Terror' Martyrs Memorial Museum
MUSEUM
(የቀይ ሽብር ተጠቂዎች ማስታወሻ ሙዚየም; Map p38; Meskal Sq; by donation; ⊗8.30am-6.30pm) 'As if I bore them all in one night, they slew them in a single night.' These were the words spoken by the mother of four teenage children all killed on the same day by the Derg, as she officially opened the small but powerful 'Red Terror' Martyrs Memorial Museum in 2010. Over a couple of rooms the museum reveals the fall of Emperor Haile Selassie and the horrors of life under Mengistu's Derg regime.

The museum is well laid out and incredibly moving, nothing more so than the walls of photos and names of just some of the estimated half a million killed under the Derg,

or the display cabinets filled with human belongings dug out of mass graves. Some of the skulls and other bones are displayed alongside a photo of the victim and the personal artefacts they had on them when they died. The watch hanging in one display case was given by its owner to his wife just as he was led away by the soldiers of the Derg. His words: 'Keep this safe. One day you will need it'. When the museum opened, his wife brought the watch here.

Excellent English-speaking guides are often available, although you may prefer to just look on in silence.

The museum is funded by donations only.

★ Ethnological Museum
MUSEUM
(ብሄራዊ ሙዚየም; Map p34; ☑011 123 1068; Addis Ababa University, Algeria St; adult/student Birr100/50; ⊗8am-5pm Mon-Fri, 9am-5pm Sat & Sun) Set within Haile Selassie's former palace, and surrounded by the beautiful gardens and fountains of the university's main campus, is the enthralling Ethnological Museum. Even if you're not a museum fan, this one is worth a bit of your time – it's easily one of the finest museums in Africa, showing the full sweep of Ethiopia's cultural and social history across two floors.

The show starts before you even get inside: facing the entrance, look for the intriguing set of 13 stairs spiralling skyward. Each step was placed by the Italians as a symbol of Fascist domination, one for every year Mussolini held power (starting from his march to Rome in 1922). A small Lion of Judah (the symbol of Ethiopian monarchy) sits victoriously atop the final step, like a jubilant punctuation mark at the end of a painfully long sentence.

Within the entrance hall you'll find a small exhibition dedicated to the history of the palace, and the doorway to the Institute of Language Studies library.

The museum truly comes into its own on the 1st floor, where superb artefacts and handicrafts from Ethiopia's peoples are distinctively displayed. Instead of following the typical static and geographical layout that most museums fall into, these displays are based upon the life cycle. First comes Childhood, with birth, games, rites of passage and traditional tales. We particularly enjoyed the 'Yem Tale', a story of selfishness, dead leopards and sore tails! Adulthood probes into beliefs, nomadism, traditional medicine, war, pilgrimages, hunting, body culture

Addis Ababa is massive and incoherent. To navigate the city, it's best to break it down into distinct districts.

The **city centre** is at the end of Churchill Ave, the southern section of which is named Gambia St. Here you'll find many government and commercial buildings.

To the north is **Piazza**, a district whose legacy and architecture are owed to the Italian occupation. It is found atop the hill at Churchill Ave's north end and houses budget hotels, as well as many cafes and bars.

To the east of Piazza is **Addis Ababa University**, several museums and the landmark roundabouts of **Arat Kilo** and **Siddist Kilo**. South from there is **Menelik II Ave**, which boasts the National Palace, Africa Hall, a series of new urban parks and, at its southern end, the huge **Meskal Sq**.

Thanks to the ring road, the southeast of the city – on and around **Bole Rd** between Meskal Sq and the airport – is thriving with exciting development, such as high-quality restaurants, bars, cafes and shopping centres. It contrasts sharply with the rest of the city.

and handicrafts. The last topic is Death and Beyond, with burial structures, stelae and tombs. The exhibition gives a great insight into Ethiopia's many rich cultures.

Other rooms on this floor show the preserved bedroom, bathroom and exorbitant changing room of Emperor Haile Selassie, complete with a bullet hole in his mirror courtesy of the 1960 coup d'etat.

The 2nd floor is home to two drastically different, but equally delightful, displays. The vibrant hall focuses on religious art, with an exceptional series of diptychs, triptychs, icons, crosses and magic scrolls. Magic scrolls, like the Roman lead scrolls, were used to cast curses on people or to appeal to the gods for divine assistance. The collection of icons is the largest and most representative in the world. Senses of another sort are indulged in the small cavelike corridor that sits next to the hall. Inside, the black surrounds leave you nothing to look at besides traditional musical instruments from across Ethiopia. If you're lucky you might have a soundtrack accompany you.

It's well worth coming to this museum twice; once at the start of your journey through Ethiopia and once at the end when you'll be able to put everything into context.

After you've lapped up the treasures in the museum, stop by the double-decker London bus next to the university entrance gates. Brought to Addis by Haile Selassie, it's now a bar and packed with students.

★**National Museum** MUSEUM
(ብሔራዊ ሙዚየም; Map p34; ☑ 011 111 7150; King George VI St; Birr10; ⊙ 8.30am-5.30pm) The collection on show at the National Museum is ranked among the most important in

sub-Saharan Africa, but sadly many of its exhibits are poorly labelled, lit and displayed. Far and away the highlight is the palaeontological exhibition in the basement, the home of world-famous Lucy. Her 1974 discovery in the Afar region of northwestern Ethiopia changed our understanding of human origins forever. This section is well labelled in English, so if your time is limited spend most of it here.

On the basement level, you'll find two remarkable casts of Lucy, a fossilised hominid and easily Ethiopia's best-known ancient inhabitant. One lays prone, while the other stands much as she did some 3.2 million years ago, truly hitting home how small our ancient ancestors were. The real bones are preserved in the archives of the museum.

Also here is the fossilized evidence of some amazing extinct creatures, like the massive sabre-toothed feline *Homotherium* and the gargantuan savannah pig *Notochoerus*.

The periphery of the ground floor focuses on the pre-Aksumite, Aksumite, Solomonic and Gonderian periods. The wide array of artefacts includes an elaborate pre-1st-century-AD bronze oil lamp showing a dog chasing an ibex, a fascinating 4th-century-BC rock-hewn chair emblazoned with mythical ibexes, and ancient Sabaean inscriptions. The middle of the room hosts a collection of lavish royal paraphernalia, including Emperor Haile Selassie's enormous (and rather hideous) carved wooden throne.

On the 1st floor, there's a vivid display of Ethiopian art ranging from early (possibly 14th-century) parchment to 20th-centu-

Addis Ababa

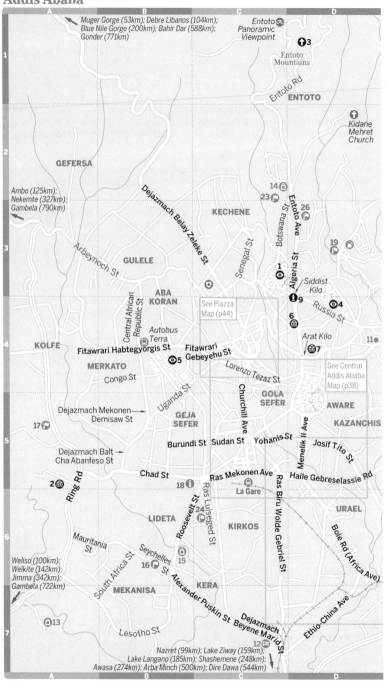

Muger Gorge (53km); Debre Libanos (104km);
Blue Nile Gorge (200km); Bahir Dar (588km);
Gonder (771km)

Entoto
Panoramic
Viewpoint

Entoto
Mountains

ENTOTO

Kidane
Mehret
Church

GEFERSA

Ambo (125km);
Nekemte (327km);
Gambela (790km)

Dejazmach Belay Zeleke St

KECHENE

Arbeynoch St

GULELE

ABA
KORAN

Senegat St

Botswana St

Entoto Ave

Algeria St

Siddist
Kilo

Russia St

Central African
Republic St

See Piazza
Map (p44)

Autobus
Terra

KOLFE

Fitawrari Habtegyorgis St

Fitawrari
Gebeyehu St

Arat Kilo

MERKATO

Congo St

Lorenzo Tezaz St

See Central
Addis Ababa
Map (p38)

Uganda St

Dejazmach Mekonen
Demisaw St

GEJA
SEFER

GOLA
SEFER

AWARE

KAZANCHIS

Churchill Ave

Dejazmach Balt
Cha Abanfeso St

Burundi St Sudan St   Yohanis St

Menelik II Ave

Josif Tito St

Chad St

Ring Rd

Ras Mekonen Ave

Ras Biru Wolde Gebriel St

Haile Gebreselassie Rd

URAEL

La Gare

Roosevelt St

Ras Luiseged St

Bole Rd (Africa Ave)

LIDETA

KIRKOS

Mauritania
St

Seychelles
St

Weliso (100km);
Welkite (142km);
Jimma (342km);
Gambela (722km)

South Africa St

Alexander Puskin St

KERA

MEKANISA

Dejazmach
Beyene Marid St

Ethio-China Ave

Lesotho St

Nazret (99km); Lake Ziway (159km);
Lake Langano (185km); Shashemene (248km);
Awasa (274km); Arba Minch (500km); Dire Dawa (544km)

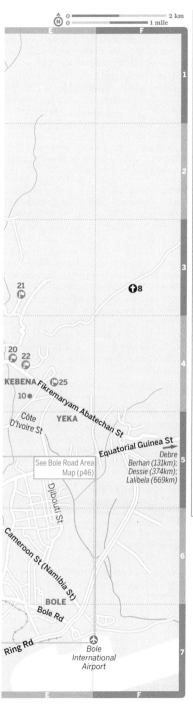

Addis Ababa

⊙ Sights

⊙ Activities, Courses & Tours

⊜ Sleeping

⊗ Eating

⊙ Shopping

⊙ Information

ry canvas oil paintings by leading modern artists. Afewerk Tekle's massive *African Heritage* is one of the more notable pieces. Another painting depicts the meeting of Solomon and Sheba. Note the shield of the soldier next to Solomon, which is engraved with the Star of David and a Christian Cross. The artist must have forgotten that this meeting is said to have occurred long before the birth of Christianity.

The 2nd floor contains a dusty and poorly labelled collection of secular arts and crafts, including traditional weapons, jewellery, utensils, clothing and musical instruments.

English-speaking guides are available for free (they should be tipped afterwards) and help to bring things alive.

★ St George Cathedral & Museum
CHURCH

(ቅዱስ ጊዮርጊስ ቤተክርስቲያን; Map p44; Fitawrari Gebeyehu St; museum Birr100; ☺ museum 9am-noon & 2-5pm Tue-Sun) Commissioned by Emperor Menelik II to commemorate his stunning 1896 defeat of the Italians in Adwa, and dedicated to St George (Ethiopia's patron saint), whose icon was carried into the battle, this Piazza cathedral is one of Addis' most beautiful churches. The grey stone exterior is easily outdone by the interior's flashes of colour and art. Sections of ceiling glow sky-blue and boast gilded stars, while the outer walls of the Holy of Holies are covered in paintings and mosaics by the renowned Afewerk Tekle (p51).

The church, built in traditional octagonal form and with a severe neoclassical style, was completed in 1911 with the help of Greek, Armenian and Indian artists. Empress Zewditu (in 1916) and Emperor Haile Selassie (in 1930) were both crowned here.

In the grounds just north of the cathedral is the museum. It's included on the church admission ticket, is well presented and contains probably the best collection of ecclesiastical paraphernalia in the country outside St Mary of Zion in Aksum. Items include beautiful crowns, crosses, prayer sticks, holy scrolls, ceremonial umbrellas and the coronation garb of Zewditu and Haile Selassie.

Entry includes a guided tour of both the museum and church. Try to get Archdeacon Mebratu to be your guide. He's very entertaining – maybe the most amusing and informative church guide we've had anywhere in Ethiopia – and liable to burst into song and dance, and get you to do likewise, at the drop of a hat.

Washa Mikael Church
CHURCH

(Tekle Haymanot; Map p34; admission/camera/guide Birr50/100/200; ☺ 8.30am-5pm) The Washa Mikael Church is a few kilometres east of Addis Ababa's town centre. Though local priests date it back to the 3rd century AD, it most probably dates back to the 12th century. If you're mad and not planning to visit the churches at Lalibela or Tigray in the north, this is definitely worth a peek as an example of the extraordinary rock-hewn architecture that Ethiopia is so famous for. Unfortunately, from July to October it's usually flooded with rainwater.

The church is tricky to find, so ask locals en route.

ADDIS ABABA IN...

Two Days

Start in Piazza with a steaming espresso at **Tomoca** (p54), before visiting **St George Cathedral & Museum**. Next, get ready to say hello to Auntie Lucy, your long-lost ancestor, in the **National Museum** (p33).

After lunch at **Lucy Gazebo & Restaurant** (p52), explore the massive **Merkato** (p41). After checking you still have all your belongings, finish the day dining and drinking *tej* (honey wine) at **Topia Tej Bet** (p55), then dine at a traditional Ethiopian restaurant, such as **Yod Abyssinia** (p53) or **Habesha 2000** (p53), while enjoying a show of song and dance.

Day two, and the morning kicks off with more culture when you marvel at the brilliant **Ethnological Museum** (p32). In the afternoon, pay your respects to Emperor Haile Selassie at the **Holy Trinity Cathedral** then be moved to tears by the powerful displays in the new **'Red Terror' Martyrs Memorial Museum** (p32). Finish your day off on a more cheerful note at the wonderful **Kategna** (p51) restaurant.

Four Days

With four days, you could complete the two-day itinerary at a slower pace (more espressos! – try **Mokarar** (p54)), squeezing in extra sights like the **Bete Maryam Mausoleum**, a meal at **Sana'a Restaurant** (p51) and some pampering at **Boston Day Spa** (p42). Another well-worthwhile alternative is to head out of town to the extraordinary **Washa Mikael Church**, get some fresh air walking in the **Entoto Mountains** and visit the **Entoto Maryam Church** (p61), or take a half-day trip out to **Debre Libanos Monastery** (p66).

Finally, a word of warning: a number of tourists have been mugged on the road up to the church, so go with a friend or two.

Holy Trinity Cathedral CHURCH

(Map p38; ☑ 011 123 3518; off Niger St; Birr100; ☻cathedral 8am-1pm & 2-6pm Mon-Fri, museum 8am-noon & 2-5pm) This massive and ornate cathedral is the second-most important place of worship in Ethiopia (ranking behind the Old Church of St Mary of Zion in Aksum). It's also the celebrated final resting place of Emperor Haile Selassie and his wife Empress Menen Asfaw. Their massive Aksumite-style granite tombs sit inside and are a sight indeed. The solemnity of the interior design contrasts sharply with highly the charged emotions of many pilgrims. It's a fascinating place.

The cathedral's exterior, with its large copper dome, spindly pinnacles, numerous statues and flamboyant mixture of international styles, provides an interesting and sometimes poignant glimpse into many episodes of Ethiopia's history.

Inside, there are some grand murals, the most notable being Afewerk Tekle's depiction of the Holy Trinity, with Matthew (man), Mark (lion), Luke (cow) and John (dove) peering through the clouds. There are also some brilliant stained-glass windows (those on the north depict scenes from the Old Testament, those to the south from the New) and two beautifully carved imperial thrones, each made of white ebony, ivory and marble.

The entrance fee also includes admission to a small but impressive museum of ecclesiastical artefacts in the grounds out the back.

To the south of the cathedral is the memorial and graves of the ministers killed by the Derg for their opposition in 1974. Due to the prime minister's compound being behind this memorial, photographs are strictly forbidden.

The churchyard also hosts the graves of many patriots who died fighting the Italian occupation, including the great Resistance fighter Ras Imru. To the west of the cathedral is the **tomb of the famous British suffragette Sylvia Pankhurst** (Map p38). Sylvia was one of the very few people outside Ethiopia who protested Italy's occupation; she moved to Addis Ababa in 1956. On the north side is the tomb of Meles Zenawi, prime minister of Ethiopia until his sudden death in 2012.

Purchase tickets at the administration office 20m west of the main gate. Guides charge Birr20 to Birr30 per person.

Lion of Judah Monument MONUMENT

(ዯቅር አንበሳ ሐውልት; Map p38; Gambia St) Long the symbol of Ethiopia's monarchy, the Lion of Judah is ubiquitous throughout the country – and although images of the almighty animal abound in Addis Ababa, it's the storied history of the Lion of Judah Monument that makes this statue significant.

After being erected on the eve of Haile Selassie's coronation in 1930, it was looted by Italians in 1935 and placed in Rome next to the massive Vittorio Emanuele II Monument. In 1938, during anniversary celebrations of the proclamation of the Italian Empire, Zerai Deress, a young Eritrean, spotted the statue and defiantly interrupted proceedings to kneel and pray before it. After police verbally and physically attempted to stop his prayers, he rose and attacked the armed Italians with his sword while screaming 'the Lion of Judah is avenged!' He seriously injured several officers (some reports say he killed five) before he was shot. Although he died seven years later in an Italian prison, his legend lives on in Ethiopia and Eritrea.

The Lion of Judah Monument was eventually returned to Addis Ababa in the 1960s.

Bete Maryam Mausoleum CHURCH

(ቤተ ማርያም መቃብር; Menelik's Mausoleum; Map p38; Itegue Menen Rd; Birr50; ☻9am-6pm) The Bete Maryam Mausoleum is located just south of Menelik's palace and offers what could be an enchantingly eerie experience for travellers (were it not for security personnel at every turn). If you're lucky, after the priest has rolled up the carpet and pried open the large metal door in the floor, you will descend into the thick air of the creepy crypt. There you find four elaborate marble tombs of Empress Taitu, Emperor Menelik, Empress Zewditu and Princess Tsehai Haile Selassie.

At least that's how a visit should go. The reality is that – thanks to the prime minister's residence being next door – the whole complex is guarded by an inordinate number of very surly and unhelpful soldiers, who, if our last visit was anything to go by, try to make visiting the church as problematic as they possibly can.

Central Addis Ababa

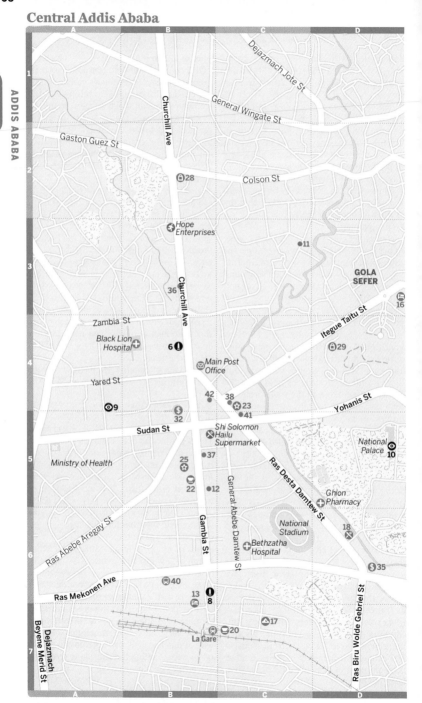

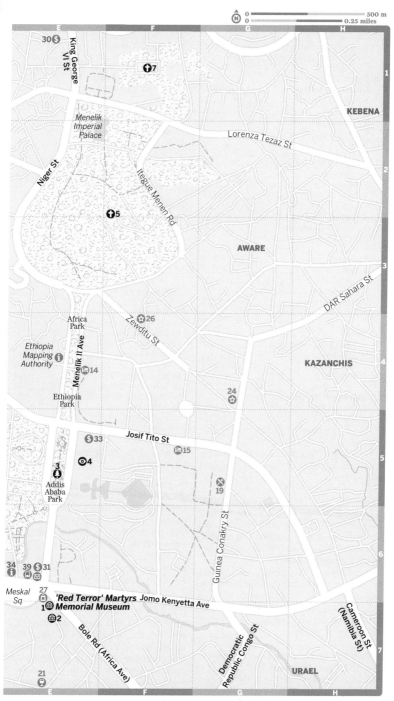

Central Addis Ababa

◎ **Top Sights**
1 'Red Terror' Martyrs Memorial
Museum E7

◎ **Sights**
2 Addis Ababa Museum E7
3 Addis Ababa Park E5
4 Africa Hall E5
5 Bete Maryam Mausoleum F2
6 Derg Monument....................................B4
7 Holy Trinity Cathedral F1
8 Lion of Judah Monument......................B6
9 National Archives & Library of
Ethiopia A4
10 Presidential Palace D5
Tomb of Sylvia Pankhurst ....(see 7)

Activities, Courses & Tours
11 Mon Pays Tours C3
12 Smiling Ethiopia B5

Sleeping
13 Buffet de la Gare B6
14 Hilton Hotel...E4
15 Radisson Blu F5
16 Sheraton Hotel......................................D3
17 Wim's Holland House C7

Eating
18 China Bar & Restaurant D6
19 Lime Tree..G5
Shaheen ....(see 16)
Stagioni ....(see 16)

Drinking & Nightlife
20 Choche Fine Coffee Plc C7
Club Illusion ....(see 23)

21 Memo Club E7
22 National Café B5

✪ **Entertainment**
23 Ambassador Cinema C4
24 Fendika Azmari Bet..............................G4
25 National Theatre...................................B5
26 Yewedale F4

Shopping
27 Bookworld E6
28 Gallery 21 ....B2
29 St George Interior Decoration
& Art Gallery....................................D4
Tourist Information Shop.............(see 34)

ⓘ **Information**
30 Commercial Bank...................................E1
31 Commercial Bank..................................E6
32 Commercial Bank..................................B4
33 Commercial Bank..................................E5
Dashen Bank...................................(see 16)
34 Tourist Information Centre E6
United Bank.....................................(see 14)
35 Wegagen Bank......................................D6

ⓘ **Transport**
36 EgyptAir B3
Ethiopian Airlines ....(see 14)
37 Ethiopian Airlines B5
Kenya Airways ....(see 14)
KLM ....(see 14)
38 Saudi Arabian Airlines C4
39 Selam Bus Office E6
40 Short-distance Bus Station B6
41 Sudan Airways C5
42 Yemenia..B4

On Wednesdays and Fridays the mausoleum closes for prayers between 12.30pm and around 2pm.

Afewerk Tekle's Home & Studio   GALLERY
(የአፈወርቅ ተክለ ቤት እና ስቱዲዮ; Map p34) A member of several international academies and with a drawer full of international decorations – about 100 at last count, including the British Order of Merit – Afewerk Tekle is considered among Africa's greatest artists. His former home and studio was closed to the public after his death in 2012. Renovations were still taking place as of late 2016, but we were assured that there are still plans to reopen...one day.

Entoto Panoramic Viewpoint   VIEWPOINT
(Map p34; Entoto Mountains) High on Entoto Mountain, there's a terrific but windy panoramic view of Ethiopia's modern capital spread out below through the towering eucalyptus trees.

Derg Monument   MONUMENT
(የድል ሐውልት (ድላችን); Map p38; Churchill Ave) The towering Derg Monument is one of the more poignant reminders of the country's painful communist rule. Topped by a massive red star and emblazoned with a golden hammer and sickle, the cement obelisklike structure climbs skyward in front of Black Lion Hospital.

Institute of Ethiopian Studies   LIBRARY
(የኢትዮጵያ ጥናትና ምርምር ተቋም; Map p34; ☑ 011 123 9740; Addis Ababa University, Algeria St) Inside the grounds of Addis Ababa University, this institute boasts the world's best collection of books in English on Ethiopia. It's free for a half-day's casual use. If you're having trouble finding it, ask at the ticket office for the Ethnological Museum.

Merkato
MARKET

(መርካቶ; Map p34; ⊙ 6am-7pm Mon-Sat) Wading into the market chaos known as Merkato, just west of Addis' centre, can be as rewarding as it is exasperating. You may find the most eloquent aroma wafting from precious incense. You may also find that your wallet has been stolen and that you've got stinky excrement on your shoe. Some people say it's the largest market in Africa, but as its exact boundaries are as shady as some of its characters, this is a little hard to verify.

What should be noted, however, is that this isn't one of those nicely photogenic markets with goods laid out on the ground or in little stalls. Most vendors now have permanent tin shacks to house their wares, so in many eyes this changes the market from a scene of exotica to just a slum.

The mass of stalls, produce and people may seem impenetrable, but on closer inspection the market reveals a careful organisation with sections for each product. You can spend your Birr on pungent spices, silver jewellery or anything else that takes your fancy. There's even a 'recycling market', where sandals (made out of old tyres), coffee pots (from old Italian olive tins) and other interesting paraphernalia can be found.

Kidane Mehret Church
CHURCH

(Map p34) The unremarkable new church on this site is far less interesting than the reconstructed original, complete with Aksumite architectural traces, alongside it.

Africa Hall
NOTABLE BUILDING

(አፍሪካ አዳራሽ; Map p38; ☑ 011 551 7700; Menelik II Ave; ⊙ 8am-1pm & 2-5pm Mon-Fri) Built in 1961 by Emperor Haile Selassie, Africa Hall (near Meskal Sq) is the seat of the UN's Economic Commission for Africa (ECA). The Italian-designed building isn't very interesting, apart from the friezelike motifs that represent traditional Ethiopian *shamma* (shawl) borders. It's well worth a visit, but this is only possible by prior appointment (call the number above). You'll need to bring your passport and they generally prefer it if you visit as part of a group.

Of greatest interest is 'Africa: Past, Present and Future', a monumental stained-glass window by the artist Afewerk Tekle. Measuring 150 sq m, it fills one entire wall and is one of the biggest stained-glass windows in the world. During some hours of the day, the white marble floor of the foyer is flooded with colour.

Addis Ababa Museum
MUSEUM

(አዲስ አበባ ሙዚየም; Map p38; Meskal Sq; Birr10; ⊙ 8.30am-12.30pm & 1.30-5.30pm Tue-Fri, 8.30-11.30am Sat) Despite only being founded on Addis' centenary in 1986, the Addis Ababa Museum is the city's scruffiest museum. That said, perusing candid portraits of the redoubtable Empress Taitu, rakish Lij Iyasu and the very beautiful Empress Zewditu, along with pictures of the capital in its infancy, is still worth an hour or so. It's unbelievable that the raucous city outside was nothing more than tents on a hill just over a century ago.

There's also a 'first-in-Ethiopia' room, with pictures of Menelik with Bede Bentley in Addis Ababa's first motor car (1907) and the first telephone in Ethiopia. This was brought from Italy by Ras Makonnen in 1890, and it's said that local priests, when they first heard the disembodied voices, thought telephones the work of demons.

Natural History Museum
MUSEUM

(የተፈጥሮ ታሪክ ሙዚየም; Map p34; ☑ 011 111 9496; Queen Elizabeth II St; still/video camera Birr20/60; ⊙ 9am-4.30pm Tue-Sun) Unless you've a particular interest in Ethiopia's animals and birdlife, this is more a case of rainy day tourism. Go eye to eye with a bloated leopard – sometimes the stuffers just don't know when to stop stuffing! – and other stuffed wildlife, but sadly there's neither Ethiopian wolf nor lion. Of most interest are the bird specimens – reportedly around 40% of the country's 862 species are represented here.

Yekatit 12 Monument
MONUMENT

(የካቲት 12 መታሰቢያ ሐውልት; Map p34; Siddist Kilo) Rising dramatically from the roundabout Siddist Kilo is this moving monument, dedicated to the thousands of innocent Ethiopians killed by the Italians as retribution for the attempt on Viceroy Graziani's life on 19 February 1937. 'Yekatit 12' is a date in the Ethiopian calendar roughly equivalent to 19 February.

National Archives & Library of Ethiopia
LIBRARY

(ብሔራዊ መዝገብ እና መፃህፍት ቤት; Map p38; www.nala.gov.et; off Sudan St; ⊙ 9am-5pm Tue-Fri, noon-5pm Mon) Shelves groan under the weight of 20,000 books on Ethiopia. The English-language section is quite good.

Jan Meda Sports Ground STADIUM
(Map p34; Russia St) Stadium in the north of Addis Ababa, where major celebrations and horse races take place.

Addis Ababa University UNIVERSITY
(Map p34) Addis Ababa's expansive university is the country's largest and most prestigious. The academic year runs roughly from October to May. The university also houses within its ground the excellent Ethnological Museum (p32).

Addis Ababa Park PARK
A thin stand of greenery opposite the **presidential palace** (Map p38; Menelik II St).

🏃 Activities

Activities in Addis are generally pretty sedate and are aimed more at business people than backpackers. Then again, who can complain about a heavenly massage, steam bath or sauna? Swimming and horse riding are also possible. Cooling swims are also justifiably popular.

Hope Enterprises (Map p38; ☑011 156 0345; www.hopeenterprises.org; Churchill Ave; ⊙8am-noon & 1-5pm Mon-Sat) is one of the best places to do some volunteering while in Addis, from teaching (if you're a qualified teacher) to helping out in Hope Enterprises' soup kitchens for the homeless.

Massage, Steam Bath & Sauna
Sheraton Hotel (p49) offers a sublime massage from Birr450. There's a full range of reflexology, Swedish, deep-tissue and neck and shoulder massages, as well as mineral body scrubs.

Boston Day Spa (Map p46; ☑011 662 3808, 093 229 5209; http://kurifturesortspa.com/boston; Bole Rd (Africa Ave); ⊙8am-8.30pm) is Addis Ababa's best day spa beyond the big international hotels.

Running
If you want to run where the best of the best used to train, head to Meskal Sq to jog up and down the square along the concrete, terraced seating. If you complete the entire circuit, running up and down each aisle, you'll have sweated through 42km.

Swimming
Beat the heat with some underwater action. The sweetest swims in town are to be had at the Sheraton Hotel (Birr200/250 weekday/weekend) and the Hilton Hotel (Birr200, Mon-Thu, Birr250 Fri-Sun).

Tours

There are no scheduled tours of the city itself; however, if you contact one of Addis Ababa's many travel agencies, most can usually arrange something.

★ Go Addis Tours TOURS
(☑094 307 6240; www.goaddistours.com; per person US$60-135) This fantastic new kid on the block is your window into the best Addis has to offer. Run by Eliza and Xavier, they offer a range of city tours, with a particular focus on the capital's best Ethiopian food. Their five-hour Highlights tour is probably our pick with a good mix of sightseeing, a fine lunch stop and good coffee.

Do spend time perusing their website, as you'll find market tours, food tours (which take in three restaurants and a coffee ceremony) and full-day tours (which combine elements of the other tours). Go Addis are also happy to customise tours to your interests.

🍴 Courses

Destino Dance Company DANCING
(www.destinodance.org; adult/child Birr120/80; ⊙adult/child classes noon/11am Sat) A fabulous and all-too-rare opportunity to learn a key aspect of Ethiopian culture, this excellent dance troupe runs classes in Ethiopian contemporary dance every Saturday at Galani Cafe (p54).

Institute of Language Studies LANGUAGE
(Map p34; ☑011 123 9702; Addis Ababa University, Algeria St) The Institute of Language Studies teaches three Ethiopian languages (Amharic, Tigrinya and Orominya). Classes last four months and start from US$150. Head immediately left after entering the main university gates. The office is on the 2nd floor, room 210.

🎉 Festivals & Events

Although Addis doesn't boast any major festivals of its own, it's a great place to catch some of the national festivals.

For minor festivals and upcoming cultural events, check out www.addisallaround.com.

Leddet CHRISTMAS
(⊙6-7 Jan) Ethiopian Christmas is a powerful affair – all-night church services are the

norm. Head to Jan Meda Sports Ground in the north of the city where the most exuberant celebrations take place. Festivities also include a traditional game of *genna* (hockey without boundaries).

Timkat RELIGIOUS
(☺ Jan) This celebration of the Epiphany (Christ's baptism) is a colourful, three-day affair. As with Leddet, Jan Meda Sports Ground is the best place in Addis to see the procession.

Meskel RELIGIOUS
(☺ 27-28 Sep) Celebrating the Finding of the True Cross, Meskel involves bonfires, priests in full ceremonial robes and plenty of festivities around the suitably named Meskal Sq.

Great Ethiopian Run SPORTS
(☺ Nov) Inaugurated in 2001, the 10km run is now the biggest mass-participation race on the continent. It takes over the city on the last or second-to-last Sunday of November and attracts over 20,000 runners. Whether running or watching, it's a fun time and it's a great chance to see some of East Africa's elite athletes in action.

🛏 Sleeping

Accommodation runs the gamut in Addis – brandish your flip-flop and do battle with almighty insects, or sink into a sumptuous suite. It's all up to you, your budget and the strength of your shoes.

Hotel owners quote their rates in a mixture of Birr and US dollars, though all accept payment in Birr. We have quoted prices using the currency the hotel uses. All hotels listed here have hot water unless otherwise indicated.

The Bole area southeast of Addis' centre is where you'll find dozens of midrange hotels. With so many restaurants nearby, it's a good area to base yourself.

Around Mike Leyland St and Haile Gebreselassie Rd are plenty of budget hotels, although you should keep your wits about you if venturing out after dark. The midrange hotels in the area generally inhabit more salubrious surrounds. There are plenty of budget hotels just down the hill from Piazza – con artists are known to hang around waiting for gullible new arrivals but it's not as bad as it used to be.

Ankober Guest House HOTEL $
(Map p44; ☎ 011 111 2350; Mundy St; r Birr420; ☎) The most salubrious of the cheap Piazza-area hotels, this place has smart rooms with polished floors and good showers. On the flip side, the echoey corridor means sound travels, the wi-fi never seems to work and the beds can be soft in the middle.

Selam Pension HOTEL $
(Map p46; ☎ 091 051 1083; Gabon St; d incl breakfast Birr350-430, tw Birr 480; ☎) This shining white place offers one of the better budget deals in Addis. It's all very clean, though the bathrooms are a little cramped. It's also well run and far enough from the road to mean honking horns won't interrupt your sleep (too much)! The sign is in Amharic only, so ask someone to point it out.

Wim's Holland House CAMPGROUND $
(Map p38; ☎ 091 188 7770; wimshollandhouse@gmail.com; campsites from Birr100; P ☎) Hidden in the maze of lanes to the east of the train station, this campground, the sole overlanders' party in the city, is a cramped area occasionally overflowing with hardened road warriors talking about oil filters. There's a busy bar, frequent party nights and a kitchen for guest use.

Wutma Hotel HOTEL $
(Map p44; ☎ 011 853 4267; wutmahotel@yahoo.com; Mundy St; r Birr260) The city's backpacker hotel of choice for years. The smallish

---

ℹ **STREET NAMES**

Finding a street sign in Addis Ababa can be something of an art form and then, when you do find one, it's likely that no local will actually know the street by that name. In fact, aside from a couple of streets (Churchill Ave, Bole Rd, Meskal Sq and a few others) it's highly unlikely that locals will have any idea what the street is called. Most people, taxi drivers included, use landmarks in order to enquire about the location of something. When trying to get to a specific place, asking for the nearest big hotel, shopping centre or well-known restaurant, is more likely to garner a result than merely giving a street name.

We have included the names of the major streets on our maps, but it's likely that locals will have half-a-dozen different names or no name at all for the same road. The moral of the story? Think creatively when trying to locate something!

Piazza

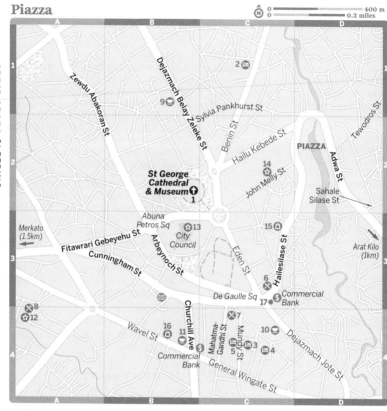

Piazza

grey-walled rooms at the Wutma are simple but satisfying but the bathrooms are *tiny*. The downstairs restaurant is popular with travellers.

Buffet de la Gare
HOTEL $

(Map p38; off Ras Mekonen Ave; d Birr350) Once upon a time the chuff-chuffing of steam trains would have soothed you to sleep here, but with the trains no longer functioning, peace, quiet and a pervasive sense of neglect prevails. The handful of rooms, set around a garden, are clean but old with thin, sagging mattresses. Service often goes missing. The on-site restaurant is simple but adequate.

Henok Guest House
HOTEL $

(Map p46; ☎ 011 662 4234; off Mike Leyland St; r Birr165-330) The rooms here are set around a sun-baked courtyard and are clean and as well-cared for as you can hope to find in this price range in Addis. It's tucked away up a maze of dusty tracks, so it stays nice and quiet, but be careful walking this area at night.

Baro Hotel
HOTEL $

(Map p44; ☎ 011 155 1447; barohotel@ethionet.et; Mundy St; s from Birr230, d Birr230-400; P ⚹) Traditionally one of the better backpacker hang-outs of Ethiopia; the cheaper rooms at the Baro are decidedly skanky, but opt for one of the more expensive options and you'll be the proud resident of a large and fairly well-maintained room (some with a bath tub). The whole place has lost some of the buzz of former years, but it's still good when full. The garden can be a fantastic place to meet other travellers, but falls flat when things are quiet.

Polaris Pension
HOTEL $

(Map p46; ☎ 092 022 4499; off Mike Leyland St; r from Birr300; ⚹) This relatively new guesthouse is a reasonable deal. Peach-pink rooms, OK bathrooms (some with showers, some with bath tubs), a TV...it ticks all the boxes, although the surrounding streets are a touch dodgy after dark.

★ Arequ Guest House
B&B $$

(Map p34; ☎ 011 896 3843; www.arequbandb. com; off Dejazmach Beyene Merid St; d/f/ste US$78/90/108) With a real family feel that we found nowhere else in town, Arequ comes heartily recommended. It's like staying in someone's home, with lovely, warmly furnished rooms, but with friendly and professional service that never gets in your way. Our only criticism is that it's not really

MENELIK BUYS A NEW CHAIR

If Emperor Menelik II (r 1889–1913), the founder of Addis Ababa, was alive today he'd have been the first in the queue for the latest mobile phone or technological gadget. If it was new and flashy he just had to have one. So, when he first heard about a new invention in America called the electric chair, he decided that Ethiopia just had to have a couple of these ingenious death machines. After months of waiting, the new contraptions arrived in Addis. When he first saw them the emperor was delighted with the craftsmanship that had gone into them and asked for a demonstration. It was only then, and no doubt to the great relief of the chosen 'demonstrator', that Menelik's technicians suddenly realised that electricity hadn't yet been turned on in Ethiopia...

close to anywhere, but it's so good we reckon that's worth overlooking.

★ Caravan Hotel
HOTEL $$

(Map p46; ☎ 011 661 2297; www.caravanaddis. com; off Mike Leyland St; s/d from US$56/66; P ⚹) Travellers rave about this place for its friendly service, good rooms, strong wifi and all-round excellence. The carpeted rooms are far classier than you usually get for this price in Addis and the buffet breakfast is outstanding.

★ Stay Easy
BUSINESS HOTEL $$

(Map p46; ☎ 093 886 5555, 011 661 6688; www. stayeasyaddis.com; off Haile Gebreselassie Rd; r US$45-55; P @ ⚹) With its minimalist, modern design, this budget business-class hotel is hands down the best place to stay in Addis in this price bracket. It has art on the walls, high-quality mattresses, soundproofed rooms, flat-screen TVs with satellite channels, great service and an OK in-house restaurant.

★ La Source Guest House
GUESTHOUSE $$

(Map p46; ☎ 011 466 5510; lasourceguesthouse@ gmail.com; off Meskal Flower Rd; r incl breakfast US$19-36; @ ⚹) Finally, Addis has produced a guesthouse with style. It's sparkling clean, with constant hot water, and even has that rare thing – character in abundance. All rooms have local textiles and artworks; some have furnishings made of twisted tree

Bole Road Area

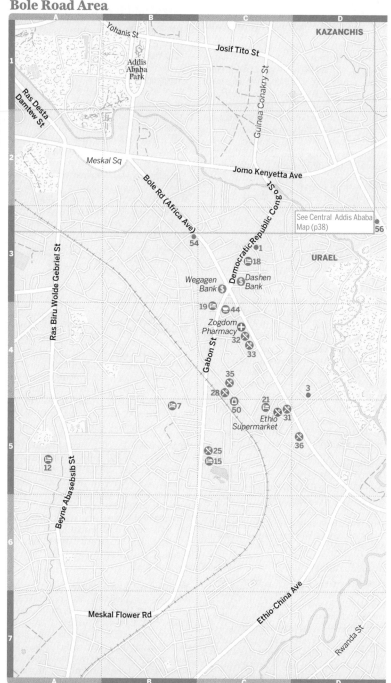

KAZANCHIS

Yohanis St

Josif Tito St

Addis
Ababa
Park

Ras Desta
Damtew St

Guinea Conakry St

Meskal Sq

Jomo Kenyetta Ave

Bole Rd (Africa Ave)

Democratic Republic Congo St

See Central Addis Ababa
Map (p38)

56

54

URAEL

1

18

Wegagen
Bank

Dashen
Bank

Ras Biru Wolde Gebriel St

19

44

Zogdom
Pharmacy

32

33

Gabon St

35

28

3

50

21

7

31

Ethio
Supermarket

36

12

25

15

Beyne Abasebsib St

Meskal Flower Rd

Ethio-China Ave

Rwanda St

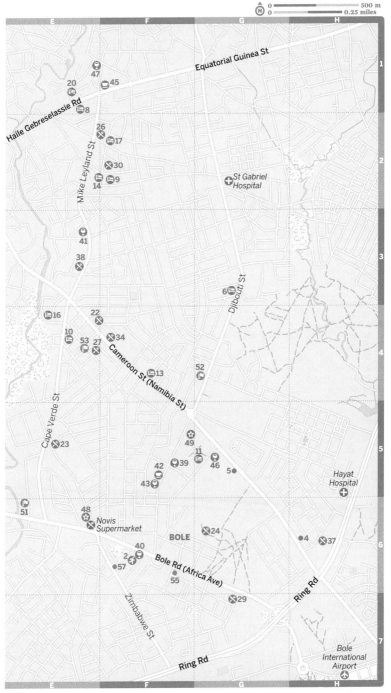

Bole Road Area

🟢 Activities, Courses & Tours

🔵 Sleeping

🟠 Eating

🟢 Drinking & Nightlife

🟣 Entertainment

🟡 Shopping

🔵 Information

🔵 Transport

branches. Service is friendly and, very unusually in this price bracket, it offers a free airport shuttle. The front-facing rooms can be very noisy.

★ Itegue Taitu Hotel   HISTORIC HOTEL $$
(Map p44; ☑ 011 156 0787; www.taituhotel.com; r Birr410-830, without bathroom Birr199-450; P 🖱) Appear in the dream of an empress! Built at the whim of Empress Taitu in 1907, and nearly burned down in 2015 (most of the rooms survived), this is the oldest hotel in Addis: the main building is virtually a museum piece full of beautiful old furniture and high ceilings. The rooms upstairs in the main building are large and easily the best.
   The newer block contains a wide range of rooms, including some passable doubles.

There are plenty of facilities, a lovely garden in which breakfast is served and an excellent restaurant. All up it offers a cash-strapped overlander a classy experience for very little coin.

GT Guesthouse   GUESTHOUSE $$
(Map p46; ☑ 093 001 1199; www.gtguesthouse. com; Sierra Leone St; r US$35-55, apt US$100; 🖱) It may be way out in the west of Addis and not really close to much, but GT is a terrific place to stay. Lee is a memorable host and the rooms are excellent value by any standards, but especially so for Addis. Rooms are immaculate, breakfasts are excellent and things like flat-screen TV, are extras you rarely get in this price category.

Bow Hotel B&B
B&B $$

(Map p46; ☑ 093 866 8800; www.bowaddis.com; off Gabon St; r US$36-48, ste US$54; ☎) Rooms here are nothing to write home about, but this place has that certain something that travellers can't get enough of. In short, it's a combination between friendly staff (Raz and Aster are fine hosts), good food, quiet and well-tended rooms. At this price, who could ask for more?

Mr. Martin's Cozy Place
HOTEL $$

(Map p46; ☑ 091 088 4585, 011 663 2611; www.mmcozyplace.com; Cape Verde St; s/d with shared bathroom US$25/30, d with private bathroom US$30-40; ☎) This quiet and well-run place has gained a name for itself as one of the better-value cheapies in town. All the rooms are impeccably clean. Wi-fi is in the lobby only and the best rooms are in the main building, with Room 101 our pick. Breakfast included.

Rita's Guest House
HOTEL $$

(Map p46; ☑ 011 553 0979; www.ritaguesthouse.com.et; Democratic Republic Congo St; r US$38-45; ☎) Cosy (read: small) rooms in a good central location. Even though the rooms are tiny they are well cared for and contain everything you might require. It's down a little dirt track off the main road.

Weygoss Guest House
HOTEL $$

(Map p46; ☑ 011 551 2205; www.weygossguesthouse.com; d incl breakfast US$50-75; ☎) Lacking a sign and hidden up an alley just north of **Ethio Supermarket** (Map p46; ⊘ 8am-8pm Mon-Sat), this five-storey guesthouse is well looked after and friendly, if a little overpriced. It's popular with foreigners looking to adopt an Ethiopian child.

★ Addissinia Hotel
HOTEL $$$

(Map p46; ☑ 011 662 3634; www.addissiniahotel.com; Djibouti St; s/d/tw from US$89/99/129) Getting consistently good reviews from travellers both for service and room quality, the Addissinia is one of the best deals in town. The corner deluxe rooms are outstanding, with terrific views from the upper floors, and there's also a reasonable restaurant. The location is a little out of the way, but that's our only complaint.

★ Sheraton Hotel
BUSINESS HOTEL $$$

(Map p38; ☑ 011 517 1717; www.sheratonaddis.com; Itegue Taitu St; d/ste from US$275/600; ✳@☎☒) One of Africa's elite hotels, the Sheraton has long been the standard bearer for luxury accommodation in the capital. Its rooms are uber-luxurious and its facilities mean you barely need to leave your hotel, with every need – spa, restaurants etc – serviced on site. Whether or not that's a good thing is entirely your call, but needless to say, it's an absolute treat to stay here.

Radisson Blu
HOTEL $$$

(Map p38; ☑ 011 515 7600; www.radissonblu.com; Josif Tito St; r from US$210; ℗✳@☎☒) One of the top hotels in town, the Radisson lacks the Sheraton's scale but it's still one place we never hear a bad word about. Rooms are large and luxurious, there are some fine onsite restaurants and the central location is nicely suited to exploring. The room style is sophisticated with a pleasing blend of the traditional and the contemporary.

Golden Tulip
HOTEL $$$

(Map p46; ☑ 011 618 3333; www.goldentulipaddis.com; off Cameroon St; s/d from US$115/145; ✳@☎) It may be part of an international chain, but this appealing hotel has sophisticated rooms with more character than most in this price range.The location in the heart of the Bole neighbourhood and close to the airport is good, plus you're down a quiet side street. The breakfast is good for the price. Those here to work will appreciate the large desks.

Desalegn 2 Hotel
BUSINESS HOTEL $$$

(Map p46; ☑ 011 662 4524; www.desalegnhotel.com; Cape Verde St; r incl breakfast from US$71; @☎) Refurbished in 2012, this large business hotel is already showing signs of age. The rooms are large and we like the balconies with reasonable city views (ask for a north-facing room), but they're wearing faster than they should and the lobby is crowded and comes with kitchen smells. Yes, the rooms are slightly overpriced, but it's still not a bad deal for Addis.

Addis Regency Hotel
HOTEL $$$

(Map p44; ☑ 011 155 0000; www.addisregencyhotel.com; off Benin St; r incl breakfast US$75-99, tw US$95-105, ste US$170; ℗@☎) Friendly, immaculately well kept, supremely comfortable with beds that seem custom designed to give sweet dreams, endless piping-hot water and a quiet side-street location make this place a cut above the competition. The only drawback is that the Addis Regency is quite far from the city's more interesting dining and nightlife options, so it's a good job they have a reasonable in-house restaurant.

Adot-Tina Hotel
BUSINESS HOTEL $$$

(Map p46; ☑ 011 467 3939; www.adottinahotel. com; off Meskal Flower Rd; s/d incl breakfast from US$125/150; @ 🛜) The small, attractive rooms of this intimate business-class hotel, which come with either a deep, relaxing bath or a space-age shower far too complicated for us to work out, are really good value. However, the seal on the deal might be the free sauna and gym. It's a popular choice with tour groups and people coming to Ethiopia to adopt a child. Discounts are common.

Hilton Hotel
HOTEL $$$

(Map p38; ☑ 011 551 8400; www3.hilton.com; Menelik II Ave; r incl breakfast US$210; 🅿 @ 🛜 🏊) Something of an institution, the Hilton still attracts the conference crowd but it lost its crown as Addis' top hotel long ago. It's starting to show its age and there are better top-end deals in town.

Capital Hotel & Spa
HOTEL $$$

(Map p46; ☑ 011 667 2100; www.capitalhotel andspa.com; Haile Gebreselassie St; s/d from US$107/135; 🅿 ❄ @ 🛜) Vying for the title of Addis' best top-end hotel, the Capital is a classy establishment with a soothing wellness spa, good restaurants and stylish rooms decked out in a muted but classic five-star style. Service, too, rarely misses a beat.

Haimi Apartment Hotel
APARTMENT $$$

(Map p46; ☑ 011 618 1834; www.haimihotel.com; Namibia St; s/d from US$108/126; 🅿 🛜) For those who value a little more space and perhaps even your own kitchen, Haimi has great rooms. While the style might be a little overdone for some tastes, we hear very few complaints from travellers about this place.

✖ Eating

You lucky, lucky souls...you've either just stepped off a plane (Welcome to Ethiopia! Lucky you!) and can experiment with your first genuine Ethiopian meals, or you've just arrived from several weeks in Ethiopia's wilds (How amazing was that? Lucky you!) and can now say goodbye to repetitive *injera* and *wat* (stew) and sloppy pasta. Middle Eastern or Italian? French or Ethiopian? It's all here for you to enjoy.

The area taking in Bole Rd, Cameroon St (sometimes called Namibia St) and environs is the undisputed culinary centre of the cap-
ital. This is where the city's well-to-do and expats like to hang out, so you can expect high quality and higher than normal prices. Food types from around the world are represented here as well as flash Western-style coffee shops by the dozen.

For an insider's take on the capital's eating scene, take a tour with Go Addis Tours (p42).

For self-caterers, well-stocked supermarkets include Ethio (p49), **Shi Solomon Hailu** (Map p38; Yohanis St; ⊙ 8am-8pm Mon-Sat) and **Novis** (Map p46; Bole Rd).

Sangam Restaurant
INDIAN $

(Map p46; ☑ 091 121 4183; Bole Rd (Africa Ave); mains Birr60-130; ⊙ 11.30am-3.30pm & 6-10pm; ☑) If you've developed a craving for a cracking curry, try this atmospheric and upmarket Indian restaurant. There's plenty to choose from but the *mughali biryani* (fragrant rice), tandoori dishes or butter-chicken masala are all absolutely delicious. There are also great lunchtime *thalis* (mixed meals; Birr150 to Birr180) available every day but Sunday.

እፎይ (Efoy)
PIZZA $

(Map p46; ☑ 091 1213 4811; Mike Leyland St; pizzas Birr85-125; ⊙ noon-midnight) If Addis has a vaguely 'boutique' pizza place then this is it. It's small, warm and welcoming, with thin-crust pizzas popping out of the pizza oven to satisfy a young and cool local crowd. Upstairs is an equally intimate bar. The sign is written in Amharic only – the rough translation is 'efoy', which is the sort of sighing noise a contented person makes.

Makush Art Gallery & Restaurant
ITALIAN $

(Map p46; ☑ 011 552 6848, 091 141 8602; Bole Rd (Africa Ave); mains Birr80-140; ⊙ 9am-10pm) Surrounded by vivid paintings and wood-carvings from the 70 artists this gallery-restaurant supports, and watched over by attentive waiters and your genial host Nati, this place does reasonable Italian food and has a casual ambience. It's in an office tower above Ethio Supermarket.

New York, New York
BURGERS $

(Map p46; Bole Rd (Africa Ave); burgers Birr62-132; ⊙ 7am-1am) We wouldn't cross town for it, but New York, New York has a vaguely diner-like feel to it (although it's more Addis than Queens) and does pretty good burgers, as well as steaks, pasta and a handful of Ethiopian dishes.

Roomi Burger BURGERS $

(Map p46; Cameroon St; burgers from Birr80, pizzas from Birr90; ⊙9am-10pm) Supersized burgers are the obvious highlight of this place, which is a cross between a fast-food joint and a pavement cafe, but pizzas and other dishes also light up the menu if you're craving an *injera*-free day.

Raizel Café INTERNATIONAL $

(Map p44; ☑011 1157 1641; Hailesilase St; breakfast Birr30-39, mains Birr35-65; ⊙7am-9.30pm) This slick modern cafe speedily serves pastries, pizza and sandwiches to a fashionable, young crowd; canoodling local couples hide in the shadows upstairs. It's one of several similar places around here.

★Galani Cafe CAFE $$

(☑091 144 6265; www.galanicafe.com; Salite Mehret Rd; breakfast Birr75-110, brunch Birr170, mains Birr85-170; ⊙8.30am-7pm Thu-Sun; ☑) Best known as Addis' coolest cafe, Galani also serves up fabulous food such as raw cauliflower salad, sweet and savoury crepes, tacos and the city's best brunch (10am to 1pm weekends). The setting is classy and casual.

★Lime Tree INTERNATIONAL $$

(Map p38; Guinea Conakry St; mains Birr78-130, Sun brunch Birr270; ⊙7am-9pm) It may have moved locations but Lime Tree remains one of the hippest places to have a light lunch. Lunch specials range from chicken shwaram (Monday and Wednesday) to Asian wok dishes (Tuesday), Mexican (Thursday) or pad-Thai (Friday\). The Sunday buffet brunch (10.30am to 2pm) is an expat institution. They also do great pastries, panini, felafel, juices and pizzas all day Saturday.

★Kategna ETHIOPIAN $$

(Map p46; ☑091 152 0183; off Bole Rd (Africa Ave); mains Birr60-160; ⊙8am-10pm) A pleasingly modern take on the traditional Ethiopian restaurant, Kategna feels like a classy urban cafe with its soothing colour scheme, low wooden stools and well-to-do young crowd. The menu covers all corners of the Ethiopian culinary scene and does so exceptionally well – their special *kitfo* (like an Ethiopian version of steak tartare) is one highlight among many.

★Sana'a Restaurant MIDDLE EASTERN $$

(Map p46; ☑091 151 1899; Gabon St; mains Birr65-285; ⊙8am-10pm) For both the local Muslim and Christian communities, this busy place is a lunchtime institution – queues for a table can form out the door. The reason they all flock here? Good, honest Yemeni fare, including spicy hot *salta* (a highland stew/soup) and the house special, Yemeni-style chicken and rice. The service is fast and furious and the food is worth crossing town for.

★La Mandoline FRENCH $$

(Map p46; ☑092 132 8507, 011 662 9482; off Mike Leyland St; mains Birr130-280; ⊙closed Mon) This upper-crust French restaurant serving superb and authentic, traditional French dishes is still one of the best restaurants in the capital. Try an excellent salad for starter, a delicious steak with Roquefort sauce for main and crème brûlée for dessert, and you won't know you're not in La Belle France.

ARTIST AFEWERK TEKLE

Born in 1932, Afewerk Tekle was one of Ethiopia's most distinguished and colourful artistic figures. Educated at the Slade School of Art in London, he later toured and studied in continental Europe before returning to work under the patronage of Emperor Haile Selassie. A painter, sculptor and designer, he was also a master fencer, dancer and toastmaster.

Proud to have 'survived three regimes' (when friends and peers did not), Tekle's life was hardly without incident. In almost cinematic style, a 'friendly' fencing match turned into an attempt on his life, and a tussle over a woman led to his challenging his rival to a duel at dawn. In the royal court of the emperor, he once only just survived an assassination attempt by poisoned cocktail.

The artist famously made his own terms and conditions: if he didn't like the purchaser he wouldn't sell, and his best known paintings must be returned to Ethiopia within a lifetime. He even turned down over US$12 million for the work considered his masterpiece, *The Meskel Flower*.

Afewerk Tekle died in Addis Ababa at the age of 80 in April 2012.

The French owner works in the kitchen and stalks the dining area checking everything is just perfect. And, frankly, it pretty much is. Take a taxi to/from the restaurant after dark.

★ Itegue Taitu Hotel
ETHIOPIAN $$

(Map p44; ☑ 011 156 0787; www.taituhotel.com; mains Birr44-120, lunch buffet Birr70; ☺ 7am-10pm, buffet noon-3pm; ☑) If you've travelled overland to Addis Ababa, and eaten in a succession of cheap local restaurants serving less-than-inspiring *injera*, then reward yourself with high-quality, delicious Ethiopian fare served up in the refined and stately atmosphere of this hotel's renovated dining room. Its bargain-priced vegan lunchtime buffet is immensely popular with both foreigners and well-to-do locals.

Kuriftu Diplomat Restaurant
INTERNATIONAL $$

(Map p46; ☑ 011 618 4363; Bole Rd (Africa Ave); mains Birr99-245; ☺ 11am-11pm) Feel on top of the world and enjoy the views over the city at this 5th-floor restaurant inside the Boston Day building. The menu, which takes in Ethiopian dishes as well as steaks, Mexican and pastas, spans the world in all its culinary loveliness. Sadly, it also has the world's most uncomfortable chairs!

Lucy Gazebo & Restaurant
INTERNATIONAL $$

(Map p34; ☑ 011 111 8156; King George VI St; mains Birr90-190; ☺ 8am-10pm; ☑) Next to the National Museum and a favourite haunt of locals, expats and museum-visiting tourists, this bright and airy restaurant with alfresco garden dining serves pastas (some vegetarian options), curries and good Ethiopian fare – among the 15 local dishes, we recommend the special *kitfo* or the *Beg tibs* (sauté lamb with vegetables). However, you do pay for the location.

They sometimes have live music in the evenings from Thursday to Saturday, plus they win the prize for one of the strangest mottos we've come across – 'the food is nice but watch out for the bones'.

17 17
ETHIOPIAN $$

(Map p46; Cameroon St; 1kg of meat Birr175; ☺ noon-midnight) Come dinner and lunch, this local option sees few tourists and is alive with action. Tables spill onto a large courtyard topped by flowering vegetation. Buy a big hunk of meat from the butcher out front, then have it barbecued and served with spice and *injera* (or you could just eat it raw). Wash it all down with a beer or three.

Antica Restaurant
PIZZA $$

(Map p46; ☑ 091 174 8675; off Cape Verde St; pizzas Birr80-205, mains Birr140-210; ☺ noon-10pm) Watch chefs manoeuvre airborne dough while you wait for your thin-crust pizza – we reckon they're Addis' best. There are two-dozen pizzas on the menu – toppings range from anchovies and capers to prosciutto and sausage – but there are also dishes like pasta, grilled fish and pork ribs. They also do home delivery and there's a bar downstairs that comes alive in the evening.

China Bar & Restaurant
CHINESE $$

(Map p38; ☑ 011 551 3772; Ras Desta Damtew St; mains Birr81-160; ☺ 11.30am-3pm & 6-10pm Mon-Sat, 11.30am-10pm Sun) If you're craving something sweet or sour, this central Chinese restaurant, just around the corner from Meskal Sq, is the most convenient place in town. The atmosphere is slightly stilted and the food good without rocking our world, but you're not exactly spoilt for choice when it comes to Asian cooking around here.

Jewel of India
INDIAN $$

(Map p46; ☑ 011 557 2510; www.jeweladdis.com; off Gabon St; mains Birr80-250; ☺ 11.30am-11pm; ☑) This Indian-run restaurant specialises in tandoori dishes – with more than 150 menu items to choose from, it's difficult to know where to start, but whatever you opt for is certain to tickle your taste buds in just the right way. And what a treat it is to taste spicy food with texture and form rather than just heat!

Elsa Restaurant
ETHIOPIAN $$

(Map p46; ☑ 091 250 2274; Mike Leyland St; breakfast Birr40-80, mains Birr50-130, 1kg of meat Birr75; ☺ 7am-10pm; ☑) This simple outdoor restaurant receives high marks from locals, expats and tourists alike for its quality Ethiopian fare. The *yetsom beyaynetu* (variety of fasting foods) is perfect for vegetarians, while *yedoro arosto* (roast chicken) and *gored gored* (raw, cubed and unmarinated meat) or *tere sega* (raw meat) assuage carnivorous cravings. Half the neighbourhood comes here for an afternoon drink. After dark, take a taxi to and from the door.

Backyard
INTERNATIONAL $$

(Map p46; ☑ 011 467 3501; Meskal Flower Rd; mains Birr80-175; ☺ 7am-11pm) In an unpromising building by the side of a busy road, Backyard surprises with its softly lit interior, light pastas and salads, and with the steaks for which it's most renowned – they're heaven indeed during the fasting period. Prices are reasonable, too.

Serenade
MEDITERRANEAN **$$**
(Map p44; ☑ 091 120 0072; off Ummar Semetar St; breakfast Birr30, mains Birr125; ⊘ 8.30am-8pm Mon-Sat) Having moved to a tranquil location in the grounds of Addis' Alliance Française complex, this classy Mediterranean eatery does a creative menu of Beirut-meets-Milan dishes – try the ginger-garlic fish or the baked duck. The setting, with a gallery of revolving art works next door, is lovely.

Rico's Restaurant, Pizzeria & Bar
INTERNATIONAL **$$**
(Map p46; ☑ 011 553 9462; Bole Rd (Africa Ave); mains Birr75-135; ⊘ 9am-10pm) A brightly lit place serving everything from Moroccan kebabs to minestrone soup, plus the oddly named 'farmer's wife' steak. Rico's also does a handful of Ethiopian staples.

★ Yod Abyssinia
ETHIOPIAN **$$$**
(Map p46; ☑ 091 121 6127, 011 661 2985; www.yodethiopia.com; off Cameroon St; mains Birr160-385; ⊘ 10am-midnight) Yes, it's touristy, but they sure put on a show at Yod Abyssinia. The large dining area is crammed with low wooden stools that all face a stage; at around 7.30pm, musicians, dancers and singers perform traditional acts from around Ethiopia. The food, too, is some of the best traditional food and it's a good place to try *tej* (honey wine).

All the Ethiopian staples are here with photos to help you decipher your *tibs* from your *kitfo,* but there are some rarely seen dishes as well, such as the goat cooked with onions, garlic and seasoned butter. Friendly service, too.

★ Avanti Restaurant & Wine Bar
ITALIAN **$$$**
(Map p46; ☑ 091 152 2660; off Bole Rd (Africa Ave); mains Birr170-255; ⊘ noon-2.30pm & 6-11pm) Recently moved to an unprepossessing suburban back street, Avanti is a quiet and classy place that serves some of the best Italian food in the city. There's much on the menu to turn the head, but we particularly enjoyed the baked tortellini with smoked chicken and ricotta. There's an impressive wine list (Birr500 for the average bottle).

Habesha 2000
ETHIOPIAN **$$$**
(Map p46; ☑ 091 283 8383; www.2000habesha.net; off Cameroon St; mains Birr230-350; ⊘ 10am-midnight) One of a handful of traditional theatre-restaurants in town, the excellent Habesha 2000 has low-slung wooden seating, a full portfolio of traditional Ethiopian (and, refreshingly, only Ethiopian) dishes to choose from, and live traditional musicians, singers and dancers from 8pm every night; you could come here for lunch, but you'd be missing half the fun.

Shaheen
INDIAN **$$$**
(Map p38; ☑ 011 517 1717; www.shaheenaddis.com; Sheraton Hotel, Itegue Taitu St; mains Birr300-900; ⊘ noon-3pm & 7-11.30pm; ☑) Set within the Sheraton's confines, Shaheen is Addis Ababa's most sophisticated Indian restaurant. The decor in the restaurant is grand and the melange of Indian curries and tandooris is vast. The Ajwani Machi Curry (tandoor-grilled Nile perch in a carom-seed-tempered onion-and-tomato curry) is as good as it sounds.

Stagioni
ITALIAN **$$$**
(Map p38; ☑ 011 517 1717; www.stagionirestaurant.com; Sheraton Hotel, Itegue Taitu St; mains Birr300-850; ⊘ noon-3pm & 7-11.30pm) If either Nile perch, artichoke, capsicum, olives, white wine sauce, basil polenta and vegetables, or linguine served with mixed seafood, garlic, chili and Pinot Grigio make your stomach quiver with excitement, slide into this great Italian restaurant. Quite simply, you won't find better Italian food outside the motherland.

Ristorante Castelli
ITALIAN **$$$**
(Map p44; ☑ 011 157 1757; Mahatma-Gandhi St; mains Birr140-300; ⊘ noon-2.30pm & 7-10.30pm Mon-Sat) Very much an Addis institution, this Italian restaurant has fed Swedish royalty, Bob Geldof, Brad Pitt, Angelina Jolie and US presidents. The food is (of course) good, perhaps even the best Italian in Addis. Wines from the owners' Piedmont region dominate with a rogue Chianti in the mix, while direct-from-Italy cured meats nicely complement the pasta. Reservations recommended.

The atmosphere can be a tad stuffy, and service can be offhand – in the finest Italian tradition.

ADDIS ABABA EATING

🍷 Drinking & Nightlife

You won't go thirsty in Addis Ababa. Sip some of the world's best (and cheapest) coffee, down a healthy juice or simply sway home after swallowing your share of *tej*.

Cafes

Addis is currently experiencing a mass spawning of cafes. At the centre of the scene are the Piazza and Bole Rd areas. Many are cookie-cutter rip-offs of Western-style coffee shops, but among the dross are some fine places – some recalling bygone days in small-town Italy, others are cool and hip hangouts for the city's growing middle class.

★Tomoca   CAFE
(Map p44; Wavel St; coffee from Birr10; ⊙ 6.30am-8.30pm Mon-Sat, 6.30am-6pm Sun) Ahh, if only all cafes were like this! Coffee is serious business at this great high-stooled Italian cafe (around since 1953) in Piazza. The beans are roasted on site (you can literally smell them from a block away) and Tomoca serves what's likely the capital's best coffee. Beans are also sold by the half-kilo and there's an Ethiopian coffee map on the wall.

★Galani Cafe   COFFEE
(☑ 091 144 6265; www.galanicafe.com; Salite Mehret Rd; coffee Birr27-40; ⊙ 8.30am-7pm Thu-Sun) This one's worth taking a taxi across Addis for. A refreshingly cool and contemporary space, Galani serves up Ethiopia's finest barista-poured coffees, from espresso to picolino and from hand-drip filter coffee to cold coffees. It's also a fine restaurant and dynamic cultural space with art exhibitions, a shop selling coffee, honey and the like, and coffee tastings or 'cuppings'.

Choche Fine Coffee Plc   CAFE
(Map p38; off Haile Gebreselassie Rd, Old Train Station; coffee from Birr12; ⊙ 8am-7pm) In a quiet garden next to Addis' delightfully decaying old train station, Choche does great coffee and is for those who like to enjoy it outdoors. Service could be friendlier.

Mokarar   COFFEE
(Harar; Map p44; Belay Zeleke Rd; coffee from Birr9; ⊙ 7am-9pm) Another of Piazza's cool old coffee haunts, Mokarar (the sign in Amharic says Harar – it's opposite Hotel Soramba) has stand-up stools and serves nothing but great coffee, all roasted right here. It's as simple and as wonderful as that.

La Parisienne   CAFE
(Map p46; Gabon St; pastries Birr15-30; ⊙ 6am-8pm) If you're staying in the Bole Rd part of town (in fact, even if you're not), then there's only one place for breakfast and that's this megapopular terrace cafe with superb coffee, fair impersonations of croissants and freshly squeezed orange juice. There are several other branches throughout the city but this one is considered the best.

THE ABYSSINIAN LIONS OF ADDIS

The rather grim enclosures of Addis Ababa Zoo (which was closed for reconstruction works at the time of research) may seem like an unusual place from which to receive exciting news from the world of lions. But in 2012 researchers made a remarkable discovery: the zoo's lions may represent the last of a genetically distinct sub-species of lion – the Abyssinian lion.

Scientists had long thought the Addis lions to be different – they are generally smaller and stockier than other lions, and the Addis males have manes that continue down under their torso and along the belly. When scientific samples were taken, the results, published in the *European Journal of Wildlife Research,* revealed that no other known lions possess the same DNA.

The lions descend from five male and two female lions that came from Emperor Haile Selassie's private collection when he established the zoo in 1948. Controversy surrounds where the lions originally came from. The royal palace was adamant at the time that the zoo's lions derived from a source population in southwestern Ethiopia, although scientists have always disputed the claim. While calling for better protection and a captive breeding program for these, the last lions of their kind, scientists have also begun the search for similar populations in the wild. One promising possibility is the lion population of **Babille Elephant Sanctuary** (p200) and surrounding areas in the east of the country – the lions from Babille are known for their black manes – although no results have yet emerged from the scientific quest to track down wild Abyssinian lions.

If the waitresses could only develop more of a Gallic 'I can't be bothered to serve you' shrug then you'd think you were on the Champs-Élysées.

Cup Cake Delights Cafe   CAFE
(Map p46; ☑ 094 735 9279; off Bole Rd (Africa Ave); cupcakes Birr28-32; ⊙ 8am-8pm) Red Velvet. Caribbean Breeze. Vanilla Fever. Brunette. The bright-and-bubbly names and flavours of the cupcakes on sale here are highly appropriate for a cafe that is in itself a bright-and-bubbly place full of Addis' hopeful and young. However, if we have one criticism it's that they've gone a little overboard with the amount of icing atop each cake.

If you can't face a cupcake, the peanut-butter cookies rock.

National Café   CAFE
(Map p38; Gambia St; coffee Birr10; ⊙ 7am-9pm) An ever-popular coffee institution that's little more than a dark hole in the wall. For those not afraid of daylight, there's also a few sun-grabbing tables out on the pavement.

Oslo Cafe   CAFE
(Map p44; Dejazmach Jote St; pastries Birr16-28; ⊙ 7am-8.30pm) It's painted luscious lip-gloss red and is easily the most popular of the numerous bright, modern Western-style coffee shops around the Piazza area.

Pubs & Bars
Addis Ababa's bar scene is becoming ever more cosmopolitan and diverse, though remember this is still no Nairobi when it comes to the quantity and quality of bars – many are hole-in-the-wall dives where all but the most thick-skinned would feel uneasy. However, a growing middle class and increasing numbers of expats have led to some swanky joints, the majority of which are found in and around Bole Rd.

Small local drinking holes charge Birr30 for a bottle of beer, while established bars can charge up to Birr50. Most places are open until 2am during the week, and 5am on the weekend.

Black Rose   BAR
(Map p46; ☑ 011 663 9884; Bole Rd (Africa Ave); ⊙ 5.30pm-2.30am Mon-Sat, to 12.30am Sun) Hiding in a modern building above the Boston Day Spa and downstairs from Kuriftu Diplomat Restaurant, this plush bar possesses a cool vibe and a refined clientele. Music ranges from Ethiopian to Western and Indian, and it's a really classy place to spend an evening.

Beer Garden   BAR
(Map p46; off Bole Rd (Africa Ave); ⊙ 11am-11pm Sun-Thu, to midnight Fri & Sat; 🖈) If your tipple is beer then at the German-flavoured Beer Garden you can sit on a long bench and get 3L of the golden liquid for Birr181 or a 1L for Birr63. They also do German bar snacks like bratwurst. Parents will appreciate the (slightly overgrown) children's play park out front.

Juice Bars
Most of Addis Ababa's cafes serve freshly squeezed juices or slushy blends of everything from strawberries to avocado, but you'll also come across some dedicated juice bars in the city.

Prime Juice House   CAFE
(Map p46; off Haile Gebreselassie Rd; juices from Birr35) Bored of avocado and mango juices? Then you'll think this place, with such exotics as Energiser (banana, strawberry and yogurt), rocks. We'd even go so far as to say it has the best juice in town.

Tej Bets
If authentic experiences are what you're after, there's no better place than a *tej bet* to down the famed golden elixir (honey wine). Most are open from 10am to around 10pm, but are busiest in the evening. They're the traditional haunt of men, so women should keep a low profile. They never have signs, so you'll have to ask locals to point them out.

★ Topia Tej Bet   BAR
(Map p46; off Haile Gebreselassie Rd; half/full litre tej Birr60/120; ⊙ 10am-9.30pm) Off Haile Gebreselassie Rd, tucked up an alley behind the Axum Hotel, this is Addis' top *tej bet* and the only one to serve pure-honey *tej*. Signposted only in Amharic (as one local assured us, 'after one glass, foreigners start talking Amharic') but with menus in English, it's a congenial place with tables surrounding a tiny garden. The smallest serve is a half litre...

Nightclubs
Club Platinum & Lounge   CLUB
(Map p46; off Cameroon St; Birr50; ⊙ 9pm-dawn Thu-Sat) Packed every weekend with teenagers and 20-somethings, this place plays the usual mix of hip-hop, reggae, African and other music. Beers are a hefty Birr100.

It's close to the Edna Mall (where the Matti Multiplex is).

Memo Club
CLUB

(Map p38; Birr50; ⊙ 9am-2am Sun-Thu, 9am-dawn Fri & Sat) About 200m west of Bole Rd (Africa Ave), this is another of Addis Ababa's hot spots. Cosy seats, red lights and the odd full-length mirror surround the circular dance floor, which usually reverberates with African and Western tunes. Sadly, it's also popular with expats shopping for prostitutes.

Club H2O
CLUB

(Map p46; ☎ 011 663 2828; www.clubh2oaddis. com; Mike Leyland St; Birr50; ⊙ 7pm-late Tue-Sun) A pulsating nightclub downstairs from Yoly Hotel, Club H2O kicks things off with a more sedate Happy Hour: 7pm to 10pm with live jazz to keep things down tempo. Things get going after that with live bands then DJ-spun tunes until close to dawn. Friday is African night – otherwise, the music is the usual Afro-Western mix.

Stockholm
CLUB

(Map p46; off Cameroon St; Birr50; ⊙ 9am-late) One of the coolest clubs of the moment, Stockholm has a languid lounge atmosphere early in the night with the usual blend of Western (hip-hop, R&B, Reggae), Indian and African music as the night wears on. There's occasional live music, too.

Club Illusion
CLUB

(Map p38; cnr Ras Desta Damtew & Itegue Taitu Sts; Birr50; ⊙ 9pm-dawn Thu-Sat) This is Addis Ababa's most raucous club and you need to be pretty thick skinned to survive! It's in the basement of the Ambassador Cinema. There's occasional live music. Beer costs an outrageous Birr100.

Flirt
CLUB

(Map p46; off Cameroon Rd; ⊙ 9pm-2am Sun-Thu, to 5am Fri & Sat) A pulsating club, playing a little bit of this and little bit of that in rather plush surrounds.

☆ Entertainment

The free publication *What's Out!* and the website Addis All Around (www.addis allaround.com) highlight upcoming events on the city's entertainment scene. *What's Out!* is available (haphazardly) at large hotels, smart restaurants, art galleries and the Tourist Information Centre.

Jazz Clubs

La Gazelle Piano Bar
JAZZ

(Map p46; Bole Rd (Africa Ave); ⊙ 7pm-late) This dark and moody bar has live jazz every night and it's far more mellow than most other Addis nightspots, even after the band finishes and a DJ takes over.

Traditional Music, Dance & Theatre

Music and dance are perhaps the most accessible entry points into traditional Ethiopian culture, with restaurants putting on shows in the evenings – try Yod Abyssinia (p53) or Habesha 2000 (p53).

An *azmari bet* is also atmospheric places to catch both music and dance. What in the world is an *azmari bet*? It's a place where interactive live performances take place by a performer similar to a minstrel who improvises amusing song and poetry.

★ Fendika Azmari Bet
LIVE MUSIC

(Map p38; ☎ 091 154 7577; Zewditu St; ⊙ 7pm-late) This *azmari bet* rivals any in Addis. It's littered with Ethiopian cultural items and always offers a good time (whether you understand what's going on or not). They also do live jazz as well as DJ-spun Ethiopian music.

Yewedale
LIVE MUSIC

(Map p38; Zewditu St; ⊙ 7pm-late) Thanks to some of the city's best *azmaris* performing here, Yewedale is resoundingly popular and you may have trouble finding a seat. The sign is in Amharic only, but it's opposite the Samsung shop and next to the Canon shop.

Destino Dance Company
DANCE

(☎ 091 114 5571, 093 669 0954; www.destinodance. org) This innovative social project trains young local dancers from underprivileged backgrounds (including some with disabilities) in traditional Ethiopian dance. They put on occasional performances (check the website for details) and have plans for a new dance festival in 2017. They also run classes in Ethiopian contemporary dance.

City Hall Theatre & Cultural Centre
THEATRE

(Map p44; ☎ 011 155 0520; Fitawrari Gebeyehu St; tickets Birr60-100) A plush 1000-seat place in the Piazza, which shows productions on Tuesday and Friday. Sometimes there's traditional Ethiopian music on public holidays.

National Theatre
THEATRE

(Map p38; ☎ 011 515 8225; Gambia St) This impressive building, with its massive marble and bronze entrance hall (and the odd pigeon), hosts theatre most weekends at 5pm.

Hager Fikir Theatre THEATRE
(Map p44; ☑ 011 111 9820; John Melly St; tickets Birr50) Hager Fikir occasionally stages theatre, musicals and dancing.

Cinema

Cinema is more popular than ever in Addis Ababa – even pushing theatre out of most theatres. Most films are in English or have English subtitles (some have both!).

There is no more atmospheric place than the imposing National Theatre to catch a film. Hollywood showings are normally fairly old.

★**Alliance Éthio-Française d'Addis-Abeba** CINEMA
(Alliance Française; Map p44; ☑ 011 155 0213; www.allianceaddis.org; Wavel St; free-Birr80) As is almost always the case with French cultural centres, this centre hosts an exciting and diverse range of art-house films, experimental theatre, gallery exhibitions, opera and world music. There's also a French-language library, French lessons and, for French speakers, Amharic lessons.

Matti Multiplex CINEMA
(Edna Mall; Map p46; www.ednamall.net; off Cameroon St; Birr80) The multiplex cinema inside the Edna Mall shows all the big-ticket Hollywood, Bollywood, Nollywood and local films, including those in 3D.

Ambassador Cinema CINEMA
(Map p38; Ras Desta Damtew St; Birr30) An institution, this central cinema puts on the usual diet of action-packed and slightly passé Hollywood movies. Films are shown daily in three sessions.

🛍 Shopping

The spectrum of prices and quality of goods for sale in the Ethiopian capital is vast. You'll find most of the cheap souvenir stalls along or around Churchill Ave and in Piazza – haggling is always recommended.

★**St George Interior Decoration & Art Gallery** ARTS & CRAFTS
(Map p38; ☑ 011 551 0983; www.stgeorgeofethiopia.com; Itegue Taitu St; ⊙9am-1pm & 2.30-6.30pm Mon-Sat) One of Addis Ababa's classiest places to shop, St George has everything from antique silver crosses and contemporary textiles to wide-ranging books about Ethiopia and designer jewellery. Everything here, both modern and traditional, is exquisite and it's worth a wander.

Gallery 21 ARTS & CRAFTS
(Map p38; Churchill Ave; ⊙10am-6pm Mon-Sat) Of all the shops/stalls north of Haileselassie Alemayehu on Churchill Ave, this gallery has the biggest selection (if you ask to see the back room) and the best-quality pieces, including a fine range of Ethiopian silver crosses and some nice replicas of Ethiopian religious art. Prices are higher than most.

Makush Art Gallery & Restaurant ARTS & CRAFTS
(Map p46; ☑ 091 141 8602; Bole Rd; ⊙9am-10pm) This gallery and restaurant has an excellent, carefully selected collection of high-quality furniture and paintings created by around 70 emerging and well-known Ethiopian artists.

Alert Handicraft Shop ARTS & CRAFTS
(Map p34; ☑ 011 321 1518; ⊙8am-noon & 1-5pm Mon-Fri, 8am-noon Sat) Here the Berhan Taye Leprosy Disabled Persons Work Group produces and sells beautiful handbags, pillow covers and wall hangings, each emblazoned with vibrant embroidery. The items are so Ethiopian. The shop is off Ring Rd, southwest of the city centre in the Alert Hospital compound; follow the signs to the canteen.

DON'T MISS

SOLEREBELS FOOTWEAR

Designer Bethlehem Tilahun Alemu set up **soleRebels Footwear** (Map p34; ☑ 091 059 1180; www.solerebels.com; 2nd fl, Adams Pavilion, Sar Bet; ⊙9.30am-7pm Mon-Sat) as a way of helping the unemployed but tremendously talented artisans in her Addis neighbourhood. Just eight years later, soleRebels is one of Ethiopia's best-known companies internationally and the world's first shoe company to have been certified by the World Fair Trade Organization (WFTO). All its shoes are made using locally sourced natural fibres, handmade fabric and, for soles, old car and truck tyres, and staff are paid up to four times the average wage in Ethiopia.

SoleRebels shoes are available in around 55 countries, including a flagship shop in Addis Ababa.

Abyssinia Honey King FOOD
(Map p46; ☑ 093 500 8727; Off Gabon St; ◷ 7am-9pm) ✈ Stocking local, naturally produced honeys with not a chemical in sight, this place is as good for your breakfast as it is for an unusual but authentically Ethiopian gift.

Bookworld BOOKS
(Map p38; ☑ 011 155 6200; Cnr Bole Rd (Africa Ave) & Haile Gebreselassie Rd; ◷ 9am-7pm Mon-Sat) City-centre branch of Addis' best bookshop chain, with a small but good selection of books on Ethiopia.

Shiro Meda Market MARKET
(Map p34; Entoto Ave; ◷ 8am-8pm) If you're interested in blankets, Ethiopian wedding attire or traditional clothing like a *shamma* (shawl worn by highlander men), head to this group of stalls lining Entoto Ave, a few hundred metres north of Botswana St and the Spanish embassy. This is where Addis locals do their shopping.

Bookworld BOOKS
(Map p44; Wavel St; ◷ 9am-7pm Mon-Sat) Branch of Addis' best bookshop chain, just north of the city centre.

Tourist Information Shop BOOKS, HANDICRAFTS
(Map p38; Meskal Sq; ◷ 8.30am-1pm & 2-5pm) This small, dusty shop has little to inspire but it does offer a handful of birding and other natural history books, which is quite the rarity here.

Africans Bookshop BOOKS
(Map p44; Hailesilase St; ◷ 9am-1pm & 2.30-7pm Mon-Sat) An OK place for second-hand books on Ethiopia, particularly those out of print. That said, selection is *very* limited.

ℹ Information

DANGERS & ANNOYANCES
Violent crime in Addis Ababa is fortunately rare, particularly where visitors are concerned. However, petty theft and confidence tricks are problematic.

The Merkato has the worst reputation for pickpockets abound – targeting not just *faranjis* (white foreigners) but Ethiopians as well. You are advised to leave hand luggage and jewellery in your hotel if you plan on visiting the Merkato.

Other spots where you should be vigilant include Piazza, where many foreigners get pickpocketed or mugged; Meskal Sq; minibus stands; outside larger hotels; and Churchill Ave, where adult gangs have been known to hang

around the National Theatre. Common gang ploys are to feign a fight or argument and, when one man appeals to you for help, the other helps himself to your pockets.

Don't let any of this scare you, though – Addis is very safe compared with many other African capitals. On a personal note, in all the time this author has spent in Addis he has never once felt even remotely threatened.

GAY AND LESBIAN TRAVELLERS
In Ethiopia (and Addis is no exception), homosexuality is severely condemned – traditionally, religiously and legally – and remains a topic of absolute taboo. Needless to say, Addis has no openly gay or lesbian bars or other establishments. For more information see LGBT Travellers (p282) in the Directory A-Z chapter.

INTERNET ACCESS
Every midrange and top-end hotel and an ever-increasing number of budget hotels in Addis has good wireless internet or a computer or two for guest use. There are also numerous internet cafes, but due to the fact that these places close, reopen and change their name at the speed of a megabyte we have refrained from naming specific cafes here. If you're in a hotel without internet then ask at reception for the nearest internet cafe.

MEDICAL SERVICES
Bethzatha Hospital (Map p38; ☑ 011 551 4470; ◷ 24hr) This quality private hospital, off Ras Mekonen Ave, is recommended by most embassies.

Black Lion Hospital (Map p38; ☑ 011 111 1111; ◷ 24hr) Public hospital

Ghion Pharmacy (Map p38; ☑ 011 551 8606; Ras Desta Damtew St; ◷ 8am-6pm Mon-Sat)

Hayat Hospital (Map p46; ☑ 011 662 4488; Ring Rd; ◷ 24hr) A reliable option near the airport.

St Gabriel Hospital (Map p46; ☑ 011 661 3622; Djibouti St; ◷ 24hr) This private hospital has good X-ray, dental, surgery and laboratory facilities.

Zogdom Pharmacy (Map p46; Bole Rd (Africa Ave); ◷ 8am-5.30pm Mon-Sat)

MONEY
You will have no trouble finding a bank in Addis to change cash and most Dashen Bank branches have ATMs that accept foreign Visa and MasterCard (but not Plus or Cirrus).

An increasing number of bank ATMs also accept international Visa cards. When withdrawing cash through an ATM with a foreign card you should select the Credit Card option (whether or not you actually have a credit card) otherwise the ATM may not issue funds.

Commercial Bank The branches at Arat Kilo, (Map p38; off Atwa St; ⊙8.30am-3.30pm Mon-Fri, 8.30am-11am Sat) Bole International Airport (Bole Rd (Africa Ave); ⊙24hr), **Haile Gebreselassie St** (Map p44; ⊙8.30am-3.30pm Mon-Fri, 8.30am-11am Sat), Churchill Ave (Map p38; cnr Churchill Ave & Sudan St; ⊙8.30am-11am & 1.30-3.30pm Mon-Fri, 8.30am-11am Sat), Josef Tito St (Map p38; ⊙8.30am-11am & 1.30-3.30pm Mon-Fri, 8.30am-11am Sat), Generapl Wingate St (Map p44; ⊙8.30am-3.30pm Mon-Fri, 8.30am-11am Sat) and Meskal Sq (Map p38; ⊙8.30am-11am & 1.30-3.30pm Mon-Fri, 8.30am-11am Sat) all change cash (US dollars and euros).

Dashen Bank (Map p46; Bole Rd (Africa Ave); ⊙8.30am-11am & 1.30-3.30pm Mon-Fri, 8.30am-11am Sat) Changes cash. Also offers Visa and MasterCard cash advances. Most have ATMs accepting international cards. Also a branch at Sheraton Hotel (Map p38, Itegue Taitu St; ⊙7-11am, noon-7pm & 8-11pm).

United Bank (Map p38; Menelik II Ave; ⊙6am-10.30pm) At the Hilton Hotel.

Wegagen Bank Bole Rd (Map p46; Bole Rd (Africa Ave); ⊙8.30am-11am & 1.30-3.30pm Mon-Fri, 8.30am-11am Sat); Meskal Sq (Map p38; ⊙8.30am-11am & 1.30-3.30pm Mon-Fri, 8.30am-11am Sat)

TOURIST INFORMATION

The useful, monthly magazine What's Out! lists restaurants, shopping venues, nightclubs and events in Addis Ababa.

Tourist Information Centre (Map p38; ☑011 551 2310; Meskal Sq; ⊙8.30am-12.30pm & 1.30-5.30pm) This office does its best to provide information about the city and elsewhere. It also has a few informative brochures about the rest of Ethiopia.

ℹ Getting There & Away

AIR
Domestic Flights

All domestic flights to/from Addis are operated by Ethiopian Airlines, with offices at **Bole Rd** (p290), **Gambia St,** (Map p38; ☑011 551 7000; www.ethiopianairlines.com; off Gambia St; ⊙8.30am-5pm Mon-Fri), **Hilton Hotel** (Map p38; ☑011 551 1540; www.ethiopianairlines.com; Hilton Hotel, Menelik II Ave; ⊙7am-8.30pm Mon-Sat, 8am-noon Sun) and **Piazza** (Map p44; ☑011 156 9247; www.ethiopianairlines.com; Hailesilase St; ⊙8.30am-5pm Mon-Sat). There are more offices scattered across the city.

Be alert: schedules change quite frequently and flight durations vary depending on which stopovers the plane is making en route.

ℹ ADDIS SCAMS

One scam that still seems to be snagging tourists is the 'siren scam'. It takes various forms, including offering you a 'cultural show' or a traditional coffee ceremony. Approaches are made to couples or groups, as well as to single males. Most commonly, the person approaching you is a young, well-dressed Ethiopian male, often claiming to be a student.

The venue is usually somebody's living room, where a hostess will promptly dish out copious quantities of *tej* (honey wine) and, perhaps, traditional dancers and musicians will perform. Suddenly the 'entertainment' comes to an end and an amount upwards of Birr1500 is demanded.

If you end up in a situation like this, offer to pay for anything you've consumed (a litre of quality *tej* shouldn't be more than Birr65), and if it's not accepted, threaten to call the police. The area around the hotels in the Piazza and Churchill Ave seem to be prime hunting grounds for potential victims.

An old ploy at the Merkato is for someone to step blindly into you, while another gently lifts your belongings in the subsequent confusion. A less subtle tactic now being used involves one person diving at your feet and holding your legs while another pilfers your pockets.

Another increasingly popular scam involves the delightful technique of a passer-by 'accidentally' spitting on you. He then makes a big fuss trying to wipe it off and in the process he (or an accomplice) relieves you of your wallet.

Another one involves someone waving a packet of tissues in your face pretending to sell it to you. As you're distracted the accomplices pilfer the contents of your pocket or bag. Still, at least you'll have some tissues with which to wipe off the spit!

International Flights

International flights and international airlines serve Addis Ababa, connecting the city with destinations across Africa, the Middle East and further afield.

BUS
Long-Distance Bus

Numerous long-distance buses depart from Addis' **Autobus Terra** (Long-Distance Bus Station; Map p34; Central African Republic St), northwest of Merkato. They're significantly cheaper than the newer 'luxury' services, but as most travel extremely fast and often at night, you take your life in your hands by travelling in them. Departures for most destinations leave around 5am, but you should be at the station by 4am if you've any hope for a ticket. Be very wary of pickpockets and bag snatchers.

'Luxury buses' now fly down the country's highways and they are proving immensely popular with both foreign visitors and locals. These services have reclining seats, air-con, on-board toilets and even free snacks and drinks. Book tickets up to a week beforehand if possible.

The best-established company is **Selam Bus** (Map p38; ☎ 011 554 8800, 011 554 4831; Meskal Sq; ⊙ 5am-5pm), whose station and ticket office is on Meskal Sq. It has the following daily services (all departing at 4.30am or 5am).

DESTINATION	FARE (BIRR)	DURATION (HR)
Bahir Dar	340	10
Dessie	245	8
Dire Dawa	320	8½
Gonder	420	13
Harar	330	8½
Jijiga	300	14
Jimma	205	5
Mekele	485	36

Possibly even slicker is **Sky Bus** (Map p44; ☎ 011 467 3331, 011 156 8080; http://skybus-ethiopia.com; Itegue Taitu Hotel; ⊙ 4.30am-5pm), which also leaves from Meskal Sq, but the ticket office is inside the Itegue Taitu Hotel. These buses are air-conditioned and have toilets, and breakfast is included in the ticket price. Book tickets up to a week beforehand if possible.

Sky Bus runs to the following services:

DESTINATION	FARE (BIRR)	DURATION (HR)	TIME
Bahir Dar	340	10	5am
Dire Dawa	293	8½	6am
Gonder	422	13	4.30am
Harar	300	8½	4.30am
Jimma	220	5	9.30am Tue, Thu, Fri & Sat

Short-Distance Bus

Short-distance buses run when full from Addis' **short-distance bus station** (Map p38; Ras Mekonen Ave) to Awasa (Birr165, four to five hours), Debre Zeyit (Birr75, 45 minutes), Lake Langano (Birr38, 4½ hours), Nazret (Birr90, two hours) and Shashemene (Birr165, four to five hours). For both Lake Langano and Ziway, take a bus to Shashemene and jump off at the turn-off. Awasa and Shashemene are also serviced from the **long-distance bus station**.

There are several services to Shashemene and Awasa after the first 6.30am departure, though they all leave before noon.

CAR & 4WD

Although it's possible to hire a self-drive car, you're usually restricted to driving only in Addis itself. Hiring a chauffeured 4WD, although expensive, removes most limits on where you can travel. Four-wheel drives are rented by almost all of Addis' travel agents.

MAJOR DOMESTIC FLIGHTS FROM ADDIS ABABA

DESTINATION	FARE (BIRR)	DURATION (HR)	FREQUENCY (DAILY)
Aksum	5200	2	1 direct, several nondirect
Arba Minch	3274	1½	2
Bahir Dar	4192	1	up to 6
Dire Dawa	3248	1	up to 5
Gambela	3791	1½	2
Gonder	4515	1½	2 direct, several nondirect
Jimma	2621	1	2
Lalibela	4295	2-2½	1 direct, several nondirect
Mekele	4026	1	3-5

WORTH A TRIP

ENTOTO MOUNTAINS

These mountains, just north of the city, are the site of Menelik's former capital. You'll find a couple sights of interest and a great viewpoint. At the summit you're close to 3200m above sea level. On the way up you may pass by the Women Fuel Wood Carriers Project, an organisation set up to protect the rights of women gathering firewood on the mountain. Traditional clothing items, hats and baskets can be purchased. They can be difficult to find and there are no signs – the only way is to ask.

The octagonal **Entoto Maryam Church** (Map p34; Entoto Mountains; combined ticket for church compound, palace & museum per person Birr100; ☉ for Sunday Mass, compound gate 8.30am-6pm) hosted Menelik's coronation, but sadly for a church of such historical significance, the only time you can catch a glimpse of the interior is during Sunday Mass, and even then, casual visitors (as opposed to genuine worshipers) are not welcome. Down the hill on the back side of the building are the remains of Menelik's rather modest palace.

The rather dusty **Entoto Maryam Museum** (Map p34; Entoto Mountains; combined ticket for church compound, palace & museum per person Birr100; ☉ 8.30am-6pm) has the usual collection of royal garments, valuable coins, ceremonial drums, poor lighting and bored-looking attendants, but there are some highlights which include the royal bed and royal crown once used by Menelik II.

To get to Entoto, take a taxi or minibus to the terminus of Entoto Ave from Arat Kilo. From there another minibus will take you to Entoto Maryam Church. You might also be able to flag a minibus from Shiro Meda Market. If you're in Ethiopia on an organised tour and your time here involves a tour of Addis, your driver may well bring you up here – if not, ask.

MINIBUS

With sealed roads now all but connecting Addis Ababa with Bahir Dar and Gonder, private minibus services are starting to crop up. They're very fast (not always a good thing!) and cut journey times down to eight hours for Bahir Dar and 10 hours for Gonder. Head to **Autobus Terra** for services.

Minibuses from Piazza, Mexico Sq and Meskal Sq serve the airport daily from 6am to 8pm (Birr10). Some charge an additional Birr5 for excess luggage.

ⓘ Getting Around

Though a sprawling city, Addis Ababa is – with a little patience – fairly easy to get around.

TO/FROM THE AIRPORT

Bole International Airport (Map p34; ☎ 011 551 7000; www.addisairport.com) lies 5km southeast of the Addis city centre; both international and domestic flights depart from here. Most hotels, including many midrange hotels, offer a free shuttle service to/from the airport – always ask when making your hotel reservation.

Otherwise, from the airport, prices for foreigners are much higher than they are for locals and are normally quoted in US dollars (though they accept Birr). Heading about halfway along Bole Rd will cost around US$30 and to Piazza around US$40. A taxi association has a booth at the airport's exit. Taxi drivers belonging to this association have yellow taxis and they're probably your best bet for reliability.

BUS

Addis buses are considered poor man's transport. They're cheap but slow, run less regularly than the minibuses and are notoriously targeted by pickpockets. The minibuses are a much better bet.

CAR

Parking isn't usually too much of a problem in Addis Ababa. Most of the larger hotels and restaurants have guarded parking spaces and don't usually mind you leaving your car there. In other places, it's worth paying for a guard.

Whenever you park on the street a 'parking warden' (we're not sure how genuine they are) appears and leaves a little note on your windscreen noting the time of arrival and they then charge you based on that (per hour Birr1 to Birr2).

There are plenty of petrol stations scattered around town, including one on **Angola St**, near the French embassy.

MINIBUS

Addis Ababa is served by an extensive network of little blue-and-white minibuses, which are fast, efficient, cheap and a great way of getting around.

Minibuses operate from 5.30am to around 9pm (till 8pm Sunday). Journeys cost roughly Birr2 (though exact prices depend on the distance).

Minibus stops can be found near almost every major intersection. Major ones include Arat Kilo, De Gaulle Sq in Piazza, Meskal Sq, Ras Mekonen Ave near La Gare and in front of the main post office on Churchill Ave.

To catch the right minibus, listen to the destinations screamed by the *woyala* (attendants) hanging out the windows. 'Bole!', 'Piazza!' and 'Arat Kilo!' are the most useful to travellers. If confused, ask and someone will point you in the right direction.

TAXI

Most taxis in Addis operate from 6am to 11pm. Short journeys (up to 3km) usually cost foreigners Birr60 to Birr80 (more at night). Medium/long journeys cost Birr100/140. If you share a taxi with strangers, the normal fare is split between the group.

If you want to visit a lot of places in Addis Ababa, negotiate with a driver for a half- or full-day fare (Birr600 for a full day is pretty reasonable).

A 'city tour' lasting a couple of hours should cost around Birr300 to Birr350.

Taxis can be found outside larger hotels, as well as the National Theatre, national stadium and on De Gaulle Sq in the Piazza. At night, many line up outside the nightclubs.

Uber has yet to arrive in Addis, but the word is that they're not far away and will probably be operational some time in 2017.

TRAM

Addis Ababa's newly minted tram or light-rail system is little used by tourists, but it can be a useful way to avoid traffic congestion on the streets down below or alongside. Two lines – one roughly north–south, the other east–west – cross the city centre with 39 stations. Many of the stations are aimed more at locals than tourists, but it's worth knowing where they go just in case. Tickets cost between Birr2 and Birr6, depending on the distance you travel, and can be purchased at the stations. Be careful, however, as pickpockets are known to work the carriages.

North–South (Blue) Line Runs 16.9km from Menelik Square (north) to Kaliti (south). Useful stations at Menelik II Square, Meskal Square and Merkato.

East–West (Green) Line Runs 17.4km from Ayat in the east to Tor Hailch in the west. Stations include Meskal Square and Mexico Square.

Northern Ethiopia

Why Go?

For most visitors to Ethiopia, it's all about the north. More than anywhere else on Earth, northern Ethiopia has the ability to wow you day after day after day.

Known as the Historical Circuit, there are over two millennia's worth of ancient treasures scattered about, from giant obelisks and hidden tombs at Aksum to a collection of castles in and around Gonder, to unique churches in Lalibela, Tigray, Lake Tana and many other places. Not to be outdone by human mastery, Mother Nature really let her creative juices flow here. The Danakil Depression, an esteemed destination among adventure travellers, features a permanent lava lake and a bright-yellow sulphuric plain, while the Simien Mountains wrinkle the land with canyons and peaks with a beauty you'll struggle to find anywhere else in Africa.

Best Places to Eat

➜ Four Sisters (p83)

➜ Ben Abeba (p129)

➜ Wude Coffee (p70)

➜ Black Rose (p118)

➜ Karibu Kitchen & Bar (p118)

Best Places to Sleep

➜ Limalimo Lodge (p92)

➜ Gheralta Lodge (p115)

➜ Wukro Lodge (p115)

➜ Korkor Lodge (p115)

➜ Hotel Maribela (p129)

When to Go
Gonder

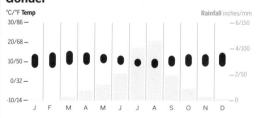

Jan Time for Timkat, the festival celebrating Jesus' baptism. Big in Gonder and Aksum.

May–Sep The rainy season doesn't stop travel, but it makes trekking tough.

Oct The best time to travel. The rain's mostly gone, but the land remains green and gorgeous.

Northern Ethiopia Highlights

1 Lalibela (p120) Immersing yourself in the mind-blowing rock-hewn churches.

2 Simien Mountains (p86) Trying not to lose your balance as you trek along the endless Abyssinian abysses with gelada monkeys for company.

3 Danakil Depression (p119) Smelling the sulphur and staring in disbelief at the thermometer in this otherworldly land.

4 Aksum (p93) Dreaming of hidden treasure in the gloom of ancient Aksumite tombs beneath glorious stelae.

5 Debre Damo (p106) Marvelling at the enduring power of faith as you climb to this ancient monastery.

6 Gonder (p75) Roaming the hallowed halls of the royal retreats, admiring the church paintings at Debre Berhan Selassie then dining at Four Sisters.

7 Rock-hewn Churches of Tigray (p107) Staring from Abune Yemata Guh then climbing to the monastery at Maryam Korkor.

8 Menz-Guassa Community Conservation Area (p131) Seeing an Ethiopian wolf in pristine habitat on a community trek far from the crowds.

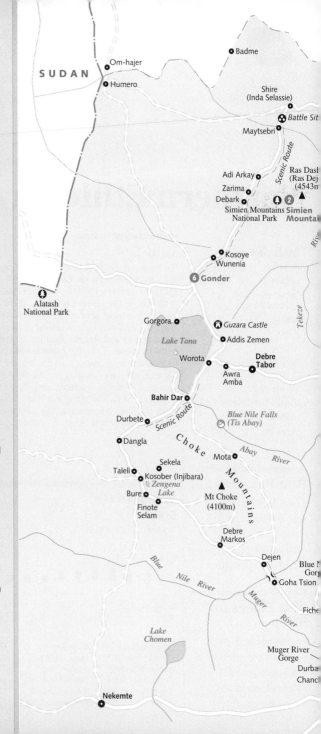

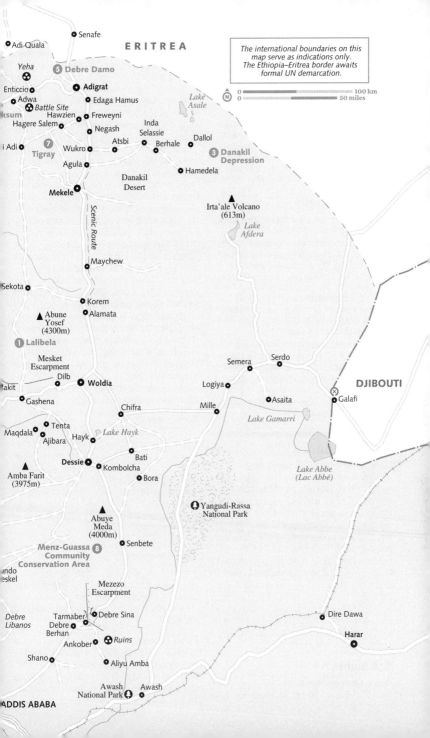

ℹ️ Getting There & Away

Ethiopian Airlines (p290) connects Addis Ababa with Bahir Dar, Gonder, Lalibela, Aksum and Mekele.

Most people who enter northern Ethiopia overland are travelling by bus or car (minibus or 4WD) from Addis Ababa, which sits conveniently at the bottom of the Historical Circuit. It's also possible to come from the Asaita region in eastern Ethiopia via roads to Woldia and Dessie. A rare few people access the Addis Ababa–Bahir Dar road from the western town of Nekemte. The only open border crossing is from Sudan at Metema, but it's sometimes closed to travellers.

ℹ️ Getting Around

Ethiopian Airlines has flights connecting Bahir Dar, Gonder, Lalibela, Mekele and Aksum.

The 2500km circular drive through the north is now nearly all sealed (though still expect some rough sections). The exception is the 45km from Debark to Zarima. This stunning stretch of road, along with a further 30km on to Adi Arkay, snakes down the western end of the Simien Mountains and is one of Africa's most beautiful roads. It makes the Blue Nile Gorge seem like a Sunday drive in comparison.

The only areas in which you'll have trouble finding regular public transport are the Simien Mountains National Park and around the rock-hewn churches of Tigray, though it's possible in both.

To visit the Danakil Depression, you must travel with a tour company.

Debre Libanos

Lying 100km north of Addis Ababa is one of Ethiopia's holiest sites. The original Debre Libanos (ደብረ ሊባኖስ) monastery was founded in the 13th century by Tekla Haimanot, a priest credited not only with the spread of Christianity in the highlands, but also the restoration of the Solomonic line of kings. Today he's one of Ethiopia's most revered saints. Since his time Debre Libanos has served as the principal monastery of the old Shoa region, and remains one of Ethiopia's largest and most important monasteries. Many Ethiopians make pilgrimages and some seek out its curative holy waters, said to be good for warding off evil spirits and for stomach disorders.

🅾 Sights

Debre Libanos Monastery　　　MONASTERY
(Birr200; ⊙8am-5.30pm) Although no trace of the 13th-century monastery remains (a casualty of the Muslim–Christian Wars), the modern site is set impressively beneath a waterfall-rich cliff (many of the monks live in caves up there) on the edge of the large Jemma River Gorge and is a peaceful place to wander. The present church was built in 1961 by Haile Selassie, against the wishes of the local priests, after hearing a prophesy that a new church would ensure a long reign.

The church is monumental and pretty awful on the outside, but the stained-glass windows are attractive.

Debre Libanos has one of the most interesting church museums in Ethiopia. Besides the usual ecclesiastical items there are Italian guns, giant cooking pots, crowns of past emperors and their wives, musical instruments and an old wooden shackle. Fifteen minutes up the hill from the monastery is the cave of Tekla Haimanot (the monastery's founder), where the saint is said to have done all his praying. It's also the source of Debre Libanos' famed holy water.

A monument in front of the church memorialises the hundreds of innocent priests, deacons and worshipers who were massacred here by the Italians following an assassination attempt on the notoriously brutal viceroy Graziani in 1937 (he was later imprisoned by the Italians as a war criminal for crimes against humanity).

Portuguese Bridge　　　BRIDGE
(Birr22) Though local guides insist the small stone-arch Portuguese bridge near Debre Libanos was erected by the Portuguese in the 16th century, it was actually built at the turn of the 19th century by Ethiopians, albeit in the old Portuguese style. The narrow span makes a pretty picture and the gushing (in the rainy season) cascade just below it is even more impressive.

🛏 Sleeping

Most people visit Debre Libanos on a day trip from Addis or as a stop en route between Addis and Bahir Dar. There is one decent place to stay if you decide to buck the trend.

Ethio-German Park Hotel　　　HOTEL $$
(☑ 0922-383490, 0911-978834; www.ethiogerman-park.com; r without/with view US$25/40; P 🛜) Just past the turn-off to the monastery along the main Addis–Bahir Dar road, this simple lodge makes the most of its gorge views and

is a popular pit stop for those driving north, and serves as a weekend getaway for residents of Addis Ababa. The more-basic-than-you'd-expect rooms have solar lights and hot water and those facing the gorge sport little porches.

❶ Getting There & Away

The monastery is 4.2km off the Addis–Bahir Dar road. Usually four minibuses run daily from Addis Ababa to the monastery (Birr105, two hours).

Bahir Dar

POP 348,529 / ELEV 1880M

Some people like to describe Bahir Dar (ባሕር ዳር) as the Ethiopian Riviera. The moniker sounds strange, but when you pull into town and see the wide streets shaded by palm trees and sweeping views across Lake Tana's shimmering blue waters, you'll perhaps understand. More than a block back from the shore, however, Bahir Dar is just another busy Ethiopian city.

The main reason to come here is to launch a boat excursion out onto Lake Tana (p72) to visit its monasteries, and to see the Blue Nile Falls (p81).

History

In the 16th and 17th centuries, various temporary Ethiopian capitals were established in the vicinity of Lake Tana. It was here that Jesuits attempted, with disastrous consequences, to impose Catholicism on the Ethiopian people. One moss-covered Jesuit building, which was built by the well-known Spanish missionary Pedro Páez, can still be seen in the compound of St George's monastery.

◉ Sights & Activities

Lounging lakeside is an essential part of the Bahir Dar experience. You'll often glimpse the flimsy, yet unsinkable *tankwa* canoe. Made from woven papyrus, they can take huge loads, including oxen! They're exactly the same as the papyrus boats depicted on the walls of ancient temples in Egypt. They're made in the village of **Weyto**, 4km northwest of town, but the men here will ask for ludicrous fees to watch them being made. You can also sometimes see the canoes being made at Debre Maryam monastery (p75).

Main Market   MARKET

(⊙ from 7am) If you can tear yourself away from the lake, visit the large and lively main market. It's busiest on Saturday – market day – when people stream into town from nearby villages. The delightful *agelgil* (goat-skin lunch boxes) are no longer sold in the market – try the **craft kiosks** near the main mosque – but just about everything else is, and getting lost is half the fun.

Blue Nile Bridge   BRIDGE

(Gonder Rd) You can only reach the famous outlet of the Blue Nile by boat, but you can get pretty close along the Gonder road, 2km out of town, where a bridge spans the river. You can see the dam that has ruined Blue Nile Falls and keep an eye out for hippos and crocodiles.

Martyrs Memorial Monument   MONUMENT

(Birr15; ⊙ museum 8.30am-5.30pm) Just past the bridge is a large Martyrs Memorial Monument dedicated to those who died fighting the Derg. Its fountain cascading down to the Blue Nile is quite the sight, especially if someone is having a wedding here and has paid to turn it on. The museum is full of photos, some labelled in English, from the resistance in Amhara Region.

Fish Market   MARKET

(⊙ from 6am) There's a one-table fish market in the mud-hut deacon's village behind St George's Church. The catch is brought in by *tankwa* in the morning and pelicans come to feed on the scraps in the afternoon.

WORTH A TRIP

BLUE NILE GORGE

Blue Nile Gorge Around 200km from Addis Ababa, one of Ethiopia's most dramatic stretches of road begins its serpentine descent to the bottom of the Blue Nile Gorge (አባይ ሸለቆ), 1km below. The gorge is traversed by a tortuous road with spectacular views in places, and a pair of bridges cross the river – the new Japanese suspension bridge handles traffic while the Italian original is now used by shepherds. Unfortunately the beauty on the southern side is frequently marred by cement-company quarries.

Bahir Dar

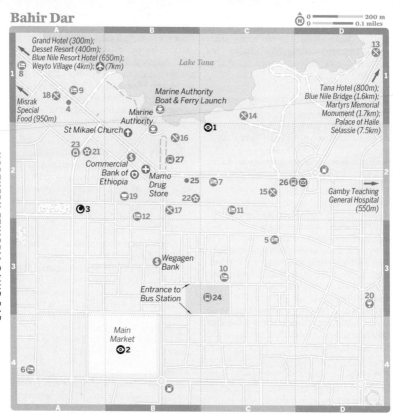

Bahir Dar

⊙ Sights
1 Fish Market	C2
2 Main Market	B4
3 Main Mosque	A2

⊕ Activities, Courses & Tours
4 Zelalem Memory	A1

⬚ Sleeping
5 Blue Nile Hotel	C3
6 Delano Hotel	A4
7 Dib Anbessa Hotel	C2
8 Jacaranda Hotel	A1
9 Kuriftu Resort & Spa	A1
10 Menen Hotel	C3
11 RahNile Hotel	C2
12 Tsehay Pension	B2

⊗ Eating
13 Castel-Kuriftu Wine House	D1
14 Lakeshore	C1
15 Lemat Restaurant	C2
16 Mango Park	B2
17 Wawi Pizzeria	B2
18 Wude Coffee	A1

⊙ Drinking & Nightlife
19 Karibu Cafe	B2
20 Pelican Wine House	D3

⊕ Entertainment
21 Amsal Mitike	A2
22 Balageru Cultural Club	B2

⬚ Shopping
23 Craft Kiosks	A2

ⓘ Transport
24 Bus Station	C3
25 Ethiopian Airlines	B2
26 Post Bus	C2
Selam Bus	(see 24)
27 Sky Bus	B2

★**Zelalem Memory** BOATING
(☑0913-122671; zelalemtadele@gmail.com) Our pick of the operators for boat trips to the monasteries on Lake Tana and to Blue Nile Falls. Has an office a few doors up from Wudu Coffee, but it's best to contact the owner, Zelalem Tadele, in advance of your arrival in town.

🛏 Sleeping

Bahir Dar has some excellent places to stay, and with older places closing down and newly built hotels springing up all the time, the possibilities just keep getting better.

Tsehay Pension HOTEL $
(☑0582-221550; s/d Birr230/280, with shared bathroom Birr150/200) Meticulous housekeepers and excellent prices make this city-centre spot popular. All rooms have satellite TV and the private showers have hot water. Unusually for Ethiopia, you don't need to be a couple to share a double room. The rooms with shared bathrooms are a little cell-like, but that's our only complaint.

Menen Hotel HOTEL $
(☑0582-263900; d Birr230-300; P) A reasonable place very near the bus station that offers clean rooms, fair value and offhand service. It's ideal if you've an early morning departure from the bus station, although check that's where your bus is leaving from before you make your booking. The lowest-priced rooms lack TVs and hot water and rooms in front can be very noisy.

Dib Anbessa Hotel HOTEL $
(☑0582-201436; d/tw incl breakfast Birr350/450; P@🛜) An older hotel with lots of carved wood giving it character. This doesn't extend into the rooms, but overlook the frayed carpets and you'll find that with their soft beds, satellite TV and balconies, they offer fair value.

★**Grand Hotel** HOTEL $$
(☑0582-208005; www.grandresortspabahirdar. com; s/d/ste US$40/60/110; P❄@🛜) Opened in 2015, this 16-floor, 125-room skyscraper has the best views in Bahir Dar – whether facing the lake or the town, you'll find it hard to tear yourself away from the window. The rooms are large, lovely and filled with light, and best of all, prices have fallen as much as threefold since the place opened – outrageous value.

RahNile Hotel HOTEL $$
(☑0582-207575; www.rahnilehotel.com; s/queen/king incl breakfast US$29/39/53; 🛜) Opened in 2015 with a decent city-centre location, RahNile gets the important things right. Modern, well-sized rooms are rather lovely, especially those with a king-sized bed, which come with a free 30-minute massage. All rooms include a buffet breakfast, free tea and coffee and a free airport shuttle. There's an on-site restaurant.

Delano Hotel HOTEL $$
(☑0582-200622; www.delanohotelbahardar.com; Addis Rd; s/d/tw from Birr780/845/990; P❄🛜) If you don't mind being a few blocks from the water, Delano is an excellent choice. The modern, immaculate and supremely comfortable rooms are some of the best in this price range and the rooms on the upper floors have views that stretch for miles. Service, too, is excellent.

Abay Minch Lodge LODGE $$
(☑0582-181039; www.abayminchlodge.com; off Gonder Rd; s/d from US$45/55; P🛜) In a lovely garden location 2km west of town (the turnoff is just after the Blue Nile Bridge if you're coming from town), Abay Minch Lodge has stone-and-thatch rondavels with smallish rooms. You get mosquito nets, satellite TV, hi-tech showers and friendly service, but the quoted rates are double what it used to charge – the current rates are about right.

Jacaranda Hotel HOTEL $$
(☑0582-209899; www.jacarandahotelbahirdar. com; s/d/tw/tr Birr762/1099/1199/1599; 🛜) Across the road from the lake, this fine modern place has nicely turned-out modern rooms, most with a balcony. The ones in the front building are best but noisier, while some in the back can be a tad claustrophobic – ask to see a few. It's an excellent midrange choice away from the city-centre scrum, but within easy walking distance of it.

Blue Nile Hotel HOTEL $$
(☑0582-202028; www.bluenilehotel.com; s/d Birr500/600; 🛜) Filling a niche between the real budget cheapies and pricier midrange options, the Blue Nile (not to be confused with the waterfront behemoth of similar name) has good rooms at a fair price in a decent location. Prices include breakfast, wifi and a free airport shuttle.

Tana Hotel HOTEL $$
(☏ 0582-200554; s/d US$38/51; P 🛜) Known for its sunset views, Tana's top selling point is the forested lakeside setting. Some funky touches, such as the goat-skin wall in the restaurant, brighten up the older building. Maintenance may not be Tana's strong point, and the hot water is only turned on mornings and early evenings, but you're here for the location. Birdwatchers will love the gardens.

⭐**Kuriftu Resort & Spa** RESORT $$$
(☏ 0582-264868, 0920-959797; www.kurifturesortsspa.com; s half board incl massage & reflexology session US$157-195, d US$194-228; P ❄ @ 🛜 ☃) There's lots of new luxe lodging going up in Bahir Dar, but this attractive spot will surely remain one of the best. Kuriftu's large, refined stone-and-wood cottages are filled with lovely furnishings and artistic touches. Be sure to request a lake-view room: they hardly cost any extra. The service is excellent and the shady grounds ooze relaxation.

Blue Nile Resort Hotel HOTEL $$$
(☏ 0582-222207; www.bluenileresorthotels.com; d/ste from US$137/171; P ❄ @ 🛜) Inhabiting its own peninsula, this expansive 127-room place has a prime location. You pay extra for a waterfront room (although all have some sort of lake view), but the walls that separate each room to provide privacy also block out much of the lake. The rooms are passable, motel-style affairs; the duplex suite is our pick, but you're still paying over the odds.

🍴 Eating

This being Bahir Dar you should have at least one meal lakeside. Desset Resort, Castel-Kuriftu Wine House and Lakeshore, which put you right on the shore, are our favourite lakeside spots; Tana Hotel has the best sunsets.

⭐**Wude Coffee** CAFE $
(mains Birr30-60; ⊘ 6am-10pm) For high-class Ethiopian fare in a chic city-style garden cafe, come to Wude Coffee, although it's just as good for a stiff macchiato. While the indoor tables are intimate and cosy, we prefer the outdoor perches.

Lemat Restaurant ETHIOPIAN $
(☏ 0918-706475; mains Birr40-130; ⊘ 7am-9.30pm) You don't see many tourists in here and the menu is only in Amharic, but that's precisely the point. Excellent local food brings the locals here in droves and you won't find better *tibs, kitfo* or *doro wat* anywhere in Bahir Dar. It's a simple place, but it's all about the food.

Wawi Pizzeria ITALIAN, ETHIOPIAN $
(mains Birr40-70, pizza Birr54-115; ⊘ 10am-9pm) You take your life in your hands climbing the rickety spiral staircase up to this 1st-floor pizzeria. Once there, as long as you're not in a hurry, join the crowd on the balcony for a pretty good pizza. There's also lasagne and chicken *tibs*.

Mango Park ETHIOPIAN $
(mains Birr30-80; ⊘ 6.30am-8.30pm) A popular lakeside spot for an afternoon drink, this rundown place is usually packed with local students and families, though the pelicans that once joined them have fled and the persistent boat touts in the area can soon wear thin.

Castel-Kuriftu Wine House ETHIOPIAN $$
(☏ 0582-263889; mains Birr40-120; ⊘ 9am-midnight) Right by the water and affiliated with the Kuriftu Resort, this fine place does excellent Ethiopian dishes with all the usual suspects – *tibs, firfir, kitfo* et al – present and nicely prepared. The soaring ceiling of the main dining area is an architectural stunner, but we prefer the more intimate, open-sided pavilions overlooking the lake from the garden.

Lakeshore ETHIOPIAN $$
(☏ 0918-760429; mains Birr55-110; ⊘ 6am-10pm) Down a rough dirt track and right by the lake, Lakeshore looks a little past its prime, but still serves what some locals claim to be the city's best seafood – order the grilled fish or fish *kitfo* and make up your own mind. Grab a table in the garden rather than the cavernous main dining area.

Misrak Special Food ETHIOPIAN $$
(☏ 0911-946034; mains Birr35-150; ⊘ 1-3pm & 7-10pm) Out in the west of town, far from the main tourist trail, Misrak Special Food has a lovely traditional setting on the 1st floor and excellent Ethiopian cooking. It does everything from *tibs wat* to meatball curry, and while there's not much English spoken, there is great coffee and a real air of authenticity.

Desset Resort EUROPEAN, ETHIOPIAN $$
(mains Birr35-110; ⊘ 7am-10pm) This popular restaurant really makes the most of its long landscaped shoreline. Both the *habesha*

(Ethiopian – try the fish *firfir*) and *faranji* (foreigner) dishes (try the roasted lamb or pizza) are quite good and the menu is bigger than normal. It's immediately northwest of the Grand Hotel.

Drinking & Nightlife

The Balageru Cultural Club serves *tej bet* (honey wine), along with laughs. If you want a drink that will knock you off your feet, visit the hole-in-the-wall *araki* (grain spirit) bars in the blocks north of the bus station.

For coffee, it's hard to beat Wude Coffee.

Karibu Cafe　　　　　　　　　　CAFE
(☺6.30am-9pm) One of Bahir Dar's best places for coffee, Karibu has low wooden stools, excellent coffee (from Birr9), tempting cakes and an overwhelmingly local clientele.

Pelican Wine House　　　　　WINE BAR
(☺5.30-10pm) A chemistry degree from Bahir Dar University led owner Yordanos into a life of wine and she now makes her own honey, date, mango, apple and grape varieties. The place is not quite what it was, but is still worth a look. It's signed only in Amharic, 500m south from the university gate on your left.

☆ Entertainment

Amsal Mitike　　　　　DANCE, LIVE MUSIC
(☺6pm-late) Unlike other more touristy places around town, this fine venue should do the trick. The focus here is more on live music and dance by well-known local performers and the crowd's almost entirely local.

Balageru Cultural Club　　　　COMEDY
(☑0918-784844; ☺7pm-2am) `FREE` If you'd like an entertaining cultural experience and a good laugh, visit this place. Various *azmari* (local minstrels who perform a mix of music and humour) do their thing nightly (from around 7.30pm to 2am) to the rapturous joy of locals. If you're brave enough to dance – if you're not, order a *tej bet* (honey wine) and you'll find all inhibitions drift away – you'll win lots of friends.

❶ Information

Women, accompanied by male companions or not, should not walk along the waterfront path as there can be serious hassle from men hanging out here. Don't walk anywhere in town after about 8pm.

Tourist hustlers can be a problem. Most 'know' the best place to stay or the 'cheapest' boat operators: thankfully you know better.

MEDICAL SERVICES
Gamby Teaching General Hospital (☑0918-143195; ☺24hr) The town's best medical facility.

Mamo Drug Store (☑0918-760909; ☺8am-9pm Mon-Sat, 11am-9pm Sun) City-centre pharmacy.

MONEY
There are plenty of banks with ATMs along the main roads in the centre of town.

Wegagen Bank (☺8.30am-11am & 1.30-3.30pm Mon-Fri, 8.30am-11am Sat) Has a branch along the main road.

Commercial Bank of Ethiopia (☺8.30am-11am & 1.30-3.30pm Mon-Fri, 8.30am-11am Sat)

❶ Getting There & Away

AIR
Ethiopian Airlines (☑0582-200020; ☺8am-1pm & 2-6pm Mon-Sat) has two (some days three) daily flights to Addis Ababa (Birr4192, one hour) from Bahir Dar airport and at least one daily flight to Lalibela (Birr1781, 35 minutes).

BOAT
For the record, a ferry sails every Sunday at 7am for Gorgora (Birr278, 1½ days), on the northern shore of Lake Tana, from the Marine Authority Boat & Ferry Launch, but there are far better ways to get there and to see the lake. It stops for loading at Dek Island (with enough time to wander around) and overnights in Kunzula, where there's food and a couple of grotty hotels. It's far from luxe, with a toilet and limited seating in what they call '1st class'. Snacks and drinks are sometimes available, but it's best to bring your own. Buy tickets from 2pm to 4pm the day before at the **Marine Authority office** (☑0582-200730).

BUS
From the bus station, two ordinary buses travel to/from Addis Ababa (Birr125, 12 to 15 hours, 6am), while the Post Bus (Birr248) departs at 5.30am three days a week.

Minibuses travel at night (which makes them dangerous) and can do the trip in as little as eight hours. Your hotel can reserve a seat for you, or ask around for an agent at the north gate of the bus station to avoid the hotel's commission. There are two more comfortable options:

➡ **Sky Bus** (☑0924-440428) Has a ticket office near the lake and uses Dib Antessa as its 5am and 7am departure points (Birr340).

➪ **Selam Bus** Has a ticket office at the bus station, but the buses park in front of St George's Church and depart at 5.30am (Birr340).

Two buses travel to Gonder (Birr75, three hours) at 6am and minibuses (Birr90) go about hourly. For a steep fee, most hotels will call and have the minibus pick you up so you can avoid the chaotic bus station. Some travellers prefer to band together and hire a private minibus to Gonder, which can cost as little as Birr1200.

There's nothing direct to Lalibela, but you can take one of about five morning minibuses (Birr150, three hours) or the 6am bus (Birr145, 3½ hours) to Woldia and get off at Gashena to catch a connection there.

ⓘ Getting Around

If you're in a hurry, flag a passing *bajaj* (auto-rickshaw). A normal trip is Birr5, but nowhere in the city should cost more than Birr10.

Most of the pricier hotels provide a free shuttle to/from the airport. By *bajaj*/taxi the trip will set you back Birr120/250.

Lake Tana & its Monasteries

Lake Tana's beauty can only be truly appreciated when you get out beyond the city to enjoy azure waters, a lush shoreline and rich birdlife. But even the lake's natural beauty plays second fiddle to its centuries-old monasteries, full of paintings and treasures, and some pretty impressive numbers: Tana is Ethiopia's largest lake, covering more than 3500 sq km, and its waters are the source of the Blue Nile, which flows 5223km north to the Mediterranean Sea.

◉ Sights

While the boat engine's buzz is anything but a throwback to ancient times, your first meetings with the cross-wielding priests after stepping onto the islands just may be. Most monasteries date from the late 13th and 14th centuries, though the current church buildings were erected later. These are no architectural wonders like those at Lalibela and Tigray, but the murals adorning the monasteries' walls are full of all the colour, life, wit and humanity of Ethiopian art at its best and provide a compendium of Ethiopian saints, martyrs and lore.

Although it's possible to see all the monasteries over several long days, one day is enough for most travellers, not least because admission fees quickly add up and many monasteries are quite similar. Women can visit all but a few of the monasteries.

Although last-minute arrangements are possible, it's best to organise things at least the day before.

Planning ahead also helps to make sure that you see the monasteries you wish to see. If we had to choose, we'd make sure that we didn't miss Ura Kidane Meret, Azuwa Maryam, Narga Selassie, Dega Estefanos and, if time permits, Bete Selassie. To see all of these you'll need a full-day excursion.

Note that most of the monasteries close to tourists during Mass – you'll simply have to wait until they're finished.

Outlet of the Blue Nile RIVER

The Blue Nile outlet, a 20-minute boat ride east of Bahir Dar, has far greater geographical significance than it does natural beauty, although there's plenty of birdlife and you might see the odd hippo. From here, the Blue Nile snakes its way, eventually tracking north and 5223km to the Mediterranean; it joins the White Nile in Khartoum, Sudan. Although you can organise a dedicated boat excursion here, most visitors come as part of a boat trip that takes in nearby monasteries.

◉ Zege Peninsula

Walking between the monasteries on this forested peninsula, full of birds and vervet monkeys, is an enjoyable way to spend half a day...better, in our opinion, than spending long hours sitting in a boat visiting distant islands. It's about 40 minutes from Bahir Dar, and most people only visit the four monasteries near the shore. Most paintings are from the 18th century or later, not the 14th century like the guides will tell you.

If visiting monasteries on the Zege Peninsula, you'll be required to take a local guide (Birr150 per group of one to three people). Generally speaking they're among the most annoying guides in Ethiopia.

Bete Selassie and Tekla Haimanot are among the few monasteries you can reach by road (4WD only). It's a 1½-hour drive from Bahir Dar to a parking area close to Ura Kidane Meret, from where it's a further 40-minute walk to Azuwa Maryam.

★**Ura Kidane Meret** CHRISTIAN MONASTERY

(ኡራ ኪዳነምረት; Birr100, video camera Birr100; ⊙7am-6pm) The Zege Peninsula's largest and most famous monastery is hard-

Lake Tana & its Monasteries

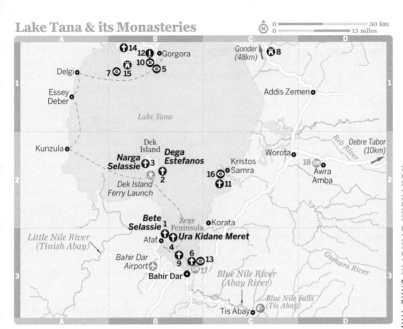

Lake Tana & its Monasteries

ly the most attractive on the outside, but its *maqdas* (inner sanctuary) is beautifully painted and it holds an important collection of 14th- to 20th-century crosses and crowns that will one day be displayed in a big new museum. Outside its gate is the private **Zeghie Satekela Museum** (admission Birr20; ⊙8am-5pm), with a collection of household items displayed in a 300-year-old home. The monastery is a 20-minute walk from the landing.

Bete Maryam   CHRISTIAN MONASTERY
(ቤተ ማርያም; Birr100, video camera Birr100; ⊙7am-6pm) Founded in the 13th century, Bete Maryam, near the tip of the peninsula, is the oldest monastery on Zege and its attractive church has some excellent murals that, unfortunately, have suffered water damage. It's a short walk from the landing through lemon and coffee trees.

Bete Giorgis   CHRISTIAN MONASTERY
Just uphill from Bete Maryam, Bete Giorgis is being rebuilt from scratch following a fire.

THE PURSUIT OF A PERFECT WORLD: AWRA AMBA

'Education is our source of income and helping each other is our culture.'

Awra Amba tour guide.

Awra Amba village is like no other in Ethiopia. The residents have a utopian world vision of total equality (regardless of gender, age, race, social standing etc), shared responsibility based on ability, and hard work and education as the best path to a good life. They also reject formal religion, though they do believe in a creator. The village's founder, Zumra Nuru, began imagining this sort of society as a child. Most people in his village thought he was crazy, but over time he met some like-minded people and, in 1986, 18 of them joined him in founding this village. It's since grown to nearly 500 residents (in over 140 households) and has attracted respect from around the country. For more information, check out www.visitawraamba.com.

Ninety-minute guided village tours (Birr10) start with the preschool, where ethics and human rights are taught alongside the ABCs, and also visit the village's libraries, retirement home and weaving workshop. There's not enough land to go around so weaving is one of the ways the village stays self-sufficient. Note that there's no weaving every other Saturday. You may also have the chance to speak to the humble founder. Begging is very shameful here so please avoid giving handouts. Some visitors choose to help out by buying the villagers' products or giving some books to the library.

The simple **guesthouse** (d/tw without bathroom Birr50/100) (earthen walls, sheet-metal doors and a bathroom out back) has about the cleanest shoestring lodging you'll ever see. The small **restaurant** (mains Birr20-35) has pasta and national dishes.

Awra Amba is 73km from Bahir Dar on the Woldia road, 10km after Worota. Several minibuses from Bahir Dar (Birr42, one hour) pass the signposted junction, from where it's a 2km walk.

Its small museum, with an important collection of crowns, is still open.

Azuwa Maryam CHRISTIAN MONASTERY
(አዙዋ ማርያም; ⊙7am-6pm) The thatch roof atop the church at Azuwa Maryam helps make it the best-looking church on Zege (currently Bete Maryam is the only other church with thatch), though its paintings and small museum are more ordinary. Don't miss the religious school for priests and deacons here. Azuwa Maryam is a two-minute walk from the ferry landing – the same landing used for Ura Kidane Meret.

★ **Bete Selassie** CHRISTIAN MONASTERY
(Birr100, video camera Birr100; ⊙7am-6pm) Bete Selassie (men only) is a 30- to 45-minute walk inland from the Lake Tana shore at Zege Peninsula. The simple exterior of the church (rebuilt in 1858) gives no clue to the wonderfully vivid paintings (arguably the best on the lake) inside, most of which date from the 1930s.

Tekla Haimanot CHRISTIAN MONASTERY
(Birr100, video camera Birr100; ⊙7am-6pm) On top of the Zege Peninsula's highest point, 10 minutes' walk from Bete Selassie, the church at Tekla Haimanot is similar but smaller than Bete Selassie's. It has paintings by the same artists, but lacks the historic atmosphere. It has the potential for great views, but the forest prevents it. Guides consider the walk up here very difficult (it's not!) and you'll probably have to negotiate a higher price.

◉ Islands

There is nowhere to sleep on any of the islands – Bahir Dar is the best base for exploring the monasteries.

★ **Narga Selassie** CHRISTIAN MONASTERY
(ናርጋ ስላሴ; Birr100, video camera Birr100; ⊙7am-6pm) Set in the middle of the lake on Dek Island, Narga Selassie is peaceful, atmospheric and little visited. Built in the mid-18th century, it has a Gonderian influence and the fine original paintings include a portrait of Mentewab; there's also a bas-relief of James Bruce (smoking his pipe) at the main entrance. It's three hours by boat and a two-minute walk from the landing.

★ **Dega Estefanos** CHRISTIAN MONASTERY
(ደጋ እስጢፋኖስ; Birr100, video camera Birr100; ⏰7am-6pm) One of the lake's most sacred monasteries, Dega Estefanos (men only) was rebuilt in the mid-19th century. Though the church isn't too interesting, it holds a good selection of treasures (including a 16th-century painting of the Madonna) and the mummified remains in glass coffins of five former Ethiopian emperors (13th to 17th centuries). One of the bodies is Zara Yaqob, one of the most important Ethiopian emperors.

The founder of this monastery, locals believe, was a saint who sailed to the island in 1268 on a stone boat. The 'boat' is still visible halfway along the trail to the monastery.

The monastery is about 2½ hours from Bahir Dar and 45 minutes from Narga Selassie, 30-minutes' walk up a steep trail.

Kebran Gabriel CHRISTIAN MONASTERY
(ክብራን ገብርኤል; Birr100; ⏰7am-6pm) Though the 17th-century church at Kebran Gabriel is beautiful, it's no longer open to the public and the museums (one each for men and women) have nothing you won't see elsewhere. It's 20 minutes away from Bahir Dar by boat, directly on the way to Zege Peninsula, which is why guides encourage people to stop here. The tiny treasury has a few old books and pictures.

The small island next door hosts the completely modern and, frankly, uninteresting **Entos Eyesu** (Birr100; ⏰7am-6pm), which offers the novelty of monks and nuns living together.

Debre Maryam CHRISTIAN MONASTERY
(ደብረ ማርያም; Birr100, video camera Birr100; ⏰7am-6pm) The original 14th-century (some say 12th-century) church at Debre Maryam was rebuilt by Tewodros in the 19th century. It's unattractive both outside and in and the treasury is meagre. The main reason to visit is that sometimes men make *tankwas* here. Also, it's across from the outlet of the Blue Nile. It's 15 minutes by boat and a short walk through coffee, mango and fig trees.

In the dry season you can visit Debre Maryam by *tankwa*. Head north of Bahir Dar to just before the Nile bridge and then walk west about 1km to the lake on the road with the family-planning sign. Locals pay Birr2 return, but you're unlikely to get it for less than Birr20.

Tana Cherkos MONASTERY
(ጣና ጨርቆስ; Birr150, video camera Birr100; ⏰7am-6pm) It's said the Ark of the Covenant was hidden at Tana Cherkos for 800 years, which would seem to indicate it's an interesting destination, but the present 19th-century church and its modern paintings are rather modest. Its unique feature is its ancient Judaic sacrificial stones. Tana Cherkos is 2½ hours from Bahir Dar by boat. From the landing it's a 30-minute walk uphill.

Mitsele Fasiladas CHRISTIAN MONASTERY
(Birr100; ⏰7am-6pm) Because most of the treasures of Mitsele Fasiladas (on an island just south of Tana Cherkos and a short walk from the landing) were stolen in the 1990s, and the church is ordinary, few people visit, though the setting is attractive.

❶ Getting Around

There's no shortage of boat operators in Bahir Dar, and shifty commission agents lurk everywhere. One agency we recommend is **Zelalem Memory** (p69).

Prices are always negotiable, but the standard half-day tour costs Birr950 for a group of five people. Half-day excursions usually last from 4½ to five hours and take in Ura Kidane Meret, Azuwa Maryam, Kebran Gabriel, Debre Maryam and the Blue Nile outlet. A shorter, 2½-hour trip that includes Debre Maryam and the Blue Nile outlet is around Birr750, while a full-day trip out to distant islands will likely cost Birr3000, or Birr3600 if you include lunch – most full-day excursions don't include food, which you'll need to bring yourself. Always ask if a guide is included in the cost. Bottled water should also be part of the rate. Before departing, always ensure your boat has life jackets and spare fuel.

Entry fees for the monasteries are not included in the tour prices.

A ferry to the Zege Peninsula (Birr54) departs Bahir Dar at 7am (come at 6.30am to buy tickets), arriving at the landing near Ura Kidane Meret monastery around 8am and Afaf village 15 minutes later. It departs Afaf at 4pm. There are also a few minibuses to Afaf (Birr12, 1½ hours), the last returning to Bahir Dar around 4pm.

Gonder

POP 323,900 / ELEV 2300M

It's not what Gonder (ጎንደር) is, but what Gonder was that's so enthralling. The city lies in a bowl of hills where tall trees shelter tin-roofed stone houses, but rising above these, and standing proud through the

NORTHERN ETHIOPIA GONDER

Gonder

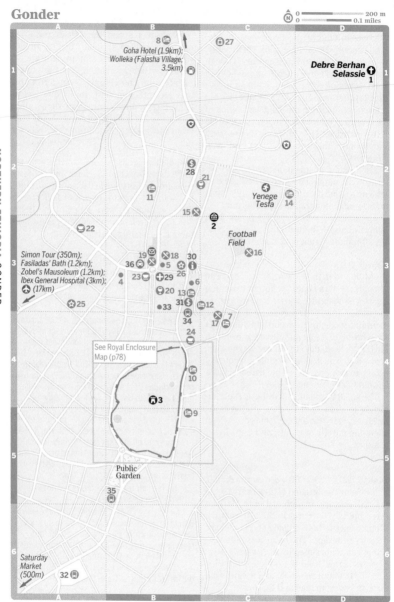

Goha Hotel (1.9km);
Wolleka (Falasha Village;
3.5km)

Debre Berhan
Selassie 1

Yenege
Tesfa

Football
Field

Simon Tour (350m);
Fasiladas' Bath (1.2km);
Zobel's Mausoleum (1.2km);
Ibex General Hospital (3km);
(17km)

See Royal Enclosure
Map (p78)

Public
Garden

Saturday
Market
(500m)

centuries, are the walls of castles bathed in blood and painted in the pomp of royalty. It's often called the 'Camelot of Africa', a description that does the royal city a disservice: Camelot is legend, whereas Gonder is reality.

History

Surrounded by fertile land and lying at the crossroads of three major caravan routes, it's easy to understand why Emperor Fasiladas (r 1632–67) made Gonder his capital in 1636. To the southwest lay rich sources of gold,

Gonder

civet, ivory and slaves, to the northeast lay Massawa and access to the Red Sea, and to the northwest lay Sudan and Egypt.

At the time of Fasiladas' death, Gonder's population already exceeded 65,000 and its wealth and splendour had become legendary. Drifting through the old palaces, banqueting halls and former gardens, it's not difficult to imagine the courtly pageantry, ceremony and intrigue that went on here.

The city flourished as a capital for well over a century before infighting severely weakened the kingdom. In the 1880s what remained of Gonder was extensively looted by the Sudanese Dervishes. Despite this, and further damage sustained by British bombs during the liberation campaign of 1941, much of Gonder remains intact.

⊙ Sights

Although Gonder is fairly spread out, it's still a great place to navigate on foot. The Italian-built piazza marks the centre of town and packs in most shops and services that travellers need. The Royal Enclosure is just south of the piazza, while the road leading north is dotted with restaurants and hotels.

★ **Debre Berhan Selassie**   CHURCH
(Birr100, video camera Birr75; ⊙ 7.30am-12.30pm & 1.30-5.30pm) Welcome to one of Ethiopia's most beautiful churches. Appealing as it is on the outside with its stone walls, arched doors and two-tiered thatch roof, it's the inner sanctuary of Debre Berhan Selassie, with its glorious frescoes, that really shines. But it was very nearly destroyed like most of Gonder's other churches. When the marauding Sudanese Dervishes showed up outside the church gates in the 1880s, a giant swarm of bees surged out of the compound, chasing the invaders away.

The ceiling, with its rows and rows of winged cherubs representing the omnipresence of God, draws most eyes. There's space for 135 cherubs, though 13 have been erased by water damage. Aside from the cherubs the highlights have to be the devilish Bosch-like depiction of hell. Although local tradition attributes most paintings to the 17th-century artist Haile Meskel, this is unlikely because the building only dates back to the late 18th century. The original circular church, created in the 1690s by Iyasu I, was destroyed by lightning.

A large stone wall with 12 rounded towers surrounds the compound and these represent the 12 apostles. The larger 13th tower (entrance gate) symbolises Christ and is shaped to resemble the Lion of Judah. If you have a keen eye, you'll be able to spot the lion's tail above the doorway in the wall west of the church. Flash photography inside the church is forbidden. Priests offer tours, but a small contribution for the church should be left afterwards.

Royal Enclosure CASTLE

(adult/student Birr200/100, video camera Birr75; ☉ 8.30am-12.30pm & 1.30-6pm) The Gonder of yesteryear was a city of extreme brutality and immense wealth. Today the wealth and brutality are gone, but the memories linger in this amazing World Heritage site. The entire 70,000-sq-metre compound containing numerous castles and palaces has been restored with the aid of Unesco. Knowledgeable guides (Birr200) are well worth it.

➡ **Fasiladas' Palace**

By far the most impressive, and also the oldest, building is Fasiladas' Palace, just inside the entrance gate. It stands 32m tall and has a crenulated parapet and four domed towers. Made of roughly hewn stones, it's reputedly the work of an Indian architect and shows an unusual synthesis of Indian, Portuguese, Moorish and Aksumite influences. The main floor was used as dining halls and a formal reception area. Note the wall reliefs, including several Stars of David, which trumpet Fasiladas' link to the Solomonic dynasty. The small room in the northern corner boasts its original beam ceiling and some faint frescoes. On the 1st floor, Fasiladas' prayer room has windows in four directions, each overlooking Gonder's important churches. Religious ceremonies were held on the roof, and it was from here that he addressed his people. Above Fasiladas' 2nd-floor bedroom was the watchtower, from where it's (apparently) possible to see

Royal Enclosure

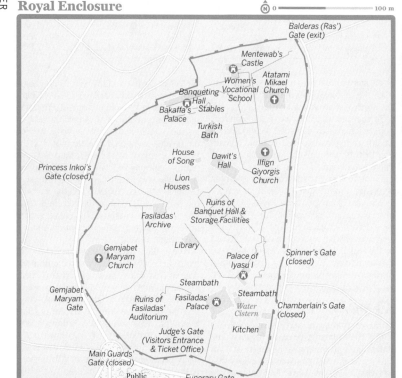

Ⓝ 0 ━━━━━━━━━━━━━━━━ 100 m

Balderas (Ras') Gate (exit)

Mentewab's Castle

Women's Vocational School

Atatami Mikael Church

Banqueting Hall

Bakaffa's Palace

Stables

Turkish Bath

House of Song

Dawit's Hall

Ilfign Giyorgis Church

Princess Inkoi's Gate (closed)

Lion Houses

Ruins of Banquet Hall & Storage Facilities

Fasiladas' Archive

Library

Palace of Iyasu I

Spinner's Gate (closed)

Gemjabet Maryam Church

Steambath

Gemjabet Maryam Gate

Ruins of Fasiladas' Auditorium

Fasiladas' Palace

Steambath

Water Cistern

Chamberlain's Gate (closed)

Judge's Gate (Visitors Entrance & Ticket Office)

Kitchen

Main Guards' Gate (closed)

Public Garden

Funerary Gate (closed)

all the way to Lake Tana. Behind the castle are various ruined buildings, including the kitchen (domed ceiling), steam bath and water cistern.

⇒ **Palace of Iyasu I**

To the palace's northeast is the saddle-shaped Palace of Iyasu I, with its unusual vaulted ceiling. The son of Yohannes I, Iyasu I (r 1682–1706) is considered the greatest ruler of the Gonderine period. The palace used to be sumptuously decorated with gilded Venetian mirrors and chairs, with gold leaf, ivory and beautiful paintings adorning the walls. Visiting travellers described the palace as 'more beautiful than Solomon's house'. Although a 1704 earthquake and British bombing in the 1940s have done away with the interior and most of the roof, its skeletal shell reeks of history.

⇒ **Other Southern Buildings**

North of Iyasu's palace are the relics of its banquet hall and storage facilities. To the west is the quadrangular library of Fasiladas' son, Yohannes I (r 1667–82), which was plastered over by the Italians in a nonhistoric renovation. (In fact, all plaster found in the Royal Enclosure compound was added by the Italians.) Once an impressive palace decorated with ivory, only the tower and walls of Fasiladas' Archive remain. It sits northwest of the library.

⇒ **Northern Buildings**

The compound's northern half holds vestiges of Dawit's Hall, known as the House of Song, in which many religious and secular ceremonies and lavish entertainments took place. Emperor Dawit (r 1716–21) also built the first of two Lion Houses (the second was built by Haile Selassie) where Abyssinian lions were kept until 1990. When Dawit came to a sticky end (he was poisoned in 1721), Emperor Bakaffa (r 1721–30) took up the reins and built his palace with a huge banqueting hall (the current ceiling was added by the Italians) and the impressive stables. Between the stables and Dawit's Hall is the Turkish bath (*wesheba*), built by Iyasu I at the advice of a French physician to deal with his skin conditions. It apparently also worked wonders for those suffering from syphilis! At the southern end you'll see the fire pit and the ceiling's steam vents. The Italians added windows and made it a kitchen.

Bakaffa's consort was responsible for the last palace, Mentewab's Castle, a two-storey structure that's now the site's office. Note the Gonderian cross being used as a decorative motif. Mentewab (r 1730–55) also built the women's vocational school to the front, where classes included facial tattooing and chicken cutting.

⇒ **Atatami Mikael Church**

Atatami Mikael church, just outside the Royal Enclosure's exit gate, was built by Emperor Dawit III. The church itself is off-limits, but the interesting little museum (Birr25) has lots of beautiful illustrated manuscripts and a few other items such as giant pots for making beer.

Saturday Market   MARKET
(የቅዳሜ ገበያ; ⊙7am-3pm) Originally the city's weekly market, Kidame Gebya is now packed throughout the week, although Saturday remains the biggest day and Sunday is rather quiet. Traditional clothes vendors are right at the top, while the vegetable sellers use ancient-looking dirt perches in the back. It's 500m southwest of the bus station.

Ras Gimb   MUSEUM
(ራስ ግምብ) Though its early history is murky (it was likely built in the 17th century, though some say the 18th), this attractive palace once served as a retreat for Haile Selassie, a residence for Italian generals and a torture chamber for the Derg. It's now under renovation (don't hold your breath) to serve as a museum of Gonder's history that will include some of Haile Selassie's furniture and objects found at the palace and Portuguese Cathedral at Gorgora.

Empress Mentewab's
Kuskuam Complex   PALACE
(Birr100, video camera Birr75; ⊙8am-6pm) It mightn't be as well-preserved as the Royal Enclosure, or as sacred as Debre Berhan Selassie, but what this royal compound, known as Kuskuam, lacks in order and holiness it more than makes up for in melancholy. The complex was built in 1730 for the redoubtable Empress Mentewab after the death of her husband (Emperor Bakaffa).

Fasiladas' Bath   HISTORIC SITE
(included in Royal Enclosure ticket; ⊙8.30am-6pm) Around 2km northwest of the piazza lies Fasiladas' Bath, which has been attributed to both Fasiladas and Iyasu I. The large rectangular pool is overlooked by a charming building, thought by some to be a vacation home. It's a beautiful and peaceful spot, where snakelike tree roots digest sections of the stone walls. Minibuses (Birr3) from

near the piazza pass here. A contract *bajaj* is Birr20. You must obtain your ticket at the Royal Enclosure before visiting Fasiladas' Bath. Although the complex was used for swimming (royalty used to don inflated goat-skin life jackets for their refreshing dips!), it was likely to have been constructed for religious celebrations, the likes of which still go on today. Once a year, it's filled with water for the Timkat celebration. After the water is blessed by the bishop, the pool becomes a riot of splashing water, shouts and laughter as a crowd of hundreds jumps in. The ceremony replicates Christ's baptism in the Jordan River and is seen as an important renewal of faith.

Just east of the main compound is **Zobel's Mausoleum**. Local legend states it's named after Yohannes I's horse, which ran so fast that he was able to escape some bandits he encountered while out hunting buffalo. Another tale says that the horse heroically brought Iyasu (Yohannes' son) back from Sudan after his father's death. Not only was the horse a good walker, but it could, it is said, jump 25m in a single leap.

Wolleka (Falasha Village) VILLAGE

(ወለቃ (የፈላሻዎች መንደር)) Around 3km north of Gonder, several craft stalls with 'Stars of David' and 'Falasha Village' signs signal what's really the *former* Falasha village of Wolleka. Once home to a thriving population of Falashas (Ethiopian Jews), most were airlifted to Israel in the 1980s and today none remain. There are a few original houses with interesting artwork on their fronts and the small **synagogue**; for Birr10 you can look inside, but be prepared for an entourage of persistent sales kids.

🏃 Activities

Yenege Tesfa VOLUNTEERING

(☎0918-774745; www.yenegetesfa.org) A local NGO working with Gonder street kids. It has an orphanage and also provides educational programs for the town's children as well as medical facilities. Following the success of Hope Enterprises (p289) in Addis, Yenege Tesfa also sells meal tickets that you can distribute to the town's street children. Tickets are available from most of the bigger hotels for Birr0.50.

👉 Tours

The guides at the Royal Enclosure can also be hired for any other place in town. The prices are fixed and posted at the entrance and you can walk, ride bikes, hop on local minibuses or charter a *bajaj* (around Birr80 an hour).

A number of reliable agencies can arrange everything from city tours to Simien Mountains treks. Prices vary and negotiations are always in order.

Explore Abyssinia Travel WALKING, HORSE RIDING

(☎0581-111917; www.exploreabyssinia.com) This excellent company, which also owns Lodge du Chateau (p82), leads walking and horse-riding trips to the villages around Gonder. It also has a book exchange.

Trek in Ethiopia Tours TREKKING

(☎0911-904792; www.trekinethiopia.com) Run by former Simien Mountains trekking guide Alebachew Abebe. There is no office; call with questions or to arrange a meeting.

Explore Simien Tours TOURS

(☎0581-119066; fasilm_675@yahoo.com) A do-it-all agency with an excellent reputation.

Simon Tour TOURS

(☎0911-733479; www.simonethiopiatour.com) Decent Gonder-based company.

Simen Fox Trekking TREKKING

(☎0918-770887; www.simenfoxtrekking.com) Trekking specialist.

🎓 Courses

⭐ Four Sisters COOKING

(☎0581-122031; www.foursistersrestaurant.com; cooking class per person from Birr100) If you call ahead to this wonderful restaurant (p83), you can join it in the morning for a short session where you learn how to cook *injera* and make honey wine. At night, staff are also on hand to teach you how to dance Ethiopian Eskista during the traditional live performances, or initiate you into the world of Ethiopian coffee ceremonies.

⭐ Lodge du Chateau COOKING

(☎0911-021025; www.lodgeduchateau.com; per person US$35) This excellent place to stay also offers two fine programs that provide a real window on local life. The most popular is a traditional cooking class (followed by a meal) in the home of a local family. For women travellers, there's also a traditional hair-styling session with a local expert.

BLUE NILE FALLS (TIS ABAY)

The Blue Nile (ጢስ አባይ; adult/student/child Birr50/30/free, personal video cameras Birr50, mandatory guide Birr100; ☉7am-5.30pm) looks like a sluggish beast as it meanders out of Lake Tana, but not far out of Bahir Dar you'll see the Nile in a very different mood. The river pours over the side of a sheer 42m-high chasm and explodes into a melange of mists and rainbows (best at 10am) before continuing on its tumultuous path to Khartoum, where it finally gets to kiss the White Nile.

The catch to this impressive scene is that hydroelectric projects upstream have stolen most of the energy from Tis Abay, the 'Nile that Smokes'. Though far smaller than its natural 400m-wide flow, the three-pronged waterfall is still jaw-droppingly huge in August and September. From around January or February until March it's now known as 'Blue Nile Shower' and it's not really worth a visit. The in-between time is still beautiful enough that most people enjoy the trip (though note that one of the hydro plants only operates on standby and if it's turned on during this time the waterfall gets turned off). You may want to ask fellow travellers who've recently been to the falls about the flow, as tourist-industry operators won't always give you a straight answer.

The ticket office is at the very end of the road through the town of Tis Abay. The road to the falls starts 50m west of here and it's 1.5km to the start of a rocky footpath that leads down to a 17th-century Portuguese bridge (which was the first bridge to span the Blue Nile) along the so-called eastern route. From here the trail climbs up through a small village and a gauntlet of children selling souvenirs to reach the main viewpoints. Some people backtrack from here, but the better option is to take the suspension bridge over the narrow Alata River and walk down to the base of the falls. In the dry season you can swim at the bottom and walk behind the watery curtain. You can complete a circuit by using a bridge above the falls and crossing the river by motorboat. The boat service usually operates 7am to 6pm, but when the river runs too fast the boats can't cross. Look for crocs during dry-season mornings. The entire walk is about 5km and takes about 2½ hours with lots of gawping time. As it's not very steep, less energetic or mobile people may want to approach and return from the falls along this western route.

The falls are located 28km southeast of Bahir Dar down a bad dirt road; the first 10km were being sealed at the time of writing. Buses from Bahir Dar leave about hourly for Tis Abay village (Birr15, one hour). The last bus back usually leaves about 4.30pm, but to be safe, plan to return around 3.30pm. You don't need to pay anyone to hold a seat for you. If you miss the bus, hitching back isn't tough, though it will probably be expensive.

Zelalem Memory (p69) in Bahir Dar can organise excursions here for Birr1200, which includes a vehicle, fuel and a driver; a guide costs Birr400 extra. It's pricey, but less so if you can get a group together.

✨ Festivals & Events

Timkat   RELIGIOUS
(☉Jan) This three-day celebration of the Epiphany, or Christ's baptism, is marked with special fervour in Gonder. White-robed faithful throng the streets and churches in solemn processions, with a less-solemn event at Fasiladas' Bath (p79).

Meskel   RELIGIOUS
(☉Sep) Gonder is a fine place to be for this important national festival that marks the 'finding of the True Cross'. Expect bonfires, priests in full regalia and much pageantry.

🛏 Sleeping

Gonder's accommodation scene has plenty at the budget and midrange end of things, while top-end travellers have a couple of OK options, but are generally less well-catered for.

Zozamba Hotel   HOTEL $
(☎0582-110131; s/d Birr300/400; P) Between the piazza and Debre Berhan Selassie, this quiet, newish hotel is excellent value – the rooms are tidy and large enough to put your backpack down without tripping over it. It has a decent kitchen where it can rustle up simple but hearty Ethiopian meals.

JAMES BRUCE: IN SEARCH OF THE SOURCE

Half undressed as I was by the loss of my sash, and throwing my shoes off, I ran down the hill towards the little island of green sods, which was about two hundred yards distant...

...It is easier to guess than to describe the situation of my mind at that moment – standing in the spot which had baffled the genius, industry and enquiry of both ancients and moderns, for the course of near three thousand years.

James Bruce, Travels to Discover the Source of the Nile (1790)

One of the first European explorers in this part of Africa was a Scot named James Bruce. After serving as consul general in Algiers, he set off in 1768 in search of the Nile's source, a puzzle that had preoccupied people since the time of the Egyptian pharaohs. After landing in Massawa, Eritrea, he made his way to the powerful and splendid court of Gonder, where he became close friends with Empress Mentewab.

In 1770 he reached the source of the Abay, the main river that empties Lake Tana. There he declared the mystery of the Nile's source solved. He dedicated his discovery to King George III and returned home to national acclaim.

In fact, Bruce had traced only the source of the *Blue* Nile River, the main tributary of the Nile. Not only that, but he'd been beaten to his 'discovery' (as he very well knew) more than 150 years earlier by a Spanish Jesuit, Pedro Páez.

Of greater interest was the account of his journey, *Travels to Discover the Source of the Nile*, published in 1790. It remains a useful source of information on Ethiopia's history and customs. His contemporaries considered much of it a gross exaggeration, or even pure fiction. Given his earlier claims, it's no wonder.

Queen Taytu Pension   PENSION $
(✆ 0581-122898; d d/tw Birr250/350, d with shared bathroom Birr150; 🛜) This popular backpacker spot has the usual broken doors and toilet seats you expect at cheaper places. It's worth considering, however, for its central location.

L-Shape Hotel   HOTEL $
(✆ 0918-770272;   s/d/tw   Birr200/280/400; P🛜) Rooms here are in better shape than the hallways would lead you to believe and they're a reasonable in-town choice, especially if you score a room with a view; some rooms on the back side look straight into a wall. The restaurant (serving a good pizza) below is popular with university students.

Belegez Pension   PENSION $
(✆ 0918-772997; d Birr200, with shared bathroom Birr150; P) Formerly wearing the crown of best-value cheapie in Gonder, the small and simple rooms here have turned the corner towards decay. But the location is OK and the traveller-aware staff mean it still rates a mention.

★**Lodge du Chateau**   HOTEL $$
(✆ 0918-152001; www.lodgeduchateau.com; dm/s/d & tw incl breakfast US$20/45/55; @🛜) Doing things its own way, this owner-managed spot next to the Royal Enclosure has the friendliest service in town, attention to detail and a real commitment to community involvement. The rooms are nicely decorated and have good mattresses, renovated bathrooms and Gonder's best breakfast served in a dining-room-lounge perched high to make the best of the valley views.

Ask about its innovative local excursions. It also has a small book exchange and sells its own honey.

Gonder Landmark Hotel   HOTEL $$
(✆ 0581-122929; www.gonderlandmark.com; s/d/tw US$60/68/72/85) Lording it over the town's northern end and with terrific city views from most rooms (avoid the 'Mountain View' rooms), the Landmark is an excellent choice if you like modern, light-filled rooms. The suites may look like they didn't quite know what to do with all that space, but even the standard rooms are some of the nicest in town.

Florida International Hotel   HOTEL $$
(✆ 0581-112260;   www.floridainternationalhotel. com; s/d US$42/49; P🛜☒) If only this place was closer to the centre (it's 5km east of town, on the road from Bahir Dar), it would be a top choice. The excellent rooms are modern and among Gonder's best, there's an enormous pool out the back, a spa and massage centre in the basement and the views from the roof terrace are terrific.

Taye Hotel
HOTEL **$$**

(✆ 0581-112180; www.tayebelayhotel.com; s/d/ste incl breakfast US$60/66/85; @ 🛜) Once Gonder's top in-town digs, and the choice of most NGO and UN workers, the Taye lords over the heart of the city. Some of the front-facing rooms have enormous balconies with great sunset views, but little space left for anything other than the tiniest of bathrooms. All rooms feature satellite TV but the wi-fi is restricted to the lobby.

Lodge Fasil
HOTEL **$$**

(✆ 0581-110637; s/d & tw incl breakfast US$35/45; P 🛜) A stone's throw from the Royal Enclosure's exit, this well-run place features eager staff and spotless rooms with satellite TV that are set back from traffic noise among plenty of trees. Those on the upper level have partial views of the valley below. Overall it has a good vibe.

Goha Hotel
HOTEL **$$$**

(✆ 0581-110634; www.gohahotel.com; s/d incl breakfast US$71/82; P @ 🛜 🏊) Perched on a high natural balcony providing a lammergeyer's-eye view, the stone-walled Goha has the highest perch in all the land. The pool terrace and the bar are the best vantage points, but sadly the rooms, which are overpriced and rather simple, are set back among the trees. If you don't spend much time in your room, it's a good choice.

🍴 Eating

⭐ Four Sisters
EUROPEAN, ETHIOPIAN **$**

(✆ 0581-122031; www.thefoursistersrestaurant.com; mains Birr70-100; ⊙ noon-10pm) Now here's something special. One of the best places in northern Ethiopia for both food and atmosphere, Four Sisters has brilliant traditional food (order 'national food' for an overview of what it's capable of), a lovely, leafy setting with stone walls and Debre Berhan Selassie–inspired paintings and nightly traditional music and dance.

Tele Café
ETHIOPIAN **$**

(breakfast Birr18-35, mains Birr35-90; ⊙ from 7am) Although it serves food all day, we rather like this spot for breakfast and for people watching. When it comes to the former, it serves good *ful* (an Egyptian staple of broad bean and butter puree), including a version with avocado.

Quara Hotel
EUROPEAN, ETHIOPIAN **$**

(mains Birr40-100; ⊙ noon-11pm) While the menu doesn't break the mould, it does offer a few meals not often available in Ethiopia, such as curry-spiced noodles, as well as the usual Ethiopian and European staples. The balcony is good for watching Gonder life pass by.

Alliance
ETHIOPIAN **$**

(✆ 0918-773637; mains Birr32-82; ⊙ 7am-10pm) Several locals recommended this newish place for traditional Ethiopian food and, while we couldn't quite see what all the fuss was about, it does serve up good honest local food, albeit in a rather anodyne dining area.

Lodge Fasil
ETHIOPIAN, INTERNATIONAL **$$**

(✆ 0581-110637; mains Birr55-120; ⊙ 7am-10pm) With an agreeable garden setting (there's a more formal dining area inside), Lodge Fasil in the hotel of the same name does a good mix of Ethiopian dishes with European comfort food such as steak sandwiches and pizzas. Nothing special, but a reliable central choice.

Masterchef
ETHIOPIAN, EUROPEAN **$$**

(✆ 0581-192440; mains Birr75-120; ⊙ 8am-9pm) This bamboo-walled restaurant, a short walk from the Royal Enclosure exit, is a good place for lunch, with grilled fish a speciality. It also does lamb *tibs* and pasta.

🍷 Drinking & Nightlife

⭐ Senait Coffee Shop
COFFEE

(⊙ 9am-5pm) Serving up Gonder's best coffee, Senait is brought to you by the same people who run Four Sisters and it shows. With a small but lovely, character-filled outdoor setting opposite the exit to the Royal Enclosure, it's a nice place to rest during your exploration of the city. The coffee is strong and traditional and of the highest quality.

Ethiopia Café
CAFE

(⊙ 7am-10pm) This classic, though subtle, art deco Italian cafe in the heart of the piazza is a throwback to the days of yesteryear – it's easily the most atmospheric of Gonder's traditional coffeehouses.

EEPCO Coffee House
CAFE

(⊙ 7am-9pm) You'd be hard-pressed to find a Gonderian who doesn't consider the brew here the city's best, and we think it serves the best cake.

Goha Hotel   BAR
(☎) There's nowhere better in town for a sunset drink than this hotel's lofty garden terrace. Besides the overpriced beers, there's a variety of local and imported wines and the views are superlative.

Camelot House   CLUB
A dark and cosy modern club where the band plays and the people dance until at least 2am.

Dashen House   BEER GARDEN
(☺noon-11pm) The large outdoor terrace here is indisputably the town centre's most popular beer joint.

☆ Entertainment

Elilta   LIVE MUSIC
(free) There's traditional Amharic music and dance on stage here nightly from 7pm to midnight.

Shewe Beye   COMEDY
(free) Gonder produces Ethiopia's best *azmaris* (local minstrels who perform a mix of music and humour). While many end up starring in Addis Ababa, there are still some good *azmari bets* (bars) here. This is one among many and usually packed. Look for the signs with the lutes.

🛍 Shopping

Project Ploughshare Women's Crafts Training Center   ARTS & CRAFTS
(tesfalemabera@gmail.com) This centre in Wolleka is helping disadvantaged women rekindle local pottery traditions, along with traditional Amhara weaving and basketry. You can watch the women working Monday to Saturday and buy the high-quality pottery every day.

Kindu Trust   ARTS & CRAFTS
(www.kindutrust.org; ☺8.30am-noon & 2-5pm) This child-sponsorship charity has a small store selling baskets, banana art and beads made from recycled magazines. Some items are also sold at Lodge du Chateau (p82).

ℹ Information

DANGERS & ANNOYANCES
Various 'guides' will seek you out, but it's rare that they have any historical knowledge and they aren't allowed inside the Royal Enclosure. Their favourite scam is a half-day trip to the Simien Mountains, but this is impossible and they'll only take you to Wunenia or Kosoye.

MEDICAL SERVICES
Goha Pharmacy (☑0581-113978; ☺8.30am-9.30pm) Helpful and well stocked.
Ibex General Hospital (☑0581-118273) Gonder's best medical facility has a 24-hour casualty department and pharmacy.

MONEY
Dashen Bank (☺8.30am-11am & 1.30-3.30pm Mon-Fri, 8.30-11am Sat) The branch north of the piazza has an ATM, as do some others further out of town.
Wegagen Bank (☺8.30-11am & 1.30-3.30pm Mon-Fri, 8.30-11am Sat) Also has an ATM (☺24hr) inside Taye Hotel.

TOURIST INFORMATION
Gonder City Tourist Information Centre (☑0581-110022; ☺8.30am-12.30pm & 1.30-5.30pm Mon-Sat, 8.30am-12.30pm Sun) Officially there's a tourist office but if it bothers to open at all, it's not much help.

ℹ Getting There & Away

AIR
Ethiopian Airlines (☑0581-117688; ☺8am-1pm & 2-6pm Mon-Sat) flies twice daily to Addis Ababa (Birr4516, one hour) and once to Aksum (Birr2113, two hours) via Lalibela (Birr1781, one hour).

BUS
Ordinary buses leave from the bus station.
Addis Ababa Few travellers go direct to/from Addis, but it can be done in 15 hours with the luxury buses. Options include Sky Bus (Birr422, 5am), which departs from the Royal Enclosure entrance gate, and Selam (Birr420, 5.30am), which, just to be different, departs from the Royal Enclosure exit gate.
Aksum For Aksum, you'll need to change in Shire (Birr160, 10 to 11 hours, 5.30am).
Bahir Dar Two daily buses make the trip between Gonder and Bahir Dar (Birr75, three hours).
Debark (Simien Mountains) Minibuses and an early morning bus connect Gonder with Debark (Birr65, 2½ hours).
Lalibela There are no direct buses to Lalibela so take the 5.30am bus (Birr115, four to five hours) or one of the minibuses (Birr210, four hours) headed to Woldia and get off in Gashena, where you can catch a connection as long as you don't arrive too late in the day.

ℹ Getting Around

A shared taxi from the airport, which is 17km from town, costs Birr60 per person. Many hotels have free airport shuttles.

Chartering a *bajaj*/taxi to see Gonder's sights costs about Birr80/130 per hour, but you'll have to negotiate hard for this. Minibuses charge between Birr2 and Birr3 for hops around town. *Bajaj*, taxis and minibuses congregate just west of the piazza.

Gorgora

POP 4783 / ELEV 1830M

The little lakeshore town of Gorgora (ጎርጎራ), 60km southwest of Gonder, has a slow, tropical vibe. It provides the chance to see rarely visited monasteries and makes a good excursion for birders. Mostly it offers an easy, comfortable escape from well-trodden tourist trails. If you've already visited the monasteries from Lake Tana's southern shore, these will struggle to impress – come instead for the quiet natural beauty of the place.

◉ Sights

With the exception of Debre Sina, you'll need a local guide to find the surrounding sights. Guides usually hang out at the Gorgora Port Hotel and charge Birr200 per day for a small group. Andrayano Tesema, who speaks pretty good English (he's probably the only one), can also do birdwatching trips; ask for him at the hotel.

Church of Debre Sina   CHURCH

(Birr100, personal video cameras Birr100; ⊙ 7am-6pm) The most interesting relic of Gorgora's former days as a short-lived capital is the attractive Debre Sina church. Built in 1608 by Emperor Susenyos' son and future founder of Gonder, Fasiladas, on the site of a 14th-century monastery, it's decorated with fading original paintings. These are older and thus less vivid and complex than the paintings in the monasteries on the southern side of the lake, and interesting because of the difference.

Locals believe the 'Egyptian St Mary' painting, which is supposed to have come from Egypt but looks no different than the other paintings, has the power to heal. The church's thatch roof and surrounding stone buildings lend this monastery a more ancient feel than most.

Mandaba Medhane Alem   MONASTERY

(Birr100, men only; ⊙ 7am-6pm) Of Tana's four far-northern monasteries, all west of Gorgora, Mandaba Medhane Alem, which hosts ancient biblical manuscripts and some of Ethiopia's most dedicated priests, is the only one that most consider worth a trip, even though its paintings only date to 1991. It takes 30 minutes by boat, 90 minutes by *tankwa* (available at Tim and Kim Village lodge) or two hours walking from town.

Birgida Maryam   MONASTERY

(by donation, men only; ⊙ 7am-6pm) The most rewarding of the monasteries is known for its jungle and dedicated monks. The building itself is fairly standard, but the highlight is a lovely 16th-century painting of the Virgin Mary.

Galila   MONASTERY

(admission by donation, men only; ⊙ 7am-6pm) The oldest monastery, Galila is a one-hour boat journey southwest of Gorgora. Although destroyed by invading armies in the 16th century, the church was rebuilt using the original stones.

Susenyos' Old Palace   PALACE

FREE Emperor Susenyos (r 1607–32) built his palace, known by locals as Susenyos Ghimb, on a peninsula (called Old Gorgora) 10km west of town. It can be reached in an hour by boat. Compared with Gonder, it's a shambles, but historical architecture buffs should make the trip.

> ### THE LIONS OF ALATASH
>
> Ethiopia has long been considered by big-cat conservationists as an important lion stronghold, but in 2016 it became even more so. A team led by Oxford University's Wildlife Conservation Research Unit discovered a hitherto undocumented population of between 100 and 200 lions in an area of northwestern Ethiopia, along the Ethiopia–Sudan border. The population is shared between Ethiopia's Alatash National Park, with possibly more than 50 lions, and Sudan's Dinder National Park. Alatash, which lies northwest of Bahir Dar and southwest of Gonder, is a relatively new national park – so new, it's yet to be marked on most maps of the country. It's not open to tourists without special permission from the **Ethiopian Wildlife Conservation Authority** (Map p34; www.ewca.gov.et; Chad St; ⊙ 9am-12.30pm & 1.30-5pm Mon-Fri) in Addis.

Portuguese Cathedral
CATHEDRAL

Near Susenyos' palace is the Portuguese Cathedral he funded. The decrepit state (due largely to a 1995 earthquake) illustrates his failed attempt to force Catholicism on his people. The Spanish government has funded some restoration and research. Except in the rainy season, you can drive close to it or walk (three to four hours each way) the whole way from town. The road begins 7.4km north of Gorgora in Abrecha village, the one with the tourism sign at the junction.

Mussolini's Stele
MONUMENT

Gorgora was a hard-fought prize during the Italian occupation and on the way into town you'll pass Mussolini's stele, high on a hill, which commemorates the capture. In town, the historic-looking ruins on a much lower hill are nothing more than a recent, never-completed hotel.

🛏 Sleeping

You could visit on a day trip from Gonder, but you'll really appreciate being here when the sun starts to near the horizon and when the lakeshore falls silent for the night. There are two places to stay.

Gorgora Port Hotel
HOTEL **$**

(☑ 0583-467000; campsites Birr100, s/d/tw with shared bathroom Birr100/170/250, d/tw Birr300/450, 3-bedroom cottage Birr550; **P** 🛜) An old, rather than historic, hotel with a range of rooms, but all except Mengistu's old cottage are tired and the epitome of government-hotel neglect. Electricity and water (cold showers only) are sporadic. It's the relaxing flower garden and lakeshore setting that are the real reason to come.

The restaurant (mains Birr30 to Birr70) has decent food; the catfish cutlet is the speciality of the house.

★ Tim & Kim Village
LODGE **$$**

(☑ 0920-336671; www.timkimvillage.com; camping/mud house per person Birr95, s/d or tw Birr700/850; **P**) Just over the hill west of Gorgora, this Dutch-run spot is in an idyllic lakeside valley. The six solar-powered, thatch-and-stone cottages are cosy and the welcome is warm. Tim leads day and overnight canoeing and trekking trips and you can paddle your own *tankwa*. Meals are normally only available for guests, but with notice day guests (Birr120) are usually welcome.

ℹ Getting There & Away

A daily bus departs Gonder (Birr42; two to three hours) at 5.30am and another when full, usually around noon. The second bus sometimes takes up to five hours. The buses depart Gorgora at 5.30am and 8am.

The ferry sails to Bahir Dar every Thursday at 6am (Birr278, 1½ days). Buy tickets at the Lake Tana Transport Enterprise office (next to Gorgora Port Hotel) up to two days before.

ℹ Getting Around

Boats for touring the monasteries out on the lake are available through the Lake Tana Transport Enterprise office alongside the Gorgora Port Hotel. Ask your guide or someone at your hotel to call. It's Birr1400 out to the palace and monasteries. Fishermen will charge less, but their boats won't have roofs or life vests.

Wunenia & Kosoye

Despite what anyone may tell you, the Simien Mountains are not visible from either of these two ridgetop viewpoints, 22km and 29km northeast of Gonder respectively, but the views are awesome nonetheless. At both Wunenia (ዉኗኒያ) and Kosoye (ኮሶዬ), friendly local guides will lead you on walks of about an hour for a small tip. The guides aren't mandatory at Wunenia, but they know the best viewpoints and can help you find gelada monkeys. Longer treks are also possible.

The **Befiker Kossoye Ecology Lodge** (☑ 0911-250828; www.semienkossoye.com; campsites US$20, s US$65, d or tw US$80, tr US$120, incl breakfast; **P**) at Kosoye is a fine hideaway, though rooms are much simpler than you'd expect at these prices. The three-course set lunch or dinner (Birr150) in the attractive restaurant is welcome post-walk. Any minibus en route between Gonder and Debark can drop you off.

Simien Mountains National Park

No matter how you look at it, the Unesco World Heritage–listed Simien Mountains National Park (የስሜን ተራሮች ብሔራዊ ፓርክ) is one of Africa's most beautiful ranges. This massive plateau, riven with gullies and pinnacles, offers tough but immensely rewarding trekking along the ridge that falls sheer to the plains far below. It's not just the scenery (and altitude) that will leave you speechless, but also the excitement of sitting among a group of gelada monkeys, or watching magnificent walia ibex joust on rock ledges. Whether you come for a stroll or a two-week trek, the Simiens make a great companion to the Historical Circuit's monument viewing.

Geography & Geology

Comprising one of Africa's principal mountain massifs, the park extends from 1600m to 4543m in elevation and much of its 412 sq km lies within the 'Afro-alpine' zone, above 3200m, but there's also heath forest and high montane landscapes.

A number of peaks rise above 4000m, including Ethiopia's highest, 4543m-tall Ras Dashen. (It's actually Ras Dejen, though to avoid confusion we use the common-but-incorrect name.) It's touted by Ethiopian tourism officials as the fourth-highest mountain in Africa; it's actually the 10th.

The Simiens' landscape is incredibly dramatic. It was formed by countless eruptions some 40 million years ago; layer upon layer of molten lava piled up. The subsequent erosion produced the mountains' jagged and spectacular landscapes. The famous pinnacles that sharply and abruptly rise from the surrounding landscape are volcanic necks, the solidified plumbing of the ancient volcanoes.

Wildlife

The highlands are home to three of Ethiopia's larger endemic mammals: the walia ibex (population estimated around 1100), the gelada monkey (5000) and the elusive Ethiopian wolf (100). While wolves are rarely encountered (Bwahit and Ras Dashen offer the best chances), you're nearly guaranteed to meet hundreds-strong troops of gelada monkeys (often erroneously called gelada baboons). These gregarious monkeys, said to be the most sociable of all primates, are also the highest-dwelling primates on the planet, ranging up to 4500m above sea level (it's a close-run thing: mountain gorillas are thought to make it up to 4300m). Other possible primate sightings include black-and-white colobus, Hamydra baboons and others.

You also stand a good chance of seeing the walia ibex (especially around Chenek), which is found only in the Simien Mountains. Other notable mammals are rock hyraxes, jackals, Menelik's bushbucks, klip-springers and leopards; the last is extremely difficult to see.

The often-seen thick-billed raven and the less common black-headed siskin, wattled ibis, spot-breasted plover and Abyssinian woodpecker are some of the 16 Ethiopian–Eritrean endemic birds. Though common, one of the most memorable sights is the soaring lammergeyer.

When to Go

➡ December to March is the driest time.

➡ In October, after the rains, the scenery is greenest.

➡ During the main rainy season, between June and September, mist often obscures the views and trails can be slippery. However, you'll usually get several hours of clear, dry weather for walking since the rain tends to come in short, sharp downpours.

➡ Wildflowers come out in August and last until October, except the ivory-coloured Abyssinian rose, an Ethiopian endemic, which blooms March to May.

➡ Daytime temperatures are consistently between 11.5°C and 18°C, while 3°C is typical at night. Between December and April night-time temperatures often dip below freezing.

Maps

The most useful trekking map is produced by the Institute of Geography, University of Berne, Switzerland: the *Simen* [sic]

ℹ **SIMIEN MOUNTAINS NATIONAL PARK**

Why Go?
This is one of the most beautiful mountain ranges in Africa, with world-class trekking and fabulous wildlife watching.

Gateway Towns
Gonder, Debark

Practicalities
Pay park fees and organise compulsory scouts and (possibly) guides at park headquarters.

Budget Tips
Get a small group together to minimise per-person costs for scouts and guides.

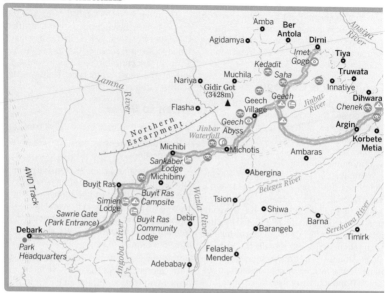

Mountains Trekking Map (2003; 1:100,000). It's getting increasingly hard to find – ask around in Gonder, or your hotel. If you do find it, the cost is Birr300.

◉ Sights

Jinbar Waterfall   WATERFALL
The 15-minute walk from the roadside to the lookout across the chasm to Jinbar Waterfall is well worth taking. The views are vertiginous and they're at their best in the rainy season when water cascades down a sheer cliff across the other side of the valley.

🏃 Trekking

'The foot that is restless, will tread on a turd.'
Ethiopian proverb

When trekking in the mountains you'll mostly be following centuries-old paths that crisscross the slopes and connect villages with pasture lands, but sometimes you'll also use the main park road. On some stretches the walking is fairly level, but there are long, steep climbs and descents in many places.

Organising trekking yourself at **park headquarters** (📷 0581-170016; Debark; ⏰ 8.30am-12.30pm & 1.30-5.30pm) in Debark is straightforward, but it can take up to two hours so it's best to arrive the afternoon before you plan to trek, or to book through a reputable agency in advance of your visit.

Park fees are payable at the park headquarters in Debark.

Entrance fees won't be refunded once paid. However, if mules, cooks, guides and scouts aren't used (because of bad weather or acclimatisation difficulties), their fees can be refunded.

Also be sure to allow time for acclimatisation, particularly if you fly to Gonder right after arriving in Ethiopia.

Guides, Scouts, Cooks & Mule Men
Cooks, scouts, mules and guides are all organised at park headquarters. 'Scouts' (armed park rangers) are compulsory (Birr150 per day). Guides (Birr330 per day) are only required for people travelling with an agency, but are highly recommended for their knowledge of the mountains and command of English. Some trekkers, unable to communicate with the scout, end up regretting not having a guide along. Guides are trained by the national park on courses established by an Austrian team.

In general the guides are excellent. We've heard, however, that some try to rush their clients on the final day to get home sooner.

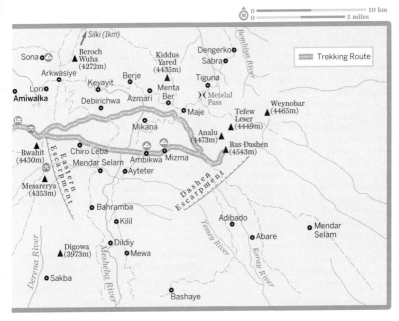

Should this happen, refuse to play along and report it when you return. The guides work on a rota basis directly with the park, but you can request a particular guide if, for instance, you hear a good report from a fellow traveller.

Cooks cost Birr350 to Birr400 per day (cooking for one to six people), a welcome luxury for some. Porters aren't available, but mules (Birr120 per day) with handlers (Birr120 per day) are. Two handlers can handle three mules and each mule can carry 45kg. If you plan on covering two days' worth of trekking in one, you'll have to pay your team double for the day.

Guides, scouts, cooks and mule handlers should bring their own food and they usually do when the trekkers aren't hiring a cook. Regardless, you should make sure the park official organising your trip and/or your guide ensures the team is not going to look to you for sustenance. Or just bring extra packets of rice etc and make the team happy.

Equipment

Mattresses (Birr50 per day), sleeping bags (Birr50 per day), two-person tents (Birr100 per day), rain jackets (Birr50), walking sticks (to hire/buy Birr50/400) and cooking equipment, including gas stoves (Birr100 per day for two people), can be hired at park headquarters. Check tents carefully and use two sleeping bags to ensure a warm night.

Organised Treks

There are numerous tour operators and travel agencies in Addis Ababa and several more in Gonder that can arrange transport, guides, equipment rental and food. However, they charge you more for similar services that you can easily arrange yourself at park headquarters. On the other hand, they probably have higher-quality camping gear.

Some of the park's top guides, such as Shiferaw Asrat (p91) and Nurlign Hassen (p91), also organise all-inclusive trips starting in Gonder or Addis, which should be cheaper than going through one of the bigger agencies.

Choosing a Trekking Route

Most people trek for four or five days and begin in Debark. In four you can trek to Geech and back; with an extra day you could get to Chenek, taking in Mt Bwahit. If time is of the essence then in two days you could walk from Debark to Sankaber and back; add a third day and you can get to Geech, which has the most spectacular scenery. With eight days to play with, you could summit Ras Dashen.

Many people maximise their mountain experience by using vehicles to access Sankaber and/or Chenek. A minibus can get you to Sankaber year-round, but you'll need a 4WD to reach Chenek during the rainy season. Arranging pick-up or drop-off at Chenek allows a long but satisfying three-day trek to/from Debark.

If you have time, strong legs and a hatred of doubling back, you could finish your trek at Adi Arkay, 75km north of Debark. This allows a mix between highland and lowland scenery and the views up the valleys are just as amazing as the views down into them. Note that since it takes the guides, mules and other members of your team two days to return to Debark from Adi Arkay, you must pay two days' extra fee.

Though it's rarely done, guides can even take you all the way to Lalibela. You'll need to swim across some rivers, carry food for nearly the entire 15 to 17 days and will probably have to purchase rather than hire the mules. An epic trip.

Debark-to-Chenek Trek

The following Debark-to-Chenek trek is the classic five-day route. The times have been estimated in consultation with local guides, but vary from person to person and also depend on whether exact routes are followed.

Debark to Buyit Ras (10km; Three to Four Hours)

Sankaber can be reached in a single day, but many trekkers prefer to (or, if they arrive from Gonder that day, *must*) break at Buyit Ras, where there's an abundance of gelada monkeys. There's also a community lodge and camping spot with beautiful views, or the expensive Simien Lodge (p92). Some people prefer to drive to Buyit Ras, bypassing the heavily populated areas outside the park, and trek to Sankaber (13km; three to four hours) from there.

Buyit Ras to Geech Camp via Sankaber (25km; Seven to Eight Hours)

The road will take you straight to Sankaber, but the scenic route along the escarpment isn't to be missed. There are particularly good views between Michibi and Sankaber. From Sankaber to Geech is between four and five hours' walk.

Geech Camp to Chenek via Imet Gogo (20km; Seven to Nine Hours)

Geech to Chenek could take about five to six hours, but you'd be crazy not to take in Imet Gogo, around 5km northeast of Geech. This promontory, at 3926m, affords some of the most spectacular views of the Simien Mountains. It adds about 1½ hours one way. To make a day trip of it, you could also visit the viewpoints at Saha and Kedadit (2.5km) and then return to Geech camp.

From Imet Gogo you have two choices: the first is to return to Geech by your outward route, then head directly south and back across the Jinbar River to where you'll meet the dirt road that leads to Chenek. The alternative, which is harder but more scenic, is to follow the escarpment all the way to Chenek. Chenek is probably the best spot in the Simien Mountains for wildlife. A short walk often brings you to a herd of walia ibex and near Chenek is **Korbete Metia**, a stunning spot where lammergeyers are often seen.

Chenek to Mt Bwahit & Return (6km; Five to Six Hours)

If you can spare more time, the ever-tempting summit of Mt Bwahit (4430m) lies southeast of Chenek camp.

Return Routes

For the return journey you can retrace your steps (Sankaber is seven to eight hours away from Chenek), though most people just hike back along the road.

Climbing Ras Dashen

Ras Dashen, frankly, doesn't offer a great deal beyond the satisfaction of 'bagging it'. And thanks to an odd perspective from its summit, nearby peaks actually look higher. This has led disgruntled trekkers to drag their guides up the other peaks, repeatedly musing the 'one over there' is higher! It's not.

If you want to skip the initial trek, you can drive to Chenek and start the climb there. But even though that trek only takes three days, the park will charge you for six!

Chenek to Ambikwa (22km; Eight to Nine Hours)

Heading on from Chenek, the first day takes you along a track leading eastward and then southeastward up towards a good viewpoint on the eastern escarpment north of Mt Bwahit. To the east, across the valley of the Mesheba River, you can see Ras Dashen.

Ambikwa to Ras Dashen & Return (17km; Eight to 10 Hours)

Most trekkers stay two nights at Ambikwa and go up to the summit of Ras Dashen on the day in between. It's a good idea to start at first light. If you don't have a mule man, it's recommended that you hire another scout here to guard your tent for the day.

At Ras Dashen there are three distinct points, and much discussion about which is the true summit. The total walk from Ambikwa to reach the highest summit is about five to six hours. If you want to knock off the others, add two to three hours for each. Returning by the same route takes about three to four hours. Although there's some scrambling at the very end, overall the trek isn't very difficult.

Return Routes

Most trekkers return from Ambikwa to Debark (77km; three days) along the same route to Chenek and then follow the road to Sankaber.

One alternative is to trek from Ambikwa to Arkwasiye, northeast of Chenek, taking in the nearby peaks of Beroch Wuha (4272m) and Silki (4420m). From Arkwasiye to Adi Arkay will take two to three days of strenuous walking. The total route from Ambikwa to Adi Arkay is about 65km (three to five days). Note that facilities down here are very basic and you may end up sleeping in villages. From the last campsite it's two hours to Adi Arkay, which lies 75km north of Debark. From there you can continue to Aksum in stages using minibuses or hitchhiking.

Day Trips

It's only a two-hour drive (in dry season) to Chenek, which leaves lots of time for strolling, taking photos and lounging with gelada monkeys at various spots along the way. During the rainy season the narrow **Jinbar Waterfall** (p88), estimated to drop 500m, is an almost-mandatory stop. It's unsigned 4km after Sankaber, down a short (15-minute), muddy trail.

The six- or seven-hour round-trip walk from the road near Ambaras to the amazing Imet Gogo viewpoint would be a popular day trip if park authorities didn't insist on charging tourists the price of a two-day trip. (Park guides, knowing this policy is taking away business from them, have protested, but to no avail.)

Although there will be precious little time actually in the park, you can drive to it and back from Gonder in a day.

Tours

★ Argin Village Visits
TOURS

(discoversimien@gmail.com; per person short/long tour Birr200/300) A fabulous initiative worth supporting is the guided visits to Argin village, in the heart of the park a few kilometres southwest of Chenek. There are two options. One starts at 10am, runs for four hours and includes a 1½-hour trek with a local guide, *injera* baking, beer making and a coffee ceremony. Revenues go straight to the local community.

There's a shorter, 2½-hour version that begins at 11am, although we strongly recommend the longer version.

★ Shiferaw Asrat
TOUR

(☑ 0918-776499; www.simientrek.com) One of the park's top guides, with very professional organisation.

★ Nurlign Hassen
TOUR

(☑ 0910-373904; www.simienmountainstour.com) One of the park's top guides.

SimienEcoTours
TOUR

(☑ 0918-731724, 058-2110044; www.simienecotours.com) Good company for trekking in the Simiens.

🛏 Sleeping

The standard of accommodation in the area is improving, but outside of the two main lodges in the park, the hotels and campsites are simple.

🛏 Debark

Hotels in Debark range from very basic to simple but fine – sadly, it doesn't get much better than that.

★ Pension Everlasting
GUESTHOUSE $

(☑ 0581-171173, 0918-724558; simienpension everlasting@gmail.com;; s/d/tw/tr Birr300/400/500/600; 🛜) Our pick of the budget options in Debark, Pension Everlasting has a friendly English-speaking owner and a fine little restaurant where mostly local, organic ingredients are used. The rooms are fairly similar to those elsewhere, but the quiet location and friendly service are what stand out.

Jaint Lobelia Hotel
HOTEL $

(☑ 0918-763002; s/d/tw Birr320/450/550) Similar in standard to the other places around town, but with slightly older furnishings, this place only warrants a mention because it has bathtubs.

Unique Landscape Hotel
HOTEL $

(☎0581-170152; www.uniquelshotel.com; s/d/tw Birr350/400/500; ℗) One of the quieter options along Debark's main street, the Landscape has basic but generally OK rooms out the back, but a pretty ordinary restaurant, so you may want to eat elsewhere.

Simien Park Hotel
HOTEL $

(☎0581-170005; s/d/tw Birr300/400/450, s/d with shared bathroom Birr150/200; ℗ 🛜) About 1km north of park headquarters, this is one of Debark's more popular hotels, but that has more to do with a lack of choice than any innate quality. The rooms out back are fine, if a touch basic and overpriced, while all sorts of hangers-on seem to congregate out front. The restaurant (mains from Birr60) is fine, but nothing more.

★ Sona Hotel
HOTEL $$

(☎0581-170627, 0918-350967; www.sonahotel ethiopia.com; s/d/tw/tr/f US$25/35/35/45/55; ℗ 🛜) With undoubtedly the best rooms in Debark, Sona Hotel is a good choice. It has a bar, probably the town's best restaurant (mains Birr80 to Birr120) and the rooms at the front have views out over the town.

🛏 On The Mountains

With a few exceptions, you're required to camp at the official campsites (Birr10 per person). The three busy highland camps have showers and all the camps have long-drop loos as well as huts for your guides and scouts.

Sleeping and eating with locals used to be normal for trekkers, but it's now actively discouraged by guides because they've dealt with so many trekkers complaining about the basic conditions. Your bed will most likely be the floor and you'll share space with children, chickens, cows and fleas.

Funded by the Austrian government and managed by locals, the community lodges (Birr120) are simple two-room, four-bed dorms (at Buyit Ras, Geech and Chenek) offering an alternative to camping, though you should still bring a sleeping bag. Guests staying in them must still pay the park camping fee. Local meals (pasta, tibs etc) and drinks are available.

There are also two excellent privately run lodges that make a priority of clean environmental practices.

★ Limalimo Lodge
LODGE $$$

(☎0918-776499,0931-688062;www.limalimolodge. com; s/d/tr full board Oct-Apr US$220/320 /410, May & Jun US$185/270/360, Sep US$150/220/310; ⊘ closed Jul & Aug) Now here's something really special – one of the best places to stay in Ethiopia. The location is the best in the Simiens, with incredible views from the terrace; the architect-designed look is clean-lined and contemporary, and the lodge supports local development projects and was built by members of the local community. Rooms are supremely comfortable with massive windows and lovely day beds.

Local building materials (eucalyptus poles in the ceiling, rammed-earth soils for the walls to keep the heat in) were used throughout. Meals are also outstanding, and there are plenty of activities on offer, from half-day visits to the local village (per person US$5) to early-morning yoga, traditional Ethiopian foot massages and walks in the vicinity for fine views and the chance to see five primate species. A US$10 conservation fee (included in the room rate) goes towards a newly built local school. Shiferaw and Julia are warm, welcoming and knowledgeable hosts.

Simien Lodge
LODGE $$$

(☎0582-310741; www.simiens.com; s incl breakfast US$98-205, d US$105-215, f US$148-300; ℗) At 3260m this is Africa's highest hotel. The thatch-and-stone tukuls (cone-shaped mud huts) are large and comfy, although many travellers feel they don't get nearly enough for the price. Despite the location, rooms are on the dark side and the under-floor heating does little to take the edge off freezing nights. But the food is excellent and its commitment to local projects is admirable.

🍴 Eating

Basic trekking supplies are available in Debark, but we strongly recommend stocking up in Gonder. Debark also has a bakery. Outside Debark there are no shops, though you can buy eggs, chickens and sheep at villages. Water is available during the trek, but should be treated.

There is a handful of passable hotel restaurants in Debark, while the two mountain lodges have excellent restaurants for guests.

Great Work Cafe BREAKFAST $
(📋 0918-156035; Debark; breakfast Birr35-50; ⏱ from 6am) Just up the hill and opposite the bus station, this simple cafe does excellent breakfasts, including *ful* (an Egyptian staple of broad bean and butter purée), eggs and other excellent choices. The rest of the day it has cakes to choose from and not much else.

Limalimo Lodge INTERNATIONAL $$
(📋 0918-776499; www.limalimolodge.com; 3-course meals per person US$15; ⏱ noon-3pm) High on a hilltop north of Debark, with some of the best views you'll find in the Simiens, the stylish and uber-contemporary Limalimo Lodge opens its restaurant for nonguests and it's well worth the trip. The cooking (from a menu that changes daily) is accomplished and the service excellent. For dinner you'll need to book and see if it has room.

Simien Lodge INTERNATIONAL $$$
(📋 0582-310741; www.simiens.com; lunch set menu US$15, dinner buffet US$18; ⏱ 11.30am-2pm & 7.30-9.30pm) The best place for passing travellers to eat in the park, the restaurant at Simien Lodge does lunch set menus and dinner buffets most nights, with an emphasis on well-prepared international dishes in the lodge's agreeable stone-and-thatch *tukul* restaurant.

❶ Getting There & Away

Two morning buses and lots of minibuses run from Debark to Gonder (Birr40, 2½ hours). The only bus to Shire (for Aksum) is the Gonder service that passes through Debark around 8am, but it's often full. If you want to guarantee a seat, the national park office, your guide or hotel will reserve you a place by getting somebody in Gonder to ride in your seat between Gonder and Debark. They charge Birr300 to Birr350 for this service; arrange it a day in advance. Hitching is possible, but you may need more than one day to reach Shire.

❶ Getting Around

There's usually a bus at 6am from Debark to Janamora, which can drop trekkers anywhere along the way, though you'll probably need to pay Birr100 no matter where you get off. It can't be used on the return trip because there's almost no chance of a free seat. Convincing your guide to let you use the occasional Isuzu supply trucks is likely to be tough since it's illegal, but some trekkers who get to Chenek and find they've had their fill of the mountains manage to do it, albeit at an extortionate rate.

The park gate opens at 6am and driving is not permitted before this or after 6pm. Guides can arrange minibus and 4WD hire, though the latter can be very expensive because it usually comes from Gonder. Minibuses can reach everywhere most of the year, but 4WD is required to go beyond Sankaber between July and September.

Aksum

POP 56,500 / ELEV 2130M

Aksum (አክሱም) is a riddle waiting to be solved. Did the Queen of Sheba really call the town's dusty streets home? Does the Ark of the Covenant that holds Moses' 10 Commandments reside in a small Aksum chapel? Is one of the Three Wise Men really buried here? And what exactly do those famous stelae signify?

Dr Neville Chittick once described Aksum (often incorrectly spelled Axum) as 'the last of the great civilisations of Antiquity to be revealed to modern knowledge'. Yet even today, despite being one of the most important ancient sites in sub-Saharan Africa, this Unesco World Heritage site has revealed only a tiny fraction of its secrets, and an exploration of its ruined tombs and palaces is sure to light a spark of excitement.

History

The early history of Aksum, like most Ethiopian history, is shrouded in such a fog of legend that the truth remains largely unknown. While debate continues between historians and the majority of Ethiopians about whether or not Aksum really was the Queen of Sheba's capital in the 10th century BC, what's certain is that a high civilisation started to rise here as early as 400 BC.

By the 1st century AD, Greek merchants knew Aksum as a great city and the powerful capital of an extensive empire. For close to 1000 years, Aksum dominated the vital seaborne trade between Africa and Asia and the kingdom was numbered among the ancient world's greatest states. But then, quite suddenly, the power of Aksum collapsed and the city turned into a forgotten backwater. Only now, a millennium later, are archaeologists starting to take a serious interest in the city.

⊙ Sights

Ancient Aksum obelisks pepper the area, and whether you're looking down on a small specimen or staring up at a grand tower, you'll be duly bowled over. The closer you

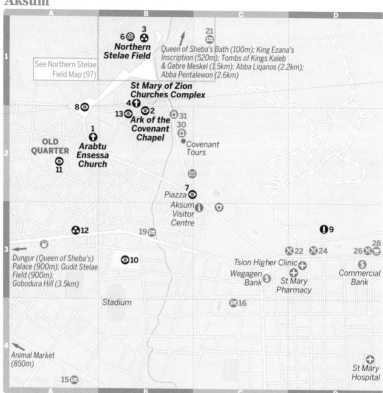

Queen of Sheba's Bath (100m); King Ezana's
Inscription (520m); Tombs of Kings Kaleb
& Gebre Meskel (1.5km); Abba Liqanos (2.2km);
Abba Pentalewon (2.6km)

**St Mary of Zion
Churches Complex**

**Ark of the
Covenant
Chapel**

Covenant
Tours

Piazza

Aksum
Visitor
Centre

Dungur (Queen of Sheba's)
Palace (900m); Gudit Stelae
Field (900m);
Gobodura Hill (3.5km)

Tsion Higher Clinic

Wegagen
Bank

St Mary
Pharmacy

Commercial
Bank

Stadium

Animal Market
(850m)

St Mary
Hospital

get, the more amazing they are. A full day
is a minimum for seeing everything worth
seeing. And carry a torch for the tombs.

If you can get your hands on Stuart
Munro-Hay's *Ethiopia: The Unknown Land*
you'll find an excellent compendium to Aksum's history, archaeology and major sites
and monuments.

The brand new Aksum Visitor Centre
(p105) was due to open in the weeks after
our visit and it's a welcome addition to the
traveller's experience. Aside from information on the town, the centre will offer some
streaming documentaries on Aksum's history and it is here that you can buy your ticket
that covers many of the city's historic sites.

One admission ticket (adult/student
Birr50/25) covers Aksum's archaeological
sites, but not the St Mary of Zion church
compound and the monasteries of Abba
Pentalewon and Abba Liqanos. The ticket is
good for three days.

★**St Mary of Zion Churches
Complex**   CHURCH
(Birr200, video camera Birr100; ⊙8am-12.30pm
& 2.30-5.30pm Mon-Fri, 9am-noon & 2.30-5.30pm
Sat & Sun) Though religions have come and
gone, Aksum has always remained a holy
city – welcome to the centre of the universe
for Christian Ethiopians. A church of some
form has stood here since the earliest days of
Ethiopian Christianity and it was God himself who, descending from heaven, indicated
that a church should be built here, though
the original church is long gone. The complex includes the new church, old church,
museum and the chapel said to house the
Ark of the Covenant.

★**Ark of the Covenant Chapel**   LANDMARK
In between the old and new St Mary of Zion
churches is the real reason for most people's
devotion: a tiny, carefully guarded chapel
that houses what most Ethiopians believe

is the legendary Ark of the Covenant. Don't think you can take a peek: just one specially chosen guardian has access to the Ark, and even he is not allowed to look at it.

Nobody else is allowed in the chapel and foreigners aren't even allowed to approach the fence guarding the chapel grounds because previously some foreigners tried to scale the fence and rush into the chapel! No matter what you think of the legend, there's no denying that to be in this church compound during a major service or festival, when thousands of pilgrims pour into the city, is an experience of pure devotion and faith that will leave you spellbound.

Note that the building currently has a leaky roof and the ark may be moved, at least temporarily.

New Church of St Mary of Zion   CHURCH
(combined ticket with Old Church of St Mary of Zion Birr200, video camera Birr100; ⊙8am-12.30pm &

2.30-5.30pm Mon-Fri, 9am-noon & 2.30-5.30pm Sat & Sun) The huge new church of St Mary of Zion was built in the 1960s so women had a place to worship and it displays Haile Selassie's usual hideous taste. Still it does cut a dramatic silhouette on the skyline. Beside it, a disproportionately tall bell tower, inspired

AKSUM'S FALL

After Aksum lost its grip on the Red Sea trade due to the rise of Islamic Arabs' fortunes, the society quickly imploded and sent Ethiopia into the dark ages for five centuries. Why this happened when it was still rich in natural resources is the subject of many theories.

The environmental argument suggests that Aksum's ever-increasing population led to overcropping of the land, deforestation and eventually soil erosion. The climatic explanation claims that a slight 'global warming' took place, which finished Aksum's agriculture and eventually led to drought and famine. The military argument claims that Aksum was undermined by continual incursions from neighbouring tribes.

According to tradition, Aksumite power was usurped around the 9th century by the dreaded warrior Queen Gudit (or Judit), a pagan or Jew, who killed the ruling king and burnt down the city. This legend seems to be borne out by at least two documents written at about this time, and may represent a rare case of Ethiopian tradition meshing, at least partly, with reality.

by the stelae, sprouts heavenwards, while the ruins of the original church sit south of the new church and museum.

Old Church of St Mary of Zion CHURCH
(combined ticket with New Church of St Mary of Zion Birr200, video camera Birr100; ☺ 8am-12.30pm & 2.30-5.30pm Mon-Fri, 9am-noon & 2.30-5.30pm Sat & Sun) The rectangular, men-only old church at the southern end of the complex of churches here is a remarkable example of traditional architecture built by the Emperor Fasiladas, the founder of Gonder, in 1665. Inside there are fine original murals, including a painting of the Nine Saints. Some say the foundation on which it sits may belong to Africa's first church, supposedly erected by King Ezana in the 4th century and destroyed in the 9th century during Queen Gudit's devastating raid.

A rebuilt version was destroyed during the incursions of Ahmed Gragn the Left-Handed in 1535, and some remains lie just south of the museum.

Also of historical interest, at the top of the stairs in front of the old church, is the **Throne Stone** where the coronation of 261 Aksumite kings took place.

★ Abba Pentalewon MONASTERY
(አባ ጰንጠሊዎን; men/women Birr100/75, personal video camera Birr20; ☺ 8am-5.30pm) High above Aksum, on top of a tall, narrow peak, is Abba Pentalewon monastery. Tradition states it was built by Abba Pentalewon, one of the Nine Saints and a man who is said to have prayed nonstop for 40 years, and that this is where King Kaleb retired to after abdicating his throne. The views, the monastery itself and the treasures are all worth

the climb, although women may feel a little short-changed by the experience.

The site of the monastery was sacred to pagans and it's thought the monastery was built here to bolster Christianity and eradicate pagan beliefs. The original church, the foundation of which can still be seen, may date to the 6th century but the attractive 'old' church (men only) is from the 1940s. Some centuries-old paintings hang amid the new. Women can enter the new church to see similar but only new paintings. There's no museum for the treasures (which include crowns of King Kaleb and Gebre Meskel), but an unusually friendly monk will bring them out to show you – his show is kind of fun.

The main access path (walking only) is past the tombs of Kings Kaleb and Gebre Meskel. For the return trip you can head downhill to Aksum's main road near the Consular International Hotel.

★ Arabtu Ensessa Church CHURCH
(አርባዕቱ እንስሳ ቤተክርስቲያን; combined ticket with St Mary of Zion Church Birr200; ☺ 8am-12.30pm) The 'Four Beasts' Church, named after the writers of the Biblical Gospels, was rebuilt in the 1950s and is worth a look for the wonderful murals (most modern, but a few old) covering nearly every centimetre of the interior. The saints and angels on the ceiling are particularly delightful, while there's a rather scary representation of the devil. You may find it open in the afternoon, but don't count on it.

★ Northern Stelae Field ARCHAEOLOGICAL SITE
(archaeological sites combined ticket Birr50; ☺ 8am-5.30pm) Despite the dizzying gran-

deur of the numerous rock needles reaching for the stars, it's what's under your feet here that's most important. Amazingly, about 90% of the field hasn't yet been dug, so no matter where you walk, there's a good chance there's an undiscovered tomb with untold treasures beneath. This is part of Aksum's appeal: the thought that fascinating finds and secrets lurk in the depths. That said, these are some of the ancient world's most striking monuments.

All of the tombs excavated to date had been pillaged by robbers, so very little is known about Aksumite burial customs or the identities of those buried.

➤ Tomb of the False Door

In 1972 the unique Tomb of the False Door was discovered. It lies in the western extremity of the Northern Stelae Field and is thought to date around the 4th century AD. Complex in structure, its stone blocks are also larger and more finely dressed than those found in some other tombs. Comprising an antechamber and inner chamber, it's surrounded on three sides by a passage.

Above the tomb, at ground level, a rectangular, probably flat-roofed building would once have stood (measuring some 12 sq metres by 2.8m high). Above the stairs descending into the tomb's chamber was a stone slab

carved with a false door almost identical to those found on the stelae. Look for the iron clamps fixing blocks of stone together like giant staples.

Judging from the lengths to which the grave robbers went to gain access, it's thought to have contained objects of great value. A single stone base that held the sarcophagus can still be seen.

➤ Mausoleum

The so-called mausoleum has a monumental portal (hewn from a single slab of granite) marking the tomb's entrance and is carved with the stelae's curious false-door motifs. The portal leads into a passageway with 10 chambers. In total the tomb covers some 240 sq metres. Part of the tomb was disfigured at some unknown date by robbers, who succeeded in digging through 1.5m of solid masonry.

➤ Tomb of the Brick Arches

Dating from the end of the 3rd century, this tomb is remarkably well preserved and contains four rock-cut chambers, subdivided by a series of brick arches built with lime mortar. These arches are the same as those that had been in the mausoleum before the grave robbers damaged it.

The tomb was first excavated by archaeologists in 1974, and though tomb robbers had

Northern Stelae Field

N   0 — 100 m

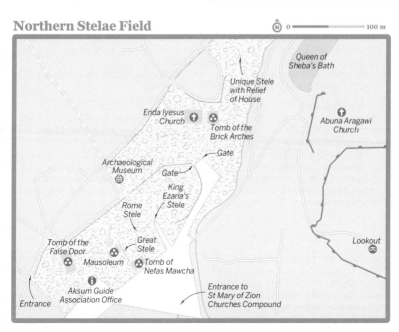

- Queen of Sheba's Bath
- Unique Stele with Relief of House
- Enda Iyesus Church
- Tomb of the Brick Arches
- Abuna Aragawi Church
- Gate
- Archaeological Museum
- Gate
- King Ezana's Stele
- Rome Stele
- Great Stele
- Lookout
- Tomb of the False Door
- Mausoleum
- Tomb of Nefas Mawcha
- Aksum Guide Association Office
- Entrance
- Entrance to St Mary of Zion Churches Compound

A QUICK GUIDE TO AKSUM'S STELAE

For as long as 5000 years, monoliths have been used in northeast Africa as tombstones and monuments to local rulers. In Aksum this tradition reached its apogee. Like Egypt's pyramids, Aksum's stelae were like great billboards announcing to the world the authority, power and greatness of the ruling families. Aksum's astonishing stelae are striking for their huge size, their incredible state of preservation and their curiously modern look. Sculpted from single pieces of granite, the later ones come complete with little windows, doors and even door handles and locks that make them look remarkably like tower blocks.

Despite granite being famously hard, Aksum's masons worked it superbly, often following an architectural design that mirrored the traditions seen in Aksumite houses and palaces.

Metal plates, perhaps in the form of a crescent moon and disc (pagan symbol of the sun), are thought to have been riveted to the top of the stelae, both at the front and back. The crescent is also an ancient pagan symbol, originating from southern Arabia. In 1996 a broken plate that could have matched the rusty rivet holes atop a stele was excavated from the Tomb of Brick Arches. It bore the effigy of a face, perhaps that of the ruler to whom the plate's stele was dedicated. It's on display in the Archaeological Museum. Despite locals having long ago assigned king's names to each stele, nobody knows who they were dedicated to. (Though it *is* certain the kings chosen by locals are incorrect.) For this reason, historians only use numbers to identify each stele.

Ethiopian traditions have it that the Ark of the Covenant's celestial powers were harnessed to transport the mighty monoliths 4km from the quarries, and raise them – the largest weighed no less than 520 tonnes! Archaeologists are confident that the earthly forces of elephants, rollers and winches were responsible.

Gudit Stelae Field   የጉዲት የመቃብር ትክል ድንጋዮች መስክ

Though they're far less arresting than those found in the centre of town, the stelae in the Gudit Stelae Field are still worth a visit.

The field is named after Queen Gudit, and most stelae here are small, undressed and lie on the ground. Locals suggest the largest stele, alongside the road to the east, marks the Queen of Sheba's grave. But neither of these associations seem possible since the stelae date to the 2nd century AD.

Despite excavations in the 1970s and 1990s, little is known about the field. Though some mark graves, neither rock-hewn nor constructed tombs have been found. Finds here did include a set of fine 3rd-century glass goblets, which has led scholars to suggest the area was the burial site of Aksumite society's lesser nobles.

The entire field is cropland, so from June into October you can only walk on the footpath through the middle and along the road.

Northern Stelae Field   የሰሜን የመቃብር ትክል ድንጋዮች መስክ

The Northern Stelae Field is Ethiopia's biggest and most important stelae field. It contains 66 stelae from the 3rd and 4th centuries AD, though the original number was higher – some have been removed, others may lie buried.

The stelae range from 1m to 33m in height and from simple slabs of stone (the majority) to finely dressed rectangular blocks, usually with flat sides and a rounded or conical apex. Though they were undoubtedly connected with the practice of human burial, it's not yet certain if every stele marks a tomb. The three largest and most famous stelae (King Ezana's Stele, Great Stele and Rome Stele) are found here.

beaten them to it by centuries, they still discovered fragments of gold jewellery, beads, bronze objects, weapons and glass objects. Nobody knows who was buried here, but archaeologists surmise that the tomb contained the bodies of an elderly woman, a man and one other person and that the treasures found within indicate that they were people of high standing.

The tomb remains closed because archaeologists think further excavation is warrant-

KING EZANA'S STELAE

Although standing slightly off kilter, the magnificent 23m-high, 160-tonne Stele 3 has done something no other stele of similar stature has done: remained standing (albeit today it's aided by a sling). Henry Salt, the British traveller and first foreigner to describe it in 1805, proclaimed it 'the most admirable and perfect monument of its kind'. The stone platform at its base is believed to have served as an altar. Within the platform are four 30cm-deep cavities, which probably collected blood during sacrificial offerings. It's older than both the Great Stele and Rome Stele and only has carvings on three sides.

GREAT STELE

Lying like a broken soldier, the massive 33m Stele 1, also known locally as King Ramhai's Stele, is believed to be the largest single block of stone that humans have ever attempted to erect, and overshadows even the Egyptian obelisks in its conception and ambition.

Scholars theorise that it fell during its erection sometime early in the 4th century. Comparing the unworked 'root' (only 2.7m long) with the sleek, carved base and the intricate walia ibex carvings near its top gives you a vivid idea of the precision, finesse and technical competence of Aksum's stone workers.

As it toppled it collided with the massive 360-tonne stone sheltering the central chamber of Nefas Mawcha's tomb. This shattered the upper portion of the stele and collapsed the tomb's central chamber, scattering the massive roof supports like toothpicks. Seeing that no other stele was ever raised here, it seems likely that the collapse sounded the death knell on the long tradition of obelisk erection in Aksum. Some scholars have even suggested that the disaster may have actually contributed to the people's conversion to Christianity. More controversially, some propose it may have been sabotaged deliberately to feign a sign of God. Whatever the origin of its downfall, the stele remains exactly where it tumbled 1600 years ago, a permanent reminder of the defeat of paganism by Christianity.

ROME STELE

At 24.6m high and 170 tonnes, Stele 2 is the second-largest stele ever produced at Aksum. Like the Great Stele, its ornate carvings of multistoreyed windows and doors adorn all four sides. Pillagers raiding the site are believed to have accidentally caused its collapse sometime between the 10th and 16th centuries. It broke into three pieces with the cracks visible.

In 1937 the stele's remains were shipped to Italy on Mussolini's personal orders. On arrival it was reassembled and raised once more in Rome's Piazza di Porta Capena, where it was known as the Aksum Obelisk. It remained in Rome until 2005, when decades of negotiations were finally victorious over diplomatic feet-dragging. It was returned to Aksum that year and Unesco raised it in 2007, just in time for the Ethiopian millennium celebration. It's now the most impressive of all the stelae.

OTHER STELAE

Lying prone between the Mausoleum and Tomb of the False Door is another important stele, albeit unfinished...hence it's known as the unfinished stele. The fact it's unfinished is evidence that the final carving of stelae was finished on site and not at the quarries.

Although none still stand, there are several large stelae in the field east of Enda Iyesus church. The most notable boasts decoration near the top, and is sometimes called the unique stele. The large relief of a house-like object, formed by a rectangle surmounted by a triangle, is claimed by some to be early proof of Aksum's claim to house the Ark of the Covenant; look underneath for further intricate relief carvings. There are always plans to raise this stele once again, but they remain just plans.

NORTHERN ETHIOPIA AKSUM

ed, but you can clearly see one of the arches through the gate.

➡ Tomb of Nefas Mawcha

The megalithic Tomb of Nefas Mawcha consists of a large rectangular central chamber surrounded on three sides by a passage. The tomb is unusual for its large size, the sophistication of the structure and the size of the stones used for its construction (the stone that roofs the central chamber measures 17.3m by 6.4m and weighs some 360 tonnes!). The force of the Great Stele crashing into its roof caused the tomb's spectacular collapse.

Locals believe that under this tomb is a 'magic machine', the original implement the Aksumites used to melt stone in order to shape the stelae and tombs. The same type of machine was apparently also used to create some of the rock-hewn churches of Tigray.

St Mary of Zion Church Museum   MUSEUM

(combined ticket with Churches of St Mary of Zion Birr200, video camera Birr100; ⊘ 8am-12.30pm & 2.30-5.30pm Mon-Fri, 9am-noon & 2.30-5.30pm Sat & Sun) The museum inside the St Mary of Zion Church complex contains an impressive haul of treasure, including an unsurpassed collection of former Ethiopian rulers' crowns and a dazzling display of gold and silver chalices, crosses, jewellery and even drums. It clearly demonstrates the immense wealth of the Church.

Gobodura Hill   HILL

(ጎቦዱራ ተራራ) A site known as Wuchate Golo is one of Aksum's four ancient quarries, the birthplace of the famous stelae. Several stelae (all unmarked) were almost completely freed from the rock, but then abandoned. Just as interesting is the Lioness of Gobodura (የጎቦዱራዋ እንስት አንበሳ). It was here that the Archangel Mikael fought a tremendous battle with a fierce lioness. The fight ended when the saint hurled the beast into a massive boulder with such force that its outline is still visible.

Mystery still surrounds the exact tools that were used by the master craftsmen of Aksum, but in the quarry you can see clearly the process by which they cut the hard stone from the rock. After the intended break was mapped out, a row of rectangular sockets was cut. Then, perhaps, dry wooden wedges were inserted into the sockets and made to expand by the use of water.

The parking area is signed 3km west of Aksum, off the Shire road. It's quite a rough walk from the road over boulders and through scrub, and you'll need a guide to help you find anything. It's typically a one-hour circular trip, but it's a beautiful spot for walking and some choose to wander here for hours.

Lioness of Gobodura   MONUMENT

(archaeological sites combined ticket Birr50; ⊘ 8am-5.30pm) Despite being the crudest of tombs, roughly hewn into solid rock instead of constructed with fine masonry, this place has a slightly magical feel. According to local beliefs, King Bazen is thought not just to have reigned at Christ's birth, but to have been Balthazar, and it was he who carried news of Christ's birth to Ethiopia. Whether true or not, judging from the number of tombs and stelae found nearby, the burial site may once have been quite large and important.

A rectangular pit above the tomb contains a row of burial chambers, including a few that appear to be unfinished.

King Ezana's Inscription   MONUMENT

On the way up to the tombs of Kings Kaleb and Gebre Meskel, you'll pass a small shack containing a remarkable find that three farmers stumbled upon in 1988: an Ethio-

---

AKSUMITE COINS

Aksumite coins are valuable not just for their beauty: they also provide a vital source of information on the ancient kingdom. The coins bear the names, effigies and sometimes lineage of 23 different kings, providing a rare factual record of who ruled and when. The historians who studied them found something that rocked the foundations of traditional Ethiopian history. Many of the kings of the traditional history failed to appear on the coins, while those on the coins failed to appear in the historical lists.

Beautifully struck, the coins depict the royal crowns, clothing and jewellery of the kings (even the large earrings worn by some monarchs) and probably served propagandist purposes. A curiosity still unexplained by historians is the fact that almost all the coins are double-headed: on one side the king is depicted with his crown; on the other he dons a modest head cloth.

Farmers frequently find coins in their fields and because the Ethiopian government lacks the budget to buy them, most are sold illegally to collectors and tourists. Both the sale and purchase is illegal and airport staff are trained to look for them during security searches. Don't even think of buying them.

pian version of the Rosetta Stone. The pillar, inscribed in Sabaean, Ge'ez and Greek, dates from between AD 330 and AD 350 and records the honorary titles and military victories of the king over his 'enemies and rebels'.

One section thanks the God of War, thus placing the stone's age before Ezana's conversion to Christianity.

The guardian who opens the hut expects a small tip (Birr10 to Birr20).

Dungur (Queen of Sheba's) Palace   RUINS

(ደንጉር (የንግስተ ሳባ) ቤተ-መንግስት; archaeological sites combined ticket Birr50; ☺8am-5.30pm) The structure at Dungur is popularly known as Queen of Sheba's Palace, though archaeologists are divided over whether it was the great woman's palace or the 6th-century-AD mansion of a nobleman. Most leaned towards the latter, but the find during recent excavations of a relief carving depicting a beautiful woman (in the museum at St Mary of Zion Church) has caused some to wonder whether her palace may lie beneath the current ruins.

Climb the observation tower at the back of the site for a view out over the 50-room layout. It has small undressed stones and walls recessed at intervals and unusually tapering with height. The well-preserved flagstone floor is thought to have belonged to a throne room. The palace also contains hidden treasure rooms, a private bathing area and a kitchen, where a large brick oven can still be seen. The stairwells suggest the existence of at least one upper storey.

Old Quarter   AREA

It's worth taking a wander around the old quarter surrounding the Northern Stelae Field and stretching west to Ta'akha Maryam. It's in these dusty streets that it really hits you how Aksum is more than just a collection of dead ruins; rather it's a living, breathing community where the past persists. Camels and donkeys carting heavy loads trudge past homes that feel as ancient as the ruins, and pilgrims in white come in from the countryside.

Basket Market   MARKET

(☺8.30am-2.30pm Sat) Aksum has two interesting markets that burst to life on Saturday; both are best between 10.30am and noon. This one takes place under the massive fig tree shading the heart of the piazza. It's absolutely huge at festival time when visiting Ethiopians stock up on high-quality Tigrayan workmanship.

Main Market   MARKET

(☺8am-6pm) The main market, with spices and the like, runs all week, but is busiest on Saturday.

Tombs of Kings Kaleb & Gebre Meskel   MONUMENT

(archaeological sites combined ticket Birr50; ☺8am-5.30pm) Set on a small hill 1.8km northeast of the Northern Stelae Field and offering views of the jagged mountains of Adwa are these two tombs that local tradition attributes to the 6th-century King Kaleb and his son, King Gebre Meskel. Although the twin tombs' architecture resembles the Tomb of the False Door, they show more sophistication, using irregular-shaped, self-locking stones that don't require iron clamps.

The Gebre Meskel (south) tomb is the most refined. The precision of the joints between its stones is at a level unseen anywhere else in Aksum. The tomb consists of one chamber and five rooms, with one boasting an exceptionally finely carved portal leading into it. Inside that room are three sarcophagi, one adorned with a cross similar to Christian crosses found on Aksumite coins. This points towards an age around the 6th century AD, which, as seldom happens, corresponds with local tradition... though the rest of the story has Meskel buried at Debre Damo.

Like Meskel's tomb, King Kaleb's is accessed via a long straight stairway. Inside you'll notice the stones are larger, more angular and less precisely joined. Of those who attribute the making of the tomb to Kaleb, few accept that he was actually buried here. The common theory is that his body lies at Abba Pentalewon monastery, where he lived after abdicating his throne. The tomb's unfinished state fits with the theory. Local rumour has it that there's a secret tunnel leading from here to the Red Sea.

Above ground, a kind of raised courtyard combines the two tombs. Some scholars have suggested that two parallel churches with a basilica plan lay here, probably postdating the tombs.

Archaeological Museum   MUSEUM

(archaeological sites combined ticket Birr50; ☺8am-5.30pm) This well-laid-out museum inside the Northern Stelae Field contains an interesting variety of objects found in the tombs, ranging from ordinary household

NORTHERN ETHIOPIA AKSUM

objects, such as lamps and incense burners, to quite sophisticated glassware. This is one museum that you may want to save for the end of your visit to Aksum when so many of the items will make more sense.

Animal Market
MARKET

(⊙ 8.30am-3.30pm Sat) The animal market, south of town, is one of the biggest in the north. It's ripe with donkeys, goats, sheep and cows, but no camels. These are only sold straight from the huge caravans that pass through the nearby countryside from the Danakil to Sudan.

Ta'akha Maryam
RUINS

(ተክአ ማርያም) This is one site where the past very much outweighs the present, at least for now. Early excavations revealed that Ta'akha Maryam was a magnificent palace, probably dating from the 6th century AD or earlier. Covering a vast 120m-by-80m area, Ta'akha Maryam is bigger than Dungur and would have been far larger than medieval European palaces of the time. The Archaeological Museum (p101) has a model of how it may have looked. Sadly it's closed to the public pending excavations.

Queen of Sheba's Bath
HISTORIC SITE

(የንግስት ሳባ መዋኛ) Despite the colourful legends, this large reservoir probably wasn't where Sheba came to bathe. It was an important reservoir rather than a swimming pool or gargantuan bath. Nobody is totally sure of its age, but it's certainly been used as a water source for millennia. Its large size is even more impressive considering it's hewn from solid rock. It's also known as Mai Shum, which translates to 'Chief's Water'. It's used for Timkat celebrations, just like Fasiladas' Bath (p79) in Gonder.

Sadly, the outer portion of the bowl was coated with concrete in the 1960s, making it look more like a modern trough than an ancient relic.

Abba Liqanos
MONASTERY

(አባ ሊቃኖስ; Birr100; ⊙ 8am-5.30pm) On the way to Abba Pentalewon you'll pass Abba Liqanos (men only), which was supposedly built by one of the Nine Saints (p109) and boasts excellent views. *But* there's no treasure to see; the modern church (a replacement for the one destroyed by the Derg when the area was occupied by rebels) is uninteresting and there's little return for the price.

✨ Festivals & Events

Aksum's calendar is filled with Christian celebrations – if you're in Ethiopia for any of the most important dates in the Orthodox calendar, make your way to Aksum (but make sure you've booked your hotel well in advance).

Hosanna
RELIGIOUS

As you'd expect in such a spiritually charged city, Hosanna (Palm Sunday) is a big deal here with religious processions and much pageantry. It all happens the Sunday before Easter Sunday (according to the Orthodox calendar).

★ Festival of Maryam Zion
RELIGIOUS

This is one of Ethiopia's largest festivals. In the days leading up to the event on 30 November, thousands of pilgrims arrive and sleepy Aksum truly awakens. Celebrations start in front of the Northern Stelae Field, where the monarchs of the Orthodox church line the steps and watch performers in the street below.

For an unforgettable experience make your way to the compound of the St Mary of Zion church between 1am and sunrise on the day of the festival and witness a sea of white-robed pilgrims curled up asleep. Standing among the slowly shifting sea are a few scattered priests reading by candlelight.

Mehelela
RELIGIOUS

On the first seven days of each month (according to the Ethiopian calendar), St Mary of Zion's replica Ark (the original replica) is paraded through the streets surrounding the church compound to request forgiveness from God. The procession starts at 5am and includes a short 'special mass' in front of **Da'Ero Ela fig tree**.

Timkat
RELIGIOUS

(⊙ Jan) Though smaller than those in Gonder, Aksum's Timkat celebrations, which mark the Epiphany or Christ's baptism, are held at Queen of Sheba's Bath and are just as interesting.

⌲ Tours

Although you can see the monuments on your own, an official guide (Birr402 per day for one to four people, Birr517 to Birr617 for larger groups) adds greatly to the experience. All are trained and many are history students, so you'll get much more out of your visit than if you simply wander around unaided.

The Aksum Guide Association (p105) is next to the Northern Stelae Field entrance.

Three guides we recommend are:

Rufael Fitsum (☑0913-125540; rufael12@yahoo.com)

Tedros Girmay (☑0910-081534; tedrosaxum21@gmail.com)

Solomon Belay (☑0914-743768)

Covenant Tours TOURS
(☑0913-709926, 0347-752642; www.covenant ethiopia.com) Reliable and with many years of experience, Covenant Tours can take you most places in Ethiopia, including the Tigray rock-hewn churches and the Danakil Depression. It also has a handy (free) town map and owner Dawit Tesfay is a mine of information.

Abune Yemata Tours & Travel TOURS
(☑0911-532526; www.abuneyematatours.com) At Africa Hotel, Abune Yemata is good for budget travellers looking to join others to share costs. It runs trips all across Ethiopia's north.

🛏 Sleeping

Aksum has excellent budget and midrange choices, but there's nothing at the top end. Rooms become scarce and prices rise during major festivals, when reservations are essential. When things are quiet, it's always worth asking for a discount.

Kaleb Hotel HOTEL $
(☑0911-546823, 0347-752222; s/tw Birr300/600; P☎) With quiet rooms set around possibly Aksum's loveliest garden courtyard and with a popular pizza restaurant, Kaleb has the nicest budget setting. The rooms are large and uninspiring, but the setting makes up for it. Its twin rates are just silly – ask for a discount. Although signposted off the main road, it's only in Amharic at the property itself.

Damat Pension PENSION $
(☑0939-050473; s/d Birr250/300) With probably the best budget rooms in Aksum, Damat does have a few drawbacks – it's over in the new town, quite a distance from the main attractions, and there's not much English spoken. But the rooms are large and comfortable and a steal at this price. Lone women travellers may feel uncomfortable here.

Tekla Haimanot Pension PENSION $
(☑0346-752240; d/tw Birr120/250; P☎) Clean, functional rooms on the west side of town, a convenient walking distance to Aksum's main attractions. They've just built a new wing at the back, so expect prices to rise a little. Look for the green-and-yellow 'clean bed rooms' sign.

Africa Hotel HOTEL $
(☑0347-753700; africaho@ethio.net; s/d/tw/tr Birr200/250/300/350; P☎) The word on the street is that this place is not what it was, but the rooms are simple (some are a bit cell-like) with big, clean bathrooms and OK for the price. There's also a restaurant with mediocre food. Call for a free airport transfer.

Yared Zema Hotel HOTEL $$
(☑0347-754817; www.yaredzemainternational hotel.com; incl breakfast s US$40-55, d or tw US$50-65, ste US$65-80; ☎) One of a clutch of new hotels along the main road through town, the Yared Zema has some of Aksum's best beds. Attractive wood-floored rooms are easy on the eye with comfy beds and some of the bathrooms have bathtubs. There's a reasonable on-site bar and restaurant.

Sabean International Hotel HOTEL $$
(☑0347-751224; www.sabeanhotel.com; s/d incl breakfast US$50/60) The rooms at this new place are among Aksum's best – wooden floors, decent bathrooms and pretty good service. The walls are a tad thin and you've a right to expect a better breakfast for this price, but otherwise it's a good choice.

Remhai Hotel HOTEL $$
(☑0347-751501; www.remhaihotel.com; r/ste Birr760/1160; P☎🏊) The rooms here are fairly standard Ethiopian midrange fare – large, comfortable, a few questionable furnishing choices but otherwise unexciting. The real draw is the large swimming pool.

Consolar International Hotel HOTEL $$
(☑0348-750210; www.consolarhotelaxum.com; s/d or tw/tr/f US$55/65/75/85; P@) This six-storey tower at the Adwa end of town has big rooms that can seem a little cavernous. They're a touch overpriced, but they're still comfortable.

Yeha Hotel HOTEL $$$
(☑0347-752377; www.yehahotelaxum.com; s/tw/ste US$60/81/106) Perched atop a bluff overlooking the stelae and the Mary of Zion churches, this hotel has the most enviable

location. Sadly the rooms – carpeted, tired and overlooking either the ragged garden or parking – are difficult to recommend. Come here instead for a sunset drink on the terrace.

Eating

Aksum has plenty of good restaurants, including a number that are approximations of traditional Ethiopian eating dens.

Lucy Traditional Restaurant ETHIOPIAN $
(☑ 0914-768399; mains Birr35-80; ☉ 7am-11pm) Slightly cheaper than some of the other traditional restaurants around town, Lucy has low wooden stools and attracts a predominantly local crowd who come for the soups, grilled fish or lamb *tibs*. There's occasional live music in the evenings.

AB Traditional Restaurant ETHIOPIAN $
(☑ 0920-877382; mains Birr50-120; ☉ 7am-11pm) Decorated with bamboo and crafts and with traditional low-stool seating, this restaurant is calm, peaceful and a great spot to dig into *shekla tibs,* with goat fresh from the butchery inside the dining room (don't look too closely at the flies...), or *doro wat.* Give the pasta and rice dishes a pass: they can take forever to prepare and can be disappointing.

Ezana Café ETHIOPIAN $
(mains Birr7-45; ☉ 6am-10pm) An awesome, down-to-earth breakfast spot with excellent *ful* and 'special *fata*' (bread *firfir* with yogurt and egg). Complete your meal with a juice from Axum No-Name Cafe (p104) next door and you'll be well set up for the day.

Abyssinia Hotel BAKERY $
(cakes Birr10; ☉ 6.30am-10pm) Locals swear that the Abyssinia does Aksum's best cakes. That's probably true, although they're OK rather than oh-my-God. In the morning, everything's fresh and there's more to choose from.

Antika Cultural Restaurant ETHIOPIAN $$
(☑ 0914-172003; mains Birr50-120; ☉ 7am-11pm) Dimly lit and with a nightly 7pm show of traditional music and dance on stage, Antika is a welcome addition to Aksum's culinary offerings. It does some international dishes, but stick to the Ethiopian specialities and it's difficult to go wrong – the *shekla tibs,* served spicy, is a good choice.

Empire Restaurant & Bar ETHIOPIAN $$
(☑ 0913-620125; breakfast Birr35-80, mains Birr50-120; ☉ 7am-11pm; 🛜) Under new management but still a great place to eat, Empire does excellent Ethiopian food – its *doro wat* (chicken stew) is a cut above the average. There's also free wi-fi, a bright, modern dining area (in contrast to most places in town) and Seble is a welcoming host.

🍷 Drinking & Nightlife

For something entirely different, seek out a *tella bet* (local bar serving home-brewed barley and millet beer; *suwa* in Tigrinya) in the tiny streets around town. They're marked by cups on top of small poles, but you'll need a local to decode the various colours.

★**Kuda Juice** JUICE BAR
(☑ 0911-117746; juice Birr20-30; ☉ 6am-10pm; 🛜) This cool little juice bar has free wi-fi, a modern feel and terrific juices. Ask for its special of the day – we loved the mango, avocado and guava – or try the *shek* (juice with milk). It was in the process of expanding into an outdoor area next door, so chances are it's even better by the time you get here.

★**Yeha Hotel** BAR
(☑ 0347-752377; ☉ 7am-11pm) The hotel may be past its prime, but the Yeha remains the best place in town for a sundowner. The terrace faces the setting sun and overlooks the Northern Stelae Field, St Mary of Zion Church and surrounding hills.

Axum No-Name Cafe CAFE
(☑ 0912-141254; ☉ 6am-10pm) One of the most enduringly popular cafes along the main road, Axum No-Name has split-level seating overlooking the street and a loyal local clientele who like to watch the world go by for hours on end while nursing macchiatos. It also does teas.

🛍 Shopping

Aksum has more souvenir shops than any other town in Ethiopia and the road between the piazza and Northern Stelae Field is lined with them; the main road through town also has its fair share. Most feature basketry and weavings, but you can also buy silver crosses and old triptych paintings.

★**St George Gallery Axum** ARTS & CRAFTS
(☑ 0914-744109; ☉ 7.30am-8.30pm) One of the best shops in northern Ethiopia, St George

has that rare combination of simple tourist items and fine pieces of art and antiques, although the quality tends towards the latter. Religious paintings (including triptych and on goat skin), silver crosses and jewellery make up the bulk of the collection.

Abyssinia Handcraft Shop-Sunlight Fitsum   ARTS & CRAFTS
(☑0913-125540; ⊙7am-9pm) Has a good selection of old triptych paintings as well as a few silver crosses.

❶ Information

Aksum Guide Association Office (☑0348-759034) The Aksum Guide Association office is next to the Northern Stelae Field entrance. If you've arrived in town with a guide lined up, contact this group.

Aksum Visitor Centre (☑0347-753924; aksumtourismoffice@ethionet.net; ⊙8am-5.30pm) One of the country's most helpful offices. Also knows about the rock-hewn churches to the east.

Commercial Bank (⊙8.30am-11am & 1.30-3.30pm Mon-Fri, 8.30-11am Sat)

Wegagen Bank (⊙8.30am-11am & 1.30-3.30pm Mon-Fri, 8.30am-11am Sat) For the time being, has the only ATM in town.

St Mary Pharmacy (☑0347-752646; ⊙8am-noon & 2-10pm Mon-Fri, 8am-10pm Sat & Sun) Helpful and well stocked.

St Mary Hospital (☑0347-752013; ⊙24hr)

Tsion Higher Clinic (☑0347-754455; ⊙4.30-10pm Mon-Fri, 8.30am-noon & 2-10pm Sat, 3-10pm Sun) Helpful clinic and the doctor speaks decent English.

❶ Getting There & Away

Aksum is well connected by air and road to the rest of the country.

AIR

Ethiopian Airlines (☑0347-752300; www.ethiopianairlines.com) flies twice daily to Addis Ababa (US$240, one to three hours), sometimes direct and sometimes via Lalibela (US$130, 45 minutes) and Gonder (US$130, 40 minutes).

BUS

For buses to Gonder and Debark (for the Simien Mountains), go to Shire (Birr45, 1½ hours) first. There's only one bus (6am) and few minibuses to Adigrat (Birr58, 3½ hours), but services are more frequent from Adwa (Birr10, 30 minutes). There are two morning buses to Mekele (Birr85, seven hours, 6am), as well as minibuses (Birr120), any of which can drop you in Wukro (Birr70, six hours). All buses leave from the bus station.

THE BATTLE OF ADWA

In September 1895, as the rains began to dwindle, Emperor Menelik II issued a decree: all the able-bodied men of his empire should gather for a march north, a march for all of Ethiopia. Behind the vast army trundled 40 cannons, hundreds of mules and 100,000 rifles. In the north, the Italians were ready.

Initial skirmishes followed and amazingly the Ethiopians and their sturdy mules captured the Italian strongholds at Amba Alage and Enda Iyesus. Serious shortages of food soon followed, leading both sides to sue for peace, but Italy's continued insistence on its protectorate claim meant an agreement couldn't be reached.

In February 1896 Francesco Crispi, Italy's prime minister, sent his famous telegram to General Baratieri. In it he declared the motherland was 'ready for any sacrifice to save the honour of the army and the prestige of the monarchy'.

In the early morning hours four days later, the Italians made their move. Stumbling over difficult terrain, with inaccurate maps and no communication between the three offensive brigades, the surprise attack was a disaster. Menelik, whose spies had long before informed him of the forthcoming attack, met the Italians with thundering artillery and fierce fighting on every front.

Nearly half the Italian fighting force was wiped out (more than 10,000 soldiers were injured, captured or killed) and of the five Italian field commanders, three were killed, one was wounded and another was captured. Finally, laying down their arms, the Italians ran. Though the Ethiopians had lost almost equal numbers, the day was clearly theirs.

To this day the Battle of Adwa is celebrated annually and, like the Battle of Hastings in Britain or the Declaration of Independence in America, it's the one date (1 March 1895) every Ethiopian child can quote.

CAR & MOTORCYCLE

Aksum's travel agencies and numerous free-lance agents rent vehicles (including driver and guide) for trips to Yeha, Debre Damo and the rock churches of Tigray.

ⓘ Getting Around

A taxi to/from the airport, 5.5km from town, costs Birr100 'shared'. Almost all the popular hotels have vans waiting to meet incoming flights, though you may want to call just to be sure yours will be there.

Contract *bajaj* charge foreigners Birr30 to Birr40 from the Africa Hotel area to the Northern Stelae Field. A shared *bajaj* is Birr3 to cross town.

Adwa

POP 49,000 / ELEV 1907M

Like Aksum, unassuming, urban Adwa (አድዋ) belies its status. For Ethiopians the town holds huge significance. It was in the dramatic mountains surrounding Adwa that Emperor Menelik II inflicted the biggest defeat ever on a colonial army in Africa, thus saving Ethiopia from colonisation. Later, many key figures in the Ethiopian People's Revolutionary Democratic Front (EPRDF) came from Adwa, including long-time prime minister Meles Zenawi. Even so, Adwa is very missable.

OFF THE BEATEN TRACK

DEBRE DAMO MONASTERY

Debre Damo (ደብረ ዳሞ; Birr200 (men only), guide Birr200, helpers Birr100; ⊘6am-6pm) is one of Ethiopia's most important monasteries and is thought to date back to Aksumite times and the 6th-century reign of King Gebre Meskel. The monastery's formidable cliffs make for one of Ethiopia's most memorable experiences (for men, at least – women aren't allowed up). To reach the monastery, you'll need to scale a sheer 15m cliff; there's a thick leather rope to help you climb and the monks will tie a second line around your torso and help pull you up.

The whole experience takes some nerves and a good head for heights. (If you're short of confidence, don't look at the laces holding the strips of rope together until after you've come down!)

It was Abuna Aregawi, one of the most revered of the Nine Saints (p109), who established Debre Damo monastery atop a sheer-sided *amba* (flat-topped mountain). It may seem like it would have been impossible for the first person to reach this island in the sky, but Abuna Aregawi had God on his side, and God, knowing this was a fine place for a saint to find peace, made a giant snake lower its tail down the mountain, allowing Aregawi to clamber up it to the summit.

The remarkable **Abuna Aregawi church** is likely the oldest standing church in the country (10th or 11th century AD) and possibly all of Africa. Thanks to a major restoration in 1948 it's in excellent condition, but still has a truly ancient feel. It's an almost prototypical example of Aksumite architecture and features the same style of doors and windows found on Aksum's stelae. Notable are the beams and ceiling, famously decorated with carved wooden panels depicting Ethiopian wild animals. Debre Damo has long been used as a safeguard for religious treasures and its collection includes some of Ethiopia's oldest **illuminated manuscripts**.

The monastery's location once allowed Aksumite monarchs to coop up excess male members of the royal family here, thus removing possible threats to their reign. Today it hosts some 150 monks, who are entirely self-sufficient. They grow their own crops, raise their own livestock (all male) and have water reservoirs hewn deep into the rock.

There's no public transport to Debre Damo, although any transport on the Aksum–Adigrat road can drop you at the well-signposted junction. From there it's a toasty 14.5km (around three hours) walk. Catching rides to Adwa, Adigrat or Aksum from the junction is tough in the late afternoon. If there's a group of you, it's easiest to hire a minibus in Aksum or Adigrat. Debre Damo is usually a first-day stop on Tigray rock-hewn church tours out of Aksum.

Passing deep canyons and terraced barley fields, the road running southeast of Debre Damo towards Adigrat, with its distant views of the Adwa Mountains, is a contender for Ethiopia's most beautiful drive.

In the mountains about 5km due east of Adwa, the **Monastery of Abba Garima** (Birr150, men only; ⊘8am-5.30pm) is said to have been founded by one of the Nine Saints (p109) in the 6th century. It's known for its collection of religious artefacts, including what may be Ethiopia's two oldest manuscripts, perhaps dating to sometime between AD 330 and AD 650. They're kept in a proper museum in glass cases along with a few old crosses, crowns, robes etc.

The main church has modern paintings, mostly behind plastic sheeting, but the geometric ceiling paintings are an unusual sight. Head 6km south of Adwa before turning east for the final 2.5km.

On the Aksum side of town is a **monument** to the victims of, and victors over, the Derg.

Most travellers stay at Aksum, 25km away. **Setit Humera Hotel** (☑0914-301627; r Birr350-680; P 🛜) is in the town centre, not far from the bus station. It's fine for a night but if you're here because Aksum is full, you'll likely be paying inflated prices, which aren't good value at all.

Numerous minibuses connect Adwa to Aksum (Birr10, 30 minutes). There are 10 buses or minibuses to Adigrat (Birr49, three hours) and six to Yeha (Birr18, 50 minutes).

Adigrat

POP 76,400 / ELEV 2475M

Tigray's second-largest town is situated on what was Ethiopia's most important junction with Eritrea before the border was closed. Adigrat (አዲግራት) is a humdrum place and mostly used as a lunch-stop on the way from Aksum to Hawzien or Mekele.

🛏 Sleeping & Eating

Adigrat can be a good place to break up the journey between Aksum and the Tigray churches, and it has at least one excellent choice just outside town. Otherwise, it's a pretty uninspiring mix of fairly standard in-town Ethiopian hotels by the roadside.

Hohoma Hotel　　　　　　　　HOTEL $

(☑0344-452469; r Birr250; 🛜) Probably the best of Adigrat's cheapies, Hohoma has basic, simple rooms with satellite TV and slow wi-fi. The downstairs cafe does an excellent version of that Tigrayean speciality, *tihlo* (barley balls dipped in a spicy sauce; Birr90).

★**Agoro Lodge**　　　　　　　LODGE $$

(☑0348-450202; www.agorolodge.com; sd or tw incl breakfast Birr850/1062; P @ 🛜) Easily Adigrat's best place to stay, Agoro Lodge sits high on a hill 4km south of town. The rooms and public areas are built of sandstone and are large and comfortable; put a desk in the rooms and they'd look even better. There's a good restaurant (mains Birr58 to Birr80) and all profits are invested back into the community.

★**Geza Gereslase Cultural Restaurant**　　　　　　ETHIOPIAN $$

(mains Birr80-120; ⊘7am-11pm) If it's Ethiopian food you're after, the big *tukul* across the street from Eve Hotel is easily Adigrat's best. Traditional decoration and well-priced dishes such as *mahberawi* (an Ethiopian meat platter served with *injera* – we challenge you to finish it all) make it the ideal place for lunch or, if you're staying in town, dinner.

❶ Getting There & Away

There are at least 10 daily buses to Mekele (Birr48, 2½ hours) and countless minibuses. Use the latter for Freweyni (Birr18, 45 minutes) and Wukro (Birr32, 1½ hours).

Going west, there are several buses and minibuses to Adwa (Birr49, three hours) and Aksum (Birr62, 3½ hours).

Rock-hewn Churches of Tigray

The landscapes of northern Tigray seem to spring from some hard-bitten African fairy tale. The luminous light bathes scattered sharp peaks that rise into the sky out of a sandy, rolling semidesert. The stratified plateaus, particularly between Dugem and Megab in the Gheralta region, lead to inevitable comparisons with the USA's desert southwest.

The 120-odd churches are as intriguing as the landscape is beautiful. Very different from the more famous monolithic (carved out of the ground and only left attached to the earth at the base) churches of Lalibela, the Tigrayan churches are carved from cliff faces, built into pre-existing caves or constructed high atop some improbable perch – getting to some of them may not be for the faint-hearted, but getting there is almost always half the fun. And beyond a few famous churches, you'll likely get to explore on your own, even in the high season.

Rock-Hewn Churches of Tigray

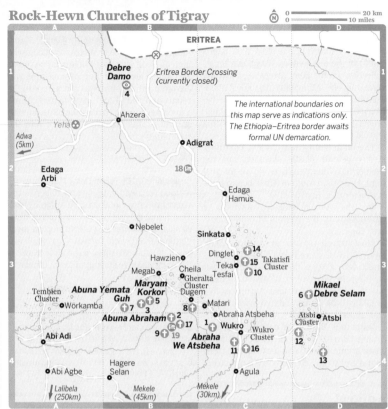

Rock-Hewn Churches of Tigray

History

Until the mid-1960s, the churches were almost unknown outside Tigray itself and still very little is known about their real history, as opposed to their oral histories. Their remote and precarious positions have led scholars to think they were built in such inaccessible places in order to remain hidden from invading Muslim armies.

While local tradition attributes most of the churches to 4th-century Aksumite kings Abreha and Atsbeha, as well as to 6th-century rulers, most historians confidently date them between the 9th and 15th centuries.

Thus the early churches represent an artistic, cultural and technical link between Aksum and Lalibela.

◉ Sights

Most churches are spread out across the eastern Tigray region and it helps when planning to group them together. Hawzien and the surrounding area is generally the base/starting point of choice for most travellers.

Guides can be arranged through the Gheralta Local Guide Association (p116). One guide we recommend is Tewelde Hileselassie (☏ 0914-616851).

Gheralta Cluster

The Gheralta cluster is home to the most famous, most visited and simply the most (about 30) rock-hewn churches. It's the gloriously high and remote locations as much as the churches themselves that provide the attraction, and visitors must be properly fit to reach many of them. Since it gets by far the most visitors, there are more reports of hassles, but in our experience it's rarely enough to ruin the experience.

There's no public transport, and little traffic at all, between Wukro and Megab, where most of the churches lie. The exception is on Wednesday – market day – when two buses leave Wukro for Hawzien (Birr32, two hours) in the morning and return (completely full, so you can't rely on them stopping to pick you up) in the afternoon. If you need a vehicle to get around, ask at your hotel or the guide office.

★ Abuna Abraham   CHURCH
(አቡነ አብርሃም; Birr150; ⊗ 8am-5.30pm) Rectangular in shape, with six massive freestanding pillars, this large and impressive 14th-century church (also known as Debre Tsion) is known for its diverse architectural features, including decorated cupolas, bas-reliefs and carved crosses on the walls and ceiling. It also has beautiful, though faded and damaged, 16th-century murals and an unusual, large 15th-century ceremonial fan. It sits like a fortress on a hill about 500m south of Dugem.

It can be accessed either from Dugem or the same parking area as Yohannes Maequdi (p110). Either way it's a steep one-hour walk up the back of the mountain.

★ Abuna Yemata Guh   CHURCH
(Birr150; ⊗ 8am-5.30pm) There's nowhere on earth quite like Abuna Yemata Guh. Although less impressive architecturally than most, the church is spectacularly sited within a cliff face, halfway up a sheer rock pinnacle 4km west of Megab. The first 45 minutes of the climb is mildly challenging, with a couple of tricky sheer sections requiring toehold action; guides carry ropes (Birr150) for the final push. The last two minutes require nerves of steel to make the final scramble and precarious ledge walk over a 200m drop. Even if you don't make it all the way, it's still worth getting to where the ledge begins as the views from the baptism chamber are astounding. Inside are beautiful and well-preserved frescoes that adorn two cupolas, while the bones of monks from the open-air tombs lie around.

★ Maryam Korkor   CHURCH
(ማርያም ቆርቆር; Birr150; ⊗ 8am-5.30pm) Although an unsightly green from the outside, this impressive, cross-shaped church is known for its architectural features (cruciform pillars, arches and cupolas), fine 17th-century frescoes and church treasures. It's also one of the largest churches in the area. The path begins around 1km from the road just southeast of Megab and involves a fairly steep one-hour ascent. Maryam Korkor is easily combined with nearby Abuna Yemata Guh (p109) into an all-day trek from Megab.

Daniel Korkor   CHURCH
(combined ticket with Maryam Korkor Birr150; ⊗ 8am-5.30pm) Just a couple of minutes' walk from Maryam Korkor (p109) is the seldom-used church of Daniel Korkor. It sits

---

THE NINE SAINTS

Though it was Abba Salama who first brought the Christian faith to Ethiopia in AD 330, he didn't make great inroads into converting the masses. Instead this task was left to a group of wandering holy men who were eventually to become known as the Nine Saints. In the 5th century they arrived in Ethiopia from the Middle East and each chose a mountaintop on which to construct a monastery and preach the new religion. All nine are frequent subjects of church paintings.

THE TROUBLE WITH TIGRAY

The rock-hewn churches of Tigray are spectacular, but visiting them comes with strings attached. Years of tourists handing out coins, pens, sweets etc around the Gheralta cluster created a climate of aggressive begging that's now so rotten that kids sometimes throw stones at people who don't hand over bounty. All locals we talked to insist the situation is improving, in part because police visit schools to teach kids not to hassle tourists. Our experience is that things have improved, but the frequency of reports from travellers and tour guides contradicts this. Hiring a local Tigrinya-speaking guide is a good, but only partial, defence. Making things more frustrating is the attitude among many locals that if you go alone and have trouble it's your own fault.

But kids aren't the only problem. Some priests expect, and often demand, extra money. Many visitors balk at tipping priests because the admission fees are so high, but fees go to the church bureaucracy (unless a receipt is not issued, in which case it *might* go to the church or priest). True, with the huge profits being made from tourism the church should compensate the priests for this extra work, but it doesn't. Priests here are not full-time preachers. They have homes, families and farms just like everyone else who lives near the churches, so a tip for opening their church (Birr50 is usually fine) is entirely justified. (Anyone who goes to find a priest or walks you to a church deserves a small tip, too.)

But when they won't turn on lights or point anything out unless even more money is donated, the whole experience becomes frustrating. In fact, one of our writers was locked inside a church by a priest who refused to let him go until he handed over more money!.

atop a paralysing precipice, offers astounding views and has fine paintings.

Dugem Selassie
CHURCH

(ዱግም ስላሴ; Birr150; ⊘8am-5.30pm) Built into a small outcrop rather than a big hill, this church feels like a tomb and may have been one before being converted. The 19th-century 'new' church alongside it is partially cut from the rock and topped by plastered stone construction, which is easily distinguished because it's painted white. It's easily accessible along the road on the eastern edge of the village of Dugem.

Yohannes Maequdi
CHURCH

(ዮሀንስ መቁዲይ; Birr150; ⊘8am-5.30pm) High atop the mountain and not visible from the ground below, this rectangular chapel has six freestanding pillars that support a ceiling carved with geometrical designs. While it's best known for well-preserved murals, it's less striking overall than Abuna Abraham and most visitors remember the intense atmosphere rather than the architecture. It's accessed from the village of Matari (park by the school) and is around a one-hour walk via a steep footpath.

Abuna Gebre Mikael
CHURCH

(Birr150; ⊘8am-5.30pm) Though not visited very often, this is considered one of Gher-

alta's finest churches. The cruciform plan is hewn into a dome-like rock and it has good unfaded frescoes and carefully carved columns, pillars, cupolas and arches. It's around 15km southwest of Abuna Yemata Guh and requires a steep climb, negotiating a few obstacles on the way; plan on a 3½-hour trip up to the church and back.

Maryam Papaseit
CHURCH

(Birr150; ⊘8am-5.30pm) In a pretty valley south of Hawzien and signposted off the Megab–Wukro road, Maryam Papaseit is one of the most accessible and rewarding churches in the region. It's a semimonolithic structure (only the 'Holy of Holies' is hewn from the rock), while the main sanctuary has some exceptional paintings, most of which date from the 17th century. The church is a moderate one-hour walk from the end of the road.

Painting subjects include the usual mix of Old and New Testament scenes, with Mary and St George prominent – those of the '24 elders of the apocalypse' and Jesus washing Peter's feet are particularly finely rendered.

Wukro Cluster

Both of Wukro Cluster's churches are very easy to reach.

★**Abraha We Atsbeha**　　　　CHURCH
(አብርሃ ወ አጽብሃ; Birr250; ⊘8am-5.30pm)
Architecturally speaking, this 10th-century
church is one of Tigray's finest. It's large and
cruciform in shape, with cruciform pillars
and well-preserved 17th- and 18th-century
murals and a wonderful wooden door. Some
of the church treasures, including what's believed to be King Atsbeha's golden shoes are
properly displayed in glass cases in the adjacent museum. It's by the road 15km west of
Wukro or 23km from Megab.

The obtrusive portico was an attempt by
Italians to win over locals by proving they
weren't Muslims.

Wukro Cherkos　　　　　　CHURCH
(ዉቅሮ ጨፍርቆስ; Birr150; ⊘8am-5.30pm)
This crooked cruciform sandstone church is
semimonolithic and boasts beautiful cruciform pillars (notice the swirling sandstone
laminae), cubical capitals, an outstanding
Aksumite frieze and a barrel-vaulted ceiling.
In 1958 Haile Selassie himself, apparently,
ordered the angular roof squared with concrete for either aesthetic reasons or to protect the church from water seepage (which
has severely damaged the geometric ceiling
designs), depending on who you ask. It's on
the northern edge of Wukro, making it the
most easily accessible church.

Wukro Museum　　　　　　　MUSEUM
(🖉0910-292927; Birr50; ⊘9am-12.30pm &
2-4.30pm Mon-Sat) One of the best museums
in Ethiopia's north, Wukro Museum begins with some displays on generators and
electricity in Wukro, which are interesting
enough, but head instead for the southern
wing with its fine exhibition hall covering
archaeological finds from the 7th-century
Sabean site of Meqaber Ga'ewa and elsewhere. There are tablet inscriptions, Axumite coins and a fine sacrificial altar. The
labelling and information panels in English
are outstanding, and there's no real need for
a guide here.

Meqaber Ga'ewa　　　　　　CHURCH
This ancient site is little more than a barely
accessible archaeological dig, but it's an important piece of the puzzle when it comes to
the 7th-century-BC Sabean civilisation. Far
more interesting than the site itself are the
finds in Wukro Museum.

Takatisfi Cluster
With four churches in easy walking distance
of each other just 2km off the highway,

Takatisfi is the perfect cluster for independent travellers. As an added bonus, the priests
are, most often, easily found. The best approach is from the village of Dinglet (a
minibus from Wukro is Birr15, 30 minutes),
which is just 2.2km from Petros We Paulos.
From there, head south to the other two
churches and then take the southwest-run-
ning road back to the highway south of Teka
Tesfai, 5km south of Dinglet. If you're travelling by vehicle, it needs to be 4WD. You
can drive to within a 10-minute-or-less walk
of all the churches. Mikael Meka'e (Takatisfi
Cluster) is a minor, rarely visited church 15
minutes' walk north of Petros We Paulos.

Medhane Alem Kesho　　　　CHURCH
(Birr150; ⊘8am-5.30pm) Also known as
Adi Kesho, after its location, this is one of
Tigray's oldest, tallest and finest rock-hewn
churches. Its exterior and interior walls are
roughly hewn, which only makes the elaborately carved coffered ceiling that much
more special. Ask to watch them unlock
the door from the inside: rather ingenious
indeed! From the end of the 4WD track,
it's a steep-but-easy 10-minute climb to the
church. From the highway, you can walk
there in about an hour.

Petros We Paulos　　　　　CHURCH
(ጴጥሮስ እና ጳውሎስ; Birr150; ⊘8am-5.30pm)
Only partly hewn, this wood, stone and
mortar church, now out of service, is built
on a steep ledge and is more interesting
from the outside than in, though the old,
rapidly deteriorating murals of saints and
angels are delightfully unsophisticated. Behind the church the skulls of some former
monks are lying around enjoying the view.
It's a five-minute climb up a rickety wooden
ladder, much like those used at Ethiopian
construction sites.

The new Petros We Paulos, carved into
the rock after God told a local man to do it,
is down below. Note that the priest's home
is closer to the highway than the church. He
usually sends one of his children to open the
doors.

Mikael Milhaizengi　　　　　CHURCH
(ሚካኤል ምልህ፤ዘንጊ; Birr150; ⊘8am-5.30pm)
This tiny church, with its stooped doorway,
is hewn into the top of a small bleached hill
and is thought to date from the 8th century.
It's known for its 3m-high carved dome ceiling that resembles a *himbasha* (a favourite
round bread of Tigrayans) and it's believed
by locals to be the stamp of God. It's about

30 minutes' walk from Medhane Alem Kesho and 15 minutes' walk from Petros We Paulos.

Atsbi Cluster

A seldom-visited but very rewarding cluster with plenty of public transport between Wukro and Atsbi (Birr18, one hour) town. Market day is Saturday. If you're looking for a guide to this cluster from Wukro, try Mearg Abay (p114).

★ Mikael Debre Selam   CHURCH

(ሚካኤል ደብረ ሰላም; Birr150; ⊘8am-5.30pm) This church or 'church within a church' has an exceptional brown-and-white, Aksumite-style facade fronting its inner rock-hewn section. The bright, modern paintings at the front and its beautiful carved arch add an odd but interesting contrast. The setting is lovely and it's one of our favourites. The 45-minute, one-way climb is strenuous but otherwise not difficult.

The church is clearly visible in the distance, so you could walk there on your own, but finding a direct path would be tough, so hiring a guide is recommended. The walk usually begins 8km northwest of Atsbi. Stay left at the first junction and then turn west at the sign (6km north of Atsbi) until you hit the river; in the growing season you'll have to stop at the school, 1km before the river. The four daily minibuses from Atsbi to Dera can drop you at the signed junction (Birr10, 10 minutes), but you'll almost certainly have to walk back to town.

Mikael Barka   CHURCH

(ሚካኤል ባርካ; Birr150; ⊘8am-5.30pm) Atop a small but panoramic hill and behind an ugly 1960s facade sits this better-than-average rock-hewn church. It has thick cruciform pillars, small carved ceiling domes, a few paintings so faded you wouldn't even see them if the priest didn't point them out, and a solitary carving of a foot. Be sure to pop into the adjoining nunnery. It's 18km from Wukro – you'll instinctively know which hill it is when you round the bend. Reaching it involves a 15-minute climb.

Mikael Imba   CHURCH

(ሚካኤል እምባ; Birr150; ⊘8am-5pm) Of all Tigray's rock-hewn churches, Mikael Imba, possibly dating from the 11th century, most resembles those seen at Lalibela. A three-quarter monolith, the interior is huge (16.6m wide and 9m deep) with 25 pillars (nine freestanding) holding up the 6m-high ceiling. The view from here is great. It's 9km south of Atsbi and has an easy 20-minute ascent, which is finished with a short ladder. There's no public transport here.

Tembien Cluster

Isolated from the other clusters, Tembien receives so few visitors that on our last visit no children asked us for anything... Abi Adi, the nearest town, sits gorgeously in a half-ring of mountains. It's best approached from Adwa or Mekele. The direct road from Hawzien is often impassable, requiring a 135km drive through Nebelet. Market day is Saturday.

Abba Yohanni   CHURCH

(አባ ዮሃኒ; Birr150, men only; ⊘8am-5.30pm) Impressively located halfway up a 300m-high sheer cliff face, this church is reached by a 15-minute climb using steps, tunnels and little bridges. The crooked carving and large cracks make the three-aisled, four-bayed interior as fascinating as the facade and the bright afternoon light makes it easy to photograph. As a bonus, it's an active monastery, so the key is never far away. On the downside, it means women are prohibited.

Architecturally it can't compete with many others, but all things combined, it's still worth a visit. It sits 13.5km from Abi Adi on the back of the mountain. The last 7.5km is on a 4WD-only road that gets very little traffic, except on market day.

If the church has captured your imagination, you'll be pleased to know that another 42 churches founded by Yohannes are in the vicinity. The only problem is that not only are they all invisible, some are also guarded by a sword-wielding Yohannes...

Gebriel Wukien   CHURCH

(ገብርኤል ውቄን; Birr150; ⊘8am-5.30pm) In a grove of trees on the other side of the same mountain as Abba Yohanni this architecturally interesting 15th-century church, is entered through a rock-hewn trench. Unfortunately the priest lives an hour away, meaning unless you're lucky and he's at the church when you come, you need to plan on up to a two-hour wait to get inside.

It's 14km northwest of Abi Adi, just 1km off the main road (plenty of public transport passes the junction), and involves a not-too-tough 10-minute climb.

If you do get inside, the church has three aisles and four bays with well-carved details, six massive, finely hewn freestanding pillars and three cupolas.

YEHA

Yeha (ቤሃ; Birr200, guide Birr220, personal video cameras Birr50; ⊘8am-5.30pm) is considered the birthplace of Ethiopia's earliest known civilisation nearly three millennia ago. Many features here, such as the immense, windowless, sandstone walls of the so-called Great Temple, are identical to those found in temples in Saba, Yemen, and debate continues among scholars as to whether it was founded by Sabaean settlers from Arabia or by Ethiopians influenced by Sabaean ideas. The current thinking is that it was created by a mix of the two groups.

Now in the midst of restoration, the ruins are impressive for their sheer age as well as their stunning construction. The 7th-century-BC Great Temple's limestone building blocks, measuring up to 3m in length, are perfectly dressed and fitted together without a trace of mortar. The whole temple is a grid of perfect lines and geometry.

Just northeast, behind a little restaurant that has some photos of the site from 1906 on its walls, are the remains of **Grat Be'al Gebri**, a monumental structure where the oldest sections date to the 8th century BC. Perhaps once a palace, it measured 2500 sq metres and it's distinguished for its unusual, square-sectioned, monolithic pillars (which could have been taller than the tallest known in South Arabia at the Temple of the Moon in Ma'rib in Yemen). Important rock-hewn tombs have also been found in the vicinity.

Next to the temple is the new **Church of Abuna Aftse**, which was built in the 1940s over the 6th-century-AD original. Incorporated into its walls are stones removed from the temple, and in the west wall there are reliefs of ibexes, a sacred animal of southern Arabia. Entry is not allowed to tourists. The tiny **museum** contains a collection of beautifully incised ancient Sabaean inscriptions believed to originate from the temple, as well as some similarly ancient pottery plus the usual church paraphernalia.

Guides are compulsory, although if you insist you *may* be allowed to wander around alone. One guide we recommend is **Hawaz** (☑0910-932155) – it's worth ringing ahead to make sure he's free.

The last minibus back to Adwa leaves the village at about 4pm.

Hawzien

If you're in Hawzien on a Wednesday, take time for a stroll through the **market**. It's one of Tigray's most important and between mid-October and May it sometimes receives camel caravans bringing salt from the Danakil.

You may also want to look at the patch of ruined houses and bomb craters at the west end of town that remain from an attack by the Derg in 1988 that killed 2500 people. An obelisk-style monument to the victims sits in the middle of the roundabout in the centre of town.

Cheila

Around 8km southeast of Megab, the village of Cheila is well worth a visit. The small collection of houses represent some of the best examples of stone-built Tigrayan architecture you'll find anywhere. Locals here take a real pride in keeping their village tidy, and there's usually someone around (especially if you come with a local guide) willing to show you their stone-built houses with rooms arrayed around an internal courtyard. It's also a terrific way to meet local people and provides an alternative to visiting the rock-hewn churches.

🏃 Activities

Because most of the Tigray churches are in remote places, short treks are required to reach them. Until recently there were no organised overnight treks; luckily, for adventurous travellers, this has changed.

Although the locally inspired architecture is different, the set up of the new trekking program is otherwise nearly identical to the excellent one around Lalibela. There are currently four community-run camps (at altitudes between 2200m and 3000m) spread out in the remote mountains southwest of Adigrat. Most people begin trekking near Hawzien, but the guides can also meet you at Adigrat or Aksum and start closer to these towns. Treks run year-round and booking is through Tesfa Tours (p298) in Addis Ababa.

Two options that you can arrange with a guide on arrival:

➡ **Full or Half-Day** Climb up to Maryam Korkor (p109) and then climb down off the escarpment (not for the faint hearted...) and then up to Abuna Yemata Guh (p109). Have a driver pick you up at the base of the latter, or walk to the main road to flag down a (rare) passing minibus.

➡ **Two Days** Begin at Abraha We Atsbeha (p111) and trek all the way to Yohannes Maequdi (p110); you'll be able to camp nearby. On day two, trek via Abuna Abraham (p109) and finish the day at Maryam Papaseit (p110), where you'll need to arrange return transport.

Tours

Mearg Abay TOURS
(☑ 0910-292927; mearg.abay@yahoo.com) A local guide in Wukro.

🛌 Sleeping

There's accommodation in many towns around the churches, but only Wukro, Abi Adi and Hawzien provide a level of comfort and cleanliness that most people expect.

🛏 Hawzien

This is the base for most tour companies and the region's best accommodation is either in the town or just outside.

★**Vision Hotel** HOTEL $
(☑ 0924-293314; Main Rd; s/d/tw/tr incl breakfast Birr329/429/459/699; 🛜) If only all Ethiopian budget hotels were this good. Overseen by the professional Geshu, and with one of the faster wi-fi connections we came across in Ethiopia, it's an excellent place. The rooms are clean, well-sized and reached via a courtyard with more greenery than most places at this price. All in all, it's excellent value for money.

CHURCH VISITS – PRACTICALITIES

Before setting out in the morning, remember the following and plan accordingly:

➡ Good walking shoes are essential.

➡ Bring a torch, but don't take it out too fast; letting the priests show you around by candlelight can be wonderful.

➡ Bring lots of small notes (priests never have change).

➡ Carry more water than you think you'll need for the day.

Costs

Visiting the Tigrayan rock-hewn churches and monasteries doesn't come cheap, and the following is a rough guide to how much you can expect to pay for the following:

Most churches cost Birr150 per person to enter. The only exception is **Abraha We Atsbeha** (p111), which costs Birr250.

In addition to the church admission fee, you'll be expected to pay:

➡ Guide – Birr385 per group of one to three people; Birr600 for four to six people.

➡ The man with the key who opens the church (usually the priest) – Birr50.

➡ Scouts who attach themselves to climbing parties and help them up/down the tricky bits – Birr100.

➡ Rope if required (for Abuna Yemata Guh, for example) – Birr150 per group.

➡ If you arrive without a vehicle, you can rent a minibus (ask at the **Guide Association** in Magab) – Birr1300 per day.

Finding the Priest

Patience and a positive attitude are essential for your enjoyment as it can take up to an hour to locate some priests. Also remember that when a local person tells you they know where the priest is, they only really know where the priest last was or is supposed to be, so if someone takes you up a mountain with a promise that the priest is there but he isn't, the person was probably not lying. But always make it clear that payment to a guide is dependent on getting inside the church: no entry, no money.

Tsego Gebre Gergis Pension PENSION $
(☑0920-073602; s/d Birr250/350) One of Hawzien's better cheapies, this pension sits around a concrete courtyard and has tidy and large rooms. They're building a further storey so there should be some new rooms as well. It's in front of Geralta Restaurant.

Green Hotel HOTEL $
(☑0914-730722; Main Rd; r Birr250) An OK choice along the main road through town, the basic Green Hotel has a busy little bar-restaurant and rooms with smallish beds and garish bedspreads.

Habesha Hotel HOTEL $
(☑0920-429668; off Main Rd; s/d/tw Birr250/330/430) With run-of-the-mill rooms with service that often goes missing, Habesha is a relatively new place that attracts a predominantly local clientele. It's just off the main road, behind Green Hotel.

★**Gheralta Lodge** LODGE $$$
(☑0346-670344, Addis Ababa office 0116-632893; www.gheraltalodgetigrai.com; per person incl breakfast Birr950; ☑) In a word: fantastic. This lovely Italian-owned, African-themed lodge has great facilities and service and many guests declare it their best night in Ethiopia. Rooms in the stone buildings are large and lovely. Don't miss eating at the restaurant, which provides a set Italian-inspired menu (lunch/dinner Birr210/250) that may be some of the finest food you eat in Ethiopia.

Book as far ahead as possible.

🛏 Wukro

Wukro is by far the biggest town in the rock-hewn church zone. It doesn't have the same breadth of accommodation choices as Hawzien or the Gheralta cluster in general, but it does have an excellent lodge, a handful of decent restaurants and several small supermarkets. Water shortages are endemic here and while you can rely on running water every day at the big hotels, you can't expect it all day.

Lwam Hotel HOTEL $
(☑0348-430042; www.lwamhotel.com; s Birr380, d & tw Birr470; ☑☎) Once a very nice place to stay, Lwam is slipping fast and many of the ensuite rooms are a little on the nose; ask to see a few. However, the *faranji* food (mains Birr30 to Birr80) here isn't bad at all and the upstairs dining area is an agreeable place to eat.

★**Wukro Lodge** LODGE $$
(☑0921-117028, 0115-150698; www.wukrolodge.com; s/d/tw incl breakfast Birr880/1020/1150; ☑☎☒) Finally nearing completion during our recent visit, Wukro Lodge has been worth the wait. The rooms feature traditional designs – split levels like many local homes, walls carved from the rock like the region's churches, traditional building materials and even 'soil' ceilings – and all have fabulous views over the surrounding valleys. Add in eminently reasonable prices and we're already hooked.

🛏 Abi Adi

Abi Adi suffers regular water shortages. Don't count on being able to have a shower. If there is one and it happens to be hot, you've hit the jackpot.

Mylomine Botanical Garden Lodge LODGE $$
(☑0910-040893, 0344-460754; r in new/old bldg US$50/45; ☑) An unexpectedly relaxing spot, Mylomine has five too-expensive but otherwise decent Sidamo-style (the owner is from Awash) bamboo huts in a quiet garden. There's pleasant dining (meals from Birr40) on the large verandah. It's signposted above town on the Adwa Rd.

🛏 Dugem

Kuriftu Resort LODGE
Still under construction at the time of our visit, the new Kuriftu Resort (part of a chain with excellent hotels elsewhere in Ethiopia) is one to watch. With its back to sheer cliffs and expansive views, the resort will have large rooms built from ferrous stone and thatched roofs. It's well signposted off the road from Megab to Dugem.

🛏 Megab

★**Korkor Lodge** COTTAGE $$$
(☑0912-912305; www.korkorlodge.com; s/d full board US$150/200) Set on a rise southwest of Megab, this lovely place has stone cottages built from local materials (sandstone walls, olive-wood floors, eucalyptus ceilings) and fabulous views of the surrounding mountains. Luigi and Françoise are warm and knowledgeable hosts and while the place was a work-in-progress when we visited, it's already a fine choice and will just get better with time.

✖ Eating

Hawzien has the best selection of restaurants. Gheralta Lodge is the best place to eat in town. Wukro also has a few good choices.

Tesfay Restaurant ETHIOPIAN **$**
(☑0914-784425; Hawzien; mains Birr50-100; ⊙7am-9pm) Opened in 2016, this friendly place is a good, simple choice. It does all the usual Ethiopian staples, as well as sandwiches. It's not signposted – take the road heading south down the hill off the main road through Hawzien, around 100m east of the local guide association office; once on this road, it's 200m down the hill on your right.

Fisseha Hotel ETHIOPIAN **$**
(☑0914-730898; Wukro; mains Birr55-150; ⊙7am-10pm; ☜) The main reason to come here is not the large and loud TV screen in the dining room, but the roast goat served with rice – it's a great meal and easily our favourite dish in town. Get your hands all greasy, pick it up and tuck in. The rooms here are rather nondescript, and if you can work out their pricing system (rooms from Birr400), let us know.

Geralta Restaurant ETHIOPIAN **$**
(☑0912-172659; Hawzien; mains Birr40-130; ⊙6.30am-10pm) In this centre of Hawzien, this basic eatery does decent Ethiopian food that's popular with a local crowd.

ⓘ Information

Tigray Tourism Commission (☑0344-430340; ⊙8am-noon & 1.30-5pm Mon-Sat) The helpful staff at the tourist offices in Wukro, **Aksum** (p105) and **Mekele** (p118) advise on itineraries and provide brochures.

Gheralta Local Guide Association (☑0914-616851; 1-3/4-6 people per day Birr250/350) Official guides are mandatory for Abuna Yemata Guh and Maryam Korkor (where going alone is potentially dangerous), but they can be hired for other places too, which we recommend. This office is at the main junction in Megab. You can also hire local scouts (Birr100) to carry bags and chase away children.

ⓘ Getting There & Away

Quite good gravel roads now connect the villages with the trailheads to most churches. Contract minibuses (per group per day Birr1300) are available in Hawzien, Wukro and Abi Adi, or ask at the Gheralta Local Guide Association office in Megab.

If you're patient, exploration by public transport is possible. There are many minibuses from Adigrat (Birr35, 1½ hours) to Wukro and also from Mekele to Wukro (Birr26, one hour) and Hawzien (Birr48, 2½ hours) via Freweyni. There's always much more traffic on market days.

Mekele

POP 219,818 / ELEV 2062M

The rapidly expanding university city of Mekele (መቀሌ), Tigray's capital, owes its importance to Emperor Yohannes IV, who made it his capital in the late 19th century. Though hardly anyone comes to see the town itself, there's enough here to pass the time waiting for your Danakil tour to depart or en route between Lalibela and the north.

◉ Sights

There are several churches, both old and new, dotting the city and their towers are visible throughout. Southwest of the 'bazaar', the intriguing monument in the roundabout is a memorial to the victims of the Derg bombing in Hawzien.

Camel caravans still arrive from the Danakil on Monday mornings, but they no longer come inside the city and the bars of salt are brought to market by truck.

Martyrs' Memorial MEMORIAL
(የሰማዕታት መታሰቢያ ሐውልት; www.haweltisemaitat.com; Birr50; ⊙8am-5.30pm) From a distance, this memorial to the victims of the Derg could be mistaken for the world's biggest golf ball and tee. From up close it's another story, with larger-than-life statues flanking the tower that illustrate the true cost of war. The domed building just to the north is a museum that exalts the successes and sacrifices made by the Tigrayan People's Liberation Front (TPLF) during the 1970s and 80s.

Yohannes IV Museum MUSEUM
(ዮሐንስ አራተኛ ሙዚየም; Birr50; ⊙8am-5pm Mon-Sat) The Italian-designed stone palace built for Emperor Yohannes IV (r 1872–89) is now an interesting museum. Although the palace itself is undergoing a thorough restoration, the three-part collection (royal regalia, religious paraphernalia and Tigrayan crafts) is on display in another building.

☞ Tours

Mekele is a possible launch pad for trips to the Danakil Depression and tours to the rock-hewn churches of Tigray (p107).

Mekele

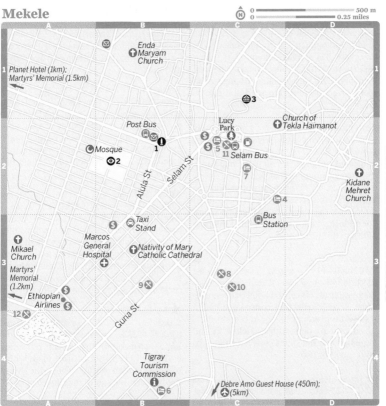

Mekele

◉ Sights
1 Derg Bombing Monument B2
2 New Market B2
3 Yohannes IV Museum C1

🛏 Sleeping
4 Atse Kaleb Hotel C2
5 Atse Yohannes Hotel C2
6 Axum Hotel B4

7 Yordanos Hotel C2

✕ Eating
8 Black Rose C3
9 Geza Gerlase B3
10 Karibu Kitchen & Bar C3
11 Nur Supermarket C2
12 Yordanos Restaurant A4

Covenant Tours   TOURS
(☑ 0911-185279; www.covenantethiopia.com) Although its main offices are in Axum and Addis, this is a good company for the Danakil.

Magma Flow Tours   TOURS
(☑ 0914-721601;   www.magmaflowtoursethiopia.
com) Recommended for tours to the Danakil
Depression in particular.

🛏 Sleeping

Atse Kaleb Hotel   HOTEL $
(☑ 0344-415255; r Birr250, with shared bathroom
Birr90; ⓟ 🛜) Simple but clean: even most of
the toilet seats remain firmly attached. It's
quieter than other similar nearby options,
although some rooms are a little dark.

Debre Amo Guest House
GUESTHOUSE $$

(☎0344-409251; www.debreamoguesthouse.com; s/d from US$60/80, r with shared bathroom US$40) Although it's a bit out on a limb, this place has excellent rooms that punch well above their midrange weight. The look is modern and immaculate, although most rooms overlook the main road and can be noisy.

Atse Yohannes Hotel
HOTEL $$

(☎0344-406762; atseyohanneshotel@yahoo.com; s/tw/ste US$38/41/73; P@) Not so much renovated as given a complete makeover, the Atsey Yohannes has excellent rooms overlooking one of the main roundabouts in town. The white colour scheme with muted tones gives the place a refreshingly contemporary look you don't see in many Ethiopian hotels in this price range.

Yordanos Hotel
HOTEL $$

(☎0344-413722; s/d/tw incl breakfast US$40/50/45; P@) You'll find decent mid-range value at this central hotel that features some clever Tigrinyan decoration, although it's a little overdone in the reception area. All rooms have desk, fridge, satellite TV and large bed and the suites even have hot tubs with room for two.

★Planet Hotel
HOTEL $$$

(☎0344-405660; www.planetinternationalhotel.com; r US$80-120, ste US$140-210; P🛜🗙) With Mekele's classiest hotel rooms (at least for now – there's a five-star hotel under construction next door), the four-star Planet looks out over the new stadium. Warm colour schemes in the rooms as well as comfortable beds and strong wi-fi.

Axum Hotel
HOTEL $$$

(☎0344-406760; www.axumhotels.com; r US$76-120; P🛜) The hotel of choice for many tour groups and certainly the best that straddles midrange and top-end price categories, Axum has a professional air, with good, modern, business-standard rooms. The wi-fi works most of the time and there's a good on-site restaurant and central location.

✖ Eating

Mekele has a handful of excellent places to eat – the only problem in a town where most travellers stay only a night is which one to choose.

If you're stocking up on supplies for a camping expedition into the Danakil or elsewhere, Nur Supermarket (⊙8am-6pm Mon-Sat) is Mekele's best-stocked grocery. Seti Supermarket (⊙8am-6pm Mon-Sat) is also good.

Yordanos Restaurant
EUROPEAN, ETHIOPIAN $

(mains Birr60-90; ⊙11am-11pm) Tucked away up a side street off the main road, this surprisingly stylish place has a casual open courtyard popular with local couples and a more stylish inside restaurant where thin-based pizza is the undoubted highlight of a varied menu.

★Black Rose
EUROPEAN, ETHIOPIAN $$

(☎0911-513984; mains Birr81-107; ⊙9am-midnight) This stylish outpost of an Addis lounge bar is one of Mekele's more intriguing dining options. Downstairs it serves excellent pizza, pasta and Ethiopian dishes in a quietly sophisticated setting with world music playing in the background, while upstairs it shakes cocktails (Birr48 to Birr199) until late.

★Karibu Kitchen & Bar
EUROPEAN, ETHIOPIAN $$

(☎0344-402788; mains Birr39-82, pizza Birr67-115; ⊙7am-midnight) This garden restaurant is the first choice for *faranji* food, with a pleasing garden setting where the wood-fired pizza is the star of the show.

Geza Gerlase
ETHIOPIAN $$

(Guna St; 1kg beef/lamb Birr280/320; ⊙7am-11pm) This cultural restaurant within a cavernous traditional *tukul* is a great place to enjoy excellent Ethiopian dishes. Specialities include *zilzil tibs* (strips of lamb, fried and served slightly crunchy with mustard-and-chilli *awazi* sauce) and *kitfo*. Vegetarians steer clear – it's *all* about meat here. There's a cultural dance show at 7.30pm on Tuesday, Thursday, Saturday and Sunday nights.

❶ Information

There are numerous ATMs in Mekele, especially in the city centre.

Marcos General Hospital (☎0344-409220; ⊙24hr) A reliable clinic with a diagnostic laboratory.

Tigray Tourism Commission (☎0914-721280; Axum Hotel; ⊙8.30am-noon & 2-6pm) Can advise on Danakil and rock-hewn-church visits, but don't expect more than high-level information.

ℹ Getting There & Away

Ethiopian Airlines (📞 0344-400055; ⊗ 8am-5.30pm Mon-Sat) flies three times daily to Addis Ababa (Birr4027, one to 1½ hours).

Numerous minibuses run from the bus station to Adigrat (Birr48, 2½ hours), while one bus runs to Aksum (Birr85, seven hours, 6am). For the Tigray churches, vehicles leave from the bus station daily for Abi Adi (Birr45, 3½ hours), Wukro (Birr22, one hour) and Hawzien (Birr48, 2½ hours) via Sinkata.

There's no direct transport to Lalibela, so you must transit through Woldia. With a bit of luck, it's usually possible to make it in one day by public transport. To get to Woldia either take an Addis Ababa–bound bus (Birr178, six hours), or take a minibus to Alamata (Birr62, four hours) and continue to Woldia (Birr43, 1½ hours) from there.

To Addis Ababa, you have the choice of normal service (Birr300, two days, 5am daily), deluxe Selam Buses (Birr485, 1½ days, 6am daily) or Post Bus (Birr365, 1½ days, 6am thrice weekly).

Danakil Depression

Bubbling volcanoes light up the night sky, sulphurous mounds of yellow contort into otherworldly shapes, and mirages of camels cross lakes of salt. Lying 100m and more below sea level, the Danakil Depression (ዳ ናክል ጠለል ቦታ) is about the hottest and most inhospitable place on Earth. In fact it's so surreal that it doesn't feel like part of Earth at all. If you want genuine, raw adventure, few corners of the globe can match this overwhelming wilderness. But come prepared because with temperatures frequently saying hello to 50°C and appalling 'roads', visiting this region is more an expedition than a tour.

Some companies will take you year-round, but between July and early October there's a good chance of flooding and you may not be able to make it to Irta'ale or Lake Afdera. Travellers with heart conditions shouldn't visit at any time of the year and everyone should heed signs of heat exhaustion.

There are no hotel or restaurants – tour operators set up mobile camps.

◉ Sights

Irta'ale Volcano

The Danakil's most amazing site is Irta'ale Volcano (613m), which has been in a state of continuous eruption since 1967. Its small southerly crater is one of the only permanent lava lakes on the planet. The climb is long (15km; three to four hours) but not steep; the heat and darkness (you climb after dinner) create the difficulty. Camels will transport the gear for the night and riding one is an option. You'll need a torch and it can get cool enough at the summit that you may want a light jacket or sleeping bag – make sure the operator organising your expedition has all of these covered.

Dallol

One of the Danakil's must-sees is Dallol (125m below sea level at its base), about 20km north of Hamedela, where great warts of twisted sulphur and iron oxide paint a yellow-and-orange landscape that looks more like a coral reef than anything you've ever seen above the waterline. The base of the hill is the lowest place in Ethiopia and the hottest place on Earth, with a year-round average temperature of 34.4°C. The dry, cracked bed of Lake Asale alongside Dallol is where the Afar people hack blocks of salt out of the ground. The famous camel caravans load up here and you can stop to watch.

Lake Afdera

Seldom visited (usually only by tours starting in Addis) is Lake Afdera (102m below sea level), sometimes called Afrera, which is 60km (up to six hours by 4WD!) south of Irta'ale. Salt is extracted from its green waters and you can swim in it or the nearby hot springs.

NORTHERN ETHIOPIA DANAKIL DEPRESSION

ℹ DANAKIL DEPRESSION

Why Go?
Quite simply, one of the most unearthly landscapes in Africa.

Gateway Towns
Mekele's main base is the half-village, half-tourist camp of Hamedela where you'll sleep outdoors or inside simple shelters against the wind, if necessary.

Budget Tips
Mekele companies are in the habit of joining travellers together into large groups and, in high season at least, you can usually just show up and find a trip departing in a day or two.

Practicalities
You can only visit the Danakil as part of an organised tour and a minimum of two 4WD vehicles is required.

☞ Tours

Just about every tour operator in Ethiopia will happily take you out into the Danakil Depression. We recommend the following as the most professional:

GETTS Ethiopia (p298)

Smiling Ethiopia (p298)

Magma Flow Tours (p117)

Abeba Tours Ethiopia (p298)

ℹ Information

The Danakil has a reputation as a largely lawless area and there have been killings and kidnappings in recent years, so do check the situation carefully before going. That said, the Ethiopian government now has a major military presence in the region and all organised tours should travel with a military escort. If you're coming from Addis, you'll pick up your security detail in Serdo or Semera. From Mekele, it should happen in Berhale.

ℹ Getting There & Away

Trips to the Danakil Depression can be organised through tour operators in Addis Ababa, Mekele and elsewhere. Tours starting in Addis usually enter or exit from the south via Serdo, with formalities handled in Semera. From the Mekele side, registration and hiring of security is done in Berhale. The going rate in Mekele is US$600 per day with a big-enough group, but all prices are negotiable – remember, however, that obtaining a discount may be a false economy as

the operators may then be forced to cut back on essentials such as food and water.

Two days is a minimum for visiting the Danakil, including a visit to Irta'ale Volcano, but three- and four-day excursions are also possible; the latter will enable you to visit Irta'ale, Dallol and Lake Asale.

Private travel is no longer allowed.

Lalibela

POP 25,000 / ELEV 2630M

Lalibela (ላሊበላ) is history and mystery frozen in stone, its soul alive with the rites and awe of Christianity at its most ancient and unbending. No matter what you've heard about Lalibela, no matter how many pictures you've seen of its breathtaking rock-hewn churches, nothing can prepare you for the reality of seeing it for yourself. It's not only a World Heritage site, but truly a world wonder. Spending a night vigil here during one of the big religious festivals, when white-robed pilgrims in their hundreds crowd the courtyards of the churches, is to witness Christianity in its most raw and powerful form.

History

Lalibela, initially known as Roha, was the Zagwe dynasty's capital in the 12th and 13th centuries. In a rare consensus, scholars and local tradition both claim that the churches

---

SALT FOR GOLD

Since earliest times and right up to the present day, salt, a precious commodity for people and their animals, has been used as a kind of currency in Ethiopia. According to Kosmos, a 6th-century Egyptian writing in Greek, the kings of Aksum sent expeditions west to barter salt, among other things, for hunks of gold.

Mined in the Danakil Depression, the mineral was transported hundreds of kilometres west across the country to the Ethiopian court in Shoa. Later the salt was cut into small, rectangular blocks, which came to be known as *amole;* their value grew with every further kilometre they travelled from the mine.

To this day, Afar nomads and their camels continue to follow this ancient salt route. Cutting the bars by hand from the salt lakes in eastern Ethiopia, they spend weeks travelling by caravan to market, where the bars will be bartered.

Though nowadays the people of the Danakil Depression mine salt in order to earn gold in the highland markets, once upon a time it was, according to local legend, the other way around. Long ago – so long that nobody really remembers – the salt of the Danakil was all gold...endless thousands of tonnes of pure gold. People say that Danakil had more gold than anywhere else on earth and its people lived like royalty. Wealth made them greedy, lazy and forgetful of God. In order to punish them, God turned all the gold to salt. But one day, so the locals say, when the people are no longer greedy, God will turn it all back into gold again and then the people of Danakil will once more be able to swap gold for salt.

date from around the time of King Lalibela (r 1181–1221), but the consensus is thrown out the window for everything else.

True believers say all work was completed in 23 years and this was possible because every night the earthly workforce was replaced by a celestial one. However, regardless of angelic intervention, the buildings are so different from each other in style, artisanship and state of preservation that they surely span a far longer period than even Lalibela's reign. It's also possible that not all were originally churches.

In many of Lalibela's churches, the exceptional masonry skills that had been refined during the days of Aksum were deployed here, and indeed most of the churches show clear Aksumite characteristics, in particular in the doors and windows.

One of the many local legends about the site's origin states that the king wanted to make a new Jerusalem so pilgrims didn't have to make the long, dangerous journey to the real one. Another claims that Lalibela was poisoned by his brother (or half-brother or half-sister) and while in a coma he went on a journey to heaven where God commanded him to return to Ethiopia and re-create the holy city of Jerusalem there. A multitude of sites, from Calvary to the Jordan River, have taken names from the Holy Land and local tradition also has decided that the northwestern group represents the real Jerusalem, while the southeastern group is the 'heavenly' Jerusalem.

⊙ Sights

Lalibela's rock-hewn churches, all built below ground level, aren't just carved into the rock but freed from it. And the carving, both inside and out, is exceptionally refined. Although time has treated most with gentle gloves, Unesco has built protective roofing. Fortunately, despite the intrusive design, this won't detract much from your enjoyment.

There are two main church clusters around the town, and it will take you the best part of a day to visit them all. There are also some wonderful churches and monasteries outside of town that can be explored on day trips.

The **ticket office** (⊙ 8am-noon & 2-5.30pm) lies at the northwestern group (which makes the southeastern group less busy in the morning). Tickets are valid for five days and can be paid in either US dollars or the Birr

equivalent; the exchange rate used to calculate the latter is the official bank rate.

Some people rush through in a half-day, but this simply isn't enough time. A second day allows proper appreciation. A 6am visit to see the locals in private worship can be enchanting, although you won't be allowed into the churches themselves in most cases. Many of the priests are more than happy to show off their church's treasures and pose obligingly beside them for photos. Since they get a cut of the entry fee, it's not necessary to tip for this and the whole Lalibela experience is refreshingly free of people asking for money at every turn. Note that camera flashes inside churches cause great damage to the paintings, so please resist using one.

Bringing a torch can be a good idea.

★ **Bet Giyorgis**   CHURCH
(በ·ት ጊዮርጊስ; adult/child 9-13yr with combined Lalibela church ticket US$50/25; ⊙ 8am-noon & 2-5.30pm) When you think of Lalibela, you're thinking of Bet Giyorgis. Resting off on its own, St George's Church is Lalibela's masterpiece. Representing the apogee of the rock-hewn tradition, it's the most visually perfect church of all, a 15m-high three-tiered plinth in the shape of a Greek cross – a perfectly proportioned shape that required no internal pillars. Due to its exceptional preservation, it also lacks the obtrusive roofing seen over the other churches.

Inside, light filters in from the windows and illuminates the ceiling's large crosses – beauty in simplicity. Peer over the curtain to see the maqdas' beautiful dome. There are also two 800-year-old olive-wood boxes (one with opposing corkscrew keys) that locals believe were carved by King Lalibela himself and now hold the church's treasures. Some of the cavities in the walls surrounding the church hold mummified corpses, and note the exquisite 16th-century canvas depicting St George slaying the dragon.

Plan to visit a number of times, including in the hour before sunset for good photos from above.

Northwestern Group of Churches

This group contains seven of Lalibela's 12 churches. From a size perspective, as well as the quality of the interior art, this group is easily the most impressive.

★ **Bet Medhane Alem**   CHURCH
(በ·ት መድኃኔዓለም; adult/child 9-13yr with combined Lalibela church ticket US$50/25; ⊙ 8am-

Lalibela

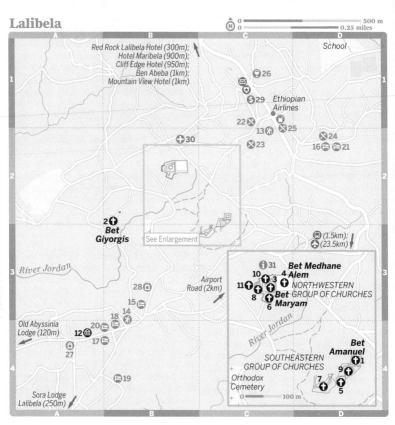

NORTHERN ETHIOPIA LALIBELA

noon & 2-5.30pm) Resembling a massive Greek temple more than a traditional Ethiopian church, Bet Medhane Alem (House of the Saviour of the World) is impressive for its size and majesty. Said to be the largest rock-hewn church in the world, it measures 33.5m by 23.5m and is more than 11.5m high. Some scholars have suggested it may have been a copy in rock of the original St Mary of Zion church (p96) in Aksum.

The building is surrounded by 34 large, rectangular columns (many are replicas of the originals). The three jointed at each corner are thought to represent the Holy Trinity. The interior consists of a barrel-vaulted nave and four aisles with 38 columns supporting the gabled roof. The three empty graves in one corner are said to have been prepared symbolically for Abraham, Isaac and Jacob. On Sundays worshipers come hoping to be blessed or healed by the famous 7kg gold Lalibela Cross.

⭐ **Bet Maryam**   CHURCH

(ቤተ ማርያም; adult/child 9-13yr with combined Lalibela church ticket US$50/25; ⊘8am-noon & 2-5.30pm) Connected to Bet Medhane Alem by a tunnel is a large courtyard containing three churches. The first, Bet Maryam, is small, yet designed and decorated to an exceptionally high standard. It's also the only church with porches extending off it. Dedicated to the Virgin, who's particularly venerated in Ethiopia, this is the most popular church among pilgrims. Some believe it may have been the first built by Lalibela.

On its eastern wall you'll see two sets of three windows. The upper set is thought to represent the Holy Trinity, while the lower three, set below a small cross-shaped window, are believed to represent the crucifixion of Jesus and the two sinners. The lower right window has a small opening above it, a signal that this sinner was accepted to heaven after repenting his sins and asking

Lalibela

for Jesus' help. The lower left window, which represents the criminal who went to hell, has the small opening below it.

Above the western porch and squeezed beneath the roof is a rare and beautifully carved bas-relief of St George fighting the dragon.

Inside, the ceilings and upper walls are painted with very early frescoes, and the columns, capital and arches are covered in beautifully carved details, including a curious two-headed eagle and two fighting bulls, one white, one black (thought to represent good and evil). At the eastern end of the tall nave, surrounded by seven galleries, is a holy column with inscriptions in Ge'ez, Hebrew and Greek kept permanently wrapped in cloth. Christmas celebrations here on 7 January are a wonderful thing to behold.

Bet Golgotha & Bet Mikael   CHURCH
(ቤተ ጎልጎታ እና ቤተ ሚካኤል; adult/child 9-13yr with combined Lalibela church ticket US$50/25; ⊗8am-noon & 2-5.30pm; men only Bet Golgotha) A trench at the southern end of the Bet Maryam courtyard connects it to the twin churches of Bet Golgotha and Bet Mikael (also known as Bet Debre Sina). The pair have the only cruciform pillars of Lalibela's churches and relief-carved crosses proliferate in Bet Mikael. The entrance leads first to Bet Mikael and then to Bet Golgotha, which women can't enter.

Bet Golgotha is known for containing some of the best early examples of Ethiopian Christian art, including some amazing life-size depictions of the 12 apostles carved into the walls' niches. Four are visible, with the other eight behind the curtains in the off-limits Selassie Chapel, one of Lalibela's holiest sanctuaries, home to more fantastic art and also the reputed tomb of King Lalibela himself.

Bet Meskel   CHAPEL
(ቤተ መስቀል; adult/child 9-13yr with combined Lalibela church ticket US$50/25; ⊗8am-noon & 2-5.30pm) Carved into the courtyard's northern wall at Bet Maryam is the tiny semichapel of Bet Meskel. Four pillars divide the gallery into two aisles spanned by arcades.

Bet Danaghel   CHAPEL
(ቤተ ደናግል; adult/child 9-13yr with combined Lalibela church ticket US$50/25; ⊗8am-noon & 2-5.30pm) To the south of the Bet Maryam courtyard is the pleasingly primitive and grotto-like chapel of Bet Danaghel (House of the Virgins), said to have been constructed in memory of the maiden nuns martyred on the orders of the 4th-century Roman emperor Julian in Edessa (modern-day Turkey).

Bet Uraiel
CHURCH

(ቤተ ኡራኤል; adult/child 9-13yr with combined Lalibela church ticket US$50/25; ⊘8am-noon & 2-5.30pm) In the trench fronting the western facade of Bet Golgotha, past the symbolic Tomb of Adam (a giant, hollowed-out block of stone), Bet Uraiel opened as a church in 1998 in what may have been a storeroom. Its rough-hewn rooms are rarely visited by worshippers or tourists.

Southeastern Group of Churches

Although smaller in size than the north western group, the southeastern cluster offers Lalibela's most finely carved exteriors. After visiting the final church (most likely Bet Abba Libanos), climb up to Mt Tabor, from where most of Lalibela's churches are visible.

Bet Gabriel-Rufael
CHURCH

(ቤተ ገብርኤል እና ቤተ ሩፋኤል; adult/child 9-13yr with combined Lalibela church ticket US$50/25; ⊘8am-noon & 2-5.30pm) Its entrance flanked by a sloping sliver of rock known as the 'Way to Heaven', this imposing twin-church marks the main entrance to the southeastern group. Unlike most Lalibela churches its entrance is at the top and it's accessed by a small walkway, high over the moat-like trench. This, along with its curious, irregular floor plan and non-east–west orientation, has led scholars to propose that it may have been a fortified palace for Aksumite royalty as early as the 7th century.

The entrance takes you into Bet Gabriel and then another doorway accesses Bet Rufael. Although the section of Bet Rufael's roof that collapsed has been rebuilt, services only take place in Bet Gabriel. Once inside the surprisingly small complex you'll realise its monumental facade was its most interesting feature.

Bet Merkorios
CHURCH

(ቤተ መርቆርዮስ; adult/child 9-13yr with combined Lalibela church ticket US$50/25; ⊘8am-noon & 2-5.30pm) Reached via a series of trenches and tunnels (one is long, narrow and pitch-black) that starts from Bet Gabriel-Rufael, this church may have started as something altogether different. The discovery of ankle shackles among other objects has led scholars to believe it may have served as the town's prison or house of justice.

Due to a large section collapsing, the interior is a fraction of its former size and the brick walls are an unfortunate necessity. Don't miss the beautiful fresco (maybe 15th century), sometimes said to represent the Three Wise Men, though since they're holding crosses, this can't be correct. With their little flipper hands and eyes that look askance, they're delightful. The 12 apostles are represented below in a less attractive and probably later fresco. The Passion of the Christ painting on cotton fabric next to the frescoes probably dates from the 16th century. Formerly, such paintings were plastered to the church walls with a mixture of straw, ox blood and mud.

The 35m pitch-black tunnel to the church as you come from Bet Gabriel-Rufael is said to represent hell and, according to local tradition, should be walked without any light – mind your head!

★ Bet Amanuel
CHURCH

(ቤተ አማኑኤል; adult/child 9-13yr with combined Lalibela church ticket US$50/25; ⊘8am-noon & 2-5.30pm) Freestanding and monolithic, Bet Amanuel is Lalibela's most finely carved church. Some have suggested it was the royal family's private chapel. It perfectly replicates the style of Aksumite buildings, with its projecting and recessed walls mimicking alternating layers of wood and stone seen at places such as Yemrehanna Kristos and Debre Damo. The most striking feature of the interior is the double Aksumite frieze atop the nave.

Although not accessible, there's a staircase to an upper gallery. In the southwest corner, a hole in the floor leads to a (closed) subterranean tunnel that connects the church to Bet Merkorios. The chambers in the walls are the graves of pilgrims who requested to be buried here.

Bet Abba Libanos
CHURCH

(ቤተ አባ ሊባኖስ; adult/child 9-13yr with combined Lalibela church ticket US$50/25; ⊘8am-noon & 2-5.30pm) Hewn into a rock face, Bet Abba Libanos is unique among Lalibela's churches because only the roof and floor remain attached to the strata. Many of its architectural features, such as the friezes, are Aksumite. Curiously, although it looks large from the outside, the interior is actually very small. The carved corners of its cubic capitals represent angel eyes. Legend says it was constructed in a single night by Lalibela's wife, Meskel Kebra, with a little help from angels.

Churches & Monasteries Around Lalibela

Many fascinating churches and monasteries lie in the stunning countryside within a day's striking distance of Lalibela. They vary greatly in style, design and age and offer a different experience from the churches in town. Tucked away and still absent from most modern maps, many require a guide to find them. The journey, whether by foot, mule or vehicle, to these sites is rewarding. If you didn't arrive in Lalibela with a 4WD and driver, ask your hotel or guide about renting one.

Yemrehanna Kristos   CHURCH

(ይመርሃነ ክርስቶስ; Birr300, personal video cameras Birr50; ⊙8am-5.30pm) Despite Yemrehanna Kristos being one of Ethiopia's best-preserved late-Aksumite buildings, few people reward themselves with a visit. And a reward it is. The church is different because it's built rather than excavated. Seeing the stepped exterior facade, created from alternating wood and stone layers, you'll understand why so many of Lalibela's rock-hewn churches look like they do. And knowing that Yemrehanna Kristos may predate Lalibela's churches by up to 80 years, you have before you a virtual blueprint of greatness.

Incredibly, the whole church sits on a foundation of carefully laid olive-wood panels, which 'float' it perfectly above the marshy ground below. The carving and decoration are exceptional, especially the cruciform windows and the elaborate nave ceiling. Behind the church lies a pile of mummified bodies: some are those of pilgrims who've come here to die over the centuries; others are said to be those of the workmen. This entirely inspiring and slightly spooky complex sits within a cave roofed by basalt lava flows. The ugly brick wall at the front was built in 1985 to improve the church's security.

The church is about 1½ hours (45km) north of Lalibela by 4WD. It can easily be visited along with Arbatu Ensessa, Bilbila Giyorgis and Bilbila Chirkos. It's also possible to get here by foot or mule. Both options take about five hours to cover the shorter 20km distance. The climb up to the church through a forest of juniper trees alive with vervet monkeys takes around 20 minutes.

If you're in the area on 10 October (19 October in the Ethiopian calendar), the site throngs with pilgrims and is an unforgettable experience.

Arbatu Ensessa   CHURCH

(አርባቱ እንሳሳ; Birr200; ⊙8am-5.30pm) On the way to Yemrehanna Kristos, around 35km from Lalibela, is this three-quarter monolith church in a wild, overgrown but rather beautiful setting. It's thought to have been built by King Kaleb in AD 518. *Arbatu ensessa* means 'the four beasts' after the four Evangelists: Matthew, Mark, Luke and John. It's five minutes' walk from the road.

Bilbila Giyorgis   CHURCH

(ቢልቢላ ጊዮርጊስ; Birr200; ⊙8am-5.30pm) Lying west of Arbatu Ensessa, around 32km from Lalibela, Bilbila Giyorgis is also attributed to King Kaleb. It resembles Bet Abba Libanos in design. According to tradition, five swarms of bees took up residence shortly after the church was completed. They still reside here and their sacred honey is said to have curative properties, particularly for psychological disorders and skin problems. The priest will let you taste it. It's 20 to 30 minutes' walk up the hill from the road.

Bilbila Chirkos   CHURCH

(ቢልቢላ ጨርቆስ; Birr200; ⊙8am-5.30pm) Also near Arbatu Ensessa, 41km off the Yemrehanna Kristos road, this is an interesting three-quarter monolith known particularly for its ancient frescoes. Also attributed to King Kaleb, it's thought to date from AD 523. It's a three-minute walk from the road.

Ashetan Maryam   CHURCH

(አሸተን ማርያም; Birr200; ⊙8am-5.30pm) Set at 3150m, atop Abune Yosef mountain, is this monastery where the local priests believe they're 'closer to heaven and God' here, and it's easy to see why. The monastery's construction is believed to span Lalibela's and Na'akuto La'ab's reign, although local tradition claims it as King Lalibela's first attempt at church construction. Although the architecture here compares pretty poorly with Lalibela, it's the extraordinary mountain scenery for which you really come. The five-hour climb (one way) from Lalibela is quite steep; it's a 30-minute climb from the car park. Church treasures include parchment and some icons. The most important local festival is on 12 September.

Na'akuto La'ab

(ናአኩቶ ለአብ; Birr200; ⊙8am-5.30pm) Lying 7km from Lalibela, just off the airport road, this is a simple but attractive church (apart from the outer security wall). It's attributed to King Lalibela's successor and shelters in

NORTHERN ETHIOPIA LALIBELA

a natural cave. It was almost certainly the site of a much older shrine and Empress Zewditu built the inner red-brick building. Some very old stone receptacles collect the precious holy water that drips from the cave roof. The church boasts various treasures said to have belonged to its founder, including crosses, crowns, gold-painted drums and an illuminated Bible.

Geneta Maryam CHURCH
(ገነተ ማርያም; Birr200; ◷8am-5.30pm) Thought to have been built around 1270 by Yekuno Amlak, who restored the Solomonic line. With its rectangular shape and 20 massive rectangular pillars that support it, Geneta Maryam resembles Lalibela's Bet Medhane Alem. It's also known for its remarkable 13th-century paintings, though most are very faded. There's a moon-shaped face of Christ on the western wall. Whoever built the hideous protective roof over it should be ashamed. It's about five hours by foot from Lalibela or 1½ hours by vehicle.

Mekina Medane Alem CHURCH
(መኪና መድኀኒኀዓለም; Birr200; ◷8am-5.30pm) Two to three hours' walk from Geneta Maryam and six hours' walk from Lalibela, this remote church was, according to Ethiopian tradition, constructed by three virgins during the reign of King Gebre Meskel in AD 537. The church is constructed under an overhanging rock in a natural cave. It rather resembles Yemrehanna Kristos in design and many features are Aksumite, but its beautiful frescoes, some of hunting scenes with one-eyed lions, are the main attraction.

Other Sights
Lalibela Cultural Center MUSEUM
(Birr30; ◷8am-12.30pm & 1.30-5.30pm) This excellent new museum has beautifully presented displays about Lalibela's history, both past and present. The exhibits range from cultural artefacts to ancient manuscripts and other archaeological finds from Lalibela's sites. But the real stars are the 11 detailed information panels around the walls outlining Lalibela's history and archaeology. A museum guide is included in the entry fee.

🏃 Activities

Trekking through the villages and valleys surrounding Lalibela is a wonderful experience that mixes astounding scenery, historical riches and a fascinating insight into the life of Ethiopian highlanders. You'll likely meet gelada monkeys and there's a small chance of Ethiopian wolves in the highest reaches. Plus there's a good variety of birdlife, from lammergeyers to bee-eaters. The treks were originally set up by a now-defunct NGO called TESFA (www.community-tourism-ethiopia.com) and many people refer to trekking here as 'tesfa trekking'. Responsibility has now passed to the Frankfurt Zoological Society – visit www.abuneyoseph tourism.org.

Treks are typically three to five days long and routes can be designed based on time, fitness, churches, chances of animal encounters or whatever you want. The Lasha area northwest of Lalibela, home to Abuna Yosef, Ethiopia's third-highest peak (4300m), and the part of the Meket Plateau to the southeast offer rugged treks with some heavy-duty climbs. Further away, the part of the Meket Plateau west of Gashena has low gradients and the walking is fairly easy.

There are 11 community-run lodges (and an additional seven lunch stops) near villages, each consisting of traditional yet comfortable mud-and-stone *tukuls* and loos with views. Most have showers.

Information & Booking

Bookings can be made through Addis Ababa–based Tesfa Tours (p298), under an agreement with the local communities, or via www.abuneyoseph tourism.org. It's best to book as far in advance as possible, especially at peak seasons: October, December and early January. At other times of the year you can usually just show up and head out the next day, but maybe not on the route you had in mind. Make arrangements locally with the guides in Lalibela through the Lasta Lalibela Community Tourism Guiding Enterprise (LLCTGE; ☏0913-244479).

The treks, including guides, pack mules, accommodation, meals, tea and coffee (beer, soft drinks and water are sold at each lodge), cost Birr1493.50 per person per 24 hours. Any transport to and from trailheads, if necessary, costs extra. Solo trekkers pay an additional Birr250 per night and there's a Birr60 fee per group per night if booking less than three days in advance. There are discounts for children.

Though a few of the community lodges are open year-round, during the heaviest rains from mid-July to late-September most are closed and you won't likely have much fun anyway. During this time it would be better to head to the drier Tigray region.

Lalibela-based company Highland Trekking (0912-130831; www.highlandtrekking.com) and some of the licensed church guides, such as Girma Derbie (0913-513763; girmaderbie123@yahoo.com) or Zenebe Minale (0913-420383; zenebeminale2017@yahoo.com), can also lead trekking trips at slightly lower prices because they have their guests sleep in villages (it's not as romantic as it sounds and many people don't enjoy the rough, hectic conditions; others love it, though) or use tents instead of the community lodges. This may be your only option if you book late during the high season.

Tours

Local licensed guides are best arranged at the ticket office. One guide who we warmly recommend is Zenebe Minale.

Although visiting without a guide is possible (getting lost in the warren of tunnels and trenches is quite memorable), we consider it a false economy as you'll miss out on many of the amazing subtleties each church has to offer. The guides also know many good photo viewpoints.

Guide fees are divided into two different categories:

➡ A guide to all of Lalibela's 12 churches costs Birr500 for groups of one to five, Birr800 for six to 10 people, and Birr1000 for larger groups. These are usually covered in one full day.

➡ Guides charge Birr500 for *each* of the churches outside the town.

Courses

★ **Unique Restaurant** COOKING
(0333-360125; per person US$20) It's difficult to imagine simpler surrounds, but Sisaynesh inspires confidence and plenty of laughs as she takes you through the process of making *injera, shiro* and other Ethiopian dishes.

★ **Lalibela Cooking School** COOKING
(0338-362758; per person US$25) In the classes at Lalibela Cooking School at Old Abyssinia Restaurant (p129), you'll learn how to make *injera, shiro* and other vegetarian options. It's a lovely way to spend an afternoon in an appealing setting, but you'll need to book in advance to make sure it's set up.

Festivals & Events

The most exciting time to visit is during a major festival, when thousands of pilgrims crowd in. Timkat and Leddet are the biggest, but Lalibela draws masses for all the major ones. Outside these periods, try to attend at least one church's monthly saint day.

Sleeping

Lalibela's sleeping choices are improving all the time, especially in the midrange.

Discounts, often very large ones, are negotiable in most hotels from April through August. Vacancies are almost nonexistent during the festival period and European Christmas, so reservations are essential. However, prices for reserved rooms during these times can quintuple or more. If you arrive during a festival without reservations, look for brokers who work the centre of town hiring out rooms in people's homes.

Asheton Hotel HOTEL $
(0333-360030; hailu_mher@yahoo.com; s/d/tw Birr300/400/500; P ♠) This classic budget-traveller haunt offers older whitewashed rooms – don't be fooled by the intricately carved doorways as what lies within is far simpler. The whole place is running down slowly, so the doubling of prices since we were last here is most unwelcome. One big plus: it's across the road from Unique Restaurant.

★ **Old Abyssinia Lodge** BUNGALOW $$
(0338-362758; www.oldabyssinia.com; incl breakfast s US$55-75, tw US$65-85; P ♠) There were just three *tukul*-style rooms here when we visited, but they certainly caught our eye. Stunning wood furnishings, many with intricately carved traditional local designs, inhabit stone-walled rooms that are lovely and large and come with well-sized bathrooms. The balconies have wonderful views. It's *very* quiet.

Sora Lodge Lalibela HOTEL $$
(0911-637211; www.soralodgelalibela.com; s/d/tw incl breakfast main bldg US$45/55/60, d/f tukul cottages US$65/99; P ♠) A friendly place out on the tip of one of Lalibela's many ridges, Sora Lodge has a modern main building with tidy rooms and sweeping views from the upper floors, as well as nicely decorated *tukul*-style rooms, also with terrific views. It grows many of its own vegetables for the on-site restaurant.

Tukul Village Hotel
LODGE **$$**

(☎ 0333-360564; www.tukulvillage.com; s/d or tw incl breakfast US$49/67; P@☎) The prices here haven't risen in years and that makes them even better value. While many *tukul*-rooms in Ethiopian hotels are dark, here they're filled with light and look out over a lovely garden area. The traditional furnishings and decor are nicely deployed, the bathrooms are large and the location is central.

Lal Hotel
HOTEL **$$**

(☎ 0333-360008; www.lalhotelsandspa.com; s/d incl breakfast US$40/45; P☎☎☎) Ask many locals which is Lalibela's best hotel and they'll tell you this place. It's certainly the biggest with 100 rooms, and while it does have a swimming pool and a small spa and sauna, we reckon the *tukul*-style rooms are fairly average and rather dark. That said, a recent fall in prices makes it reasonable value for the overall package.

Lalibela Hotel
HOTEL **$$**

(☎ 0911-095004; www.lalibelahotels.com; s/d/tr US$25/30/45; ☎) Nothing to write home about, but you won't mind being here while you do so. Rooms are simple but reasonable for the price and the setting, just back from the road, keeps things nice and quiet.

Cliff Edge Hotel
HOTEL **$$**

(☎ 0333-360606; www.cliffedgehotel-lalibela.com; s/d or tw/tr incl breakfast US$45/55/85; P☎) This is one of the better deals among the places lined up along the edge of the ridge, with fine views and nicely decorated rooms – the traditional Ethiopian bedspreads we've seen elsewhere, but the intricately carved bed frames are a lovely local touch. It also has a restaurant.

Selam Guest House
PENSION **$$**

(☎ 0333-3600374; s old/new rooms US$20/25, d or tw old/new rooms US$30/35) An all-round good deal in the centre of town, this place has recently built an entirely new wing and the rooms are spick and span and really rather good for the price. The on-site owner and his family keep things nice and friendly. A good choice with a price that's very fair for Lalibela.

PRESTER JOHN OF THE INDIES

I, Prester John, who reign supreme, exceed in riches, virtue and power all creatures who dwell under Heaven...In our territories are found elephants, dromedaries and camels and almost every kind of beast. Honey flows in our land, and milk abounds... No poison can do harm here and no noisy frogs croak, no scorpions are there, and no serpents creep through the grass. No venomous reptiles can exist or use their deadly power.

Prester John

The letter the mysterious Christian ruler Prester John wrote to the Byzantine Emperor Manuel Comnenus I in 1165 went on to inform of how his kingdom contained 'Centaurs, Amazons and shrinking giants'. There was a river that flowed from Paradise 'and in it are found emeralds, sapphires and many other precious stones'. His palace, so he said, was a 'palace of crystal with a roof of ebony and everyday 30,000 sit down to eat at tables of gold supported by columns of amethyst'. The great ruler himself wore robes spun from gold by salamanders that lived on a mountain of fire.

It was impressive stuff, but what really grabbed the attention of medieval Europe was Prester John's promise that he would ride forth from his kingdom with 10,000 cavalry and 100,000 foot soldiers and, alongside the armies of Western Europe, they would re-take the Holy Land from the Muslims.

The Christian Crusaders had lost much of the Holy Land and were on the verge of losing Jerusalem itself. News of Prester John's letter spread like wildfire throughout Christian Europe. It was partially in order to find Prester John's kingdom that the Portuguese launched the age of European exploration that changed the world forever.

Having first looked unsuccessfully in Asia, the focus turned to Ethiopia. When the Portuguese finally reached Gonder, they found a Christian kingdom that was a far cry from the glorious legend, and certainly in no position to aid the reconquest of Jerusalem.

And of Prester John? It turned out that one of the most intriguing figures of medieval Europe was nothing more than collective imagination, and the letter that started it all was a fake created by a German monk.

Red Rock Lalibela Hotel
HOTEL $$

(☑0333-361030; www.redrocklalibelahotel.com; s/tw/tr US$28/35/40; ☎) One of a number of lower-midrange places scattered around the centre of town, the Red Rock is typical of the genre – it won't win any style awards but it's kept clean, some rooms have city views and the predominantly female staff are friendly.

Alief Paradise Hotel
HOTEL $$

(☑0911-556211, 0333-360023; alparahotel@ya-hoo.com; old block d/tw US$15/20, new block d/tw US$25/35; ℗) Alef's reasonable new rooms are bright, tiled and clean, with bathtubs and partial views. The older rooms, though dark and uninspiring, are still decent value. The location is pretty central as well.

★Hotel Maribela
HOTEL $$$

(☑0333-360345; www.hotelmaribela.com; s/d or tw/ste US$65/99/110) Of all the hotels lined up along the ridges that face out over the valleys and mountains, this is the one we like best. With just 15 rooms, it has a more intimate feel than most and the rooms are filled with light and a light touch that gets the mix of modern and traditional just right.

The balconies, some with day beds and cushions, are perfect. It also has a good restaurant and friendly service.

Lalibela Hudad
HOTEL $$$

(☑0944-143690; www.lalibelahudad.com; campsites incl breakfast US$35, s/d/tr without bathroom incl breakfast US$65/80/90; ☑Sep-Jul; @) This peaceful ecolodge in the hills above Lalibela (five hours by foot: many people use mules, and it's possible to drive to within an hour's walk) has stone-and-thatch *tukuls,* incredible views and resident gelada monkeys. Despite the high price, the *tukuls* are very simple (shared drop toilets) though hot showers and decent food (lunch and dinner Birr100) are available.

Mountain View Hotel
HOTEL $$$

(☑0333-360804; www.mountainview-hotel.com; s/d or tw/tr incl breakfast US$64/77/100; ℗☎) Built by two former tour guides who received a miraculous business loan from a generous tourist, this comfortable hotel has an enviable perch with great views and a lovely stone-and-glass design. Rooms, all with balconies, are rather ordinary and some are a little cramped, but you'll love the balconies and their views.

✗ Eating & Drinking

Old Abyssinia Restaurant
ETHIOPIAN $

(☑0338-362758; www.oldabyssinia.com; mains Birr40-95; ☑6am-10pm) The combination of excellent food (mostly Ethiopian with a few European dishes), fine views and an on-site cooking school (p127) means you can take care of all of your culinary needs in one go here. It's lovely and quiet, not least because it's a fair hike out of town (downhill on the way here, uphill the way back...).

Unique Restaurant
EUROPEAN, ETHIOPIAN $

(☑0333-360125; breakfast Birr30-40, mains Birr40-70; ☑6am-10pm) This basic but cosy little restaurant ('bad house, good food' is what the charming and irrepressible owner Sisaynesh tells people who hesitate outside her door) serves the usual mix of national and *faranji* dishes. It's the kind of place you'll wonder about as you enter, then find yourself staying to take cooking classes (p127).

John Café
ETHIOPIAN $

(mains Birr30-45; ☑6am-9pm) A great little local breakfast spot in the town centre.

Zewditu Bar & Restaurant
EUROPEAN, ETHIOPIAN $

(mains Birr35-80; ☑6am-10pm) The partners behind this restaurant used to work in other restaurants before striking out on their own. Both the pastas and the *tibs* are tasty and the simple traditional dining room is popular with locals.

★Ben Abeba
EUROPEAN, ETHIOPIAN $$

(☑0922-345144, 0333-360215; www.benabeba.com; mains Birr45-110; ☑6am-10pm) Easily one of Ethiopia's coolest restaurants, this Ethio-Scottish–owned, Dali-esque jumble of walkways, platforms and fire pits is perched on the edge of the ridge for 360-degree views. The food is tasty – we especially like that it makes its own traditional bread and uses it to make an excellent goat burger. Stop by at 11am to see *injera* being made.

XO Lalibela
EUROPEAN $$

(☑0333-361010; mains Birr55-150; ☑6am-10pm) With a classier dining area than most (but with no views), XO Lalibela serves up a fresh modern menu that does have some Ethiopian dishes, but it put most of its attention into its roast chicken, burgers, fajitas and paninis. It's one of Lalibela's better dining options, especially for dinner when you can't see anything outside anyway.

NORTHERN ETHIOPIA LALIBELA

Seven Olives Hotel EUROPEAN, ETHIOPIAN $$
(☎ 0333-360020; www.sevenoliveshotel.com; mains Birr40-175; ⊙ 6am-10pm; P 🛜) We don't recommend staying here, but it's a popular lunch spot where travellers enjoy the leafy, bird-filled terrace. It does the usual mix of local and *faranji* food – the fried Nile perch or tilapia served with a spicy Awaze sauce caught our eye.

Torpido Tej House BAR
(⊙ 7am-midnight) Also known as Askalech, Torpido serves *tej* (honey wine) along with traditional *azmari* song and dance after 8pm. It gets a lot of tourists, but locals usually outnumber them. And unlike the more earthy *tej* houses, you are ensured good-quality wine – it comes in three strengths. Everyone is expected to dance – it's all in the shoulders...

🛍 Shopping

House of the Lalibela Artisans ARTS & CRAFTS
(⊙ 8.30am-12.30pm & 1.30-5.30pm Mon-Sat) Set up to help local artisans market their work, this modest collection has some textiles, basketry, figurines and paintings. You can sometimes see some of the weavers at work in the courtyard.

Fine Art Gallery ART
(⊙ 2-6pm) The one shop that stands out from Lalibela's throng of souvenir shacks. Inside are beautiful watercolour and sepia paintings created by local artist Tegegne Yirdaw. He's often around outside normal shop hours.

ℹ️ Information

Lalibela has its share of would-be guides and hangers-on, but the hassles are not what they were and you'll rarely be disturbed at the sites themselves.

There are banks, some with ATMs, all across the town centre.

Dashen Bank (⊙ 8.30am-11am & 1.30-3.30pm Mon-Fri, 8.30-11am Sat) Has an ATM.

Lalibela Health Center (☎ 0333-360416; ⊙ 24hr)

Tourism Information Centre (⊙ 8.30am-12.30pm & 1.30-5.30pm Mon-Fri) Unsigned behind the church ticket office and of limited use.

ℹ️ Getting There & Away

AIR

Ethiopian Airlines (☎ 0333-360046; ⊙ 8am-5pm Mon-Sat) flies between Lalibela and Addis Ababa (Birr3224, 45 minutes, twice daily), Aksum (Birr2190, 45 minutes), Bahir Dar (Birr1781, 30 minutes, weekly) and Gonder (Birr4298, two hours, daily).

BUS & MINIBUS

There are two morning buses (Birr75, four hours) and usually four minibuses (Birr95) to/from Woldia, the last leaving about 2pm. If you're travelling to/from Bahir Dar or Gonder, you'll need to change in Gashena.

A bus departs daily for Addis Ababa (Birr295, two days, 6am), overnighting in Dessie (Birr125, eight to nine hours).

CAR & MOTORCYCLE

The more direct route from the north from Mekele was undergoing major works at the time of writing, but when finished it should cut travel times considerably. Until then you're better off going via Woldia, from where it's a tortuous three-hour slog on a potholed gravel road.

ℹ️ Getting Around

The bus station is an inconvenient couple of kilometres out of town. Sometimes buses will continue into the centre and some hotels will pick you up if you have a reservation. Otherwise you can take a contract minibus (Birr120) or make the long, hot walk.

Minibuses (starting at Birr100) meet every flight at the airport, which is 23km south of town, and trips to the airport can be booked at all hotels. Increasingly, some hotels offer a free shuttle pick-up service, although some charge a fee – check when making your hotel reservation.

Dessie

POP 279,423 / ELEV 2470M

The tall and solid city centre of Dessie (ደሴ), surrounded by a vast city of rusted roofs, appears to offer the promise of something interesting, but it doesn't. The main reason people stop here is to break up the journey between Lalibela and Addis.

🛏 Sleeping & Eating

Qualiber Hotel HOTEL $
(☎ 0331-111548; d/tw Birr275/325; P 🛜) Exceptionally clean and well cared for, Qualiber defies the norm for older hotels. We can't quite call it cosy, but this whitewashed spot on a quiet secondary street above the city centre is one of the best in its price range.

Hotel Melbourne HOTEL $$
(☎ 0333-124949; www.melbourneht.com.et; r/ste Birr750/1400; P 🛜) Dessie's best midrange hotel has well-appointed rooms (ask for one

at the back to avoid the considerable street noise), a good restaurant and decent service.

Time Hotel HOTEL **$$**
(☏0338-119056; s/d or tw Birr700/900; 🛜) Bland modern rooms at the northern end of town may not sound all that appealing, but they're fine for a night and the restaurant's one of the better places to eat in town. Rooms at the front can be very noisy.

ⓘ Information

There are many banks along the main drag. The Dashen Bank in the unmissable Hajji Mohammed Yassin tower at the southern roundabout has an ATM.

ⓘ Getting There & Away

The bus station is located smack in the city centre. Normal buses leave for Addis Ababa (Birr156, nine hours, 10 daily), or you can treat your battered bottom to Selam (Birr245, eight hours, 5.30am) or Sky Bus (Birr245, eight hours, 6am), both of which have ticket offices near the bus station. There's one daily bus to Lalibela (Birr128, eight to nine hours, 6am) and Mekele (Birr135, eight hours, 7am) and frequent buses and minibuses to Woldia (Birr65, 2½ hours) and Kombolcha (Birr12, 30 minutes).

Kombolcha

POP 109,000 / ELEV 1850M

Aside from serving as base for nearby Bati's Monday Market, Kombolcha (ኮምቦልቻ) is really just a place to break up the journey between Addis and the north. If coming from nearby Dessie, the dramatic and curvaceous descent into Kombolcha outdoes anything the twin towns have to offer. Kombolcha is less of a transport hub than Dessie, but it's also less dirty and noisy.

🛏 Sleeping

Given its importance to travellers as an overnight way station, Kombolcha lacks good hotels, and at the time of writing there were better options in Dessie, 25km away. That said, a couple of large new hotels were nearing completion in Kombolcha, which will hopefully improve things a little.

Hikma Pension HOTEL **$**
(☏0335-510015; d/tw Birr300/450) This simple spot on the town's top traffic circle (where the road to Bati enters town) has good rooms on the top (2nd) floor, but the rest are cramped, musty, have peeling lino floors and

are not averse to the occasional questionable smell in the bathroom.

Sunny Side Hotel HOTEL **$$**
(☏0335-513016; s/d/tw incl breakfast Birr850/1000/1200; 🅿🛜) It takes some chutzpah to let your hotel decay over the years and still boldly raise your prices. This once-appealing hotel is overpriced, not always clean and the maintenance staff gave up long ago. Despite all of this, and only because of a distinct lack of choice elsewhere in town, it still attracts tour groups.

ⓘ Getting There & Away

Frequent minibuses serve Dessie (Birr12, 30 minutes). Two buses leave daily for Addis Ababa (Birr175, seven hours, 6am).

Bati

POP 19,263 / ELEV 1502M

The little town of Bati (ባቲ), 39km east of Kombolcha, is renowned for its massive Monday market, which attracts thousands from far and wide.

Attracting up to 10,000 Afar, Oromo and Amhara, and even some traders from Djibouti, the Monday Market (☉9am-3pm Mon) is epic. It's Ethiopia's largest after Addis Ababa's Merkato, but it far eclipses the capital's for interest and exotica. Within the market is an old gallows (dating from the emperor's day) and on the other side of town are the livestock and chat markets. Guides can be extremely pushy here.

Kombolcha, 39km away, is a better place to stay than Bati. If you want an early start though, Vasco Tourist Hotel (☏0335-530548; d Birr200) is the pick of a basic bunch.

Two buses and many minibuses serve Kombolcha daily (Birr28, one hour), with many more on market day. Five buses head to Logiya (Birr95, four hours).

Menz-Guassa Community Conservation Area

Truly off the beaten track, the 98-sq-km Menz-Guassa Community Conservation Area (የመንዝ-ጓሳ ማህበረሰብ የአካ ባቢ ጥበቃ) has one of the smallest but best-protected Afro-alpine habitats in Ethiopia. In fact, it's been a locally managed natural resource management area since the 17th century. Trekking and village visits can be arranged, but must be booked in advance.

For more information, check out www.guassaarea.org.

A quarter of Ethiopia's endemic mammal species are found here. The most notable wildlife on the plateau are the three dozen Ethiopian wolves (best seen 6am to 7am and 4pm to 7pm) and the many gelada monkeys. There are also some leopards, spotted hyenas, servals, klipspringers and honey badgers, but these are difficult to spot.

The locally common Auger buzzard, golden eagle and lammergeyer (among the many raptors) are birding highlights here. Some 114 bird species have been recorded in the area, with the spot-breasted plover and the endangered Ankober serin the real prize for birders.

Activities

A community-run **trekking program** (0116-851326; www.guassaarea.org; per person per 24hr Birr100, guide per group Birr200) initiated by the Frankfurt Zoological Society (www.fsz.org) has made tourism in the area much easier – reservations are required. Treks range from two-day/one-night walks up to four-day/three-night options.

Mules for riding or carrying gear are available for Birr150 per day; a muleteer (who can handle two mules) costs another Birr70 per day.

Note that as elsewhere in the north, July and August are the rainiest months, but here October is third rainiest. In the cold season temperatures can drop to -10°C.

Sleeping & Eating

Accommodation choices out here are few and far between, but the two campsites are wonderfully wild and the simple community lodge is welcoming.

Guassa Community Lodge LODGE $
(0116-851326; www.guassaarea.org; dm per person Birr300; P) This place has four simple but almost-cosy upper-floor bedrooms, plus a lounge with fireplace and a kitchen. It's still quite rustic, but small improvements (hot showers, solar electricity and meals) are planned and the view over the plain is superb. For now you must bring all your own food; it costs an additional Birr100 to use the kitchen. Reservations required.

Campsite CAMPGROUND $
(camping Birr100) At this basic camping area out in the wild there are two campsites with no facilities. As long as you're self-sufficient in everything from food and water to camping equipment, it can be one of Ethiopia's most rewarding wilderness experiences.

Getting There & Away

From Tarmaber, 45km east of Debre Berhan, a rocky, seldom-travelled road begins south and takes you over the highway tunnel. It passes huge valleys for 80km (at least two hours' driving) to the headquarters.

Buses from Addis Ababa (Birr145, seven hours, 6am) and Debre Berhan (Birr88, four hours) to Mehal Meda pass the lodge/headquarters.

Debre Markos

Roughly equidistant between Addis and Bahir Dar, Debre Markos is a convenient place to break up the long 11- to 12-hour journey, either for a meal or overnight.

Sleeping

For anyone who left Addis or Bahir Dar late (much later than 7am and you'll be pushing it), or is choosing to mosey rather than motor up north, Debre Markos is the most logical place to overnight, with a couple of good in-town options.

Tilik Hotel HOTEL $
(0587-712203; d/tw/f Birr300/350/425; P) This place paints a fairly unimpressive picture from the outside, but don't be deterred. All rooms have minifridges, satellite TVs, little balconies, better maintenance and cleaning and lower rates than other hotels in town.

Gozamen Hotel HOTEL $$
(0935-983930, 0581-780053; Nigus Teklehaimanot Sq; s/d incl breakfast Birr880/1100; P) Easily Debre Markos' best, this newish hotel has large, immaculate rooms that still look as new as when they opened in 2014. Windows in some of the rooms look out over the town and surrounding hills.

Getting There & Away

Debre Markos is a roughly six-hour (or 300km) drive to/from Addis, while Bahir Dar is five hours (about 255km) in the other direction. Buses and minibuses pass along the main road at regular intervals – catching one early in the morning greatly increases your chances of not driving at night.

Southern Ethiopia

Best Places to Eat

➜ Paradise Lodge – Abaya Restaurant (p157)

➜ Venezia (p145)

➜ Dolce Vita Bar & Restaurant (p145)

➜ Harena Coffee (p152)

➜ Lem Cafe (p153)

Best Places to Sleep

➜ Paradise Lodge (p157)

➜ Bale Mountain Lodge (p152)

➜ Buska Lodge (p172)

➜ Haile Resort (p144)

➜ Aregash Lodge (p152)

➜ Sabana Beach Resort (p139)

Why Go?

Southern Ethiopia is a canvas ripped in two. Its landscape is being torn apart by the Great Rift Valley, leaving a trail of lakes where you can go see crocodiles, hippos and birds – or just drink in the scenery from your hotel.

Move east and the Bale Mountains offer rewarding treks across a plateau amid Afro-alpine plants and rare wildlife. It's here you'll encounter the world's rarest canid, the Ethiopian wolf.

But it's the seemingly timeless tribes of the Lower Omo Valley, such as the lip-stretching Mursi and body-painting Karo, that leave the deepest impression on visitors. To meet them 20 years ago was nearly unheard of. To travel here today is very easy, but still a privilege. And if you really want to get away from it all, you can cross the Omo River and explore the Omo National Park, which feels like the world's end.

When to Go
Arba Minch

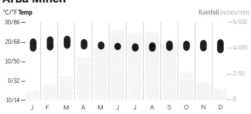

Jan–Apr Prime months for Jumping of the Bulls ceremonies.

Apr–May & Oct The rainy season around the Lower Omo Valley; travel to some villages is impossible.

Aug–Oct The wettest months in the Bale Mountains; trekking can be difficult.

Southern Ethiopia Highlights

1 **Bale Mountains National Park** (p147) Spotting the world's rarest canid, the Ethiopian wolf, while trekking this sublime national park.

2 **Key Afar** (p170) Bartering for an inscribed calabash at the lively tribal market.

3 **Konso Villages** (p163) Getting lost in labyrinthine traditional villages.

4 **Dodola** (p146) Imagining you're in a fairy-tale forest while horse trekking on the edge of the Bale Mountains.

5 **Dorze** (p161) Seeing how the Dorze people weave their houses.

6 **Lake Chew Bet** (p154) Marvelling at the strength of the men who work the black ooze at this spectacular lake.

7 **Mursi Villages** (p169) Experiencing African tribal life at its most raw and wild.

8 **Omo National Park** (p175) Exploring this remote but newly accessible park before the crowds discover it's not so hard to reach after all.

9 **Awasa** (p142) Dining on grilled fish and recharging the batteries in southern Ethiopia's most enjoyable city.

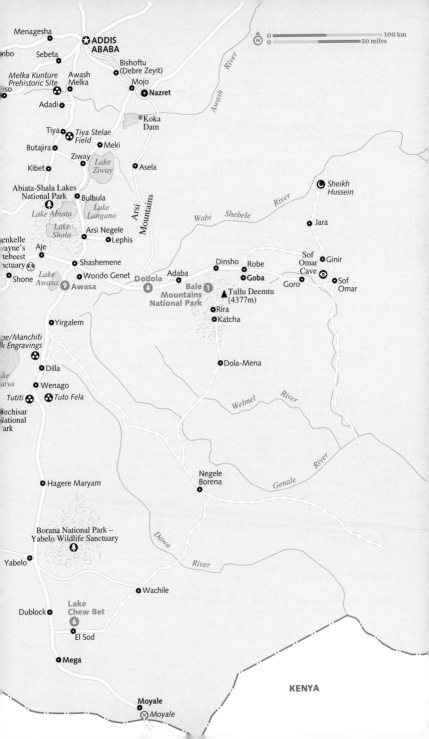

❶ Getting There & Away

Ethiopian Airlines (www.ethiopianairlines. com) connects Addis Ababa with both Arba Minch and Jinka.

Overland, there are three routes from Addis Ababa into southern Ethiopia. The shortest option to the Lower Omo Valley is the recently paved Hosaina road, which still feels remote with facilities fewer and further between and more basic than along the long-standing Rift Valley route. The latter heads southeast out of Addis and departs the Harar road 70km later at Mojo. Lastly, the paved Asela route takes you direct to the Bale Mountains.

There are also direct links from the western towns of Jimma (to Sodo) and Welkite (to Hosaina and Butajira) and from Kenya via Moyale and Omorate. Note that access from the southwest to the Lower Omo Valley has improved since the completion of two road bridges over the Omo River (in Omorate and Kangaten).

There's public transport available along all routes except through Omorate.

❶ Getting Around

All three routes into the south are almost completely paved (the pavement ends in Jinka) and in generally good condition, as are the Butajira–Ziway, Shashemene–Sodo and Sashemene–Goba roads. The road between Turmi and Omorate has also been recently asphalted, and the road between Konso and Yabelo is being upgraded. Most other roads are seriously rough and can be problematic during rain.

Daily buses and minibuses cover most major routes including most in the Lower Omo Valley. Jinka to Turmi, served only on market days, is the notable exception, though trucks may fill the gap. Most people visiting isolated areas hire 4WDs from tour operators in Addis Ababa, although they can also be rented in Arba Minch and Jinka.

Butajira

POP 34,000 / ELEV 2131M

There's not much to catch the eye in Butajira (በታጂራ), but there's a fair chance you'll stop here for lunch if you're driving without haste between Addis Ababa and Arba Minch.

Minibuses run frequently to/from Ziway (Birr20, one hour) and Addis Ababa (Birr50, two hours).

❂ Sights

Lake Hare Sheitan   LAKE
(ሀሬ ሽይጣን ሐይቅ; Butajira) Lake Hare Sheitan (Devil's Lake), about 9km south of Butajira, is an incredibly photogenic circular crater lake with the rim soaring perhaps 150m above the deep-green waters. The turn-off is not signed; ask for directions.

🛏 Sleeping & Eating

Butajira comes too early to be a convenient overnight stop for most people journeying south from Addis Ababa, but if you're one of the exceptions, there's a surprisingly good selection of hotels.

Kasetch Fekadu Asore Hotel   HOTEL $
(☑ 046 115 0443; Butajira; d Birr150-270; ⓟ ⓢ) This old-timer is an OK runner-up if other accommodation options in Butajira are full, although the cheaper rooms could do with a makeover. The real draw is the restaurant (mains Birr30 to Birr90), which serves a variety of local and international specialties.

Rediet Hotel   HOTEL $$
(☑ 046 115 0803; Butajira; d incl breakfast US$48-84; ⓟ ⓢ) This efficient and welcoming hotel is a popular midrange option right in the centre. It offers a broad choice of modern, well-appointed rooms and the added benefit of English-speaking staff. The attached restaurant (mains Birr80 to Birr170) is recommended.

Hosaina

POP 76,000 / ELEV 2400M

Travellers rarely stop in Hosaina (ሆሳዕና), a bustling, fairly prosperous town between Addis Ababa and Sodo, but if you happen to be there at lunch or dinnertime it's a great place for a restorative meal.

If you need to break up your journey, Hosaina has a couple of good lodging options in the centre.

Beside the busy bus station, **Lemma International Hotel** (☑ 046 555 4453; s/d/tw Birr350/400/500; ⓟ ⓢ) is a safe bet, with yawn-inspiring but clean rooms, billiards tables, a sauna (Birr160 per hour), a good restaurant (mains Birr35 to Birr70) and scenic views from front-facing rooms.

Tranquil, competent and professional, **Shambalala Hotel** (☑ 046 178 0142; www.shambalalahotelethiopia.com; d/tw incl breakfast Birr630/1260; ⓟ ⓢ) offers one of the most relaxing experiences in Hosaina, with a vast garden, an excellent restaurant (mains Birr80 to Birr130) and 36 spacious, tidy rooms with all mod cons.

BUTAJIRA SITES

Tiya Stelae Field The World Heritage–listed Tiya Stelae Field is an important stelae cluster at the south end of Tiya village, about 35km after the turn-off to Adadi. Tiya contains 41 stelae up to 5m in height (including the buried portions), engraved with enigmatic symbols including swords. They mark graves of individuals aged between 18 and 30 who died around 700 years ago and were buried in the foetal position, though little is known about the culture that carved them.

Melka Kunture (መልካ ቆንጡሬ; ☑ 011 157 3102; www.melkakunture.it; Awash Melka; Birr70; ⏲ 8.30am-12.30pm & 1.30-4.30pm) An hour from Addis, just over the Awash River, is the Melka Kunture prehistoric site, where many stone tools and fossils, dating back 1.8 million years, have been found. Examples are displayed in four *tukuls* (huts), and include tools used by the Homo erectus who once inhabited the area. There's also an open excavation site down a sometimes muddy path. It's modest but interesting. Find it a couple of kilometres west of Awash Melka town.

Adadi Maryam Ethiopia's southernmost rock-hewn church, Adadi Maryam is believed to date from the 12th or 13th century. It's fairly crude in comparison with its counterparts in Lalibela, but if you won't be travelling north, don't miss it. It sits on the far side of Adadi village, 12km west of the main Addis Ababa–Sodo road.

There are regular buses and minibuses to Addis Ababa (Birr70, two hours) and Sodo (Birr40, two hours).

Sodo

POP 86,000 / ELEV 1600M

There's not much to detain you in Sodo (ሶዶ), the hillside capital of Wolaita Zone, but it makes for a convenient overnight stop on your way to Arba Minch and southern Ethiopia.

If you're not in a rush, visit the low-key **Sodo Museum** (Birr100; ⏲ 8.30am-12.30pm & 1.30-5pm Mon-Fri). It has various objects on display in the big main hall – the metal and brick exterior covers a traditional-style king's palace – including 2m-long musical horns, elephant-skin shields and a typical family's home. It's just past the southern roundabout on the new road. Someone from the Tourism Bureau (the building by the painted trees) will open the door, turn on the lights and spray air freshener for you.

🛏 Sleeping & Eating

Sodo has a couple of well-equipped hotels, making it a good stop-off between Addis Ababa and Arba Minch.

Abebe Zeleke Hotel HOTEL $$
(☑ 046 180 1127; s/d/tw incl breakfast Birr650/750/850; P ☎) An excellent addition

to Sodo's sleeping scene, this professionally run outfit is kept in top nick and features a fine selection of cheerful rooms with all the creature comforts plus a working lift for easy access. If you're feeling peckish and don't fancy venturing out, there's an on-site bar and restaurant (mains Birr100 to Birr150).

Day Star Cafe & Restaurant ETHIOPIAN $
(☑ 091 184 4018; mains Birr30-90; ⏲ 8am-9pm) With few exceptions, the lunch stop of choice for tours passing through is this lively restaurant with an attractive courtyard on the Arba Minch road. The menu boasts fairly standard fare (burgers, sandwiches, soups, pasta and steaks) but it's the buzz and atmosphere that most come to ingest. The adjacent hotel section, which opened in 2016, features modern, clean rooms (Birr500).

ℹ Information

Dashen Bank (Sodo; ⏲ 8.30am-5pm Mon-Fri) On the Arba Minch road; has an ATM and changes currency.

ℹ Getting There & Away

There are frequent buses to Arba Minch (Birr50, 3½ hours) and Awasa (Birr60, 2½ hours), plus two morning departures to Addis Ababa (Birr120, six or seven hours).

RIFT VALLEY LAKES

The traditional route to southern Ethiopia heads southeast out of Addis and departs the Harar road 70km later at Mojo. The many shade houses you'll pass supply the European market with flowers and vegetables.

The route follows one of our planet's grandest geographical features: the massive Great Rift Valley. A 4000km scar that stretches from the Red Sea to Mozambique, it's a work in progress, and millions of years from now the rifting process will have split Africa in two. The most visible manifestation of the subterranean forces in this area is a string of five lakes along the road.

Lake Ziway

Surrounded by volcanic hills and covering a massive 425 sq km, Lake Ziway (ዝዋይ ሐይቅ) is the largest of the northern group of Rift Valley lakes. Typically the lake earned just a quick hit on a southern sojourn, for its prolific birdlife, but there are also now some great boat trips available, as well as excellent amenities, that warrant an extended stay.

🏃 Activities

Birdwatching

From the jetty near Haile Resort, you can spot a healthy population of white pelicans, hamerkops, sacred ibises, African fishing eagles and marabou storks – they all wait to feed on fishermen's cast-offs. Access to the jetty costs Birr200. For dedicated birdwatching tours you can hire guides at the Lake Ziway Tourism Ticket Office.

Boat Trips

Boat trips are booked at the Lake Ziway Tourism Ticket Office (☑ 092 734 0309; ziwayboatservice@gmail.com; Lake Ziway; ☺ 8am-5pm), near Haile Resort. The most popular outing is the half-day Short Boat Tour (one to four people Birr750, plus Birr200 for the mandatory guide), which visits the historic monastery on Galila island, takes a close look at the residents of Bird Island, finds the hippo pods and stops to climb up to a viewpoint.

Another half-day trip (Birr2750, plus Birr200 for the mandatory guide) goes out to the largest island, Tullu Gudo, to visit the Zay village and the legendary Maryam Tsion monastery. According to tradition it housed the Ark of the Covenant for 70 years when priests, fleeing the destruction of the city of Aksum at the hands of Queen Gudit in the 9th century, brought it here. A full-day Tullu Gudo trip (Birr3700) provides enough additional time to climb up to the ruins of the original monastery. A small community-run restaurant on Tullu Gudo serves fresh tilapia.

🛏 Sleeping & Eating

The town of Ziway is a pleasant, laid-back little place, with good, reasonably priced hotels scattered along the Addis Ababa–Shashemene road.

⭐ **Haile Resort**   RESORT $$
(☑ 046 441 2828; www.hailehotelsandresorts.com; Ziway; d/tw incl breakfast US$45/55; P 🎧 🏊) Popular with weekending families, this well-managed resort is widely praised for its attractive setting – in large manicured gardens that open onto a stretch of lakeshore – and numerous facilities, including a modern restaurant, a small pool and a kids' playground. Rooms are comfortable, if a bit blandly decorated. Be sure to book a room with a lake view.

Bethlehem Hotel   HOTEL $$
(☑ 046 441 4104; bethlehemhotelzewaye@yahoo.com; Ziway; d/tw Birr450/700, bungalow d/tw Birr700/900; P 🎧) A well-run little number with a quiet location, the Bethlehem offers neat rooms, well-furnished and spacious bungalows, sparkling bathrooms, a good restaurant and a small flower-filled garden.

⭐ **Castel Kuriftu Wine House & Restaurant**   INTERNATIONAL $$
(☑ 046 441 2705; www.kurifturesortspa.com; Ziway; mains Birr120-200; ☺ 8am-10pm; 🎧) Surprise! Easily one of the most characterful restaurants in Ethiopia, the Castel Kuriftu is a huge venture built from stone, wood and thatch. On top of its eye-catching architecture, it is noteworthy for the superb selection of wines from the Rift Valley and the delicious food, especially the grilled tilapia.

Ziway Tourist Hotel   ETHIOPIAN, EUROPEAN $$
(☑ 091 177 3063; Ziway; mains Birr70-150; ☺ 8am-9pm) Towards the southern end of town, the Ziway is the lunch stop of choice for those on their way to or back from the south. It serves juices and draught beer along with an extensive selection of national and Western dishes best enjoyed in the courtyard.

ℹ️ Information

There's a Dashen Bank with an ATM north of the telecommunications office.

ℹ️ Getting There & Away

Transport runs regularly to Shashemene (Birr35, 1½ hours), Butajira (Birr25, one hour) and Addis Ababa (Birr55, three hours). For Lake Langano you may have to pay the full Shashemene fare, even in a minibus. If driving, use the Hosaina route to Lake Ziway rather than the Rift Valley route – it adds about 20km, but saves an hour.

Shared *bajaj* (autorickshaws) run up and down the highway, but for the jetty you'll have to charter for Birr20.

Lake Langano

Lake Langano (ላንጋኖ ሐይቅ) resembles a giant puddle of milky English tea set against the blue curtain of the Arsi Mountains. The water may be brown and unappealing, but it's one of the few Ethiopian lakes to be declared bilharzia-free and thus safe for swimming. And, as with all the Rift Valley lakes, the birdwatching is good. Langano is also the obvious base from which to explore Abiata-Shala Lakes National Park.

🛏️ Sleeping & Eating

Accommodation options around Lake Langano are limited to large, expensive resort-style establishments. Our best advice: avoid the weekends, when every man and his boom box make the 180km trip from Addis Ababa. Weekend prices (Friday and Saturday) are also up to 20% higher than weekday rates.

Simbo Beach Resort RESORT $$
(📞011 558 0046; www.simbobeachlangano.com; camping per person US$10, tent hire US$20, d/ tw from US$55/65; 🅿️🛜) Don't be put off by the bland exterior of the bungalows. Inside they have been spruced up and feature good beds, tiled floors and neat bathrooms. What sets this family-oriented venture apart is its appealing sandy beach, with safe swimming. The on-site restaurant gets good reviews.

⭐ **Sabana Beach Resort** RESORT $$$
(📞046 119 1180; www.sabanalangano.com; incl breakfast d US$66-91, f US$95-130; 🅿️🛜) Occupying an elevated position with oh-my-god views over the lake, this sprawling property

sets the standard for Langano. The modern bathrooms, refined colour scheme, woven ceilings, landscaped gardens and pavilion-like restaurant make these 25 cottages an obvious choice for those who can afford it. There's direct access (via a steep footpath or a funicular) to a swimmable beach.

Amenities include a wellness centre, free kayaks and a kids' playground.

Afrika Vacation Inn RESORT $$$
(📞046 119 1586; www.africavacationclub.net; d from US$75; 🅿️🛜🏊) This smart resort has a spectacular location on Lake Langano's northeastern shore and is set in beautifully landscaped gardens. It comprises 29 well-sized *tukuls*, three beach villas and four standard rooms – all well equipped and comfy. The beach here is suitable for swimming and sunbathing, and the on-site restaurant serves toothsome Ethiopian and Western dishes. Activities include kayaking and horseback riding.

ℹ️ Getting There & Away

To get to/from Lake Langano, take any bus or minibus plying the Addis Ababa–Shashemene road, and ask to be dropped off/picked up at the turn-off to your hotel, from where you'll need to walk two to three kilometres, depending on the hotel you're staying at. For a bus, you'll likely have to pay full fare to either Shashemene or Ziway.

Abiata-Shala Lakes National Park

West of Lake Langano lie the twin lakes of Abiata and Shala, which form part of the national park. They're vastly different lakes: Shala has a 410-sq-km surface that sits within a collapsed volcanic caldera and depths exceed 260m in some areas, making it the deepest lake in Ethiopia, while Abiata's highly alkaline waters rest in a shallow pan no more than 14m in depth.

Abiata is shrinking dramatically as water is diverted to irrigation projects and a soda-ash factory. The increased salinity has killed off the fish and forced most birds to go elsewhere to feed. The land has suffered along with the lake, and this is now a national park in name and decree only. Illegal settlers have invaded nearly its entirety, turning the thick woodland into charcoal and replacing much of it with villages and farm fields. Despite the destruction, a short visit remains enjoyable.

Camping is permitted anywhere in the park, though there are no facilities and you must have the scout with you. Don't leave your camp unattended.

◉ Sights

A typical visit to Abiata-Shala Lakes National Park lasts about two hours and starts with a drive (or walk) through the fenced land around the headquarters. Living here are semitame ostrich, gazelle and warthogs (almost certainly the only nonwinged wildlife you'll encounter). Then you drive 5km to an **overlook** of the two lakes, followed 3.5km later by a spread of gurgling sulphurous **hot springs** on the northeast shore of Shala, where locals wash clothes and bathe. A futher 7km will take you to the shrunken shore of Abiata. Here flocks of flamingos in their thousands can be seen, especially from October to February; their numbers have increased dramatically since the fish die-off (because they feed on algae).

There's a second hot spring and a stunning, pint-sized crater lake at Shala's southwestern shore. Looking 80m down from the rim to **Lake Chitu** and spotting its 2000 or so semiresident flamingos is a sight worth the effort. The south shore is accessed via Aware or Aje, but admission can only be paid at the main park entrance and at Horakelo.

Abiata-Shala Lakes National Park

❶ Getting There & Away

The main park entrance, where the headquarters is, lies right along the highway. Buses doing the Addis Ababa–Shashemene run can drop you off, as can many minibuses.

A 4WD is essential for driving inside the park.

Shashemene

POP 125,000 / ELEV 1700M

Shashemene (ሻሸመኔ) is a crossroads town and most travellers prefer nearby Awasa. Shashemene does have one trick up its sleeve, however: it's the Rastafari capital of Africa and if this interests you, you're going to love it.

◉ Sights

Rastafarian Community   AREA
(Shashemene) Shashemene's Rastafarian community, known locally as Jamaica, straddles the main road just north of town. It's readily distinguished by its tri-coloured buildings, dreadlocked inhabitants and rounded vowels of Caribbean English. If you want to really meet and learn about the 'Jamaicans', the Zion Train Lodge and Banana Art Gallery are two good places to start.

Various local teenagers (none of them real Rastas) serve as unofficial, and often unwelcome, guides. They'll take you to see some churches and the defunct Black Lion Museum, which is just a family's home with paintings of the Emperor on the walls, but their real aim is to sell you *ganja* (marijuana), which is held sacrosanct in Rastafarianism but is illegal in Ethiopia. You've been warned.

Wondo Genet   SPRING
(Birr25; ⊘ hot springs pools 6am-10pm) The name of this hot springs resort 16km southeast of Shashemene translates as 'Green Heaven', which was more applicable before the hills were cleared of most of their forest. The cement hot springs pools have more the feel of a water treatment plant than a resort, but it's a great place to enjoy a slice of local life.

Banana Art Gallery   GALLERY
(☑ 091 110 4856; Jamaica; Birr20; ⊘ 7am-6pm) This place is the home-cum-workshop-cum-museum of Haile Selassie medals and memorabilia of Ras Hailu Tefari (Bandy), originally from St Vincent in the Caribbean. His extraordinary collages use only material

from banana plants, without additional colouring. They can be purchased for around Birr700 per item.

Tours

Wondo Genet Ecotourism Guide Association HIKING
(☏ 091 661 5476; Wondo Genet) This well-trained guide association offers a variety of one-hour to four-hour forest walks in the area. Guides are knowledgable about flora and fauna and charge from Birr100 to Birr450 per party. You may spot deer, hyenas, colobus monkeys, baboons and numerous species of birds. The office is by the Wondo Genet Resort Hotel.

Sleeping & Eating

There's no shortage of places to stay in Shashemene but most travellers stay in Awasa, which has more tourist-oriented options.

Rift Valley Tourist Hotel HOTEL $
(☏ 046 110 5710; riftvalleytouristhotel@gmail.com; Shashemene; d Birr193-385, tw Birr380-480; P🛜) This hotel has three levels of rooms in an old and a more recent building. They're old-fashioned and a bit overpriced, but you're paying a premium for the multi-level garden full of trees and art, which takes you a world away from the rest of the town. The restaurant (mains Birr35 to Birr60) has a larger than normal roster of local and international fare. The first-class rooms, with tiled floors, have a fresher feel and are more spacious than others.

Mana Sire Bareentuma PENSION $
(☏ 091 682 1736; Shashemene; d Birr160, with shared bathroom Birr120; P) Right by the bus station (go out the south exit and turn right), this two-storey building is a good bet for backpackers. It features sparse yet cleanish rooms, some with shared toilets that shouldn't make your squirm.

★ Zion Train Lodge GUESTHOUSE $$
(☏ 091 188 7680; www.ziontrainlodge.com; Jamaica; camping per person Birr120, d with shared bathroom Birr450, hut d/q Birr1000/2000; P) Behind the gates here hides a good surprise. Run by a French Rastafarian family, this haven of peace shelters three large Sidamo-style huts as well as three rooms with shared bathrooms in the main building, all comfortable and embellished with a few exotic bits and bobs. The restaurant (mains Birr30 to Birr85) has healthy offerings using some organic ingredients. It's signposted 1km from Jamaica. No wi-fi.

Framont Hotel HOTEL $$
(☏ 046 211 5010; framonthotel12@gmail.com; Shashemene; d incl breakfast US$40-60; P🛜) If you want no surprises and no hassles, you'll strike gold at the Framont. Service is everything it should be – no more, no less – while the unadventurous, motel-style rooms are exactly what you'd expect. It's along the old main road (noise!). The on-site restaurant gets appreciative reviews. No lift.

Wondo Genet Resort Hotel RESORT $$
(☏ 046 119 0705; Wondo Genet; incl breakfast s Birr550-680, d Birr650-775; P) Wow, the set-

SOUTHERN ETHIOPIA SHASHEMENE

SENKELLE SWAYNE'S HARTEBEEST SANCTUARY

Senkelle Swayne's Hartebeest Sanctuary (ሰንቀለ የስዋይን ቆርኪዎች መጠለያ; per person Birr100, vehicle Birr20, park guide Birr150) was established to protect Ethiopia's endemic Swayne's hartebeest, and though the population of around 700 is a far cry from the huge herds of the past, it's large enough to make a visit enjoyable. A typical visit, whether driving or walking, goes through the savannah, where Swayne's and oribi antelope are sure to be seen, and then up to Borena Hill, 6km from the headquarters, for views of Lake Awasa and likely wildlife encounters with warthogs, olive baboons, vervet monkeys and bushbuck.

Don't count on seeing any of the few remaining leopards, cheetahs, spotted hyenas or caracals. The globally threatened greater spotted eagle is one of 191 bird species documented, and swallow-tailed kites are often seen. There are lakes and hot springs deeper into the 57-sq-km park. Wherever you go, a park guide is mandatory. Camping is permitted, though there are no facilities or food.

The road towards the park lies 2km west of Aje and then the turn-off is after 10.3km at Debu, from where you follow the signs 4.6km to the headquarters.

ting! Ouch, the rooms. The Wondo Genet sits in a wonderfully exuberant park, but its run-down rooms make it a contender for most overpriced lodgings in Ethiopia. For visitors, it's nothing more than an agreeable place to relax over a cuppa in the shade.

Bolt House   CARIBBEAN $
(☑091 176 2830; Jamaica; mains Birr45-80; ☺9am-10pm; ☁) Yes, it's possible at the Bolt House. Run by a Jamaican couple, this colourful eatery about 100m off the main road (it's signposted) has a wonderful green feel. It's noted for its selection of stews, fish dishes, goat curry and fruit juices. There's (theoretically) wi-fi here, too.

❶ Getting There & Away

Shashemene is the principal transport hub of the south, and the huge bus station is located along the new bypass, northeast of the city centre. Buses run frequently to Sodo (Birr48, three hours), Addis Ababa (Birr95, four hours) via Ziway (Birr35, 1½ hours), and Goba (Birr80, three hours) via Dodola (Birr30, one hour). There's also one early-morning bus direct to

RAS TAFARI

When Ras Tafari was crowned Emperor Haile Selassie in 1930, he gained subjects far beyond his own kingdom. In Jamaica, Marcus Garvey's 'return to Africa' movement saw the emperor's coronation as fulfilment of the ancient biblical prophesy that 'Kings will come out of Africa'. Identifying themselves passionately with Ethiopia's monarch, as well as with Ethiopia's status as an independent nation, Garvey's followers created a new religion. In it, the emperor was accorded divinity (the Messiah of African Redemption) and the new faith given his precoronation name. What did the Emperor think of all this? Well, it was said that he was rather embarrassed. That is until 1963, when he overcame his bashfulness and granted the Rastafarians land in Shashemene.

Although nothing came of it in the end, much to the thanks of the entire population of Jamaica, Shashemene was briefly in the news when Bob Marley's wife announced that she was going to have his remains moved here.

Moyale (Birr165, 11 to 12 hours) via Dilla (Birr48, three hours), and two to Negele Borena (Birr130, 10 to 11 hours). Minibuses to Awasa (Birr10, 30 minutes) depart almost constantly.

Awasa

POP 300,000 / ELEV 1708M

Perfectly poised at Lake Awasa's edge, the capital of the Southern Nations, Nationalities and People's Region (SNNPR) is large, modern, well organised and a bit of a shock to the system for those who've been slogging it through the south for a long time. While Awasa (አዋሳ; officially Hawassa, but this new name hasn't completely caught on yet) has no major sights, the scenic Lake Awasa and its lush surrounds and good amenities offer a relaxing respite from the rigours of southern travel or the hectic pace of life of Addis – small wonder it's such a popular resort town.

◉ Sights

★**Lake Awasa**   LAKE
(ሀዋሳ ሐይቅ) With its mountainous backdrop, Lake Awasa is a lovely sight. You could easily spend a few pleasant hours strolling the lakeshore trail at the end of town, watching men fishing from papyrus rafts, seeing the various shorebirds feeding in the reeds and stopping for fried tilapia and a coffee ceremony at one of the many rustic restaurants. To gain a pelican's perspective of Awasa's shimmering waters, clamber into a boat at the base of the main drag. The boatmen will take you anywhere you request, but most people choose Tikur Wuha (Black Water) to see the hippos. Count on Birr500 for a party of up to five people for a one-hour excursion.

★**Fish Market**   MARKET
(ዓሣ ገበያ; Birr20; ☺7.30-10.30am) Lake Awasa's fishermen head out in their little wooden boats in the afternoon and return the next morning laden with tilapia and catfish. The men are amazingly deft at gutting, scaling, skinning and flicking the eyes out of their catches. Massive marabou storks do janitorial duty while vervet monkeys beg around the nearby bar. It's an incredibly photogenic place, but you'll need a guide to walk around it – contact Tesfaye from Paradise City Tours, who charges Birr50 per person.

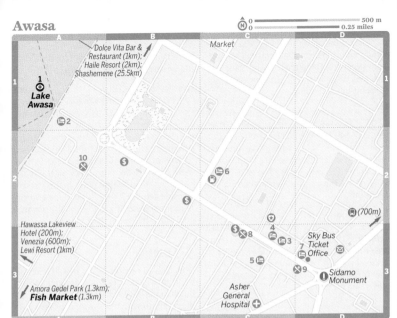

Awasa

Amora Gedel Park　　　　　　　PARK

(አሞራ ገደል መዝናኛ Guduma Park; Birr20; ☉8.30am-6pm) These lovely grounds west of the fish market provide a green haven for nature lovers and are also popular with newlyweds. You'll see plenty of vervet and colobus monkeys as well as a rich variety of forest and woodland birds amid the majestic ficus trees. The park opens onto the lake, and boat rides are available (from Birr700 for a party of five people).

Sidamo Monument　　　　　MONUMENT

Awasa's most prominent landmark, this cylindrical monument lies on a large roundabout east of the main avenue. It is said to represent the leaf of the false banana plant and is decorated with colourful mosaics.

👉 Tours

Paradise City Tours　　　　　　TOURS

(📞091 677 8650) Friendly guide Tesfaye runs tours of Awasa's fish market, various cultural tours in the Sidamo area and arrange birdwatching trips. There's a Facebook page.

🛏 Sleeping

A great place to break up the journey between Addis Ababa and more southerly destinations, Awasa boasts a good range

Awasa

of accommodation to suit most tastes and budgets. Awasa sprawls for kilometres and no matter where you stay you'll need wheels to get anywhere.

Circle of Life Hotel　　　　　　HOTEL $

(📞091 094 3559; d Birr250, with shared bathroom Birr150; 🅿🛜) Though the rooms are dark and a tad rank, this place deserves consideration for being so near the lake and having such a vivid garden. The shared bathrooms are a bit grungy. Angle for rooms 1 to 8, which are substantially better.

Kasech Pension
PENSION **$**

(☎ 046 221 4593; d Birr280; **P**) The rooms here are fairly standard Ethiopian budget fare – bland, unexciting, simply furnished but perfectly acceptable if you're counting your birr. The real draw is the central location, one block off the main drag.

★ Hawassa Lakeview Hotel
HOTEL **$$**

(☎ 046 220 8080; www.hawassalakeviewhotel.com; d US$40-70; **P** 🛜) The Lakeside has a professional air to it, with good, modern, business-standard rooms, all with balconies and great lake views. The wi-fi works most of the time and there's a good on-site restaurant.

Tadese Enjory Hotel
HOTEL **$$**

(☎ 046 220 0101; s/d/tw incl breakfast Birr400/550/800; **P** 🛜) Though the rooms aren't large, they are comfortable, well furnished and tidy. The affable staff help in any way they can and the on-site restaurant enjoys a fine reputation.

Lewi Hotel Piazza
HOTEL **$$**

(☎ 046 220 1654; www.lewihotelandresort.com; d/tw incl breakfast Birr715/865; **P** 🛜) In a busy location off the main drag in central Awasa, this large, multistorey place has been thoughtfully spruced up and shelters a mix of neat, well-equipped rooms with sparkling bathrooms as well as an excellent restaurant. A sweet deal.

Hotel Pinna 2
HOTEL **$$**

(☎ 046 221 0336; d/tw incl breakfast Birr570/680; **P** 🛜) One of a clutch of midrange hotels along the main avenue through town, the Pinna 2 has some of Awasa's cleanest rooms, although furnishings feel a bit tired. There's a good restaurant next door.

Hotel Pinna 1
HOTEL **$$**

(☎ 046 221 0335; d/tw Birr520/750; **P** 🛜) The word on the street is that this place is not what it was, but the rooms are well maintained and OK for the price. Rooms at the back are much quieter. There's no lift – worth knowing if your backpack weighs a tonne.

★ Haile Resort
HOTEL **$$$**

(☎ 046 220 3847; www.hailehotelsandresorts.com; incl breakfast d US$70-150; q US$180-230; **P** @ 🛜 ⛱) A project of famed distance runner Haile Gebrselassie, this lakeside place on the Addis-side of town is a tasteful, art-filled international-standard hotel. There are plenty of extras, like tennis courts, spa, gym, swimming pool, banking facilities and ATMs, plus top-notch dining. Paying extra for a lake view is well worth it. Boat trips can be arranged (from Birr500).

Lewi Resort
RESORT **$$$**

(☎ 046 221 4143; www.lewihotelandresort.com; d incl breakfast US$45-110; **P** 🛜 ⛱) This sprawling place serves four-star luxury in a completely Ethiopian way – think dated design and uninspiring architecture. There's a large variety of rooms, from the basic 'garden view' to the tacky bungalows with circular beds. The main selling point is the forested lakeside setting. Amenities include two restaurants (mains Birr50 to Birr120), a gym, a pool and a playground for kids.

✗ Eating

Gourmands, rejoice! Awasa is well endowed with stand-alone eateries as well as top-notch hotel restaurants. Fans of fresh fish may want to sample a simple fish stew at the fish market (morning only). For self-caterers, there's no shortage of well-stocked supermarkets as well as plenty of fruit stalls.

★ Luwa Bar & Restaurant
ETHIOPIAN **$**

(mains Birr40-80; ⊘ 8am-10pm) Far more welcoming than some of the other traditional restaurants around Awasa, Luwa attracts a predominantly local crowd who come for the freshly prepared Ethiopian food – their lamb *tibs* is a cut above average. Sit under the woven bamboo parasols or inside the traditional hut in the middle of the courtyard – it can't get more atmospheric than that. The sign is in Amharic only; find it next to the Wegagen Bank on the main drag.

What A Burger
BURGERS **$**

(mains Birr50-100; ⊘ 8am-11pm) One of the best spots to chill in Awasa, this lively eatery near the main jetty boasts an attractive setting, with a large, shady courtyard. Foodwise, the emphasis is on burgers (easily the best in town), pasta and Ethiopian dishes.

Time Café
ETHIOPIAN, EUROPEAN **$**

(mains Birr35-90; ⊘ 7am-9pm; 🛜) A stylish cafe popular with young Awasians. Coy couples come here to giggle under the patio umbrellas and share luscious fruit juices and plates of fries. It also has good burgers, salads, omelettes and pizzas as well as appetising cakes.

★ **Dolce Vita Bar & Restaurant**   ITALIAN $$
(☑ 046 220 5050; mains Birr90-170; ⊘ 8am-10pm;
☜) Many people, apparently decompressing
after a long time travelling in the south, rave
about this Italian kitchen, and we share
their unbridled enthusiasm. The food here
(and the shady terrace) is clearly above av-
erage for Ethiopia, with an assortment of
toothsome Italian dishes as well as delicious
Ethiopian specialities. There's also a bright,
modern dining area (in contrast to most
places in town).

Hi-Life Bar & Grill   EUROPEAN $$
(☑ 046 221 1118; mains Birr70-150; ⊘ 11am-
9.30pm; ☜) On the ground floor of Hawassa
Lakeview Hotel, this buzzy eatery is a great
choice for a quick bite in modern surrounds.
The generous chicken wraps and satisfying
pasta dishes are best enjoyed at the tables
out front, allowing premium lake views.
Keep your fluids up with a juice concoction
or a cold beer.

Pinna   ETHIOPIAN, EUROPEAN $$
(☑ 046 221 0336; mains Birr60-150; ⊘ 8am-9pm;
☜) If the cakes in the ground-floor pastry
shop don't sidetrack you, head upstairs to
a very *faranji* (foreigner)-friendly menu.
Specialities include ravioli with spinach,
home-made tagliatelle, veal steak with garlic
butter and grilled fish. Safe choice.

★ **Venezia**   ITALIAN $$$
(☑ 046 220 0955; mains Birr110-320; ⊘ 7am-
10pm; ☜) Run by an Italian-Ethiopian
couple, this upmarket trattoria-like venue
wouldn't be out of place in Roma, and gets
top marks for its flawlessly prepared Italian
specialities. You'll find it hard to choose between the wide range of salads, bruschetta,
pasta, grills and woodfired pizzas. Wash it
all down with a glass of Italian or South African wine, and leave with a smile.

❶ Information

Banks with ATMs can be found between the
Sidamo Monument and the lake.

Commercial Bank (Awasa; ⊘ 8.30-11am &
1.30-3.30pm Mon-Fri, 8.30-11am Sat) Changes
currency and has an ATM. On the main drag.
Dashen Bank (Awasa; ⊘ 8.30-11am & 1.30-
3.30pm Mon-Fri, 8.30-11am Sat) Also changes
currency and has an ATM.
Wegagen Bank (Awasa; ⊘ 8.30-11am & 1.30-
3.30pm Mon-Fri, 8.30-11am Sat) Has an ATM

at its downtown branch, and another at Lewi
Resort.
Asher General Hospital (☑ 046 220 6153;
Awasa; ⊘ 24hr) Awasa's best medical facility.
Includes a pharmacy.

❶ Getting There & Away

Around 10 buses daily run to Addis Ababa
(Birr85 to Birr101, four to five hours) and Sodo
(Birr56, three hours), plus two to Arba Minch
(Birr101, six hours). There are many buses
and minibuses to Dilla (Birr50, three hours)
and nearly constant minibus departures to
Shashemene (Birr10, 30 minutes). For Moyale,
go to Shashemene or Dilla and get a bus direct
from there.

The deluxe Sky Bus departs to Addis Ababa
from in front of the bus station at 6am. The **ticket office** (Awasa; Birr170; ⊘ 8am-6pm) is in the
Alliance Marketing Centre building downtown.
The bus station lies about 1km northeast of the
centre. A contract *bajaj* to the centre should cost
no more than Birr30.

Lephis

Up against the Duro Mountains north of
Shashemene is the lovely and relatively
pristine Lephis Forest, home to Menelik's
bushbuck, mountain nyala, leopard, spotted
hyena, warthog, black-and-white colobus
and olive baboon. The rich birdlife includes
the beautiful white-cheeked turaco and Abyssinian oriole. If you have one day to spare,
this is a great spot to get away from it all.

Trekking trips, either on horseback (must
be booked in advance) or foot, are offered
by the **Lephis Ecotourism Cooperative**
(☑ 092 882 8530; Lephis) based in Lephis village. The two- to three-hour waterfall trail
(Birr75) climbs to the lovely 45m-tall Lephis
Waterfall, passing several smaller falls as it
loops back on the other side of the Lephis
River. Treks on the Dungago Trail (per group
Birr400, horse per person per hour Birr150)
can last a full day and it's the trail of choice
for birdwatchers.

A **campsite** (2 people Birr250) 6km up the
Dungago Trail allows early morning and
late afternoon wildlife watching. Otherwise, you can visit Lephis as a day trip from
Shashemene.

The 'welcome *tukul*' is 17.5km east of Arsi
Negele (Birr10, 45 minutes) and buses run
about hourly.

BALE MOUNTAINS

Once one of the country's worst roads, the fresh pavement on the mountain-tracing highway east of Shashemene has opened up the Bale Mountains, though visitors have yet to descend in any great numbers. This unique region offers great trekking amid rare wildlife, a surreal underground river and a fertile countryside lorded over by rugged horsemen.

Dodola

POP 25,000 / ELEV 2475M

Resting between Shashemene and Bale Mountains National Park, the diminutive town of Dodola is a great base for hikers, nature lovers or indeed anyone who is receptive to the untamed beauty of a wilderness environment. Superb treks (on horseback or on foot) can be organised in the area.

🏃 Activities

Due to the high altitudes and steep gradients, most people trek on horseback (no riding experience is necessary), but this isn't mandatory and those with large lungs and legs of steel can trek on foot.

The trekking territory lies adjacent to Bale Mountains National Park and many people choose to trek at both. The national park offers significantly better wildlife watching, but most people find the scenery here superior and enjoy the cultural exchange with villagers along the way. The ecosystem and climate are essentially the same as Bale Mountains National Park.

Planning

Thanks to five cosy lodges built along the route, trekking here is perfect for those without camping gear; however, bringing your own sleeping bag is recommended. Typical camping food (pasta, lentils, biscuits, tomato paste etc) can be purchased in Dodola, while bread, porridge, sheep and goats can be obtained en route. Stoves, cooking utensils, beer and soft drinks are all found at the lodges. Optional cooks cost Birr250 per day.

Guides, Horses & Handlers

In Dodola, the **Dodola-Adama Tour Guide Association** (☏022 666 0700; www.facebook.com/BaleTrek; ⊙8.30am-12.30pm & 1.30-5.30pm) organises horses (Birr120 per day), horse handlers (one per two horses, Birr120 per day) and mandatory guides (Birr400 per day). Visitors must also pay Birr60 entry.

Treks

Treks typically start from Dodola and follow a dirt road to the tented camp at Changiti

Dodola Trekking

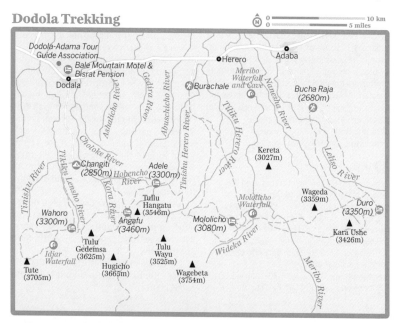

(2850m; 11km, 2½ hours), but if you start by 9am you can ride straight to the first lodge, Wahoro (18km, five to six hours), either following the thick, fairy-tale forest along the Tikiku Lensho River or taking a higher route with good views. From here you work your way eastward to the lodge Angafu (3460m; 10km, three to four hours); typically it's a short trip, but there's the option to trek (sans horse) the long way via the Wagabeta Ridge, which has lots of wildlife, including Ethiopian wolves. The ridge can also be visited the next day before the easy ride to Adele (3300m; 5km, 1½ to two hours). Then it's a long, lovely ride to Mololicho (3080m; 18km, five to six hours) and finally the last lodge at Duro (3350m; 20km, six to seven hours), which most agree has the best vistas. From here it's a 20km (five to six hours) descent to the town of Adaba, 22km east of Dodola.

To complete the full circuit, stopping one night at each lodge, takes seven days, but many people skip Changiti and Adele and do it in five. Shorter rides are also possible or you can extend the journey into the Sanetti Plateau in Bale Mountains National Park; your Dodola guides will hand you over to a new guide and horse at the border. In the rainy season, when rivers flow fast and high, Duro may be blocked and you'll need to descend from Mololicho to Herero (20km, four to five hours).

🛏 Sleeping

There are five simple but self-contained and comfortable lodges built along the route, making it perfect for those without tents and camping gear to explore the Bale Mountains' western range. Hot showers cost Birr10. Changiti is a more basic permanent tented camp.

In Dodola itself you'll find a few eateries. If you're trekking, you'll need to bring your own supplies.

Bale Mountain Motel   HOTEL $
(☏ 022 666 0016; camping Birr100, d/tw Birr200/300; 🅿) Set in a quiet garden with many birds, this long-running place has simple yet clean rooms with good mattresses. Showers are cold. Meals cost Birr25 to Birr80.

Bisrat Pension   PENSION $
(☏ 091 294 4942; d Birr300, with shared bathroom Birr200; 🅿) The rooms at this family-owned place are about as spotless as a budget hotel's can be. Meals can be prepared on request.

❶ Getting There & Away

Public transport is frequent along the main road and you won't have to wait long for transport to Adaba (Birr10, 20 minutes), Dinsho (Birr25, one hour) or Robe (Birr45, two hours).

To/from Addis Ababa (Birr120, five hours) you can ride the Robe or Goba buses, since no buses to Addis start here. They'll be full when they arrive so either go to Shashemene (Birr35, one hour) and catch a connection there or ask your guide to call Robe and have the conductor hold a seat for you.

Bale Mountains National Park

The Bale Mountains National Park (የባሌ ተራሮች ብሔራዊ ፓርክ; Birr90, vehicles Birr20) is known for its wildlife more than any other park in Ethiopia, but it's a very beautiful place, too. Approaching from Dodola, ridges to the east are punctuated with fortress-like escarpments, standing out from the gentler, rounded rock pinnacles to the north, and great wildlife watching begins as soon as the road cuts through the Gaysay Grassland in the valley between them, which is home to Ethiopia's densest concentration of large mammals.

Up in the hills are deep gorges, alpine lakes, rushing streams, several waterfalls, lava flows and views that go on almost forever. It would probably be as popular as the Simien Mountains if it wasn't located in such a remote corner of the country. For hikers, nature lovers, birders and wildlife watchers, the Bale Mountains National Park is a must.

Climate & Geography

Bale can be rewarding at any time. Although the nights are cold, November to March is dry and visibility is at its best, thus it's the ideal time to trek. August to October is the wettest time and wildflowers are most abundant, though the rain usually comes only in the afternoon and the fog can last for days. Negative temperatures are normal at night on the Sanetti Plateau, whose name means 'where strong winds blow' in Oromo.

The park stretches over 2400 sq km and ranges in altitude from 1500m to 4377m. It covers the largest area above 3000m in

Map labels:
- 0 — 10 km
- 0 — 5 miles
- Boditi (3543m)
- Gaysay Grassland
- Gaysay Valley
- Robe
- Web Waterfall
- Adelay Ridge
- Adelay Campsite
- Dinsho
- Nyala Guide Association; Park Headquarters & Museum; Dinsho Lodge
- Sof Omar Cave (100km)
- Gasuray (3325m)
- Dodola (55km)
- Web Valley
- Denka River
- Shaya River
- Kotera Plain
- Finch' Abera Waterfall
- Sodota Campsite
- Mararn Campsite
- Worgona Mineral Springs
- Shaya Valley
- Goba
- Weshema (4010m)
- Wosema River
- Worgona
- Worgona Campsite
- Tegona Valley
- Morobawa Campsite
- Keyrensa Campsite
- Webu River
- Wasema
- Tegona River
- Morobawa (3843m)
- Keyrensa Valley
- Batu (4203m)
- Garba Guracha Campsite
- Garba Guracha Lake
- Rafu Valley
- Harenna Escarpment
- Sanetti Plateau
- Sanetti Campsite
- Konten (4132m)
- Rafu Campsite
- Tullu Deemtu (4377m)
- Crane Lakes
- Dimtu Tika (4130m)
- Rira River
- Rira
- Harenna Escarpment
- Harenna Forest
- Rira Campsite
- Harenna Forest Hotel & Cultural Lodge
- Bale Mountain Lodge (5km); Dola-Mena (40km)

Africa. The Harenna Escarpment splits the park in two, running fracture-like from east to west. North of the escarpment lies the high-altitude plateau known as the Sanetti Plateau (4000m), which is dotted with several peaks, including Tullu Deemtu (4377m), the second-highest in Ethiopia. To the south, the land falls away from the plateau, and a thick heather belt gives way to the 4000-sq-km Harenna Forest.

Ecology

The park can be divided into three main ecological zones. The northernmost area, the Gaysay Grassland, near the park headquarters at Dinsho, consists of grassy, riverine plains and bushland. From 2500m to 3300m, woodland of mainly *Hagenia abyssinica* and *Juniperus procera* is found. The abundant wildflowers in the area include geranium, lobelia and alchemilla. Higher

up, montane grassland gives way to heather, which here rarely grows tall.

The second zone, the Sanetti Plateau, is home to the continent's largest swath of Afro-alpine plants, some of which have adapted to the extreme conditions by either remaining very small or becoming very large. The best known is the curious-looking giant lobelia *(Lobelia rhynchopetalum)*, which can soar to 9m in height. The silver *Helichrysum* ('everlasting' flowers) are the dominant wildflowers. Keep an eye out for the indigenous Abyssinian rose.

The third habitat, the moist, tropical Harenna Forest, is the second-largest remaining forest in Ethiopia, and its only cloud forest. It's little explored and scientists are still revealing new species. At the southern end of the park, there are some enormous podocarpus and fig trees, and wild coffee still grows in their shadows. At its highest reaches, around the Harenna

Escarpment, the giant heather stands, with twisted trunks draped in 'old man's beard' lichens and thick moss, and with cloud swirling around, the forest is straight out of a Grimm brothers fairy tale.

Wildlife

Seventy-eight mammal species reside here, but none excites like the Ethiopian wolf; sightings are almost guaranteed on the Sanetti Plateau. The rare mountain nyala is also likely to be seen. Other common sightings include Menelik's bushbucks, Bohor reedbucks, grey duikers, spotted hyenas, warthogs, the giant molerat, black-and-white colobus and the only recently defined bamboo-eating Bale monkey. The area around the park headquarters and the nearby Gaysay Grassland are two of the best places to see many of the larger mammals.

The Bale Mountains are a hot spot for endemic wildlife and there are more endemic mammals (including giant molerats and the bamboo-eating Bale monkey) in this spot than in any other area of equal size in the world. There are also many endemic amphibians.

In the Harenna Forest reside giant forest hogs, black-and-white colobus, leopards, lions and African hunting dogs. The last three are rarely seen.

The Bale Mountains' bird list is 280 species strong, but, again, it's the nine Ethiopian-Eritrean endemics (including the locally endemic Bale parisoma) that set Bale apart. On the plateau, sightings of the blue-winged goose, wattled ibis, thick-billed raven, black-headed siskin, spot-breasted plover and Rouget's rail are almost guaranteed. The birdlife in the juniper forests around

the park headquarters is outstanding, too, where Abyssinian catbirds and Abyssinian longclaw are two top ticks.

🏃 Activities

★ **Dola-Mena Road**   SCENIC DRIVE
There's no need to trek at Bale Mountains National Park. Awesome scenery and abundant wildlife can be seen along the highest all-weather road in Africa. It takes you right through the park, up over the Sanetti Plateau and down into the Harenna Forest. With your own vehicle, the summit of Tullu Deemtu (4377m) can also be reached by 4WD from the Sanetti Plateau.

It's best to leave early; pay park fees in Dinsho the day before. The long climb takes about 30 minutes from Goba and if you reach the plateau by 7am, you're almost guaranteed to see Ethiopian wolves while they are out searching for food. They're also usually visible from 10am to 4pm. Guides aren't needed here, unless you plan to get out and walk, but they're good at spotting wolves so you may want to bring one anyway.

Trekking

Trekking is the number-one activity in Bale Mountains National Park, with most of it fairly gentle and undemanding, and following well-trodden paths. But don't forget to factor in the altitude. Various routes, from one-day hikes to multiday treks, can be arranged – just ask your guide, who can put together a trek of any length to any place.

Planning

Entry fees must be paid and treks arranged at **park headquarters** (www.balemountains.

THE ETHIOPIAN WOLF

The Ethiopian wolf (*Canis simensis*) is the rarest canid (dog-family member) in the world. Found only in the Ethiopian highlands, it's teetering on the verge of extinction with only about 300 believed to be remaining. The Bale Mountains are home to the largest population, with approximately 150.

In Amharic, the wolf is known as a *key kebero* (red jackal), and indeed it does outwardly resemble one. Living in family groups of around 13 adults, the wolves are highly territorial and family oriented. When the dominant female in the pack gives birth to her annual litter of between two and six pups, all members chip in to rear the young. When it comes to hunting, however, the wolves forage alone, favouring giant molerats and other rodents.

The main threats to the wolves are rabies and canine distemper, caught from the domestic dog population. These days wolves and dogs are vaccinated. Lack of genetic diversity is also a problem.

Visit Ethiopian Wolf Conservation Programme (www.ethiopianwolf.org) to learn more.

org; entry Birr90, vehicles Birr20; ☺8.30am-5.30pm), which sits 1km from Dinsho village. All fees are good only for a single day (not the normal 24 hours) and include entry to the small **museum** (ᎧᎧ·ᎥᏆᎥᎧᎧᏦᏊ; Dinsho; ☺8.30am-5pm Mon-Fri) **FREE** nearby, which has information on the natural history of Bale. A trekking map (Birr100) and the dated *Bale Mountains: A Guidebook* are available at the headquarters. There are banks with ATMs in Robe and Goda.

A few stores in Dinsho and Robe sell the basics (instant noodles, pasta, rice, tomato paste, canned sardines, jam, biscuits etc), so if you're planning elaborate menus stock up in Awasa or Addis Ababa. Guides supply their own food (as do the horse handlers), but they'll often agree to be your cook if you feed them. Professional cooks can be hired for Birr400 per day. Water is available in various places on the mountain, but it should be treated.

Some guides hire out tents, sleeping bags and camping stoves, but there aren't many to go around so it's best to bring your own. They can also fix you up with rods for trout fishing.

Be sure to bring wet-weather gear, a warm top, trousers, a hat, gloves, sunscreen and sunglasses.

Guides, Horses & Handlers

Organising the 'team' (guide, horse and horse handler) is done through the **Nyala Guide Association** (Dinsho; ☺8.30am-6.30pm) at park headquarters and should be arranged the day before you plan to start. Guides are compulsory and cost Birr250 per day. They have a good reputation.

Porters aren't available, but horses (Birr120 per day) and horse handlers (Birr170 per day) can be hired. You must take a minimum of two horse handlers, even if you're trekking alone. If you are using horses, the trek needs to start at Dinsho (or you have to pay to get the horses to your trailhead of choice), though if you are schlepping your own bags you can begin anywhere.

Treks

➤ Quick Trip (Three Days)

Bale's most popular route covers diverse landscapes in a short time and is even better for wildlife watching than treks concentrating on higher altitudes.

Day one (4–6 hours) Walk southwest from Dinsho up the lovely Web Valley, usually following a dirt road, to Finch' Abera Waterfall and on to the Sodota campsite.

Day two (4–5 hours) Head to the Kotera Plain, a good wolf habitat, and loop back past Gasuray Peak (3325m) to Adelay campsite. The good visibility here makes this the best birdwatching spot in the north of the park.

Day three (6–8 hours) Descend to the flat Gaysay Grassland for excellent wildlife viewing and the small Web Waterfall before returning to Dinsho. The Gaysay Grassland can also be done individually as a day trek from Dinsho.

➤ Mountains & Lakes (Seven Days)

This trek, usually done in a week, focuses on the desolate highlands, and your challenge won't be spying wolves, it'll be keeping count of how many you've seen. There's the option of adding a night or two in the Harenna Forest after day five, either by walking or hitchhiking along the Dola-Mena road. You could also cut the trek short and hitch out of the park.

Day one (4–6 hours) Dinsho–Sodota via the Web Valley and Finch' Abera Waterfall.

Day two (5–6 hours) Continue southwest up the Web Valley to Keyrensa campsite, in an area home to many klipspringers and rock hyraxes.

Day three (4–5 hours) Head east past many viewpoints to the Rafu campsite, surrounded by rock pillars caused by a lava flow.

Day four (5–6 hours) Under the shadow of Tullu Deemtu (Bale's highest mountain; 4377m), head across the Sanetti Plateau to Garba Guracha campsite, with its picture-perfect view of its namesake lake.

Day five (6–7 hours) Trek over to the seasonal Crane Lakes, which attract thousands of birds from July to October, and up to the summit of scree-covered Tullu Deemtu. Return to Garba Guracha.

Day six (4–5 hours) Head north across Shaya Valley, bagging Mt Batu (4203m) if you wish, before arriving at Worgona campsite.

Day seven (5–6 hours) Follow the Denka River back to Dinsho.

🛏 Sleeping & Eating

Hikers usually stay at Dinsho Lodge, located above park headquarters, while travellers heading up to the Sanetti Plateau or Harenna Forest prefer to spend the night in Robe or Goba, 30km and 42km east of Dinsho respectively, for an early morning start. Campsites (Birr40 per tent) are spread throughout the park, and a few can be reached by road. For a splurge, head to Bale Mountain Lodge, south of the park.

Siko Mendo Hotel
HOTEL **$**

(☑ 022 665 3060; Robe; d/tw incl breakfast Birr265/400; ℗ 🛜) If fancy decor is not the question, but hygiene, location and solid amenities are high on your list, then this salmon three-storey edifice near the main roundabout in Robe could be worth it. It offers well-appointed rooms with crisp sheets, clean-smelling bathrooms and a satisfying breakfast. The on-site restaurant dishes up Ethiopian and Western specialties.

There's a bit of street noise but nothing to lose sleep over.

Tweens Pension
GUESTHOUSE **$**

(☑ 091 341 0272; Goba; d with shared bathroom Birr200; ℗) The most obvious choice for tight-fisted travellers, not so much because of its inherent merits, but because of the lack of competitors in this price bracket. Rooms are unflashy but clean, secure and well organised, and the shared facilities are thoroughly scrubbed. It's just off the main roundabout, with various cafes and eateries within staggering distance.

Abadma Hotel
HOTEL **$**

(☑ 092 020 2543; Robe; d/tw Birr200/300; ℗ 🛜) This simple pile on the Goba road 500m south of the bus station won't win any medals for design or comfort, but as far as Robe goes it's not bad for the price. It features a leafy compound and there's an attractive cafeteria on the premises.

Harenna Forest Hotel & Cultural Lodge
GUESTHOUSE **$**

(☑ 092 456 9160; Rira; s/d with shared bathroom Birr300/500; ℗) In the village of Rira, just north of the Harenna Forest, this family-run spot has a few rudimentary woven bamboo huts. It's grossly overpriced, the ablution block is basic and there's little English and no electricity, but the welcome is warm and it's the only budget option within Bale Mountains National Park. Someone will cook meals if you ask.

Dinsho Lodge
LODGE **$$**

(☑ 091 231 5073; Dinsho; camping per tent US$10, s/d/tw with shared bathroom incl breakfast US$45/55/70; ℗) Dinsho Lodge is located above park headquarters (park fee applicable) and surrounded by endemic species; a stay here is a no-brainer. It feels more like an old ski chalet than a proper lodge but

SOUTHERN ETHIOPIA BALE MOUNTAINS NATIONAL PARK

OFF THE BEATEN TRACK

SOF OMAR CAVE

Around 100km east of Robe, the fast-flowing Web River runs through a deep gorge and then cuts straight through a limestone hill. Though underground for only 1.5km, the aeons of erosion have carved 15km of passages known as Sof Omar Cave (የሶፍ ኦማር ዋሻ). Proposed for World Heritage listing, the vaulted chambers, flying buttresses, massive pillars and fluted archway sometimes resemble an Antonio Gaudí cathedral. The cave is venerated by area Muslims due to Sheikh Sof Omar Ahmed reputedly taking refuge here in the 11th century. There's a pilgrimage every November.

If you walk through you'll cross the river seven times, either wading or swimming. It takes about two hours. You can also ride a four-passenger boat. Some Sof Omar villagers (none of whom speak English) act as guides and, though prices aren't fixed, you can expect to pay Birr200 to walk through and Birr100 just to look around the entrance. They have torches, but for safe spelunking one is never enough; bring your own. From August to October the water is usually too high to get through, though the beautiful rock formations near its mouth can be seen any time. The guides at Bale Mountains National Park know about the cave's water levels, and if you want someone who speaks English, you can hire one to come with you.

From the village of Goro, 60km east of Robe, buses leave for Sof Omar (Birr28, two hours) at 6am on market days (Thursday, Friday and Saturday), and return about 4pm. Other days you'll have to rely on sporadic pick-up trucks. A few daily buses connect Goro to Robe (Birr35, two hours).

WORTH A TRIP

AREGASH LODGE

Aregash Lodge (☎ 046 225 1136; www.aregashlodge.com; Yirgalem; s/d/tr incl breakfast US$70/80/105; ℗ 🛜), about 50km south of Awasa, is the only thing of interest in Yirgalem (ይርጋለም), One of Ethiopia's most lauded lodges. The 16 Sidamo-inspired thatched huts are rustically plush with bamboo furniture and lots of space, while the grounds are home to 100-plus species of bird and black-and-white colobus. Hyenas come to feed during the evening coffee ceremony.

The excellent buffet meals, with vegies from the garden, cost Birr260. Walks to local villages are available. It's outrageous value.

has plenty of rustic charm, and the wonderfully bucolic setting is hard to beat. The restaurant (mains Birr55 to Birr90) is set in a lounge with a smoky fireplace. Hot water is available. Book early as there are only six rooms.

Goba Wabe Shebelle Hotel HOTEL $$
(☎ 022 661 0041; Goba; d/tw incl breakfast Birr455/600; ℗ 🛜) Long the top dog in these parts, this one-time classy place isn't bad, but it simply charges way too much for its unadorned rooms with soft mattresses and ageing bathrooms. Its best features are the quiet setting away from the road and the area's best restaurant (mains Birr50 to Birr90), though service can be lethargic.

★**Bale Mountain Lodge** LODGE $$$
(☎ 091 279 0802; www.balemountainlodge.com; Bale Mountains National Park; d with full board US$170-320; ⊙Sep-Jun; ℗ 🛜) 🌿 What a find! This exquisite lodge, a favourite with nature lovers, is set in the Harenna Forest at an altitude of 2400m. It features three well-proportioned stone cottages and five rustically chic 'forest cottages' in a lush property. They're all sensibly furnished and have views of Mt Gushuralle. Another plus is the cosy restaurant, which serves excellent Western dishes.

The ethos here is laid-back, ecological and activity-oriented. Prices include one guided activity (birdwatching, walks to a nearby waterfall or to Mt Gushuralle) per day. Game drives cost extra; knowledgable guides will

take you to the Sanetti Plateau for some serious wolf-spotting.

★**Harena Coffee** CAFETERIA $
(Goba; mains Birr40-110; ⊙7am-9pm; 🛜) There's no more pleasant spot to hang out and grab some food and drinks than this surprisingly snappy cafeteria on the main drag in Goba. Expect zesty salads, well-prepared burgers and sandwiches, toothsome pasta dishes and generous breakfasts.

❶ Getting There & Away

If coming from Addis Ababa, catch an early morning bus to Robe or Goba and leap off in Dinsho (Birr143, nine hours). The return buses will surely be full when passing Dinsho so either have your guide reserve you a seat the day before or head to Shashemene (Birr65, three hours) and continue from there.

Minibuses run roughly every 15 minutes between Robe and Goba (Birr5, 20 minutes) and less frequently from Robe to Dinsho (Birr12, 40 minutes).

Dola-Mena

POP 14,100

The intense heat of Dola-Mena (ዶሎ መና), along with the striking Somali herdsmen bringing camels to market on Thursday and Sunday, are novelties after the Bale Mountains. Apart from its atmospheric market there is little to visit, but getting here is half the fun – the 110km journey south from Goba is truly captivating.

Few visitors stay here, but if you're travelling without your own wheels and are planning to carry on to the wilds further south, you'll likely need to wait until the morning to find transportation. **Hotel Genet** (☎ 091 091 1966; d with shared bathroom Birr120; ℗) is Dola-Mena's only dependable hotel. Shamble Habti, the owner, speaks good English.

There are usually three buses to Goba (Birr55, four hours), the last out the gate about 1pm. If you're not going to backtrack, there are buses to Negele Borena (Birr95, six hours) on Thursday and Sunday (Dola-Mena's market days), arriving from Negele Borena the day before. Trucks travel most days: try to strike a deal for a front seat with the driver the day before. From Negele Borena, there are occasional buses to Shashemene (Birr125, 10 to 11 hours) via Awasa. You may also find a truck heading to Yabelo.

SOUTH TO KENYA

The northern half of this route takes you through verdant *enset* ('false-banana' trees), maize and coffee fields and past two minor archaeological sites. Minutes after Hayere Maryam, there's a rapid change from lush, fertile farms to the dusty, sparsely populated cattle country of the Borena people, where you can witness singing wells and salt-filled craters before wiping sweat from your brow as you enter the baking plains and desolate glory that continues into northern Kenya.

Dilla

POP 79,900 / ELEV 1570M

From a traveller's perspective the most important thing about Dilla (ዲላ), the capital of Gedeo Zone, is that within its sphere of influence lie three of southern Ethiopia's most important archaeological sites. And those who've been in the south for some time may relish the chance to enjoy plush beds, trendy cafes and some urban vibes.

🛏 Sleeping & Eating

Lalibela Pension   PENSION $
(☑ 046 331 2300; d Birr210, with shared bathroom Birr150; 🅿) While the unexceptional rooms don't set hearts aflutter, the quiet Lalibela is a decent option if the bottom line counts. It's 50m off the main drag, near Delight Hotel.

⭐ **Delight Hotel**   HOTEL $$
(☑ 046 331 2808; www.delighthotelethiopia.com; s/d/tw incl breakfast Birr500/700/900; 🅿 🛜) This supercentral multistorey abode is regarded as the best option in Dilla. It is well arranged and has tidy rooms filled with light. Freshen up in the big bathrooms after a dreamy slumber in the comfy beds. The attached restaurant (mains Birr90 to Birr150) serves excellent Ethiopian and international dishes. There's no lift, but this is our only gripe.

Afomiya Pension   PENSION $$
(☑ 091 366 5759; s/d/tw Birr500/600/700; 🅿 🛜) Afomiya Pension is a good, safe bet with a ramshackle charm. Though very simple, rooms are well looked after. Facilities include a small restaurant and well-tended gardens in which to curl up with a book.

⭐ **Lem Cafe**   CAFE $
(mains Birr30-50; ⊙ 8am-9pm) Hands-down the best bakery/cafe in Dilla, with such a tantalising array of cakes and pastries that we almost made ourselves a nuisance here. It also has salads, burgers and pizzas, as well as excellent breakfasts and luscious fruit juices. An added bonus is the streetside

---

WORTH A TRIP

THE STELAE FIELDS & ROCK ENGRAVINGS AROUND DILLA

The region around Dilla is the southern end of a string of ancient burial sites marked by mysterious stelae that stretch all the way north to Tiya. The two most interesting sites at this end of the chain lie near the highway and are easy to reach.

The nearly 1500 tapered stones at **Tutiti** (Dichika; Birr125; ⊙ 8am-5pm) are up to 7.5m tall, though few remain standing. The Tutiti field is on a hill in Dichika village, 3.4km west of the highway; the turn is signposted 5.4km south of the Tuto Fela turn-off. Due to their smaller size, the 267 (or so they say) densely packed stelae at **Tuto Fela** (Birr125; ⊙ 8am-5pm) are less impressive, but they are variously carved with facial features, ribs and breasts. It's accessed from a turn-off 2.5km south of Wenago. Head 2km east and then uphill at the Protestant church behind the big fence for another 1km.

Both sites have caretakers, but they're neither knowledgable nor able to speak English.

Splendid rock engravings can also be seen at a site known as **Shape/Manchiti**, about 7km west of Dilla, and feature a herd of cattle on a vertical granite slab located atop a steep river gully. Get there by motorbike taxi (Birr60 including waiting time).

Since the archaeological sites are tricky to find, your best bet is to organise a guide at the **Gedeo Tourist Office** (p154) in Dilla or, for the rock engravings, at the **Abbaya Cultural Tourism Office – Oromia District Office** (p154) in the village of Guangwa, about 7km south of Dilla. For the rock engravings, you'll also need to pay an entrance fee of Birr350 per car at this office.

open-air terrace, which allows for a dash of people-watching panache.

One Net Cafe & Restaurant
CAFE $

(📞 093 027 9044; mains Birr40-70; ⏰ 7.30am-9pm; 📶) Step into this trendy, shady and airy spot for an escape from the busy street. Get things going with well-presented salads, soups, pasta or pizzas. There's also a pastry corner – hmm, the tiramisu...

ℹ Information

Abbaya Cultural Tourism Office – Oromia District Office (📞 091 704 3893; Guangwa; ⏰ 8.30am-12.30pm & 1.30-5.30pm Mon-Fri) If you want to visit the Shape/Manchiti rock engravings, you'll first need to pay an entrance fee of Birr350 per car at this office located in the village of Guangwa, about 7km south of Dilla. It's also possible (and recommended) to hire a guide (Birr200) – ask for Habetamu, who can get by in English.

Gedeo Tourist Office (📞 046 331 4482; ⏰ 8.30am-12.30pm & 1.30-5pm Mon-Fri) Can arrange an English-speaking guide for the Tutiti and Tuto Fela archaeological sites (Birr200). It's in a ramshackle building off the main drag in Dilla, not far from Delight Hotel – look for the sign 'Gede'l Inxxe Zoonekaaada Tuurizimenna'.

ℹ Getting There & Away

A 6am bus departs for Yabelo (Birr100, six hours) and Moyale (Birr130 to Birr170, nine to 10 hours) and at least one goes to Addis Ababa (Birr170, 10 hours). You can also go south by minibus in stages.

Minibuses are the best option north for Shashemene (Birr60, three hours) and Awasa (Birr50, 2½ hours).

Yabelo

POP 20,700 / ELEV 1857M

The Borena town of Yabelo (ያቤሎ) is a base for visiting the Borana National Park – Yabelo Wildlife Sanctuary and also offers road access to the Omo Valley via Konso. No traveller comes for the town itself, though it's not an unpleasant place.

🛏 Sleeping

Almost everyone stays at the Yabelo/Moyale–Shashemene road junction, 5km east of town, where you'll find a variety of lodging options.

Wabe Pension
PENSION $

(📞 092 819 3726; d Birr500; 🅿) One of Yabelo's most commendable pensions, with a dozen fair-sized, simply furnished rooms opening onto a flowering courtyard, a stone's throw from the Moyale–Shashemene road junction.

Pension Ahuz
PENSION $

(📞 091 175 7060; d Birr400-500; 🅿) The cheeriest of several pensions near the Moyale–Shashemene road junction; rooms are on the small side but are serviceable and open onto a neat courtyard.

Green Pension
PENSION $

(📞 094 808 4459; d Birr250-300; 🅿) A good place to spend the night if you're counting your pennies, this family-run venture just north of the Moyale–Shashemene road junction features ordinary rooms clustered around a courtyard draped with greenery. There's also a little grocery shop.

WORTH A TRIP

LAKE CHEW BET

Lake Chew Bet (ጨው ቤት ሐይቅ; El Sod; Birr100, per vehicle Birr50, compulsory guide Birr200) is a bizarre crater lake about 800m across and 600m below the crater rim – it is so dark in colour that it looks like an oil slick amid the ruddy rocks. Valuable and muddy, black salt has been extracted from the lake for centuries, carried up on the backs of donkeys. It's a half-hour, knee-trembling walk down and a full-hour, thigh-burning slog back up. It's best to visit during the morning's cooler temperatures when the salt gatherers are actually working.

Don't expect to learn much about this fascinating endeavour from the guides; their English is very limited.

The lake sits beside the village of El Sod ('Chew Bet' in Amharic), 35km south of Dublock. Many buses and even more minibuses plying the Yabelo and Moyale road can drop you off at the turn-off for El Sod, from where you'll need to hitch the 14km to the village.

Yabelo Motel HOTEL **$$**
(☑046 446 0785; www.mazethiopia.com.et; d US$44-50, tw US$61-72; P) The most obvious choice for NGOs and travellers, for lack of competition. Its main selling points are the leafy garden and the attached restaurant serving burgers, pasta and Ethiopian staples (mains Birr30 to Birr55). Rooms are unimaginative (and overpriced) but kept clean.

ℹ Getting There & Around

All buses (including those starting elsewhere and passing through) use the bus park in town, while the more frequent minibuses leave from the Total station out at the junction. There are many minibuses throughout the day and one 6am bus to Moyale (Birr80, four hours). The bus to Shashemene (Birr120, seven hours) departs every other day at 6am. Legally, minibuses can't travel all the way to Shashemene or Awasa (though many do), so you may have to do it in stages, changing at Hagere Maryam and Dilla. Buses to Konso (Birr80, two hours) leave at about 7am and 1pm.

Locals pay Birr3 for a *bajaj* between the town and the Moyale–Shashemene road junction.

Borana National Park – Yabelo Wildlife Sanctuary

The 2496-sq-km Borana National Park – Yabelo Wildlife Sanctuary (ያቦሎ የዱር አራዊት ፓርክ; per person Birr90, vehicle per day Birr20, camping per tent Birr20) was originally created to protect Ethiopia's endemic Swayne's hartebeest. Along with most other wildlife, hartebeests have since been poached out of the preserve, with cows the only large mammal in abundance (Burchell's and Grevy's zebras are likely to be seen by visitors as well). Birdwatchers are pretty much the only visitors these days, here to add the locally endemic Ethiopian bush crow, Abyssinian hornbill and white-tailed swallow to their life lists.

The park is devoid of lodging options, but camping is allowed. Most people visit the park as a day trip from Yabelo, which has numerous hotels and guesthouses.

Visitors must hire a scout (Birr175 per day) from the Borana National Park – Yabelo Wildlife Sanctuary Headquarters (☑046 846 0212, after hrs 091 632 5008; Yabelo; ⊙8.30am-12.30pm & 1.30-5.30pm Mon-Fri) in the town of Yabelo. The main entrance is on the road to Dilla, about 10km north of Yabelo.

Getting here by public transport is not convenient – you'll need your own wheels to explore the park.

Moyale

POP 41,600 / ELEV 1090M

There's only one truly compelling reason to visit Moyale (ሞያሌ): Kenya. A porous border cuts the one-street town in two and the difference between the sides is immediately palpable. The Kenyan half, with dust-swept dirt streets, exudes a true wild-frontier atmosphere while the Ethiopian side is more of a proper town with better facilities.

🛏 Sleeping & Eating

There are a couple of pleasant places to stay on the Ethiopian side of Moyale.

There are plenty of fruit stalls and small groceries along the main drag.

Eda Pension Moyale GUESTHOUSE **$**
(☑046 444 0090; s/d Birr200/300; P) The Eda Pension is as no-frills as it gets but the rooms are well kept and the staff pleasing, making it an obvious choice for budget-minded travellers. Find it at the northern entrance to town, almost opposite the Total petrol station.

Koket Borena Hotel HOTEL **$$**
(☑091 348 7500; camping per tent Birr100, d Birr500-1000; P🛜) With some simple but cute bamboo *tukuls*, a mix of ordinary yet perfectly serviceable concrete rooms, friendly staff and an excellent attached restaurant (mains Birr40 to Birr80), this large place offers the best lodgings on either side of the border. Oh, and there's strong wi-fi.

ℹ Information

There are banks on both sides of the border. On the main drag, the Commercial Bank (on the Ethiopian side) has an ATM. If you need to change between shillings and birr, ask at your hotel.

The border is open from 6am to 6pm daily. Three-month Kenyan tourist visas are available at the border for most Western nationalities for US$50. You *cannot* get an Ethiopian visa at the border.

ℹ Getting There & Away

A bus leaves Ethiopian Moyale for Addis Ababa (Birr240) each morning at around 6am. The two-day journey is broken with a night's sleep

THE SINGING WELLS OF THE BORENA

The Borena are seminomadic pastoralists who occupy lands that stretch from northern Kenya to the dry, hot plains around Yabelo. Their lives revolve entirely around their cattle and during the dry season it's a constant struggle to keep their vast herds alive. To combat the problem, the Borena developed a unique system of deep wells. A long channel drops about 10m below the ground and funnels the cattle to troughs dug close to each well's mouth. When it's time to water the cattle, the men create a human chain down the well (which can be 30m deep), tossing buckets of water between one another from the bottom up to the top, where the troughs are gradually filled. The men often sing to keep rhythm as they pass up the buckets, hence the name. Several hundred or even thousand cattle come to drink at a time. For travellers, it's certainly a memorable and unique sight, though new pumps are slowly ending the tradition.

Delve into Borena territory near Dublock, about 70km south of Yabelo, where there's a big Friday market and some of the famous 'singing wells'. They're only genuinely worked during the dry season (December through April), but the men are glad to demonstrate at other times, for a hefty fee: tour companies usually pay Birr150 per person and another Birr150 for the guide to arrange it.

at Awasa (Birr170). Many buses go to Yabelo (Birr80, four hours).

For those heading south into Kenya, get ready for some teeth-rattling rides.

For those driving, petrol is cheaper and more reliable on the Ethiopian side.

ARBA MINCH & AROUND

Bordered by verdant mountains and home to two of Ethiopia's largest Rift Valley lakes, this region is more than a convenient overnight stop on the southern circuit. With Nechisar National Park and the highland Dorze villages on its doorstep, it deserves to be a destination on its own.

Arba Minch

POP 120,000 / ELEV 1285M

Arba Minch (አርባ ምንጭ) is actually two cities in one. Its dual settlements of Shecha and Sikela, separated by 3km of virtual no-man's land, have distinct personalities. Larger Sikela is more commercial and chaotic than her slightly more refined sibling up the hill. Shecha also offers fantastic views over the lakes.

⊙ Sights

Lake Chamo   LAKE

(ጫሞ ሐይቅ) Lake Chamo supports a very large population of crocodiles and, unlike neighbouring Lake Abaya, the waters are not rusty in colour.

Lake Abaya   LAKE

(አባያ ሐይቅ) Divided by the lyrical 'Bridge of God' from Lake Chamo, beautiful Abaya is Ethiopia's second-largest lake. Its peculiar reddish-brown waters are a result of elevated natural concentrations of suspended sediments, and it has a large population of crocodiles, which are said to be aggressive towards people and animals because the lake has few fish, their preferred food.

Arba Minch Crocodile Ranch   ZOO

(አርባምንጭ ዓዞ እርባታ; US$10; ☺8.30am-noon & 1.30-5.30pm) Walking between the masses of crocs in their concrete tanks at this government-run facility is more humdrum than it sounds, except during feeding, which usually happens Monday and Thursday between 3pm and 5pm. It's signposted almost 6km from Sikela. There's no public transport here.

The crocodiles are either hatched from eggs collected in the lakes or pulled out as youngsters and reared on the farm. Most of the hapless crocs are killed when they're about 2m length (five years old), when their skin is the best quality, and will end up as handbags or belts in European stores – Italy and Greece, mostly.

⚐ Tours

See Us Tour Guide Association   TOURS

(☏046 881 0117; https://seeusarbaminch.wordpress.com; Shecha; ☺7.30am-5.30pm) A guide for the Crocodile Market, Lake Abaya or Lake Chamo will cost you Birr300 a day.

Tuti Mesfin   ADVENTURE

(☎091 180 5971; tutiman_utd@yahoo.com; Arba Minch) This knowledgable guide can arrange fully outfitted multiday trips down the Omo River.

🛏 Sleeping

Arba Minch has a variety of hotels that cater for a range of budgets. Overall, Shecha's accommodation options outgun Sikela's. Shecha is significantly cooler in the hot season.

Romi Hotel   HOTEL $

(☎091 176 1890; Sikela-Shecha Rd; d/tw Birr400/600; P🖧) This well-managed hotel-cum-guesthouse has a great feel about it from the moment you enter its pretty plant-filled courtyard. All rooms have a bright, modern appearance and are very clean. Angle for one of the upstairs rooms (rooms 12 to 16), which have partial lake views. There's a modest on-site restaurant.

Forty Springs   HOTEL $

(☎046 881 0392; https://fortysprings.wordpress. com; Shecha; d/tw Birr400/500; P🖧) The Forty Springs gets good marks for its spruce, colourful rooms with tiled bathrooms. Upstairs rooms get more natural light. Ethiopian staples and sandwiches are available at the attached restaurant.

Zebib Pension   PENSION $

(☎046 881 4788; Shecha; d Birr400-500, tw Birr600-700; P🖧) Offering good value, the Zebib has bright and cheerful tiled rooms and a welcoming coffee shop that serves snacks, pastries and fruit juices. A safe choice.

Mora Heights   HOTEL $$

(☎046 881 2158; s/d/tw incl breakfast US$45/60/65; P🖧) The fantastic clifftop location is a big selling point here, although many rooms have obstructed views – ask for one with a lake view as they cost the same. There are only 24 units, which ensures intimacy. The hotel's enticing dining room plays host to a menu laden with inspired Ethiopian and Western dishes (mains Birr50 to Birr150). Prices include airport transfers.

Arba Minch Tourist Hotel   HOTEL $$

(☎046 881 2171; Sikela; d Birr550-600; P🖧) The Tourist Hotel would not be your ideal honeymoon hotel but the amenities are fine, the location very convenient (if busy) and the oasis-like garden pure bliss after a day's driving. Plus it boasts a well-patronised restaurant. The nearby church may enforce an early wake-up.

Swayne's Hotel   LODGE $$

(☎046 881 1895; Shecha; camping per tent US$20, d/tw incl breakfast US$50/60; P🖧) This place is a real heartbreaker. It boasts a wonderful clifftop location, with unbeatable lake views. Alas, most of the 77 bungalows, although they are prettily decorated with colourful artwork and equipped with hand-carved wooden furniture, need a freshen-up. There are plans to renovate them – stay tuned. Facilities include a well-regarded restaurant (mains Birr50 to Birr100) with breathtaking views.

★**Paradise Lodge**   LODGE $$$

(☎046 881 2914; www.paradiselodgeethiopia.com; Arba Minch; camping per tent US$20, s/d/tw incl breakfast US$74/85/99; P🖧🏊) This upmarket lodge staring straight at the national park's 'Bridge of God' features comfortable Konso-inspired huts (many of which have lake views) built from stone and wood; the most sought-after have a terrace right on the clifftop and cost the same. Amenities include two top-notch restaurants, a swimming pool, steam baths, a gift shop and ATMs. Prices include airport transfers.

It's perched between Sikela and Shecha, up a very rough 1.9km road.

🍴 Eating & Drinking

Fish has long been a staple in the diet here, though overfishing means it's a lot more expensive these days. Unlike with lodging, Sikela holds its own against Shecha in the dining department.

Zebib Café & Snack   CAFE $

(☎046 881 3676; Sikela; mains Birr20-40; ☉7am-8pm) Near the main roundabout in Sikela, this quick-eat establishment is safe for a sandwich and a mixed-fruit juice. It also has a tempting array of sweet-tooth nibbles.

Fruit Supermarket   SUPERMARKET $

(Sikela; ☉8am-6pm) Althought small, it's the best-stocked grocery in town and has a few exotic items like peanut butter and imitation Cocoa Puffs.

★**Paradise Lodge – Abaya Restaurant**   EUROPEAN $$

(☎046 881 2914; Arba Minch; mains Birr90-170; ☉8am-9.30pm; 🖧) Inside Paradise Lodge,

Arba Minch

N 0 ———————— 500 m
0 ———————— 0.25 miles

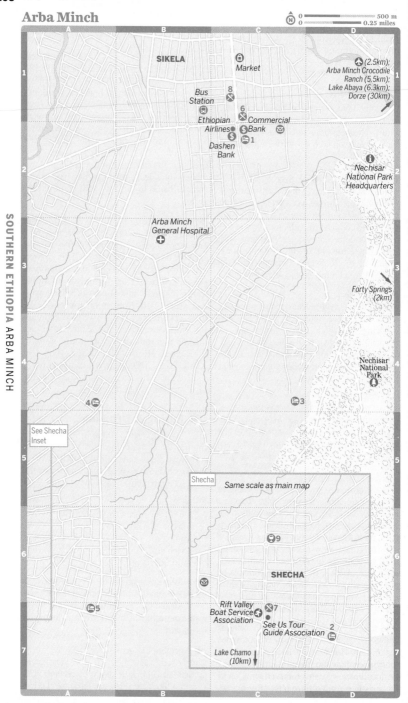

SIKELA

Market

Arba Minch Crocodile
✈ (2.5km);
Ranch (5.5km);
Lake Abaya (6.3km);
Dorze (30km)

Bus
Station
8 ⊗

6 ⊗
Ethiopian
Airlines ● Commercial
$ Bank ✉
$ 1
Dashen
Bank

ℹ Nechisar
National Park
Headquarters

Arba Minch
General Hospital ✚

Forty Springs
(2km)

Nechisar
National
Park

See Shecha
Inset

4 ⊟

3 ⊟

5 ⊟

Shecha — Same scale as main map

⊕ 9

SHECHA

✉

Rift Valley
Boat Service ⊕ ⊗ 7
Association
● See Us Tour
Guide Association 2 ⊟

Lake Chamo
(10km) ↓

Arba Minch

🛏 Sleeping
1 Arba Minch Tourist Hotel C2
2 Forty Springs D7
3 Paradise Lodge C4
4 Romi Hotel A4
5 Zebib Pension A7

🍴 Eating
Arba Minch Tourist Hotel
Restaurant .... (see 1)
6 Fruit Supermarket C1
Paradise Lodge – Abaya
Restaurant .... (see 3)
7 Soma Restaurant C7
8 Zebib Café & Snack C1

🍷 Drinking & Nightlife
9 Lemlem Bar & Restaurant C6

the lovely ridgetop dining room, together with menu choices like poached fish or beef stroganoff, make this the most atmospheric restaurant and best sundowner spot in Arba Minch. There's outdoor seating.

⭐ Arba Minch Tourist Hotel Restaurant
EUROPEAN, ETHIOPIAN $$
(☎ 046 881 2171; Sikela; mains Birr90-150; ☺ 8am-10pm) Though the wait staff can be a touch clueless at times, this leafy compound with resident dik-dik roaming around looking for hand-outs is a great place to dine, and the food is tasty. Western dishes are popular, but the large menu makes this a good place to try some new Ethiopian foods.

Soma Restaurant
SEAFOOD $$
(Shecha; mains Birr140-220; ☺ 8am-9pm) This unassuming restaurant (charging much higher *faranji* prices than it used to) has made quite a name for itself with its mouth-watering grilled fish dishes, most of which are big enough to share.

Lemlem Bar & Restaurant
BAR
(Shecha; ☺ 8am-9pm) For a good local beer and a solid dose of local gossip, there's no better place than this super-popular garden bar. The standard Ethiopian fare is useful for lining the stomach with all that beer flowing freely.

Market
MARKET
(Sikela; ☺ 8am-5pm) Has a range of products, including fruit and vegetables.

ℹ Information
You'll find a few banks with ATMs in Sikela. Another option is Paradise Lodge, which has three ATMs and also changes currency.
Commercial Bank (Sikela; ☺ 8am-5pm Mon-Sat) and **Dashen Bank** (Sikela; ☺ 8am-5pm Mon-Sat) both change currency and have an ATM.

ℹ Getting There & Away
Ethiopian Airlines (☎ 046 881 0649; www.ethiopianairlines.com; Sikela; ☺ 8am-noon & 2-5pm) flies between Addis Ababa and Arba Minch (US$145, one hour) three times a week.

At least two buses leave Sikela's **bus station** (Sikela) for Addis Ababa (Birr145, nine hours) and there's one daily to Jinka (Birr110, six hours) and Awasa (Birr100, six hours), all departing at 6am. Many minibuses serve Konso (Birr35, two hours).

Though most people contract with a tour agency in Addis Ababa, it's possible to begin Lower Omo Valley tours in Arba Minch. Some hotels, including Paradise Lodge, hire out 4WDs for US$160 to US$180 per day, including fuel and driver. One local guide with several solid recommendations is **Tuti Mesfin** (p157), who offers both 4WD and cheaper minibuses, which can get to most Omo destinations. With notice he can also arrange fully supported boat trips on the Omo River.

Nechisar National Park

This 514-sq-km national park (ነጭ ሳር ብሔራዊ ፓርክ; Birr90, vehicle Birr20, armed scout per day Birr200) spans the narrow yet mountainous 'Bridge of God' that separates Lakes Chamo and Abaya, and ranks among the most scenic national parks in East Africa. It contains diverse habitats ranging from wide-open savannah and acacia woodland to thick bush and sections of riparian forest. The bleached savannah grasses actually spawned the park's name, which means 'white grass' in Amharic. It's the scenery that makes Nechisar special, but there's still wildlife left, despite the government's refusal to tackle the rampant land encroachment and poaching.

◎ Sights

On the Nechisar Plain (where animals are most easily seen), the Burchell's zebra is the most conspicuous, sometimes gathered in herds of 100-plus. Visitors usually also see Swayne's hartebeest, greater kudu and

Nechisar National Park

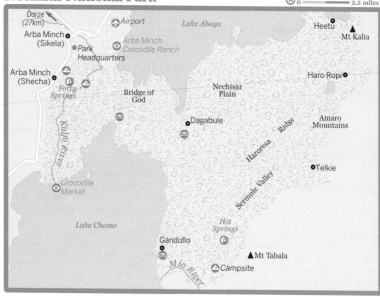

Grant's gazelle. A small population of lions still roams the park, too, but don't expect to meet them. Olive baboons, black-and-white colobus and Guenther's dik-dik can often be seen between the headquarters and Forty Springs. The birdlife is more diverse: 351 species have been counted and there isn't a birder alive who doesn't want to see the Nechisar nightjar, but you'll probably have to settle for Abyssinian ground hornbills and Kori bustards.

Crocodile Market   VIEWPOINT

(ግዞ ገበያ; Nechisar National Park; Birr90, vehicle Birr20; ⊘8am-5pm) Where the Kulfo River empties into Lake Chamo you'll find oodles of crocodiles sunning themselves. Both the size of the congregation and the size of the crocs (6m is common) make this one of Africa's best crocodile displays. There are also plenty of hippos, fish eagles and shore birds.

The **Rift Valley Boat Service Association** (☑046 881 4080; ⊘7am-4pm) holds a monopoly on the trips, so prices are high. The cost of the boat (which has a roof) for a group of up to six people is Birr800, and hiring a mandatory guide is between Birr250 and Birr300. You also have to transport the guide and boat driver to the launching point, 11km from Shecha.

While it's only a 20- to 30-minute boat ride to the crocs (there's actually not a single spot – their preferred perch changes with the seasons), allow two hours for the trip. It's best to visit mid-afternoon or early morning.

Nechisar Plain   NATIONAL PARK

(ነጭ ሣር ሜዳ; Nechisar National Park; Birr90, vehicle Birr20, armed scout per day Birr200; ⊘6.30am-5.30pm) The main wildlife-watching circuit crosses the Bridge of God to the park's namesake savanna, but the road is so atrocious that many tour companies prefer not to come here; nobody will attempt it when it's wet. It takes about three hours to reach so there's no chance of wildlife watching during the morning hours unless you camp.

Another option is to boat across and then walk, though because of past armed robberies the park turns permission for this on and off with some regularity. You'll need to bring an armed scout from the park headquarters. A boat from the association costs Birr1800 for up to six people and can cross in about 90 minutes.

Forty Springs   SPRING

(አርባምንጭ; Nechisar National Park; Birr90, vehicle Birr20; ⊘6.30am-5.30pm) Arba Minch, which is Amharic for 'Forty Springs', is named after the innumerable little springs that bubble up right at the base of the ridge below the town. All the development (the city pumps its water from here) and the fact that it's not especially scenic to begin with make it only worth visiting if you've already paid park fees. The 3km road there from the headquarters, however, *is* beautiful and is a good, easy walk.

Sleeping & Eating

The park has three official campsites: one on the road to Forty Springs, another nearby along the Kulfo River and one at the back of the park in the Sermule Valley. There are no facilities and the last of these lacks a water source in the dry season. Of course you can also hunker down in a comfy hotel in Arba Minch and visit the park as a day trip.

Information

Whether entering by land or water, you must pay park fees at the **Nechisar National Park Headquarters** (Nechisar National Park; Birr90, vehicle Birr20, armed scout per day Birr200; ◷6.30am-5.30pm). Armed scouts are mandatory for everywhere except the Crocodile Market and Forty Springs.

Getting There & Away

The park headquarters is 800m beyond Sikela. If you don't have your own wheels, it's easily reached by *bajaj* from Arba Minch (about Birr150).

Dorze

High up in the Guge Mountains, northwest of Arba Minch, is cold and cloudy Dorze territory. Dorze (ዶርዜ) people are famous for their towering homes and fine cotton weaving. Experiencing a cultural immersion in a Dorze village is one of the highlights of any trip to southern Ethiopia – not to mention the journey up here, which affords some spectacular views over Arba Minch and the Rift Valley lakes.

Sights & Activities

Near Dorze, the Guge Mountains are trekking territory. A 30m-tall waterfall is an hour's walk away, with others further afield. A longer option is the five-day trip up Mt Guge (4200m) and then down to Arba Minch. A guide for overnight trips is Birr500 per day. Pack horses are also available.

Hayzo   VILLAGE

(ሃይዞ; per person Birr100) Hayzo is one of the few Southern Nations' villages that has succeeded in turning the influx of tourists into a positive experience for all concerned. You can see the traditional way of life with few hassles from begging kids and without the need to pay for photos. Guides (Birr200) are mandatory and can be found at the **Besa Gamo Chencha Local Guide Association** (☑094 398 9013, 091 670 1460; Dorze; ◷8am-5pm) in Dorze, though most people hire a guide (same price) from Mekonen Lodge further up the hill.

The standard short tour usually kicks off with a look inside one of the famed Dorze huts, followed by visits to the weaving cooperative (women spin the thread and men work the looms) and pottery workshop. You'll probably also get to bake and eat *kocho*, a delicious, fermented, unleavened bread made from *enset*. It's eaten with honey or *data* (a delicious hot sauce). With more time you can see and do pretty much anything else, like visiting coffee plantations, fruit farms and local hooch stills. A dance demonstration can also be arranged.

A colourful market can be found at Hayzo on Monday and Thursday.

DORZE HUTS

Standing 12m high when first built, Dorze homes are essentially massive upturned baskets. Woven from bamboo and thatched with *enset* leaves, they don't use a central pillar for support and can be picked up and moved to a new location. On the inside a partitioned area is reserved for livestock (which provide heat), while the section that juts out at the entrance serves as a small reception room. If you imagine this as the trunk and the upper vents as eyes, the homes resemble massive elephant heads.

Though fragile-looking, the huts can last 60 to 80 years. Smoke from the central fire helps keep them dry (preventing rot) and largely termite free, though termites do slowly eat the homes from the base up. As they do, the lower portion is sliced off, resulting in a progressively shorter home.

Chencha Market MARKET

(ጨ.ንቻ ገበያ; ⊘8am-5pm Tue & Sat) The village of Chencha, 8km further up the road from Hayzo, has a vibrant market on Tuesday and Saturday.

🛏 Sleeping

★**Mekonen Lodge** GUESTHOUSE $

(☑091 670 9533, 091 627 0294; camping per person Birr200, tent hire Birr400, hut per person Birr200; ℗) Dorze's original lodge is set in an attractive family compound in Hayzo village, making it ideal for those looking for cultural immersion. The 15 huts are arranged around a central courtyard that doubles as the restaurant (dinner buffet Birr100). Huts share rudimentary external bathrooms. Mekonen offers 4WD hire (US$150 per day including fuel).

★**Tsehay Dorze Lodge** BUNGALOW $$

(☑091 682 5205, 091 155 8344; tsehab@yahoo.com; Dorze; camping per tent US$10, new hut s/d/q US$40/50/70, old hut with shared bathroom s/d US$25/30, incl breakfast; ℗) Perched on the edge of a cliff peacefully away from any village, this lodge boasts a sensational setting. It comprises four well-equipped new huts with views that are, without a hint of hyperbole, amazing. The old ones are more basic and, frustratingly, don't have views. Meals cost Birr130. The 1km-long 4WD-only access road is signposted 2km before Hayzo.

❶ Getting There & Away

A series of switchbacks affords some spectacular views over Lake Abaya. Although, be warned; the road is slippery when it rains.

Buses (Birr22, one hour) leave Arba Minch's Sikela bus station about hourly. They return when full, with the last departing at about 6pm, but aim to leave by 5pm to be sure.

Konso

POP 5200 / ELEV 1650M

The gateway town for the Lower Omo Valley, Konso (ኮንሶ; also known as Karat-Konso) boasts a lofty ridge-top setting, but it's the ancient, complex and fascinating culture of the Konso people and their architecturally inspiring villages around the town that make it a must-stop. The stone walls, terraced fields and ceremonial structures comprise such a unique lifestyle that the whole Konso Cultural Landscape was declared a Unesco World Heritage site.

⊙ Sights

Konso Museum MUSEUM

(ኮንሶ ሙዚየም; Birr20; ⊘8am-noon & 1-5pm) High above the town, this venture provides a very brief introduction to Konso culture, but it's the excellent collection of totemistic *waga* that makes it a must-see. These carved wooden sculptures are raised in honour of Konso warriors after their death and not only depict the 'hero' but also his family, and the enemies and dangerous animals he has killed. You must pay at the tourist office.

This collection is so important because most *waga* have been stolen for sale in Addis Ababa, and erection of new *waga* is dying out due to the influence of missionaries who oppose ancestor worship.

Komaya Heart of Konso Cultural Handicraft Market ARTS CENTRE

(የኮንሶ ልብ ኮማያ ባህላዊ እጅ ጥበብ ስራ ገበያ; ⊘8am-5pm) This beautiful hilltop spot is a developing project to provide an income for local craftspeople. There's a weaving workshop and other craft demonstrations, a cafe and, of course, a shop. The turn-off is across from the Dokatu Market, from where it's another 1km.

Dokatu Market MARKET

(ዶካቱ ገበያ; Dokatu; ⊘10am-4pm Mon & Thu) Perched on a ridge 2km west of Konso, this atmopheric market proffers grand views over the Rift Valley. For sale, you'll find women's traditional skirts, cassava, *cheka* (home-brewed sorghum beer) and *etan* (the incense used in coffee ceremonies).

Konso Cultural Centre ARTS CENTRE

(ኮንሶ ባህላዊ ማህበል; ⊘8.30am-12.30pm & 1.30-5.30pm Mon-Sat) Though more a local resource centre than tourist attraction, there's a pottery display (ask staff to unlock the rooms) and occasional special exhibitions. It's 500m before the roundabout.

🛏 Sleeping & Eating

For such a small town, Konso has a surprisingly dynamic accommodation scene, with a smattering of well-priced hotels. Note that Konso's electricity is often offline and hotels only run generators from 6pm to 10pm.

New Edget Hotel HOTEL $

(☑046 773 0034; www.konsoedgethotel.com; s/d/tw Birr330/360/400; 🛜) Don't be put off by the odd location, above the Commercial Bank; this well-priced abode shelters sunny rooms that are perfectly serviceable.

Green Hotel HOTEL $
(☑046 773 0151; d/tw from Birr250/400; **P**)
Rooms at this budget hotel on the way into town from Arba Minch are crude but acceptable for a night's kip if other hotels are full. Showers are cold.

★**Kanta Lodge** LODGE $$
(☑046 773 0403; camping per person US$10, d/tw incl breakfast US$45/65, d/tw cottage incl breakfast US$55/78; **P** 🛜) Kanta Lodge is a friendly, comfortable place with lovely valley views and two types of rooms. The tightly packed *tukuls* are simply designed but attractively decorated and the standard rooms are unadorned but functional. Kanta is also the top spot to dine in Konso, with a tempting menu (mains Birr80 to Birr120) and an outstanding stone terrace.

Edget Hotel ETHIOPIAN $
(mains Birr25-50; ⊙8am-9pm) On the main roundabout, this is a basic place where you can fuel up with *tibs* and other Ethiopian staples.

ℹ Information

Commercial Bank (⊙8am-5.30pm Mon-Fri, 8am-noon Sat) Changes currency and has an ATM. On the main roundabout.

Konso Tourist Information Centre (☑046 773 0395; www.konsotourism.gov.et; ⊙8.30am-5.30pm) Stop here before visiting Konso Museum or Konso villages – this is where you must pay entrance fees and pick up a guide (from Birr200). It can also arrange trekking trips (from Birr300 per day). It's on the road to Jinka.

ℹ Getting There & Away

Several daily minibuses run in each direction between Arba Minch (Birr40, two hours) and Jinka (Birr60, 3½ hours). There are also two buses to/from Yabelo (Birr60, three hours).

Konso Kantas

Walking through the narrow maze of paths inside the defensive walls of Konso *kantas* (villages) feels like entering another world. The twisting stone-walled walkways connect family and clan compounds, each with a clutch of thatched-roof homes, communal *mora* (where young men sleep at night to serve as watchmen and community servants for the village) and public squares where generation poles (one pole is raised every 18 years) and sometimes battle stones

(commemorating victories over and defeats by enemy tribes) stand tall. These squares traditionally also contain the famous Konso *wagas*. Any *wagas* found inside a family compound were carved only to earn birr from snap-happy tourists.

◉ Sights

The most visited village, simply because it's the easiest to reach, is Gamole, 6km west of Konso town. Just as interesting architecturally, and better overall because of the much lower number of visitors, is Machekie, 14km southwest of Konso. It still has three original sets of weathered *wagas* and also a rare newly erected set. Near Machekie, the village of Gesergio itself gets few visitors, but the oddly eroded valley alongside it does. Thanks to the towering pinnacles that someone decided resemble skyscrapers, it's now commonly known as 'New York'. One local legend explaining the landscape states that it's the result of a magic spell cast by village elders to reveal the location of a chief's stolen sacred drums.

Fasha, between Gesergio and the turn-off to Machekie, hosts the biggest market (ፋሻ ገበያ; Fasha; ⊙11am-6pm Sat) in Konso-land; Tuesday is a smaller affair. The road to Machekie and Gesergio passes the home of Chief Kalla Gezahegn (የካላ አለቃቃ(መሪ) ገዛኸኝ ቤት; Birr50), one of the nine Konso clan chiefs. A former civil engineer in Addis Ababa, he speaks fluent English and welcomes (paying) visitors.

Though seldom visited because it requires walking or riding a motorcycle 4km, Busso (5km southwest of Konso) is perhaps the loveliest village, as it surrounds a rocky point. It's also home to some original *wagas*. Dekatu, about 1km off the main road near the Dokatu Market, is the nearest traditional village to Konso town and also very interesting. It's best accessed by foot because the road is so bad. Usually a stop on the way to the Lower Omo Valley, Arfaide (አርፋይድ; per person Birr100), 20km out of town along the Jinka road, has a large collection of old *waga* that were recovered after being stolen.

Gersale is the one village of note along the Arba Minch road. It's just north of town and is visited for a new tree-planting program (plant a tree for US$20), where a small plaque with your name is placed in front of your tree, and for the half-hour traditional dance performances rather than its architecture. Inquire at the tourist office.

SOUTHERN ETHIOPIA KONSO KANTAS

Before visiting any of these villages (except Arfaide) you must pay fees (village fee per day Birr100, vehicle Birr50) and hire a guide (per group Birr200) at the Konso Tourist Information Centre. You'll likely be charged an additional Birr20 to enter individual compounds and Birr5 per picture of people.

The children's *faranji* frenzy (a result of previous visitors handing out sweets, pens, etc) gets irritating at times, but it's only truly aggressive at Gesergio. If you want to give something, ask your guide to take you to the local school.

🛏 Sleeping & Eating

The obvious base is Konso, which has a couple of hotels. Camping is allowed at the villages for Birr20 per person.

You won't find any restaurants in the Konso villages; bring some supplies. The nearest places to eat are in Konso.

ℹ Getting There & Away

There's no public transport. Your guide can go to Konso with you to hire a motorcycle if you're travelling without your own wheels.

THE LOWER OMO VALLEY

If there's anything in southern Ethiopia that can rival the majesty of the north's historical circuit, it's the people of the Lower Omo Valley. The villages are home to some of Africa's most fascinating ethnic groups and a trip here represents a unique chance for people to encounter a culture markedly different from their own. Whether it's wandering through traditional Daasanach villages, watching Hamer people performing a Jumping of the Bulls ceremony or seeing the Mursi's mind-blowing lip plates, your visit here will stick with you for a lifetime. This is quite a beautiful region, too. The landscape is diverse, ranging from dry, open savannah plains to forests in the high hills and along the Omo and Mago Rivers. The former meanders for nearly 800km, from southwest of Addis Ababa all the way to Lake Turkana on the Kenyan border.

When to Go

➡ Decent roads allow year-round visits, though even one rainy day (April, May and October are the wettest months) can render roads south of the main Konso–Jinka route temporarily impassable due to mud and lack of bridges.

➡ Most of the park is below 500m elevation, so temperatures can soar over 40°C, but some nights get cool enough to necessitate a light jacket.

➡ For a cultural insight into the region, the best time to visit is January to April when many celebrations take place, including marriages and initiation ceremonies.

➡ The driest period (January and February) increases the odds of animal sightings in Mago National Park.

➡ While Jinka and most of the northern half of the region are relatively cool, the southern towns around Turmi have burning hot days.

Planning

Most towns are completely ordinary, with modern buildings that look no different from elsewhere in Ethiopia because they were built and populated mostly by Ethiopians from elsewhere in the country. Tribal peoples generally only visit on market days and you should try to coincide with as many markets as you can. Likewise, the surrounding villages have few people on those market days, at least until late afternoon when they return home.

The towns of Jinka and Turmi have the bulk of tourist infrastructure. Standards of

PRESSURES ON THE LOWER OMO VALLEY

The Lower Omo Valley, or South Omo, as it's also known, is not a land frozen in time as many visitors with visions of *National Geographic* articles imagine it. While ancient traditions still form the backbone of daily life, this is perhaps not for much longer. Outside factors such as huge hydroelectric dams, sugarcane and palm-oil plantations, road construction, oil exploration and laws aiming to 'civilise' the people (like outlawing stick-fighting) are forcing rapid change. Tourism, though not without its problems, is about the last stabilising influence on tribal culture because tourists are generally interested in and respectful of it.

Lower Omo Valley & its Tribes

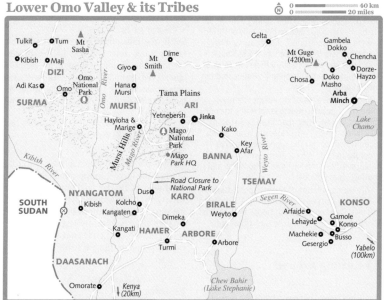

accommodation have improved over recent years, but don't expect the Ritz – even the 'luxury' places here are prone to electricity (and sometimes water) failures. Generators usually only run from 6pm to 10pm. Reservations are recommended for January to February and September to December.

Standalone restaurants are in short supply in the Lower Omo Valley, and the dining scene is pretty low-key. The best eateries are generally found at your accommodation. Jinka and Turmi have the widest selection, but still there's little to get the heart racing – expect the standard diet of *tibs, shiro* and pasta dishes.

Dangers & Annoyances

Because there are many tourists, '*faranji* frenzy' is as bad here as it is in northern Ethiopia. Just keep smiling and remember that the stress will pass.

Photography can also be stressful. Locals love having their photo taken – because they charge you for the privilege. Posing for photos is the best and sometimes only source of cash the villagers have. (Keep in mind that, generally speaking, women are more likely to spend the money on useful things like plastic buckets or flashlights; men mostly buy *areke,* home-made liquor.) They'll often aggressively approach you, demanding that you start snapping. In fact, most of the face and body painting and elaborate headgear were once worn only for battle or special occasions, but it's now done daily to prompt tourists to snap photos. The clothing (or lack of it in the case of the Mursi), however, is genuine. The price is always negotiable but Birr5 for a quick pose or Birr10 for a longer one is normal. The days of your model counting camera clicks is mostly over. During village-wide celebrations your guide will negotiate a flat fee for photography, but this is very rarely acceptable during normal village visits because when the money is paid to the chief, he will generally keep it all.

In an attempt to get you to stop and take their picture, many kids have taken to dancing, selling whistles and doing acrobatics alongside the road, which is dangerous enough. Some even do their shtick in the middle of the road to force you to slow down. In either case, please don't promote this behaviour (which also encourages them to skip school) by giving them anything.

For many ethnic groups, raiding is a part of life. Camps should never be left unattended.

ⓘ Getting There & Away

Most people visit with a tour agency from Addis Ababa, though you can also book fully outfitted tours in Arba Minch and Jinka. If you want to join with others to reduce costs, Addis Ababa is best. Most companies will try to do this for you. A minimum of six nights should be allocated for such a journey.

Whether you're travelling independently or with a tour operator, Konso is currently the only gateway, though a new road from Sodo to Jinka will change things. Two bridges have also been recently built across the Omo River – one in Omorate and one in Kangaten – which will facilitate travel between the Lower Owo Valley and southwestern Ethiopia.

With the completion of a new airport in Jinka in 2017, it's also possible to fly from Addis Ababa to Jinka. Some visitors also choose to fly to Arba Minch where they are met by their guide and 4WD.

ⓘ Getting Around

BUS

If you don't have your own wheels, it's feasible (but fairly impractical) to visit parts of the region independently, as long as you're not in a hurry or in need of comfort. Buses run daily from Konso and Arba Minch to Jinka, and on market days from Jinka to Turmi and Omorate. You'll almost surely pay much more than bus prices quoted (which are for locals).

CAR

On days when there's no bus, the local guide associations can arrange rides in private cars for a fee. Just be sure what kind of vehicle you're getting; 4WDs hired in the Lower Owo Valley are generally in poorer repair than anything you'd be offered in Addis Ababa (but are as expensive).

Note that the government has closed the direct Jinka–Omorate road south of Mago National Park because of the oil exploration taking place.

Jinka and Konso have petrol stations, but they're often dry. Do as all tour companies do; fill your tank and jerry cans in Arba Minch.

BOAT

It's now possible to avoid the growing masses of tourist 4WDs crowding into the Omo Valley and visit villages by boat instead. From September to February, fully outfitted three- to five-day trips head down the Omo River from near the Karo village of Dus. It's still something unusual and off the beaten track. Contact **Tuti Mesfin** (p157) in Arba Minch for more information.

The Omorate Local Guide Association offers simpler, overnight trips out of Omorate.

Jinka

POP 25,800 / ELEV 1500M

Set in the hills above Mago National Park, fast-growing Jinka (ጂንካ) is the biggest town in the region, although its facilities and services remain limited. Because it's the only practical base for visiting the Mursi villages, it's often bursting at the seams with tour groups.

◉ Sights & Activities

Market   MARKET

(⊙7am-4pm Sat) Jinka's famous Saturday market, the largest in the region, sits 300m northwest of the roundabout. It attracts a variety of ethnic groups including Ari, Banna, Mursi and sometimes Bashada. Though smaller and significantly less colourful the rest of the week, when it's mostly just the local Ari people trading, it's still worth a long wander.

South-Omo Museum & Research Centre   MUSEUM

(☑046 775 0332; Birr100; ⊙8am-noon & 2-5.30pm) Perched on a hill northeast of town (look for the green roof), this museum hosts an interesting exhibition on the region's cultures. There's also a collection of ethnographic DVDs to view.

Pioneers Vision   CULTURAL

(☑092 710 4109; Jinka; ⊙6.30am-4pm) Contact this association in Jinka to hire the mandatory guide for day visits to Mursi villages, multiday treks between Ari and Mursi villages as well as village stays. There are about 25 guides; some of them are competent and knowledgable while others are completely unqualified. If you're coming via a tour operator based in Addis Ababa it should hire the most reliable ones.

⏩ Sleeping & Eating

Jinka has a good selection of accommodation choices, making it an optimal launching pad for exploring the Mago National Park and the Mursi villages. Note that even in the rainy season the town can run out of water and power cuts are common.

Eyob Hotel   HOTEL $

(☑046 775 1508; camping per tent Birr100, d/tw Birr400/500; 🅿🛜) The pluses at this budget set-up are its leafy surrounds and its peaceful location in a side street south of the centre. Rooms are utterly without frills but it's a good base for unfussy travellers. Thanks to a canopy of trees the camping area gets plenty of shade and the on-site restaurant gets good reviews.

Goh Hotel HOTEL $

(☎046 775 0033; d/tw Birr350/460; ⓟ 🛜) This shoestringer's haunt has seen better decades but remains an acceptable fallback if you're not too fussy about things like, well, comfort and style. Staff here are friendly and there's hot water in the evening (or so they claim).

Orit Hotel HOTEL $$

(☎046 775 0045; incl breakfast s Birr250-530, d Birr300-840; ⓟ 🛜) The Orit has been smartened up and is now a favourite among tour operators. The cheaper rooms are quite spartan, but the ones in the newer two-storey wing are unsurprisingly more cheerful and overlook a mango-shaded garden. With its shady outdoor seating, the attached restaurant is the perfect salve after a day spent in the Mago National Park.

Jinka Resort HOTEL $$

(☎046 775 0143; camping per tent Birr300, d/tw incl breakfast Birr775/840; ⓟ 🛜) Jinka Resort's best asset is its leafy grounds – it's set in a lovely section of forest just east of the town centre. Rooms are no-frills yet cleanish; the ones at the back are larger. The camping area is beautiful, but there are no cooking facilities. The attached restaurant serves up simple Ethiopian dishes and spaghetti.

Eco-Omo Safari Lodge LODGE $$$

(☎095 920 0706; www.eco-omo.com; camping per person US$5, s/d incl breakfast US$69/110; ⓟ 🛜) Jinka's fanciest (though least friendly) address is 4km out of town on the road to Mago. Simple safari tents on thatched-roof platforms are in a large patch of green sloping down to the Neri River. They're equipped with fans and private facilities, but lack privacy – you can hear everything in the neighbouring tent. There are also four bungalows, including two family units.

Hot water is available mornings and evenings only, but unlike at hotels in town you can count on it being available. Top marks go to the pricey yet attractive traditional-style restaurant (mains Birr140 to Birr250) with an atmospheric wooden deck, soothing views and tasty Italian specialities. A pool is planned.

Redu Café & Restaurant ETHIOPIAN $

(mains Birr50-90; ⊘8am-10pm) This restaurant-cum-cafe serves pastas, burgers and excellent Ethiopian fare – among the 15 or so local dishes, we recommend the *kwanta fir fir* (strips of beef served with *injera*). The walls are adorned with posters of various South Omo tribespeople, and there's an atmospheric coffee corner. It's on the 1st floor of an office block on the main road.

Besha Gojo Restaurant ETHIOPIAN $

(☎046 775 0568; mains Birr70-100; ⊘7am-10pm) Right on the main drag, this popular place has won accolades for its eclectic menu, which includes Ethiopian classics – think *shiro* (chickpea purée) and *tibs* – as well as roasted lamb, salads and soups. The congenial outdoor dining area with covered bench tables boasts a kind of ramshackle charm.

Sipara Restaurant ETHIOPIAN $

(☎091 183 5431; mains Birr70-110; ⊘8am-9pm; 🛜) This attractive option slap bang in the centre of town is high on atmosphere, with

SOUTHERN ETHIOPIA JINKA

MAKE IT MEANINGFUL

Far too often, people treat their visits to Omo Valley villages like human safaris. The villagers line up, the tourists pick some out, cameras click, birr flies, and the tourists jump back into their Land Cruiser to rush off to the next stop. It doesn't have to be this way, but to avoid it you'll probably need to take the initiative because most guides do little more than negotiate the photography fees.

Village visits are so much better when there's genuine interaction. Commence your visit by *not* starting with the photos. Stroll through the village first. Visit some houses and ask questions. (Have your guide translate your questions to the villagers rather than answer himself.) The answers will often surprise you, and you'll not only learn interesting things about their lives, you might gain new perspectives on your own. Another great way to immerse yourself in local culture is to spend a night or two in a village (bring your own tent and supplies); thus you'll have the chance to experience village life at its best – early morning and late afternoon, when no other visitors are around and when all villagers – men, women and kids – are around and busy.

PEOPLES OF THE LOWER OMO VALLEY

The Lower Omo Valley is unique in that it's home to so many peoples in such a small area. And despite the close confines, many of the 16 ethnic groups are dramatically different from their neighbours. Historians believe that this region served for millennia as a kind of cultural crossroads, where Cushitic, Nilotic, Omotic and Semitic peoples met as they migrated from the north, west, south and east.

The Ari (አሪ)

By far South Omo's largest tribe, almost 290,000 Ari live around Jinka. Most are farmers (sorghum and coffee) but cattle-raising remains important and all villages have full-time blacksmiths and potters. They also produce large amounts of honey from beehives made with bark and dung, often for trade. The women wear skirts made from the *enset* ('false-banana' tree), but now only on special occasions.

The Banna (በና)

Numbering around 27,000, the Banna inhabit the higher ground around Key Afar. Most practise agriculture, though their diet is supplemented by hunting. Culturally, they're closely related to the Hamer and they dress quite similarly. The easiest way to tell them apart (though this isn't foolproof) is that the Banna wear beads that include the colour blue, while the Hamer don't. After killing a buffalo, they decorate themselves with clay for a special celebration and feast for the whole village.

The Daasanach (ዳሰነች)

Roughly 48,000 Daasanach people live along both sides of the Omo River between Omorate and Lake Turkana. They're closely related to the Arbore and the languages are mutually intelligible. Originally purely pastoralists, the villagers now all raise maize, sorghum and tobacco, and some have adopted fishing, though cows are still the mainstay of life. They are one of the poorest peoples of the valley.

Like their enemies, the Nyangatom, women make beads from scraps of plastic, but Daasanach women wear fewer necklaces.

The Hamer (ሃመር)

The Hamer, who number around 46,500, are subsistence agropastoralists. They cultivate sorghum, vegetables, millet, tobacco and cotton, as well as rear cattle and goats. Honey is also an important part of their diet.

The people are particularly known for their remarkable hairstyles. The women mix together ochre, water and a binding resin before rubbing it into their hair. They then twist strands again and again to create coppery-coloured tresses known as *goscha*. These are a sign of health and welfare.

Traditionally if they've recently killed an enemy or dangerous animal, men are permitted to don clay hair buns that sometimes support magnificent ostrich feathers. With the help of *borkotos* (special headrests) for sleeping, the buns last from three to six months, and can be 'redone' for up to one year. These days they're done for decoration.

The Hamer are also considered masters of body decoration, much of it improvised: nails, mobile phone cards and wristwatch bands are all incorporated into jewellery. The women wear iron coils around their arms, and bead necklaces. The *ensente* (iron torques) worn around the necks of married and engaged women indicate the wealth and prestige of their husband. Unmarried girls wear a metal plate in their hair that looks a bit like a platypus bill.

The iron bracelets and armlets are an indication of the wealth and social standing of the young girl's family. When she gets married, she must remove the jewellery; it's the first gift she makes to her new family.

Hamer territory is concentrated around Turmi and Dimeka.

The Karo (ካሮ)

With a population of about 1500 people, the Karo are one of the Omo Valley's smallest groups. Inhabiting the Omo's eastern bank northwest of Turmi, some of these traditional pastoralists turned to agriculture (growing sorghum and maize) after disease wiped out their cattle.

In appearance, language and tradition, they somewhat resemble the Hamer, to whom they're related. The Karo are considered masters of body painting, using white and sometimes coloured chalk to create bold patterns.

The Mursi (ሙርሲ)

The 7500 or so Mursi are mainly pastoralists who have been relocated out of Mago National Park to the drier hills west of it. Traditionally the Mursi would move during the wet and dry seasons and practise flood-retreat cultivation along the Omo River, though raising cattle is the most important part of their life.

The most famous Mursi traditions include the fierce stick-fighting between the men (now illegal and so never done for tourists), and the lip-plates worn by the women. Made of clay and up to 12cm in diameter, the plates are inserted into a slit separating their lower lip and jaw. Due to the obvious discomfort, women only wear the lip-plates occasionally, leaving their distended lips swaying below their jaw. The hole is cut around age 15 and stretched over many months. At this time the women also have their four lower front teeth pulled out, while men remove only the lower two. The origin of the practice is no longer known, but it probably began as a purely aesthetic practice done to mark entry into adulthood. Women's large ear holes are cut at about age five.

The Nyangatom (ያንጋቶም)

Inhabiting the land west of the Omo River all the way to South Sudan (but sometimes bringing their cows to the Omo's east bank to graze) are around 25,000 Nyangatom. Related to the Turkana in Kenya, the Nyangatom are agropastoralists, growing sorghum and maize as well as rearing cattle and goats. They also hunt, and those along the river smoke bees out of their hives for honey. Known as great warmongers, they used to be the enemies of just about everybody, but today only have significant cattle-raid conflicts with the Daasanach.

Nyangatom women are best known for their distinctly thick pile of necklaces. In the past the beads were made of ostrich egg (still used to decorate their goat-skin skirts) but these days they mould round beads from melted scraps of plastic such as broken jerry cans.

The Surmi (ሱርሚ)

Formerly nomadic pastoralists, the Surmi (sometimes wrongly called the Surma) now largely depend on the subsistence cultivation of sorghum and maize. The Surmi have a fearsome reputation as warriors, in part inspired by their continual search for grazing lands. Fights against the Bumi, their sworn enemies, still occur.

It's believed that the Surmi once dominated the area, but their territory has been reduced to the western parts of the Omo National Park and surrounding areas. The population of 45,000 is split into three subgroups: the Chai, Tirma and Bale. Like the related Mursi, the Surmi men stick-fight and the women don distending lip plates. However, stick-fighting is now technically illegal – and, as in the main Omo Valley area, you should not put pressure on a guide or driver to take you to one of the illegal flights. Also, wearing lip plates is dying out among the young generation.

The Surmi are also known for their white, almost ghost-like body painting. White chalk is mixed with water to create a kind of wash. The painting is traditionally much less ornamental than that found in other tribes and it is intended to intimidate enemies in battle. (Tourism is starting to change this, and children in Kibish and other popular tourist villages now routinely paint themselves up like prancing peacocks in order to gain camera attention.) Sometimes snake and wave-like patterns are painted across the torso and thighs.

The Tsemay (ፀማይ)

The 15,000 or so Tsemay are agropastoralists, growing sorghum and millet as well as raising cattle and gathering honey. They inhabit the land between Konso and Weyto.

an attractive compound and a verdant setting. The menu covers enough territory to please most palates, including salads, meat dishes, sandwiches and the best spaghetti this side of the Omo River.

ℹ Information

Commercial Bank (◎8am-5pm Mon-Fri, 8-11.30am Sat) Changes cash and has an ATM.
Dashen Bank (Jinka; ◎8am-5.30pm Mon-Fri, 8am-noon Sat) Changes cash and has an ATM.
Jinka Zonal Hospital (☏046 775 0046; ◎24hr)

ℹ Getting There & Away

A new airport was inaugurated in Jinka in 2017, and **Ethiopian Airlines** (p136) has resumed flights between Addis Ababa and Jinka.

The 150km road between Konso and Jinka is fully asphalted. There are three daily buses to Arba Minch (Birr95, six hours), several daily minibuses to Konso (Birr55, 3½ hours), and one bus to Omorate (Birr100, 3½ hours) via Turmi (Birr100, 2½ hours) on Tuesday and Saturday, returning the next day.

The guide association in Jinka rents out 4WDs with drivers and fuel for an outlandish US$190 a day (definitely try to bargain). For anything more than a day, it's better to deal directly with **Bereket Tadesse** (☏092 831 0295; meetthetribes@gmail.com), who is half-Mursi, and **Lalo Dessa** (☏091 336 3077; www.lalo-tours.com) – these two Jinka-based guides can organise total Omo packages starting in Addis Ababa or anywhere else for reasonable prices.

Mago National Park

In the dramatically beautiful 2162-sq-km Mago National Park (የማጎ ብሔራዊ ፓርክ; Birr200, per vehicle Birr40) wildlife is fairly abundant by Ethiopian standards, however, there's no chance of an East African-safari-style experience. Poaching remains a problem and the thick acacia woodland dominating the plains makes seeing what wildlife remains quite tough. You can expect to see dik-diks, baboons and guinea fowl, and, if you're lucky, Burchell's zebras, lesser kudus, defassa waterbucks, gerenuks and black-and-white colobus. Most travellers visit the park on their way to the Mursi villages (the park's major attractions), which lie along the Mago River – you can leave Jinka very early and spend several hours in the park before visiting the Mursi by arranging this with your guide the day before. Pay the entrance fee when leaving, as the ranger sta-

tion at the entrance to the park is usually closed in the morning.

Most travellers visit Mago National Park as a day trip from Jinka on the way to the Mursi villages, but if you want to overnight in the park there are a few basic campsites. Mursi village stays can also be organised through Pioneers Vision (p166) in Jinka.

Even though buses now pass through Mago National Park, they're of no use to visitors so you'll have to rent a 4WD from a tour operator in Addis Ababa or Jinka.

Key Afar

Key Afar (ቀይ አፋር) rests on a lush plateau along the Konso–Jinka road. A rather large modern town, what it lacks in atmosphere for six days out of the week it more than makes up for on Thursday with one of the best markets around. Thousands of Banna, Hamer and Tsemay descend on the town, along with every tourist in the vicinity!

All visitors must hire a guide (Birr200) from the **Anomba Local Tour Guide Association** (☏093 731 7414; ◎8am-5pm), across from the Nassa Hotel. They can take you to visit surrounding Banna villages (Birr150 per-person entrance fee for each), some of which are within easy walking distance. Jumping of the Bulls ceremonies and *evangadi* (Hamer night dances; Birr300 per person) take place in these villages. The guide fee doubles if they take you to see the bulls.

🛏 Sleeping

Key Afar has two spartan hotels, but most visitors prefer to stay in more comfortable lodgings in Jinka.

Sami Hotel   HOTEL $
(☏091 160 8751; d Birr300; ℗) If you're stuck in Key Afar, Sami Hotel is the most acceptable accommodation option in town (which is not saying a lot).

Nassa Hotel   HOTEL $
(☏046 271 0021; r Birr100-150; ℗) An ultra-basic sleeping option with scruffy rooms. Meals can be ordered.

ℹ Getting There & Away

The frequent buses and minibuses between Jinka (Birr30, 45 minutes) and Konso (Birr55, two hours) can drop you here, but there are rarely empty seats when you want to get on. Buses go to Turmi (Birr55, two hours) via Dimeka on Tuesday, Thursday and Saturday afternoons.

Turmi

POP 1000 / ELEV 925M

Despite being an important transit and tourist hub, Turmi (ኦፐርሚ) is just a speck of a town. It's surrounded by Hamer villages and on Monday the villagers, along with nearly every tourist in the valley, descend on the large market. Hamer women, with their shimmering coppery-coloured tresses, sell vegetables, spices, butter, milk and traditional items like incised calabashes, head stools, metal arm bracelets and fantastically smelly goatskins decorated with beads and cowrie shells – it doesn't get more atmospheric than this. The smaller Thursday market is almost tourist-free. Turmi is also a handy base from which to arrange day trips to Omorate.

No guide is required for the market, but you do need one to visit villages, several of which are within walking distance. Try the Evangadi Local Guide Association (☑ 091 682 5037; Turmi), which can also do multiday treks and sometimes arrange motorbike hire. They can also take you to see a Jumping of the Bulls ceremony (Birr600, plus Birr200 village entrance fee) or *evangadi* (dancing; Birr400 per person). While the bull jumping is never done especially for tourists, the *evangadi* usually is. It's still fun, though.

Sleeping

As Turmi lies at an important crossroads – not only for travellers, but also for locals – a number of hotels have sprouted up around this dusty settlement. Compared with similar establishments in other Ethiopian towns they feel overpriced, but they're in high demand and reservations are wise. Generators usually don't fire up until 6pm.

Kaske Mango Campsite CAMPGROUND $
(☑ 092 816 2836; camping per tent Birr150, d Birr300; P) Thanks to a canopy of lush mango trees, there's plenty of shade at this attractive campsite next to the Kaske River. The ablution block is cleaner than average, though showers (and toilets) come in buckets. It also has a few grubby rooms that are best avoided. It's 4km east of Turmi, a long hot walk to town for meals.

Otherwise, it's a short walk to Buska Lodge, which has an excellent attached restaurant.

Green Hotel GUESTHOUSE $$
(☑ 092 710 5422; d/tw Birr500/700; P) With quiet rooms set around a garden courtyard, the Green Hotel has the nicest budget setting. The rooms in the more recent wing cut the mustard but are unreasonably priced, especially given showers are cold; it's worth negotiating if it's quiet.

SOUTHERN ETHIOPIA TURMI

MARKET DAY IN THE OMO VALLEY

Since most people have long journeys to and from the towns, markets are best visited between 10.30am and 3pm. Notable markets include the following:

TOWN	DAY	TRIBE
Arbore	Mon	Arbore & Tsemay
Dimeka	Tue & Sat	Banna, Bashada, Hamer, Karo & Tsemay
Jinka	Tue & Sat	Ari, Banna, Bashada & Mursi
Giyo	Thu	Ari, Bacha, Dime, Mursi & Surma
Hana Mursi	Sun	Ari, Bacha, Dime, Mursi & Surma
Kako	Mon	Ari & Banna
Kangaten	Tue & Sat	Nyangatom & Karo
Key Afar	Thu	Banna, Hamer & Tsemay
Omorate	Tue & Sat	Daasanach
Turmi	Mon & Thu	Bashada & Hamer
Weyto	Sat	Tsemay

The markets at Dimeka (Saturday), Key Afar (Thursday) and Turmi (Monday) are among the biggest and best. Market days do change, so it's wise to inquire before making your schedule.

WORTH A TRIP

BULL JUMPING

Whipping, teasing, screaming, horn-blowing and leaping are part of the Jumping of the Bulls ceremony. It's a rite of passage into manhood for all Hamer and Banna boys and is truly a sight to behold. After 15 to 30 bulls have been lined up side by side, each naked boy taking part must cross the line of bulls, jumping on the beasts from back to back. If they fall, they're whipped and teased by women. If they succeed, they must turn around and complete the task three more times!

Before the bulls, young female relatives of the boys beg to be whipped with sticks; the deeper their scars, the more love they show for their boy. It's as disturbing as it is intriguing.

Ceremonies typically take part between January and early April, July through September and the first half of December. The whole event lasts more than a day, but the main activities happen between 2pm and 6pm. You must, of course, go with a guide, from either Turmi or Dimeka. Prices are up to the chief and so you may not know the cost until you get to the village, but it's not going to be less than Birr500 per person (plus the guide's fees).

★ **Buska Lodge**   LODGE $$$
(☑ 046 899 1178; www.buskalodge.com; camping own tent s/d US$7/12, tent with bed s/d US$23/33, bungalows with half-board s/d/tr US$84/110/118; P 🛜) By far the best place to stay in the Lower Omo Valley, Buska has well-built, stone-and-thatch green *tukuls* and rooms amid plenty of trees and flowers. It's ideal for camping as well; the campsite also has 'islands' with concrete pads, thatched roofs and beds, and there are excellent facilities. It's east of town, 1km off the Weyto road.

Another drawcard is the widely acclaimed restaurant (mains Birr60 to Birr120), which provides an enjoyable dining experience with well-executed food. Massage is available. The generator runs from 6.30am to 8am and from 6.30pm to 11pm.

Turmi Lodge   LODGE $$$
(☑ 011 663 1481; camping s/d US$15/20, incl breakfast s/d/tw US$72/83/85, budget r s/d US$45/55; P) The pink concrete pavilions are plain and overpriced but well maintained. If you're counting the birrs, the budget rooms in a separate block are smaller but better value. The restaurant (mains Birr70 to Birr110) is a long walk from the bungalows and features à la carte dishes and buffets (Birr230). It's 1km north of town.

Overall, it lacks charm and personality, but is a good plan B.

❶ Getting There & Away

The Tuesday and Saturday buses between Jinka (Birr90, three hours) and Omorate (Birr30, one hour) stop in Turmi. On other days it's easy to find a truck to both towns.

The direct route to Weyto sees little traffic other than tour-company 4WDs. Those driving themselves should inquire about the road before heading out because when it rains in the highlands, some of the dry riverbeds can fill up and become too high to cross.

Arbore

POP 1200

Arbore (ኣርቦሬ) rests 50km south of Weyto on the Turmi road and remains a traditional village with only a few scattered modern buildings. The Arbore people are a mixed bunch, with ancestry linking back to both the Omo Valley and Konso highlands. With their beads and aluminium jewellery, they almost resemble the Borena people. Locals outside the village know it as 'mosquito town'. To escape the notorious pests many Arbore sleep on platforms high in their houses rather than on the ground.

To visit an Arbore village, a guide must be hired through **Arbore Grevy's Zebra Local Guide Association** (☑ 092 601 1754). It charges some of the highest fees in the valley (Birr350 per vehicle and Birr200 for the guide), even though visits are usually less than an hour. Guides speak minimal English.

There's no public transport along this road, and not much traffic at all since it's actually faster to drive the long way between Konso and Turmi via Key Afer. Additionally, there are some dry riverbeds that can fill and block the route when it rains.

Dimeka

POP 2200

Dimeka (ዲመካ), 28km north of Turmi, is the biggest town in Hamer territory and its Saturday market (Tuesday is smaller) is said to be the most atmospheric and liveliest of the big ones. It has a great crafts section, with jewellery, woodcarvings, masks and pottery. Ask your guide to take you to the *tej bets* that are just behind the market – around noon they're full of Hamer men and women enjoying calabashes of honey wine or sorghum beer. The cattle market, which is held in the morning about 400m further north, is also not to be missed. There's little reason to stop here besides the markets.

Tours

Dimeka Negaya Local Guides Association CULTURAL

(8.30am-12.30pm & 1.30-4pm) Provides mandatory guides to visit the Dimeka market (Birr300 per group), as well as to take you to surrounding villages, including the Bashada village of Argude (with Hamer who make pottery, to oversimplify things), 5km away (also Birr300 per group). Staying in Banna villages and watching bull-jumping ceremonies can also be arranged here. It's based at the National Tourist Hotel.

If you have your own camping gear, the association can also organise trekking overnight up Mt Busca, the area's highest peak (Birr700 per day).

Sleeping & Eating

Few foreigners sleep here, and when you see the state of the pensions (each with grubby common toilets and lack of showers) you'll probably want to join the masses and head to Turmi, which have better facilities.

National Tourist Hotel ETHIOPIAN $

(mains Birr 20-40; 8am-8pm) This is usually where tourists have lunch after visiting the markets. It's a modest affair, with a very limited menu featuring a few Ethiopian dishes and, if you're lucky, pasta.

Getting There & Away

The market-day buses between Jinka (Birr50, three hours), Key Afar (Birr30, two hours) and Turmi (Birr20, 30 minutes) pass through. At other times, it's usually not tough to hitch a ride.

Kangaten & Kolcho

This pair of Omo River–side destinations makes an excellent day trip out of Turmi. Both Kangaten (ካንጋተን) and Kolcho (ቆልቾ) are largely hassle-free, though it's best to visit Nyangatom villages in the morning because many men are quite drunk by the afternoon. This way you also avoid the morning caravan of 4WDs occupying Kolcho.

The Nyangatom, whose women wear massive stacks of beaded necklaces, only inhabit lands west of the Omo River and many villages lie within a few kilometres of the regional town of Kangaten.

Only a few kilometres northeast of Kangaten (an hour by car), the clifftop village of Kolcho is the smallest of three Karo villages. And with its lofty views over a U-bend in the Omo River, it's one of the most beautifully set in all of Ethiopia. The village remains very traditional, and Hamer women routinely come daily to trade milk for sorghum or *cheka* (local beer).

In Kangaten you'll lighten your wallet of a Birr100 parking fee, a Birr200 per-person village fee, a Birr300 per-group guide fee and a Birr60 per-person round-trip boat fare.

In Kolcho guides charge Birr150 per group and Birr450 per vehicle. Dance demonstrations (at least Birr1500 per group) can be arranged.

Sleeping & Eating

Kolcho has no lodgings, but camping (Birr100) on the clifftop is magical. Kangaten has one basic hotel.

Yeshi Hotel HOTEL $

(092 514 8186; Kangaten; d with shared bathroom Birr250; P) The only acceptable accommodation option in Kangaten, the Yeshi has some basic yet relatively clean rooms arranged around a courtyard. Meals can be prepared on request.

Getting There & Away

Each of the villages is about 65km from Turmi and can be reached in less than two hours. A high-clearance vehicle is a must. You'll need to come with someone who knows the way since there are no signs and the roads to these villages pass through something of a no-man's land, so there's no chance to ask directions. Also note that heavy rains in the highlands can fill the normally dry Kizo River, temporarily blocking access.

A bus runs from Jinka to Kangaten (Birr100, six hours) on Monday and Saturday (leaving around lunchtime) and departs Kangaten on Sunday and Tuesday as early as 10am.

Truck traffic is so scarce that hitching to either village is simply not a realistic option.

Omorate

POP 2500

The region's hottest and dustiest town hugs the eastern bank of the Omo River, 72km southwest of Turmi. Omorate (አሞራተ) is visited almost exclusively as a morning trip out of Turmi. The town itself is rather unsightly; the real attractions are the Daasanach villages located just across the river.

Omorate's Tuesday and Saturday markets aren't very big, but differ from others in that there are many products, like bed sheets and beads, imported from Kenya.

To visit a Daasanach village, a guide must be hired through the Omorate Local Guide Association, which has a makeshift office at the dugout-canoe jetty. It charges some of the highest fees in the valley (village fee per person Birr150, and Birr400 for a guide). You'll have to pay for the return boat trip across the river as well. It can also arrange overnight boat trips on the river (Birr7600 per day for a party of four).

ℹ Information

Ethiopian Immigration Office (⊘7.30am-5pm) As Omorate is considered a border area,

SCAR TISSUE

For many tribes of the Lower Omo Valley, scarification serves as a distinction for brave warriors; the men were once not allowed to scarify themselves until they'd killed at least one foe. For women, the raised texture of the skin is considered highly desirable, and is said to hold sensual value for men.

Scarification is achieved using a stone, knife, hook or razor blade. Then ash is applied to the wound, creating an infection and promoting scar-tissue growth. As the wound heals, the scar creates the desired knobbly effect on the skin's surface.

travellers need to register their passport here upon arrival. The office is near the dugout-canoe jetty.

ℹ Getting There & Away

The road between Turmi and Omorate has been asphalted and is in good condition. Getting to Omorate by public transport is an extremely impractical option. There's only one bus that connects Omorate to Jinka (Birr100, 3½ hours) via Turmi (Birr30, one hour), heading south on Tuesday and Saturday and back north the following day.

The road north to Jinka through Mago National Park has been closed, and likely won't reopen any time soon.

Following the construction of a new bridge across the Omo River, it's now possible to continue your journey towards Omo National Park.

ℹ Getting Around

To cross the river you'll need to take a dugout canoe (per person Birr150) or a more reassuring motorboat (per person Birr250) from the makeshift jetty, about 500m east of the new bridge.

Weyto

POP 1500

Weyto (ወይጦ) is the first town you'll encounter coming from Konso – it's in the territory of the Tsemay (part farmers, part pastoralists who dress similarly to the Banna, but are culturally different). No guide is needed to visit the market, which is a very laid-back experience.

Unless your vehicle has broken down, it's hard to imagine why you'd want to stay in Weyto – Jinka, which is the epicentre of tourism in the Lower Omo Valley, is only 80km away.

Weyto Lodge – Meheret Hotel (☏091 654 7506; d Birr200-250; P) has some rudimentary rooms and local food (mains Birr30 to Birr55).

You can bus to/from Jinka (Birr52, two hours) and Konso (Birr50, 1½ hours) but there's no public transport to Turmi.

SOUTHWEST OMO VALLEY

Prepare to be amazed! The Omo Valley and its fascinating ethnic peoples is nowadays one of the biggest tourist attractions in Ethiopia. The vast majority of visitors to this region focus on the easier to reach, safer and ethnically more diverse eastern side of the valley, but two new bridges across the Omo River have opened up this area that was, until very recently, a region filled with the spirit of pure, raw Africa.

This near roadless wilderness is the home of the Surmi – a people adorned with lip plates and spirit-like white paint, whose cattle-herding lifestyle remains, for the moment at least, fairly untouched by outside influences. To spend time with these people, experiencing a genuine slice of tribal African life, is an honour and a privilege.

Planning

There are almost no tourist facilities here. Unless you are prepared to put up with one of the exceedingly rough local 'hotels' (think barn) in Kibish village then you will need to bring camping gear, food, water and everything else you need with you. There is no infrastructure at all in Omo National Park.

Dangers & Annoyances

The southwest Omo Valley is an area with a highly volatile security situation. Cattle rustling and tribal fighting are very common and can lead to significant loss of life (indeed, a week or so before one of our recent visits, around 200 people were rumoured to have been shot in the market place of Kibish village). There is also a not-insignificant risk of banditry. This is a particular problem along the Mizan Tefari to Kibish route where a sparsely inhabited 50km stretch has seen a number of attacks on passing vehicles.

And when we were last in Ethiopia, a group of tourists was attacked along the track from Tum to Kibish. In what appears to have been a robbery gone wrong, a local driver for the group was shot and killed and others in the party were injured. Although reports were still sketchy at the time of writing, it appears that the group was travelling without an armed escort. As a result of this tragedy, the government closed all access to Kibish for an indefinite period. When it reopens, you should always check the security situation in the area before travelling and *always* travel with an armed escort.

Be aware that the situation changes very fast here. It's rare for foreign embassies to have much in the way of solid information on the current security situation and Addis-based tour companies often have only fairly old news. Having said that they should be your first port of call for the latest, along with tour operators, but do be prepared for plans to change at the last second in this region due to the fluid security situation.

Kibish

The main settlement in this area is the colourful village of Kibish (ኪቢሽ; village fee per day Birr10, government fee per day Birr200, guide fee per group per day Birr350, compulsory armed guard per day Birr250, camping per tent Birr30, guardian fee Birr100). Set in a bowl in the forested hills, it is a fascinating place populated by the striking Surmi people. Photographing the Surmi attracts a fee of Birr5 per photo of an adult and Birr4 per photo of a child. Photographers likely to take a lot of photos will be better off negotiating a fee for unlimited photos over a set period of time (Birr40 for 10 minutes per person is fair).

Days spent in Kibish will be filled with visits to small surrounding villages (extra village entry fees apply) and evenings bathing in the river. It might not sound like much, but trust us. It is.

Most people pitch a tent in the campsite on the southern edge of the village – there's nowhere else to stay. However, camping under the African stars makes up for a lot!

You'll need to bring everything with you out here. There are few facilities: no mains electricity or water and just a handful of poorly stocked shops. There's a hut with a fire pit in which to cook, but no other facilities whatsoever.

No public transport connects Kibish with the outside, and such is the security situation around Kibish, that most travellers come as part of an organised 4WD expedition from Addis. It takes around six hours to drive from Tepi or Mizan Tefari.

Omo National Park

Omo National Park (ኦሞ ብሔራዊ ፓርክ) has long been one of the most remote parks in Ethiopia and travelling here can be incredibly tough – but never less than fascinating. But getting *to* the park has just got a whole lot easier – with two new bridges over the Omo River, the park can now be reached from the rest of southern Ethiopia, making it more accessible than ever before.

The park consists of grasslands, hot springs and riverine forests, which provide good wildlife habitat. Surveys of what

ℹ️ OMO NATIONAL PARK

Why Go?
The park is thought to have excellent wildlife possibilities and terrific birding and, having just become more accessible, is about to become more popular. Get there before that happens.

Gateway Towns
Jinka

Budget Tips
It's impossible to visit Omo National Park on a tight budget, although joining an organised tour may reduce per-person costs.

Practicalities
The park has no infrastructure so you must bring everything with you.

Wildlife

Like other parks in Ethiopia, wildlife here has come into conflict with the indigenous tribes who live here, among them the Surma, Mogudge and Dizi. Even so, the best wildlife areas are close to the Omo River in the park's east. The park's wildlife portfolio is believed to be broadly similar to Mago National Park across the river, where you can find eland, buffalo, elephant, giraffe, Burchell's zebra, lesser kudu, topi and oryx, as well as predators (cheetah, lion, leopard) and primates (including deBrazza's and colobus monkeys).

animals exist here are still underway, but birding is excellent with 312 recorded species. Highlights include the blue-breasted kingfisher, red-naped bush shrike, bare-eyed thrush (burdened with the rather unfortunate scientific name *Turdus tephronotus*...), Boran cisticola, violet wood hoopoe and Donaldson Smith's sparrow-weaver among others.

🛌 Sleeping & Eating

An EU-funded program, still in its infancy, is looking at ways to develop the park's potential, but until the plan progresses, there is almost no tourism infrastructure, not even designated campsites within the park. Either way, you'll need your own camping equipment.

You'll need to bring your own supplies and be entirely self-sufficient in food and water.

ℹ️ Getting There & Away

Getting to the park is now possible from the east bank of the Omo River, but there's no public transport into the park and you'll need a fully equipped 4WD to get here and around. The park is 870km southwest of Addis.

Eastern Ethiopia

Best Places to Eat

➡ Paradiso Restaurant (p189)

➡ Al-Hashimi Sweets (p189)

➡ Asham Africa (p181)

➡ Fresh Touch Restaurant (p199)

➡ Hirut Restaurant (p198)

➡ Awash Falls Lodge (p183)

Best Places to Sleep

➡ Doho Lodge (p183)

➡ Asham Africa (p180)

➡ African Village (p188)

➡ Rawda Waber Harari Cultural Guesthouse (p197)

➡ Grand Gato (p198)

Why Go?

Most of eastern Ethiopia is a stark landscape of dust-stained acacia scrub and forgettable towns. But scattered around this cloak of the commonplace are gems of genuine adventure. Undoubtedly, the east's pièce de résistance is the walled city of Harar. There's still a patina of myth about this ancient town, handed down from the days when its markets served as the Horn's commercial hub and attracted powerful merchants and Islamic scholars. The colonial-rural melange that is the modern city of Dire Dawa delights in its own odd way, while nature lovers can get their kicks at Babille Elephant Sanctuary and Awash National Park, where the volcanic landscape takes top billing over the wildlife. The truly intrepid can follow the seemingly endless ribbon of asphalt north to the desolate southern Danakil Desert, territory that remains virtually unexplored since legendary adventurer Wilfred Thesiger first thrilled the world with tales of the proud Afar.

When to Go
Harar

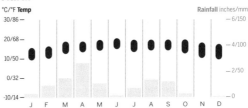

May–Sep Rainy and hot season sends lowland temperatures up to 45°C.

Sep–Oct The seemingly barren Asaita road is painted yellow by the meskel flower.

Nov–Feb Driest months; best time to see elephants at Babille, the lakes near Asaita and Harar.

❶ Getting There & Away

Ethiopian Airlines (www.flyethiopian.com) flies from Addis Ababa to Dire Dawa and Jijiga, and also between Dire Dawa and Djibouti. You can enter eastern Ethiopia overland from Djibouti City by bus and, as of 2017, by train to Dire Dawa thanks the new railway line that connects Djibouti City to Addis Ababa. There's a bus-minibus combination from Djibouti City to Logiya, and connecting minibuses from Hargeisa (Somaliland) to Jijiga.

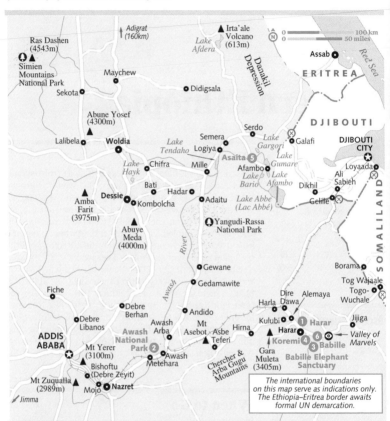

The international boundaries on this map serve as indications only. The Ethiopia–Eritrea border awaits formal UN demarcation.

Eastern Ethiopia Highlights

❶ Harar's Old Town (p193) Exploring the magical jumble of alleyways of the old walled town, and witnessing the famous feeding of the hyenas after nightfall.

❷ Awash National Park (p181) Taking a tour of this popular park known for its outstanding birdlife and variety of landscapes.

❸ Babille Elephant Sanctuary (p200) Getting out of the car and tracking elephants on foot around this underrated wildlife reserve.

❹ Koremi (p200) Soaking up the chilled-out atmosphere in an unspoilt village endowed with traditional houses.

❺ Asaita (p186) Following in the footsteps of Wilfred Thesiger around several salt lakes blessed with stark beauty.

❻ Babille Market (p200) Dreaming of purchasing your own ship of the desert at a lively livestock market.

Bishoftu (Debre Zeyit)

POP 171,000 / ELEV 1920M

There's no love at first sight with Bishoftu (ቢሾፍቱ), formerly known as Debre Zeyit (ደብረ ዘይት). But turn off the highway and you'll find a dishevelled necklace of maars (flat-bottomed, steep-sided volcanic crater lakes) strung around the town, and these make it a favourite playground for frazzled Addis Ababans in search of tranquillity. With some of the best lodging options in the country, Bishoftu is also a great place to spend a few days and recharge the batteries after your epic adventures around the country.

◉ Sights

Lake Babogaya　　　　　　　　　LAKE
(ባቦ.ጋያ ሐይቅ) Lake Babogaya (formerly named Bishoftu Guda) is the site of most of Bishoftu's high-end resorts. With its beautiful backdrop of volcanic Mt Yerer, this circular lake is scenic to boot.

Lake Kuriftu　　　　　　　　　　LAKE
(ኩሪፍቱ ሐይቅ) The tiniest of the lakes dotted around town, pretty Lake Kuriftu is notable for the sprawling Kuriftu Resort and Spa (p181) that hugs the north shore.

Lake Hora　　　　　　　　　　　LAKE
(ሆራ ሐይቅ) Lying just north of the town centre, Lake Hora is the wildest of Bishoftu's lakes and features some outstanding birdlife along its lushly vegetated slopes. There's a footpath around the lake, but never go alone as theft is a real concern. Sadly there's no reliable local guide that can be recommended in the area.

On the first Sunday following Meskel, the Oromo people celebrate Irecha here. Thanks are given to Waka (One God) and good fortune is sought for the upcoming planting season. Devotees gather around an ancient fig tree to smear perfume, butter and *katickala* (a distilled alcohol) on the trunk and share ceremonial meals.

Lake Bishoftu　　　　　　　　　LAKE
(ቢሾፍቱ ሐይቅ) The best way to appreciate this scenic body of water is from the crater rim at one of the hotels, drink in hand. The view is sensational. According to local lore, this, the second-deepest lake in Ethiopia, is home to a sleeping devil. From time to time his evil gases kill the fish and send them bobbing to the surface to be scooped up by delighted waterbirds.

Lake Chelekleka　　　　　　　　LAKE
(ጨለቅለቅ ሐይቅ) Shallow Lake Chelekleka, 2km west of the main roundabout, is a birdwatcher favourite, and lesser flamingos as well as pelicans and various species of waterfowl are sometimes seen. As it's not a crater lake, Chelekleka lacks the dramatic scenery of other lakes in the area.

🛏 Sleeping & Eating

Bishoftu is well endowed with quality accommodation options, including a few boutique-style hotels – bliss if you come from southern or eastern Ethiopia. To avoid disappointment, particularly on weekends, it's wise to book your accommodation well in advance. Truly budget options are nonexistent, but a couple of simple ventures offer perfectly acceptable double rooms with private bathroom at affordable rates.

Bishoftu Afaf Hotel　　　　　RESORT $
(☑ 011 437 8892; Lake Bishoftu; d Birr215; ℗) The Afaf won't inspire romance but has a low-key backpacker vibe and is deservedly popular with budget travellers. The rooms are ordinary, but a steal at this price considering it's perched on Lake Bishoftu's crater rim. The terrace restaurant overlooks the lake, but is enclosed by dirty glass windows.

Viewpoint Lodge　　　　　　LODGE $$
(☑ 091 146 5693; lakebabogaya@live.com; Lake Babogaya; s/d incl breakfast Birr850/1050; ℗ 🛜) If you're looking for a casual place to unwind, then look no further. Refreshingly out of the ordinary, the nine rooms have a semitraditional theme and are set in lush gardens. The stilted rooms below the rim have the best views, though their bathrooms are up above, and there's also a 'treehouse' for those not afraid of heights.

That said, Viewpoint Lodge is not for everybody. Some travellers have found the rooms a bit too rustic, and access to the two stilted units a bit tricky (read: steep stairs). Simple meals (mains Birr45 to Birr100) can be prepared on request.

Dreamland Hotel & Resort　　HOTEL $$
(☑ 011 437 1520; www.ethiodreamland.com; Lake Bishoftu; d incl breakfast Birr930-1380; ℗ 🛜) Once the town's flashiest digs, Dreamland has lost some of its sheen but provides some of the best Bishoftu views. All rooms have richly polished furniture and private

EASTERN ETHIOPIA BISHOFTU (DEBRE ZEYIT)

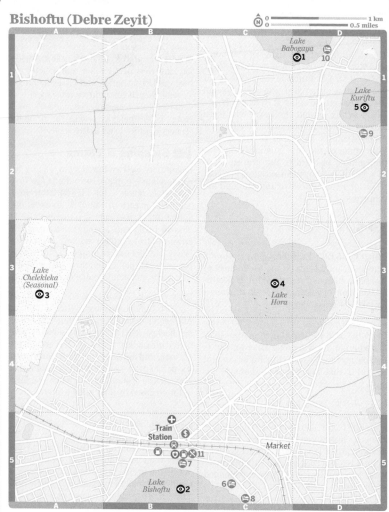

balconies facing the lake. Its positive is the on-site restaurant: its lofty perch on Bishoftu's crater rim and a serenade of birdsong make this the place to dine (mains Birr80 to Birr140).

★ **Asham Africa**   HOTEL **$$$**
(☎ 0114-370021; www.ashamafrica.com; Lake Bishoftu; d incl breakfast US$80-150; P🛜❄) This boutique-style venture is the epitome of a relaxing cocoon, with 32 opulent, over-sized rooms named after different African countries. All overlook Lake Bishoftu and come with parquet floors, four-poster beds

and private balconies. Amenities include a pool, spa, gym and a widely acclaimed restaurant with cracking lake views. The icing on the cake? A large African art gallery.

Adulala Resort & Spa   RESORT **$$$**
(☎ 011 667 0226; www.adulala.com; Lake Babogaya; d incl breakfast from US$140; P🛜❄) Spread out over three hectares along the sloping shores of Lake Babogaya, this sprawling resort features enormous stone-and-wood bungalows scattered in a sea of spruce greenery. Amenities are solid, with two restaurants, spa, pool, tennis courts

Bishoftu (Debre Zeyit)

and a kids' playground. Activities include boat trips on the lake and horse riding. One blemish: not all bungalows come with lake views.

Babogaya HOTEL $$$
(☎011 433 7677; www.babogayaresort.com; Lake Babogaya; d incl breakfast from US$80; P🛜) This well-regarded venture provides an excellent level of comfort and service and is a more intimate alternative to a resort. The 45 sun-filled rooms boast pristine bathrooms, well-sprung mattresses, fancy decorative touches and cardiac-arresting lake views. Prices include a boat ride. A new wing is under construction and a pool is planned.

Kuriftu Resort & Spa RESORT $$$
(☎011 433 6860; www.kurifturesortspa.com; Lake Kuriftu; d incl breakfast from US$99-175; P@🛜🏊) Popular with Addis Ababa's elite, this is a massive but attractive resort – the only one on Lake Kuriftu. There's a wide variety of spacious, spick-and-span rooms in several stone-and-timber buildings right on the shore; not all rooms come with lake views, though. The atmospheric, fancy restaurant (mains Birr130 to Birr250) overlooking the lake is a joy.

Hoteela Gabarewoochi ETHIOPIAN $
(Bishoftu; mains Birr50-80) If you're in an *injera* mood you can't do better than this spot on the main road, though the menu is only in Amharic. It also churns out pasta dishes.

★ **Asham Africa** EUROPEAN, ETHIOPIAN $$
(☎0114-370021; Lake Bishoftu; mains Birr80-180; ⊙11.30am-2.30pm & 6.30-10pm) It's all about tasteful African chic in this respectable ho-

tel restaurant with an airy feel and unsurpassed lake views. Bounteous wood-fired pizzas are also available.

ⓘ Information

You'll find banks with ATMs in the centre.
Commercial Bank (Bishoftu) Changes currency and has an ATM.

ⓘ Getting There & Away

Buses and minibuses leave roughly every 20 minutes for Addis Ababa (Birr12, 45 minutes) and Nazret (Birr20, 40 minutes).

From the bus station to the turn-offs for the Lake Bishoftu or Lake Babogaya hotels, a contract *bajaj* costs about Birr70.

Awash National Park

Easily accessible from Addis Ababa, 756-sq-km Awash National Park (አዋሽ ብሔራዊ ፓርክ; per person per day Birr90, vehicle Birr20; ⊙6am-6pm) is one of Ethiopia's most visited parks. However, if you're here for the thrill of staring slack-jawed at lions crunching through bones, you'll be seriously disappointed. It's more low-key than that and ongoing incursions by Kereyu pastoralists have done little to help wildlife numbers. Nevertheless, it's a must for birders and the volcanic landscape of blister cones and fissures is interesting and beautiful.

◉ Sights

Filwoha Hot Springs HOT SPRINGS
(ፍልውሃ) At Filwoha Hot Springs, in the far north of the park, around 30km from the highway, you can swim in the turquoise-blue pools, but they're not as refreshing as they look: temperatures touch 45°C and crocodiles lurk in the cooler areas. The beauty around the springs is boosted by the doum palms, used by the local people to make mats. After 5pm the area comes alive with birds, and lions can sometimes be heard at night. Beware of treacherous quicksand – always go with a guide or an armed scout.

Fantale Crater VOLCANO
(ፈንታሌ) Towards the west end of the park, 600m above the plains, lies Fantale Crater (2007m). With its terrific vistas, total quiet and cool air, this dormant volcano makes a great trek. At the top (a three-hour walk uphill; the 4WD track is no longer driveable) the 360-degree view is phenomenal and the

Awash National Park

elliptical caldera, which measures an enormous 3.5km in diameter, is quite an eerie sight in the morning when the steam vents can be seen.

Awash Falls
WATERFALL

(አዋሽ ፏፏቴ; ◷ museum 6am-6pm) Just past the headquarters at Awash Falls Lodge, there are viewpoints above this mighty waterfall, which tumbles into the magnificent Awash Gorge along the park's southern boundary. The gorge is 150m deep and at its most beautiful by the abandoned Kereyou Lodge, about 10km east of Awash Falls Lodge.

Near the park headquarters is a very modest museum filled with dusty skins, skulls and stuffed animals, plus good written information about the wildlife.

Hyena Den
CAVE

(የጅብ ጐሬ) Below Fantale, a few kilometres north of the village of Metahara, you can routinely see dozens of spotted hyenas exit their dens around dusk.The Birr300 per car fee is paid to the community and your park scout gets an extra Birr150 for going with you.

🏃 Activities

Awash National Park lies on an important migratory route between the north and the south, bestowing an astonishing amount of birdlife. More than 460 species have been recorded, among them the extremely rare yellow-throated seedeater and somber rock chat, both found only in and near Awash.

Two especially good spots to observe birds are around Filwoha Hot Springs and around the Awash River campsites, where francolin, barbets and hoopoes are all seen. On the plains, kori bustards are quite easily spotted, and sometimes secretary birds. An ostrich reintroduction program has recently begun. Among the many raptors are fish eagles, lammergeyer and pygmy falcons.

In the south of the park, the grassy Illa-la Sala Plains is the one place devoid of the dominant thick acacia scrub that makes wildlife spotting tough. The beautiful beisa oryx and Soemmering's gazelles are usually seen here. Also present are salt's dik-dik, greater and lesser kudus (particularly in the area called Kudu Valley), defassa waterbucks, warthogs and black-and-white colobus, which prefer the riverine forest. Lions, leopards, cheetahs, black-backed jackals, caracals, servals, wildcats and aardwolves are also found in the park, but thank your lucky stars if you manage to spot one of them: they're virtually never seen.

All wildlife drives start at the main gate. An armed scout (Birr100, plus an extra Birr150 for the Filwoha Hot Springs) is compulsory.

🛏 Sleeping & Eating

Most visitors stay in Awash, which offers a wide range of facilities and is a mere 15-minute drive to the east, and visit the park as a day trip. There are also two good lodges inside the park as well as a few basic campsites along the Awash River and near Filwoha Hot Springs.

Meridian   HOTEL $

(☑ 096 369 8620; Awash; d with fan Birr200, with air-con Birr400-500; P ❋ ☏) This large, multistorey place in the centre of Awash has straightforward, spacious rooms with balconies overlooking a shady courtyard. There's also a restaurant. Avoid the older, cheaper rooms that occupy a separate building.

Buffet d'Aouache   HOTEL $

(☑ 091 187 2379, 022 224 0008; Awash; d with shared bathroom Birr120, d Birr350-400; P) This delightfully old-fashioned relic of French railway days (1904) is without frills but it's high on atmosphere, with whitewashed walls, birds in the rambling garden and a pot-plant-filled courtyard. The rooms with shared bathrooms are pretty spare; treat yourself to one of the two generous-sized 'presidentielle' rooms. Greek, Italian or French-style dishes (Birr50 to Birr100) can be ordered in advance.

Rooms back across the railway tracks, in a more modern building, feature fans and plumper beds, but have less atmosphere. One downside: both the nearby Orthodox church and Islamic mosque employ loudspeakers to broadcast their prayers at ungodly hours.

Camping   CAMPGROUND $

(Awash National Park; per tent Birr40) A great camping option is the area around the Filwoha Hot Springs in the northern extreme of the park, with its shady fig trees.

Camping   CAMPGROUND $

(Awash National Park; per tent Birr40) The shady sites along the Awash River in the area known as 'Gotu', 400m south of the park headquarters, are muddy but attractive and shady. Bring everything you need because there are no facilities.

Genet Hotel   HOTEL $$

(☑ 022 224 0040; Awash; d with fan Birr200-510, d with air-con Birr620; P ❋ ☏) This solid, no-frills four-storey option is deservedly popular with tour operators. Rooms in the main building are comfortable, serviceable and fairly priced, and the ambience is relaxed. However, they catch a bit of road noise. The older, cheaper rooms in a separate wing are quite scruffy. There's an excellent restaurant (mains Birr60 to Birr130) here – try the delicious roasted chicken.

★ Doho Lodge   LODGE $$$

(☑ 022 899 2224; www.doholodge.com; Awash National Park; s/d incl breakfast US$80/110-115; P ☒) If you're looking to rehabilitate your travel-worn body and mind, a surprisingly relaxing retreat is this small lodge just outside the northeast park boundary. Opened in 2014, Doho Lodge feels wonderfully secluded, with nine well-designed, Afar-style cottages on a low ridge overlooking a tiny reed-fringed lake.

Food (Birr90 to Birr160) is a plus and is served in an atmospheric open-air restaurant with top-notch views. There's electricity in the evening only. Activities include swimming, boating on the lake, bathing in a pair of artificial pools fed by hot springs, wildlife watching, guided walks and village visits.

Awash Falls Lodge   LODGE $$$

(☑ 091 277 0965, 0116-530245; http://awash fallslodge.net; Awash National Park; camping own/ hired tent US$12/20, s US$80, d US$90-110, incl breakfast; P) This attractive place right above the falls has rustic yet serviceable wood-and-stone *tukuls* and a restaurant with awesome views. Aside from the setting, a highlight is the food (mains Birr100 to Birr200), with a wide selection of well-prepared Ethiopian and Western dishes. A variety of wildlife and village walks can be organised from the lodge.

There's 24-hour power and tepid water. Note that the walls in the bathrooms don't make it to the ceilings and there's no air-con (only fans). Units 23, 24 and 25 come with breathtaking views of the gorge and the falls. Low-season discounts are usually available.

ℹ️ Getting There & Away

The park gate is 14km before Awash and the headquarters and waterfall lie 10km south of the gate. There are no Awash buses from Addis (four hours); you'll either need to pay the full Dire Dawa fare (Birr160 to Birr290) or use two vehicles, changing in Nazret (Birr40, 2½ hours). For Harar and Dire Dawa, head to Asbe Teferi (Birr50, 1½ hours) and catch a connection there. Waiting for a bus to Harar or Dire Dawa that started in Addis and has a free seat is likely to prove futile, but if you want to try, wait along the main road in front of the bus station.

Except for climbing the volcano, strolling along the river or short jaunts from your vehicle to get better photos, walking is not allowed in the park, nor are bikes and motorcycles. A 4WD is necessary to get around the park.

Djibouti Road

Known as the Djibouti road (ጂቡቲ መንገድ), the asphalt road that connects Awash to Djibouti City crosses a hauntingly bleak landscape of parched plains, ferocious sun and barren scenery. Besides some occasionally beautiful vistas, a fistful of unassuming towns and a rifle-toting Afar tribesman or two picking their way through acacia scrub,

there's little to stop the perpetually curious spiralling into a free fall of boredom.

This is not the road less travelled: countless Ethiopian trucks ply this route to and from Djibouti, and because it is such an important corridor the road is in excellent condition.

For visitors the Djibouti road is mostly used as an access route to the Danakil Depression or Djibouti. It also provides access to a series of beautiful but underrated shallow lakes that lie south of the town of Asaita.

👁️ Sights

The road branches north just after Awash (officially Awash Sabat: 'Awash Seven') and crosses Awash Arba (Awash Forty) 10km to the north. It's then 107km to the featureless town of Gewane, which doesn't warrant a full stop, just a slow-down to admire Mt Ayele looming to the east. After Gewane, the country begins to resemble Djibouti more and more: arid and desolate. The road passes through Yangudi-Rassa National Park but, frankly, don't expect much wildlife other than ostriches and gazelle; there's probably less here than in any national park in Ethiopia.

One hundred and twelve kilometres north of Gewane is Adaitu. Built mostly of sticks and sheet metal, it's one of three Issa (a tribe often in deadly conflict with the dominant Afar) towns along the road. Both peoples are traditionally pastoralists and live in domed thatch huts that are light and easy to transport. As you'll see, plastic sheeting is now part of the standard design. Just after town, the road crosses the Awash

---

THE AFAR

'The Danakil invariably castrated any man or boy whom they killed or wounded, removing both the penis and the scrotum. An obvious trophy, it afforded irrefutable proof that the victim was male...'

Sir Wilfred Thesiger, The Life of My Choice

Fuelled by early accounts from European travellers and explorers, the Afar have gained an almost legendary reputation for ferocity. And, as they are one of the few tribes capable of surviving the harsh conditions of northeastern Ethiopia, perhaps that aura of myth is deserved.

On your journey north, look out for Afar men striding along in simple cotton *shirits* (sarongs), with their famous *jile* (curved knives), water-filled gourds hanging at their side and a rifle slung casually across a shoulder. Even today many Afars still lead a nomadic existence and when the herds are moved in search of new pasture, the huts in which the Afars live are simply packed onto the backs of camels and carted away. In the relatively fertile plains around the Awash River, some Afars have turned to cultivation, growing cotton and maize. Interclan rivalry is still alive and conflicts occasionally break out.

River. Mille, 30km after Adaitu, is spread between an upper and lower town on opposite sides of its eponymous river.

Southwest of Mille is Hadar, the famous archaeological site where the fossilised remains of the hominid Lucy were discovered.

The second half of the 48km stretch of road north of Mille takes you through a virtually lifeless expanse of rust-coloured volcanic boulders and, just after Lake Tendaho (the impoundment of which feeds sugar-cane fields), the road deposits you in Logiya, the most developed town along the highway and the region's transport hub.

Atop the plateau 6km north of Logiya, it's a shock to come suddenly upon Semera, the Afar region capital. With its soulless mix of workers barracks, administrative buildings, sheet-metal shacks and petrol stations, it looks like a crummy little desert version of Brasília, and about the only people who live here are government workers and university students. Semera makes a convenient stopover on your way to the Danakil.

Eight kilometres past Semera, the easy-to-miss asphalt road to Asaita branches off to the right.

🛌 Sleeping & Eating

If you need to break your journey, the choice of reliable accommodation is very limited. Most hotels are scruffy and spartan and cater primarily to Ethiopian truck drivers on their way to and from Djibouti port. Your best bet is to base yourself in Semera, which has a handful of quality hotels.

Nazret 2 HOTEL $
(Naazret Ixximak No2; ☑094 551 5614; Logiya; bed in courtyard Birr40, d Birr290-460, with shared bathroom Birr100; ⓟ❄🛜) On the Mille end of Logiya, Nazret 2 is a reliable and well-managed venture. The cheapest rooms are fan cooled and very simple; the more expensive ones have air-con and better beds. You can also sleep outdoors under a net. Nazret 2 serves good food (mains Birr30 to Birr100), though there's no menu. And there's wi-fi.

Tareke Hotel HOTEL $
(☑091 182 3700; Mille; d Birr300-500, with shared bathroom Birr120; ⓟ❄) This unsigned establishment is a dependable budget choice with three types of clean and generally decent rooms. The rooms in the green section have air-con (and bathrooms); rooms in the

yellow and blue sections don't. It's in Upper Mille, across from the tall brown minaret.

Agda Hotel HOTEL $$
(☑033 666 0839; Semera; d incl breakfast Birr750-1250; ⓟ❄🛜🏊) Semera isn't overrun with upmarket accommodation, but this well-managed venture on the road to Logiya just about works out. It scores high on amenities, with a modern restaurant serving tasty local and Western dishes, a swimming pool and well-presented rooms set in various low-slung buildings dotted around a vast property. A safe choice.

Erta-Ale Motel HOTEL $$
(☑091 221 3532; Semera; d Birr530-580; ⓟ❄🛜) This three-storey building on the main road is no architectural beauty queen, but it sports functional rooms with plump bedding and there's a good on-site restaurant. No alcohol is served.

ℹ️ Information

You'll find banks with ATMs in Logiya and Semera.

Culture & Tourism Bureau (☑033 666 0488, 091 181 9338; saahisto@gmail.com; Semera; ⏰7am-noon & 3-5.30pm Mon-Fri) Permission papers (Birr500 per person for the whole Afar region) to visit the lakes around Asaita and to enter the Danakil Depression are handed out at this office in the large administrative building on the way into Semera. If you only want to visit the lakes around Asaita, it costs Birr200. This can be processed in advance by emailing your application. If you're on an organised tour, your operator will handle the application on your behalf.

ℹ️ Getting There & Away

Public transport is thin on the ground but it's usually possible to get from Awash to Asaita in a day – you'll need to travel in stages, though. From Awash's bus station up to three early morning buses go to Logiya (Birr150, six to seven hours). Logiya is the region's main transport hub and minibuses go at least hourly to Semera (Birr4, 10 minutes) and Asaita (Birr30, one hour). A contract *bajaj* to Semera can cost Birr60. Minibuses to Galafi (Birr60) at the border with Djibouti run early in the morning.

From Logiya, there's also one morning bus to Dessie (Birr140, six to seven hours) via Woldia (Birr90, 5½ hours) where you can continue to Addis Ababa and Lalibela respectively. These buses pass through Mille, but there's virtually no chance of them having an empty seat when they do.

It's possible to hitch a lift with one of the legions of Ethiopian trucks that ply the route between Awash and Djibouti City; be sure to negotiate the price.

Asaita

POP 22,700 / ELEVATION 300M

Asaita (አሳይታ) is a cul-de-sac at the end of the world. This is the starting point from which to explore the salt lakes in the area, but Asaita itself has a look and feel all its own, so it's worth a visit even if you aren't planning to be a modern-day Wilfred Thesiger. No matter what your reason for coming, be prepared: the heat is unbearable for most of the year and the swarms of flies are bigger than even those in the towns you passed on your way here.

Tuesday is market day – a must if you're in town.

◉ Sights

Lakes Afambo & Gumare   LAKE

The little-explored territory and salt lakes scattered around Asaita are something of a holy grail for serious adventurers. This area remains one of the Horn's most inhospitable corners, appearing much the same as when explorer Wilfred Thesiger laid eyes upon it in the 1930s. Here the Awash River disappears into a chain of lakes, including Lakes Gumare and Afambo, which can be fairly easily visited from Asaita. The scenery is as stark, desolate and surreally beautiful as it is foreboding.

The easiest way to do things is as a day trip from Asaita using your own vehicle or the public buses from Asaita to Afambo (Birr15, one hour) that leave between 6am and 9am and return around 4pm. It's possible to drive a couple of kilometres beyond Afambo; then you'll have to hike the remainder.

Start by obtaining permission papers from the tourist office in Semera, which is easy enough. Then you'll have to arrange armed Afar escorts (who almost certainly won't speak English) in the village of Afambo near the lakes – expect to fork out Birr200 per armed guard. There'll be other monetary demands at the start and along the way, including a necessary boat crossing on a reed raft. Buy everything you'll need in Asaita, or better still in Addis, as there are no real shops after this, and bring camping gear as there's no lodging.

The legendary Lake Abbe, the ultimate destination of the Awash River's waters, is at least a three-day trip. Called Lac Abbé in French-speaking Djibouti, it can be approached much more easily from that side.

🛏 Sleeping

Apart from a couple of basic hotels, there's not much in the way of accommodation in Asaita. Semera has a wider choice.

Basha Amare Hotel   HOTEL $

(☑ 091 345 5341, 033 655 0119; bed in courtyard Birr175, d with shared bathroom Birr175) The friendliest option by far is this family-run hotel on the cliff above the Awash River, where you might see crocodiles in the day. Rooms are small and basic and shared facilities are rudimentary, but the atmosphere is congenial. If the slow-mo fans can't cool you, use the natural air-con and sleep in the courtyard – beds with mattresses are provided.

Omelettes, rice and *tibs* (sliced lamb) are available in the restaurant (mains Birr20 to Birr40) out front. It's a short stagger south of the bus station.

Lem Hotel   HOTEL $

(☑ 091 107 0560; d with shared bathroom Birr50, d with shower Birr60, d with shower & air-con Birr450; ❋) This cheapie on the main road, right in the centre, has benefitted from an upgrade (read: some rooms have been equipped with air-con). The swing-a-cat-sized rooms at the rear are set around a pretty courtyard and boast clean sheets and tolerable shared toilets of the squat variety.

ℹ Information

Commercial Bank (⊙7-11.30am & 3-5pm Mon-Fri, 7-11.30am Sat) Next to Basha Amare Hotel. Changes cash and has an ATM.

ℹ Getting There & Away

Leaving from the main square, near the lighthouselike minaret, buses and minibuses go about hourly to Logiya (Birr28, one hour) via Semera. There's one early morning bus to Dessie (Birr150, 10 hours) and a couple of morning buses to Afambo (Birr15, one hour). For Djibouti you'll have to go back to Logiya; trucks won't pick up hitchhikers along the highway.

Dire Dawa

POP 256,800 / ELEV 1200M

The fourth-most populous city in Ethiopia, Dire Dawa (ድሬ ዳዋ) usually elicits strong reactions. Its colourful storefronts, tree-lined streets, neat squares and foreign influence (look for Arab, French, Italian and Greek styles in some of the architecture and design) are a refreshing change from the filthy disorder and lack of character in most Ethiopian towns. Others just consider it a more vibrant version of tedium.

Dire Dawa is made up of two distinct settlements, divided by the trash-strewn Dechatu Wadi (seasonal river). Lying to the north and west is the European-influenced 'new town', known as Kezira. To the east is the more colourful 'old town', known as Megala, which has a distinctly Muslim (and, co-incidentally, a slightly Mexican) feel.

◉ Sights

Dire Dawa's main highlights are its thriving markets.

Kafira Market
MARKET

(ቀፊራ ገበያ; Megala) With its Babel-like ambience, the enormous Kafira Market, sprawling way beyond its Moorish-style arches, is the most striking of Dire Dawa's markets. Delving into the organised chaos of its narrow lanes is an assault on the senses. This market attracts people from miles around, including Afar and Somali herders, Oromo farmers and Amhara merchants. Charcoal and firewood is brought in from the hinterlands by camel; look for them in the *wadi*.

Ethiopia-Djibouti Rail Yard
MUSEUM

(ኢትዮጵያ – ጅቡቲ ባቡር ማቢያ ገበ; ☑0915-154557; Kezira; ⊘8am-noon & 3-5.30pm Mon-Fri, 7am-noon Sat) Rail fans can clamber through what remains of the once-great Imperial Railway Company of Ethiopia. Ask for Kadra Ali – she can get by in English and will happily take you around the rail yard (tip expected). You'll see plenty of rusty carcasses of disused engines, the still-operational roundhouse and Haile Selassie's private carriage.

Ashawa Market & Livestock Market
MARKET

(አሽዋ ገበያና ከብት ገበያ; Kezira) With its numerous sheet-metal shacks in the back, the chaotic Ashawa Market is well worth a gander. In the wadi behind Ashawa you'll find the livestock market, which is usually held in the morning.

Dire Dawa Market
MARKET

(ድራደዋ ገበያ; Megala) Also known as 'Taiwan', this is a modern, orderly covered market mostly full of clothing and fabric, though some of the cheap electronic goods that used to dominate this space remain.

Chattara Market
MARKET

(ጫት ተራ ገበያ; Megala) *Chat* is sold all over town, but the trade at the Chattara Market is so frenetic it deserves a look.

Old Palace
PALACE

(አሮጌ ቤተመንግስት) This large building is the former imperial residence of Haile Selassie. It's not open to the public and difficult to see from outside.

Bete Mikael Church
CHURCH

(ቤተ ሚካሄል ቤተክርስቲያን; Kezira) This colourful church, which lies near the Old Palace, is noted for its octagonal shape.

Juma'a Mosque
MOSQUE

(ጁማ መስጊድ; Megala) Juma'a Mosque is the city's largest mosque and a prominent landmark in the Megala neighbourhood.

Greek Orthodox Church
CHURCH

(ግሪክ አርቶዶክስ ቤተክርስቲያን; Kezira) This modern, well-proportioned church is most notable for its two spires and yellow facade.

☞ Tours

Yige Tour
CULTURAL

(☑0915-732313; yigeremut@yahoo.com) Yigeremu Tadess is the man behind the business, and he charges Birr500 a day for guided tours around Dire Dawa. For the cave-art sites of Lega-Oda, Goda-Awaja and Porc-Epic, he'll ask Birr500 per archaeological site. If you don't have your own wheels, he can provide a 4WD for an extra Birr2500. Just be sure you know what kind of vehicle you're getting; 4WDs are hard to come by.

🛏 Sleeping & Eating

Dire Dawa has no shortage of quality accommodation options, with a wide range of well-run, business-like ventures offering loads of facilities. Reliable budget digs are harder to find. Most of Dire Dawa's accommodation is concentrated in the centre, but there are also several good midrange places on the road to the airport.

Dire Dawa

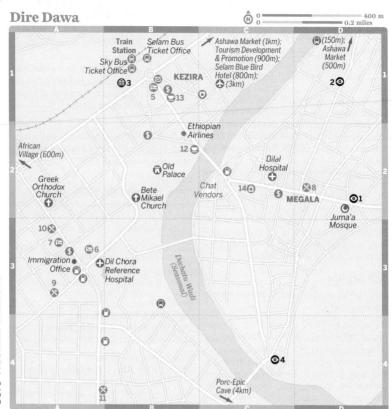

When celebrations are taking place in Kulubi (around 26 July and 28 December), hotels here are booked out months in advance.

Mekonnen Hotel
HOTEL $

(☎091 573 2927; Kezira; d with shared bathroom Birr100) A good deal for shoestringers, this faded glory is housed in an Italian colonial building opposite the train station. Most rooms have plenty of space to strew your stuff around, and some have balconies overlooking the square. Shared bathrooms (with cold showers) are a tad scummy but still do the trick. The proximity of cafes and restaurants is another bonus.

★ African Village
HOTEL $$

(☎025 112 6006; www.african-village.com; Kezira; incl breakfast s Birr380-450, d Birr450-600; P 🛜) An attractive mesh of traditional and modern, the comfortable rooms with satellite TV surround a communal courtyard and excellent restaurant (mains Birr45 to Birr90). The only real knock is the lack of air-conditioning, though the traditional construction does help cool the rooms. It's in a quiet neighbourhood west of the centre, signposted down a side street.

The kitchen turns out expertly cooked Ethiopian dishes and the clear explanations on the menu will guide you along. There are also burgers, salads, soups, pastas and pizzas. One grumble: service is a bit slow. The Swiss owners prohibit alcohol.

★ Samrat Hotel
HOTEL $$

(☎025 113 0600; www.samrathoteldire.com; Kezira; s/d incl breakfast with fan US$33/43, with air-con US$37/51; P ❄ @ 🛜 ☒) The dour exterior of Dire Dawa's best lodging hides a classy lobby, well-appointed rooms (though not all have air-con) and a prolific list of amenities, including a swimming pool, top-notch restaurant, nightclub, business centre, an ATM and two well-stocked bars. Efficient service, too.

Dire Dawa

◉ Sights
1 Chattara Market D2
2 Dire Dawa Market D1
3 Ethiopia-Djibouti Rail Yard.................B1
4 Kafira Market C4

🛏 Sleeping
5 Mekonnen Hotel B1
6 Ras Hotel..A3
7 Samrat Hotel..A3

🍴 Eating
8 Al-Hashimi Sweets D2
9 Asefah Roasted Chicken.....................A3
10 Elga Café A3
11 Paradiso Restaurant A4
   Samrat Hotel................................(see 7)

🍸 Drinking & Nightlife
12 Dini Paradise.......................................B2
13 Hamdail Coffee House B1
   Mekonnen Hotel ....(see 5)

🛍 Shopping
14 Bashanfer Trading..............................C2

Ras Hotel   HOTEL **$$**
(📞 025 111 3255; www.rashotel.com; Kezira; s/d US$40/50; 🅿❄🛜🏊) Ras Hotel is back with a vengeance. After a top-to-bottom makeover, it now ranks as one of the swankiest options in Dire Dawa. Sure, its exterior look doesn't really scream holidays, but who cares when you can enjoy attractive rooms with excellent bedding, a well-regarded restaurant, a bar, an ATM and a swimming pool. Another selling point is the large garden (full of birds), which is a great spot to chill out.

Selam Blue Bird Hotel   HOTEL **$$**
(📞 025 113 0219; Kezira; d/tw/ste incl breakfast Birr500/600/600; 🅿❄🛜) You'll go giddy over the ever-so-slightly OTT doubles and suites, with ornately carved beds and wardrobes. There's not a speck of dirt to be found in this blue-glass spot along the road to the airport. It also features a well-regarded restaurant.

★ Al-Hashimi Sweets   SWEETS **$**
(Megala; sweets from Birr10; ⊙8am-8pm) This perpetually busy joint has been spoiling customers and waistlines for several years with its irresistible baklava – all freshly made on the premises. Heaven on earth for the sweet-toothed. Expect long queues. It's on the main thoroughfare in Megala.

★ Paradiso Restaurant   ITALIAN **$**
(📞 025 111 3780; Kezira; mains Birr50-90; ⊙11am-9.30pm) Haven't had a slap-up meal for a while? Don't look past Paradiso, the most respected restaurant in town. The menu roves from flavoursome Italian dishes to more traditional gut-busters such as *kitfo* (raw meat) and *tibs*. Add friendly staff, wallet-friendly prices and an enticing setting – an Italian mansion with old-world charm and outdoor seating – and you have a winner.

Asefah Roasted Chicken   CHICKEN **$**
(Kezira; mains Birr55-110; ⊙8am-9pm) This lively eatery specialises in one thing and one thing only: roast chicken. There's an agreeable terrace with plenty of shade.

Elga Café   CAFE **$**
(Kezira; snacks Birr35-60; ⊙6.30am-noon & 3.30-8pm) A little corner of tranquillity, Elga Café is a great spot to refuel over coffee, pastries and snacks.

Samrat Hotel   INDIAN **$$**
(📞 025 113 0600; Kezira; mains Birr90-200; ⊙7am-10.30pm; 🛜) Besides the usual European dishes and some token Ethiopian ones, this venture inside Samrat Hotel concocts delicious Indian dishes (the chef is Indian) that will satisfy the pickiest of appetites. Get things going with tasty tandoori specialities or well-presented biryanis. Chinese specialities and a wide choice of veggie options are also on offer.

🍷 Drinking & Nightlife

Dini Paradise   TEA GARDEN
(Kezira; ⊙7am-9pm) This ramshackle place near the bridge is a great place to relax over a cup of coffee or a delicious frappé. Food is only so-so.

Hamdail Coffee House   CAFE
Brimming with good cheer, this large place with a modernish feel is an ideal refuelling stop after a walking tour in the area. It serves excellent macchiatos, cappuccinos and fresh juices (from Birr15) and has an appetising selection of pastries.

Mekonnen Hotel   BAR
(Kezira; ⊙8am-10pm) Cheap beers and great people-watching. From around 6pm the footpath tables are packed with men talking politics and sipping coffee and beer.

🛍 Shopping

Bashanfer Trading　　　　　COFFEE
(Megala; ◎8am-noon & 3-6pm Mon-Fri, 8am-noon Sat) You can buy fresh, export-quality Ethiopian coffee at this well-stocked shop on the main drag in Megala. It sells 1kg (Birr90) and 500g (Birr46) packets of excellent whole and ground beans.

ℹ Information

Commercial Bank (Kezira; ◎8am-4.30pm Mon-Fri) Changes cash and has an ATM.

Dashen Bank (Kezira; ◎8am-4.30pm Mon-Fri, 8am-noon Sat) Changes currency and has an ATM.

Dashen Bank (Megala; ◎8am-4.30pm Mon-Fri, 8am-noon Sat) Changes cash and has an ATM. It's in the heart of Megala.

Immigration Office (📋 025 111 2497; Kezira; ◎8am-noon & 2-5pm Mon-Fri) You can renew your visa here, saving the long trip back to Addis Ababa. It costs US$100 for one month and payment must be made in US dollars. You need to supply one photo and a copy of your passport. It's issued the same day.

Tourism Development & Promotion (Dire Dawa Administration Council Bldg, 1st fl; ◎7.30am-noon & 2-5pm Mon-Fri) Issues permission papers for cave paintings near Dire Dawa (Lega-Oda, Goda-Ajawa and Porc-Epic). It costs Birr50 per cave.

Wegagen Bank (Kezira; ◎7.30-11.30am & 2-5pm Mon-Fri, 7.30-11am Sat) Has an ATM. Near Samrat Hotel.

ℹ Getting There & Away

AIR

There are two daily **Ethiopian Airlines** (📋 025 111 3069; www.ethiopianairlines.com; Kezira; ◎7.30-noon & 3-5.45pm) flights between Addis Ababa and Dire Dawa (US$143, one hour), one

---

CAVE ART

Dire Dawa is known for its many prehistoric cave paintings. Dating back an estimated 5000 years, the crude red, white and black figures depict humans and animals. They're important to archaeologists, though lay visitors may end up disappointed.

You'll need to find the man with the key, who'll take you to the caves. The price for this service is not fixed, but Birr100 to Birr150 should do it. The guards at the gate will also expect a tip and others may have their hands out along the way. You can also expect some hassles from village kids at some point. It's highly recommended to go with a guide and a police escort from town, which will smooth things considerably.

You first need to go to the Tourism Development and Promotion (p190) office in the building next to Selam Blue Bird Hotel and get a permission paper for Birr50 per cave. Public transport to these sites is virtually nonexistent – you'll need your own wheels.

Goda-Ajawa　　　　　ጎዳ-አጃዋ
Though the paintings, including some palm prints, in this lofty cave are good, they're fewer and less varied than at Lega-Oda, and graffiti around the paintings mars the site. It's 28km (about one hour) southeast of Dire Dawa on a much rougher road than to Lega-Oda. The man with the key is usually in Awale, but he could be off in one of several other villages that you'll pass as you drive there. The long, uphill-almost-the-whole-way walk takes about an hour (less if you come with a 4WD and can park closer).

Lega-Oda　　　　　ለጋ-ኦዳ
By far the best cave-art site around Dire Dawa, this 70m-long rock shelter holds some 600 paintings. The figures clearly show humans, antelope, anteaters, camels and groups of lines and dots. The cave is 38km (one hour's drive) southwest of Dire Dawa, and an easy 20-minute walk from the road. You'll find the man with the key in Wuchale village, about 1km from the trailhead.

Porc-Epic　　　　　ፖርሲክ ኤፒክ
The best-known and easiest to reach cave has a few rock formations, making it the most geologically interesting of the three, but the paintings are largely obscured by soot. It's 4km past the bus station to a wadi, the last 2km of which is on a very rough road, and then a 30-minute climb takes you 140m up to the cave. The man with the key will likely be out shepherding his goats and will find you after you arrive.

continuing to Jijiga (US$49, 25 minutes) and the other to Djibouti (from US$80, 50 minutes).

BUS

A few regular buses depart daily to Addis Ababa (Birr158, 10 hours) between 4.30am and 5.30am from the **bus station** (Kezira). For better comfort, use the daily **Sky Bus** (Kezira; Birr275) and **Selam Bus** (Birr305 to Birr325), both with 5am departures and ticket offices in front of the train station. Stopping anywhere along the way requires paying the full Addis fare.

Ee City (☑ 092 281 3751) operates a daily bus to Gelille (Birr185) at the border with Djibouti, where you'll find onward connection to Djibouti City. It leaves around 7pm.

Minibuses run every 10 minutes or so to Harar (Birr21, one hour).

TRAIN

Trains to Djibouti City resumed in 2017. The new railway station is about 11km north of the city. From the old railway station, there's also a twice-weekly service to the border town of Gelille (Birr155, seven hours), from where you can catch a minibus to Djibouti City.

Around Dire Dawa

Harla (ሀርላ), the former capital of Harla Kingdom, was a 13th-century walled city that excavations have shown did much trade with the Middle East. A few minor remnants of its glory days are still around, but don't hold your breath. It's 15km out of Dire Dawa. Catch a minibus (Birr11, 20 minutes) from in front of the NOC petrol station instead of the bus station.

Twice a year, tens of thousands of pilgrims converge on the little town of Kulubi (ቁልቢ) and its hilltop cathedral, Kulubi Gabriel, built by Ras Mekonen to thank St Gabriel for the victory over the Italians at Adwa. Many people come to express thanks for fulfilment of a wish, and babies feature prominently: up to 1000 infants may be christened during celebrations. If you're in the area around 26 July and 28 December, it's an amazing experience.

Harar

POP 196,000 / ELEV 1850M

World Heritage–listed Harar (ሀረር) is a place apart. With its 368 alleyways squeezed into just 1 sq km, it's more reminiscent of Fez in Morocco than any other city in the Horn.

> ## CHAT
>
> The region around Dire Dawa and Harar (and especially the town of Awaday, about 13km northwest of Harar) is the reputed origin of the addictive stimulant *chat*. It's not only a major export commodity, replacing coffee on many farms (look for the slender trees with shiny, dark-green leaves planted in neat rows), but a huge percentage of the population spends most afternoons lying on the ground in a drunken-like stupor. Driving through Awaday on your way to Harar, you'll see why it's dubbed the '*chat* capital of the world'.

Its countless mosques and shrines, animated markets, crumbling walls and charming people will make you feel as if you've floated right out of the 21st century. It's the east's most memorable sight and shouldn't be missed. As if that wasn't enough, there are many chances to get up close and personal with wild hyenas. It's a rare traveller who doesn't enjoy it here.

History

Harar is steeped in history, though its origin is unknown. Evidence suggests it was founded by Arabian immigrants, including Sheikh Abadir, in the 10th century, though local legend declares the sheikh arrived in the 13th century. Other sources date the first settlement all the way back to the 7th century. Regardless, it grew into a crossroads for commerce between Africa, India and the Middle East and a place where great dynasties of rich and powerful merchants grew and the arts flourished. European merchants eventually joined the mix and though it did decline in importance over the years, it was still significant enough that the Egyptians came and conquered it in 1875 and held on for 10 years.

In the 17th and 18th centuries, Harar became known as an important centre of Islamic scholarship and spearheaded Islam's penetration into the Horn. There's an oft-repeated myth that Harar is the fourth holiest city in Islam (after Mecca, Medina and Jerusalem), but this is purely a local invention.

In 1854 British explorer Richard Burton, disguised as an Arab merchant, was the first non-Muslim to penetrate the city. French poet Arthur Rimbaud (p197) later spent

EASTERN ETHIOPIA AROUND DIRE DAWA

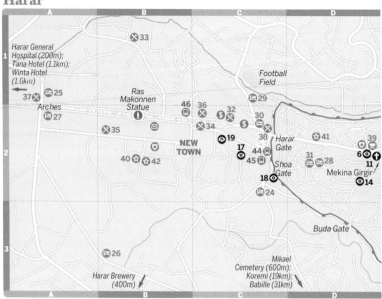

many years here. In 1887 the city surrendered to Emperor Menelik, who sought to expand and unify his empire, but the Hararis retain their own ethnic identity, language and culture to this day.

◉ Sights

Markets

No visit to Harar would be complete without wading through its shambolic markets. They're packed with Oromo people from the surrounding countryside coming to town to sell their goods (mostly firewood) and then spend their earnings on food and household goods. All the fresh markets are busiest after 3pm and are pretty quiet on Sundays.

Smugglers' Market   MARKET
(የኮንትሮባንድ ገበያ; New Town) The Smugglers' Market is chock-full of counterfeit clothing and electronics (some real stuff, too) from China. Most of it is smuggled in from Somaliland either by night caravans of camel and donkey across the remote desert frontiers or cleverly concealed in trucks. The whole area is undergoing a major urban revamp, and most shops are expected to be relocated inside modern shopping malls.

Shoa Gate Market   MARKET
(ሸዋ በር; Shoa Gate) Elbow your way through the Shoa Gate Market (also known as the Christian Market) to find *etan* (incense) from the Jijiga area; it's used in the famous coffee ceremonies. This odoriferous market also has spices and bark, roots and twigs used in the preparation of traditional medicine plus heaps of vegetables.

Recycling Market   MARKET
(ያገለገሉ ዕቃዎችን በአዲስ መልክ መሠጫ) Near the Shoa Gate Market is the Recycling Market where men repair metal materials and beat scrap into useful utensils. The area is undergoing a serious makeover, and most stalls will be relocated in modern mall-style buildings in the next few years.

Erer Gate Market   MARKET
(Oromo Market ኤረር በር ገበያ; Old Town) At the eastern end of the old town, Erer Gate was the one Richard Burton entered in 1854, disguised as an Arab merchant. The *chat* market is found here.

Fallana Gate Market   MARKET
(ፈላና በር ገበያ; Old Town) This attractive gate to the north is the site of a colourful market. A *chat* market, one of many in the city, is also found here.

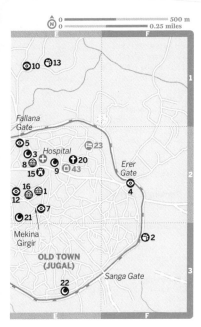

Livestock Market MARKET
(ከብት ገበያ; New Town; ⊙9am-2pm Mon-Fri)
North of Fallana Gate the weekday livestock
market features cows, goats and sheep, but
no camels – these are sold at Babille.

◉ Old Town

Harar's old walled town (known as Jugal;
በግንብ የታጠረ ከተማ) is a fascinating place
that begs exploration. The thick, 5m-high
walls running 3.5km around town were
erected in the 16th century in defensive response to the migrations northwards of the
Oromo, and little development occurred outside them until the early 20th century. There
are six gates: five 16th-century originals and
the car-friendly **Harar Gate**, also known as
Duke's Gate after Ras Makonnen, the first
Duke of Harar, who added it in 1889. The
photograph on this gate is of Emir Abdulla-
hi, the last of Harar's 72 emirs and the city's
last Muslim leader. The nearby **Shoa Gate**
and the **Buda Gate** (Bedri Bari) are also
attractive, though they no longer have their
wooden doors. **Erer Gate** (Argob Bari), the
one Richard Burton entered through, and
the little-used **Sanga Gate** (Suqutat Bari)
lie to the east. To the north is busy **Fallana
Gate** (Assum Bari). Within the walls the city
is a maze of narrow, twisting alleys replete
with historic buildings, including 82 mostly
tiny mosques (two dating back to the 10th
century), more than 100 shrines and tombs,
and about 2000 traditional Harari houses.

Fear not: you can't get lost in the old town
for too long. It is so compact that no matter
how deep you get into the maze of alleyways
you'll eventually come to a wall or a larger
street that will lead you to the bustling central square, Feres Magala (Horse Market).

What breathes life into these landmarks
is the community that still lives within the
city walls. Prepare to encounter the magnificent Adare (Harari) women, known for
their colourful dress, and the sweat-soaked
blacksmiths near Buda Gate who still labour
over open fires.

You'll also find a number of shrines devoted to local religious leaders. They're peaceful, interesting and well-kept places, but
they're unsigned and so hard to find. Most
are under large trees. The caretaker will expect a Birr20 tip for unlocking the door.

Arthur Rimbaud Center MUSEUM
(የሪምባ ቤት; Old Town; Birr50; ⊙8am-noon &
2-5pm Mon-Sat, 8am-noon Sun) Near the middle of the walled city, and often mistakenly called Rimbaud's House, is this museum
dedicated to French poet Arthur Rimbaud
with a series of illustrated wall panels about
his life. It's in an attractive Indian merchant
house built on the site of an earlier house
where it's said Rimbaud lived. There's an
excellent photographic exhibition of turn-
of-the-20th-century Harar – with several of
the photos taken by Rimbaud – that show
some similarities to the city of today but also
significant differences.

In front is a women's association where
you can sometimes see basket weaving. If
you're looking for gifts, there are colourful
baskets for sale.

Feres Magala SQUARE
(ፈረስ መጋሪ; Old Town) The main square is a
bustling place with several minor points of
interest. Most conspicuous is the monument
to those who died fighting against Menelik's
conquest of Harar. It shows the five original
gates. To the east is the rather unimpressive
Medhane Alem Cathedral, built by Ras Makonnen on the site of an Egyptian mosque.

Queen Taitu's Palace ARCHITECTURE
(የንግስት ጣይቱ ቤተመንግስት; Old Town)
What is called Queen Taitu's Palace, next
door to Ras Makonnen's Palace, was neatly

Harar

restored and now shelters a training centre for craft makers.

Gidir Magala
MARKET

(ጊደር መጋላ; Old Town) Gidir Magala (previously known as the Muslim market) is the main market and the city's biggest butchery. Watch how the locals hide their meat purchases from the black kites that fearlessly swoop down trying to steal them.

Mekina Girgir
STREET

(መኪና ጊርጊር; Old Town) Leading southeast from Feres Magala, this narrow, atmospheric street is jam-packed with tailors' workshops, which is how it came to be called 'Sewing Machine Sound St'.

Jamia Mosque
MOSQUE

(ጃሚያ መስጊድ; Old Town) Harar's great mosque is the only one inside the wall big enough to host both men and women. The mosque was built in the 16th century, though according to local tradition a mosque has stood on the site since the 12th century. While not architecturally distinct, its white-tile minarets can be seen from all over the city. It's off-limits to non-Muslims.

Ras Makonnen Statue
STATUE

(ራሱ መኮንን ሀውልት) In the centre of Ras Makonnen Sq stands a rather Italian-looking, equestrian statue of the *ras* (duke) cast in bronze by the well-known Amhara artist Afewerk Tekle. The *ras* is said to look towards Somalia and the lands conquered here. Ras Makonnen was Emperor Menelik's cousin and was appointed first ruler of Harar after the emperor's occupation of the city. The *ras* is also known as the father of the Emperor Haile Selassie.

Ras Tafari's House & Sherif Harar City Museum
MUSEUM

(የራሱ ተፈሪ ቤቶችና ሸሪፍ ሐረር ከተማ ሙዚየም; Old Town; Birr50) Close to Rimbaud's House, the conspicuous Ras Tafari's House was built by an Indian trader and many of its features, such as the Ganesh carving above the door, are Eastern in origin. Haile Selassie spent his honeymoon here: hence the house bears his precoronation name. It's now home to a well-organised museum that houses a private collection of weaponry, coins, jewellery, household tools, old manuscripts and cultural dress. The owner will probably offer to show you his book-restoration workshop upstairs.

Ras Makonnen's Palace
PALACE

(የራስ መኮንን ቤተ መንግስት; Old Town) Don't expect a fairy-tale castle. This late-19th-century 'palace' is a sharp-edged, charmless building. You can climb to the top floor and soak up the views.

St Mary Catholic Church
CHURCH

(ቅድስት ማርያም ካቶሊክ ቤተርርስቲያን; Old Town) One of just two churches in Old Harar, St Mary Catholic Church is a haven of peace and a good spot if you need to unwind. It's a French Catholic mission dating from 1889. The carved wooden door is particularly attractive.

Harar National Museum
MUSEUM

(የሐረር ብሔራዊ ሙዚየም; Old Town; Birr30; ☉8am-noon & 2-5pm Mon-Fri, 8am-noon Sat & Sun) This modest museum across the road from Ras Makonnen's Palace hosts household artefacts, traditional costumes, weapons and jewellery.

Tomb of Sheikh Abadir
ISLAMIC TOMB

(የሼክ አባድር መቃብር; Old Town) The tomb of Sheikh Abadir, Harar's legendary founder and second emir, is an important pilgrimage site. His tomb still attracts worshippers seeking solutions to daily struggles, and if their prayers are answered devotees return with gifts of rugs, incense or expensive sandalwood. Non-Muslims are usually refused entry, but might be allowed in during the Thursday night gatherings (around midnight) when devotees come to play drums, read the Quran and pay respect.

Tomb of Said Ali Hamdogn
ISLAMIC TOMB

(የሰዒድ አሊ ሀምዶኝም መቃብር; Old Town) Said Ali Hamdogn was an important 12th-century religious leader. His whitewashed tomb can easily be visited; it looks a little like a miniature mosque without the minaret. Local tradition has it that below his tomb lies a well that can sustain the whole city in times of siege.

Medhane Alem Cathedral
CATHEDRAL

(መድህኒዓለም ካቴድራል; Feres Megala) On the east side of Feres Megala is this rather unimpressive cathedral, built by Ras Makonnen in 1890 on the site of an Egyptian mosque.

Emir Nur's Tomb
ISLAMIC TOMB

(የኢሚር ኑር መቃብር; Old Town; Birr30; ☉7am-6pm) Emir Nur's Tomb resembles a spiky green beehive. It's devoted to the ruler

EASTERN ETHIOPIA HARAR

ADARE HOUSES

A distinct architectural feature in Harar, the *gegar* (traditional Adare house) is a rectangular, two-storey structure with a flat roof. The house is carefully constructed to remain cool whatever the outside temperature: clay reinforced with wooden beams that is then whitewashed. Sometimes bright colours adorn the facades, but the old style of uncovered stone remains common. A small courtyard, usually facing east, is often shared by several families.

The upstairs room used to serve as a food storeroom; today it acts as a bedroom. The main living room consists of five raised platforms of different levels, which are covered in rugs and cushions. Guests and members of the household sit on the platform befitting their status. These platforms are usually painted bright red to symbolise the blood that every Harari was prepared to shed during the resistance against Menelik.

Hung on the walls are colourful baskets and black wooden bowls. Eleven niches are built into the wall for cups, pots, plates, Qurans and, these days sometimes, expensive electronics. One shelf always holds four *aflala* (tall clay containers) that are used to store money, gold, medicine and seeds. Every house also has a rack for spears.

A rolled carpet on the rack above the front door indicates an eligible daughter resides within. After marriage, newlyweds retire to a tiny room that lies to the left of the living quarters. They remain there for one whole week, during which time they are passed food and water through a hatch.

who built the city's walls, and his wife is also buried inside. You enter the tomb normally, but when leaving, you should back out.

◎ New Town

Everything outside the walls counts as the new town; most of it sits alongside the avenue heading west from Harar Gate.

Eastern Hyena
Feeding Site
WILDLIFE ENCOUNTER

(ጅብ መመገቢያ ስፍራ; Birr100; ⊙ from 6.30pm) One of Harar's two infamous hyena feeding sites, it is located about 1.5km east of Erer Gate (near the garbage dump). This site is usually more productive than the other one because of its isolation and location near the garbage dump (although there's no guarantee).

The first sight of Africa's second-largest predator is usually of vague shadows and luminous green eyes as they skulk in and out of the shadows. As the pack grows more confident, they dart forward with their peculiar gait until all reservations are lost and they approach the hyena men to be fed, literally climbing on top of them to make a show of it. If you're game you can feed them yourself, holding the meat stick in your hands or mouth. Most people go with a guide, but it's not required. If you don't have your own wheels, take a taxi (from Birr150) – it costs more than a *bajaj* but it's worth it because they have brighter headlights.

Northern Hyena
Feeding Site
WILDLIFE ENCOUNTER

(ጅብ መመገቢያ ስፍራ; Birr100; ⊙ from 6.30pm) A highlight of any visit to Harar, this impressive spectacle at the Fallana Gate begins around 6.30pm. There are generally two to four hyenas that make an appearance after the 'hyena man' calls them. If none turn up, you'll be taken to a nearby hyena den where hyenas can be seen with their pups.

Harar Brewery
BREWERY

(ሐረር ቢራ ፋብሪካ) Built by the Czechs in 1984 and purchased by Heineken in 2011, this is a very modern brewery. Tours are sometimes available in the morning – contact local Harar guides to arrange a visit.

Mikael Cemetery
CEMETERY

(ሚካኤል መካነ-መቃብር) You don't come to this place below Mikael Church for the graves, but for the excellent views of the old town from the road below them. Photography is best in the afternoon. A contract *bajaj* should cost Birr30. If the driver doesn't know it, tell him Deker Condominium.

☞ Tours

Good city maps are sold at most of Harar's museums, but for your first foray it's quite a good idea to hire a guide. Guides know the location of less-visited corners and the best Harari houses and arts-and-crafts shops. They can also arrange vehicles for out-of-town excursions, but note that hire costs are high here and 4WDs are rare.

Although there are official guides (ask to see their ID), there's no official price. Birr500 a day is standard for a small group. Most people arrange a guide through their hotel and most hotels only work with good guides. Three guides that come particularly recommended are:

Biniyam Woldesemayat (☑ 091 344 8811; biniym.weld@yahoo.com)

Hailu Gashaw (☑ 091 307 2931; hailu_harar@yahoo.com)

Abdul Ahemed (☑ 091 574 0864)

⊨ Sleeping

For a town so touristy, there's a dearth of quality places to stay, but there are plans to build tourist-class hotels with modern amenities. Alternatively, you could base yourself in Dire Dawa, which has better facilities.

Most of the commendable places are outside the walled town, but if you're after an original experience, consider staying in one of the Adare homes now functioning as a guesthouse in the old town.

Belayneh Hotel
HOTEL $

(☑ 025 666 2030; New Town; d/tw Birr300/350; 🛜) The big drawcards here are the balcony views over the Shoa Gate Market and the hotel's proximity to the bus station and old town. The rooms themselves are noisy and tired, but will do for a night's kip. Give the bathrooms a smell test before choosing a room; some won't pass.

Steer clear of the top-floor restaurant – the fodder is as bland as the dining room.

Tana Hotel
HOTEL $

(☑ 091 532 1143; New Town; d/tw Birr250/270; 🅿 🛜) This large outfit up the hill on the Dire Dawa road is a solid budget choice. The odd cockroach or two aside, the rooms are cleaner, the staff friendlier and the water more reliable than others in this price range. The rooms come with squat or flush toilets, and most rooms have hot shower.

There's a restaurant specialising in grilled meat out front.

Tewodros Hotel
HOTEL $

(✆ 092 083 3295; New Town; d Birr250, with shared bathroom Birr150; P) Not many places pride themselves on their view of the local garbage pile, but guests in some of the east-facing rooms might see hyenas in the early morning, and they'll surely hear them at night. The hyenas, however, are the only thing recommendable. The rooms and service are simply bad, making this a clear second choice if others are full.

If you're staying here, opt for one of the upstairs rooms, which are marginally better and come with private facilities. There's an on-site cafeteria.

★ Rawda Waber Harari Cultural Guesthouse
GUESTHOUSE $$

(✆ 091 575 6439; Old Town; d/tw with shared bathroom incl breakfast Birr400/700) This genuine Adare house percolates tradition and history into a comfy brew of warm welcome amid exotic decorations. Set in the heart of the old town, down a nondescript side street, the four snug bedrooms share two bathrooms (hot water). The place feels a tad cramped, but that shouldn't mar the experience. Breakfast is in a wonderfully atmospheric living room.

Note that the 'honeymoon suite' has no door separating it from the common lounge. It's about 200m east of Shoa Gate; people will point you the right way.

Anisa Abdella Guesthouse
GUESTHOUSE $$

(✆ 091 533 0011; Old Town; d/tw with shared bathroom incl breakfast Birr400/800) Enter here at your own risk: you may never feel like leaving again! This cocoon-like guesthouse occupies an old Harari house at the northern end of the old town (ask somebody for directions, as it's tucked away in a side street). Rest your head in one of the four well-kept rooms, and marvel at the thoughtfully decorated common areas.

Ras Hotel
HOTEL $$

(✆ 025 666 0027; New Town; s/d/tw incl breakfast Birr550/800/950; P @ ⊛) This Harar institution has had a much-needed facelift, and its rooms are now fresh and comfortable; the corridors, though, are as bare as ever. Room numbers that start with '3' are brighter and have a balcony; avoid the downstairs rooms, which are a tad sombre. Facilities include a good restaurant, bar, ATM and an internet cafe. A new wing is under construction.

Wonderland Hotel
HOTEL $$

(✆ 025 466 1111; wonderlandhotel3@gmail.com; New Town; s/d incl breakfast Birr600/700; P ⊛) Opened in 2016, this efficiently run edifice benefits from a top-notch location, a stone's throw from the Harar Gate and restaurants.

ARTHUR RIMBAUD: A POET ADRIFT

In 1875 one of France's finest poets turned his back on his poetry, his country, his wild living and his lover to reverse his fortunes and see the world. He was just 21 years old, broke and bitter.

By 1880 Arthur Rimbaud had travelled to Germany, Italy, Cyprus and Java (with the Dutch Colonial Army, from which he later deserted) and, in the service of a coffee trader in Aden (Yemen), became the first white man to travel into the Ogaden region of southeastern Ethiopia, finally living like a local in a small house in Harar. His interest in culture, languages and people made him popular and his plain speaking and integrity won him the trust of the chiefs and Ras Makonnen, the governor of Harar. His commercial dealings were equally as colourful and included coffee trading and running guns to King Menelik of Shoa.

In 1891 Rimbaud developed a tumour on his right knee. Leaving Harar in early April, he endured the week's journey to the coast on a stretcher. Treatment at Aden was not a success and Rimbaud continued onto Marseilles, where his right leg was amputated. By this time the cancer had spread and he died later that year at the age of 37.

During his self-imposed exile to Ethiopia, Rimbaud's poetry had become increasingly known in France for its daring imagery and beautiful and evocative language. Sadly this belated recognition brought him little satisfaction and he remained indifferent to his fame until his dying day.

Rooms are bright, well-equipped and good value, especially the upstairs ones, some of which come with great views of the old town. One grumble: there's no lift.

Zubeyda Waber
Cultural Guesthouse   GUESTHOUSE **$$**
(☑ 091 028 4329, 025 666 4692; Old Town; d/tw with shared bathroom incl breakfast Birr400/700) Tucked in an old-town alleyway, this traditional Adare house oozes atmosphere, with five compact yet attractive rooms and a lovingly decorated sitting room; carpets line the floors and colourful baskets and plates adorn the walls. All rooms are different; if privacy is a priority, opt for the slightly more expensive room with private facilities (Birr500 for a couple).

Note that the courtyard here is shared by another family, which makes the experience more authentic but slightly less cosy.

Winta Hotel   HOTEL **$$**
(☑ 091 574 0050; New Town; s/d incl breakfast Birr800/900; P 🖘) Winta is a quiet, reliable, 12-room venture near the top of the hill in the new town. Rooms are clean and fine, if undistinguished, and despite the out-of-the-way location, it's an amenable choice. The attached restaurant serves inexpensive local-style meals.

Heritage Plaza Hotel   HOTEL **$$**
(☑ 025 666 5137; www.plazahotelharar.com; New Town; s/d/tw incl breakfast Birr610/810/901; P 🖘) Despite unattractive and faded yet spacious rooms (that don't come anywhere near the quality they should for the price) and lots of road noise, the 'Plaza' is an ac-

ceptable backup if you need a certain level of comfort. Aim for one of the rooms at the back, with a balcony that overlooks a lushly vegetated garden. There's an on-site restaurant.

★**Grand Gato**   BOUTIQUE HOTEL **$$$**
(☑ 025 466 0036; New Town; d/tw incl breakfast Birr1500/2000; P 🖘) This great collection of 14 stylish suites – at what is possibly the first hotel with an ounce of character in Harar – is perfect for well-heeled travellers who are after some sophistication. Spacious rooms with pristine bathroom and balcony are awash with calming tones, boldly accented by carpet or laminate floors and lavish furniture.

Ask for a room at the rear of the building, which is quieter.

🍴 Eating & Drinking

If you're pining for a beer, try a locally brewed Harar brand, a light-bodied lager, or Hakim stout. And of course, you'll want to try Harari coffee: it's hailed as among the best in the world. Cafes are plentiful in the new town, and most accommodation options have bars. If you want to rub shoulders with the locals, make a beeline for **National Hotel** (New Town; ⊙8pm-1am) or **Samson Hotel** (Old Town; ⊙9am-11pm), both of which have a nightclub.

★**Hirut Restaurant**   ETHIOPIAN **$**
(☑ 096 217 4799; New Town; mains Birr75-100; ⊙11am-11pm) Decorated with traditional woven baskets and specialising in authentic local cuisine, this is the most atmospheric place in Harar to sink your teeth into a

---

HYENA FEEDING

Possibly Harar's greatest attraction is the ritual feeding of hyena by the 'hyena men' of Harar. As night falls (beginning around 6.30pm), two sets of 'hyena men' set themselves up outside the city walls: one east of Erer Gate and the other north of Fallana Gate. The ritual starts by calling the hyena by name. Up to 10 individuals may make appearance on busy nights, but note that sightings are *not* guaranteed.

The practice of feeding scraps of meat to hyenas began in the 1950s. The original hyena man started doing it to acquire good luck, but when some tourists started showing up he realised he could make money, too. The inspiration is an older tradition in which hyenas were given porridge to discourage them from attacking livestock during a drought. Following that, an annual feeding began during a festival called Ashura, in which hyenas were fed porridge as a foretelling of the city's fortune for the upcoming year.

Many hyenas roam Harar's streets at night and if you go for an after-hours stroll, especially in Old Harar, you might just meet them. It's a frightening experience, but we've been assured multiple times that they pose no risk.

filling *kwanta firfir* (dried strips of beef rubbed in chilli, butter, salt and *berbere*) or swill a glass of Gouder wine. It also serves a selection of pizzas, salads and sandwiches.

The choice between the cosy lounge and the well-shaded garden is a difficult one.

Kim Café & Restaurant CAFETERIA $
(New Town; mains Birr50-100) This unmissable spot on the main avenue in the new town has a wide variety of cavity-inducing pastries, as well as excellent fruit juices and acceptable pizzas, burgers, spags and Ethiopian dishes. It's also a great place to grab a coffee and watch the world go by.

Tesh Café & Restaurant CAFETERIA $
(New Town; mains Birr30-120; ⊗7.30am-10pm; 🛜) This trendy cafeteria does a roaring lunchtime trade in sandwiches, burgers, salads, pasta dishes, cakes, pastries and fruit juices. Breakfast is also highly recommended, with a good selection of omelettes and pancakes.

Sherife Restaurant ETHIOPIAN $
(New Town; mains Birr30-140; ⊗7am-3pm) The speciality of this popular Muslim restaurant is *hanid* (goat; you pick which part – the feet, ribs and head are the most popular) served on rice pilaf. *Tibs* and pasta dishes are also available.

Weyzro ('Miss') Zewde INDIAN $
(Harar Gate; samosa Birr2; ⊗5-8pm Mon-Sat) This woman makes what are probably the best samosas (*sambusa* in Amharic) in Harar. Find her and her deep fryer sitting street-side across from Harar Gate.

Misrak Hotel ETHIOPIAN $
(New Town; mains Birr50-70; ⊗7am-10pm) It's the hyenas, not the food, that makes this a special night-time dining option. The animals usually arrive around 8.30pm to scavenge the nearby dumpsters, but if you have some flesh to offer them (hang it on a stick rather than use your hand, of course), they'll come dine at your footpath table. It specialises in raw meat.

★**Fresh Touch Restaurant** EUROPEAN $$
(📞091 574 0109; New Town; mains Birr80-190; ⊗7.30am-11pm; 🛜) The king of restaurants in Harar, snazzy Fresh Touch is a hot favourite among well-heeled locals and visitors. That's all thanks to four winning details: its convenient location near the old town; the uplifting ambience; the attractive open-air terrace;

and the excellent something-for-everyone menu. Try the burgers.

Negeyo Cafe CAFE
(Feres Megala) Overlooking Feres Megala, Negeyo's agreeable terrace is a good place to catch local vibes and enjoy plenty of local colour. It has an appetising selection of cakes and pastries and concocts superb fruit juices. Oh, and it serves delectable coffee.

☆ Entertainment

Tourist Hotel CLUB
(New Town; ⊗8pm-1am) On weekend nights you can barely breathe for the crowds. Expect Ethiopian pop and international hits. This real earthy hang-out can become rough-and-ready, but that's part of the fun.

🛍 Shopping

In some old-town houses, enterprising Adares have set up souvenir shops displaying beautifully made silver and (usually fake) amber jewellery and baskets. None have signs and only a few are outside the compounds (ie, visible when you walk by), but the guides know them all. If you're lucky, some of the women will be weaving when you drop by.

Nure Roasted Harar Coffee COFFEE
(Old Town; ⊗8am-noon & 2-6pm Mon-Sat) One step inside and the swoon-inducing scents will have you hooked. It sells 1kg and 500g packets of excellent whole and ground beans, and you can watch the sorting, roasting and grinding.

ℹ Information

Free wi-fi is now almost standard in most Harar hotels and some cafes and restaurants. Otherwise, you'll find a few internet cafes in the new town as well as **Ras@Internet Café** (New Town; per hr Birr24; ⊗8am-6pm Mon-Sat) inside Ras Hotel.

Banks with foreign-exchange facilities and ATMs can be found in the new town alongside the avenue heading west from Harar Gate.

Awash International Bank (New Town; ⊗8am-6pm Mon-Fri, to 2pm Sat)

Commercial Bank (New Town; ⊗8-11.30am & 1.30-4.30pm Mon-Fri, 8-11am Sat)

Tourist Office (📞025 666 9300; Ras Makonnen's Palace, Old Town; ⊗8am-noon & 2-5pm Mon-Fri) Can help with finding a guide.

WORTH A TRIP

KOREMI

With its superb architecture and dramatic setting, the clifftop village of Koremi (ኮረሚ), 19km southeast of Harar above the Erer Valley, is a definite must-see. It's the largest of several villages of the Argoba, a deeply traditional people whose ancestors arrived in these parts in the 12th century. Unlike most of the Adare homes of Harar, the old stone houses here are unpainted and unplastered.

Though some sheet-metal roofs detract from the ambience a bit, this shows what Harar looked like before modernisation.

There is no scheduled transport to Koremi so it is best to hire both a guide and a contract taxi in Harar. Expect some hassles by the local kids.

ⓘ Getting There & Away

AIR

There are no direct flights to Harar. The nearest airport is in Dire Dawa, from where you can catch a minibus to Harar.

BUS

The **bus station** (New Town) is near Harar Gate. Minibuses run frequently to Dire Dawa (Birr20, one hour) and Babille (Birr12, 45 minutes). There are also frequent buses to Jijiga (Birr42, 1½ hours).

For Addis Ababa (nine to 10 hours), **Sky Bus** (New Town; Birr300) and **Selam Bus** (New Town) (Birr330) depart around 5am from their ticket offices on the north side of the main road to Addis Ababa, between Harar Gate and Ras Makonnen Circle. The minibuses that do the capital run are less comfortable and more dangerous than the buses, but they do travel faster and they'll pick you up at your hotel. You can book minibus tickets departing for Addis with **Adil Transport** (☑ 091 195 5521; New Town). You can also buy tickets from your hotel, but you'll pay a commission. Most minibuses leave between 4am and 2pm.

Around Harar

Babille Elephant Sanctuary   WILDLIFE RESERVE
(ባቢሌ የዝሆኖች መጠለያ; Birr90, vehicle Birr20, mandatory scout Birr200; ☉ 7am-6pm)

Despite considerable tree cutting, livestock grazing and land encroachment, Babille is better protected than many of Ethiopia's national parks, and the population of elephants (which some authorities identify as a unique subspecies, *Loxodonta africana orleansi*) has risen to around 400. Also resident, though unlikely to be seen, are lions (notable for their black manes), leopards, Menelik's bushbucks, Soemmerring's gazelles and greater and lesser kudus. The bird list is at least 227 species strong.

The best way to see the elephants is to drive through the Erer Valley, which comprises the majority of the 6982-sq-km sanctuary, to near where they were last spotted and then get out and walk. With enough patience and perseverance you stand a good chance (but no guarantee) of finding them. They prefer the thick brush so are difficult to see clearly, but you can often get quite close. Wear long trousers; there are many thorn trees and cacti.

The signed turn-off is 20km from Harar on the Jijiga road at Kile, and then it's another 12km to the office. Except during heavy rain, a taxi or minibus can handle the road through the reserve.

Camping (per tent Birr20) is allowed anywhere, but there are no facilities.

★ **Babille Market**   MARKET
(ባቢሌ ገበያ; Babille; ☉ 10am-2pm Mon & Thu)
If you're travelling east of Harar on a Monday or Thursday, don't miss the super-atmospheric livestock market in the village of Babille – it's one of Ethiopia's biggest, attracting buyers of camels, cows, donkeys and goats from as far as Djibouti and Somaliland. The market runs from about 10am to 2pm, but because sales go fast it's best to visit early. Buses from Harar (Birr12, 45 minutes) are frequent.

Valley of Marvels   CANYON
(ጻከታ) In the Dakhata Valley (better known as the Valley of Marvels), tall rocks have been sculpted into strange, often phallic shapes by the elements. The name oversells things, but the 'Valley of the Pretty Cool' doesn't have the same ring. Most people just see it from the road, but a half-day ramble is the better choice (be sure to go with a guide). The best section of it starts 4km east of Babille on the drive between Harar and Jijiga.

Jijiga

POP 159,300 / ELEV 1696M

There's little to see and less to do in Jijiga (ጅጅጋ), but there's a strong whiff of edgy adventure about the place, and the atmosphere at this seldom-visited capital of the Somali region is noticeably different from the rest of the country. Signs are written in Somali, women are veiled and Arab-style mosques dominate the skyline (on a par with an increasing number of multistorey commercial buildings). Business, including the selling of contraband smuggled in from Somaliland, is unexpectedly brisk – small wonder Jijiga is one of Ethiopia's fastest-growing towns. For travellers it's a convenient stop-off point on the way to Somaliland.

If you've got time to kill, explore the **livestock market** (ከብት ገበያ; Jijiga; ⊙8am-2pm Sat-Thu), about 3km south of the bus station. Go early if you want to see camels, since they tend to sell out fast.

🛏 Sleeping & Eating

ZM Hotel HOTEL **$$**
(☑091 574 1439; Jijiga; incl breakfast d Birr850-950, tw Birr1200; ▣⬤) Opened in 2016, this high-rise on the main thoroughfare is aimed mainly at a business clientele and NGO workers, but the overall package is appealing, with moderately stylish rooms, salubrious bathrooms, professional staff and a respectable restaurant (yes, alcohol is served). What's missing? A lift.

Xamda Hotel HOTEL **$$**
(☑025 775 4678; Jijiga; d incl breakfast Birr500-700, with shared bathroom Birr370; ▣⬤) This locally recommended establishment has friendly service, well-maintained if simple rooms and a generally welcoming atmosphere. Precious perks include a cafeteria and a 1st-floor restaurant serving tasty local and international dishes. It's the sort of place that books up fast, so call ahead. It's on the western outskirts of town.

ℹ Information

Banks with ATMs can be found along the main thoroughfare. They also change currencies.

ℹ Getting There & Away

AIR

Ethiopian Airlines (☑025 775 2030; www. ethiopianairlines.com) operates two to four daily flights to Addis Ababa (US$145, two hours), direct or via Dire Dawa. The airport is 14km out of town (Birr200 in a *bajaj*).

BUS

The bus station is about 3km east of town. Minibuses and a few buses leave frequently throughout the day for Harar (Birr60, 1½ hours) and Togo-Wuchale (Wajaale on the Somaliland side; Birr32, one hour), on the Somaliland border.

There's one regular bus to Addis Ababa (Birr260, 15 hours) at around midnight. More comfortable Selam (Birr300) buses to Addis depart 5am daily from its office in the town centre.

Western Ethiopia

Why Go?

Western Ethiopia is undisturbed and seldom visited, and while its towns are nothing special, it's one of the most beautiful regions in Ethiopia. Rainforests and coffee plantations share the landscape with savannah grasslands, wildlife-rich swamps and high plateaus carpeted in fields of *tef* (an indigenous grass cultivated as a cereal, the base for making *injera*).

As impressive as the scenery is, it's the ethnic diversity that's the real attraction: white-robed highlanders flock to churches while, on the South Sudan border, ritually scarred Nuer people stride across the grasslands with their long-horned cattle. The Anuak people of the Gambela region believe that to continue travelling west is to fall off the edge of the world – they are wrong on this score: the world doesn't end in western Ethiopia, it just feels that way.

Best Places to Eat

➡ Negash Resort (p214)

➡ Baro Gambella Hotel (p218)

➡ Central Jimma Hotel (p213)

➡ Bebeka Coffee Plantation Guesthouses (p210)

Best Places to Sleep

➡ Negash Resort (p214)

➡ Kafa Development Association (KDA) Guesthouse (p215)

➡ Bebeka Coffee Plantation Guesthouses (p210)

➡ Baro Gambella Hotel (p218)

➡ Boni International Hotel (p213)

When to Go
Jimma

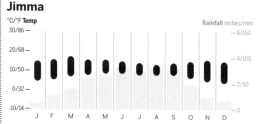

Jan–Mar Huge numbers of antelope move through Gambela National Park.

Oct–Nov Meskel flowers bloom: the countryside glows green and yellow.

Nov-Jan Ethiopia's coffee harvest takes over much of Western Ethiopia.

ℹ️ Getting There & Away

It's possible to fly from Addis to Gambela or Jimma, while the paved road extends ever further westwards with each passing year. If you're coming from the south, distances are long but access has improved since the completion of two road bridges over the Omo River.

AIR

Ethiopian Airlines (www.ethiopianairlines.com) connects Addis Ababa with both Gambela and Jimma three times a week.

BUS

Most areas of Western Ethiopia are covered by regular bus services. During the wet season, however, roads and schedules can fall by the wayside. Along the main paved roads, buses travel between Addis and Nekemte or Jimma, also serving the many towns en route.

It's possible to reach Jimma from Sodo in the south, and Nekemte from the Addis Ababa–Bahir Dar road in the north by public transport, thus letting you connect western Ethiopia with both southern and northern Ethiopia without backtracking to Addis.

CAR & MOTORCYCLE

The road network in Ethiopia's west is rapidly improving and, like elsewhere in Ethiopia, Chinese-led construction crews are in the process of upgrading many roads across the region. It may still be a few years away before they join all of the dots, but plans to provide paved roads all the way from Addis to Gambela are progressing nicely.

THE WESTERN HIGHLANDS

Carpeted in lush forests, dense patchworks of cultivation, shady coffee plantations and deep river valleys, the Western Highlands seem like an Ethiopian Arcadia.

Addis Alem

POP 18,000 / ELEV 2360M

This unremarkable agricultural town 55km west of Addis Ababa was to be the site of Emperor Menelik II's future capital – Addis Alem (አዲስ አለም) literally means 'New World' in Amharic. The emperor had sent engineers and builders to start construction here when Addis Ababa was crippled by late-19th-century firewood shortages. The introduction of eucalyptus trees ended up saving the new flower (Addis Ababa) and

killed the new world. Since then, Addis Alem has settled back into provincial obscurity, although it does have a fine little museum.

St Maryam Church (ቅድስት ማርያም ቤተክርስትያን; Birr100; ◔8am-5.30pm) is Addis Alem's most interesting building. It stands out for its lavish decoration: the basilica's exterior, as well as the *maqdas* (inner sanctuary), is entirely covered with murals. Next door the local **museum** (ሙዚየም; Birr50; ◔9am-noon & 1-3pm) displays some surprising finds for such a nondescript regional town: crowns and clothing belonging to Menelik and Haile Selassie, as well as relics from the Battle of Adwa and a gold inlaid box that local legend says once contained the Ark of the Covenant. The site sits atop a rocky hill 600m south of the main road.

Numerous depart-when-full buses pass Addis Alem heading east to Addis Ababa (Birr24, 1½ hours) and west to Ambo (Birr38, two hours).

Ambo

POP 94,342 / ELEV 2101M

The claim to fame of Ambo (አምቦ) is its mineral water, bottled here and sold throughout Ethiopia. The water is so fizzy that it continues to sparkle even after it's left overnight in a glass! You can't visit the factory, but you can take a dip in the famous **thermal pool** (የአምቦ ፍልውሃ; Mon-Thu Birr20, Fri-Sun Birr30; ◔6am-6pm) run by Ambo Ethiopia Hotel. Despite the murky green colour, the pool is cleaned weekly. The town also offers an interesting Saturday **market** where you can find brightly coloured Ambo baskets.

🛏️ Sleeping

Ambo's accommodation choices are singularly unexciting, but at least you have a handful of options to choose from, unlike many western Ethiopian towns.

Ambo Ethiopia Hotel RESORT $

(☏011 236 2002; per tent Birr120, s/d Birr175/275) Set around flowering gardens, this colonial place has bundles of old-world charm. Though it shows its age in places, notably in the rooms, it's still quite comfortable and some rooms have satellite TV. The classic dining hall (mains Birr50 to Birr90), which alone makes a stay worthwhile, serves Western and Ethiopian selections. It's 150m west of the bus station. Guests have free use of the town's thermal pool.

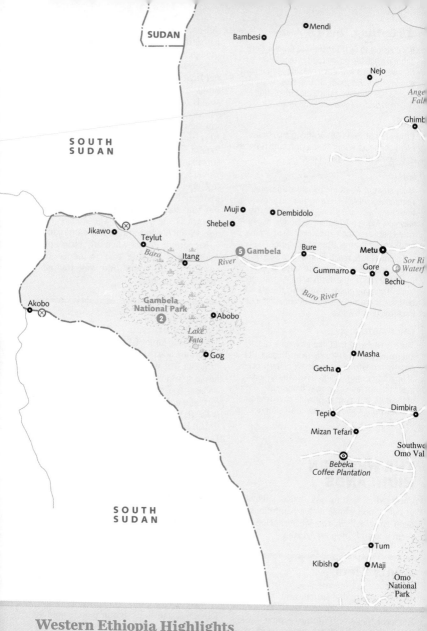

SUDAN

Mendi

Bambesi

Nejo

Ange
Fall

Ghimb

SOUTH
SUDAN

Muji

Dembidolo

Shebel

Jikawo

Teylut

Bure

Metu

Sor Ri
Waterf

Baro

Itang

River

5 Gambela

Gummarro

Gore

Bechu

Baro River

Akobo

Gambela
National Park

2

Abobo

Lake
Tata

Gog

Masha

Gecha

Tepi

Dimbira

Mizan Tefari

Southwe
Omo Val

Bebeka
Coffee Plantation

SOUTH
SUDAN

Tum

Kibish

Maji

Omo
National
Park

Western Ethiopia Highlights

1 Kafa Biosphere Reserve
(p214) Visiting Ethiopia's
first coffee museum and
trekking through wildlife-rich
forests.

2 Gambela National Park
(p220) Falling off the map
as you try to be among the
first to witness one of Africa's
greatest but least-known
migrations.

3 Mt Wenchi (p206)
Climbing aboard a scrawny
horse for a scenic descent into
this pretty lake-filled crater.

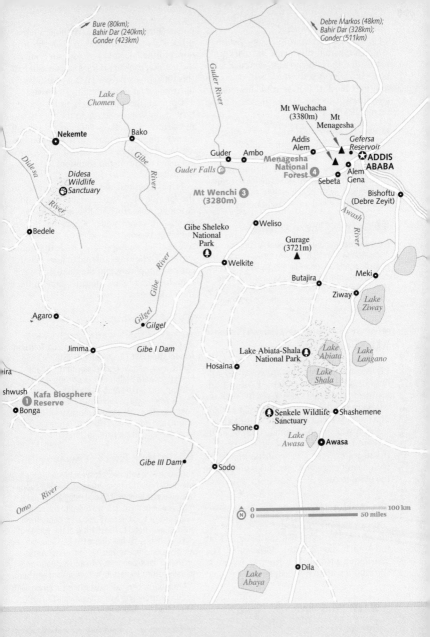

Bure (80km);
Bahir Dar (240km);
Gonder (423km)

Debre Markos (48km);
Bahir Dar (328km);
Gonder (511km)

Guder River

Lake Chomen

Nekemte

Bako

Gibe River

Didesa River

Didesa Wildlife Sanctuary

Bedele

Mt Wuchacha (3380m)

Mt Menagesha

Addis Alem

Gefersa Reservoir

ADDIS ABABA

Guder

Ambo

Menagesha National Forest 4

Sebeta

Alem Gena

Bishoftu (Debre Zeyit)

Guder Falls

Mt Wenchi 3 (3280m)

Weliso

Awash River

Gibe Sheleko National Park

Gurage (3721m)

Welkite

Butajira

Meki

Gibe River

Ziway

Lake Ziway

Gilgel River

Agaro

Gilgel

Gibe I Dam

Jimma

Lake Abiata-Shala National Park

Lake Abiata

Lake Langano

Hosaina

Lake Shala

ira

Kafa Biosphere Reserve 1

shwush

Bonga

Senkele Wildlife Sanctuary

Shashemene

Shone

Lake Awasa

Awasa

Gibe III Dam

Sodo

Omo River

N

0   100 km
0   50 miles

Lake Abaya

Dila

4 Menagesha National Forest (p217) Searching for birds, colobus monkeys and Menelik's bushbucks while meandering the forested slopes.

5 Gambela (p215) Wondering if you're still in Ethiopia (or you've crossed to South Sudan) among the Nuer and Anuak peoples in the country's sultry far west.

Hoteela Jibaatifi Maccaa HOTEL $
(☑ 011 236 2253; d Birr120-180; 🅿) Set in a large compound, this place has cheap old rooms that the cheerful (and commendably honest) owner described as 'bad', or rooms in a new block that have cold showers but are otherwise 'better'. It is located next to the turn-off for Mt Wenchi.

Abebech Metaferia Hotel HOTEL $
(☑ 011 236 2365; tw Birr200-350, d/ste Birr315/450) This modern (and rather ugly) tower, just east of the bus station houses what are feted as Ambo's smartest rooms. This might well be true, but sadly there's zero character and lots of road noise.

🛈 Getting There & Away

A dozen daily minibuses connect Ambo and Addis Ababa (Birr49 to Birr55, three hours) – the price depends on the vehicle type. One daily bus serves Nekemte (Birr85, five hours). For Guder (Birr7, 15 minutes), minibuses run approximately every 30 minutes. The bus station is centrally location on the main street.

Mt Wenchi

ELEV 3280M

Resting within the beautiful collapsed caldera of Mt Wenchi (ወንጪ ተራራ), 31km south of Ambo, is Lake Wenchi, plus an island monastery and several hot springs. The scenery, a patchwork of cultivation run through with the occasional stand of natural forest, is a tonic for the city-weary soul. If you want a quick taste of the highlands within easy reach of Addis, this is absolutely the place to come.

🏃 Activities

You can explore the crater on foot or on horseback – if you'd like the latter, ask at the Wenchi Eco Tourism Association. The association provides the compulsory guide (Birr200 for up to five people) and optional

WALK THIS WAY

There is something peculiar afoot in Ambo. If you look carefully you'll notice that locals use one side of the street for walking east and the other for walking west. This way, they say, they can easily spot out-of-towners who insist on battling the tide of human traffic.

horses (Birr150 per horse). Without a horse, it takes about 45 minutes to walk the 4km down to the lake and just over an hour for the hot slog back up. Horses can do it in half this time. If you have a 4WD it is also possible (though far less rewarding) to drive.

Once at the lake's edge, little wooden boats ferry visitors across to the tiny island monastery of Cherkos. Other than a small church, there isn't much here but you can ask to see the large 'Gonder bell', which once belonged (according to tradition) to Emperor Fasiladas.

From Cherkos the boats continue to the far side of the lake, where you begin a stunning walk (four to five hours in total) through a countryside of grazing horses, babbling brooks (not so good in the wet season) and water-powered mills to the hot springs. The springs are said to have magical curative properties and the caves in the surrounding area house pilgrims, here to treat their afflictions.

🛈 Information

Visiting Lake Wenchi is a refreshingly well-organised experience. The **Wenchi Eco Tourism Association** (WETA; ☑ 091 296 8516, 011 356 0009; www.wenchi-crater-lake.com; ⊙ 8am-5pm) is located a kilometre or so before the parking area on the Ambo side of the crater. This is where you pay your entry fee (Birr50) for boat transfers to the island monastery (Birr50 return) and hot springs (Birr100 return via the monastery), and car parking (Birr50).

🛈 Getting There & Away

For those with vehicles, Mt Wenchi makes for a wonderful day trip from Addis Ababa. For everyone else, it is best visited on Friday and Sunday from Ambo in the north or Weliso to the south, when one or two buses (Birr40, 1½ hours from either town) head to the market at the village of Haro Wenchi, which is where the Eco Tourism Association office is. Buses from either Ambo or Weliso leave between 7am and 8.30am, and usually return sometime between 4pm and 5pm.

A minibus with driver can be hired in Ambo, with a return trip costing a very negotiable Birr1000. Ask at the bus station in Ambo.

Guder

Not far west of Ambo on the road to Nekemte, Guder has little to detain you, but its waterfall is worth a look.

The journey towards Nekemte soon takes you through Guder, 11km west of Ambo.

About 1km from Guder, after crossing the river, you'll see a gate for **Guder Falls** (የጉደር ፏፏቴ; Birr30; ⊙7am-6pm). It isn't spectacular, but is worth a peek in the wet season. The ubiquitous Ethiopian red wine, Gouder, was ostensibly named after the river, and a few vineyards can still be seen covering the surrounding area.

As you climb from Guder the views open up and you'll see endless fields of quilted yellows, reds and greens. Although the views down are great, don't forget to look up, too – there are some impressive columnar basalt flows along the road cut above the town.

About 65km from Ambo you'll reach an escarpment offering westward vistas over distant volcanic landscapes. Heading further west, things become less cultivated. This area is part of the historical Wolega province and is home to gold reserves and precious frankincense. Both still fetch high prices in Middle Eastern and Egyptian markets.

If you want to stay the night, **Guder Falls Recreation Area Hotel** (☑091 189 6012; cottages Birr100) is a peaceful place set above the falls in beautifully tended gardens. Sadly, the same love hasn't been extended to the cottages themselves.

Buses and minibuses travelling between Ambo (Birr7, 15 minutes) and Nekemte (Birr35, 2½ hours) – the leave-when-full kind – pass along Guder's main street and within a short walk of the falls.

Nekemte

POP 115,000 / ELEV 2101M

Nekemte (ነቀምት), 203km west of Ambo, is the sprawling commercial and administrative centre for the Oromia region's East Wolega zone. Although there are few sights besides a museum, Nekemte has decent facilities and makes an obvious spot to break your westward journey.

◉ Sights

Worth a wander is Nekemte's **market** (ገበያ; ⊙7am-5pm Mon-Sat), which bustles most on Wednesday, Thursday and Saturday. Although the **Church of St Gabriel** casts a nice silhouette from town – you can't miss it – it can be classed as better from afar than up close.

Kumsa Moroda Palace HISTORIC BUILDING
(ቁምሳ ሞሮዳ ቤተ መንግስት; Birr50; ⊙9am-noon & 1.30-5pm Tue-Sun) Built by the King

of Wolega in the 1870s, the Kumsa Moroda Palace has only recently been opened to the public after long years of neglect. It sits 1km north of the museum and served as residence to the prominent Worra Bekere family until they were hauled off to Addis Ababa during the Derg. The compound consists of around 10 buildings, and admission includes a guide who can explain what each building was used for – expect enthusiasm but not perfect English.

Outside are a number of places to get a traditional Ethiopian coffee in a park-like setting. Note that opening hours of the palace are a little flexible and on Sunday morning everyone is likely to be at church.

Wolega Museum MUSEUM
(ወለጋ ሙዝየም; Birr50; ⊙9am-12.30pm & 2.30-5.40pm Tue-Sun) The remains of an Italian military plane shot down by the Black Lion Patriots in 1935 proudly sits in front of the Wolega Museum. Inside, displays give a good insight into the Wolega Oromo life and culture with traditional musical instruments, as well as displays of the local spinning, carving and basket-weaving industries. Admission includes a guided tour.

⌸ Sleeping

Nekemte has some of western Ethiopia's best accommodation, at least when it comes to budget variety.

Farm Land Hotel HOTEL $
(☑057 661 5150; d/tw Birr350/400; ⊛) It's not the most exciting hotel we've ever seen, but we like it because it's relatively new and has begun the long descent into decay quite slowly. Unusually for this price, the large rooms have flat-screen TVs and bathrooms you'll be happy to hang about in.

Benori Pension HOTEL $
(☑057 661 4096; brbfjerry@yahoo.com; d from Birr350; ⊛) Sitting on a quiet side street, this modern multistorey hotel has very small, but otherwise exceedingly comfortable rooms with double-glazed windows, satellite TV and good mattresses on the beds. However, compared to similar competition in town it's a smidgen overpriced.

Kebede Hotel HOTEL $
(☑057 661 2394; d Birr150-200; ⊛) The rooms in this multistorey job are kept pretty clean and light streams through the large windows and clean bathrooms. Only in the more expensive rooms have hot water.

Nekemte

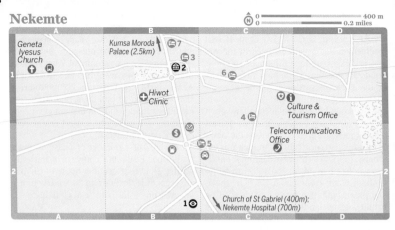

Nekemte

◉ Sights

Adugna Geleta Hotel　　　　　HOTEL **$**
(☑057 661 8225; s/d/tw Birr200/250/300; 🛜) Vast rooms with parquet flooring, well-equipped bathrooms and teeny balconies sitting atop a busy bar and cafe make this a good-value place to bed down for the night.

Desalegn Hotel　　　　　　　　HOTEL **$**
(☑057 661 6162; d with shared/private shower Birr200/300) Rooms here are rather tidy and the kind that you'll have seen often if you're travelling on a budget. Fine for a night.

❶ Information

Commercial Bank (⊙8am-noon & 1-5pm Mon-Fri, 8am-noon Sat)

Hiwot Clinic (☑057 661 2036; ⊙7am-12.30pm & 2-5.30pm) A better bet than the local hospital.

Culture & Tourism Office (☑057 661 1315; ⊙8am-12.30pm & 1.30-5.30pm Mon-Fri) Moderately useful tourist office.

❶ Getting There & Away

Half a dozen buses depart the **bus station** daily to serve Addis Ababa (Birr125 to Birr140 depending on bus quality, eight to 10 hours). Other services include Ambo (Birr85, five hours), Bedele (Birr60, four hours), Dembidolo (Birr155, nine to 10 hours) and one bus a day to Jimma (Birr128, seven to eight hours) at 6am.

Bedele

POP 26,000 / ELEV 2162M

Scrappy Bedele (በደሌ) lies 105km south of Nekemte and sits at an important crossroads linking Metu, Jimma and Nekemte. Besides a tour or tasting session at the celebrated **Bedele beer factory** (በደሌ በ.ራ 4-በረካ; ☑047 445 0134; ⊙8am-4pm Mon-Fri) **FREE**, there's little reason to stop.

If you're stuck in Bedele, try **Peensiyoonii Weqinesh** (d with cold/hot shower Birr100/120). For better options, try Metu.

Between 6am and noon several buses pass Bedele heading for Jimma (bus/minibus Birr65/70, three hours) or to Metu (Birr58, three hours). There's a couple of buses to Nekemte (Birr60, four hours) and, at 6am, a single bus each to Addis Ababa (Birr185, 10 hours) via Jimma and to Gambela (Birr140, eight hours).

Metu

POP 35,000 / ELEV 1600M

Spreading over the slope of a small hill 115km west of Bedele is Metu (መቱ), the capital of the old Ilubador province. For travellers, Metu acts as the primary gateway to the western lowlands, as well as a springboard for trips south – through some of the west's most wild and beautiful scenery – to Tepi and Mizan Tefari. The town itself has little to offer.

◎ Sights

Sor River Waterfalls   WATERFALL

(ሶር ወንዝ ፏፏቱ) A worthwhile excursion from Metu is to the 20m-high Sor River Waterfalls, one of the most beautiful falls in Ethiopia. It lies close to the village of Bechu, 13km southeast of Metu. The last 15 minutes of the one-hour walk (5km) from Bechu takes you through dense forest teeming with birds and monkeys. At the falls, Sor River suddenly drops 20m over the lip of a wide chasm into a fern-lined amphitheatre. You can take a dip in the pool below.

A daily minibus leaves Metu for Bechu (Birr19, one hour) around 7am. It returns as soon as it's full, which means you may have to walk back to Metu or battle a night of fleas in Bechu. To find the falls, enlist the help of a Bechu villager (tip expected) or ask one of the children who invariably tag along. With a 4WD you could make the return trip from Metu in less than four hours.

🛏 Sleeping

If you're going to choose between getting stuck for the night in Bedele or here in Metu, don't hesitate to choose Metu. It's not great but it's a lot better than Bedele! That said, services are still pretty basic.

Sena Hotel   HOTEL **$**

(d Birr150, with shared bathroom Birr100) Sena Hotel is more noteworthy for its restaurant-cum-bar than for its simple rooms, even though its selection of dishes is limited and vegies are few and far between. It's near the Commercial Bank, 1.4km east of the bus station.

Hoteela Antanah   HOTEL **$**

(☑ 047 441 1002; d Birr150-250) Only 50m from the bus station, this is the town's best place to rest weary heads. Its upstairs options are larger and brighter; the dingy downstairs rooms are generally clean but lack the finer touches (like light bulbs and toilet seats).

❶ Getting There & Away

Buses from Metu depart for Gambela (bus/minibus Birr82/108, three hours, several daily), Bedele (Birr58, three hours, five daily) and Addis Ababa (Birr225, 1½ to two days, 6am), all via Jimma (Birr110, eight hours).

To reach Tepi, take a leave-when-full minibus to Gore (Birr12, 35 minutes) then catch a bus to Masha (from Birr30, three hours) and go from there. If you start early enough, you can reach Tepi or Mizan Tefari in a day.

Tepi

POP 27,000 / ELEV 1238M

Tepi (ቴፒ) is famous for its state-owned and -run coffee plantation. It's Ethiopia's second largest, and stretches over 6290 hectares. Just over 20 sq km lies around Tepi, while the remainder – including Beshanwaka, a

---

METU TO TEPI SCENIC DRIVE

The road from Metu to Tepi is one of Western Ethiopia's prettiest drives. In a private vehicle the journey takes between 5½ and seven hours, depending on the season. It's also possible to do it in one day by riding local minibuses, though you'll likely have to change at Gore and Masha.

Twenty-five kilometres south of Metu is the inconsequential junction town of Gore, from where the road strikes south for Tepi and west to Gambela.

Heading south, the road snakes along a ridge and offers sublime vistas over a lush, green quilt of small fields pockmarked with thatched-roof huts, and patches of dense forest ringing with the sound of birds and monkeys. Some of the larger trees, shrouded in vegetation, seem to have ecosystems of their own. You may spot a colobus monkey or two peering from vine-draped trees.

North of muddy Masha you'll pass through rolling hills carpeted in neat tea plantations, before entering thick sections of forest and the occasional stand of bamboo south of town. After Gecha, the road winds through enset ('false-banana' tree) plantations, traditional villages and yet more jungle. As you near Tepi, you'll start to see coffee drying outside homes along the roadside.

beautiful crater lake – is in the Gambela region about 30km away. The plantation produces about 25,000kg of raw arabica coffee each year.

◉ Sights

★ **Coffee Plantation** FARM

(የቡና እርሻ; ☎0475 556 0007, 0475 556 1117) Coffee lovers will love this place and it should be possible to arrange a tour of the plantation by requesting through the **Coffee Plantation Development Enterprise** (☎011 896 2394, 011 896 2395) in Addis Ababa or at the plantation itself, close to the Coffee Plantation Guesthouse. We've never had any problem getting shown around simply by turning up. Unfortunately, it's not possible to buy coffee beans here, but you can do so in various shops around town.

🛏 Sleeping

All of the places to stay in Tepi only have cold-water bathrooms – why not drink a warming coffee straight after?

Coffee Plantation Guesthouse HOTEL $

(☎047 556 0062; d Birr300) The semidetached concrete bungalows vaunt bright-green laminate floors, frilly bedspreads, small verandahs and clean washrooms. If you order ahead, the 'workhouse club' can prepare meals; if not, the cockroaches racing across the ancient coffee machine can at least be considered a form of entertainment.

Genet Guest House HOTEL $

(☎0475 556 2145; d Birr150, with shared bathroom Birr100; P) Four-hundred metres past the main roundabout along the road to Jimma, this fairly new place has clean rooms with tiny bathrooms, built around a courtyard bar and garden.

DIDESA WILDLIFE SANCTUARY

Roughly halfway between Nekemte and Bedele is the 1300-sq-km **Didesa Wildlife Sanctuary**. Although there's currently no access, you'll have a glimpse of its beauty when crossing the Didesa River Bridge. Animals do live here, but the only larger mammals you're really likely to see are baboons on the side of the road.

ⓘ Getting There & Away

Three buses run daily from Tepi to Masha (Birr55, three hours) and onward to Gore and occasionally Gambela. From Gore there are frequent minibuses to Metu (Birr12, 35 minutes). One, sometimes two, buses serve Jimma (Birr130, seven hours) daily. For Mizan Tefari (Birr35, 1½ hours), seven buses run daily.

Mizan Tefari

POP 28,000 / ELEV 1451M

The stunningly sited small town of Mizan Tefari (ሚዛን ተፈሪ), the old capital of the Bench people, serves as a base for a visit to the Bebeka Coffee Plantation.

◉ Sights

★ **Bebeka Coffee Plantation** FARM

(በበቃ የቡና እርሻ; ☎047 111 8621) The 93-sq-km Bebeka Coffee Plantation, 28km southwest of Mizan Tefari (an hour's drive), is Ethiopia's largest and oldest coffee farm. There are no longer any official tours, but you may be able to wrangle a letter of introduction by calling the **Coffee Plantation Development Enterprise** (☎011 896 2394, 011 896 2395; Main Rd; ⊗8am-5.30pm Mon-Fri) and pleading your case once at the farm. Armed with such a letter and your own 4WD (the plantation is far too big to take in on foot), the manager will usually provide a guide

🛏 Sleeping

As impressive as Mizan Tefari's setting is, lolling across luminous green hills, the town itself is a bit of a dump and perhaps even the most unappetising town on the western Ethiopia tourist circuit. Unfortunately, though, unless you have private transport to get you to the Bebeka Coffee Plantation Guesthouses, you'll probably have to spend a night here.

★ **Bebeka Coffee Plantation Guesthouses** GUESTHOUSE $

(☎091 376 1742; campsites Birr75, d/tw Birr200/400, cottages Birr500-700) Set in the thick of the coffee plantation and surrounded by birdlife, there's little doubt that this is the best place to stay in the vicinity of Mizan Tefari. It's simply the very definition of tranquillity. Rooms are impressively clean and have high ceilings, giving them a colonial feel, but they're also fairly simple and, on the downside, only have cold-water bathrooms.

KING SOLOMON'S GOLD

The Old Testament describes King Solomon's famous temple in Jerusalem as being overlaid with the purest of gold, brought from the mines of Ophir. Just where this mysterious Ophir was located has long baffled historians and archaeologists, and over the centuries it has provided grist to the mill of thousands of dreamers, writers and explorers.

The candidates for the title of the Biblical Ophir have ranged from India to Haiti and China to Zimbabwe. But others claim that the real location of the gold mines of Ophir is close to modern day Nejo in western Ethiopia. Certainly, there is some evidence to indicate that this might just be true. The Ancient Egyptians are known to have mined gold in Nubia (close to the border with western Ethiopia) and we know that Ethiopia also has reserves of gold that have been mined for a very long time. And the oldest of all these ancient mines are thought to be the open quarries close to the small town of Nejo, northwest of Nekemte, where locals still sometimes dig up shards of pottery that point to an ancient civilisation here.

For a rollicking adventure story on this fascinating topic, get hold of a copy of Tahir Shah's book *In Search of King Solomon's Mines* (2002).

Superb Ethiopian meals (mains Birr30 to Birr60) are available in the restaurant.

Hotel Salayish HOTEL $
(☑ 047 333 0542; d Birr500, with shared bathroom Birr400) This 26-room hotel is widely considered the town's top choice; while that might well be true, it's hardly a ringing endorsement. The newer rooms are bright and far better than those in the older wing. Like the hotel, the downstairs restaurant (mains Birr35 to Birr70) is regarded by locals as the best place in town to eat.

❶ Getting There & Away

Buses from Mizan Tefari run to Tepi (Birr35, two hours, seven daily) and Jimma (Birr98, 7½ hours, one daily).

Since you require your own 4WD for a tour of Bebeka Coffee Plantation itself, there's little point arriving there on foot; don't worry about public transport.

Jimma

POP 207,573 / ELEV 1678M

Western Ethiopia's largest city, and a major university town, Jimma (ጅማ) is a raucous place with wide, dusty streets, lots of honking horns and a massive coffee pot rising from its main roundabout. The town has a fairly substantial expat community (most of whom are involved with NGOs), but for a tourist there's little real reason to linger other than to get to an ATM and break up a *long* journey.

History

For centuries, a powerful Oromo monarchy ruled the surrounding fertile highlands from its capital at Jiren (now a suburb of present-day Jimma). The region owed its wealth to its position at the crux of several major trade routes and to its abundant crops. At its height, the kingdom stretched over 13,000 sq km. When Menelik came to power in the late 1800s, he required the region to pay high tribute.

When the Italians entered the picture in the 1930s, they had grand plans to create a modern city in the heart of Ethiopia's breadbasket and Jimma was subsequently born from Jiren. Neither Italian rule nor the grand plans lasted long.

◉ Sights & Activities

Palace of Abba Jiffar PALACE
(የአባ ጅፋር ቤተ መንግስት; Birr50; ⊙ 9am-noon & 2-5pm Wed-Thu & Sat-Mon) Looking more out of America's Wild West than the Kafa kingdom, the increasingly fragile Palace of Abba Jiffar looks as if a strong wind could blow it away. It sits atop a hill 7km northeast of Jimma's town centre, near the village of Jiren, and has views back down over Jimma that are worth the price of admission alone. To get here either take a minibus (Birr8) from the marketplace in town or contract a taxi for the visit (Birr200, including waiting time).

King Jiffar (1852–1933), who was one of the most important Kafa kingdom rulers, held power at the end of the 19th century. The palace contains a private family

Jimma

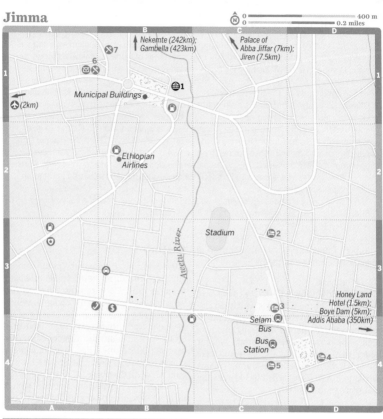

Jimma

◎ Sights
1 Jimma Museum	B1

🛏 Sleeping
2 Boni International Hotel	C3
3 Central Jimma Hotel	C3
4 Temky Pension	D4
5 Wolde Aregaw & Family Hotel	C4

✕ Eating
6 Café Variety	A1
Central Jimma Hotel	(see 3)
7 Jimma Degitu Hotel	B1
Wolde Aregaw & Family Hotel	(see 5)

mosque (still in use) and rooms that served as library, throne room, reception chamber, king's guard room, sentry tower, courthouse and guesthouse. Almost 1.6km back down the hill lies the king's tomb.

Municipal Buildings ARCHITECTURE
If you're a connoisseur of Italian Fascist architecture, take a peek at Jimma's municipal buildings.

Jimma Museum MUSEUM
(ጅማ ሙዚየም, Muuziyemii Jimmaa; ☎047 111 5881; Birr50; ☺9am-noon & 2-5pm) Admission to the Muuziyemii Jimmaa includes a guided tour in English of the museum's seven small rooms. We don't want to steal the guide's thunder (such as it is), but our favourite pieces include a ceremonial throne that cost Birr146,000 to build but was only used by Haile Selassie for 20 minutes, and a royal portable toilet that looks like a frying pan with a hole in it.

Other oddities include a poster with the entire Quran written on it in a script of almost microscopic proportions, and an Italian-made walking stick–cum-gun.

Boye Dam
BIRDWATCHING

(የቦዬ   ግድብ; Birr50, vehicle Birr100; ☺ sunrise-sunset) Located 5km southeast of Jimma off the road to Addis, the dam has some good birdwatching opportunities, but take the locals' claims of hippos with a hippo-sized pinch of salt. There are also caves and hot springs in the vicinity.

🛏 Sleeping

The choice of hotels in Jimma is arguably the best in western Ethiopia, although remember that we're starting from a pretty low base. Jimma hotels have openly embraced the *faranji* (foreigner) price scheme – the one where you pay double!

Central Jimma Hotel
HOTEL $

(☎ 047 111 8283; d with shared bathroom Birr100, d with private bathroom Birr120-200, tw Birr150-250; ⊠) The courtyard and garden bar-and-pool complex at this old-timer are abuzz with the constant activity of people coming and going (Sunday lunchtime it's simply THE place to be in Jimma). The rooms are unfussy, clean and a good size and come in an array of styles and prices. Room rates include the use of the pool (which is otherwise Birr25/50 on weekdays/weekends).

Temky Pension
HOTEL $

(☎ 047 111 2565; d with shared/private bathroom Birr140/200, tw Birr250) The large lawn, garden tables and cleanish rooms make this the best budget option in town. However, the music in the lively garden courtyard can be irritating for those needing an early night and the rooms don't warrant close contemplation if you're struggling to sleep.

Wolde Aregaw & Family Hotel
HOTEL $

(☎ 047 111 2731; d Birr200-450, tw Birr500; ☏) If you can cope with the noise of all the early buses departing town in the neighbouring bus station, blurting out their horns at 6am, then this place offers really quite decent value. The cheaper rooms are better value, although hotel staff only reluctantly rent these to 'rich *faranji*'.

Honey Land Hotel
HOTEL $$

(☎ 047 111 1515; d Birr480-800; ℗☏) Way out on the eastern fringes of Jimma's town centre, on the road to Addis, this place touts itself as the best hotel in town – with undeniably comfortable rooms that might well be true. It seems overpriced compared to other options in town.

THE ETHIOPIAN SLAVE TRADE

Ethiopia's slave trade was a lucrative one. From the 16th century right up to the 19th century, the country's main source of foreign revenue was from slaves. At the height of the trade, it's estimated that 25,000 Ethiopian slaves were sold every year..

Boni International Hotel
HOTEL $$

(☎ 047 211 5065; www.facebook.com/Boni-International-Hotel-Jimma-1450489475221394; s/d/tw US$25/35/40; ☏) One of the newest places in Jimma, the Boni is probably the pick of the in-town options. Rooms are quieter than most despite the central location and the restaurant has a wide-ranging menu.

🍴 Eating

Central Jimma Hotel
INTERNATIONAL $

(mains Birr40-90; ☺6am-10pm) For a fine view of the bus station, a cold beer and some cheap eats, stick to the hotel's roadside cafe. For shish kebab, chicken Maryland and grilled fish, head to the more upmarket poolside Sennait Restaurant. For locals this is THE place to eat at weekends.

Wolde Aregaw & Family Hotel
INTERNATIONAL $

(mains Birr35-110; ☺6am-10pm) The wood panelling and calf-skin decor give this a lived-in vibe, and if you're at a loose end you can watch the satellite TV in the bar while munching on a steak sandwich. Next door, the restaurant serves meals such as *doro arrosto* (roast chicken) and spaghetti.

Jimma Degitu Hotel
INTERNATIONAL $

(mains Birr45-95) The *faranji* food here is quite good (if you remember you're in Ethiopia) and more varied than elsewhere – think an OK cheeseburger with cold fries. The pizzas are also worthy of mention.

Café Variety
CAFE $

(light meals Birr30; ☺6am-10pm) Its shaded terrace vaunts the best selection of cakes in Jimma. It's popular with students, who flock here for the juice and coffee.

🔒 Shopping

Thursday is the main market day in town; seek out the famous three-legged stools, basketwork and locally renowned honey.

WESTERN ETHIOPIA JIMMA

COFFEE

At some point between the 5th and 10th centuries, in the Ethiopian kingdom of Kafa, an astute herder named Kaldi noticed that his goats were behaving rather excitedly each time they ate a certain plant's berries. Trying it himself, he discovered that after a few chews and a couple of swallows, he was one hyper herder! When he told the local monastery they reprimanded him for 'partaking of the devil's fruit' and flung the berries on the fire. They soon changed their minds, however, when they smelt the aroma emanating from the now-roasting coffee beans.

Soon the monks were drying the berries for transport and shipping them to Ethiopian monasteries far and wide. There, priests would rehydrate them in water, eat the fruit and drink the fluids to keep themselves awake for nocturnal prayers.

In time, Arabs began importing the bean, and in the 15th century the Turks brewed the roasted beans into the drink we know today. From Turkey, coffee spread to Europe via Italy and then to Indonesia and the Americas.

Coffee is now the top agricultural export for 12 countries, with the livelihood of over 100 million people depending on its production. It has become the world's second-most-valuable commodity after petroleum!

🛈 Information

Dashen Bank (⊘ 8am-noon & 1-5pm Mon-Fri, 8am-noon Sat) Currency-exchange services and an ATM that accepts Visa. There's another Dashen ATM outside the Honey Land Hotel.

🛈 Getting There & Away

AIR

Ethiopian Airlines (☑ 047 111 0030; www. ethiopianairlines.com; ⊘ 8am-5.30pm Mon-Sat) flies daily from Jimma to Addis Ababa (Birr2622, one hour to 2½ hours).

BUS

Selam Bus (☑ 011 554 4831) has a daily bus from Jimma to Addis Ababa (Birr205, six to seven hours) at 6am.

There are numerous ordinary buses throughout the day for Addis Ababa (Birr125 to Birr145, seven hours). The gates to the **bus station** compound usually open around 6am. Get your elbows ready and be prepared for a mad scramble.

Amid the early morning free-for-all you'll find buses for Tepi (Birr 130, eight hours), Mizan Tefari (Birr98, 7½ hours), Metu (Birr110, eight hours), Bedele (Birr66, 4½ hours) and Nekemte (Birr128, nine hours). There are up to six minibuses to Welkite (Birr98, 5½ hours).

Roads (and hence buses and minibuses) also connect Jimma to the towns of southern Ethiopia, among them Awasa and Arba Minch, but you'll usually need to change in Chida or Sodo.

🛈 Getting Around

A *bajaj* (auto-rickshaw) costs around Birr10 for hops around town, depending on distance. No buses or minibuses go to the airport, but a **taxi** will charge around Birr100.

Weliso

Around 115km from Addis is the small town of Weliso, which makes a great base for exploring the crater lake in the middle of Mt Wenchi. We can't think of any other reason to linger.

Negash Resort (☑ in Addis Ababa 011 551 1417, in Weliso 011 341 0002; www.negashresort. com; d or tw incl breakfast from Birr759; P @ 🛜 🖾) is probably the best hotel in western Ethiopia. Accommodation comes in a range of styles, from tribally decorated rondavels to stylish rooms in the 'Addis Ababa' block. The service is excellent, there's a decent restaurant serving European and Ethiopian dishes (mains from Birr120) and there's a cool bar situated halfway up a graceful old tree.

It's all centred on a swimming-pool complex fed by a hot spring (during quiet times they might empty the pool) and surrounded by lush gardens that are home to all manner of birds, monkeys, tree hyraxes and dik-dik.

Kafa Biosphere Reserve

In the heart of Ethiopia's coffee country, the 7600-sq-km Kafa Biosphere Reserve is one of the most rewarding places to visit in western Ethiopia. There's a fine coffee museum, excellent trekking and some of the west's most accessible wildlife.

The Kafa Biosphere Reserve is an ecosystem rich in wildlife. A remarkable 5000 different varieties of wild *Coffea arabica* grow here in the densely forested hillsides, while nearly 300 mammal species have been recorded; among the mammals are spotted hyenas, reedbucks, duikers, rock hyraxes, honey badgers, hippos and African buffaloes, as well as five different primate species. Although rarely seen, lions, leopards, servals and African wild cats are also known to lurk in the forest. Kafa is also excellent for birding, with more than 300 species present. Highlights include the wattled and black crowned cranes, Abyssinian longclaws, Rouget's rail, crowned eagle, olive sunbirds, yellow-fronted parrots, black-headed forest orioles and black-winged lovebirds.

Although the infrastructure is still being developed, there are plenty of trekking possibilities around the Kafa Biosphere Reserve, from leisurely walks in the vicinity of the guesthouse to longer hikes into the mountains that rise above 3300m. Both mules and horses are available for hire. The best time for hiking is in the drier months from October to March.

◉ Sights

★ Kafa Coffee Museum   MUSEUM
(ከፋ የቡና መ-ዝገዣም; ☑ 047 331 0667; Birr50; ◷ 8am-5.30pm Mon-Sat) Ethiopia's first coffee museum sits in the heart of coffee country, and is part of the Kafa Biosphere Reserve. It provides an overview of the history of coffee with a focus on Ethiopian production, as well as some archaeological finds from the area. It's a terrific place to access Ethiopia's coffee industry.

⎁ Sleeping

★ Kafa Development Association
(KDA) Guesthouse   GUESTHOUSE $
(☑ 092 466 0703; www.kafa-biosphere.com/accommodation; s/d incl breakfast Birr450/600) Run by a local NGO, this fine guesthouse has simple but light-filled rooms amid a verdant garden that captures all the reasons you came to Kafa in the first place.

❶ Getting There & Away

Bonga is the gateway town to the reserve and the town is connected by a paved road from Jimma. Numerous leave-when-full minibuses make the trip between the two towns (Birr68, two to three hours).

THE WESTERN LOWLANDS

The Gambela federal region is somewhat of an oddity within Ethiopia – its swampy lowlands stand in stark contrast to the lush landscapes seen in the western highlands. Many of its people have stronger cultural ties with neighbouring South Sudan than they do with the rest of Ethiopia.

Gambela
POP 39,022 / ELEV 526M

Set on the banks of the sluggish, chocolate-brown Baro River, at a lowly altitude of 526m, Gambela (ጋምቤላ) is muggy, swampy, sweaty and utterly removed from everything else you'll have come to associate with Ethiopia. This carries over to its people too, many of whom have stronger cultural ties with neighbouring South Sudan than they do with the rest of Ethiopia. Long-horned cattle, trailing clouds of dust and led by tall, elegant Nuer and Anuak tribesmen, sweep through the wildlife-haunted savannahs that surround Gambela. In the town itself people loll riverside under the spreading branches of giant trees. All up it's one of the more exotic (and least-visited) corners of Ethiopia.

History

Thanks to the Baro River being the only truly navigable watercourse in Ethiopia, plus the town's proximity to Sudan, Gambela's strategic and commercial significance has long dictated the fortunes of its turbulent past.

Prior to the 19th century the Baro River was principally used by raiding slave parties to transport captured men. Later, at the end of the 19th century, Menelik II dreamed of linking Ethiopia with Egypt and Sudan via the White Nile. To help create the great inland shipping service, the emperor agreed to grant the British (already in control of

THE IMPORTANCE OF GREETINGS

Although they initially appear reticent and deeply suspicious, the local people are actually incredibly hospitable. Using *daricho* (the Anuak greeting) or *male* (the Nuer greeting) helps break the ice.

Gambela

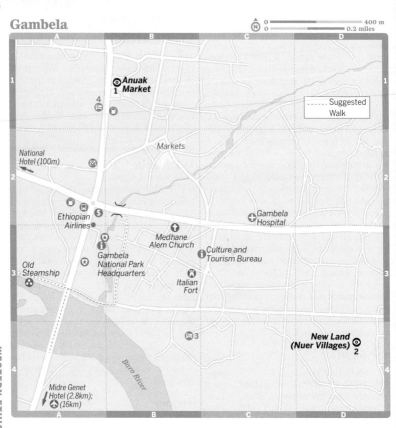

Suggested Walk

National Hotel (100m)

Markets

Anuak Market

Gambela Hospital

Ethiopian Airlines

Medhane Alem Church

Culture and Tourism Bureau

Old Steamship

Gambela National Park Headquarters

Italian Fort

New Land (Nuer Villages)

Baro River

Midre Genet Hotel (2.8km); (16km)

Gambela

⊚ Top Sights
1 Anuak Market B1
2 New Land (Nuer Villages) D4

🛏 Sleeping
3 Baro Gambella Hotel B4
4 Tadessech Hotel A1

Sudan) an enclave on the Baro River. In 1907 the site was chosen and Gambela was formally inaugurated as a port and customs station.

Soon steamers were chugging up and down the wide river, laden with valuables ranging from coffee to cotton. Commerce flourished and Gambela boomed.

The Italians briefly captured Gambela in 1936 and vestiges of their fort are still visible. The British won back the river port in 1941 and amazingly made it part of Sudan 10 years later. When Sudan gained its independence in 1956, the protectorate was given back to Ethiopia. Around this time the old shipping service formally ceased and Gambela began to sink slowly back into the mud from which it had sprung.

Interethnic tensions have plagued the region for decades. These culminated in a massacre of Anuak communities in Gambela township in 2003, resulting in the displacement of tens of thousands of people. In 2006 the Anuak attacked the Gambela police station and prison; they killed several officers, including the state police commissioner, and freed an unknown number of prisoners. More recently, in 2012, a public bus was attacked just outside Gambela town by unknown assailants, while 208 people were killed and more than 100 children were kidnapped and taken across the border into South Sudan during a raid in 2016; the fate of the children was still unknown at the time of writing. The allocations of vast areas of land for agricultural investments has further exacerbated tensions between ethnic groups, as has the arrival of large numbers of internal migrants from other areas of Ethiopia looking for new opportunities.

Dangers & Annoyances

In recent decades, there has been terrible violence across the border with Sudan and South Sudan; this has, on occasion, spilled over into Ethiopia. As a precaution we strongly suggest that you keep your eye on developments around Gambela before visiting the western lowlands.

Security issues aside, your biggest concern should be reserved for some of Gambela's smaller residents – mosquitoes. Malaria continues to kill an extraordinarily high percentage of the population here, and adequate precautions are essential. Giardia is also common.

Photographers should know that taking photos of, or from, the bridge is strictly forbidden. The Anuak and Nuer people are also notoriously camera-shy. Always ask permission before taking photos – if you don't, warm hospitality may turn to aggression.

◉ Sights

A pleasant walk around Gambela includes the riverside, where you'll find an old boat or two and a pier (visible from the riverbank), the bridge and the markets. At sunset, locals gather at the river beneath the bridge to bathe, walk or catch up on gossip. Once every few years (usually during the wet season), a villager is taken by a crocodile. Be wary not only of crocodiles – photographing the bridge is not permitted.

It's possible to visit both Nuer and Anuak villages. The Nuer villages on the outskirts of town, known as New Land, are the easiest to get to.

For those with their own wheels, a better excursion is to the large village of Itang and its satellite hamlets, some 51km west of Gambela along the excellent road leading to the South Sudan border. Itang, like Gambela itself, is home to both Nuer and Anuak peoples, and most residents live in traditional thatch-and-wattle huts of extraordinary complexity. The Nuer villages on the northern side of Itang tend to be the most receptive to visitors, but wherever you go you can expect to be the subject of extreme curiosity – foreign visitors are very rare indeed around here.

Whichever village you choose to visit, a local guide (Birr500 per group) is compulsory, as is a letter granting permission to enter a village (Birr150). Both guide and letter are provided by Gambela's Culture and Tourism Bureau and take about 15 minutes to sort out. Note that the bureau is closed at weekends and on holidays, time your stay to coincide with weekdays. If you do arrive at the weekend try calling Aychlum (p219), who works at the tourist office and will hopefully come and sort everything out for you. You'll also have to pay a little extra to the people themselves for any photos you take.

★ **Anuak Market**   MARKET
(አኙዋክ ገበያ; ⊙7am-4pm) In Gambela's north is the Anuak market. Vendors sit in the shade of the trees selling cereals,

WORTH A TRIP

MENAGESHA NATIONAL FOREST

Menagesha National Forest (መናገሻ ብሔራዊ ጫካ; Birr100) is one of the prettiest stands of forest in Western Ethiopia, and is an easy day trip from Addis. Almost a dozen trails (up to 9km in length) meander through the forest, with one even heading above the treeline to Mt Wuchacha's 3380m summit. On the crater's western slopes, some of the giant juniper and *wanza* (*Cordia africana*) trees are said to be over 400 years old.

Watch out for black-and-white colobus (monkeys) along the trails, as well as bushbucks, while birders will love the chance to see Ethiopian specialities such as the yellow-fronted parrot, Abyssinian catbird, black-winged lovebird and banded barbet.

The forest is accessed via the small town of Sebeta, roughly 30km from Addis. Just before arriving in Sebeta (if travelling east toward Addis) turn left at the green sign reading 'Dhaabbata Bosona Finfinetti' and 'Finfine Forest Enterprise', and it's a 17km drive to the park headquarters where the well-signed walking trails begin.

GIBE SHELEKO NATIONAL PARK

Gazetted in 2011, the Gibe Sheleko National Park (ግቤሸለቆ ብሄራዊ ፓርክ, Gibe Valley National Park; ☑046 220 8490, 046 221 0480; www.southtourism.gov.et; per day Birr150, walking guide per day Birr150, campsites Birr50) covers 360 sq km of upland plateau, parts of the Gibe River gorge area and patches of endemic forest. The diverse, but rather elusive, wildlife includes 17 mammal species, such as greater kudu and a few hippos in the river valley. The birdwatching is also good, with over 200 species recorded – including red-winged pytilia and white-winged cliff chat. The park headquarters is signed 178km west of Addis just beyond the town of Welkite.

Although the wildlife might be shy, the views off the plateau and down to the Wabe Plains are anything but. To make the most of the scenery get out there on foot; guides are available from the park office and they can take you on day long or multiday hikes. There are two basic campsites, or a range of accommodation is available in the nearby town of Welkite.

The park is brand new and hasn't yet received many visitors. Infrastructure is still limited but it's certainly open for business and well worth a visit.

firewood, large Nile perch and tobacco. To pass the time, many indulge in *akowyo* (water-pipe) smoking. You can taste the *borde* (traditional sorghum 'beer'), served to thirsty marketgoers from metal buckets.

Italian Fort
FORT

(የጣልያን ምሽግ) The Italians lorded it over Gambela for five years from 1936, long enough to build a fort; remnants of the fortifications can still be seen from the outside.

Medhane Alem Church
CHURCH

(መድኃኒአለም ቤተክርስትያን) An important landmark for the town's Orthodox Christian community, although it's a fairly standard modern Ethiopian church.

Old Steamship
RUINS

(አሮጌ የከሰል መርከብ) One of the old steamboats that once plied the Baro River.

🛏 Sleeping

Decent hotels are not Gambela's forte, although things have improved with some new hotels in recent years. At the cheaper places, it's cold-water showers only.

Gambela's restaurant situation is in line with its hotel scene – quality options are slim on the ground and your best bets are usually the hotels.

Baro Gambella Hotel
LODGE $

(☑091 191 8878, 047 551 0044; s/tw Birr205/267; P🗑) OK, the rooms here are worn and tired, but the birdsong-filled gardens and helpful management give this place real character. Add in the restaurant (mains

Birr40 to Birr90) serving Western and Ethiopian dishes that is hands down the best in town and all up you get a good place to stay.

It's often filled with NGO types, but note that communications is not the hotel's strong point and making advance reservations is almost impossible.

Tadessech Hotel
HOTEL $

(☑047 551 0559; d or tw Birr500) This relatively new block on the main road into town has very ordinary rooms that are overpriced, even more so with the recent hike in prices, and especially given its showers are cold water only. It's really only worth trying if everywhere else is full.

Midre Genet Hotel
HOTEL $

(☑047 551 2212; d Birr150) This fading sky-blue place, out along the road to the airport, offers (mostly) clean rooms. There's a simple bar-restaurant out the front. Its biggest drawback is its distance from town, meaning that only those with their own wheels are likely to want to stay here.

National Hotel
HOTEL $$

(☑093 205 6956; s/d US$20/25; P🗑) The lack of a restaurant here is a drawback, but the rooms are otherwise the best in this price range in town. It's close to the bus station and the leafy grounds out the back add some appeal.

🍷 Drinking & Nightlife

There is a string of coffee and tea stalls along the road following the Baro River. Perched on a log, coffee balanced precariously on one knee, surrounded by Nuer tribesman: this is travel at its rawest.

ℹ️ Information

The electricity supply in Gambela can only be described as erratic, and usually cuts out half-way through composing an email.

If you get sick in Gambela and have a choice about it, head to **Metu** (☑ 991) – Gambela's hospital is grim.

Commercial Bank (⊘7.30am-11.30am & 3-5.30pm Mon-Fri, 7.30-11.30am Sat)

Culture and Tourism Bureau (☑ 047 551 2529, 047 551 2351; ⊘7am-12.30pm & 3-5pm Mon-Fri) The bureau organises documentation for visits to Nuer villages (የኑዌር መንደሮች). A local guide (Birr500 per group) is compulsory, as is a letter granting permission to enter a village (Birr150). These will take about 15 minutes to sort out. They also offer general tourist information, as well as advice on visiting nearby villages and Gambela National Park.

Note that the bureau is closed at weekends and on holidays; time your stay to coincide with weekdays. If you do arrive at the weekend try calling Aychlum (☑ 091 780 4646), who works at the tourist office and will hopefully come and sort everything out for you.

ℹ️ Getting There & Away

AIR

Ethiopian Airlines (☑ 047 551 0099; www.ethiopianairlines.com; ⊘8.30am-5pm Mon-Sat) flies between Gambela and Addis Ababa (Birr3792, 1¼ hours) twice daily. Flights are frequently cancelled during the rainy season.

BUS

One bus leaves Gambela's **bus station** daily at 6am for Addis Ababa (Birr3750, two days) overnighting en route. Another bus goes to Bedele (Birr140, nine hours, 6am departure) and several go to Metu (bus/minibus Birr82/108, three hours). An early-morning bus occasionally leaves for Tepi (Birr215, 12 hours), although it

---

PEOPLES OF THE WESTERN LOWLANDS

The Nuer and the Anuak are the two main ethnic groups within the Gambela region. They have strong links (and ancient feuds) with peoples across the border in South Sudan, and together they form the vast majority of the population around Gambela.

The Anuak

The Anuak language closely resembles that of the Luo tribes in Kenya. Fishing is their main means of survival, though some grow sorghum. Outside Gambela proper, most Anuak live in extended family groups rather than villages, in a cluster of huts in a small compound. Anuak huts are characterised by low doorways and thickly thatched roofs. The eaves, which stretch almost to the ground, keep out both the torrential rain and the baking sun. A common practice among many Nilotic peoples of Ethiopia and Sudan, including the Anuak, is the extraction of the front six teeth of the lower jaw at around the age of 12. This is said to have served originally as a precaution against the effects of tetanus or lockjaw.

The Majang

The Majang, also known as Majangir, are the third major group living in and around Gambela (as well as up towards Metu and Tepi). The last census recorded only around 15,000 Majang, many of whom claim to feel persecuted by national and local governments and other tribal groups. They speak a Nilo-Saharan language of the Surmic cluster.

The Nuer

The Nuer people, who are relatively recent arrivals to the region, originated in the Nilotic-speaking regions of Sudan and now form the largest ethnic group in Gambela. They're largely cattle herders and much Nuer oral literature, including traditional songs and poetry, celebrates their beasts.

Unlike the Anuak, the Nuer like to live together in large villages. Very tall and dark, the Nuer women are fond of ornamentation, including bright bead necklaces, heavy bangles of ivory or bone and, increasingly rarely (around Gambela at least), a spike of brass or ivory that pierces the lower lip and extends over the chin. Cicatrising (scarification; considered sensual) is also widely practised: the skin is raised in patterns and decorates the face, chest and stomach; rows of dots are often traced on the forehead.

may be easier to go to Gore first and change there.

The border to South Sudan remains firmly closed to foreigners (but locals can cross). If it opens, buses go to the border town of Jikawo (Birr98, 4½ hours) daily at 6am.

ⓘ Getting Around

A short hop in a shared *bajaj* (auto-rickshaw) around Gambela costs Birr5, but they can be contracted for Birr25 an hour.

Ethiopian Airlines provides transport between Gambela and the airport, which is 16.5km south of town. Passengers meet at the airline office first and, if the flight hasn't been cancelled, proceed to the airport together.

Gambela National Park

Gambela National Park (ጋምቤላ ብሔራዊ ፓርክ; www.ewca.gov.et) is Ethiopia's greatest wildlife show-in-waiting. Thanks to vast herds of migrating antelope species and what are thought to be sizeable populations of predators, Gambela National Park could have wildlife numbers to rival the famous reserves of Kenya and Tanzania. It's also rather beautiful with savannah, flood plains and riverine forests.

But, for the moment at least, such bounty remains almost impossible to access. This is a very remote and swampy park with absolutely no infrastructure, which makes it an adventure of the highest order. Further, the animals are thought to be concentrated in the southwestern parts of the park – the swampiest, and hardest-to-reach area. Add to this continued local ethnic tensions and official suspicion towards anyone seeking to head out into what remains a sensitive border area, and conditions are clearly not ideal for wildlife tourism.

History

Less than 50 years ago, Gambela National Park, spreading over 5061 sq km and abutting the even larger Boma National Park of South Sudan, was considered one of Ethiopia's richest places for large mammals. Elephants, lions, leopards, giraffes, buffaloes, topis, tiang (a subspecies of tsessebe antelope), roan antelope, hartebeests, white-

eared kob, Nile lechwe and waterbucks were found here in huge numbers.

Then to both Ethiopia and neighbouring Sudan (now South Sudan) came decades of war, civil unrest and refugees, and with these Gambela National Park was largely forgotten and abandoned. War and wildlife generally don't mix well and experts quite logically assumed that the wildlife of both Gambela and Boma national parks would have been decimated. But then in 2007, as peace started to return to the wider region, conservationists from the New York–based Wildlife Conservation Society (www.wcs. org) embarked on aerial surveys of South Sudan's Boma National Park. They were shocked to find that the wildlife had not merely survived the dark years of violence but that it was flourishing.

The wildlife they found was astonishing, including over a million white-eared kob, tiang and Mongalla gazelles. In addition to the antelope species, there are thought to be over 8000 elephants, 8900 buffalo and 2800 ostrich as well as lions, leopards, giraffes, hippos and numerous other species. Between 2007 and 2012 the focus was all on Boma park, but logic always said that the wildlife would likely be following the rains and grazing over the border and into Gambela. Today surveys are also taking place here, and the first indications are that Gambela park may just be equally rich in wildlife.

ⓘ Information

If you do decide to visit Gambela National Park, you will need a local guide (Birr250 per day), and we strongly recommend that you inform the local authorities of your plans.

Gambela National Park Headquarters (✆ 047 551 0918, 047 551 0912; omotagwa@ yahoo.com; per 24hr Birr200; ⊙ 7am-noon & 3-5.30pm Mon-Fri) Unusually useful and helpful when it comes to planning a trip to Gambela National Park.

Culture and Tourism Bureau (p219) Also useful for information on the park.

ⓘ Getting There & Away

There is no public transport to or from Gambela National Park; you'll need your own fully equipped 4WD to reach and explore the park.

Understand Ethiopia

Ethiopia Today

Ethiopia prides itself on having attained political stability and has an enviable rate of economic growth thanks to huge foreign investment and the development of a manufacturing industry. Despite the apparent boom, the country faces numerous challenges as it grapples with finding job opportunities for an expanding population – not to mention the growing political dissent from the Oromo people, who feel marginalised by the ruling elites. To achieve long-term stability, Ethiopia is in need of better governance and democratic reforms.

Best on Film

In Search of Myths and Heros (2005) The first in Michael Wood's sumptuously filmed series seeks the truth behind the Sheba legend.

Lost Kingdoms of Africa (2010) Dr Gus Casely-Hayford explores ancient Ethiopian cultures and legends.

The Great Rift: Africa's Wild Heart (2010) A finely crafted portrait of the Rift Valley and its wildlife.

Lamb (2015) The story of a young orphan in rural Ethiopia. It's the first Ethiopian film to make the Cannes festival's official selection.

Best in Print

Cutting for Stone (Abraham Verghese; 2009) This absorbing novel follows the fortunes of twin brothers over five turbulent decades in Addis Ababa.

Beneath the Lion's Gaze (Maaza Mengiste; 2011) Tells a poignant story of a fictional family during the fall of Haile Selassie and the rise of the Derg.

Notes from the Hyena's Belly (Nega Mezlekia; 2002) Sheds light on the violent decades straddling the ousting of Haile Selassie.

All Our Names (Dinaw Mengestu; 2014) The story of two young students who are confronted by violence during a revolution.

Ethiopia Under Desalegn

Hailemariam Desalegn has been serving as prime minister since 2012. Desalegn is said to be competent to foster growth in the country and combat poverty but has the reputation of lacking charisma on international matters (unlike Zenawi, his predecessor). Though his party, the Ethiopian People's Revolutionary Democratic Front (EPRDF), is solidly behind him, many observers wonder if he has the political clout to hold together such a diverse country and one that, despite its progress, remains blighted with problems and surrounded by unstable neighbours – not to mention ISIS, which executed 28 Ethiopians in Lybia in April 2015. The border conflict with Eritrea is still ongoing and relations with Somalia remain tense.

Economic Progress & Improved Infrastructure

Ethiopia has been developing at an astonishing rate. In the 10 years leading up to 2016, economic growth has, thanks to a huge investment in agriculture (particularly the flower-export market), been at record highs, sometimes reaching the giddy heights of 12%. Foreign investment has been tumbling into the country and the nation's infrastructure given a much needed overhaul. This is most notable in the transport system, which has been undergoing a major makeover, with Chinese road construction crews turning what have long been pot-hole-infested tracks into super-smooth highways – not to mention the Addis Ababa–Djibouti City railway line, which was inaugurated in late 2016 and is expected to boost exports. But this has not come without a price: local farmers have complained of being forcibly removed from their land in order to make way for huge foreign-owned farming or industrial projects. And Ethiopia faces a massive challenge in ensuring that the country's improved economy benefits all Ethiopians. High youth unemployment is a major concern. Many young Ethiopians, including university students, are devoid of perspective and seek to emigrate to Europe.

Democratic Deficit & Ethnic Division

Ethiopia is often hailed as a modern development success story. But it's not all that rosy. Sure, the ambitious infrastructure programme that has been implemented since the early 2000s has driven growth, but the government's record on freedom of expression and other rights leaves something to be desired. In December 2015, protests against the government's project to expand Addis Ababa into surrounding farmland in the Oromia state were violently curbed by security forces. This led to growing resentment from the Oromo – Ethiopia's most populous ethnic group – against the state which, they claimed, is controlled by Tigrayans, who comprise only 6% of the country. Oromo people, who feel increasingly repressed and discriminated against by the ruling elite, voiced their opposition during the Irreecha Festival in Bishoftu (Debre Zeyit) on 2 October 2016. The police reacted by firing tear gas, which triggered a stampede that left at least 55 people dead. The government, which felt under threat, announced a six-month state of emergency and cracked down on opponents to quell civil unrest. There seems to be no space for political dissent and independent criticism. Experts say such simmering tensions could destabilise the country and discourage foreign investors.

Foreign Relations

That Ethiopia is now a regional powerhouse is beyond doubt. The country is increasingly flexing its military and diplomatic muscles, whether this be in Somalia where the Ethiopian military is once again tackling Islamic militants or in UN-sponsored peace-keeping missions on the disputed Sudan–South Sudan border. One problem that never seems to get solved, though, is the ongoing border dispute with arch-enemy Eritrea. The two nations fought a bitter war between 1998 and 2000 and have come close to war since. For the moment a wary calm prevails, but everyone knows that the merest spark could reignite a war that neither country can afford.

POPULATION: **102,000,000**

AREA: **1,098,000 SQ KM**

LIFE EXPECTANCY: **63 YEARS**

FERTILITY RATE: **4.6 PER WOMAN**

GDP PER CAPITA: **US$1800**

if Ethiopia were 100 people

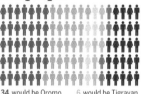

34 would be Oromo   6 would be Tigrayan
27 would be Amhara   4 would be Sidama
6 would be Somali   **23** would be other

belief systems
(% of population)

44 — Ethiopian Orthodox Christian
34 — Muslim
11 — Animist
11 — Other

population per sq km

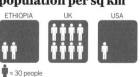

ETHIOPIA   UK   USA

≈ 30 people

Ethiopia's History

Ethiopia has a long, rich and colourful history that's generally not well known outside East Africa. Who knows that Ethiopia is one of the oldest Christian civilisations in the world? And that it has the longest archaeological record of any country on earth? From the ancient Aksumite civilisation's obelisks to the fascinating architectural wonders of medieval Lalibela to the castles of Gonder to the communist monuments of the Derg, Ethiopia wears its history on its sleeve.

Cradle of Humanity

In palaeoanthropology, where years are measured in tenths of millions, 40 years is less than a blink of an eye. However, 40 years worth of palaeoanthropological study can rock the very foundations of human history.

After Richard Leakey's discovery of skull 1470 near Kenya's Lake Turkana in 1972, which proved *Homo habilis* (the direct ancestor of *Homo sapiens*) had lived alongside *Australopithecus africanus* and therefore couldn't have evolved from them, the search was on for a new species that had branched into the genera *Homo* and *Australopithecus,* a species that would likely be Darwin's 'missing link'.

On 30 November 1974 Lucy was discovered in a dried-up lake near Hadar in Ethiopia's northeast. She was a new species, *A. afarensis,* and she miraculously walked on two legs 3.2 million years ago. Lucy's bipedal (upright walking) anatomy also shattered previous theories that hypothesised our ancestors only started walking upright after evolving larger brains. Lucy, the oldest and most complete hominid ever found, was famous and Ethiopia was tipped to claim the cradle of humanity.

After further finds in Ethiopia, including the 1992 discovery of the 4.4-million-year-old *A. ramidus,* whose foot bones hinted at bipedism, the ink on Ethiopia's claim was almost dry. However, recent computed-tomography (CT) scans on a six-million-year-old hominid skeleton *(Orrorin tugenensis)* found in Kenya in 2001, and computer-aided reconstruction of a six- to seven-million-year-old skull *(Sahelanthropus tchadensis)* in Chad seem to suggest that Lucy and *A. ramidus* may not be part of the direct line of human evolution, but rather a lateral branch of it.

TIMELINE	c 3.2 million BC	3500–2000 BC	2000–1500 BC
	Lucy collapses and awaits discovery and fame 3.2 million years down the line. Ethiopia uses her as the basis of its claim to be the birthplace of humankind.	The Ancient Egyptians trade with the Land of Punt, which many people consider to be somewhere on the Eritrean or Somalian coast.	Ge'ez, the precursor to the Amharic and Arabic languages, is developed somewhere in the vicinity of northern Ethiopia. Amazingly it is still spoken by priests in Ethiopia and Eritrea today.

Land of Punt

Though this period is shrouded in darkness, Ethiopia (and Eritrea) are believed to have formed part of the ancient Land of Punt, an area that attracted the trading ships of the Egyptian Pharaohs for millennia.

Many valuable commodities such as gold, myrrh, ivory and slaves were issued from the interior of the region and were exported from the coast.

It's thought the northern coastal region saw much migration from surrounding areas, and by 2000 BC it had established strong contacts with the inhabitants of southern Arabia.

Pre-Aksumite Civilisation

The cultural significance of the southern Arabian and the East African cultures mixing was enormous. One consequence was the emergence of a number of Afro-Asiatic languages, including Ge'ez, which laid the foundation for modern Amharic. Amazingly, Ge'ez script is still read by many Christian priests in Ethiopia.

Most significant was the rise of a remarkable civilisation in Africa's Horn in 1500 BC. The fact that the influence of southern Arabia was so clear (in the Sabaean script and in the worship of Sabaean gods), that the civilisation appeared to mushroom overnight and was very localised, and that it benefited from specialist crafts, skills and technologies previously unknown in the area, led many scholars throughout history to believe that the civilisation was actually spawned by Arabian settlers, and not Africans.

However, scholars of late argue with great conviction that this civilisation was indeed African and, while undoubtedly influenced by Sabaean ideas, it developed from within from local effort and initiative.

Whatever the origin, the civilisation was a very important one. The most famous relic of the times is the extraordinary stone 'temple' of Yeha.

Those intrigued by the ancient civilisation of Aksum should pick up Professor David W Phillipson's *Ancient Ethiopia* (2009). It's excellent and is an easy read.

ETHIOPIA'S HISTORY LAND OF PUNT

WHICH HISTORY?

The factual 'real' history presented here is what historians like to use, but it's important to remember that for the majority of Ethiopians this isn't the history they believe in. In Ethiopia, like in much of Africa, legends concerning magical deeds, ghostly creatures and possibly nonexistent folk heroes are not just legends, but are taken as solid fact, and who cares if the historians say the dates and places don't add up! History is what you make of it and how you translate it, so just because there is no historical evidence proving that the Queen of Sheba existed, the people believe she did and recount it as their history, so in Ethiopia that makes her real. It is important to keep this in mind when travelling through Ethiopia.

1500–400 BC	955–587 BC	400 BC–AD 200	200–500
An Arabian-influenced civilisation rises in northern Ethiopia; the country's first capital, Yeha, is founded, but by whom? Historians remain uncertain whether Yeha and Africa ruled Arabia or Arabia ruled Yeha.	The Ark of the Covenant, the sacred chest built by Moses containing the Ten Commandments, vanishes from Jerusalem at some point in this period.	The great Aksumite kingdom is formed and thrives on Red Sea trade and rich natural resources. It is first mentioned in the 1st-century-AD book *Periplus of the Erythraean Sea*.	The Aksumite kingdom reaches its apogee. At its height the kingdom controls lands from the Nile to Arabia and is counted among the most powerful kingdoms of the ancient world.

Kingdom of Aksum

The Aksumite kingdom, which grew to rank among the most powerful kingdoms of the ancient world, was the next civilisation to rise in present-day Ethiopia. The first written evidence of its existence (*Periplus of the Erythraean Sea*, written by a Greek-speaking Egyptian sailor) was from the 1st century AD, but by this point its realm of influence was wide, suggesting it rose to prominence much earlier. New archaeological evidence hints it may have emerged as early as 400 BC.

King Ezana is thought to be the man behind the first church in Ethiopia. Built in the 4th century its remains can still be seen next door to the St Mary of Zion church in Aksum.

Aksum, its capital, is thought to have owed its importance to its position, situated at an important commercial crossroads. To the northwest lay Egypt, and to the west, near the present-day Sudanese border, were the rich, gold-producing lowlands. To the northeast, in present-day Eritrea, was the Aksumite port of Adulis, positioned at the crux of an extensive trading route. Exports included frankincense, grain, animal skins, rhino horn, apes and, particularly, ivory (tens of thousands of elephants were reported to roam the region). Imports of dyed cloaks, cheap unlined coats, glassware, and iron for making spears, swords and axes flowed in from Egypt, Arabia and India. Syrian and Italian wine and olive oil were also imported, as was much gold and silver plate for the king. The flourishing trade allowed the Aksumite kingdom to thrive.

Aksum also benefited from its well-watered agricultural lands, which were further exploited by the use of dams, wells and reservoirs.

During its heyday between the 3rd and 6th centuries, the Aksumite kingdom stretched into large parts of southern Arabia, and west into

THE DAYS BEFORE SHEBA

Historians might like to insist that little is known about the founding of the Aksumite Kingdom, but ask the average Ethiopian and they'll tell you something very different. Aksum, they will say, was founded by none other than the Great-Grandson of Noah, Aksumawi. His new kingdom flourished for a while, but one day Wainaba, a giant snake, 170 cubits long, attacked the city, killed the king and then ruled for 400 dark years. The snake was a foul-tempered and dangerous creature and in order to placate him the people of Aksum fed him a diet of milk and virgins. Eventually salvation came in the form of a man named Angabo who, crossing the Red Sea from the land of the Sabeans, offered to kill the serpent in exchange for the throne. The people of Aksum agreed, but rather than fighting the serpent as the Aksumites expected, Angabo proved himself wise and fed the serpent a goat laced with poison.

The kingdom quickly recovered, Angabo married and had a daughter. That daughter was named Makeda and on her father's death she became the woman we today know as the Queen of Sheba.

300–325	400–500	615	640–750
Aksum's Great Stele collapses; the catastrophic event signals the end of paganism and the birth of Christianity in Ethiopia.	The famous Nine Saints, a group of Greek-speaking missionaries, arrive in northern Ethiopia. Christianity is solidified as the main religion of the region.	Prophet Mohammed's daughter and successor flee persecution in Arabia and introduce Islam to Ethiopia. Some believe that the king let them stay because he thought they were persecuted Christians.	The Aksumites lose their hold on Red Sea trade and the kingdom collapses. Ethiopia enters a long 'dark age' about which almost nothing is known.

the Sudanese Nile Valley. Aksumite society was rich, well organised, and technically and artistically advanced. During this era, an unparalleled coinage in bronze, silver and gold was produced and extraordinary monuments were built, all of which are visible in Aksum today. The kingdom also exerted the greatest influence of all on the future of Ethiopia: it introduced Christianity.

The Coming of Christianity

The Ethiopian church claims that Christianity first reached Aksum at the time of the Apostles. According to the Byzantine ecclesiastical historian Rufinus, it arrived on Ethiopian shores by accident rather than by design, when two young Christian boys from the Levant were given to the King.

Whatever the truth of the matter, what's certain is that Christianity didn't become the state religion until around the beginning of the 4th century. King Ezana's stone inscription makes reference to Christ, and his famous coins bear the Christian cross – the world's first to do so.

The end of the 5th century AD brought the famous Nine Saints, a group of Greek-speaking missionaries from the Levant who established well-known monasteries in the north of the country, including Debre Damo. At this time, the Bible was first translated from Greek into Ge'ez.

Christianity shaped not just Ethiopia's spiritual and intellectual life, but also its cultural and social life, including its art and literature. Today almost half of Ethiopia's population is Orthodox Christian.

The Coming of Islam & the Demise of Aksum

According to Muslim tradition, the Prophet Mohammed was nursed by an Ethiopian woman. Later, the Muslim Hadith (collection of traditions about Mohammed's life) recounts that Mohammed sent his daughter (and successor) along with some of his followers to Negash in AD 615, to avoid persecution in Arabia.

When things calmed in Arabia, most refugees returned home. However, Negash continues to be a crucial pilgrimage point for Ethiopia's Muslims.

Good relations between the two religions continued until at least King Armah's death. Thereafter, as the Arabs and Islam rose to prominence on the opposite side of the Red Sea, trade slowly shifted away from Christian Aksum and it eventually became isolated.

After Aksum's decline around AD 700, Ethiopia endured what is commonly known as its 'dark age'.

Check out J Spencer Trimingham's *Islam in Ethiopia* (2013) for an insight into Ethiopia's second-most popular religion.

1137–1270	1165–1600	1270	1400
The Zagwe dynasty rises from Ethiopia's 'dark ages' and produces, with a little helping hand from a gang of angels, the astounding rock-hewn churches of Lalibela.	Rumours about Prester John, a powerful Christian king based in Ethiopia, spread throughout Europe. Excitement mounts that he will help Christian Europe gain control of the Holy Lands.	Yekuno Amlak establishes the 'Solomonic dynasty' and Ethiopia enters its well-documented Middle Ages.	French aristocrat Duc de Berry sends the first European ambassador to Ethiopia. In turn, Ethiopians journey to Europe where many join churches, particularly in Rome.

Lalibela & the Zagwe Dynasty

The 12th century witnessed a new capital (Adafa) rise in the mountains of Lasta, not far from present-day Lalibela. It was established under a new power: the Zagwe dynasty.

Although the Zagwe dynasty reigned from around AD 1137 to 1270, and left the rock-hewn churches of Lalibela, this period is shrouded in mystery. Seemingly, no stones were inscribed, no chronicles written, no coins minted and no accounts of the dynasty by foreign travellers have survived.

It's not certain what brought the Zagwe dynasty to an end; it was likely a combination of infighting within the ruling dynasty and local opposition from the clergy. In 1270 the dynasty was overthrown by Yekuno Amlak; political power shifted south to the historical province of Shoa.

The Ethiopian Middle Ages

Yekuno Amlak, claiming to be a descendant of King Solomon and Queen Sheba, established the 'Solomonic dynasty', which would reign for the next 500 years. His rule would also ring in the start of what's known as the Ethiopian Middle Ages, a period that, up until the modern age, was more documented than any other in the nation's past.

With its all-powerful monarchy and influential clergy, the Middle Ages were a continuation of the past. However, unlike the past, the kingdom's capitals were itinerant and were little more than vast, moving military camps. There were no longer minted coins, and trade was conducted by barter with pieces of iron, cloth or salt.

Culturally, the period was important for the significant output of Ge'ez literature, including the nation's epic Kebra Negast. It was also at this time that contacts with European Christendom began to increase. With the rising threat of well-equipped Muslim armies in the East, Europe was seen as a Christian superpower.

Europe, for its part, dreamed of winning back Jerusalem from the 'Saracens', and realised the important strategic position occupied by Ethiopia. At the time, it was almost the only Christian kingdom outside Europe.

In the early 15th century, the first European embassy arrived in Ethiopia, sent by the famous French aristocrat Duc de Berry. Ethiopians in their turn began to travel to Europe, particularly to Rome, where many joined churches already established there.

The Muslim-Christian Wars

The first decades of the 16th century were plagued by some of the most costly, bloody and wasteful fighting in Ethiopian history, in which the entire empire and its culture came close to being wiped out.

FAST RAIDS

Mahfuz timed his annual raids to take advantage of Christian Ethiopia's weakened state during their 55-day fast before Fasika (Orthodox Easter).

1400–1600	1490–1529	1529–42	1543–59
The Kebra Negast, Ethiopia's national epic, is written. There remains much debate about the exact date it was written.	Mahfuz declares jihad on Christian Ethiopia and starts the bloody Muslim–Christian wars, the most costly in the country's history. Ahmed Gragn the Left-Handed, eventually defeats the emperor.	Ahmed Gragn the Left-Handed expands his kingdom and by 1532 has taken most of eastern and southern Ethiopia. In 1542 he defeats a Portuguese/Ethiopian army near Lake Tana.	Emperor Galawdewos, with help from Portugal, finally defeats and kills Muslim raider Ahmed Gragn. Intermittent fighting continues for years until Galawdewos is killed in an attack on Harar.

From the 13th century, relations between Christian Ethiopia and the Muslim Ethiopian emirates of Ifat and Adal were showing signs of strain.

In the 1490s animosities came to a head. After establishing himself at the port of Zeila in present-day Somalia, a skilled and charismatic Muslim named Mahfuz declared a jihad against Christian Ethiopia. Emperor Lebna Dengel finally halted Mahfuz's incursions, but not before he had carried off huge numbers of Ethiopian slaves and cattle.

An even more legendary figure was Ahmed Ibn Ibrahim al Ghazi, nicknamed 'Ahmed Gragn the Left-Handed'. After overthrowing Sultan Abu Bakr of Harar, Ahmed declared his intention to continue the jihad of Mahfuz. Carrying out several raids into Ethiopian territory, he managed in March 1529 to defeat Emperor Lebna Dengel.

Ahmed then embarked on the conquest of all of Christian Ethiopia. Well supplied with firearms from Ottoman Zeila and southern Arabia,

THE ARK OF THE COVENANT

Few other objects in history match the enduring legend of the Ark of the Covenant. But what is this Ark and is it really sitting inside a small Aksum chapel? The Old Testament says that the Ark was constructed on Mt Sinai by Moses, and that it houses the two stone tablets on which are inscribed the Ten Commandments. It is also said to contain the Rod of Aaron (Moses' brother) and a jar of manna (an edible substance that, according to Abrahamic doctrine, God provided for the Israelites during their travels in the desert). Other more recent descriptions of its contents include that of 17th-century Ethiopian Emperor Susenyos who said that it contained the 'figure of a woman with very large breasts'. Such a figure was common in ancient fertility beliefs.

In Old Testament days the Ark was housed in King Solomon's Great Temple in Jerusalem and was used by the Israelites as an oracle. It was also carried into battle. After the sacking of the Great Temple in 587 BC, the Bible falls silent as to the Ark's whereabouts – some say it was buried in a secret chamber under the Temple Mount in Jerusalem, and others say it was destroyed. But according to Ethiopian tradition, the Ark of the Covenant was carried off from Jerusalem and brought to Ethiopia in the 1st millennium BC by Menelik, the son of Solomon and Sheba. It's now believed to sit in Aksum's St Mary of Zion church compound.

Today, every other Ethiopian church has a replica of the Ark (or more precisely the Tablets of Law that are housed in the Ark) known as the *tabot*. Kept safe in the *maqdas* (Holy of Holies or inner sanctuary), it's the church's single most important element, and gives the building its sanctity.

During important religious festivals, the *tabot* is carried in solemn processions, accompanied by singing, dancing, the beating of staffs or prayer sticks, the rattling of the sistrum (a sophisticated rattle, thought to be directly descended from an ancient Egyptian instrument used to worship Isis) and the beating of drums.

1550	1582	1629	1636
The Oromo people move north from Kenya and plunge the country into 200 more years of intermittent armed conflict. It's during this period that the walls of Harar are built.	Much of the Christian world adopts the revised Gregorian calendar, but Ethiopia stays with the Julian calendar – staying seven years behind the rest of us.	Emperor Susenyos converts to Catholicism and tries to force his people to do likewise. His subjects are not happy and in the civil war that follows an estimated 32,000 die.	Emperor Fasiladas founds Gonder, the first permanent capital since Lalibela; he also expels all foreigners from the empire. The new capital flourishes and Ethiopia enters another golden age.

the Muslim leader had, by 1532, overrun almost all of eastern and southern Ethiopia.

In 1535 the Emperor Lebna Dengel appealed in desperation to the Portuguese, who were already active in the region. In 1542 an army of 400 well-armed musketeers arrived in Massawa (in present-day Eritrea), led by Dom Christovão da Gama, son of the famous mariner Vasco da Gama. They met Ahmed near Lake Tana, where he quickly routed them before lopping off the young and foolhardy head of Dom Christovão.

In 1543 the new Ethiopian emperor, Galawdewos, joined ranks with the surviving Portuguese force and met Ahmed at Wayna Daga in the west. This time, the Christians' huge numbers proved too powerful and Ahmed was killed.

Oromo Migrations & the Jesuits

A new threat to the Ethiopian empire arose in the mid-16th century. The nomadic pastoralists and warrior horsemen of the Oromos began a great migration northwards from what's now Kenya.

For the next 200 years intermittent armed conflict raged between the empire and the Oromos.

Early in the 17th century the Oromo threat led several Ethiopian emperors to seek an alliance with the Portuguese-backed Jesuits. Two emperors, Za-Dengel and Susenyos, even went as far as conversion to Catholicism. However, imposing Catholicism on their population provoked widespread rebellion. Za-Dengel was overthrown and, in 1629, Susenyos' draconian measures to convert his people incited civil war.

Eventually Susenyos backed down and the Orthodox faith was re-established. Susenyos' son and successor, Fasiladas, expelled the meddling Jesuits and forbade all foreigners from setting foot in his empire.

The Rise & Fall of Gonder

In 1636, following the old tradition of his forefathers, Emperor Fasiladas decided to found a new capital. However, Gonder was different from its predecessors: it was to be the first permanent capital since Lalibela.

By the 17th century's close, Gonder boasted magnificent palaces, beautiful gardens and extensive plantations. It was also the site of sumptuous feasts and extravagant court pageantry, attracting visitors from around the world.

Under the ample patronage of Church and state, the arts and crafts flourished. Impressive churches were built, among them the famous Debre Berhan Selassie, which can be seen to this day. Outside Gonder, building projects included some remarkable churches at Lake Tana's historic monasteries.

Recounting events over the past half a century across Africa, Martin Meredith's *The State of Africa* (2013) includes a couple of chapters on Ethiopia and is by far the best history of modern Africa currently available.

1706–21	1755–1855	1855	1855–72
The court in Gonder is thrown into turmoil as coups, assassination and court rumour become a virtual hobby for the people of the royal city.	Emperor Iyasu II dies and the central government in Gonder quickly collapses. Ethiopia slips back into the dark ages and a century of endless civil war and skirmishes follows.	Kassa Haylu outsteals, outwits and outmanoeuvres his rivals to become Emperor Tewodros; he unites a feuding Ethiopia and embarks on ambitious modernisation programs.	Tewodros builds numerous roads, establishes an army and promotes Amharic over Ge'ez as the language of use. He also makes the mistake of imprisoning a group of Britons attending his court.

But not all was sweet in Gonder's court, and between 1706 and 1721 everyone from royal bodyguards, the clergy and nobles to ordinary citizens tried their hand at conspiracy. Assassination, plotting and intrigue became the order of the day, and the ensuing chaos reads like something out of Shakespeare's *Macbeth*. No fewer than three monarchs held power during this turbulent period, with at least one meeting a sticky, poisonous end. Emperor Bakaffa's reign (1721–30) briefly restored stability, during which time new palaces and churches were built, and literature and the arts once again thrived.

However, by the time of Iyasu II's death in 1755, the Gonder kingdom was back in turmoil and the provinces started to rebel.

Between 1784 and 1855 the emperors were little more than puppets in the hands of rival feudal lords and their powerful provincial armies. The country disintegrated and civil war became the norm.

Emperor Tewodros

After the fallout of Gonder, Ethiopia existed only as a cluster of separate and feuding fiefdoms. That was until the mid-19th century, when a unique man dreamt of unity.

Kassa Haylu, raised in a monastery and the son of a western chief, had first been a *shifta* (bandit) after his claim to his deceased father's fief was denied. However, he eventually became a Robin Hood figure, looting the rich to give to the poor. This gained him large numbers of followers and he began to defeat the rival princes, one after another, until in 1855 he had himself crowned Emperor Tewodros.

The new monarch soon began to show himself not just as a capable leader and strong ruler but as a unifier, innovator and reformer as

ITINERANT COURTS

During the Ethiopian Middle Ages, the business of most monarchs consisted of waging wars, collecting taxes and inspecting the royal domains.

Obliged to travel continuously throughout their far-flung empire, the kings led a perpetually nomadic existence. And with the rulers went their armies, courtiers and servants; the judges, prison officers and priests; the merchants; the prostitutes; and a whole entourage of artisans. The camps could spread over 20km; for transportation up to 100,000 mules were required.

The retinue was so vast that it rapidly exhausted the resources of the location. Four months was usually the maximum possible length of stay, and 10 years had to pass before the spot could be revisited.

The peasantry were said to dread the royal visits as they dreaded the swarms of locusts. In both cases, everything that lay in the path of the intruders was consumed.

1872–76	1875–76	1888	1889
After helping the British dispose of Tewodros, Kassa Mercha wins the battle of succession with Emperor Tekla Giorgis and rises as Emperor Yohannes.	Egyptian forces attempt to invade the country, but Emperor Yohannes puts up a good fight and ends their ambitions.	Cattle imported by the Italians introduces a rinderpest epidemic. In combination with a severe drought and an increase in the locust population, a famine develops that was to last four years.	Yohannes' successor, Emperor Menelik, signs a friendship treaty with Italy and grants the region that is now Eritrea to Italy.

well. He chose Maqdala, a natural fortress south of Lalibela, as his base and there he began to formulate mighty plans. He established a national army, an arms factory and a great road network, as well as implementing a major program of land reform, promoting Amharic (the vernacular) in place of the classical written language, Ge'ez, and even attempting to abolish the slave trade.

But these reforms met with deep resentment and opposition from the land-holding clergy, the rival lords and even the common faithful. Tewodros' response, however, was ruthless and sometimes brutal. Like a tragic Shakespearean hero, the emperor suffered from an intense pride, a fanatical belief in his cause and an inflated sense of destiny. This would eventually be his downfall.

Frustrated by failed attempts to enlist European, and particularly British, support for his modernising programs, Tewodros impetuously imprisoned some Britons attending his court. Initially successful in extracting concessions, Tewodros overplayed his hand, and it badly misfired. In 1868 large, heavily armed British forces, backed by rival Ethiopian lords, inflicted appalling casualties on Tewodros' men, many of them armed with little more than shields and spears.

Refusing to surrender, Tewodros played the tragic hero to the last and penned a final dramatic and bitter avowal before biting down on a pistol and pulling the trigger.

Emperor Yohannes

In the aftermath of Tewodros' death, there arose another battle for succession. Using his weaponry gained from the British in exchange for his support of their Maqdala expedition, Kassa Mercha of Tigray rose to the fore. In 1871, at the battle of Assam, he defeated the newly crowned Emperor Tekla Giorgis.

After proclaiming himself Emperor Yohannes the following year, Kassa reigned for the next 17 years. In contrast to Tewodros, Yohannes staunchly supported the Church and recognised the independence of local lords.

Yohannes also proved himself a skilful soldier. In 1875, after the Egyptians had advanced into Ethiopia from the coastal area, Yohannes drew them into battle and resoundingly routed them at Gundat and then again at Gura in 1876.

But soon another power threatened: the Italians. The opening of the Suez Canal in 1869 greatly increased the strategic value of the Red Sea, which again became a passageway to the East and beyond.

In 1885 the Italians arrived in Massawa (in present-day Eritrea) and soon blockaded arms to Yohannes. The failure of the British to impede the arrival of the Italians made Yohannes furious. He accused them of

Sci-fi writer Robert Silverberg turns his hand to historical detective in the excellent book *The Realm of Prester John* (1996), about the legendary Christian ruler that is said to have lived in Ethiopia.

1889	1896	1913–16	1915
Addis Ababa, the New Flower, is founded and made capital of Ethiopia.	Emperor Menelik stuns the world by thrashing the Italian army in the Battle of Adwa. The 1889 Friendship Treaty is annulled and Italy recognises Ethiopian independence but hangs onto Eritrea.	Emperor Menelik dies and Lij Iyasu takes over the reins of power before being deposed and succeeded by Menelik's daughter, Zewditu, who rules through a regent, Ras Tafari Makonnen.	Thanks to the shoe-making skills of two engineers, the Djibouti–Addis Ababa rail line is completed, expanding Ethiopian trade and ushering in the rapid development of Addis Ababa.

contravening the 1884 Hewett Treaty. Though protesting otherwise, Britain privately welcomed the Italians, both to counter French influence on the Somali coast (in present-day Djibouti) and to deter Turkish ambitions.

Meanwhile, the Mahadists (or Dervishes) were raising their heads in the West. Dislodging the Egyptians and British, they overran Sudan before arriving in Ethiopia and eventually sacking Gonder in 1888.

Yohannes rushed to meet the Dervishes at Qallabat in 1889 but, at the close of yet another victory, he fell, mortally wounded by a sniper's bullet.

Emperor Menelik

Menelik, King of Shoa since 1865, had long aspired to the imperial throne. Confined at Maqdala for 10 years by Tewodros, he was yet reportedly much influenced by his captor, and also dreamt of Ethiopia's unification and modernisation.

After his escape from Maqdala and his ascendancy in Shoa, Menelik concentrated on consolidating his own power, and embarked on an aggressive, ruthless and sometimes brutal campaign of expansion.

Relations with the Italians were at first good; Menelik had been seen as a potential ally against Yohannes. On Yohannes' death, the Italians recognised Menelik's claim to the throne and, in 1889, the Treaty of Wechale was signed. In exchange for granting Italy the region that was later to become Eritrea, the Italians recognised Menelik's sovereignty and gave him the right to import arms freely through Ethiopian ports.

However, a dispute over a discrepancy in the purportedly identical Amharic and Italian texts – the infamous Article 17 – led to disagreement. According to the Italian version, Ethiopia was obliged to approach other foreign powers through Italy, which essentially reduced Ethiopia to a lowly Italian protectorate. The Amharic version differed in its wording.

In the meantime, the Italians continued their expansion in their newly created colony of Eritrea. Soon, they were spilling into territory well beyond the confines agreed to in both treaties.

Philip Marsden tells the ultimately tragic tale of Emperor Tewodros II in his beautifully executed book on Ethiopia, *The Barefoot Emperor* (2007).

FATHER OF MODERN ETHIOPIA

Considered the father of modern Ethiopia, Amda Seyon (also known as Gebre Meskel) ruled from 1314 to 1344. Known as a military mastermind, he vastly expanded the size of the Christian Empire through the use of force, and his rule is considered something of a golden age for Ethiopia. Military mastermind he may have been, but man of morals he wasn't. He was accused of sleeping with at least one of his sisters and marrying his father's concubine!

1930	1931	1935	1936
After the death of Zewditu and years of careful posturing, Ras Tafari is crowned as Emperor Haile Selassie and dubbed the Chosen One of God.	Ethiopia gets its first written constitution, which grants Emperor Haile Selassie almost total power; his body is even declared sacred.	Italy invades Ethiopia; illegal use of mustard gas and repeated bombing of civilian targets, including Red Cross hospitals, kills 275,000 Ethiopians; Italy loses 4350 men.	The Italians capture Addis and Selassie flees the country. Mussolini triumphantly declares: 'Ethiopia is Italian'. The King of Italy is made Emperor of Ethiopia.

Despite the Italians' attempts to court Tigray's local chiefs, the latter chose to assist Menelik. Nevertheless, the Italians managed to defeat Ras Mangasha and his Tigrayan forces and occupied Mekele in 1895.

Provoked at last into marching north with his forces, Menelik shocked the international world by resoundingly defeating the Italians at Adwa. This battle numbered among the very few occasions when a colonial power was defeated by a native force in Africa. Ethiopia stood out as the only independent nation left in Africa.

Menelik then set his sights on modernisation. He abandoned the Shoan capital of Ankober and soon founded the new capital, Addis Ababa. During his reign, electricity and telephones were introduced; bridges, roads, schools and hospitals were built; and banks and industrial enterprises were established.

Iyasu

Menelik died a natural death in 1913. Iyasu, his raffish young grandson and nominated heir, proved to be very much a product of the 20th century. Continuing with Menelik's reforms, he also showed a 'modern' secularist, nonsectarian attitude.

The young prince built mosques as well as churches, took several Muslim as well as Christian wives, and supported the empire's peripheral populations, which had for years suffered at the oppressive hands of Amharic settlers and governors.

Iyasu and his councillors pushed through a few reforms, including improving the system of land tenure and taxation, but they faced ever-deepening opposition from the church and nobility.

Finally, after also upsetting the allied powers with his dealings with the Weimar Republic (Germany), Austria and the Ottoman Empire, a pretext for his removal was found. Accused by the nobles of 'abjuring the Christian faith', the prince was deposed in 1921.

Zewditu, Menelik's daughter, was proclaimed empress. Things were not plain sailing for her, though. Zewditu had a rival to the throne, Ras Tafari (the son of Ras Makonnen, Menelik's cousin, and grandson of an earlier Showan monarch). The conservative Ethiopian aristocracy largely supported Zewditu, but they had severe misgivings about other members of her family. In the end a kind of 'power sharing' agreement was reached with Zewditu being empress and Ras Tafari proclaimed the prince regent.

Ras Tafari

Prince Ras Tafari boasted more experience and greater maturity than Iyasu, particularly in the field of foreign affairs.

Donald N Levine's imaginative *Wax & Gold* (2014) provides outstanding insight into Amharic culture, though chapter six is rather far-fetched!

1936	1937	1940–50	1941–42
In June Haile Selassie makes a plea to the League of Nations asking for help, but the league lifts sanctions against Italy.	The 1700-year-old Aksum Obelisk is dismantled and removed from Ethiopia by the Italians. In 1998 Italy agrees to return it, but the Ethiopia–Eritrea war prevents it being returned until 2003.	Ethiopia establishes its first national bank, a new national currency, its first university and its first (and only) airline – Ethiopian Airlines.	British Commonwealth and Ethiopian forces liberate Ethiopia from Italian occupation; Haile Selassie reclaims his throne and Ethiopia its independence. The country modernises rapidly.

In 1923 Tafari pulled off a major diplomatic coup by securing Ethiopia entry into the League of Nations. Membership firmly placed Ethiopia on the international political map, and also gave it some recourse against the grasping designs of its European, colonial neighbours.

Continuing the tradition begun by Menelik, Tafari was an advocate of reform. A modern printing press was established as well as several secondary schools and an air force. In the meantime, Tafari was steadily outmanoeuvring his rivals. In 1930 the last rebellious noble was defeated and killed in battle. A few days later the sick empress also died. Ras Tafari assumed the throne.

Emperor Haile Selassie

On 2 November 1930 Tafari was crowned Emperor Haile Selassie. The extravagant spectacle was attended by representatives from across the globe and proved a terrific public-relations exercise. It even led indirectly to the establishment of a new faith, Rastafarianism.

The following year, Ethiopia's first written constitution was introduced. It granted the emperor virtually absolute power. The two-house parliament consisted of a senate, which was nominated by the emperor from among his nobles, and a chamber of deputies, which was elected from the landholders. It was thus little more than a chamber for self-interested debate.

Ever since the day of his regency, the emperor had been bringing the country under centralised rule. For the first time, the Ethiopian state was unambiguously unified.

Italian Occupation

By the early 20th century Ethiopia was the only state in Africa to have survived European colonisation. However, Ethiopia's position between the two Italian colonies of Eritrea and Somalia made it an enticing morsel.

From 1933, in an effort to undermine the Ethiopian state, Italian agents, well heeled with funds, were dispatched to subvert the local chiefs, as well as to stir up ethnic tensions. Britain and France, nervous of pushing Mussolini further into Hitler's camp, refrained from protests and turned a blind eye.

In 1934 a minor skirmish known as the Wal Wal incident took place between Italian and Ethiopian forces. Italy had found its pretext.

On 3 October 1935 Italians, overwhelmingly superior in both ground and air forces, invaded Ethiopia from Eritrea. First the northern town of Aksum fell, then Mekele.

The League of Nations issued sanctions against Italy, but their enforcement by various European nations was lacklustre and had little impact.

The Emperor (1989) by Ryszard Kapuscinski offers bizarre insights into Haile Selassie's imperial court through interviews with servants and close associates of the emperor. Some historians question its authenticity though.

1960	1962	1962	1972–74
In response to growing discontent over the emperor's autocratic rule, the imperial bodyguard stage a coup d'etat, which is defeated by the army and air force.	Addis Ababa is made the headquarters of the Organisation of African Unity.	Haile Selassie unilaterally annexes Eritrea; separatist Eritreans launch a bitter guerrilla war.	A dreadful famine strikes and around 200,000 people die. This further increases resentment towards the emperor, and students start protesting.

Campaigning

Terrified that the international community would impose more serious embargoes, and keen to keep Italian morale high, Il Duce pressed for a swift campaign.

Impatient with progress made, he soon replaced De Bono, his first general. Pietro Badoglio, his replacement, was authorised 'to use all means of war – I say all – both from the air and from the ground'. Implicit in the instructions was the use of mustard gas, which contravened the 1926 Geneva Convention.

Despite overwhelming odds, the Ethiopians succeeded in launching a major counter-attack, known as the Christmas Offensive, at the Italian position at Mekele at the end of 1935. However, the Italians were soon on the offensive again. Backed by hundreds of planes, cannons and weapons of every type, the Italian armies swept across the country.

Meanwhile, Emperor Haile Selassie had fled Ethiopia (some Ethiopians never forgave him for it) to present Ethiopia's cause to the world. On 30 June 1936 he made his famous speech to the League of Nations in Geneva. However, the league lifted the sanctions later that year against Italy – only the USSR, the USA, Haiti, Mexico and New Zealand refused to recognise Italy's conquest.

Occupation & Resistance

Soon Ethiopia, Eritrea and Somalia were merged to become the colonial territory of 'Africa Orientale Italiana' (Italian East Africa).

Hoping to create an important economic base, Italy invested heavily in its new colony. From 1936 as many as 60,000 Italian workers poured in to work on Ethiopia's infrastructure.

Ethiopia kept up a spirited resistance to Italian rule throughout its brief duration. Italy's response was famously brutal. Mussolini personally ordered all rebels to be shot, and insurgencies were put down using large-scale bombing, poison gas and machine-gunning from the air.

Ethiopian resistance reached a peak in February 1937 with an assassination attempt on the much-hated Italian viceroy, Rodolfo Graziani. In reprisal, the Italians spent three days shooting, beheading or disembowelling several thousand people in the capital.

The 'patriot's movement' (the resistance fighters) was mainly based in the historical provinces of Shoa, Gonder and Gojam, but drew support from all parts of the country; many fighters were women.

Graziani's response was simple: 'Eliminate them, eliminate them, eliminate them'. But Ethiopian resolve stiffened and resistance grew. Although in control of major towns, Italy never conquered the entire country.

The second edition of Bahru Zewde's widely acclaimed *A History of Modern Ethiopia 1855–1991* (2002) contains two particularly readable sections: Harold G Marcus' *Ethiopia* and Richard Pankhurst's *The Ethiopians*.

1974	1975	1975	1976–90
After years of growing discontent and increasing street protests, Haile Selassie is unceremoniously deposed as emperor on 12 September. The Derg declare a socialist state on 20 December.	The last emperor of Ethiopia, Haile Selassie, dies while in custody. The cause of death is unknown but many believe he was smothered with a pillow by Mengistu.	The Tigrayan People's Liberation Front is founded. Its first attacks are a raid on a jail and a bank robbery in Aksum. It goes on to launch a war for autonomy.	Collectivisation of agriculture begins and forced resettlement and 'villageisation' takes place. One of the stated goals is to help reduce famine. Most experts believe it had the opposite effect.

The outbreak of WWII, particularly Italy's declaration of war against Britain in 1940, dramatically changed the course of events. Britain at last reversed its policy of tacit support of Italy's East African expansion and initially offered Ethiopia assistance on the Sudan–Ethiopia border. Later, in early 1941, Britain launched three major attacks.

Though not then widely recognised, the Ethiopian patriots played a major role before, during and after the liberation campaign, which ended on 5 May 1941 when the emperor and his men entered Addis Ababa.

Postliberation Ethiopia

The British, who'd entered Ethiopia as liberators, initially seemed to have simply replaced Italy as occupiers. However, Anglo-Ethiopian treaties in 1942 and 1944 eventually marked Ethiopia's resumption of independence.

The 1940s and '50s saw much postwar reconstruction, including (with US assistance) the establishment of a new government bank, a national currency and the country's first national airline, Ethiopian Airlines.

In 1955 the Revised Ethiopian Constitution was introduced. Although for the first time the legislature included an elected chamber of deputies, the government remained autocratic and the emperor continued to hold all power.

In 1962 Addis Ababa became the headquarters of the Organisation of African Unity (OAU) and, in 1958, of the UN Economic Commission for Africa (ECA).

Discontent

Despite modernisation, the pace of development was slow, and dissatisfaction with it, and with the emperor's autocratic rule, began to grow. Finally, taking advantage of a state visit to Brazil in December 1960, the emperor's imperial bodyguard staged a coup d'etat. Though put down by the army and air force, it signalled the beginning of the end of imperial rule in Ethiopia.

Discontent simmered among the students too, who protested in particular against land tenure, corruption and the appalling famine of 1972–74 in which an estimated 200,000 died.

Meanwhile, international relations had also been deteriorating. In 1962 Ethiopia abrogated the UN-sponsored federation with Eritrea and unilaterally annexed the Eritrean state.

Then war broke out in 1964 with Somalia over joint claims to Ethiopia's Somali-inhabited region of the Ogaden Desert.

The ultimate guide to the historical treasures of the north is Stuart Munro-Hay's *Ethiopia: The Unknown Land: A Cultural and Historical Guide* (2002).

1977	1977–78	1977–78	1984
Colonel Mengistu Haile Mariam emerges as leader of the Derg. He appeals to the Soviet Union and Cuba among others for aid.	Somalia invades the Ogaden region of Ethiopia. Somali forces are eventually defeated in 1978, but only with massive help from Cuban and Soviet forces.	The Derg launch a violent crackdown on opponents; thousands die in what becomes known as the Red Terror campaign.	Israel launches 'Operation Moses', a six-week operation to secretly airlift 8000 Ethiopian Jews to Israel.

The 1974 Revolution & the Emperor's Fall

By 1973 an increasingly powerful and radical military group had emerged. Known as the Derg (Committee), they used the media with consummate skill to undermine the authority of the emperor himself. They famously flashed striking footage of starvation from Jonathan Dim-

THE BEST ETHIOPIAN BOOKS

With a country as endlessly fascinating as Ethiopia, it's little surprise that a small library of books has been written documenting Ethiopia's wonders.
The following are our favourites:

➡ *The Chains of Heaven*, by Philip Marsden (2005). If you're going to read one book on Ethiopia make it this one. The author walks across the north Ethiopian plateau and in the process reveals much about Ethiopian culture and history.

➡ *Sheba: Through the Desert in Search of the Legendry Queen*, by Nicholas Clapp (2002). Successfully blending personal travel accounts through Ethiopia, Yemen and elsewhere with thorough academic research to shed light on one of history's most famous characters.

➡ *Eating the Flowers of Paradise*, by Kevin Rushby (1998). The author travels the old trade route from Ethiopia to Yemen. Chewing *chat* leaves with everyone he meets, Rushby reveals much about the culture surrounding this drug.

➡ *The Prester Quest*, by Nicholas Jubber (2005). An entertaining voyage from Venice to Ethiopia tracing the story behind Prester John.

➡ *The Sign and the Seal*, by Graham Hancock (1992). Hancock attempts to solve the mystery of the 'disappearance' of the Ark of the Covenant. Though his research and conclusions raised an eyebrow or two among historians, this detective story is very readable – however tenuous the facts may be!

➡ *In Search of King Solomon's Mines*, by Tahir Shah (2002). A riveting quest to find the mythical gold mines of King Solomon. In typical Shah fashion it's full of magic and bizarre encounters.

➡ *The Mountains of Rasselas*, by Thomas Pakenham (1999). The author's fascination with the historical anecdotes revolving around Ethiopia's *ambas* (flat-topped mountains) is the basis of this engaging and nicely illustrated coffee-table book.

➡ *Remote People*, by Evelyn Waugh (2002). Although very dated, this book includes some wry impressions of Ethiopia in the 1930s.

➡ *Les Afars d'Éthiopie*, by Jean-Baptiste Jeangène Vilmer and Franck Gouéry (in French; 2011). Beautiful images of the Danakil, and descriptions of the Afar and other peoples who make their lives in this harshest of climates.

1984–85	1991–93	1992	1993
Famine haunts much of highland Ethiopia and up to a million people die. The reasons for the famine are climatic and political. A huge relief operation spearheaded by Bob Geldof is launched.	The Derg are defeated by the rebel EPRDF; Ethiopia's experiment with communism ends, and Mengistu scuttles off to Robert Mugabe's Zimbabwe where he remains to this day.	Haile Selassie's remains are found buried under a toilet in the royal palace. He is reburied eight years later in the Holy Trinity Cathedral. Turn out is much lower than funeral organisers predicted.	Following a referendum Eritrea finally gets its long-sought independence. Relations between the two new neighbours are excellent.

bleby's well-known BBC TV report on the Wolo famine in between clips of sumptuous palace banquets.

The result was an unprecedented wave of teacher, student and taxi strikes in Addis Ababa. Even army mutinies began to be reported. At crisis point, the prime minister and his cabinet resigned and a new one was appointed with the mandate to carry out far-reaching constitutional reforms. But it was too late.

On 12 September 1974 Emperor Haile Selassie was deposed, unceremoniously bundled into the back of a Volkswagen and driven away to prison. Ministers, nobles and close confidants of the emperor were also arrested by the Derg. The absolute power of the emperor and the divine right of rule of the century-old imperial dynasty were finished.

The Derg soon dissolved parliament and established the Provisional Military Administrative Council (PMAC) to rule the country.

Emerging as the leader of the Derg was Colonel Mengistu Haile Mariam who rode the wave of popular opposition to Selassie's regime, as well as the Marxist-Leninist ideology of left-wing students.

And what happened to the emperor? The official line at the time was that he died of 'respiratory failure' in August 1975 following complications from a prostate operation. However, many people believe he was murdered by Mengistu himself. In 1992, after the fall of the Derg, Selassie's bones were discovered buried under a concrete slab in the grounds of the palace in Addis.

The Socialist Experiment

On 20 December 1974 a socialist state was declared. Under the adage *Ityopya Tikdem* or 'Ethiopia First', banks, businesses and factories were nationalised as was the rural and urban land. However, few of the projects launched by the Derg proved to be successful and agricultural output stagnated.

In the meantime, the external threats posed by Somalia and secessionist Eritrea were increasing. The Derg responded to these threats with a wave of mass arrests and executions. In July 1977 Somalia invaded Ethiopia. Thanks to the intervention of the Soviet Union, which flooded socialist Ethiopia with Soviet state-of-the-art weaponry, Somalia was beaten back. In Eritrea, however, the secessionists continued to thwart Ethiopian offensives.

Meanwhile internal political debate also degenerated into violence. The leadership of the Derg split into two groups, with one, the Ethiopian People's Revolutionary Party (EPRP) proclaiming that the Derg had 'betrayed the revolution'. Verbal violence between the two groups quickly turned to physical violence and the then Vice-Chairman of the Derg,

Aidan Hartley's *The Zanzibar Chest* (2004) recalls his days as a foreign correspondent throughout Africa and includes chapters on the last days of the Derg. It's one of the most powerful and wonderfully crafted books you could hope to read.

1995	1996	1997	1998–2000
The Federal Democratic Republic of Ethiopia is proclaimed and elections are held. Former guerrilla leader Meles Zenawi is proclaimed prime minister.	The Italian Ministry of Defence finally admits to the use of mustard gas in the Abyssinian campaign.	Eritrea drops the birr as its national currency and introduces the nakfa. This leads to a souring of the relationship between the two neighbours.	Ethiopia and Eritrea's leaders go to war over a sliver of barren wasteland. By the close of hostilities 70,000 have died and tens of thousands are internally displaced.

Mengistu, used the unstable political situation to justify a purge of the upper echelons of the Derg. The result was the execution of a number of party leaders and the promotion of himself to undisputed leader of the Derg.

Red Terror

Shortly afterwards, in an effort to suppress all political opponents, Mengistu launched the Red Terror campaign with an infamous speech in Addis Ababa that involved him smashing three bottles filled with what appeared to be blood on the ground and proclaiming 'Death to counter revolutionaries! Death to the EPRP!'. The Red Terror turned out to be a highly appropriate name as, at a very conservative estimate, 100,000 people were killed (Amnesty International estimates the number may have been as high as 500,000) and thousands more fled the country.

Families of victims of the Red Terror were ordered to pay for the cost of the bullet that killed their relatives before the victim's body was returned. Anyone who was suspected of being opposed to the Derg was liable to arrest or execution. At the height of the Red Terror, the general secretary of Save The Children stated: '1000 children have been killed and their bodies are left in the street and are being eaten by wild hyenas. You can see the heaped-up bodies of murdered children, most of them aged 11 to 13, lying in the gutter, as you drive out of Addis Ababa'.

The Demise of the Derg

Lucy was named after the Beatles' song 'Lucy in the Sky with Diamonds'. It was playing in the archaeologists' camp when she was discovered.

Red Terror only cemented the stance of those opposing the Derg. Numerous armed liberation movements arose, including those of the Afar, Oromo, Somali and particularly Tigrayan peoples. For years, with limited weaponry, they fought the military might of the Soviet-backed Derg, which had the second-largest army in sub-Saharan Africa.

The various opposition groups eventually united to form the Ethiopian People's Revolutionary Democratic Front (EPRDF), which in 1989 began its historic military campaign towards Addis Ababa.

The Derg was doubly confronted by the EPRDF in Ethiopia and the Eritrean People's Liberation Front (EPLF) in Eritrea. With the fall of his allies in Eastern Europe, and with his state in financial ruin as well as his own military authority in doubt, Mengistu's time was up and he fled the country on 21 May 1991. Seven days later, the EPRDF entered Addis Ababa and the Derg was done.

Mengistu received asylum in Zimbabwe, where he remains to this day, despite being tried in absentia in Ethiopia and sentenced to death.

2000–01	2001	2005	2006
A formal peace agreement is signed by Ethiopia and Eritrea and a demilitarised zone is established along the border under the supervision of the UN Mission in Ethiopia & Eritrea (UNMEE).	Two Ethiopian scientists discover possible human fossils dating back some 5.8 to 5.2 million years. They are tentatively named as a subspecies of *Ardipithecus ramidus kadabba*.	After 15 May elections, mass protests turn deadly when government troops fire on unarmed demonstrators. Thousands of people, including opposition politicians, journalists and newspaper editors are detained by police.	Construction begins on the controversial Gibe III dam, the biggest dam project in Africa. Debate rages over whether the dam will bring advantages or disadvantages.

The Road to Democracy (1991–95)

After the war of liberation Ethiopia showed zeal and determination to rebuild the country.

In July 1991 a transitional charter was endorsed, which gave the EPRDF-dominated legislature a four-year, interim rule under the executive of the TPLF leader, Meles Zenawi. First and foremost, Mengistu's failed socialist policies were abandoned, and de facto independence was granted to Eritrea.

In August 1995 the Federal Democratic Republic of Ethiopia was proclaimed, a series of elections followed, and the constitution of the second republic was inaugurated. Meles Zenawi formed a new government.

Ethiopia–Eritrea War

Despite being friends and having fought against the Derg side by side for more than a decade, Meles Zenawi and Eritrea's president, Isaias Afewerki, soon clashed. The cause? Eritrea's introduction of the nakfa currency to replace the Ethiopian birr in November 1997.

In early May 1998 a number of Eritrean officials were killed near the border. On 12 May Eritrea upped the stakes by occupying the border town of Badme. Over the next month there was intense fighting between the two sides. In early June the Ethiopians launched air raids on the airport in Asmara to which the Eritreans retaliated by bombing Mekele airport. In both cases civilians were killed.

In February 1999 a full-scale military conflict broke out that left tens of thousands dead on both sides before it finally ceased for good in mid-2000. During this time there were mass exportations of Eritreans from Ethiopia and Ethiopians from Eritrea.

Although Ethiopia had agreed to peace earlier, it wasn't until Ethiopia recaptured all territory and went on to occupy parts of central and western Eritrea that Eritrea finally agreed to a ceasefire.

In December 2000 a formal peace settlement was signed in Algiers. In April 2001 a 25km-wide demilitarised strip, which ran the length of the internationally recognised border on the Eritrean side, was set up under supervision of the UN Mission in Ethiopia and Eritrea (UNMEE).

In late 2005 a commission at the Permanent Court of Arbitration in the Hague ruled that Eritrea broke international law when it attacked Ethiopia in 1998 and triggered the war.

Since the guns fell silent there have been periods of extreme tension between the two nations that have seen forces massed on both sides of the border, and today the two armies continue to eye each other suspiciously over the desert.

In the past, the causes of famine have had less to do with environmental factors – Ethiopia has abundant natural resources – and more to do with economic mismanagement and inequitable and oppressive governments.

ETHIOPIA'S HISTORY THE ROAD TO DEMOCRACY (1991–95)

2006–09	2006–09	2007	2008
Ethiopia invades Somalia in order to dislodge the Islamic Courts Union. It becomes embroiled in a guerrilla war and finally pulls out in early 2009.	Tensions between Ethiopia and Eritrea come close to boiling over and both sides begin massive troop build-ups in the border region. Fortunately tensions subside and war is averted.	In September Ethiopia celebrates the new millennium. Why is it seven years 'late'? It uses a different calendar to Western countries.	The UNMEE mandate expires after 'crippling restrictions' from Eritrea, and UN troops withdraw from the border region, leaving the two nations eyeing each other nervously.

ETHIOPIA'S HISTORY PROTESTS & INVASIONS

Protests & Invasions

The 15 May 2005 elections returned the EPRDF and Zenawi to power, but while the election run-up and the voting polls were witness to few irregularities, there were numerous reports by EU observers about questionable vote counting at the constituency level and the announcing of the results by state-run media.

In the years leading up to the elections, discontent with the government had been growing and then, during the election campaigning, opposition parties alleged cases of intimidation and arrests of their supporters. On the morning of 15 May, when the first results were first announced, it appeared that the opposition parties had made sweeping gains, but then later that afternoon the EPRDF announced that, aside from in Addis itself, it had in fact won a majority of seats. Straight away opposition parties and supporters cried foul play and mass protests broke out in Addis. Government troops arrested thousands of opposition-party members and killed 22 unarmed civilians. Similar protests and mass strikes occurred in early November, which resulted in troops killing 46 civilians and arresting thousands more. Leaders of political party Coalition for Unity and Democracy, as well as owners of private newspapers, were also arrested and charged with inciting the riots. The government's actions were condemned by the EU and many Western governments, but the election result stood.

In 2006 Ethiopia launched an invasion of Somalia in order to dislodge the Islamic Courts Union (ICU), which had gained control of much of the country (and ironically brought the first semblance of peace Somalia had seen in years). By the end of the year Ethiopian troops had pushed the ICU back to the far south of Somalia, but they soon found themselves tangled up in a messy guerrilla war, with the ICU slowly beginning to win back lost ground. Many observers suspected that Eritrea was secretly arming and aiding the ICU in its war with Ethiopia. Unwilling to get bogged down in a long and bloody battle in Somalia, Ethiopia called for an African Union (AU) force to take its place and the Ethiopians began to withdraw in early 2009.

Despite the official withdrawal, the Ethiopian military made repeated incursions over the border to fight al-Shabaab (the Islamic militant group which rapidly replaced the ICU after their demise, and quickly came to control much of southern Somalia) throughout the remainder of

Ethiopia was named by the Greeks, who saw the country as a far-off realm, populated by remarkable people and extraordinary animals. It means 'Land of the Burnt Faces'.

When the EPRDF rolled into Addis Ababa it was navigating with photocopies of the Addis Ababa map found in Lonely Planet's *Africa on a Shoestring*.

2010	2011	2012	2012
Colonel Mengistu Haile Mariam announces he is writing his memoirs. In 2012 a leaked version, entitled *Tiglatchn*, appears on the internet.	In late 2011 Ethiopian forces, in an effort to support the government of Somalia in their battle against al-Shabaab militants, re-enter Somalia alongside African Union and Kenyan troops.	Ethiopia jails prominent journalist Eskinder Nega for 18 years for violating the country's antiterrorism legislation after he wrote an article questioning arrests under that very same act.	Ethiopia's most acclaimed modern artist, Afewerk Tekle, dies.

2009 and up to 2011. Many of these incursions were denied by the Ethiopian government. In late 2011 the Ethiopian military, working with the transitional government, AU forces and the Kenyan military, officially re-entered Somalia as part of a concerted drive to destroy al-Shabaab.

The End of an Era

The elections of 2010 saw Zenawi and the EPRDF returned to power. This time there was none of the violence that marked the 2005 election but international observers criticised the elections saying they fell short of international standards. Human Rights Watch claimed the government had a strategy of systematically closing down space for political dissent and independent criticism.

In July 2012 rumours began to circulate that Zenawi, who hadn't been seen in public for some weeks, had died. The government denied these rumours but admitted that Zenawi had been hospitalised, but that his condition was not serious. On 20 August 2012 it was announced that after 21 years of leading Ethiopia, Zenawi, the man who had led the country since the overthrow of the Derg regime in 1991, had died of an infection contracted after an operation to remove a brain tumour. Zenawi had

Although only published locally, *Eritrea's War* by Paul Henze (2002) delves into the 1998–2000 Ethiopia–Eritrea War.

FAMINE IN ETHIOPIA

If there's one word everyone associates with Ethiopia it's 'famine'. The country has regularly been plagued by drought, food shortages and famine. The famine of 1972–74 in Wolo and other northern provinces, and the government's mishandling of it, added greatly to the general dissatisfaction with the government, and this contributed to the fall of Selassie and the imperial government.

The most infamous famine of all was that of 1984–86, in which between 400,000 and a million people died. Though the conditions that led to famine are widely blamed on drought, it's been shown that widespread drought conditions actually occurred only some months after the famine was underway and that for many areas the harvest of 1982 delivered something of a bumper crop. Instead, the major cause was the civil unrest and rebellions taking place in many parts of the country, the failed government resettlement campaigns, communal farms and 'villageisation' programs – all of which aggravated the disaster in many areas. In addition, Derg leader Mengistu's disinclination to help the province of Tigray – the worst affected region and home to the powerful Tigrayan People's Liberation Front (TPLF) – caused thousands more to die.

Drought continues to haunt the Horn of Africa today. A severe drought, said by many to be the worst in 60 years, affected (and at the time of writing continues to affect) a large part of eastern Africa. However, with a much more organised national and international response, the death toll has been far lower and famine was declared only in parts of war-torn Somalia.

2012	2012	2012	2012
The Patriarch of the Ethiopian Coptic Church, Abune Paulos, dies unexpectedly.	On 20 August it is announced that Meles Zenawi, the man who has dominated the Ethiopian and regional political scene for 21 years, has died.	The government announces that Hailemariam Desalegn, from southern Ethiopia, is to be the acting prime minister until elections in 2015.	The Ethiopian national football team qualifies for the 2013 Africa Cup, the first time it has managed this in 31 years. Ethiopians celebrate as if they've already won the cup!

made economic growth and development his number-one priority and during his 21-year rule the country changed for the better, beyond all recognition of the Ethiopia Zenawi had inherited.

Hailemariam Desalegn, the deputy prime minister and former President of the Southern Nations, Nationalities, and Peoples' Region, took office as prime minister. His party (the EPRDF) won another overwhelming victory in the general elections in 2015.

According to the Greek poet Homer (800 BC), the Greek gods, including Zeus himself, visited Ethiopia. Homer refers to the people as 'blameless Ethiopians'.

Despite a slightly condescending view of the 'primitive negroes' Alan Moorehead's *The Blue Nile* (2000), which depicts the history of the river, land and those who sought its source, remains a classic of the genre.

ANTON IVANOV / SHUTTERSTOCK ©

Church and bell tower, Aksum (p93)

2015	2015	2015	2016
Hailemariam Desalegn is re-elected prime minister.	The controversial Gibe III dam begins generating electricity.	The (controversial) government's plans to expand Addis Ababa into surrounding Oromia state triggers civil unrest.	Following violence and civil unrest sparked by the death of 55 people during a religious festival on 2 October, the government declares a state of emergency and restricts civil liberties.

Ethiopian Culture

More than any other country in sub-Saharan Africa, Ethiopia is known for its culture. With its long and prestigious history and early connections with the Christian church, its culture is ancient and rich. Additionally, it was the only country on the continent to escape colonialism; its culture has survived largely intact.

The People of Ethiopia

Ethiopia's population has squeezed past the 100-million mark, an astounding figure considering the population was just 15 million in 1935. Ethiopia has one of the fastest growing populations in the world. This population explosion is arguably the biggest problem facing Ethiopia today. In 2015 its population growth rate was estimated at a worryingly high 2.5%; which, if growth rates continue at around that level, will leave Ethiopia bursting at the seams with almost 120 million people in 2025. However, AIDS, which affects 2.1% of the population, will inevitably slow future growth.

Although 84 languages and 200 dialects are spoken in Ethiopia, the population can be broken down into nine broad groups.

According to Homer, the ancient Greek Gods often travelled to the edges of the Hellenic world to enjoy the company of a people who, unlike Mediterranean man and his gods, were renowned for their grace and virtue: the blameless Ethiopians.

The Oromo

Although traditionally most of the Oromo were nomadic pastoralists, it was the skilled Oromo warrior horsemen who put fear into Ethiopians when they migrated north from present-day Kenya in the mid-16th century. It was the Oromo who inspired Harar's leaders to build a wall around the city and even led Ethiopian emperors to (briefly and much to the disgust of the general population) accept Catholicism in order to gain Portugal's military support.

Today, most Oromo are settled, making a living as farmers or cattle breeders. They are Muslim, Christian and animist in religion, and are known for their egalitarian society, which is based on the *gada* (age-group system). A man's life is divided into age-sets of eight years. In the fourth set (between the ages of 24 and 32), men assume the right to govern their people.

They are the largest ethnic group in the country, making up 34.5% of its population. Over 85% of the massive 350,000-sq-km Oromia region's population are Oromo. Many Oromo resent the Tigray-led national government, and the Oromo Liberation Front (OLF) continues to lobby for separation from Ethiopia.

The Amharas

As great warriors, skilful governors and astute administrators, the Amhara have dominated the country's history, politics and society since 1270, and have imposed their own language and culture on the country. In the past this was much resented by other tribal groups, who saw it as little more than a kind of colonialism.

Amhara tend to be devoutly Christian, although there are some Muslim Amhara. They're also fanatical about their land and 90% of them are traditional tillers of the soil: they produce some of the nation's best *tef* (endemic cereal grain used for *the* national staple, *injera*).

Making up 26.9% of Ethiopia's population, they're the second-largest ethnic group. Over 90% of the Amharaland region's people are Amhara.

The Tigrayans

Much like the Amharas, the Tigrayans are fiercely independent and zealously attached to their land. They disdain all manual labour with the single exception of agriculture.

Most live in the Tigray region, where both Christianity and Islam were introduced to Ethiopia. Ninety-five per cent of Tigrayans are Orthodox Christian, and most devoutly so. Tigrayans are Ethiopia's third-largest ethnic group, comprising around 6.1% of the population.

As a result of the Tigrayan People's Liberation Front (TPLF) playing the major role in the bringing down of the Derg, many Tigrayans feature in Ethiopia's government. This has caused resentment among other groups.

The Somali

The arid lowlands of the southeast dictate a nomadic or seminomadic existence for the Somali. Somali society is 99% Muslim, strongly hierarchical, tightly knit and based on the clan system, which requires intense loyalty from its members. In the harsh environment in which they live, ferocious competition for the scant resources leads to frequent and sometimes violent disputes (thanks to an abundant supply of AK-47s) over grazing grounds and sources of water.

The Somali make up 95% of the Somali region's people and 6.2% of Ethiopia's population.

A staggering 13% of Ethiopian children are missing one or both parents. Nearly a quarter of these parents have been lost through AIDS.

The Sidama

The Sidama, a heterogeneous people, originate from the southwest and can be divided into five different groups: the Sidama proper, the Derasa, Hadiya, Kambata and Alaba. Most Sidama are farmers who cultivate cereals, tobacco, *enset* (false-banana tree found in much of southern Ethiopia) and coffee. The majority are animists and many ancient beliefs persist, including a belief in the reverence of spirits. Pythons are believed to be reincarnations of ancestors and are sometimes kept as house pets. The Sidama social organisation is based on an age-group system.

The Sidama comprise about 4% of Ethiopia's population and most live in the Southern Nations, Nationalities and People's region.

The Gurage

Semitic in origin, the Gurage practise herding or farming, and the *enset* (false-banana tree) is their favoured crop. They are known as great workers, clever improvisers and skilled craftspeople. Many work as seasonal labourers for the highlanders. Their faith is Christian, Muslim or animist, depending on the area from which they originate.

They comprise only 2% of Ethiopia's population, but make up more than 10% of the population in the Southern Nations, Nationalities and People's region.

The Afar

The Afar, formerly also known as the Danakils, inhabit the famous region of Dankalia, which stretches across Ethiopia's east, Djibouti's west and into Eritrea's southeast. It's considered one of Earth's most inhospitable environments. Rightly or wrongly, they've latched onto early-20th-century adventurer Wilfred Thesiger's portrayal of them as famously belligerent and proud. Thesiger wrote of the Afar winning social prestige in the past for murdering and castrating members of an opposing tribe. Fortunately for male travellers this is somewhat rarer today!

The Afar comprise 1.7% of Ethiopia's population.

The Harari

Like the Gurage, the Harari people (sometimes known as Adare) are also Semitic in origin. They have long inhabited the walled Muslim city of Harar. The people are particularly known for their distinct two-storey houses, known as *gegar*, and for the very colourful traditional costumes still worn by many Harari women today. In the past, the Harari were known as great craftspeople for their weaving, baskets and bookbinding. They're also renowned Islamic scholars.

The Falashas

Falashas (Ethiopian Jews) have inhabited Ethiopia since pre-Christian times. Despite actively engaging in wars over the years to defend their independence and freedom, few now remain: war, some persecution (though much less than seen elsewhere) and emigration in the latter part of the 20th century have greatly reduced their numbers.

In 1984 around 8000 Falashas fled Ethiopia and walked on foot to Sudan, where the Israeli and US secret services surreptitiously airlifted them to Israel. A further operation took place in 1991, when 34 Israeli aircraft secretly transported some 14,325 Jews to Israel over a 36-hour period (by the time the planes had landed, there were actually two extra passengers as two women gave birth during their flights!).

Tiny populations of Falashas remain north of Lake Tana in the northwest of Ethiopia; their beliefs combine a fascinating mixture of Judaism, indigenous beliefs and Christianity.

The Ethiopian Way of Life

Other than religion, which undoubtedly plays a huge role in almost all Ethiopians' daily life, it's agriculture and pastoralism that fill the days of well over 80% of the country's population. Everyone is involved, right down to stick-and-stone-wielding four-year-old children who are handed the incredible responsibility of tending and herding the family's livestock.

With almost everyone toiling out in the fields, it's not surprising that only 42.7% (CIA figures; note that other sources give lower, or higher, figures) of the population is literate. Since young children are needed to help with the family plots and animals, only 82% (Unicef figures) of

Every Ethiopian emperor (bar one) since Yekuno Amlak established the Solomonic dynasty in 1270 has been Amhara. Yohannes (r 1872–89), who was Tigrayan, is the only exception.

ETHIOPIA'S STREET KIDS

Throughout Ethiopia there are a range of charities working to help the country's many street children. In many cases working with these charities involves a considerable commitment of time as well as having a certain skill to offer. In these cases it's usually easiest for a short-term visitor to just donate money to their chosen charity after they've returned home.

A more hands-on approach is the distribution of meal tickets. Some local centres sell booklets of meal tickets that are then distributed to needy children. Each day hundreds of children redeem the tickets for a meal at the centre.

Addis Ababa–based **Hope Enterprises** (p289) sells booklets of eight meal tickets.

In Gonder, local NGO **Yenege Tesfa** (p80) runs an orphanage and provides educational and medical programs. Tourists are encouraged to visit some of its project sites. It sells 'bread coupons' that children can exchange for a loaf of bread. Tickets are available from most of the bigger hotels for Birr0.50 per ticket.

children attend primary school. If all children under 16 were forced to attend school, Ethiopia's workforce would be ravaged and almost half of the country's entire population would be attending classes.

Ethiopian families are incredibly close and most people live with their parents until marriage. After marriage, the couple usually joins the household of the husband's family. After a couple of years, they will request a plot of land from the village, on which to build their own house.

Divorce is relatively easy in Ethiopia and marriage can be dissolved at the request of either party (adultery is usually given as justification). In theory, each partner retains the property he or she brought into the marriage, though sometimes allowances are made for the 'wronged' partner.

WHO DOES SHE THINK SHE IS?

The most beautiful and alluring woman ever to live had hairy legs and the cloven foot of the devil. Her fame has lasted 3000 years, yet nobody remembers her name. She's a player in the ancient legends of Judaism, Christianity and Islam, yet no one knows where she lived. She's the mother of the throne of Ethiopia, the most famous daughter of Yemen and the original Jerusalem pilgrim. She is, of course, the Queen of Sheba, but she may never even have existed.

Though she appears in the writings of all three monotheistic religions, it's the Ethiopian story (in which she is known as Makeda) of her life that is most famous in the West, while for Christian Ethiopians the story is virtually the very cornerstone of their culture, history and lifestyle.

According to the Kebra Negast (Ethiopia's national epic), the Queen of Sheba's first public appearance was when she paid a visit to the court of King Solomon in Jerusalem in the 10th century BC.

The Ethiopian legend reveals how after her arrival Solomon became enraptured with her beauty and devised a plan to have his wicked way with her. He agreed to let her stay in his palace only on the condition that she touched nothing of his. Shocked that Solomon should consider her incapable of such a thing, she agreed. That evening Solomon laid on a feast of spicy and salty foods. After the meal, Sheba and Solomon retired to separate beds in his sleeping quarters. During the night Sheba awoke, thirsty from all the salty food she had consumed, and reached across for a glass of water. The moment she put the glass to her lips Solomon awoke and triumphantly claimed that she had broken her vow. 'But it's only water', she cried, to which Solomon replied, 'And nothing on earth is more precious than water'.

Ethiopian tradition holds that the child that resulted from the deceitful night of passion that followed was to become Menelik I, from whom the entire royal line of Ethiopia claims direct descent (in truth the line, if it ever existed, has been broken a number of times).

But there's more to this tale than just the birth of the Ethiopian royal line. This is also the story of the arrival of the Ark of the Covenant in Ethiopia and the conversion of its people to Judaism. It's said that the centrepiece of Solomon's famous temple was the Ark of the Covenant, and that as long as the Jews had the Ark nothing bad could come of them. However, when Menelik travelled to Jerusalem to meet his father, his luggage was a little heavier on his return trip. Secreted away among his dirty laundry was the Ark of the Covenant.

Finding out whether Sheba existed and where her capital was located has not proved easy. The strongest claims have come from both Ethiopia, which claims that Aksum was her capital, and Yemen, which says it was Ma'rib. Both cities were important trade and cultural centres and it's quite likely that both were, if not ruled by the same monarch, then certainly closely tied through trade. However, so far neither has yielded any evidence to suggest that the Queen of Sheba ever existed. Whatever the truth, the legend persists, and every Ethiopian will swear to you that Aksum was the home of the most beautiful cloven-footed woman to ever live.

Although women continue to lag behind men economically, they are highly respected in Ethiopian society. The same can't be said for gay men and lesbians. Homosexuality is severely condemned – traditionally, religiously and legally – and remains a topic of absolute taboo.

Women in Ethiopia

Legally, women in Ethiopia enjoy a relatively equitable position compared with some African countries. They can own property, vote and are represented in government, though there are still some cases in which women's rights are impeded.

Life for many women is extremely hard; to make ends meet many have to resort to extreme actions. Many foreigners are shocked to see just how many prostitutes there are in Ethiopia and just how openly it's practised. Put simply, prostitution doesn't have the same social stigma as it does in the West. Often prostitutes are just students trying to get by. Others are widows, divorcees or refugees, all with little or no hope of finding other forms of employment. With no social security system, it's often their only means of survival. Though not exactly a respected profession, prostitution is considered a perfectly viable means of making a living. HIV-AIDS levels among prostitutes is thought to be close to 50% in Addis Ababa (although no official figures exist). Outside the city, men should be warned that almost all women in bars are prostitutes.

Many Ethiopian women also have to endure the practice of female genital mutilation (genital cutting). The UN has stated that 74.3% of Ethiopian women between the ages of 15 and 49 have undergone some form of female genital mutilation; in the Somali regions of Ethiopia this figure rises significantly. One bit of good news though is that among younger women the rate is lower and continuing to decline year on year.

Reasons given in the Horn for genital mutilation vary from hygiene and aesthetics to superstitions that uncut women can't conceive. Others believe that the strict following of traditional beliefs is crucial to maintaining social cohesion and a sense of belonging, much like male circumcision is to Jews. Some also say that it prevents female promiscuity.

Multiculturalism

Ethiopia's mix of cultures has been pretty stable over the past few centuries, with only the expulsion of Eritrean citizens after the recent Ethiopia–Eritrea War, and influxes of Sudanese refugees into the western lowlands shifting the status quo.

For a fascinating look at the cultural clash that occurs when photo-hungry tourists and lip-plate wearing Mursi meet watch *Framing the Other* (www.framing-the-other.com).

THE ETHIOPIAN 'HANDSHAKE'

Greeting one another in Ethiopia can be a complicated business. Do you just say hello? Do you offer a hand? Do you kiss the other person on the cheek? Or do you go for the 'fighters salute'? Commonly, as Ethiopians shake hands they also gently knock their shoulders together. This is known as the 'fighters salute' and traditionally was used as a greeting between those who fought the Derg. Today, it's used by almost everyone – male and female – but only in informal situations between friends. You would not use this form of 'handshake' at a business meeting!

There are plenty of other ways to greet people in Ethiopia. Multiple kissing on the cheek is also very common among friends and relatives of either sex. It's also considered polite to kiss babies or young children, even if you've just met them.

And if you do just stick with a boring old handshake then deference can be shown by supporting the right arm (near the elbow) with the left hand during shaking. When Ethiopians enter a room they try and shake hands with everyone (including children). If hands are dirty or wet, limp wrists are offered.

ETHIOPIAN HAIRSTYLES

Hairstyles in all societies form an important part of tribal identification. Reflecting the large number of ethnic groups, Ethiopian hairstyles are particularly diverse and colourful. Hair is cut, shaved, trimmed, plaited, braided, sculpted with clay, rubbed with mud, put in buns and tied in countless different fashions. In the Omo Valley, hairstyles are sometimes so elaborate and valued that special wooden headrests are used as pillows to preserve them.

In rural areas, the heads of children are often shaved to discourage lice. Sometimes a single topknot or tail plait is left so that 'God should have a handle with which to lift them unto Heaven', should he decide to call them.

Despite the nation's regions being divided along ethnic lines in 1995, there's still some resentment, particularly among the Oromo, that has led to violence over the fact that the minority Tigrayan and Amhara people largely maintain control of the national government (although the prime minister is not from either of these groups).

Many travellers also notice that some Ethiopian highlanders, regardless of their ethnic background, seem to show a slight disdain for Ethiopians from the lowlands.

Religion in Ethiopia

Faith is an extremely important part of an Ethiopian's life. Orthodox Christians bring religion into everyday conversation just as much as their Muslim counterparts. Although Orthodox believers only slightly outnumber Muslims (43.5% to 33.9%), Christianity has traditionally dominated the country's past. The vast majority of highlanders are Orthodox and the religion continues to heavily influence the highlands' political, social and cultural scene. Most Muslims inhabit the eastern, southern and western lowlands, but there are also significant populations in the country's predominantly Christian towns, including Addis Ababa.

Ethiopian Orthodox Christianity

The 1984 evacuation of Ethiopian Jews to Israel was captured in an Israeli-French film, *Live and Become* (2005).

As the official religion of the imperial court right up until Emperor Haile Selassie was deposed in 1974, the Orthodox Church continues to carry great clout among the Ethiopian people and is regarded as the great guardian and repository of ancient Ethiopian traditions, directly inherited from Aksum.

Ethiopia was the second country (after Armenia) to adopt Christianity as its state religion and it's been a truly unifying factor over the centuries. By the same measure, it's also legitimised the oppression of the people by its rulers.

Ethiopian Orthodox Christianity is thought to have its roots in Judaism – some even say that this is the home of the Lost Tribes of Israel. This Jewish connection explains the food restrictions, including the way animals are slaughtered. Even the traditional round church layout is considered Hebrew in origin. Ancient Semitic and pagan elements also persist.

Circumcision is generally practised on boys, marriage is celebrated in the presence of a priest and confession is usually only made during a grave illness.

Know Your Ethiopian Saints

In Ethiopia the air seems to be saturated with the stories of saints, magic, ghosts and monsters. For the majority of Ethiopians (of all faiths) these tales are not wild legends, but solid fact. Don't be surprised if, on asking about the history of a church, you end up listening, spellbound, to a story so unlikely that you assume it's nothing but an ancient legend, only for the storyteller to turn around and announce that the events recounted happened just a year or so ago.

As a traveller, it's important that you don't dismiss these stories out of hand. Ethiopians, like many Africans, live a life very different from those in the West. It's a life lived close to the rhythm of nature, in which the dead are never far away. Every Ethiopian has their favourite saint, and there's hardly an Ethiopian church not adorned with colourful, vibrant murals. In most cases the paintings follow a set pattern, depicting the important personalities of Ethiopia's peculiar pantheon of saints often alongside a bevy of strange creatures.

Some of the best-known saints are listed below, but first, no list of Ethiopian saints would be complete without mentioning the names of the Nine Saints who famously brought Christianity to Ethiopia: Abuna i, Abuna Tsama, Abuna Aftse, Abuna Gerima, Abuna Liqanos, Abuna Guba, Abuna Panteleon and Abuna Yemata (the ninth one is Abuna Aregawi). Here's a quick key to some others:

Abuna Aregawi One day while wandering at the foot of a cliff, Abuna Aregawi spotted a plateau high above him. Deciding it was the ideal spot for a nice, quiet hermit's life, he prayed to God for assistance. Immediately, a large python stretched down from above and lifted him onto the plateau. The famous monastery of Debre Damo was then founded. The saint is usually depicted riding up the snake. He's one of the Nine Saints.

Abuna Samuel He lived near the Takezze River, where he preached and performed many miracles, accompanied by a devoted lion. Usually depicted astride his lion.

Belai the Cannibal Although not a saint, he's a favourite theme in religious art. Devouring anyone who approached him, including his own family, Belai yet took pity one day on a leper begging for water in the Virgin's name. After Belai died – some 72 human meals later – Satan claimed his soul. St Mikael, the judge,

THE BIRTH OF CHRISTIAN ETHIOPIA

Sometimes finding out what happened in Ethiopia just last week can be tough, so when it comes to finding out what happened nearly 2000 years ago it goes without saying that fact, fiction and an utter disregard of scientific logic are part of the parcel. The story of how Christianity first arrived in Ethiopia is no exception to this rule.

The man credited with bringing Christianity to Ethiopia is a certain St Frumentius, better known in Ethiopia today as Abuna Selama. Born a Christian in early-4th-century Lebanon, legend has it that when still young Abuna and his brother Edesius travelled by boat down the Red Sea to Ethiopia. By all accounts the shores of the Red Sea at that time were filled with people up to no good. As if to prove this point, when the boat they were travelling on stopped at a harbour the locals massacred all aboard except the two boys, who were taken as slaves to the king of Aksum. Quickly gaining the trust of the king they were eventually given their freedom, but when the king died the queen begged the brothers to stay and help bring up her son, and future king, Ezana. Abuna Selama in particular used his position to influence the young Ezana and convert him to Christianity. When Ezana was old enough to become king, Selama travelled to Alexandria in Egypt where he requested the patriarch to send a bishop to Ethiopia. Instead, the patriarch consecrated Selama and sent him back to Aksum, where he baptised Ezana, built a number of churches and set about converting the masses.

Abuna Selama may have brought Christianity to Ethiopia (actually there were already Christian traders living in Ethiopia before Selama's time), but he didn't make much headway converting the rural masses. It wasn't until the 5th century when a group of wandering monks known as the Nine Saints arrived from the Levant and, using a potent mixture of magic, giant snakes and other show-stopping stunts, impressed the locals to such an extent that they quickly converted to Christianity.

balanced Belai's victims on one side, the water on the other. However, the Virgin cast her shadow on the side of the scales containing the water, and caused them to tip. Belai's soul was saved.

Equestrian Saints They are usually depicted on the north wall of the Holy of Holies and may include Fasiladas, Claudius, Mercurius, Menas, Theodorus and George.

Mary Little known outside Ethiopia are the charming legends and miracles concerning Mary, the childhood of Jesus and the flight to Egypt. A tree is often depicted hiding the holy family – and the donkey – from Herod's soldiers during the flight to Egypt; the soldiers are confused by the sound of the donkey braying. Sometimes a furious Mary is shown scolding Jesus, who's managed to break a clay water jug.

Eostateos Also known as St Thaddeus, he's said to have arrived in Ethiopia borne up the Nile from Egypt on three large stones. Apparently water continued to obey him: whenever the saint chose to cross a river or a lake, the waters parted conveniently before him.

Gabriel God's messenger is usually represented cooling the flames of a fiery furnace or cauldron containing three youths condemned by Nebuchadnezzar: Meshach, Shadrach and Abednego.

Gebre Kristos This Ethiopian prince sacrificed all his belongings to lead a life of chastity, and ended up a leprous beggar. He's usually depicted outside his palace, where only his dogs now recognise him.

Gebre Manfus Kiddus While preaching peace to the animals in the desert, this saint came across a bird dying of thirst. Lifting it, he allowed the bird to drink the water from his eye. He's usually depicted clad in furs and girded with a hempen rope and surrounded by animals.

George The patron saint of Ethiopia features in almost every church. He's depicted either as the king of saints, with St Bula – who at first refused to recognise his kingship – looking on petulantly in the background, or as the great dragon slayer on his horse.

Mikael The judge of souls and the leader of the celestial army, St Mikael evicted Lucifer from heaven. In most churches, the portals to the Holy of Holies are guarded by a glowering Mikael, accompanied by Gabriel and Raphael.

Raphael He rescued an Egyptian church from the tail of a thrashing beached whale and is usually depicted killing the whale with his spear.

Tekla Haimanot The saint stood bolt upright and prayed nonstop for 22 years until his right leg turned rotten and fell off. Nonplussed he continued praying for a further seven years standing on just one leg, until that one also withered and fell off! Throughout, a bird brought him just one seed a year for sustenance. For his devotion, God awarded him no fewer than three sets of wings. The saint is normally depicted in his bishop's attire, surrounded by bells.

Yared Ethiopia's patron saint of music is sometimes shown standing before his king with an orchestra of monks along with their sistra (sophisticated rattles), drums and prayer sticks. In the background, birds in trees learn the magic of music.

Thanks to the Orthodox calendar, Ethiopia is a full seven to eight years (depending on the exact date) behind the Western calendar. There are also 13 months in a year.

THE SECRET NAME OF GOD

Belief in talismans and charms is common among all communities in Ethiopia, whether they be Christian, Muslim or animist. Maybe the most intriguing of these is belief in *asmat*, or the secret names of God in which reside his power. God has many *asmat* and these, if invoked by a person, can protect against misfortune or illness. Because of this many Ethiopians wear a talisman around their neck containing a small piece of parchment on which are written *asmat*. When a Christian Ethiopian dies his or her body is wrapped in a shroud containing a thin, body-length strip of linen on which are written the *asmat*. This ensures a safe passage through the underworld and across a river of fire to the gates of Heaven.

Islam

Ethiopia's connection with Islam is as distinguished as its connection with Christianity. Though bloody religious wars were fought in Ethiopia in the past, Ethiopia's Christian and Muslim inhabitants generally coexist in harmony. Fundamentalism is rare in Ethiopia, and it's uncommon to see women wearing the *hijab* (veil), though the majority wear either headscarves or *shalmas* (a gauze-thin length of fabric draped around the head, shoulders and torso).

Negash, in Tigray, where Islam was introduced in 615 AD and the shrine of Sheikh Hussein in the Bale region are both greatly venerated and attract national and international pilgrims.

The famous walled city of Harar is also an important Islamic centre in its own right and is home to an astonishing number of shrines and mosques. In the past, it was renowned as a centre of learning.

Traditional African Beliefs

Traditional African beliefs are still practised either totally or in part, by an estimated 11% of Ethiopia's population, particularly in the lowland areas of the west and south. These range from the Konso's totemism to animism (associated with trees, springs, mountains and stones), in which animals are ritually slaughtered and then consumed by the people. Elements of ancestor worship are still found among the Afar people.

The Oromo traditionally believe in a supreme celestial deity known as Wak, whose eye is the sun.

Media

In many ways Ethiopia is heading squarely in the right direction, but one sphere where things are taking a decided turn for the worse is in the freedom of media.

When the Ethiopian People's Revolutionary Democratic Front (EPRDF) first came to power the severe restrictions placed on the media by the Derg regime, and before that the imperial regime, were largely lifted and the press given more freedom than it had ever really had before. However, this change of fortunes was not to last.

After the May 2005 elections, the EU had harsh criticism of the state-owned media for regularly releasing unofficial results that highlighted the government's victories and virtually ignoring the victories of opposition parties. They blasted state-owned Radio Ethiopia and Ethiopian TV for 'completely ignoring' the press conferences and important statements given by opposition parties, information that CNN and the BBC thought newsworthy.

Since 1992, when the Press Law came into effect, numerous journalists have been arrested without trial for publishing critical articles of the government. The editor of *Agere* died untried in prison in 1998. Several owners of private media were arrested and their newspapers shut down during the post-electoral violence in 2005.

More recently the situation for journalists has gotten worse. An antiterrorism law, introduced in 2009, has been used to harass and jail journalists and editors who have published antigovernment articles. According to Journalists Without Borders, in 2011 four journalists, including two Swedes, were given lengthy prison terms for 'terrorist activities'. Under pressure the Swedes were released in 2012. In mid-2012 award-winning Ethiopian journalist Eskinder Nega was imprisoned for 18 years after writing a column questioning the arrest of journalists.

The censorship and repression doesn't stop with print media. Opposition websites and websites criticising the government are frequently blocked, and in early 2012 the government even went as far as making

The world's oldest Christian manuscript is thought to be the Garima Gospels, which recent radiocarbon dating suggests dates back to sometime between 330AD and 650AD. It is kept in the Abba Garima monastery near Adwa.

the use of Skype and other VoIP software illegal on 'national security grounds' with possible prison sentences of up to 15 years. Such an uproar followed that the government later backed down on this. In October 2016, the government declared a state of emergency and again blocked many websites as well as Facebook in an attempt to control the situation.

Arts

The church, traditionally enjoying almost as much authority as the state, is responsible for both inspiring Ethiopia's art forms and stifling them with its great conservatism and rigorous adherence to convention.

Long neglected and ignored, the cultural contributions of Ethiopia's minority ethnic groups are only now receiving due credit and attention.

Music

Whether it's the solemn sounds of drums resonating from a church, the hilarious ad-libbing of an *azmari* (wandering minstrel) or Ethiopian pop blaring in a bus, Ethiopian music is as interesting as it's unavoidable.

Church Music

There is much debate as to the origin and date of the Kebra Negast. Some say it was originally written in Coptic then translated into Arabic and finally into Ge'ez. Some say there was never a Coptic version. Some insist it dates back to the 1300s; others that it was written as late as the 16th century.

Yared the Deacon is traditionally credited with inventing church music, with the introduction in the 6th century of a system of musical notation.

Aquaquam (church music) uses resonating drums – the *kabaro* – and the *tsinatseil* (sistrum; a resonating rattle, thought to be directly descended from an ancient Egyptian instrument used to worship Isis). Percussion instruments are primarily used since their function is to mark the beat for chanting and dancing. The *maquamia* (prayer stick) also plays an essential role in church ceremonies and, with hand-clapping, is used to mark time. Very occasionally a *meleket* (trumpet) is used, such as to lead processions.

Secular Music

Strongly influenced by church music, secular music usually combines song and dance, emphasises rhythm and often blends both African and Asian elements. The Amharas' and Tigrayans' highland music, as well as that of the peoples living near the Sudanese border, is much influenced by Arab music, and is very strident and emotive.

Wind and percussion instruments are used. The *begenna* is a type of harp similar to that played by the ancient Greeks and Romans. The most popular instrument in Ethiopia is the *krar*, a five- or six-stringed lyre, which is often heard at weddings or used to attract customers to traditional pubs or bars.

In the highlands, particularly the Simien and Bale Mountains, shepherd boys can be found with reed flutes. The *washint* is about 50cm long, with four holes, and makes a bubbling sound that is said to imitate running water. It's supposed to keep the herds close by and calm the animals.

TEDDY YO

Addis-born hip-hop star Teddy Yo (real name Tewodros Assefa) is the face of young cosmopolitan Ethiopia. He started rapping at the age of 14, but didn't turn heads until he took traditional Gurage music and combined it with contemporary hip-hop beats and lyrics to create his own musical style, Guragetone (which is also the name of his most famous song). Today he is Ethiopia's best known hip-hop performer.

ILLUMINATED MANUSCRIPTS

Without doubt, illuminated manuscripts represent one of Ethiopia's greatest artistic achievements. The best-quality manuscripts were created by monks and priests in the 14th and 15th centuries. The kings, the court and the largest and wealthiest churches and monasteries were the main patrons. The manuscripts were characterised by beautifully shaped letters, attention to minute detail and elaborate ornamentation. Pictures included in the text brought it to life and made it more comprehensible for the uneducated or illiterate.

Bindings consisted of thick wooden boards often covered with tooled leather. The volume was then placed into a case with straps made of rough hides so that it could be slung over a shoulder.

On the blank pages at the beginning or at the end of the volume, look out for the formulae *fatina bere* (literally 'trial of the pen') or *bere' sanay* (literally 'a fine pen'), as the scribes tried out their reeds. Some are also dated and contain a short blessing for the owner, as well as the scribe.

Sadly, due to the Muslim and the Dervish raids of the early 16th and late 19th centuries respectively, few manuscripts date earlier than the 14th century. Modern times have seen huge numbers being pillaged by soldiers, travellers and explorers.

Modern Music

Ethiopian modern music is diverse and affected by outside influences, and ranges from classical Amharic to jazz and pop. Modern classical singers and musicians include the late Assefa Abate, Kassa Tessema and the late female vocalist Asnakech Worku. The composer Mulatu Astatike is well known for his Ethiojazz.

Amharic popular music boasts a great following with the young. Unlike many other African countries, it's generally much preferred to Western music, and can be heard in the bars and discos of all the larger towns.

Among the best known is Tewodros Kassahun ('Teddy Afro') whose political album *Yaasteseryal,* which was released in 2005 during a time of heightened political tension following disputed elections, got him on the wrong side of the government, but sent his popularity sky-rocketing. Four songs from the album were eventually banned by the government. His latest album is *Ethiopia.*

Ethiopian rap is massively popular among the young in all the big Ethiopian towns. Like many forms of artistic expression in Ethiopia most performers use a certain amount of self-censorship when it comes to rapping about domestic politics, and in general Ethiopian rap seems fairly apolitical when compared to some Western rap artists. Current leaders of the Ethiopian rap race are Teddy Yo and the upcoming Yoni Yoyi, whose best-known song is the brilliantly catchy 'Gondergna'.

Female artists more than hold their own. Gonder-born, American-based Aster Aweke has produced 20 albums since the late 1970s. She's popularly known as Africa's Aretha Franklin. Her latest release is 2013's *Ewedhalew.* Hot on Aster's tail for international fame is Ejigayehu Shibabaw (known as 'Gigi'), who rose to prominence after her 1997 album *Tsehay.* Her singing was heard in the Hollywood movie *Beyond Borders.* Her most famous album is *Mesgana Ethiopia* (2010). One of the biggest female stars at the moment is Zeritu Kebede (also known as 'Baby').

Francis Falceto, an Ethiopian music expert, compiles popular Ethiopian contemporary music into great CDs known as 'Ethiopiques'. Twenty-seven volumes have been produced to date; pick them up from www.budamusique.com.

Brush up on the history, culture and latest happenings of the Ethiopian Orthodox Church on www.ethiopianorthodox.org, the Church's official website.

Dance

Dance forms an extremely important part of the lives of most Ethiopians, and almost every ethnic group has its own distinct variety. Although the *iskista* – in which the shoulders are juddered up and down and backwards and forwards, in a careful rhythm, while the hips and legs stay motionless – is the best known, there are myriad others.

Dances in praise of nature, such as after a good harvest or when new sources of water are discovered, are still found in rural areas, as are dances that allow the young 'warriors' to show off their agility and athleticism. Look out for the *fukara* (boasting dance), which is often performed at public festivals. A leftover from less peaceful times, it involves a man holding a spear, stick or rifle horizontally above his shoulders at the same time as moving his head from side to side and shouting defiantly at the 'enemy'.

Among the tribes of the Omo Valley in the south, many dances incorporate jumping and leaping up and down, a little like the dances of Kenya's Maasai.

Literature

Recent evidence from French archaeologists working in Lalibela suggests that the churches of Lalibela were not built in a very short time period as has long been thought but rather over a period of several hundred years.

Literature has a long and illustrious history in Ethiopia. Inscriptions in Ge'ez, a South Semitic language, have been found to date as far back as 2500 years; though it wasn't until Aksumite times that it became widely used as a language of literature. It was during this early period that the Bible was translated from Greek into Ge'ez.

Even though Ge'ez had long since died as a spoken language, the 13th and 14th centuries are considered to mark the golden age of Ge'ez literature, in which many works were translated from Arabic, as well as much original writing produced. It's thought that in the early 14th century the Kebra Negast was written.

During the 16th-century Muslim–Christian Wars, book production ground to a halt and copious amounts of literature was destroyed. By the 17th century, Ge'ez was in decline as a literary language, but that didn't mean the value of books had been lost. It's around this time that rumours spread of a vast library hidden on the mysterious flat-topped mountain of Amba Gishen. Inside the library's endless halls could be found every kind of book, including the works of Job and Abraham and the lost Book of Enoch. What makes this tale so extraordinary is that in 1773 a Ge'ez version of the lost Book of Enoch was discovered in Ethiopia (to this day it remains the only complete copy ever found).

Amharic, now Ethiopia's official language, was the Amharas' language. It was Emperor Tewodros who encouraged the local language in an at-

---

KEBRA NEGAST

Written during the 14th century by author(s) unknown, the Kebra Negast (Glory of Kings) is considered Ethiopia's great national epic. Like the Quran to Muslims or the Torah to Jews, it's a repository of Ethiopian national, religious and cultural sentiment.

It's notoriously shrouded in mystery, perhaps deliberately so. Some controversially suggest it may even represent a massive propaganda stunt to legitimise the rule of the so-called 'Solomonic kings', who came to power in the 13th century and who, the book claims, were direct descendants of the kings of Israel.

Its most important legend is that of Solomon and Sheba and it's in the Kebra Negast that (aside from one or two slightly earlier and rather hazy references) we first really hear mention of the Ark of the Covenant being in Ethiopia. This last part is interesting because if Menelik I really had brought the Ark from Jerusalem some 2000 years before, it seems strange that it wasn't mentioned earlier.

MINSTRELS & MASENKOS

An ancient entertainment that continues to this day is that provided by the singing *azmari* (wandering minstrel) and his *masenko* (single-stringed fiddle). In the past, *azmaris* accompanied caravans of highland traders to make the journey more amusing.

At court, resident *azmaris*, like European jesters, were permitted great freedom of expression as long as their verses were witty, eloquent and clever.

Today, *azmaris* can be found at weddings and special occasions furnishing eulogies or poetic ballads in honour of their hosts.

In certain *azmari bets* (azmari bars) in the larger towns, some *azmaris* have become celebrities in their own right. They prance around grass-covered floors and sing about everything from history to sex, to your funny haircut. Although you won't understand a word (it's all in Amharic), you'll end up laughing; the locals' laughter is simply that contagious. And remember these two things: it's all done in good fun, and really your haircut isn't that bad!

tempt to promote national unity. In a continuation of the trend begun in the 14th century, Tewodros and other emperors right up to Haile Selassie funded writers whose compositions and poetic laudatory songs were written to praise the ruler's qualities and munificence.

Under the Derg, both writing and writers were suppressed. Be'alu Girma is a well-known example of one of the many artists who disappeared during their reign.

Poetry

Written in Amharic as well as other Ethiopian languages, poetry, along with dance and music, is used on many religious and social occasions, such as weddings or funerals. Rhymed verse is almost always chanted or sung in consonance with the rhythm of music.

Poetry places great stress on meaning, metaphor and allusion. In Ge'ez poetry, the religious allusions demand an in-depth knowledge of Ethiopian religious legends and the Bible.

Folk Literature

Perhaps the source of the greatest originality and creativity is the vast folk literature of Ethiopia, most of it in oral form and existing in all languages and dialects. It encompasses everything from proverbs, tales and riddles to magic spells and prophetic statements. For a country in which most of the population have always been (and continue to be) illiterate, folk literature has been the method by which the nation's history has been passed down from one generation to the next. As a local expression goes, 'Every time an old person passes away, it's as if a whole library were lost'.

For a full translation of the Kebra Negast, check out www.sacred-texts.com/chr/kn/.

Painting

Traditionally, Ethiopian painting is largely limited to religious subjects, particularly the life of Christ and the saints. Every church in Ethiopia is decorated with abundant and colourful murals, frescos or paintings.

Much Ethiopian painting is characterised by a naive realism. Everything is expressed with vigour and directness using bold colour, strong line and stylised proportions and perspective. Like the stained-glass windows in European Gothic churches, the paintings served a very important purpose: to instruct, inspire and instil awe in the illiterate and uneducated.

Though some modern artists (particularly painters of religious and some secular work) continue in the old tradition (or incorporate ancient motifs such as that of the Aksumite stelae), many artists have developed their own style. Borrowing freely from the past, but no longer constrained by it, modern Ethiopian painting shows greater originality of expression and is now a flourishing medium.

Architecture

Ethiopia boasts some remarkable historical architecture. Though some monuments, such as the castles of Gonder, show foreign influence, earlier building styles, such as those developed during the Aksumite period, are believed to be wholly indigenous and are of a high technical standard.

More recently, the Italians left behind a few impressive bits of fascist architecture (Gonder has a couple of memorable buildings as does Dire Dawa) and the Derg left behind some Soviet-style works (check out the Derg monument in Addis).

Aksumite Architecture

The 'Aksumite style' of stone masonry is Ethiopia's most famous building style. Walls were constructed with field stones set in mortar, along with sometimes finely dressed cornerstones. In between came alternating layers of stone and timber, and protruding ends of round timber beams, known as 'monkey heads'. The latter are even symbolically carved into Aksum's great obelisks, which may just be the nation's greatest architectural achievements. The Aksumites were undoubtedly master masons.

The best examples of Aksumite buildings are seen at Debre Damo and the church of Yemrehanna Kristos.

The Aksumite style is additionally seen in Lalibela's rock-hewn churches, particularly in the shape of the windows, as well as in modern design today. Keep an eye out for the ancient motifs in new hotel and restaurant designs.

Emperor Haile Selassie had a fairly unique taste in architecture. The Church of St Mary of Zion in Aksum and the church at Debre Libanos are exceptional examples of his unusual 'vision'.

Rock-Hewn Architecture

Ethiopia's rock-hewing tradition probably predates Christianity and has resulted in nearly 400 churches across the country. The art form reached its apogee in the 12th and 13th centuries in Lalibela, where the Zagwe dynasty produced 11 churches that continue to astound. They're considered among the world's finest early Christian architecture.

The churches are unique in that many stand completely free from the rock, unlike similar structures in Jordan and Egypt. The buildings show extraordinary technical skill in the use of line, proportion and decoration, and in the remarkable variety of styles.

HOOFPRINTS & SAINTLY REMINDERS

Few would doubt that the churches of Lalibela are one of the architectural highlights of the early Middle Ages. And of all the churches none are as exquisite as the cruciform Bet Giyorgis. So perfectly composed is this church you could be forgiven for thinking that it could not possibly be the design of mere men. And according to Ethiopian tradition you'd be right.

Just as King Lalibela was finishing off his series of churches, he was suddenly paid an unexpected visit. Astride a white horse and decked out in full armour came Ethiopia's patron saint, George. However, the saint turned out to be severely piqued: not one of the churches had been dedicated to him.

Profusely apologetic, Lalibela promised to make amends immediately by building him the most beautiful church of all.

Today, the priests of Bet Giyorgis (meaning 'Place of George') point out the hoofprints left behind by the saint's horse, permanently imprinted in stone on the side of the trench.

The rock-hewn churches of the Tigray region, though less famous and spectacular, are no less remarkable.

Gonder Architecture

The town of Gonder and its imperial enclosure represent another peak in Ethiopian architectural achievement. Although Portuguese, Moorish and Indian influences are all evident, the castles are nevertheless a peculiarly Ethiopian synthesis. Some have windows decorated with red volcanic tuff, and barrel- or egg-shaped domes.

Ethiopian Houses

Ethiopian houses are famously diverse; each ethnic group has developed its own design according to its own lifestyle and resources. In general, the round *tukul* (hut) forms the basis of most designs. Circular structures and conical thatched roofs better resist the wind and heavy rain. Windows and chimneys are usually absent. The smoke, which escapes through the thatch, fumigates the building, protecting it against insect infestations such as termites.

Sometimes the huts are shared: the right side for the family, the left for the animals. Livestock are not only protected from predators, but in some regions they also provide central heating!

The Zagwe dynasty responsible for the Lalibela churches may have built them in order to legitimise their rule to the general population.

Legendary Ethiopia

Remember when you were a child tucked in bed and your parents, opening a book, read aloud the words 'Once upon a time'? Within moments you were transported to a magical world where castles were made of crystal, monks from Syria climbed serpents tails to build invisible monasteries, emperors turned solid rock into beautiful churches, a queen known only as Sheba was seduced by a king named Solomon and the words of God were hidden in a secret ark for the world to ponder. Today you are about to venture to Ethiopia. It is your wildest fairy tale brought to life.

Ark of the Covenant

Carried by the Israelites during their 40 years wandering in the desert, and a prized possession of King David and centrepiece of King Solomon's temple, the Ark of the Covenant is now the cornerstone of Ethiopian culture and history, but is it in Aksum?

The Queen of Sheba

When King Solomon first laid eyes on the Queen of Sheba, ruler of ancient Aksum, he was enraptured with her beauty. According to Ethiopian tradition every emperor up to Haile Selassie was a direct descendant of Menelik I, the son that resulted from that fateful meeting 3000 years ago.

King of Kings

A biblical prophecy proclaimed that 'Kings would come out of Africa' and for the people of Jamaica that prophecy came true with the 1930 coronation of Haile Selassie. The emperor found himself becoming not just King of Kings to millions of Ethiopians, but also the Messiah of a new religion: Rastafarianism.

A New Jerusalem

Nearly a thousand years ago a poisoned king was taken by angels to Heaven. Here he was shown a city of rock-hewn churches. Then God himself commanded him to return to Earth and, re-creating what he had seen, build a New Jerusalem. Today it's named after that king: Lalibela.

Mystical Monasteries

The mountains of northern Ethiopia are home to hundreds of ancient monasteries. Some require scrambles up sheer rock faces to reach, some are invisible and guarded by sword-wielding ghosts, some contain the bones of former monks, and one could only be built with the help of a giant snake.

Prester John

The legendary Christian king, Prester John, was said to be a descendant of one of the Three Magi. His kingdom contained the Fountain of Youth and the Gates of Alexander. And right up until the first Europeans arrived in Gonder it was widely believed that his kingdom was in Ethiopia.

....

1. Debre Damo (p106) 2. Priests carrying *tabots* representing the Ark of the Covenant, during Timkat procession (p21)

TREVOR KITTELTY / SHUTTERSTOCK ©

1. Portrait of Emporer Haile Selassie.

2. Fasiladas' Palace (p78), Royal Enclosure, Gonder

3. Pilgrim at Lalibela (p120)

4. Detail from Piero della Francesca's The Legend of the True Cross, showing the Queen of Sheba on the way to meeting King Solomon.

Ethiopian Cuisine

Ethiopia has a culture that stands apart from all the nations around it in every way, and that includes food. Ethiopian food is not only some of the most diverse on the continent, but also totally different to any other cuisine you may have encountered. Whether it's the spices joyfully bringing a tear to your eye or the slightly tart taste of the spongy *injera* (the thin pancake that accompanies most Ethiopian meals) sending your tongue into convulsions, Ethiopia's culinary offering is utterly unforgettable.

Staples & Specialities

Eating Ethiopian-style means rethinking many things you might assume about eating. That's because the foundation of almost every meal in Ethiopia is *injera*, a one-of-a-kind pancake of near-universal proportions. At seemingly every turn, plates, bowls and even utensils are replaced by *injera*. Atop its rubbery surface sit delicious multicoloured mounds of spicy meat stews, tasty vegetable curries and even cubes of raw beef.

Other staples that are ever-present on most menus are the much-heralded *wat* (stew), *kitfo* (mince meat) and *tere sega* (raw meat).

Injera

Just like your first kiss, your first taste of *injera* is an experience you'll never forget.

It's the national staple and the base of almost every meal. It is spread out like a large, thin pancake, and food is simply heaped on top of it. An American tourist is said to have once mistaken it for the tablecloth. Occasionally, *injera* is served rolled up beside the food or on a separate plate, looking much like a hot towel on an aeroplane.

First impressions of *injera* are not always positive. The tangy taste can be unsettling for those not used to it, but give it another few mouthfuls and, for most travellers at least, it should start to grow on you. The bitter, slightly sour, taste contrasts beautifully with the fiery sauces it normally accompanies. Like bread, it's filling; like a pancake, it's good for wrapping around small pieces of food and mopping up juices. It's also much easier to manipulate on the plate than rice and it doesn't fall apart as easily as bread – all up *injera* is quite a clever invention, really.

Although *injera* may look like an old grey kitchen flannel, grades and nuances do exist. With a bit of time and perseverance, you may even become a connoisseur.

ETHIOPIAN BREAKFASTS

Popular breakfast dishes include *enkulal fir fir* (scrambled eggs made with a combination of green and red peppers, tomatoes and sometimes onions, served with bread), the omelette version is known as *enkulal tibs*, *ful* (broad beans and butter purée) and *injera fir fir* (torn-up injera mixed with butter and *berbere*, a red powder containing 16 spices or more).

TASTY TRAVEL

With raw meat being a staple in Ethiopia, what dishes could possibly constitute a radical departure for those wishing to truly travel their tastebuds and try unusual local foods?

High on the exotic factor would have to be *trippa wat* (tripe stew), which still curls our toes and shakes our stomachs. And if unleavened bread that's been buried in an underground pit and allowed to ferment for up to six months suits your fancy, order some *kotcho* with your *kitfo* (minced beef or lamb served raw with local spices). *Kotcho* comes from the false-banana plant (known in Ethiopia as *enset*) and closely resembles a fibrous carpet liner.

And how about knocking back a shot of the holy water used at the Debre Libanos Monastery to wash the 1500-year-old leg of St Tekla Haimanot?

Low-quality *injera* is traditionally dark, coarse and sometimes very thick, and is made from a very dark *tef* (the indigenous Ethiopian cereal). In some areas millet or even sorghum act as a substitute for *tef*, though it's very unlikely that as a tourist you'd encounter *injera* made of either of these. Good-quality *injera* is pale (the paler the better), regular in thickness, smooth (free of husks) and *always* made from a white *tef*. Because *tef* grows only in the highlands, the best *injera* is traditionally found there, and highlanders tend to be rather snooty about lesser lowland versions.

Know Your Injera

With large Ethiopian populations living in Western countries many people will have tried Ethiopian food in their home cities, but take note that what often passes for *injera* there is not real *injera* at all. Although you *can* get real *injera* outside the Horn of Africa, most of the time you will instead be served something made from a *tef* substitute. *Injera* made like this lacks the slightly fermented, tangy taste and the rubbery feel of real *injera*.

When in Ethiopia, many foreigners quickly find themselves getting fed up with an endless diet of *injera* (and that's without taking into account the sometimes undesired 'side-effects' on your stomach that eating a semifermented bread for days on end can cause some visitors); this is especially true of those eating only in cheap, local restaurants where *injera* might not be of the highest quality. In fact, when we spoke to tour guides about this most of them thought that around 80% of foreign visitors try to avoid eating *injera* again after a week in Ethiopia!

But let's not be too hard on *injera*. Some travellers adore the stuff and happily munch it down for week after week and, being full of proteins and nutrients, it can actually help to keep you healthy on the road.

If *injera* fatigue kicks in for you, then you'll probably find it worth splashing out on an Ethiopian 'banquet' at a more expensive tourist-class restaurant in Addis or any of the big tourist towns less much less sour. After a couple of meals like this you'll probably be ready to hit the cheap stuff again. And if not, well you can always ask to have your *wat* (stew) served with bread instead of *injera*, or even just resort to the sloppy pasta and dubious sauce that's sold everywhere!

Kevin Rushby's brilliant book *Eating the Flowers of Paradise* (1998) is an entertaining and adventurous story of his journey through Ethiopia, Djibouti and Yemen in search of the perfect *chat* session.

Kitfo

Kitfo is a big treat for the ordinary Ethiopian. The leanest meat is reserved for this dish, which is then minced and warmed in a pan with a little butter, *mitmita* (a stronger version of *berbere*, an Ethiopian spice mix with up to 16 constituent elements) and sometimes *tosin* (thyme).

It can be bland, or tasty and divine. If you're ravenous after a hard day's travelling, it's just the ticket, as it's very filling. Traditionally, it's served just *leb leb* (warmed not cooked), though you can ask for it to be *betam leb leb* (literally 'very warmed', ie cooked). A *kitfo* special is served with *aib* (like dry cottage cheese) and *gomen* (minced spinach).

In the Gurage region (where it's something of a speciality) it's often served with *kotcho* (*enset*; false-banana 'bread'). *Kitfo bets* (restaurants specialising in *kitfo*) are found in the larger towns.

Another favourite meat dish of ours is *siga tibs*, which consists of small strips of fried meat served with onions, garlic and spices. It's most commonly served *derek* (dry), but you can also find a *merek yalew* version, which comes in a liquid sauce.

Tere Sega

Considered something of a luxury in Ethiopia, *tere sega* (raw meat) is traditionally served by the wealthy at weddings and other special occasions.

Some restaurants also specialise in it. Not unlike butcher shops in appearance, these places feature carcasses hanging near the entrance and men in bloodied overalls brandishing carving knives. The restaurants aren't as gruesome as they sound: the carcass is to demonstrate that the meat is fresh, and the men in overalls to guarantee you get the piece you fancy – two assurances you don't always get in the West.

A plate and a sharp knife serve as utensils, and *awazi* (a kind of mustard and chilli sauce) and *mitmita* (a powdered seasoning mix) as accompaniments. Served with some local red wine, and enjoyed with Ethiopian friends, it's a ritual not to be missed – at least not for red-blooded meat eaters. It's sometimes called *gored gored*.

Wat

The ubiquitous companion of *injera*, *wat* is Ethiopia's version of curry and can be very spicy – fortunately the *injera* helps to temper the heat.

EATING THE FLOWERS OF PARADISE

Head to eastern Ethiopia and you don't have to be there long to notice the bulging cheeks of the *chat* chewer. *Chat*, *khat*, *qat* or *miraa* are the leaves of the shrub *Catha edulis*. Originating in the hills of eastern Ethiopia the *chat* plant has spread across parts of East Africa and into southern Arabia, and for many of the inhabitants of this broad swath of land the afternoon *chat*-chewing session has become almost a pivotal point of life.

The effects of *chat* have long been debated – most users will insist that it gives an unbeatable high, makes you more talkative (at least until the come down when the chewer becomes withdrawn and quiet), suppresses hunger, prevents tiredness and increases sexual performance. Others will tell you that it gives no noticeable high, makes you lethargic, slightly depressed, constipated and reduces sex drive! Most Western visitors who try it report no major effects aside from a possible light buzz and an unpleasant aftertaste.

If you're going to chew *chat* then you need to make sure the setting is perfect in order to enjoy the experience. Ask for the sweetest *chat* you can get (most Ethiopians regard this as poor quality *chat*, but first-time chewers find even this very bitter) and get a good group of people together to chew with, because *chat* is, above all else, a social drug. Take yourself off to a quiet and comfortable room – ideally one with a view, sit back, relax and enjoy the conversation while popping leaves individually into your mouth where you literally just store them in one cheek, gently chewing them. All going well you'll be a *chat* 'addict' by the end of the day.

And if you like it enough to want to take some home, remember that chat may be legal in Ethiopia but is illegal in many Western countries, including the UK and the countries of the European Union.

THE COFFEE CEREMONY

The coffee ceremony typifies Ethiopian hospitality. An invitation to attend a ceremony is a mark of friendship or respect, though it's not an event for those in a hurry.

When you're replete after a meal, the ceremony begins. Freshly cut grass is scattered on the ground 'to bring in the freshness and fragrance of nature'. Nearby, there's an incense burner smoking with *etan* (gum). The 'host' sits on a stool before a tiny charcoal stove.

First of all coffee beans are roasted in a pan. As the smoke rises, it's considered polite to draw it towards you, inhale it deeply and express great pleasure at the delicious aroma by saying *betam tiru no* (lovely!). Next the beans are ground up with a pestle and mortar before being brewed up.

When it's finally ready, the coffee is served in tiny china cups with at least three spoonfuls of sugar. At least three cups must be accepted. The third in particular is considered to bestow a blessing – it's the *berekha* (blessing) cup. Sometimes popcorn is passed around.

Enjoy!

In the highlands, *beg* (sheep) is the most common constituent of *wat*. *Bere* (beef) is encountered in the large towns, and *fiyel* (goat) most often in the arid lowlands. Chicken is the king of the *wat* and *doro wat* (chicken stew) is practically the national dish. Ethiopian Christians as well as Muslims avoid pork. On the fasting days of Wednesdays and Fridays, throughout Lent and prior to Christmas, as well as a further couple of occasions, meat and dairy dishes are avoided and vegetarian versions of *wat* are available. Most foreigners become firm fans of fasting food.

Kai wat is a stew of meat boiled in a spicy (thanks to oodles of *berbere*, an Ethiopian spice mix) red sauce. *Kai* sauce is also used for *minchet abesh,* which is a thick minced-meat stew topped with a hard-boiled egg – it's one of our favourites, particularly with *aib* (like dry cottage cheese).

Most Ethiopians seem to be under the impression that all foreigners are terrified of spicy food and so, unless you specifically ask for *kai wat*, you'll often be served the yellow-coloured *alicha wat,* a much milder, and really rather dull-tasting *wat*.

Drinks

Coffee

Ethiopia has a well-founded claim to be the original home of coffee, and coffee continues to be ubiquitous across the country. As a result of Italian influence, macchiato (espresso with a dash of milk), cappuccino and a kind of cafe latte known as a *buna bewetet* (coffee with milk) are also available in many of the towns. Sometimes the herb rue (known locally as *t'ena adam,* or health of Adam) is served with coffee, as is butter. In the western highlands, a layered drink of coffee and tea is also popular. If you want milk with coffee, ask for *betinnish wetet* (with a little milk).

Ethiopia finally has a museum dedicated to its most famous export: the Kafa Coffee Museum (p215).

> If you become a massive fan of *kitfo* or *tere sega (raw meat),* best get tested for tape worms when you get home. Hopefully there'll be no pain to go with your tasty gain.

Tej & Other Alcoholic Drinks

One drink not to be missed is *tej*, a delicious – and sometimes pretty powerful – local 'wine' or mead made from honey and fermented using a local shrub known as *gesho*. *Tej* used to be reserved only for Ethiopian kings and their courts and comes in many varieties. It's served in little flasks known as *birille*.

There are several breweries in Ethiopia that pump out decent beers, including St George, Harar, Bati, Meta, Bedele, Dashen and Castel. Everyone has a different favourite, so explore at will.

Though no cause for huge celebration, local wine isn't at all bad, particularly the red Gouder. Of the whites, the dry Awash Crystal is about the best bet. Unless you're an aficionado of sweet red, avoid Axumite. Outside Addis Ababa, wine is usually only served in the restaurants of midrange hotels. Castel Kuriftu Wine House and Restaurant (p138) in Ziway is well worth the excursion in particular.

If you're not catching an early bus the next morning, try the local *araki*, a grain spirit that will make you positively gasp (some travellers liken it to a stronger version of Greek ouzo). The Ethiopians believe it's good for high blood pressure! *Dagem uraki* is twice-filtered and is finer. It's usually found in local hole-in-the-wall bars.

Other Drinks

In lowland Muslim areas, *shai* (tea) is preferred to coffee, and is offered black, sometimes spiced with cloves or ginger.

Most cafes also dabble in fresh juice, though it's usually dosed with sugar. If you don't want sugar in your juice or in your tea or coffee, make it clear when you order. Ask for the drink *yale sukkar* (without sugar). Bottled water is always available, as is the local favourite Ambo, a natural sparkling mineral water from western Ethiopia.

In the Somali regions in the east, camel milk is a speciality. Locals claim that it gives most foreigners the shits, but we can happily report that our stomachs are stronger than that!

Finally, in the Omo valley region of southern Ethiopia many tribal people start the day with a calabash of fresh, warm blood straight from the neck of a favourite cow. It sounds disgusting, but fans will tell you

Contrary to the myth started by 18th-century Scottish explorer James Bruce, Ethiopians don't carve meat from living animals. Whether it occurred in ancient times, remains uncertain.

DOS & DON'TS

There are a few things to remember when eating with Ethiopians:

➡ If you've been invited to someone's home for a meal, bring a small gift. Pastries or flowers are good choices in urban areas, while sugar, coffee and fruit are perfect in rural areas.

➡ Use just your right hand for eating. The left (as in Muslim countries) is reserved for personal hygiene only. Keep it firmly tucked under the table.

➡ Take from your side of the tray only; reaching is considered impolite.

➡ Leave some leftovers on the plate after a meal. Failing to do so is sometimes seen as inviting famine.

➡ Feel free to pick your teeth after a meal. Toothpicks are usually supplied in restaurants.

➡ Try and avoid putting food back onto the food plate – even by the side. It's better to discard it onto the table or floor, or keep it in your napkin.

➡ While eating, try also to avoid touching your mouth, licking your fingers, or filling your mouth too full. All are considered impolite.

Gursha

Don't be embarrassed or alarmed at the tradition of *gursha*, when someone (usually the host) picks the tastiest morsel and feeds it directly into your mouth. The trick is to take it without letting your mouth come into contact with the person's fingers, or allowing the food to fall. It's a mark of great friendship or affection, and is usually given at least twice (once is considered unlucky). Refusing to take *gursha* is a terrible slight to the person offering it!

that not only is it full of goodness it also makes you very strong. In fact, the male members of many Omo tribes frequently gorge on it in the build-up to a stick fight in order to make themselves as strong as possible. And no harm is done to the cow: they use a miniature bow and arrow to pierce a vein in the neck and the cow appears to suffer no permanent damage.

Where to Eat & Drink

Outside Addis Ababa and major towns, there isn't a plethora of eating options. You're usually constrained to small local restaurants (which in Ethiopia, as in much of East Africa, are often known as hotels or some variation of the word) that serve one pasta dish and a limited selection of Ethiopian food. In larger towns, local restaurants and hotels both offer numerous Ethiopian meals. The hotel menus also throw some (often very forgettable) Western meals into the mix.

Kitfo bets are specialist restaurants in larger towns that primarily serve *kitfo* (minced beef or lamb served raw with local spices). Similarly *tej bets* are bars that focus on serving *tej* (honey wine).

Unlike Addis Ababa, where restaurant hours vary widely, most restaurants elsewhere are open daily from around 7.30am to 10pm. *Tej bets* tend to open later (around 10am) and close about 10pm or later.

Celebrations

Food plays a major role in religious festivals of both Muslims and Ethiopian Orthodox Christians. During the month of Ramadan, Muslims fast between sunrise and sunset, while Ethiopian Orthodox Christians abstain from eating any animal products in the 55 days leading up to Ethiopian Easter.

Orthodox Ethiopians also abstain from animal products each Wednesday and Friday. There are a very large number of Orthodox feast days, of which 33 honour the Virgin Mary alone.

Habits & Customs

Eating from individual plates strikes most Ethiopians as hilarious, as well as rather bizarre and wasteful. In Ethiopia, food is always shared from a single plate, without the use of cutlery.

In many cases, with a simple *Enebla!* (Please join us!), people invite those around them (even strangers) to join them at their restaurant table. For those invited, it's polite to accept a morsel of the food to show appreciation.

In households and many restaurants, a jug of water and basin are brought out to wash the guests' outstretched hands before the meal.

When eating with locals, try not to guzzle. Greed is considered rather uncivilised. The tastiest morsels will often be laid in front of you; it's polite to accept them or, equally, to divide them among your fellow diners. The meat dishes such as *doro wat* (chicken stew) are usually the last thing locals eat off the *injera* so don't hone in on it immediately!

Vegetarians & Vegans

On Wednesday, Friday and throughout the build up to Fasika (Lent), vegetarians breathe easy as these are the traditional fasting days, when no animal products should be eaten. Ethiopian fasting food most commonly includes *messer* (lentil curry), *gomen* (minced spinach) and *kai ser* (beetroot). *Ful* (broadbean and butter purée) is another saviour for vegetarians, although this is normally only served at breakfast time.

Apart from fasting days, Ethiopians are rapacious carnivores and vegetables are often conspicuous by their complete absence. If you're vegetarian or vegan, the best plan is to order alternative dishes in advance.

If you're eager to tell your *kekel* from your *kai wat* or simply just want to learn more Amharic, pick up Lonely Planet's *Amharic Phrasebook*.

If looking for quality *tej*, ask a local. They'll know who makes it with pure honey and who cheats by adding sugar.

If not, some dishes such as *shiro* (chickpea purée) are quite quickly prepared. Note that fancier hotels and some restaurants tend to offer fasting food seven days a week.

If you're really concerned about the availability of vegetarian food, the best bet is to come during the 55 days preceding Fasika. It's also a good idea to keep a small stack of vegetarian snacks on hand.

Food Glossary

NONVEGETARIAN

alicha wat	mild stew (meat and vegetarian options)
asa wat	freshwater fish served as a hot stew
bege	lamb
bere	beef
beyainatu	literally 'of every type' – a small portion of all dishes on the menu; also known by its Italian name *secondo misto*
bistecca ai ferri	grilled steak
derek tibs	meat (usually lamb) fried and served *derek* ('dry' – without sauce)
doro	chicken
doro wat	chicken drumstick or wing accompanied by a hard-boiled egg served in a hot sauce of butter, onion, chilli, cardamom and *berbere* (a red Ethiopian spice mix)
dulet	minced tripe, liver and lean beef fried in butter, onions, chilli, cardamom and pepper (often eaten for breakfast)
fatira	savoury pastries
fiyel	goat
kai wat	lamb, goat or beef cooked in a hot *berbere* sauce
kekel	boiled meat
kitfo	minced beef or lamb like the French steak tartare, usually served warmed (but not cooked) in butter, *mitmita* (a powdered seasoning mix) and sometimes thyme
kwalima	sausage served on ceremonial occasions
kwanta fir fir	strips of beef rubbed in chilli, butter, salt and *berbere* then usually hung up and dried; served with torn-up *injera* (the thin, slightly sour pancake served with most Ethiopian meals)
mahabaroui	a mixture of dishes including half a roast chicken
melasena senber tibs	beef tongue and tripe fried with *berbere* and onion
minchet abesh	minced beef or lamb in a hot *berbere* sauce
scaloppina	escalope
tere sega	raw meat served with a couple of spicy accompaniments (occasionally called *gored gored*)

tibs	sliced lamb, pan fried in butter, garlic, onion and sometimes tomato
tibs sheukla	*tibs* served sizzling in a clay pot above hot coals
trippa	tripe
wat	stew
zilzil tibs	strips of beef, fried and served slightly crunchy with *awazi* (mustard and chilli) sauce

VEGETARIAN

aib	like dry cottage cheese
atkilt-b-dabbo	vegetables with bread
awazi	a kind of mustard and chilli sauce
berbere	a red powder containing as many as 16 spices
dabbo fir fir	torn-up bits of bread mixed with butter and *berbere*
enkulal tibs	literally 'egg *tibs*', a kind of Ethiopian scrambled eggs made with a combination of green and red peppers, tomatoes and sometimes onions, served with *dabbo* (bread) – great for breakfast
fendisha	popcorn
ful	broadbean and butter purée eaten for breakfast
genfo	barley or wheat porridge served with butter and *berbere*
gomen	minced spinach
injera	large Ethiopian version of a pancake/plate
injera fir fir	torn-up bits of *injera* mixed with butter and *berbere*
kai ser	beetroot
kolo	roasted barley
kotcho	false-banana 'bread'; a staple food
messer	a kind of lentil curry made with onions, chillies and various spices
shiro	chickpea or bean purée lightly spiced, served on fasting days
sils	hot tomato and onion sauce eaten for breakfast
tihlo	an eastern Tigray speciality consisting of barley balls dipped in a spicy sauce
ye tsom megeb	a selection of different vegetable dishes, served on fasting days

Ethiopia's Environment

Ethiopia is a land of extraordinary diversity: where cold evening winds whip across high moorland plateaus and powerful rivers tumble through deep gorges; where elegantly dressed colobus monkeys swing through dense forests; savannah grasslands shimmer in the sun and camel caravans traverse some of the most inhospitable territory on Earth. For a visitor obsessed with seeing Ethiopia's cultural highlights, the stirring landscapes and eye-catching wildlife often comes as an unexpected, and very welcome, surprise.

The Land

With a land area of 1,098,000 sq km, Ethiopia is five times the size of Britain and twice the size of Texas. Its topography is remarkably diverse, ranging from 20 peaks higher than 4000m to one of the lowest, hottest, driest and most inhospitable points on the Earth's surface: the Danakil Depression, which in parts lies almost 125m below sea level and sprawls into neighbouring Eritrea and Djibouti.

Two principal geographical zones can be found in the country: cool highlands and their surrounding hot lowlands.

Ethiopia's main topographical feature is the vast central plateau (the Ethiopian highlands) with an average elevation between 1800m and 2400m. It's here that the country's major peaks are found, including Ras Dashen (more correctly, but less commonly, known as Ras Dejen) at 4543m, Ethiopia's highest mountain and Africa's 10th highest.

The mountains are also the source of four major river systems, the most famous of which is the Blue Nile. Starting from Lake Tana and joined later by the White Nile in Sudan, it nurtures Egypt's fertile Nile Valley. The other principal rivers are the Awash, the Omo and the Wabe Shebele.

Southern Ethiopia is bisected diagonally by the Rift Valley. Averaging around 50km wide, it runs all the way south to Mozambique. The valley floor is home to many of Ethiopia's most important lakes, including a well-known chain south of Addis Ababa.

The northern end of the Rift Valley opens into the Danakil Depression, a low-lying area that extends through northern Ethiopia to the coast (where the ever-widening Rift Valley will be flooded by sea water sometime in the next couple of million years as East Africa gradually splits off from the rest of Africa).

UK-based Naturetrek (www.naturetrek.co.uk) runs a range of varied wildlife and ornithological tours to Ethiopia.

Wildlife

Ethiopia's ecosystems are diverse, from high Afro-alpine vegetation to desert and semidesert scrubland. Rounding out the roster of habitats are six more unique ecosystems: dry evergreen montane forests and grassland; small-leaved deciduous forests; broad-leaved deciduous forests; moist evergreen forests; lowland semievergreen forests; and wetlands.

The massive Ethiopian central plateau is home to several of these ecosystems, as well as a distinctive assemblage of plants and animals. Isolated for millions of years within this 'fortress environment', and unable to cross the inhospitable terrain surrounding the plateau, many highland plants and animals evolved their own unique adaptations.

Animals

Simply because it lacks large crowds of cavorting elephants, giraffes and rhinos, Ethiopia is mistakenly written off by many Westerners as purely an historical destination. What they don't know is that Ethiopia hosts 279 mammal species, 201 reptile species, 150 fish species and 63 amphibian species. And that doesn't even include the birds!

To date, more than 860 species of birds have been recorded (compared with just 250 in the UK). Of Africa's 10 endemic mainland bird families, eight are represented in Ethiopia; only rockfowls and sugarbirds are absent. Families that are particularly well represented are falcons, francolins, bustards and larks.

More noteworthy is the fact that of all the species in Ethiopia, 31 mammals, 21 birds, nine reptiles, four fish and 24 amphibians are endemic (found only in Ethiopia). The biggest thrill of all is the realisation that you have a pretty good chance of spotting some of the rarest species, including the Ethiopian wolf, which is the planet's rarest canid.

Where to Watch Birds in Ethiopia (2010), by Claire Spottiswoode et al and published by Christopher Helm Publishers, is a guide to the 50 best bird-watching sites in Ethiopia.

ETHIOPIA'S ENVIRONMENT WILDLIFE

Afro-Alpine

The Afro-alpine habitat, within the Bale and Simien Mountains National Parks, boasts the largest number of endemic mammals and hosts mountain nyalas, walia ibexes, Ethiopian wolves, gelada baboons, Menelik's bushbuck and giant molerats. In addition, 16 of Ethiopia's endemic birds are also found in these lofty confines.

THE BLEEDING HEART BABOON

The gelada baboon (*Theropithecus gelada*) is one of Ethiopia's most fascinating endemic mammals. In fact not a baboon at all, it makes up its own genus of monkey and so more correctly should be called the gelada monkey.

Of all the nonhuman primates, it's by far the most dexterous. It also lives in the largest social groups (up to 800 have been recorded), is the only primate that feeds on grass and has its 'mating skin' on its chest and not on its bottom – a convenient adaptation, given that it spends most of its time sitting!

The gelada also has the most complex system of communication of any nonhuman primate and the most sophisticated social system: the females decide who's boss, the young males form bachelor groups, and the older males perform a kind of grandfather role looking after the young.

Although the males sport magnificent leonine manes, their most striking physical feature is the bare patch of skin on their chest. This has given rise to their other popular name: the 'bleeding heart baboon'. The colour of the patch indicates the sexual condition of not just the male (his virility), but also his female harem (their fertility).

Although its population is shrinking, the gelada monkey population is the healthiest of Ethiopia's endemic mammals. Its current population is thought to number between 40,000 and 50,000.

Resented for its alleged damage to crops and pasture, it has become the scapegoat for more sinister goings-on, too. According to local police reports, gelada monkeys are responsible for local thefts, burglaries, rapes and even murders – in one case bursting into a house to drag an adult man 1.5km before shoving him off a cliff face. If in doubt, it seems, blame the bleeding heart baboon.

ETHIOPIA'S ENDEMIC BIRDS

There's no denying that the diversity and beauty of Ethiopia's astounding 862 recorded bird species could convert even the most die-hard nonbirder into a habitual and excited twitcher. It's the endemic bird species that really set Ethiopia apart.

An amazing 16 species are found nowhere else in the world. Thirteen more are semi-endemic, shared only with Eritrea.

The best time to visit Ethiopia for birding is between November and February, when some 200 species of Palaearctic migrants from Europe and Asia join the already abundant African resident and intra-African migrant populations. The most likely time to spot birds is from dawn to 11am and from 5pm to dusk, although birds can be seen throughout the day.

Desert & Semidesert Scrubland

At the opposite end of the elevation spectrum, the sprawling deserts and semidesert scrublands of Ethiopia and Djibouti host the endangered African wild asses and Grevy's zebras, as well as the Soemmering's gazelles and beisa oryx. Birds include ostriches; secretary birds; Arabian, Kori and Heuglin's bustards; Abyssinian rollers; red-cheeked cordon bleus; and crested francolins.

> The Earth's crust is rifting apart at the rate of 1cm to 2cm a year in the Danakil Depression and earthquakes here are very frequent.

Deciduous Forest

Widespread but discontinuous deciduous forests are home to greater and lesser kudus, hartebeest, gazelles, De Brazza's monkeys and small populations of elands, buffaloes and elephants. Limited numbers of Grevy's zebras and beisa oryx also inhabit these areas. Birdlife includes the white-bellied go-away bird, superb starling, red-billed quelea, helmeted guinea fowl, secretary bird, Ruppell's long-tailed starling, gambaga flycatcher, red-cheeked cordon bleu, bush petronia and black-faced firefinch.

Evergreen Forest

Wandering the evergreen forests in the southwestern and western parts of the country are bushpigs, forest hogs, Menelik's bushbucks and more De Brazza's monkeys. Around Gambela, in the lowland semievergreen forest, are rare populations of elephants, giraffes, lions and, if rumours are to be believed, massive herds of white-eared kob, a beautiful golden antelope found in larger numbers in southern Sudan. The colourful birdlife includes Abyssinian black-headed orioles, Abyssinian hill babblers, white-cheeked turacos, scaly-throated honeyguides, scaly francolins, emerald cuckoos and yellow-billed coucals.

> The ox and plough has been in use in Ethiopia for more than 3000 years. It didn't reach much of the rest of sub-Saharan Africa until colonial times.

Dry Evergreen Montane Forest & Grassland

The odd leopard, gazelle, jackal and hyena still roam the dry evergreen montane forest and grassland found in Ethiopia's north, northwest and central and southern highlands. Birds of note include black-winged lovebirds, half-collared kingfishers and several endemic species.

Wetlands

Hippos and crocodiles are found around Gambela in the wetlands along the Baro River. They also populate some of the Rift Valley lakes in the south – Lake Chamo is famous for its massive crocodiles. Rouget's rails and white-winged flufftails are found in the wetland swamps, while Senegal thick-knees and red-throated bee-eaters live in riverbank habitats.

National Parks & Wildlife Sanctuaries

In the last few years the Ethiopian government has created a flurry of new national parks and other protected areas. Currently there are 21 national parks, five wildlife sanctuaries and reserves and six community conservation areas in Ethiopia. The most famed of these is the Simien Mountains National Park, a Unesco World Heritage site. Many of the other protected areas actually receive very little protection at all (the government itself has allowed the establishment of sugarcane plantations in Omo and Mago National Parks).

Park borders continue to overlap with local communities, and conflicts over conservation continue, despite wildlife authorities trying to encourage locals' participation in the conservation of wildlife.

One unexpected bit of good news comes from Gambela National Park on the border of South Sudan in the far west of the country. Once known to harbour huge herds of antelope as well as elephants, lions, buffalo and other big mammals, it had long been assumed that conflict in South Sudan and that part of Ethiopia, coupled with an influx of refugees into the park would have devastated wildlife populations. But according to various surveys it seems that we were all wrong and that Gambela is still home to significant populations of animals.

Environmental Issues

Despite civil wars taking their toll on the environment, Ethiopia's demographic pressures have been the main culprit. About 95% of Ethiopia's original forest is believed to have been lost to agriculture and human settlement.

Ethiopia's population has almost quintupled in the last 75 years and continues to grow at 2.9%; the pressures for living space, firewood, building materials, agricultural land, livestock grazing and food will only further reduce natural resources and wipe out larger areas of wildlife habitat.

The deforestation has resulted in soil erosion, an extremely serious threat in Ethiopia because it exacerbates the risk of famine. Although hunting and poaching over the centuries have decimated the country's once-large herds of elephants and rhinos, deforestation has also played a role.

Wildlife and forests were both victims of the most recent civil war, where whole forests were torched by the Derg to smoke out rebel forces. Additionally, large armies, hungry and with inadequate provisions,

Birdwatchers will be thrilled by the guide to this region's unique birdlife, *Birds of the Horn of Africa: Ethiopia, Eritrea, Djibouti, Somalia, and Socotra* (2011) by Nigel Redman, Terry Stevenson and John Fanshawe.

ETHIOPIA'S ENVIRONMENT NATIONAL PARKS & WILDLIFE SANCTUARIES

THE STRANGE CASE OF THE VANISHING TURACO

In a remote patch in the deep south of Ethiopia lives one of the country's rarest, most beautiful and most enigmatic birds – the Prince Ruspoli's turaco, first introduced to the world in the early 1890s. It was 'collected' by an Italian prince (who gave his name to the bird) as he explored the dense juniper forests of southern Ethiopia.

Unfortunately, the intrepid prince failed to make a record of his find, and when he was killed shortly afterwards near Lake Abaya following 'an encounter with an elephant', all hope of locating the species seemed to die with him.

The turaco finally reappeared in the 1940s. Just three specimens were obtained, then the turaco disappeared again. It wasn't until the early 1970s that the bird was rediscovered.

Today, recent sightings in the Arero forest, east of Yabelo, around the Genale River off the Dola-Mena–Negele Borena road, suggest that the bird may not, after all, be as elusive as it would have us believe. You may find your own turaco in acacia or conifer woodlands in the southwestern corner of Ethiopia.

turned their sights on the land's natural resources and much wildlife was wiped out.

Up until recently, armed conflict between ethnic groups in the Omo and Mago National Parks continued to impede wildlife conservation efforts.

Today, things are more under control. Hunting is managed by the government and may even provide the most realistic and pragmatic means of ensuring the future survival of Ethiopia's large mammals. Poaching, however, continues to pose a serious threat to some animals.

In late 2005 a new conservation action plan was put in place that crafted stricter environmental regulations designed to unite previously scattered wildlife and environmental activities under the umbrella of a radically restructured Ethiopian Wildlife Conservation Authority. This action has started to pay off with new national parks, a little more money being pumped into existing protected areas and environmental issues being discussed at higher levels of government.

For more on wildlife conservation, contact the Ethiopian Wildlife Conservation Authority (p85)

Gibe III Dam

The Nechisar nightjar (Caprimulgus solala) was long known from a single wing found squashed on the road near Nechisar National Park in 1990. In 2009, after nearly 20 years' wait, the first living birds were claimed to have been seen by a group of respected ornithologists.

Essential to the development of Ethiopia or an environmental and social disaster in the making? No conversation about environmental policies in Ethiopia is complete without talk of the huge new Gibe III dam, which was completed in 2015.

The pet project of the late prime minister, Meles Zenawi, the Gibe III dam is part of a huge hydroelectric project being constructed on the Omo river. The Gibe dams I and II have already been completed and eventually five dams will be constructed along the Omo river. The project has several stated goals. Firstly, only around 2% of rural Ethiopians have mains electricity and it's hoped that this project will bring much more of the rural population onto the mains electricity grid. The government also hopes to sell about 50% of the electricity produced to neighbouring countries (though none of them have actually signed an agreement with Ethiopia to do so; Kenya has signed a Memorandum of Understanding).

It is also hoped that the construction of the Gibe III dam (which is the biggest dam in Africa) and its brothers will help reduce instances of drought and flooding as well as allowing the establishment of large scale sugarcane plantations in the Lower Omo Valley.

Well this all sounds very worthy; so what's the problem? According to the environmental and social impact assessment commissioned by the Ethiopian government (and released two years after construction of the dam began), the dam will cause minimal problems. However, almost every other independent environmental and social body disagrees. The African Resources Working Group has stated that 'Data collected in virtually all major sections of the [government environmental impact] report were clearly selected for the consistence with predetermined objective of validating the completion of the Gibe III hydro-dam'.

FUNNY FROGS

During a scientific expedition to the Harenna Forest in the Bale Mountains a few years ago, biologists discovered four entirely new frog species in the space of just three weeks. Many of the frogs appear to have made peculiar adaptations to their environment. One species swallows snails whole, another has forgotten how to hop and a third has lost its ears.

And how will it all affect people downriver? This is where things get really heated. In a BBC interview Meles Zenawi said: 'The overall environmental impact of the project is highly beneficial. It increases the amount of water in the river system, it completely regulates flooding, which was a major problem, it improves the livelihood of people downstream because they will have irrigation projects, and it does not in any way negatively affect the Turkana Lake'. Environmentalists and social-rights bodies say that thousands of people who live downstream of the Gibe III dam, and are reliant on the annual flooding to fertilise and water their crops, will be adversely affected by its construction.

There are also widespread claims of forced resettlements in order to make room for the sugarcane plantations and repeated reports of human-rights violations by the Ethiopian army against locals who oppose the establishment of these farms.

TOP PARKS & SANCTUARIES

PARK	FEATURES	ACTIVITIES	BEST TIME TO VISIT
NORTHERN ETHIOPIA			
Simien Mountains National Park	Dramatic volcanic escarpments and plateaus; walia ibexes, gelada baboons, Simien wolves, lammergeyers	Trekking, birdwatching, wildlife viewing	Oct-Jan
SOUTHERN ETHIOPIA			
Bale Mountains National Park	Steep ridges, alpine plateaus; Ethiopian wolves, mountain nyala and 16 endemic birds	Trekking, birdwatching	Oct-Jan
Abiata-Shala Lakes National Park	Crater lakes, hot springs; red-billed hornbills, Didric's cuckoos, Abyssinian rollers, superb starlings	Birdwatching, walking	Nov-Dec
Mago National Park	Savannah, open woodland; hartebeest, buffaloes, many birds	Visiting Mursi people, wildlife drives	Jun-Sep & Jan-Feb
Nechisar National Park	Savannah, acacia woodland; Burchell's zebras, Swayne's hartebeest, crocodiles, greater kudu, 320 bird species	Wildlife drives, boat trips	Nov-Feb
Omo National Park	Savannah, open woodland; elephants, buffaloes, lions	Visiting Mursi, Dizi and Surma groups	Jun-Sep & Jan-Feb
Senkelle Swayne's Hartebeest Sanctuary	Open acacia woodland; Swayne's hartebeest, Bohor reedbucks, spotted hyenas, greater spotted eagles	Wildlife drives	Nov-Feb
Yabelo Wildlife Sanctuary	Acacia woodland, savannah grasses; Stresemann's bush crows, white-tailed swallows, Swayne's hartebeest, gerenuks	Wildlife drives, birdwatching	year-round
EASTERN ETHIOPIA			
Awash National Park	Semiarid woodland; beisa oryxes, Soemmering's gazelles, kudu, six endemic bird species	Birdwatching, wildlife viewing	Oct-Feb
WESTERN ETHIOPIA			
Gambela National Park	Semiarid woodland, deciduous forests; savannah Nile lechwe, white-eared kobs, elephants	Rugged wildlife drives, trekking	Dec-Mar

SPOT THE ENDEMIC FLORA

Ethiopia has more unique species of flora than any other country in Africa. This fact is becoming abundantly clear thanks to the ongoing Flora of Somalia project, which has documented more than 400 new species of flowering plants in Ethiopia, including a newly discovered acacia tree that grows by the millions over 8000 sq km.

In September and October, look out particularly for Ethiopia's national flower, the famous yellow daisy known as the Meskel flower, which carpets the highlands; it belongs to the sunflower family, six members of which are endemic.

In towns and villages, the endemic yellow-flowered *Solanecio gigas* is commonly employed as a hedge. Around Addis Ababa, the tall endemic *Erythrina brucei* tree can be seen. In the highlands, such as in the Bale Mountain and Simien Mountain National Parks, the indigenous Abyssinian rose is quite commonly found. Also in the Bale Mountains, look out for the endemic species of globe thistle *(Echinops longisetus)*.

International Rivers called Gibe III 'the most destructive dam under construction in Africa' and Survival International claimed it would be a 'disaster of cataclysmic proportions for the tribes of the Omo valley'. The problems are not just limited to Ethiopia. Over the border in Kenya, Lake Turkana lies in an area of extreme aridity and thousands of Kenyans living in the vicinity of the lake are reliant on the lake for their crops, to water their livestock and generally to maintain their tribal lifestyles. Opponents of the dam say that water levels in the lake will drop by between 2m and 10m and that salinity will increase to such an extent that the waters will become undrinkable for people and livestock.

Survival Guide

Directory A–Z

Accommodation

Anyone who visited Ethiopia 15 to 20 years ago will recall joyous nights sleeping in rural hotels that may as well have been stables for animals, and urban hotels that were essentially brothels. No matter where you stayed, fleas were a constant companion. Fortunately, Ethiopian accommodation has come on in leaps and bounds, and it continues to get better, especially in the midrange category. Fleas and sheep mostly stay elsewhere now and hotels functioning as brothels are the exception rather than the rule.

Camping

Tents are useful in Ethiopia for trekking and the exploration of remote regions. For short treks, tents can be hired from Addis Ababa's tour operators or from businesses in Lalibela, Gonder and Debark.

Campsites have been set up in some of the national parks and in the Omo Valley, but most lack facilities and consist of little more than a clearing beside a river. It's always essential to treat drinking water at the sites and be self-sufficient in everything else.

A few upmarket hotels allow camping on their grounds, though prices are close to what you'd pay for nice budget accommodation and privacy is limited.

Hotels

In Ethiopia, hotels will generally play home to everyone who's not camping. There are very few hostels and homestays.

The standard of hotels in Ethiopia is constantly improving in areas of high tourist traffic, particularly in the north, east and south, although western Ethiopia continues to lag behind. The boom in hotel construction is particularly noticeable for midrange travellers.

And while there aren't many of them, there's a welcome trend towards top-end lodges in the national parks.

RESERVATIONS

We recommend making advance reservations throughout peak tourist season, which effectively means from October to March, and whenever there's a big festival in the town you're visiting, especially in Gonder, Aksum and Lalibela.

DUAL PRICING

Ethiopia's use of dual pricing sometimes leads to resentment from travellers, as many hotels charge substantially higher rates (many openly) for *faranjis* (foreigners, especially Western ones). Although you may take offence to a hotel owner calling you a rich *faranji*, remember that you'll always be given priority, as well as the best rooms, facilities and service.

BUDGET

There are still countless dives, but the number of clean and comfortable budget options continues to rise, especially in the north. Maintenance doesn't seem to be a high priority, so the best budget hotels are often

---

SLEEPING PRICE RANGES

The following price ranges refer to a double room with private bathroom. Some hotels (particularly government-owned ones) charge a 10% service charge and 15% tax on top of room prices but this is usually included in the quoted price. Many hotels quote their rates in US dollars, but all accept payment in both – check the exchange rate to ensure you're getting the best deal.

$ Less than US$25

$$ US$25–75

$$$ More than US$75

those that have just opened. If you hear of a new hotel in town, it may be the best place to head.

In budget hotels expect the following:

➜ In smaller, out-of-the-way towns, hotels may double as drinking dens and brothels, or often sit by the side of busy roads – all good reasons to bring earplugs.

➜ Many lack glass windows and only have a shutter to let air and light in.

➜ Not all will have wi-fi, but many do, if only in reception.

➜ Not all will still have toilet seats attached.

➜ Most (but far from all) should have hot water.

MIDRANGE

This is where repeat travellers to Ethiopia will notice the biggest change – most towns on the tourist circuit, especially in the north, will have at least one good (and usually relatively new) midrange hotel with others under

construction nearby. There are exceptions – Kombolcha, where most travellers break up the journey between Lalibela and Addis, is one, but even there new hotels were being built when we visited. Elsewhere, older midrange options, though very comfortable compared with Ethiopian budget options, would be scraping by as bare-bones budget options in the Western world. Any that are more than three or four years old typically look tired and run-down, and rarely offer good value for money.

Midrange hotels typically include the following:

➜ Private bathroom with hot water

➜ Satellite TV

➜ Wi-fi

➜ Restaurant

➜ Air-conditioning

TOP END

There are plenty of top-end options in Addis Ababa, and a small but growing number in popular tourist towns in both the north and south. In the east and certainly in the west there is very little that really qualifies as true top end.

True top-end hotels typically include everything you'd expect to find in a midrange hotel as well as the following:

➜ Gym and/or swimming pool

➜ Garden

➜ Internet and in-room wi-fi (normally works)

➜ Good-quality restaurant

➜ Travel services

Customs Regulations

There's no limit to the amount of currency that can be brought in, but no more than Birr100 can be exported and imported. You may import 2L of spirits and 200 cigarettes or 100 cigars duty-free.

Electricity

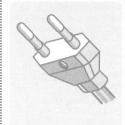

Type C
220V/50Hz

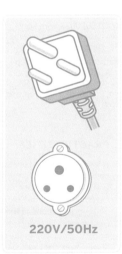

220V/50Hz

Embassies & Consulates

The following list isn't exhaustive (almost every African nation has representation in Addis Ababa), but it covers the embassies that are most likely to be needed.

Canadian Embassy (Map p34; ☏011 317 0000; www. canadainternational.gc.ca/ ethiopia-ethiopie/index. aspx?lang=eng; Seychelles St; ⊗8.30am-noon Mon-Wed & Fri) Also represents Australia.

Djibouti Embassy (Map p46; ☏011 661 3200; off Bole Rd (Africa Ave); ⊗9am-noon Mon-Thu)

French Embassy (Map p34; ☏011 140 0000; www. ambafrance-et.org; Angola St; ⊗8.30am-12.30pm & 2-6.30pm Mon-Thu, 8.30am-12.30pm Fri)

German Embassy (Map p34; ☏011 123 5139; www.ad-dis-abeba.diplo.de; off Comoros St; ⊗7.45am-1pm & 1.30-5pm Mon-Thu, 7.45am-1.45pm Fri)

Italian Embassy (Map p34; ☏011 123 5684; www.ambad-disabeba.esteri.it; ⊗9am-noon Mon-Fri)

Kenyan Embassy (Map p34; ☏011 661 0033; www.keny-aembassyaddis.org; Comoros St; ⊗9am-5pm Mon-Thu)

Netherlands Embassy (Map p34;☏011 317 0360; http:// ethiopia.nlembassy.org; Ring Rd; ⊗8am-5pm Mon-Thu, 8am-2pm Fri)

Somaliland Embassy (Map p46; ☏011 663 5921; off Djibouti St; ⊗9am-noon Mon-Thu)

Sudanese Embassy (Map p34;☏011 551 6477; sudan. embassy@ethionet.et; Ras Lulseged St; ⊗9am-12.30pm Mon-Thu)

South Sudanese Embassy (Map p46;☏011 662 0245; off Cameroon St; ⊗9am-noon Mon-Fri)

Spanish Embassy (Map p34; ☏011 122 2544; Botswana St; ⊗8.30am-4.30pm Mon-Thu, 8.30am-2.30pm Fri)

UK Embassy (Map p34;☏011 617 0100; www.gov.uk/govern-ment/world/ethiopia; Comoros St; ⊗8am-4.45pm Mon-Thu)

US Embassy (Map p34;☏011 130 6000; http://ethiopia. usembassy.gov; Entoto Ave; ⊗7.30am-5pm Mon-Thu, 7.30am-12.30pm Fri)

LGBT Travellers

In Ethiopia and the rest of the Horn, homosexuality is severely condemned – traditionally, religiously and legally – and remains a topic of taboo. Don't underestimate the strength of feeling. Reports of gays being beaten up or worse aren't uncommon. To give you an idea of how widespread such feelings are, a 2007 study found that 97% of Ethiopians thought homosexuality was not something society should accept.

In Amharic, the word *bushti* (homosexual) is a very offensive insult, implying immorality and depravity. One traveller reported expulsion from a hotel and serious threats just for coming under suspicion. If a hotel offers double beds, rather than twins, you and your companion will pay more or may even be refused occupancy.

Women may have an easier time: even the idea of a lesbian relationship is beyond the permitted imaginings of many Ethiopians! Behave discreetly, and you will be assumed to be just friends. Note that the Ethiopian penal code officially prohibits homosexual acts, with penalties of between 10 days' and 10 years' imprisonment for various 'crimes'. Although gay locals obviously exist, they behave with extreme discretion and caution. Gay travellers are advised to do likewise.

Resources

Information on homosexuality in the Horn is hard to come by, even in the well-known gay publications. Try Global Gayz (www.globalgayz. com/africa/ethiopia) or the International Lesbian & Gay Association (www.ilga.org) for more information.

Insurance

A travel-insurance policy for medical problems is essential for travel in Ethiopia, while one to cover theft is helpful but not vital.

Many insurance companies will not cover you for countries, or parts of a country, that your home government has issued a travel warning for. In Ethiopia many border regions and parts of the south can often fall under

---

PRACTICALITIES

➡ **Newspapers** The best-known English-language dailies are the government-owned *Ethiopian Herald* and the privately owned *Monitor*. Other weekly private newspapers include the *Fortune,* the *Reporter, Sub-Saharan Informer* and the *Capital*. Only the *Ethiopian Herald* is available outside Addis Ababa. The weekly *Press Digest* gives useful summaries of t important stories from the week's Amharic and English press.

➡ **Radio** Radio Ethiopia broadcasts in English from 3pm to 4pm and 7pm to 8pm weekdays. The BBC World Service can be received on radios with short-wave reception, though frequencies vary according to the time of day (try 9630, 11940 and 17640 MHz).

➡ **TV** Ethiopia's ETV1 channel broadcasts in English from 11am to 12pm Monday to Friday and 11pm to midnight daily. ETV2 broadcasts in English daily from 8pm to 9pm. Many hotels and restaurants have satellite dishes that receive BBC or CNN.

➡ **Weights & Measures** The metric system is used.

this category – check before travelling.

Worldwide travel insurance is available at www.lonelyplanet.com/bookings. You can buy, extend and claim online anytime – even if you're already on the road.

Internet Access

Internet cafes are everywhere in Addis Ababa and other major towns and are fairly easy to come by in smaller places that see few tourists. Most are open 8am to 8pm Monday to Saturday; many open with limited hours on Sunday. Most, however, come and go with monotonous regularity and few last the distance.

In-room wi-fi is increasingly common in most hotels, including most budget hotels. Before you get too excited, remember that internet connections in Ethiopia can be among the worst on the continent as bandwidth is often insufficient, although things are slowly improving.

The Ethiopian government is highly suspicious of the internet. Opposition websites and others critical of the government are frequently blocked. During the unrest in 2016, all social media (Twitter, Facebook, Skype, etc) was completely blocked, and although most Ethiopians managed to find ways around the ban, that option was not easy for casual visitors.

Legal Matters

Remember that when in Ethiopia, you're subject to Ethiopian laws. If you're arrested, you must (in theory) be brought to court within 48 hours. You have the right to talk to someone from your embassy, as well as a lawyer. For the most part, police in Ethiopia will show you as much respect as you show them. If confronted by the police, always maintain your cool, smile and be polite. Compared with some other African nations, police here rarely, if ever, ask for bribes (we're yet to experience it) and police checkpoints, for example, seem to make a point of waving tourist vehicles through.

Alcohol

Alcohol cannot be served to anyone under 18 years of age in Ethiopia. Disturbance caused by those under the influence of alcohol is punishable by three months' to one year's imprisonment. Driving while under the influence is also illegal and attracts a fine.

Drugs

Penalties for possession, use or trafficking of illegal drugs (including hashish) are strictly enforced in Ethiopia. Convicted offenders can expect both fines and long jail sentences.

Consumption of the mildly stimulating leaf *chat* is permitted in Ethiopia.

Maps

For those venturing off into the nether regions with 4WDs, a detailed map is essential. Since trekking without a guide is illegal in the Simien and Bale Mountains, additional maps aren't necessary, though topographic maps can help you plan your routes with more precision.

In Ethiopia, the map produced by the defunct Ethiopian Tourism Commission (1987; 1:2,000,000) isn't bad and can be picked up in some Addis Ababa hotels. However, the road system is now very outdated.

A more accurate map (although it lacks distance labels between cities) of the same scale is available from the **Ethiopia Mapping Authority** (Map p38; ☏ 011 551 8445; Menelik II Ave; ⏰ 8.30am-12.30pm & 1.30-5pm Mon-Thu, 8.30-11.30am & 1.30-4.30pm Fri) in Addis Ababa.

Of the maps currently available outside the country, the best by far is the Gizi Ethiopia map (1:2,000,000). It's much more up to date than other maps and includes elevations, but some of the place names are very different to how you'll see them written elsewhere.

Money

ATMs

Many banks in major towns now have ATMs that accept international Visa cards and MasterCard; some hotels have ATMs in their lobbies. Note that foreign Solo, Cirrus or Plus cards do not work in any ATM.

Black Market

Unlike 10 to 15 years ago when almost all currency exchanges were conducted on a fairly open black market that gave significantly higher rates than the banks, things have now tightened up drastically. The black market still exists (when we were in Ethiopia, US$1 was changing for around Birr22.25 in banks and around Birr24.50 on the black market, less outside Addis); ask your guide or driver for advice. Remember, however, that the black market is illegal and penalties range from hefty fines to imprisonment.

Cash

Ethiopia's currency is the birr and there are one, five, 10, 50 and 100 birr notes. The Birr1 note is slowly being replaced by the Birr1 coin. The birr is divided into 100 cents and there are 5, 10, 25 and 50 cent coins.

As with many African countries the US dollar is the preferred foreign currency in Ethiopia although the euro is also very easy to exchange. You'll have no trouble exchanging US cash wherever there are Forex facilities, but try to bring US dollar notes (especially US$100) from 2006 or more recent; earlier notes may not be accepted at banks.

Most hotels will exchange US$ cash or euros for you,

but the rates are sometimes (but not always) worse than those offered by the banks.

According to National Bank of Ethiopia regulations, all bills in Ethiopia must be paid in birr. But this isn't enforced and Ethiopian Airlines, most major hotels and most travel agencies accept US currency.

One regulation that's strictly enforced is the conversion of birr to US dollars or euros; this transaction can only be done for people holding onward air tickets from Ethiopia. This means people leaving overland must budget accordingly. There are black-market traders around the borders, but rates are poor and it can be risky.

Credit Cards

Don't come to Ethiopia and expect to rely on your credit card. Credit cards (Visa and MasterCard) are increasingly useful in Addis Ababa but are rarely accepted outside it, with the exception of some Ethiopian Airlines offices and top-class hotels. The travel agencies, airline offices and major hotels that do accept cards typically ding you 2% to 3% extra for the privilege.

Cash advances (Visa and MasterCard) are possible at branches of the Dashen Bank in the capital and elsewhere.

Tipping

Tips (*gursha* in Amharic) are considered a part of everyday life in Ethiopia, and help supplement often very low wages. The maxim 'little but often' is a good one, and even small tips are appreciated.

If a professional person helps you, it's probably better to show your appreciation in other ways: shaking hands, exchanging names or an invitation to have a coffee and pastry are all local ways of expressing gratitude.

Furnishing yourself with a good wad of small notes – Birr1 and Birr5 – is a very good idea. You'll need these for tips, taking photographs..

Opening Hours

Banks 8.30–11am and 1.30–3.30pm Monday to Friday, 8.30–11am Saturday

Cafes 6am–9pm or 10pm

Government offices 8.30–11am and 1.30–3.30pm Monday to Friday, 8.30am–11am Saturday

Internet cafes 8am–8pm Monday to Saturday, limited hours Sunday

Post offices 8.30–11am and 1.30–3.30pm Monday to Friday, 8.30–11am Saturday

Restaurants 7am–10pm; upmarket restaurants in Addis and other big towns generally open noon–3pm and 6–10pm daily

Shops 8am–1pm and 2–5.30pm Monday to Saturday

Telecommunications office 8.30–11am and 1.30–3.30pm Monday to Friday, 8.30–11am Saturday

Photography

In general most Ethiopians love having their photos taken, though in remote areas people are still suspicious of cameras and many feel seriously threatened or compromised, especially women. Be sensitive. Always ask permission, even if it is only using basic sign language. Best of all, use a local as an interpreter or go-between. Never take a photo if permission is declined.

In other areas, where people are starting to depend on tourists for income, the opposite is true. In the Lower Omo Valley, you'll be chased by people demanding their photo be taken! However, their eagerness has to do

---

TIPS FOR TIPPING

Tipping can be a constant source of worry, hassle or stress for travellers. This guide has been compiled with the help of Ethiopians.

➡ In the smaller restaurants in towns, service is included, and Ethiopians don't tip unless the service has been exceptional (up to 10%).

➡ In bars and cafes, sometimes loose coins are left. However, in the larger restaurants accustomed to tourists, 10% will be expected.

➡ In Addis Ababa's midrange and top-end hotels, staff will expect a minimum Birr20 per service.

➡ Outside Addis Ababa, midrange and top-end hotels' luggage handlers will expect around Birr2 to Birr5 per bag, and impromptu guides around Birr10.

➡ At traditional music and dance shows in bars, restaurants and hotels, an audience shows its appreciation by placing money (around Birr10) on the dancers' foreheads or in their belts.

➡ Car 'guards' (often self-appointed) expect Birr5.

➡ If the service has been good at the end of the trek, a rule of thumb for tipping guides/scouts/mule handlers might be an extra day's pay for every three days' work.

➡ A good tip for professional English-/German-/Italian-speaking guides and drivers hired from Addis Ababa travel agencies for multiday 4WD tours is around US$10 per day from each person if you're a group of two or three. Less per person per day for a larger group.

with the fee they'll claim for each snap of the shutter (around Birr2 to Birr5 per person per picture). Always agree to an amount first. The whole mercenary and almost voyeuristic affair can be rather off-putting for many travellers, but the reality is that for these people modelling is a business and they certainly don't regard it as either wrong or 'corrupting of their culture'.

Post

Ethiopia's postal system is reliable and reasonably efficient and the prices are low. Letters should take between five and eight days to arrive in Europe; eight to 15 days for the USA or Australia.

International parcels can only be sent from the main post office in Addis Ababa. All parcels are subject to a customs inspection, so leave them open until you've had their contents inspected at the counter.

Public Holidays

Ethiopia observes the following national holidays:

Leddet (Christmas) 6 or 7 Jan

Timkat (Epiphany) 19 or 20 Jan

Victory of Adwa Commemoration Day 2 Mar

Good Friday Mar or Apr

Easter Saturday Mar or Apr

International Labour Day 1 May

Ethiopian Patriots' Victory Day (Liberation Day) 5 May

Downfall of the Derg 28 May

Kiddus Yohannes (New Year's Day) 11 Sep

Meskel (Finding of the True Cross) 27 Sep

Safe Travel

Compared with many African countries, Ethiopia is remarkably safe – most of the time. Serious or violent crime is rare; against travellers it's extremely rare. Outside the capital, the risk of petty crime drops still further.

A simple traveller's tip? Always look as if you know where you're going. Thieves and con artists get wind of an uncertain newcomer in a minute.

It's very unlikely you'll encounter any serious difficulties – and even less likely if you're prepared for them.

Civil Disturbances

Most of Ethiopia is fairly trouble free, but there are a couple of areas where trouble does flare with worrying frequency. These include the Ogaden region, border regions (which can include the Danakil Depression) and parts of the south. It's generally a mixture of rebel activity and ethnic violence. Though you're highly unlikely to get caught up in it, do keep your ear to the ground for developments.

In 2016, large-scale protests against the government, particularly in Oromia and Amhara regions of central Ethiopia, prompted many foreign governments to warn foreign travellers against all but essential travel to the

country. Many demonstrators were killed in clashes with government forces, and while it seem that tourists were never the target, some foreign-owned businesses were attacked and burnt to the ground. Without such unrest, the country is usually one of Africa's safest countries in which to travel.

Always check your government's latest security reports on countries (such as those published by the British Foreign Office). Don't let these scare you away as they do tend to err on the side of caution (though if they warn you not to venture to a specific area then your travel insurance might be invalid). Try also to speak with people inside the country before making any decisions whether or not to visit.

Mobbing & Faranji Frenzy

The infamous '*faranji* frenzy', when shouts of 'You, you, you, you, YOU!' greeted you at every turn, is thankfully becoming rarer and rarer – at least in touristy parts of the country. Off the beaten track you can still expect it to be a musical accompaniment to your travels.

If it does start to get to you then just ignoring it or, even better, treating it with humour is probably the best answer. Anger only provokes children more (there can be few things more tempting than a grumpy *faranji!*). An Amharic '*hid!*' (clear off!) for a boy, '*hiji!*' for a girl or '*hidu!*' for a group is the Ethiopian response and sends children

MAJOR ISLAMIC HOLIDAYS

ISLAMIC YEAR	NEW YEAR	PROPHET'S BIRTHDAY	END OF RAMADAN	FESTIVAL OF SACRIFICE
1438	20 Sep 2017	30 Nov 2017	26 Jun 2017	1 Sep 2017
1439	10 Sep 2018	19 Nov 2018	15 Jun 2018	21 Aug 2018
1440	30 Aug 2019	9 Nov 2019	5 Jun 2019	11 Aug 2019
1441	20 Aug 2020	28 Oct 2020	24 May 2020	30 Jul 2020
1442	10 Aug 2021	17 Oct 2021	13 May 2021	19 Jul 2021

scuttling; however, it can have the reverse effect and is considered rather harsh from a foreigner.

Several travellers have reported stone-throwing children in various parts of the country.

Scams

Compared with other African countries, Ethiopia has few scams and rip-offs. Those that do exist, like the notebook scam (where kids beg for notebooks and pens for school, which, if you buy them one, are taken straight back to the shop to exchange for money), are pretty transparent and easily avoided.

In Addis in particular, reports have emerged recently of small boys selling chewing gum and the like surrounding unsuspecting visitors – in the confusion and press of bodies, pockets are often emptied. We've also heard isolated reports of a pedestrian spitting on a person's leg, pretending it was an accident and then trying to help you to clean it up (and clean out your pockets).

You'll also hear many 'hard luck' stories, or those soliciting sponsorship for travel or education in Ethiopia or abroad. Although most are

not genuine, some stories are sadly true, so don't be rude.

Also look out for fake antiques in shops.

Self-Appointed Guides

High unemployment has spawned many self-appointed and unofficial guides. You will be approached, accompanied for a while, given unasked-for information and then charged. Be wary of anyone who approaches you unasked, particularly at the exit of bus stations etc. Unfortunately, there's almost always an ulterior motive. Be polite but firm and try not to get paranoid!

Shiftas

In some of the more remote areas – these include the southeast's Ogaden Desert, near the Kenyan border; along the Awash–Mille road at night; and in the far west – *shiftas* (bandits) are sometimes reported. Tourists are very rarely targeted, but it does happen; in early 2012 five foreign tourists were killed and four people kidnapped close to the Irta'ale Volcano in the Danakil Depression. The government blamed Eritrea for the at-

tacks, but nobody has ever been brought to justice. A large Ethiopian military presence has made the Danakil area safer than before but it's still worth keeping your ear to the ground.

Check government travel-advice warnings to keep up to date with any recent trouble spots. Tour companies are also a good source of information; though remember that some less than reputable ones might tell you a place is safe when it isn't just in order to get your custom and money.

Theft

Pickpocketing is the biggest safety concern for travellers, but is a problem mainly in Addis Ababa and other large towns. Keep an eye on your belongings at bus stations and be wary of people offering to put your bags on the bus roof. Be aware that professional thieves sometimes operate at major festivals and markets, targeting Ethiopians as well as foreigners.

Telephone

All Ethiopian numbers have 10 digits. If calling an Ethiopian number from within the country, you'll need to dial the three-digit area code as a prefix to the number.

The international country code for Ethiopia is ☑251 and you need to drop the first zero from the number when calling from abroad. To call an international number from within Ethiopia, dial ☑00 followed by the number.

Mobile numbers begin with ☑09'.

Time

Ethiopia is three hours ahead of GMT/UTC.

Ethiopian daily clock sits six hours behind European time – beginning each day with sunrise, which is 12 o'clock. Also, the 24-hour clock is used occasionally in business. In short, be careful

---

GOVERNMENT TRAVEL ADVICE

The following government websites offer travel advisories and information for travellers:

Australian Department of Foreign Affairs & Trade (www.smartraveller.gov.au)

Canadian Department of Foreign Affairs & International Trade (www.voyage.gc.ca)

French Ministère des Affaires Étrangères et Européennes (www.diplomatie.gouv.fr/fr/conseils-aux-voyageurs)

Italian Ministero degli Affari Esteri (www.viaggiaresicuri.mae.aci.it)

New Zealand Ministry of Foreign Affairs & Trade (www.safetravel.govt.nz)

UK Foreign & Commonwealth Office (www.gov.uk/foreign-travel-advice)

US Department of State (www.travel.state.gov)

to ask if a time quoted is according to the Ethiopian or 'European' clock (*Be habesha/faranji akotater no?* – Is that Ethiopian/foreigner's time?). Additionally, note that instead of using 'am' or 'pm', Ethiopians use 'in the morning', 'in the evening' and 'at night' to indicate the period of day.

Toilets

Both sit-down and squat toilets are found in Ethiopia, reflecting European and Arab influences, respectively. In midrange and top-end hotels as well as budget hotels catering to foreign tourists, Western style 'sit-down' toilets are the norm. Elsewhere it's squat toilets only.

Public toilets are found in almost all hotels and restaurants, but may not form your fondest memories of Ethiopia. In small towns and rural areas, the most common arrangement is a smelly old shack, with two planks, a hole in the ground and all the flies you can fit in between. You may suddenly find that you can survive the next 1000km.

Toilet paper is very rare in any toilet outside a hotel; you're best advised to carry your own. In many budget hotels, expect the toilet seats to be missing.

Tourist Information

Ethiopian tourist offices are not especially useful and tend only to provide very general advice.

For more detailed information, contact tour operators in Addis Ababa, and local guide associations and the traveller grapevine for travel outside the capital.

The UK-based Anglo-Ethiopian Society (www.anglo-ethiopian.org) is also a good source of information before you travel. An active, nonpolitical organisation, it aims 'to foster a knowledge and

---

> ### OH, TO BE YOUNG AGAIN
>
> In addition to the Ethiopian clock system, another time-keeping idiosyncrasy that confounds many a traveller is the calendar. It's based on the old Coptic calendar, which has its roots in ancient Egypt. Although it has 12 months of 30 days each and a 13th month of five or six days, like the ancient Coptic calendar, it follows the Julian system of adding a leap day every four years without exception (which is the sixth day of the short 13th month). If you're travelling during a leap year and want to attend a specific festival check you've got the dates right – we have heard plenty of stories of people missing Christmas celebrations by a day.
>
> What makes the Ethiopian calendar even more unusual is that it wasn't tweaked by numerous popes to align with their versions of Christianity, like the Gregorian calendar (introduced by Pope Gregory XIII in 1582) that Westerners have grown up on.
>
> What does this all mean? It means the Ethiopian calendar is 7½ years 'behind' the Gregorian calendar, and you're seven years younger!

---

understanding of Ethiopia and its people'. The society publishes a tri-annual Newsfile, holds regular gatherings (including talks on Ethiopia) and has a well-stocked library open to members. Annual membership is from UK£15.

Travellers with Disabilities

Intrepid travellers with disabilities do visit Ethiopia, although the country can be something of an obstacle course and you'll end up relying on the goodwill of others rather than dedicated facilities in order to get around.

➡ For those with restricted mobility, all the cities on the Historical Route are easily reached by internal flights, but once there, many sites will extremely difficult to access. For example, only a handful of Tigray's rock-hewn churches are close to the roadside and often have a large number of steps.

➡ Car rental with a driver is easily organised. Some rough roads can be hard on the back.

➡ Taxis are widely available in the large towns and are good for getting around, but none have wheelchair access. In Addis Ababa a few hotels have lifts; at least two (the Sheraton and Hilton hotels) have facilities for wheelchair-users. Kerb ramps on streets are nonexistent, and potholes and uneven streets are a hazard.

➡ Outside the capital, facilities are lacking, but some hotels are bungalow affairs, so at least steps or climbs in such places are sometimes minimal.

➡ For those restricted in other ways, such as visually or aurally, you'll get plenty of offers of help but little else. Unlike in many Western countries, Ethiopians are not shy about coming forward to offer assistance.

➡ Before leaving home, visitors can get in touch with their national support organisation. Ask for the 'travel officer', who may have a list of travel agents that specialise in tours for people with disabilities.

Visas

Be aware that visa regulations can change. The Ethiopian embassy in your home country is the best source of up-to-date information.

➡ Currently, all visitors except Kenyan and Djiboutian nationals need visas to visit Ethiopia.

➡ Nationals of most Western countries (including the US, UK, Australia, New Zealand, South Africa and most Western European countries) can obtain tourist visas on arrival at Bole International Airport. Aside from some (usually minor) queuing, the process upon arrival is painless and a tourist visa costs US$50.

➡ Normally immigration staff automatically grant a one-month visa, but if you request it, three months doesn't seem to be an issue. Immigration officials in Addis Ababa told us that they don't require onward air tickets, though some people have been asked for them.

➡ Three- and six-month multiple entry visas are also possible. Note that visas are NOT available at any land border.

➡ Ethiopian embassies abroad may (or equally may not; it varies from embassy to embassy) require some or all of the following to accompany visa applications: an onward air ticket (or airline itinerary), a visa for the next country you're planning to visit, a yellow-fever vaccination certificate and proof of sufficient funds (officially a minimum of US$50 per day).

➡ If your citizenship isn't one that can acquire a visa at Bole and there's no Ethiopian diplomatic representation in your country, you may be able to ask Ethiopian Airlines or a tour operator to order you a visa before your arrival; otherwise contact the Department of Immigration in Addis in advance. Visas in such circumstances cannot be obtained on arrival without prior arrangement at immigration.

➡ Travellers of all nationalities can obtain transit visas on arrival or at the embassies abroad; these are valid for up to seven days. To obtain a transit visa, you will be required to show proof of onward travel or a visa for the next country you plan to visit.

➡ The Department of Immigration is unlikely to grant visa extensions to those travelling on tourist visas – rather than arguing the case, it may be easier (if far more expensive!) to fly to Nairobi and then straight back again where you should be issued with another one-month tourist visa without fuss. Business travellers can get visa extensions but will need a letter from their employer.

Other Documents

In theory a yellow-fever vaccination certificate is mandatory, as is a vaccination against cholera if you've transited through a cholera-infected area within six days prior to your arrival in Ethiopia. These are rarely checked, but you probably wouldn't want to risk it.

All important documents (passport data page and visa page, credit cards, travel insurance policy, air/bus/train tickets, driving licence etc) should be photocopied. Leave one copy with someone at home and keep another with you, separate from the originals.

Visas for Onward Travel

DJIBOUTI

Bring US$125 (48-hour service) or US$150 (24-hour service), a hotel reservation, a plane or bus ticket out of the country, and one passport photo to the **Djibouti Embassy** (Map p46; ☎011 661 3200; off Bole Rd (Africa Ave); ⊙9am-noon Mon-Thu) early in the morning and you'll usually have it by the next day. Visas can also be obtained on arrival at the airport in Djibouti.

KENYA

The **Kenyan Embassy** (Map p34; ☎011 661 0033; www.kenyaembassyaddis. org; Comoros St; ⊙9am-5pm Mon-Thu) charges US$50 for three-month tourist visas. Two passport photos are required. Applications are taken in the morning only, with visas ready the following afternoon. Visas are also easily obtained at the Moyale border and at Jomo Kenyatta International Airport in Nairobi.

SOMALILAND

The **Somaliland Embassy** (Map p46; ☎011 663 5921; off Djibouti St; ⊙9am-noon Mon-Thu) produces one-/

COMING FROM KENYA

At the time of writing the Ethiopian embassy in Nairobi was only issuing visas to Kenyan citizens or residents, a situation that has remained unchanged for a few years. Not a major problem if flying from Nairobi to Addis, where most people can get one on arrival, but a real pain for overland travellers. Note also that Ethiopian visas are not available at the Moyale border crossing. If travelling north to south across Africa then the good news is that visas were being issued without much fuss in Khartoum.

This is likely to change, so double check in advance. Lonely Planet's Thorn Tree forum (www.lonelyplanet. com/thorntree) is good for up-to-date information.

two-month tourist visas for US$40/60. It requires two passport photos and it's issued while you wait.

SUDAN & SOUTH SUDAN

Unless you're using the services of a registered Sudanese tour company, then obtaining a tourist visa at the **Sudanese Embassy** (Map p34; 011 551 6477; sudan. embassy@ethionet.et; Ras Lulseged St; 9am-12.30pm Mon-Thu) is mission impossible. Instead, apply for a transit visa, which is valid for one month from date of issue and allows up to two weeks in Sudan from the date of entry. Transit visas are relatively easy to obtain, but you will require: an onward visa for Egypt, two photos and, for most nationalities, US$100 cash. Americans, you get to pay US$200. It normally takes a day to issue.

Volunteering

There are a few volunteering opportunities in Ethiopia, although many opportunities through international agencies need to be lined up in advance of your visit, rather than offering openings for drop-in volunteers.

Keep an eye out for small, focused grassroots projects. One such organisation in Addis Ababa is **Hope Enterprises** (Map p38; 011 156 0345; www.hopeenterprises. org; Churchill Ave; 8am-noon & 1-5pm Mon-Sat).

Women Travellers

Compared with many African countries, Ethiopia is pretty easygoing for women travellers. The risk of rape or other serious offences is likely lower than in many Western countries. The best advice is to be aware of how your clothing or behaviour may be perceived by locals and remember these unspoken codes of etiquette.

➡ Drinking alcohol, smoking, and wearing excessive make-up and revealing clothes are indications to the male population of 'availability', as this is also the way local prostitutes behave. Apart from the young of the wealthier classes in Addis Ababa, no 'proper' woman would be seen in a bar.

➡ Many cheap hotels in Ethiopia double as brothels. Ethiopian men may naturally wonder about your motives for staying, particularly if you're alone. While there's no cause for alarm, it's best to keep a low profile and behave conservatively – keep out of the hotel bar and try to meet up with other travellers if you want to go out.

➡ Accepting an invitation to an unmarried man's house, under any pretext, is considered a latent acceptance of things to come. Dinner invitations often amount to 'foreplay' before you're expected to head off to some seedy hotel. Even a seemingly innocent invitation to the cinema can turn out to be little more than an invitation to a good snog in the back row.

➡ Be aware that 'respectable' Ethiopian women (even when they're willing) are expected to put up a show of coyness and modesty. Traditionally, this formed part of the wedding-night ritual of every Amhara bride: a fierce struggle with the groom was expected of them. Consequently, some Ethiopian men may mistake your rebuttals

for encouragement. The concept even has a name in Amharic: *maqderder* (and applies equally to feigned reluctance for other things). If you mean no, make it very clear from the start.

➡ If there aren't any other travellers around, here's a quick trick: pick a male Ethiopian companion, bemoan the problems you've been having with his compatriots and appeal to his sense of pride, patriotism and gallantry. Usually any ulterior plans he might have been harbouring himself are soon converted into sympathy or shame and a personal crusade to protect you!

➡ Adultery is quite common among many of Ethiopia's urban population, for both men and women. For this reason, a wedding ring on a woman traveller (bogus or not) has absolutely no deterrent value. In fact, quite the reverse.

➡ The one advantage of Ethiopia being a relatively permissive society is that Western women (in particular, white women) aren't necessarily seen as easier than local women, something that's common in many developing countries due to Hollywood cinematic 'glamour'.

Female Phobia

In some of the monasteries and holy sites of Ethiopia, an ancient prohibition forbids women from setting foot in the holy confines. But the holy fathers go strictly by the book: the prohibition extends not just to women but to all female creatures, even she donkeys, hens and nanny goats.

Transport

GETTING THERE & AWAY

The vast majority of travellers arrive in Ethiopia by air at Addis Ababa, but for those with time and a spirit of adventure it's possible to enter Ethiopia overland via Sudan, Kenya, Djibouti and even Somaliland. There are no land or air links between Ethiopia and Eritrea. Borders with South Sudan and the rest of Somalia are either closed and/or dangerous.

Flights, tours and rail tickets can be booked at www.lonelyplanet.com/bookings.

Entering Ethiopia

Entering Ethiopia by air is painless, including if you have to pick up your visa upon arrival at Bole International Airport. Departure tax is included in ticket price.

Ethiopian border officials at land crossings are more strict. While official Ethiopian visa rules suggest that visas can be obtained on arrival, in practice, they're only available for those who arrive at Addis Ababa's Bole International Airport by air. What that means is that you *must* have a valid visa to enter overland as none are available at borders. Those entering with vehicles should have all the necessary paperwork.

Air

Airports & Airlines

Addis Ababa's **Bole International Airport** (Map p34; ☑011 551 7000; www.addisairport.com) is Ethiopia's only international airport. Although modern, there's little more than a 24-hour bank, a restaurant and a few cafes in arrivals; baggage carts and wi-fi are free. There's a bar and duty-free shops in departures. Ethiopia's only international and national carrier, **Ethiopian Airlines** (Map p46; ☑011 663 3163; www.ethiopianairlines.com; Bole Rd (Africa Ave); ⊙8.30am-5pm Mon-Sat) is rated as one of the best (and largest) airlines in Africa, with a modern fleet and a good safety record.

One thing to watch out for: if you want to fly with a European airline such as Lufthansa or KLM, double-check that you will actually be on one of their planes and not on an Ethiopian Airlines plane. They route share and commonly bundle their passengers onto Ethiopian Airlines and then kindly charge you more than you'd have paid if you'd bought directly with Ethiopian Airlines.

Airlines Flying to & from Ethiopia

EgyptAir (Map p38; ☑011 156 4493; www.egyptair.com; 2nd fl, Ayeu Shashe Bldg, Churchill Ave; ⊙9am-5pm Mon-Fri)

Emirates (EK; Map p46; ☑011 518 1818; www.emirates.com; Dembel City Centre; ⊙8.30am-5pm Mon-Fri, 8.30am-12.30pm Sat)

CLIMATE CHANGE & TRAVEL

Every form of transport that relies on carbon-based fuel generates CO_2, the main cause of human-induced climate change. Modern travel is dependent on aeroplanes, which might use less fuel per kilometre per person than most cars but travel much greater distances. The altitude at which aircraft emit gases (including CO_2) and particles also contributes to their climate change impact. Many websites offer 'carbon calculators' that allow people to estimate the carbon emissions generated by their journey and, for those who wish to do so, to offset the impact of the greenhouse gases emitted with contributions to portfolios of climate-friendly initiatives throughout the world. Lonely Planet offsets the carbon footprint of all staff and author travel.

Kenya Airways (Map p38; ☎011 551 4258; www.kenya-airways. com; Hilton Hotel, Menelik II Ave; ☺8.30am-5pm Mon-Fri)

KLM (Map p38; ☎011 552 5495; www.klm.com; Hilton Hotel, Menelik II Ave; ☺9am-noon & 1-5pm Mon-Fri, 9am-noon Sat)

Lufthansa (LH; Map p46; ☎011 155 1666; www.lufthansa.com; Axum Bldg, Cameroon St; ☺9am-noon & 1-5pm Mon-Fri, 9am-noon Sat)

Saudi Arabian Airlines (Map p38; ☎011 561 4327; www. saudiairlines.com; Ras Desta Damtew St; ☺9am-12.30pm & 1.30-5pm Mon-Thu)

Sudan Airways (Map p38; ☎011 550 4724; www.sudanair.com; Ras Desta Damtew St; ☺9am-5pm Mon-Fri)

Turkish Airlines (Map p46; ☎011 662 7781; www.turkis-hairlines.com; Zimbabwe St; ☺8.30am-5.30pm Mon-Fri, 8.30am-12.30pm Sat)

Yemenia (Map p38; ☎011 552 6440; www.yemenia.com; Ras Desta Damtew St; ☺8.30am-12.30pm & 2.30-5pm Mon-Fri, 8.30am-12.30pm Sat)

Tickets

For Ethiopia, flights during August, over Easter, Christmas and New Year should be booked well in advance.

Land

Travelling to Ethiopia by land is an adventure you'll never forget, no matter where you come from or how you do it.

Djibouti

Border formalities are usually pretty painless crossing between Djibouti and Ethiopia, but you *must* have your visa prior to arriving as none are issued at the land border.

ROAD

There are two current road routes linking Djibouti and Ethiopia: one via Dire Dawa and Gelille, and one via Awash and Galafi.

ENTERING ETHIOPIA OVERLAND

The overland route from South Africa through southern Africa and East Africa to Ethiopia is quite well trodden, and should present few problems, though the last section through northern Kenya still suffers from sporadic banditry. Be aware, though, that Ethiopian visas were still only being issued in Nairobi for Kenyan citizens and residents at the time of research. If you're heading on to Cairo, things start to get more complicated after Ethiopia – the main complication goes by the name of Sudan. Tourist visas are notoriously hard to obtain (unless you employ the services of a Sudanese tour company), but transit visas, allowing a generous two weeks in Sudan, are pretty simple to get in Addis.

➡ The Gelille route is best for those without vehicles as daily buses link Djibouti City and Dire Dawa. The journey takes 10 to 12 hours, though it involves changing buses at the border. In Djibouti City, **Société Bus Assajog** (☎77671404; Parc à Bétail, Balbala) buses depart at dawn from Ave Gamel Abdel Nasser; tickets cost DFr1500 to Gelille and should be purchased at least a day in advance to be sure of getting a seat; from Gelille, you'll need to buy an onward ticket to Dire Dawa (Birr185). In Dire Dawa, buy your ticket the day of travel at the **Tibuuti Ee City** (☎092 281 3751) office north of the 'old town' of Megala by Ashawa Market. Tickets cost Birr185 and buses depart around midnight from a spot north of this office.

➡ The road between Dire Dawa and Gelille was being upgraded at the time of writing and should be fully sealed in the next few years.

➡ In the meantime, although longer, the Galafi route is best for those driving as it's sealed the entire way. For those coming from northern Ethiopia, this route can be accessed via a paved shortcut at Woldia.

➡ Those without vehicles can also travel via Galafi, although it's not straightforward. In Djibouti City, you'll have to take a

---

minibus to Galafi, 5km from the border. From Galafi, you'll have to rely on the handful of morning minibuses to Logiya (Birr60, three hours) or hitch a lift with one of the many trucks heading into Ethiopia. Those using this route to leave Ethiopia can ride trucks directly to Djibouti City. We were quoted prices of Birr400 to Birr500 for the six-hour journey from Logiya, but there are many drivers and few passengers so negotiation is in order.

TRAIN

The rail line between Dire Dawa and Djibouti has been completed but passenger services were yet to begin at the time of writing. When completed, the line will connect Djibouti with Addis Ababa via Dire Dawa.

Eritrea

There are three traditional entry points from Eritrea into Ethiopia: Asmara to Adwa and Aksum via Adi Quala; Asmara to Adigrat via Senafe; and Assab to Addis Ababa via Serdo and Dessie. However, all these border crossings have been indefinitely closed since the 1998 war.

With relations on their current path, it seems sadly unlikely that the borders will be reopened anytime soon.

The only feasible way of crossing from Ethiopia to Eritrea is by plane, travelling via a third country. Travelling via

Djibouti is the most obvious and cheapest way. A much more roundabout route is via Cairo in Egypt.

Kenya

There are usually few problems crossing between Ethiopia and Kenya. The only feasible crossing is at Moyale, 772km south of Addis Ababa by road. Moyale has two incarnations, one on either side of the border.

→ The northern, Ethiopian, version of Moyale is well connected to the north and Addis Ababa by bus, along a pretty good, but often potholed, section of sealed road. Though security is normally not a problem along the main north–south route and in and around Moyale, there are occasional flare-ups of tribal fighting.

→ Getting solid info on what the situation is like at the moment you want to cross can be a little tricky. Tour companies and government travel-advice websites will know when there has been serious and sustained fighting in the area, but for the everyday sort of clashes probably the best source of information is other travellers as well as Lonely Planet's online Thorn Tree.

→ The southern, Kenyan, side of Moyale is truly in the middle of nowhere: around 800km north of Nairobi. A daily bus connects Moyale with Marsabit from where transport is available onto Isiolo and then onward to Nairobi. Trucks servicing the same destinations pick up passengers near the main intersection.

→ For those of you in your own vehicles, the road between Moyale and Marsabit is long but the completion of the paved road has eased things considerably. Thankfully the banditry problems of the past seem to be largely under control, although outbreaks of tribal fighting and banditry do still occur. While this normally takes place well away from the main Marsabit–Moyale road, serious tribal fighting has occurred in and around Moyale. Armed convoys are sometimes used along this route, although only in times of extreme tension. The Wajir route south is still not considered safe. Either way, be sure to check the security section before setting out from Moyale. Also make sure you fill up before leaving Ethiopia as petrol is half the price north of the border.

→ The Ethiopian and Kenyan borders at Moyale are open daily. Kenyan three-month visas are painlessly produced at **Kenyan immigration** (☉6.30am-6pm) for the grand sum of US$50. It's payable in US dollars (some have managed to pay in euros), but not Ethiopian birr. Transit visas cost US$20 (valid for seven days). **Ethiopian immigration** (Moyale; ☉8am-noon & 2-6pm Mon-Fri, 9-11am & 3-5pm Sat & Sun) cannot issue Ethiopian visas; these must be obtained at an Ethiopian embassy prior to arrival at the border.

→ If you're heading south and have a serious 4WD, it's possible to cross the border near Omorate alongside

Lake Turkana. Currently the main route (a relative term since it's rarely travelled) for overlanders is a vague sandy track branching off the Turmi road about 15km outside of Omorate. Drivers must come fully prepared for a tough trip with few facilities and most people recommend taking a guide. It's about two days' travel time to Loyangalani. Rainy-season travel is not possible.

→ With the completion of the bridge across the Omo River at Omorate, the crossing west of the Omo River at Namoruputh is easier because the road is better. Kenyan immigration is in Todonyang, 7km after the border. Tribal conflicts remain common in this area, so check on the situation.

→ There's an **Ethiopian immigration post** (Omorate; ☉7.30am-5pm) in Omorate that can stamp you out; there's still no Kenyan post to issue you a visa, so you must obtain one from the Kenyan embassy in Addis Ababa beforehand. Once you reach Nairobi you'll have to get it stamped; immigration officials are used to this. Bring lots of fuel and a big sense of adventure!

Somaliland

You might brace yourself for adventure, but getting to Hargeisa, Somaliland's capital, is very easy.

→ Many buses and minibuses run along the good, paved road between Jijiga and the border town of Togo-Wuchale (Birr32, one to 1½ hours). Get stamped out at Ethiopian immigration (it's the white

BORDER CROSSINGS

TO/FROM	FROM/TO	BORDER CROSSING NOTES
Ethiopia	Djibouti	Border crossings at Gelille and Galafi
Ethiopia	Somaliland	Border crossing at Togo-Wuchale/Wajaale
Somaliland	Djibouti	Border crossing at Loyaada

Note that no visas are obtainable at borders

building with a flag and satellite dish) before walking 100m over the causeway in no-man's-land to the brightly signed Somaliland immigration office in the twin village of Wajaale. The visa must have been arranged prior to your arrival by a hotel or an agent in Hargeisa.

➡ Taxis run frequently from a muddy park next to immigration to Hargeisa (Birr140, two hours), about 90km to the southeast. The drivers will try to get you to pay extra for your bags, but you don't need to.

Sudan

The main border-crossing point with Sudan is the Metema crossing, 180km west of Gonder. The road between Gonder and Khartoum is now paved all the way. It's imperative that you've obtained your Sudan visa in Addis Ababa or elsewhere before heading this way.

➡ In Gonder minibuses leave daily for Metema (Birr105, three hours). There is also a direct bus from Addis (Birr375, two days).

➡ After reaching Metema walk across the border into the Sudanese town of Gallabat; please note that there were plans afoot in late 2016 to merge the two border posts into a single complex which should make things easier, although it was still only a plan at the time of writing. From Gallabat, transport can be found to Gedaref (three hours) and onward to Khartoum. If you set off very early and everything goes your way then you might make it from Gonder to Khartoum in a single day, but don't count on it. If you get stuck en route then try to stay overnight in Gedaref).

South Sudan

➡ At the time of research the border between Ethiopia and South Sudan at Jikawo was closed to foreigners, although it's often open for

THE EMPEROR'S NEW SHOES

Building a railway across the Horn of Africa was never going to be easy. So when two European engineers arrived in Addis Ababa in 1894 to propose such a scheme to Emperor Menelik II, they would have been prepared for the challenges of hacking a rail line through the mountains, but they probably never expected that their first challenge would involve shoes. Menelik was intrigued by the idea of a railway line, but he wanted proof that these two men knew their stuff. In order to test them, Menelik placed the men in a room under armed guard, gave them a length of twine and a sheet of leather, and ordered them to make him some shoes by dawn. Unstitching their own shoes, the engineers used these as patterns and by first light the Emperor had a fine pair of new shoes – and some years later a railway line!

citizens of the two countries. If it ever reopens, expect buses to go from Gambela to the border town of Jikawo (Birr98, 4½ hours). From there take a shared taxi to Adora (South Sudan).

➡ Another option, and one that locals in Gambela sometimes use, is to hang around the river in Gambela in the hope of securing passage on one of the small boats that occasionally travel to Akobe via the Baro River. We've never heard of any travellers doing this, but if you get the nod from immigration officials then it's going to be an interesting way to cross between Ethiopia and South Sudan.

➡ Whichever way you try to go, check the security situation in South Sudan thoroughly beforehand as at the time of research there had been a lot of fighting in southeast South Sudan.

GETTING AROUND

Air

Ethiopian Airlines (www.ethiopianairlines.com) is the only domestic carrier, with a comprehensive domestic route service and a solid safety record.

It's well worth considering a domestic flight or two, even if you're travelling on a budget. While prices cannot be described as cheap, it does eliminate long, bumpy bus rides. If you want a window seat to enjoy Ethiopia's scenic landscapes from above, check in early.

➡ Standard security procedures apply at all airports. The baggage limit is 20kg on domestic flights. Don't bring bulky hand luggage as the interiors are quite small.

➡ Most flights leave from Addis Ababa, but not all are nonstop, which means you can also jump from one town to another. For instance, most of the daily Addis Ababa–Aksum flights stop at either Bahir Dar, Gonder or Lalibela en route.

➡ Buying domestic tickets from an agency on arrival in Ethiopia is almost always cheaper than buying them online from outside the country.

➡ Booking early to ensure a seat is particularly important on the Historical Circuit and during major festivals.

➡ Technically you should reconfirm all domestic flights 72 hours in advance. This is of course a very good idea, though we've never done

Main Domestic Routes (Ethiopian Airlines)

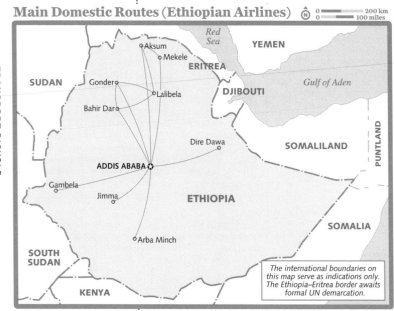

The international boundaries on this map serve as indications only. The Ethiopia–Eritrea border awaits formal UN demarcation.

this and have never had any problems. Still, it's far better to err on the side of caution.

➡ Beware that schedules are occasionally forced to change due to weather or mechanical difficulties, so try not to plan an itinerary that's so tight that it doesn't make allowances for these changes.

Bicycle

Cycling in Ethiopia is a fabulously rewarding way to explore the country. If you want to cycle across the country, come well prepared with a sturdy bike, plenty of spare parts, a good repair kit and the capacity to carry sufficient amounts of water. New and second-hand cycles can be bought in Addis Ababa, but they are not the type of bike you'd wish to conquer the Historical Circuit with!

In the past, irregular terrain and brutal roads have scared off most adventure addicts and their bicycles –

to that cyclist we saw about to climb into the clouds on the approach to the Simien Mountains, respect! But with today's greatly improving road network it may be the right time to give it a try.

➡ Cyclists should show the usual caution when travelling around the country: never travel after dark, be wary of thieves and keep the bicycle well maintained. Brakes need to be in good working order for the mountainous highland roads.

➡ Don't expect local drivers to keep an eye out for you – trucks, minibuses and other vehicles often come around corners on the wrong side of the road, so be vigilant and prepared to dodge sideways off the road at a split-second's notice.

➡ Be particularly wary of dogs; sometimes it's best to dismount and walk slowly away.

➡ Cycling in the rainy season can be very hard going.

➡ Punctures are easily repaired: just head for any *gommista* (tyre repairer) or garage. Many mechanics are more than happy to help with cycle problems, and often turn out to be ingenious improvisers.

➡ There are special customs regulations regarding the importation of a bicycle. A deposit must usually be left (amounting to the cycle's worth) at customs at the port of entry on arrival. When you leave, this will be returned. to deter black-market trading.

➡ Cycles are accepted aboard Ethiopian Airlines international flights. On domestic flights you'll need to check first in advance as it depends on what type of plane is covering the route on that given day.

➡ Check and tighten screws and nuts regularly; take a spare chain; take a front as well as rear pannier rack; and pack a water filter in case you get stuck somewhere remote.

Boat

Apart from tourist boats used for sightseeing, there are very few commercial boat operations for getting around Ethiopia. One exception, albeit one that is difficult to recommend, is the weekly ferry between Bahir Dar and Gorgora on Lake Tana.

Bus

A good network of long-distance buses connects most major towns of Ethiopia.

Recently a new breed of bus has taken to the roads of Ethiopia and these ones actually are pretty plush (air-con, reclining seats, on-board toilets, TVs and even free snacks). The biggest and best companies are **Selam Bus** (☑0115-548800) and **Sky Bus** (☑0111-568080; www.skybusethiopia.com). We strongly recommend that you pay extra to travel on one of these newer private bus operators. Apart from being much more comfortable, they rarely travel at night and are generally safer.

Otherwise, you'll find yourself at the mercy of the government buses and similar private services. A few things to remember:

➜ One government bus association and around a dozen private ones operate, though you'll rarely be able to tell the difference.

➜ Government buses sell seat-specific tickets in advance and passengers must wait in line while the bus is loaded. After that's completed, the queue is paraded around the bus before tickets are checked and the boarding barrage occurs. Private buses simply open the doors and start selling tickets to the flood of passengers as they cram in. Needless to say, private buses are usually the first to leave. They also tend to be slightly more comfortable than government ones.

➜ Unlike most African countries, standing in the aisles of long-distance buses is illegal in Ethiopia, making them more comfortable (note that we've said 'more comfortable', which is a far cry from saying comfortable) and safer. On the longer journeys, there are usually scheduled 20-minute stops for meals.

➜ In many cases, when you arrive at the bus station there'll only be one bus heading in your direction, so any thoughts about it being private or government become irrelevant. If you haven't booked through one of the new private companies, your choices will be limited to whichever bus is leaving next.

➜ Once on the road, you'll realise that all buses are slow. On sealed roads you can expect to cover around 50km/h, but on dirt roads 30km/h or less. In the rainy season, journeys can be severely disrupted. Thankfully, new roads are spreading rapidly across the land and turning many troublesome dirt sections into slick sections of sealed road. Unfortunately this has seen an increase in road accidents due to speed.

➜ Remember when asking about departure times that the Ethiopian clock is used locally (add six hours to get the Western time).

➜ In remote areas long waits for buses to fill is normal – some may not leave at all. In general, the earlier you get to the bus station, the better chance you have of catching the first bus out of town.

➜ The major drawback with bus travel is the size of the country. For the Historical Circuit alone, you'll spend a total of at least 10 days sitting on a bus to cover the 2500km.

➜ On most journeys with durations that last longer than one day, there are overnight stops en route (Ethiopian law stipulates that all long-distances buses must be off the road by 6pm, although in practice this is often ignored). In many cases you won't be allowed to remove luggage from the roof, so you should pack toiletries and other overnight items to take with you in a small bag on the bus.

➜ Smaller and more remote towns are usually served by minibuses or Isuzu trucks. They're usually faster and sometimes cheaper, but you take your life in your hands if you decide to travel in one.

Costs

Buses are very cheap in Ethiopia. Both government-run and private buses work out at around US$1.50 to US$1.75 per 100km. You will pay double or triple this for one of the newer private companies, but we think it's always worth it.

Reservations

➜ For Sky and Selam bus tickets should be booked as far ahead as possible.

➜ Tickets for most long-distance journeys (over 250km) can usually be bought in advance. If you can, do: it guarantees a seat (though not a specific seat number on private buses) and cuts out the touts who sometimes snap up the remaining tickets to resell for double the price to latecomers. Most government ticket offices are open daily from 4.30am to 6pm. For short distances, tickets can usually only be bought on the day.

➜ If you would like a whiff of fresh air on your journey, get a seat behind the driver as he tends to buck the Ethiopian trend of keeping windows firmly closed and keeps his window cracked open. If there's an accident these are often the worst seats to be in!

Car & Motorcycle

Bringing Your Own Vehicle

If you're bringing your own 4WD or motorcycle, you'll need a *carnet de passage* (a guarantee issued by your own national motoring association that you won't sell your vehicle in the country you are travelling), the vehicle's registration papers and proof of third-party insurance that covers Ethiopia.

Driving Licence

Tourists are allowed three months of using their international driving licence if driving their own vehicle, after which you need an Ethiopian one. This is rarely enforced and most overlanders we met hadn't bothered with the convoluted process of obtaining an Ethiopian licence and had yet to encounter any problems.

Fuel & Spare Parts

Fuel (both petrol and diesel) is quite widely available, apart from the more remote regions such as the southwest. Unleaded petrol is not available – the choice is between diesel and normal petrol (called Benzene in Ethiopia). Note that your vehicle's fuel consumption will be 25% higher in highland Ethiopia than at sea level because of the increased altitudes.

While there are helpful garages throughout the country (ask your hotel to recommend one), spare parts are not abundant outside Addis Ababa. It's wise to take stock while in Addis and acquire all that you may need for the journey ahead. Thanks to Toyota Land Cruisers being the choice of most tour operators, their parts are more plentiful and less expensive than those for Landrovers.

Hire

Most people hire a 4WD *with a driver*. Recent road improvements mean this isn't always necessary, but since all tour companies only offer 4WD it's something of an academic point!

➡ Despite competition between the numerous tour agents in Addis Ababa that hire 4WDs, prices are steep and start from US$180 per day. Most companies include unlimited kilometres, a driver, driver allowance (for their food and accommodation), fuel, third-party insurance, a collision damage waiver and government taxes in their rates; check all these details, and ask if service charges will be added afterwards and if there are set driver's hours. Some companies allow you to pay for fuel separately. This is almost always cheaper than paying an all-inclusive rate.

➡ Know that prices are always negotiable and vary greatly depending on the period of rental and the season. Despite the hassle, you'll always pay much less organising things yourself in Ethiopia (or dealing directly with a local company) rather than hiring an agency at home to arrange it.

➡ Drivers are mandatory – currently no agency offers self-drive 4WD outside Addis. These drivers can be very useful as guides-cum-interpreters-cum-mechanics. Although tips are expected afterwards, a nice gesture during the trip is to share food together (which costs very little).

➡ Though expensive, the chief advantage of 4WD hire over bus travel is the time that can be saved. Trip durations are at least halved and there's no waiting around in remote regions for infrequent and erratic buses. Note also that some national parks can only be entered with a 4WD.

➡ Some Addis Ababa–based agencies have branch offices in towns on the Historical Route and can rent 4WDs, but only by prearrangement.

➡ Self-drive cars are only hired for use in and around Addis and even that is rare. If you're still interested in hiring one to toot around the capital (and it's hard to see what you'd gain from doing this rather than just taking a taxi), you must have a valid international driver's licence and be between 25 and 70 years old. Vehicles cost from US$120 per day with 50km to 70km free kilometres.

➡ No companies currently offer motorcycle rental.

Insurance

Third-party vehicle insurance is required by law.

Thankfully, unlike some other African countries, which demand that vehicles are covered by an insurance company based in that country, your insurance from elsewhere is also valid in Ethiopia. If you don't have either, the numerous offices of Ethiopian Insurance Corporation (www.eic.com.et) sell third-party and comprehensive insurance.

Road Conditions

Ethiopian roads continue to improve at a rapid rate, but even so plenty remain unsealed.

➡ Roads in the south have generally improved hugely in recent years and even many parts of the Omo Valley are now accessible year-round even without a 4WD. However, there are still plenty of patches where potholes add a little bounce to your journey.

➡ Sealed roads head west from Addis Ababa and with major construction works underway, expect sealed roads all the way to Gambela in the not-too-distant future. Elsewhere in the west, many lowland roads can be diabolical in the rains.

➡ Decent sealed roads all but link Addis Ababa with most of the main towns on the northern circuit, but there are still some potholed sections.

➡ Harar and Dire Dawa, both 525km east of Addis Ababa, are connected to the capital with good sealed roads.

Road Hazards

➡ On the outskirts of the towns or villages, look out for people, particularly children playing on the road or kerbside. Unmarked speed bumps can also be an unpleasant surprise.

➡ Night driving is never recommended, as the risk of accidents escalates considerably after dark. *Shiftas* (bandits) still operate in the more remote areas. Additionally, some trucks park overnight in the middle of the road – without lights.

➡ In the country, livestock is the main hazard; camels wandering onto the road can cause major accidents in the lowlands. Many animals, including donkeys, are unaccustomed to vehicles and are very car-shy, so always approach slowly and with caution.

➡ During the rainy season, a few roads, particularly in the west and southwest, become impassable. Check conditions with local authorities before setting out.

Road Rules

➡ Driving is on the right-hand side of the road.

➡ The speed limit for cars and motorcycles is 60km/h in the towns and villages and 100km/h outside the towns.

➡ The standard of driving is generally not high; devices such as mirrors or indicators are more decorative than functional.

➡ On highland roads, drive defensively and beware of trucks coming fast the other way, sometimes on the wrong side of the road.

➡ Keep a sharp eye out for a row of stones or pebbles across the road: it marks roadworks or an accident.

➡ Seatbelts are compulsory for the driver (but nobody else), but many vehicles don't have seatbelts!

Hitching & Ride-Sharing

In the past, if someone asked for a ride in Ethiopia, it was usually assumed that it was because they couldn't afford a bus fare and little sympathy was spared for them. Many Ethiopians also suspected hitchers of hidden motives such as robbery.

However, for some towns not readily served by buses or light vehicles, hitching is now quite normal, and you will be expected to pay a 'fare'. Negotiate this in advance. The best place to look for lifts is at the hotels, bars and cafes in the centre of town.

➡ Be aware that the density of vehicles on many roads is still very low in Ethiopia; on the remote roads you'll be lucky to see any.

➡ Know that hitching is never entirely safe, and it's not recommended. Travellers who decide to hitch should understand that they are taking a small but potentially serious risk. Hitching is safer in pairs. Additionally, try to let someone know where you're planning to go. Women should never hitch alone.

Local Transport

➡ In many of the larger towns, a minibus service provides a quick, convenient and cheap way of hopping about town (from around Birr2 for short journeys). 'Conductors' generally shout out the destination of the bus; if in doubt, ask.

➡ Taxis operate in many of the larger towns, including Addis Ababa. Prices are reasonable, but foreigners as well as well-heeled Ethiopians are always charged more for 'contract services'. Ask your hotel for a fare estimate.

➡ *Bajajs* (motorised rickshaws) are common in many towns; a seat in a shared *bajaj* across town shouldn't cost more than Birr5. Hiring the vehicle for you alone will cost about Birr15 to Birr20 for the same trip.

Minibuses & Trucks

➡ Minibuses are commonly used between towns connected by sealed roads or to cover short distances. Legally they are not allowed to operate over a distance greater than 150km but plenty of drivers flout this rule. Some of these travel at night to reduce the chances of a brush with the police – or, during daylight hours, the driver merely swaps his papers halfway through the journey so as to confuse the police. Minibuses cost slightly more than buses, but they leave more often and cover the distances more quickly. A ride in one is also more likely to kill you! Avoid those travelling at night. You'll usually find them at bus stations.

➡ Some foreigners used to travel around remote regions in the back of goods trucks. The Lower Omo Valley was a popular place to do this. It's now illegal and, contrary to travellers' rumours that it's in order to make tourists pay for organised tours, it's actually for safety reasons – though yes, the rule only seems to be enforced on foreigners!

Taxi

In the towns, villages and countryside of Ethiopia taxis offer two kinds of service: 'contract taxis' and 'share-taxis'. Share-taxis ply fixed routes, stop and pick people up when hailed and generally operate like little buses. They become

TRAVELLERS' LORE

Once there was a dog, a goat and a donkey. They wanted to go on a journey together and decided to take a bus. The donkey paid and got out, the dog paid, got out but never got his change, and the goat got out but never paid. To this day, and whenever a vehicle passes, the dog still chases his change, the goat still scatters at the first approach, and the donkey just plods tranquilly on.

Ethiopian folk tale

'contract taxis' when they are flagged down (or 'contracted') by an individual or a group for a private journey. The fare is then split between all the passengers in the taxi.

Always negotiate the fare before you get in.

Tours

For the independent traveller, incorporating an organised tour into your travels in Ethiopia is useful for four things: specialised activities such as safaris; access to remote regions with limited public transport such as the Lower Omo Valley or the Danakil Depression; 'themed trips' with expert guides; and to help those with limited time who are keen to see as much as possible.

To reduce the cost of tours (few are cheap), hook up with a group of other travellers, or contact the agency far in advance to see if there are prearranged tours that you can tag onto – in such cases you may need to be flexible. The Thorn Tree forum on the Lonely Planet website can be a good place to hook up with travellers.

Agencies offer all or some of the following: guides, 4WD hire, camping-equipment hire, Historical Route tours, birdwatching and wildlife viewing, Omo Valley tours, photo safaris, Simien and Bale Mountain trekking, Rift Valley Lake trips and Danakil and Afar excursions. Some have branches in towns outside Addis Ababa, from where (if prebooked) you can hire a 4WD or guide or take a tour.

Though prices are officially fixed, most are very open to negotiation, particularly during the low season. Some agencies now accept credit cards (with a 2% to 3% commission). The following list is far from exhaustive, but it includes those recommended by travellers and Ethiopians in the tourism industry.

Abeba Tours Ethiopia (Map p46; 011 557 0881, mobile 092 781 9331; www.abebatoursethiopia.com; off Democratic Republic Congo St) Friendly and very professional, this operator seems to go the extra mile for its customers. It organises general tours throughout the country and the drivers they use are about the best in the business. If travelling by jeep is too rough, then they can also organise helicopter tours!

Ethiopian Quadrants (Map p34; 011 515 7990; www.ethiopianquadrants.com; Côte d'Ivoire St, near Adwa Bridge) Respected and well-managed tour company run by knowledgeable staff. All the standard tours as well as birdwatching, butterfly, flower and coffee tours.

GETTS Ethiopia (Map p46; 091 123 3289; www.getts.com.et; off Bole Rd (Africa Ave)) Well-regarded and professional operator, with countrywide tours with good drivers, guides and vehicles.

Green Land Tours & Travels (Map p46; 011 629 9252; www.greenlandethiopia.com; Cameroon St) Green Land is one of the biggest agencies in the city, with trips throughout Ethiopia and some pioneering tours to the remotest corners of the country.

Mandril Wenni Tour & Travel (Map p46; 091 139 3944, 092 794 9257; www.ethiomandriltour.com; Cameroon St) An excellent and relatively new company offering professionally run tours around Ethiopia.

Mon Pays Tours (Map p38; 011 655 4195; www.travels-ethiopia.com; Wendmanah St) A relative newcomer, Mon Pays has tours all across Ethiopia and can customise your itinerary. They're especially experienced in dealing with French travellers.

Red Jackal Tour Operator (Map p44; 011 155 9915; www.red-jackal.net; Itegue Taitu Hotel, Piazza) Good-value tours and used to dealing with backpackers and high-end visitors.

Simien Trek (091 877 6499; www.simientrek.com) Run by Shiferaw (Shif) Asrat, this professional outfit specialises in the Simien Mountains (p86) in northern Ethiopia, where it has its base, but staff are adept at sending you all over the country.

Smiling Ethiopia (Map p38; 091 121 8258, 011 515 0694; www.smilingethiopiatravel.com) Organises trips around Ethiopia, but we recommend trips to the Danakil Depression.

Tesfa Tours (Map p34; 011 126 0301, 092 160 2236; www.tesfatours.com; Tsehafi Tiezaz Afewerk St) With a focus on community tourism and trekking, Tesfa Tours, run by Mark Chapman, takes travellers into the heart of remote areas and local villages across Ethiopia.

Train

Major train infrastructure projects are currently underway, with the following sections completed or under construction:

Dire Dawa–Djibouti Completed but of little use.

Addis Ababa–Dire Dawa Largely completed.

Addis Ababa–Mekele Under construction.

Health

Decent health care is quite easy to access in Addis Ababa, less so elsewhere. Ethiopia certainly has an impressive selection of tropical diseases on offer, but as long as you stay up to date with your vaccinations and take some basic preventive measures, you're much more likely to get a bout of diarrhoea, a cold or an infected mosquito bite than an exotic disease such as sleeping sickness.

Before You Go

Insurance

Medical insurance is crucial, but policies differ. Check that the policy includes all the activities you want to do. Some specifically exclude 'dangerous activities' such as white-water rafting, rock climbing and motorcycling. Sometimes even trekking is excluded. Also find out whether your insurance will make payments directly to providers or will reimburse you later for overseas health expenditures (in Ethiopia many doctors expect payment in cash).

Ensure that your travel insurance will cover the emergency transport required to get you to a hospital in a major city, to better medical facilities elsewhere in Africa, or all the way home, by air and with a medical attendant if necessary. If you need medical help, your insurance company might be able to help locate the nearest hospital or clinic, or you can ask at your hotel. In an emergency, contact your embassy or consulate.

Membership of the African Medical & Research Foundation (www.amref.org) provides an air evacuation service in medical emergencies in many African countries, including Ethiopia. It also provides air-ambulance transfers between medical facilities. Money paid by members for this service goes into providing grassroots medical assistance for local people.

Medical Checklist

It's a very good idea to carry a medical and first-aid kit with you, to help yourself in the case of minor illness or injury. Following is a list of items you should consider packing.

➡ Acetaminophen (paracetamol) or aspirin

➡ Acetazolamide (Diamox) for altitude sickness (prescription only)

➡ Adhesive or paper tape

➡ Antibacterial ointment (eg Bactroban) for cuts and abrasions (prescription only)

➡ Antibiotics (see your medical-health professional for the most useful ones to bring)

➡ Antidiarrhoeal drugs (eg loperamide)

➡ Antihistamines (for hayfever and allergic reactions)

➡ Anti-inflammatory drugs (eg ibuprofen)

➡ Antimalaria pills

➡ Bandages, gauze, gauze rolls

➡ DEET-containing insect repellent for the skin

➡ Iodine tablets (for water purification)

➡ Oral rehydration salts

➡ Permethrin-containing insect spray for clothing, tents, and bed nets

➡ Pocket knife

➡ Scissors, safety pins, tweezers

➡ Sterile needles, syringes and fluids if travelling to remote areas

➡ Steroid cream or hydrocortisone cream (for allergic rashes)

➡ Sunblock

➡ Syringes and sterile needles

➡ Thermometer

Since falciparum malaria predominates in Ethiopia, consider taking a self-diagnostic kit that can identify malaria in the blood from a finger prick.

Websites

There's a wealth of travel-health advice on the internet. For further information, lonelyplanet.com is a good place to start. The World

Health Organization publishes a superb book called *International Travel and Health,* which is revised annually and is available online at no cost at www.who.int/ith. It's also a good idea to consult your government's travel health website before departure, if one is available.

Australia (www.dfat.gov.au/travel/Pages/travel.aspx)

Canada (www.hc-sc.gc.ca/index-eng.php)

UK (www.gov.uk/foreign-travel-advice)

USA (wwwnc.cdc.gov/travel)

Other websites of general interest:

Centers for Disease Control and Prevention (www.cdc.gov)

Fit for Travel (www.fitfortravel.scot.nhs.uk) Up-to-date information about outbreaks and is very user-friendly for travellers on the road.

MD Travel Health (www.mdtravelhealth.com) Provides complete travel health recommendations for every country, updated daily, at no cost.

In Ethiopia

Availability & Cost of Health Care

Health care in Ethiopia is varied: Addis Ababa has good facilities with well-trained doctors and nurses, but outside the capital health care is patchy at best. Medicine and even sterile dressings and intravenous fluids might need to be purchased from a local pharmacy by patients or their relatives. The standard of dental care is equally variable, and there's an increased risk of hepatitis B and HIV transmission via poorly sterilised equipment. By and large, public hospitals in the region offer the cheapest service, but will have the least up-to-date equipment and medications; mission hospitals (where donations are the usual form of payment) often have more reasonable facilities; and private hospitals and clinics are more expensive but tend to have more advanced drugs and equipment and better trained medical staff.

Most drugs can be purchased over the counter in the region, without a prescription. Try to visit a pharmacy rather than a 'drug shop' or 'rural drug vendor', as they're the only ones with trained pharmacists who can offer educated advice. Many drugs for sale in Africa might be ineffective: they might be counterfeit or might not have been stored under the right conditions. The most common examples of counterfeit drugs are malaria tablets

and expensive antibiotics, such as ciprofloxacin. Most drugs are available in larger towns, but remote villages will be lucky to have a couple of paracetamol tablets. It's strongly recommended that all drugs for chronic diseases be brought from home.

Although condoms are readily available (sometimes boxes – yes boxes! – are in hotel rooms), their efficacy cannot be relied upon, so bring all the contraception you'll need. Condoms bought in Africa might not be of the same quality as in Europe or Australia, and they might have been incorrectly stored.

There's a high risk of contracting HIV from infected blood if you receive a blood transfusion in the region. The BloodCare Foundation (www.bloodcare.org.uk) is a useful source of safe, screened blood, which can be transported to any part of the world within 24 hours.

Infectious Diseases

The list of diseases that you could conceivably catch in Ethiopia is lengthy, but in truth you'd be extremely unlucky to catch any of them.

DENGUE FEVER (BREAK-BONE FEVER)

Spread through the bite of the mosquito, dengue fever causes a feverish illness with headache and muscle pains similar to those experienced with a bad, prolonged attack of influenza. There might be a rash. Mosquito bites should be avoided whenever possible. Self-treatment: paracetamol and rest. Aspirin should be avoided.

HEPATITIS A

Hepatitis A is spread through contaminated food (particularly shellfish) and water. It causes jaundice and, although it's rarely fatal, it can cause prolonged lethargy and delayed recovery. If you've had hepatitis A, you shouldn't drink alcohol for up to six months afterwards, but once you've recovered, there

---

RECOMMENDED VACCINATIONS

The World Health Organization (www.who.int) recommends that all travellers be covered for diphtheria, tetanus, measles, mumps, rubella and polio, as well as for hepatitis B, regardless of their destination. The consequences of these diseases can be severe and outbreaks of them do occur.

According to the Centers for Disease Control & Prevention (www.cdc.gov), the following vaccinations are recommended for all parts of Africa: hepatitis A, hepatitis B, meningococcal meningitis, rabies and typhoid, and boosters for tetanus, diphtheria and measles. Proof of yellow-fever vaccination is mandatory for travel to Ethiopia. Depending on where you've travelled from, cholera vaccination may also be required.

won't be any long-term problems. The first symptoms include dark urine and a yellow colour to the whites of the eyes. Sometimes a fever and abdominal pain might be present. Hepatitis A vaccine (Avaxim, VAQTA, Havrix) is given as an injection: a single dose will give protection for up to a year, and a booster after a year gives 10-year protection. Hepatitis A and typhoid vaccines can also be given as a single-dose vaccine, hepatyrix or viatim.

HEPATITIS B

Hepatitis B is spread through infected blood, contaminated needles and sexual intercourse. It can also be spread from an infected mother to the baby during childbirth. It affects the liver, causing jaundice and occasionally liver failure. Most people recover completely, but some people might be chronic carriers of the virus, which could lead eventually to cirrhosis or liver cancer. Those visiting high-risk areas for long periods or those with increased social or occupational risk should be immunised.

Many countries now give hepatitis B as part of the routine childhood vaccinations. It's given singly or can be given at the same time as hepatitis A (hepatyrix). A course will give protection for at least five years. It can be given over four weeks or six months.

HIV & AIDS

HIV, the virus that causes AIDS, is an enormous problem throughout Ethiopia and Djibouti. The virus is spread through infected blood and blood products, by sexual intercourse with an infected partner and from an infected mother to her baby during childbirth and breastfeeding. It can be spread through 'blood to blood' contacts, such as with contaminated instruments during medical, dental, acupuncture and other body-piercing procedures, and through sharing

---

THE ANTIMALARIAL A TO D

➜ A – Awareness of the risk. No medication is totally effective, but protection of up to 95% is achievable with most drugs, as long as other measures have been taken.

➜ B – Bites are to be avoided at all costs. Sleep in a screened room, use a mosquito spray or coils, sleep under a permethrin-impregnated net at night. Cover up at night with long trousers and long sleeves, preferably with permethrin-treated clothing. Apply appropriate repellent to all areas of exposed skin in the evenings.

➜ C – Chemical prevention (ie antimalarial drugs) is usually needed in malarial areas. Expert advice is needed as resistance patterns can change, and new drugs are in development. Not all antimalarial drugs are suitable for everyone. Most antimalarial drugs need to be started at least a week in advance and continued for four weeks after the last possible exposure to malaria.

➜ D – Diagnosis. If you have a fever or flulike illness within a year of travel to a malarial area, malaria is a possibility, and immediate medical attention is necessary.

---

used intravenous needles. At present there's no cure; medication that might keep the disease under control is available, but these drugs are too expensive for the overwhelming majority of Africans, and are not readily available for travellers either. If you think you might have been infected with HIV, a blood test is necessary; a three-month gap after exposure and before testing is required to allow antibodies to appear in the blood.

LEPTOSPIROSIS

It's spread through the excreta of infected rodents, especially rats. It can cause hepatitis and renal failure, which might be fatal. It's unusual for travellers to be affected unless living in poor sanitary conditions. It causes a fever and sometimes jaundice.

MALARIA

Malaria is a serious problem in Ethiopia, with one to two million new cases reported each year. Though malaria is generally absent at altitudes above 1800m, epidemics have occurred in areas above

2000m in Ethiopia. The central plateau, Addis Ababa, the Bale and Simien Mountains, and most of the northern Historical Circuit are usually considered safe areas, but they're not risk-free.

For short-term visitors, it's probably wise to err on the side of caution. If you're thinking of travelling outside these areas, you shouldn't think twice – take prophylactics.

Cause

The disease is caused by a parasite in the bloodstream spread via the bite of the female Anopheles mosquito. There are several types of malaria – falciparum malaria is the most dangerous type and makes up 70% of the cases in Ethiopia. Infection rates vary with season and climate, so check out the situation before departure. Unlike most other diseases regularly encountered by travellers, there's no vaccination against malaria (yet). However, several different drugs are used to prevent malaria, and new ones are in the pipeline. Up-to-date advice from a travel-health clinic is essential as some medication is more suitable for some travellers than others. The pattern of drug-resistant malaria is changing rapidly, so what was advised several years ago might no longer be the case.

Symptoms

Malaria can present in several ways. The early stages include headaches, fevers, generalised aches and pains, and malaise, which could be mistaken for flu. Other symptoms can include abdominal pain, diarrhoea and a cough. Anyone who develops a fever in a malarial area should assume they have a malarial infection until a blood test proves negative, even if they have been taking antimalarial medication. If not treated, the next stage could develop within 24 hours, particularly if falciparum malaria is the parasite: jaundice, then reduced consciousness and coma (also known as cerebral malaria) followed by death. Treatment in hospital is essential, and the death rate might still be as high as 10%, even in the best intensive-care facilities in the country.

Medication

Many travellers are under the impression that malaria is a mild illness, that treatment is always easy and successful, and that taking antimalarial drugs causes more illness through side effects than actually getting malaria. In Africa, this is unfortunately not true. Side effects of the medication depend on the drug being taken. Doxycycline can cause heartburn, indigestion and increased sensitivity to sunlight; mefloquine (Larium) can cause anxiety attacks, insomnia and nightmares, and (rarely) severe psychiatric disorders; chloroquine can cause nausea and hair loss; and atovaquone and proguanil hydrochloride (malarone) can cause diarrhoea, abdominal pain and mouth ulcers.

These side effects are not universal, and can be minimised by taking medication correctly, eg with food. Also, some people should not take a particular antimalarial drug, eg people with epilepsy should avoid mefloquine, and doxycycline should not be taken by pregnant women or children younger than 12.

If you decide that you really do not wish to take antimalarial drugs, you must understand the risks, and be obsessive about avoiding mosquito bites. Use nets and insect repellent, and report any fever or flu-like symptoms to a doctor as soon as possible. Some people advocate homeopathic preparations against malaria, such as Demal200, but as yet there's no conclusive evidence that this is effective, and many homeopaths don't recommend their use.

Stand-by Treatment

If you're planning a journey through a malarial area, particularly where falciparum malaria predominates, consider taking stand-by treatment. Emergency stand-by treatment should be seen as emergency treatment aimed at saving the patient's life and not as routine self-medication. It should be used only if you'll be far from medical facilities and have been advised about the symptoms of malaria and how to use the medication. Medical advice should be

HEALTHCARE IN DJIBOUTI

Health care in Djibouti is varied: Djibouti City has good facilities with well-trained doctors and nurses, but outside the capital health care is patchy at best. Medicine and even sterile dressings and intravenous fluids might need to be purchased from a local pharmacy by patients or their relatives. The standard of dental care is equally variable, and there's an increased risk of hepatitis B and HIV transmission via poorly sterilised equipment. By and large, public hospitals in the region offer the cheapest service, but will have the least up-to-date equipment and medications; mission hospitals (where donations are the usual form of payment) often have more reasonable facilities; and private hospitals and clinics are more expensive but tend to have more advanced drugs and equipment and better trained medical staff.

Djibouti City is well endowed with excellent French-supplied pharmacies, and most drugs can be purchased over the counter, with or without a prescription. It's strongly recommended that all drugs for chronic diseases be brought from home.

Although condoms are readily available (sometimes boxes – yes boxes! – are in hotel rooms), their efficacy cannot be relied upon, so bring all the contraception you'll need. Condoms bought in Africa might not be of the same quality as in Europe or Australia, and they might have been incorrectly stored.

There's a high risk of contracting HIV from infected blood if you receive a blood transfusion in the region. The BloodCare Foundation (www.bloodcare.org.uk) is a useful source of safe, screened blood, which can be transported to any part of the world within 24 hours.

sought as soon as possible to confirm whether the treatment has been successful.

The type of stand-by treatment used will depend on local conditions, such as drug resistance, and on what antimalarial drugs were being used before stand-by treatment. This is worthwhile because you want to avoid contracting a particularly serious form such as cerebral malaria, which affects the brain and central nervous system and can be fatal in 24 hours. As mentioned earlier, self-diagnostic kits, which can identify malaria in the blood from a finger prick, are also available in the West.

RABIES

Rabies is spread by receiving the bites or licks of an infected animal on broken skin. It's always fatal once the clinical symptoms start (which might be up to several months after an infected bite), so post-bite vaccination should be given as soon as possible. Post-bite vaccination (whether or not you've been vaccinated before the bite) prevents the virus from spreading to the central nervous system. Animal handlers should be vaccinated, as should those travelling to remote areas where a reliable source of post-bite vaccine isn't available within 24 hours. Three preventive injections are needed over a month. If you have not been vaccinated you'll need a course of five injections starting 24 hours or as soon as possible after the injury. If you have been vaccinated, you'll need fewer post-bite injections, and have more time to seek medical help.

YELLOW FEVER

Yellow fever is spread by infected mosquitoes. Symptoms range from a flu-like illness to severe hepatitis (liver inflammation), jaundice and death. The yellow-fever vaccination must be given at a designated clinic and is

valid for 10 years. It's a live vaccine and must not be given to immunocompromised or pregnant travellers.

Travellers must carry a certificate as evidence of vaccination to obtain a visa for Ethiopia. You may also have to present it at immigration upon arrival. There's always the possibility that a traveller without a legally required, up-to-date certificate will be vaccinated and detained in isolation at the port of arrival for up to 10 days or possibly repatriated.

Traveller's Diarrhoea

Although it's not inevitable that you'll get diarrhoea while travelling in Ethiopia, it's certainly very likely. Diarrhoea is the most common travel-related illness: figures suggest that at least half of all travellers will get diarrhoea at some stage. Sometimes dietary changes, such as increased spices or oils, are the cause. To help prevent diarrhoea, avoid tap water. You should also only eat fresh fruits or vegetables if cooked or peeled, and be wary of dairy products that might contain unpasteurised milk. Although freshly cooked food can often be a safe option, plates or serving utensils might be dirty, so you should be highly selective when eating food from street vendors (make sure that cooked food is piping hot all the way through).

If you develop diarrhoea, be sure to drink plenty of fluids, preferably an oral rehydration solution containing water (lots), and some salt and sugar. A few loose stools don't require treatment, but if you start having more than four or five stools a day you should start taking an antibiotic (usually a quinoline drug, such as ciprofloxacin or norfloxacin) and an antidiarrhoeal agent (such as loperamide) if you're not within easy reach of a toilet. If diarrhoea is bloody, persists for more than 72 hours

or is accompanied by fever, shaking chills or severe abdominal pain, seek medical attention.

AMOEBIC DYSENTERY

Contracted by eating contaminated food and water, amoebic dysentery causes blood and mucus in the faeces. It can be relatively mild and tends to come on gradually, but seek medical advice if you think you have the illness as it won't clear up without treatment (which is with specific antibiotics).

Environmental Hazards

High temperatures mean that you should pay close attention to your fluid intake and make sure that you use some protection from the sun. Bites and stings from insects are common but relatively easy to prevent, while snake bites are extremely rare.

HEAT EXHAUSTION

This condition occurs following heavy sweating and excessive fluid loss with inadequate replacement of fluids and salt, and is particularly common in hot climates when taking unaccustomed exercise before full acclimatisation. Symptoms include headache, dizziness and tiredness. Dehydration is already happening by the time you feel thirsty; aim to drink sufficient water to produce pale, diluted urine. Take particular care in the Danakil Depression.

Self-treatment: fluid replacement with water and/or fruit juice, and cooling by cold water and fans. The treatment of the salt-loss component consists of consuming salty fluids as in soup, and adding a little more table salt to foods than usual.

HEATSTROKE

Heat exhaustion is a precursor to the much more serious condition of heatstroke. In this case there's damage to

TAP WATER

Never drink tap water unless it has been boiled, filtered or chemically disinfected (such as with iodine tablets). Never drink from streams, rivers and lakes. It's also best to avoid drinking from pumps and wells: some do bring pure water to the surface, but the presence of animals can still contaminate supplies.

Bottled water is available everywhere, though it's better for the environment if you treat/filter local water.

the sweating mechanism, with an excessive rise in body temperature; irrational and hyperactive behaviour; and eventually loss of consciousness and death. Rapid cooling by spraying the body with water and fanning is ideal. Emergency fluid and electrolyte replacement is usually also required by intravenous drip.

INSECT BITES & STINGS

Mosquitoes might not always carry malaria or dengue fever, but they (and other insects) can cause irritation and infected bites. To avoid these, take the same precautions as you would for avoiding malaria. Use DEET-based insect repellents. Excellent clothing treatments are also available; mosquitoes that land on treated clothing will die.

Bee and wasp stings cause real problems only to those who have a severe allergy to the stings (anaphylaxis). If you're one of these people, carry an 'epipen': an adrenaline (epinephrine) injection, which you can give yourself. This could save your life.

Scorpions are frequently found in arid or dry climates. They can cause a painful bite that is sometimes life-threatening. If bitten by a scorpion, take a painkiller. Medical treatment should be sought if collapse occurs.

Fleas and bed bugs are often found in cheap hotels. Fleas are also common on local and long-distance buses and in the rugs of some remote churches. They lead to very itchy, lumpy bites. Spraying the mattress with crawling-insect killer after removing bedding will get rid of them.

Scabies is also frequently found in cheap accommodation. These tiny mites live in the skin, particularly between the fingers. They cause an intensely itchy rash. The itch is easily treated with malathion and permethrin lotion from a pharmacy; other members of the household also need treating to avoid spreading scabies, even if they do not show any symptoms.

SNAKE BITES

Basically, do all you can to avoid getting bitten! Do not walk barefoot, or stick your hand into holes or cracks. However, 50% of people bitten by venomous snakes are not actually injected with poison (envenomed). If you are bitten by a snake, do not panic. Immobilise the bitten limb with a splint (such as a stick) and apply a bandage over the site, with firm pressure, similar to bandaging a sprain. Do not apply a tourniquet, or try to cut or suck the bite. Get medical help as soon as possible so you can get treated with an antivenene if necessary.

TAPE WORMS

These parasites are relatively common in Ethiopia and the Horn. Eating Ethiopian traditional food like *kitfo* and *tere sega* (raw meat dishes) in rural areas is usually the cause. Consider having your stool tested when you get home to avoid future health problems.

Djibouti

Djibouti

Best Places to Eat

➜ Time Out (p314)

➜ Mukbassa Central – Chez Youssouf (p314)

➜ Café de la Gare (p316)

➜ Le Pizzaiolo (p315)

➜ Hôtel-Restaurant Le Golfe (p321)

Best Places to Sleep

➜ Le Héron Auberge (p312)

➜ Atlantic Hotel (p313)

➜ Royal Plaza Hotel (p313)

➜ Hôtel Village Vacances Les Sables Blancs (p321)

➜ Campement Touristique de la Forêt du Day (p321)

Why Go?

This tiny speck of a country packs a big punch. What it lacks in size, it more than makes up for in beauty. Few countries in the world, with the possible exception of Iceland, offer such weird landscapes – think salt lakes, extinct volcanoes, sunken plains, limestone chimneys belching out puffs of steam, basaltic plateaus and majestic canyons. Outdoorsy types will enjoy a good mix of land and water activities, including hiking, diving and whale-shark spotting in the Gulf of Tadjoura.

Barring Djibouti City, the country is refreshingly devoid of large-scale development. It's all about ecotravel, with some sustainable stays in the hinterland that provide a fascinating glimpse into the life of nomadic tribes.

Travelling independently around Djibouti may not come cheap, but despite the high cost of living, you'll surely leave this little corner of Africa with new experiences and wonderful memories.

When to Go
Djibouti City

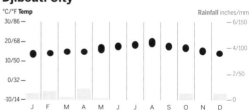

May–Sep Some like it hot...some like it *hot*.

Oct & Feb–Apr Shoulder seasons are not a bad time to visit. Calm waters for diving.

Nov–Jan Coolest months; perfect for outdoor activities. Whale sharks make their annual visit.

The international boundaries on this map serve as indications only. The Ethiopia–Eritrea border awaits formal UN demarcation.

The self-proclaimed Republic of Somaliland is currently an internationally unrecognised but de facto sovereign state.

Red Sea — YEMEN

Rahaita · Doumeïra
ERITREA · Moulhoulé · Périm Island (Yemen)
Ras Siyan · Les Sept Frères

Mt Moussa Ali (2063m)
0 — 40 km
0 — 20 miles

ETHIOPIA
Addis Ababa (500km)
Godoria

Abourma Rock Site · Obock · Ras Bir
Les Allols · Giba Gebiley ⑧ · Gulf of Aden
Goda Mountains ⑦ · Randa · Ardo · Tadjoura · Plage des Sables Blancs ⑤
Bankoualé · Dittilou · Moucha Island ⑥
Day · Forêt du Day · Maskali Island ⑥
Galafi · Lac Assal ② · Gulf of Tadjoura · Doralé · Djibouti City ①
Whale Shark Spotting ④ · Decan · Loyaada
Yoboki · Gaggadé Plain · Bay of Ghoubbet
Hanlé Plain · Petit Barra Depression · Hol Hol · Zeila
Grand Barra Depression
Lac Abbé ③ · Ali Sabieh
As Eyla · Dikhil · Gelile · Assamo
SOMALILAND
Dire Dawa (180km) · Borama (130km)

DJIBOUTI

Djibouti Highlights

① **Djibouti City** (p308) Catching local vibes while wandering through the animated streets of the capital and enjoying its culinary delights.

② **Lac Assal** (p318) Descending to the lowest point on the African continent.

③ **Lac Abbé** (p318) Wandering flabbergasted in a Martian landscape,

with hundreds of spikelike limestone chimneys.

④ **Whale-shark spotting** (p309) Sighting and swimming with whale sharks from November to January in the Gulf of Tadjoura.

⑤ **Plage des Sables Blancs** (p321) Unwinding on Djibouti's best beach.

⑥ **Diving** (p309) Exploring some superb

shipwrecks in the Gulf of Tadjoura.

⑦ **Goda Mountains** (p319) Taking a guided walk amid spectacular mountain scenery and spending a night in a traditional *campement touristique* (tourist camp).

⑧ **Abourma Rock Art Site** (p322) Looking for some well-preserved petroglyphs.

DJIBOUTI CITY

POP 610,000

Djibouti's capital is evolving at a fast pace, and there's a palpable sense of change in the air. Today's city is vastly different from the battered French outpost to which it was reduced in the 1980s and 1990s. Thanks to its geostrategic importance and its busy port, Djibouti City has been transformed from a sleepy capital to a thriving city. Yet under its veneer of urban bustle, the city remains a down-to-earth place, with jarring cultural and social combinations. Traditionally robed Afar tribesmen, stalwart GIs, sensuous Somali ladies and frazzled businessmen with the latest mobile phones stuck to their ear all jostle side by side.

Djibouti City boasts good infrastructure, including hotels, bars, clubs and restaurants – it's *the* place in the Horn of Africa to treat yourself to a fine meal. It's also the obvious place to organise forays into the fantastic hinterland or boat excursions.

◉ Sights

The centre can be divided into two quarters: the European Quarter, laid out on a grid system to the north, and the African Quarter, which spills out to the south.

The pace of life is confusing for newcomers. It's buzzing in the morning and evening, while in the afternoon the centre looks like a ghost town, with most shops and offices closed.

African Quarter   AREA
The vast **Place Mahmoud Harbi** (Place Rimbaud), which is dominated by the minaret of the great **Hamoudi Mosque** (Pl Mahmoud Harbi), Djibouti City's most iconic building, is considered the real soul of the city. Eastward, the chaotic **Quartier 1** is a crisscross of alleyways where stalls and shops are lined cheek by jowl. Spreading along Blvd de Bender are the stalls of **Les Caisses Market** (Blvd de Bender; ⊘ 8am-10pm Sat-Thu). Crammed with every type of souvenir from woodcarvings to clothing, it's a colourful place for soaking up the atmosphere.

European Quarter   AREA
The focal point of the European Quarter is **Place du 27 Juin 1977** (Place Ménélik). With its whitewashed houses and Moorish arcades, this vast square is a strange mix of Arab and European influences. It's lined with cafés, bars, restaurants and shops.

The European Quarter is connected to the Plateau du Serpent area to the north by the Blvd de la République, along which many of the principal administrative buildings can be found.

Plateau du Serpent &
Îlot du Héron   AREA
These adjoining neighbourhoods north of the centre are residential areas where you'll find many of the foreign embassies and residences, as well as lavish villas and Djibouti's swankiest hotels.

L'Escale   HARBOUR
In the early evening, the walk along the causeway northwest of the centre makes a very pleasant stroll. The Moorish-inspired **presidential palace** (not open to the public) marks one end, the harbour of L'Escale, the other. The little marina is home to a variety of boats, from the traditional and picturesque Arab dhows to the simple local fishing skiffs and ferries to Tadjoura and Obock.

Further north, running almost parallel to L'Escale, is the city's port proper, access to which is restricted. From the marina you can see the imposing cranes and cargo boats.

Cathedral   CHURCH
(Blvd de la République) The cathedral has been restored and is one of the most eye-catching buildings along Blvd de la République.

Église Éthiopienne Orthodoxe
Tewahido St Gabriel du Soleil   CHURCH
(Orthodox Church; off Rue Bourhan Bey) In a street running parallel to Blvd de la République, this Orthodox church, which is popular with the Ethiopian community, is well worth a peek.

BEACHES

For a capital that's surrounded by water, Djibouti City is not well endowed with beaches. The only decent stretch of sand is at the **Djibouti Palace Kempinski** (p313), but there's an entrance fee of DFr4000, and the swimming is not *that* tempting, with shallow waters and a profusion of algae. South of the Djibouti Palace Kempinski, the **Plage du Héron** is much wider but is average. There's also a postage stamp–sized beach at the **Sheraton Djibouti Hotel** (p313). For a dip, your best bet is to use the pools at both hotels.

Activities

Diving, whale-shark spotting and hiking can all be organised from Djibouti City.

Diving

Although it's less charismatic than Egypt, Djibouti has its fair share of underwater delights. You'll be positively surprised: there's a wide choice of shallow dives for novices and deeper dives for more experienced divers in the Gulf of Tadjoura. Wreck fans will be spoilt here, too, with a handful of atmospheric shipwrecks.

Although Djibouti is diveable year-round, the best season for diving is from November to March. During July and August, the seas may be too rough for diving.

Visibility is not the strong point of diving in Djibouti – it rarely exceeds 10m to 15m (and can drop to 5m in some places at certain periods of the year). Current conditions vary, but are generally imperceptible to mild. During the coolest months (December through March), water temperatures are between 25°C and 27°C. Summer water temperatures range from 27°C to 29°C.

Most diving takes place off the islands of Maskali and Moucha in the Gulf of Tadjoura where you'll find a variety of dive sites for all levels. Wreck enthusiasts will make a beeline for monster-sized **Le Faon**, a 120m-long cargo ship that lies in 27m of water on a sandy floor. Other shipwrecks worthy of exploration include **L'Arthur Rimbaud**, a tugboat that was scuttled in 2005, and the nearby **Nagfa**, a small Ethiopian boat that lies in about 32m of water. If you need a break from wreck dives, some excellent reef dives beckon, including **Tombant Point**, where you'll see a smorgasbord of reef fish; and the **Canyon**, a relaxing site suitable for novices.

There's also an array of spectacular sites scattered along the southern shoreline of the Gulf of Tadjoura and the Bay of Ghoubbet, furthest west.Most sites around the Gulf of Tadjoura can be accessed with organised boat trips from the capital, particularly at the weekend (Friday).

If you're interested in a live-aboard tour (outside the hot season, from around October to April only), there's a choice of at least two large motorised sailing boats offering different facilities and prices. Reservations should be made several months in advance, particularly for tours during holiday periods. Occasionally it's possible to fill spaces on a tour at short notice.

Snorkelling is also superlative. The local dive shop runs snorkelling trips in parallel with its dive excursions.

Dolphin   DIVING, WHALE-SHARK WATCHING
(☑21347807, 77103395; www.dolphinservices.com; Haramous; ⊙7am-5pm) This highly recommended operator and dive centre can organise all kinds of tours throughout the country, on land and at sea, including diving and snorkelling trips, whale-shark spotting (between November and January), excursions to Lac Abbé and Lac Assal, as well as live-aboard dive boats to the Gulf of Tadjoura and Les Sept Frères archipelago. It's staffed with qualified instructors who speak English.

Dolphin's live-aboard dive trips come highly recommended. Trip lengths vary from two to eight days and usually include Les Sept Frères archipelago.

Whale-Shark Spotting

Whale sharks (*Rhincodon typus*) migrate annually from their usual feeding grounds to the warm waters of the Gulf of Tadjoura to mate and give birth. The Bay of Ghoubbet, at the western end of the Gulf of Tadjoura, is one of the most dependable locations in the world to swim alongside a massive whale shark, the world's largest fish. The peak season runs from November to January. There are usually between two and 10 individuals close to the shore, and it's very easy to snorkel with these graceful creatures.

Djibouti City

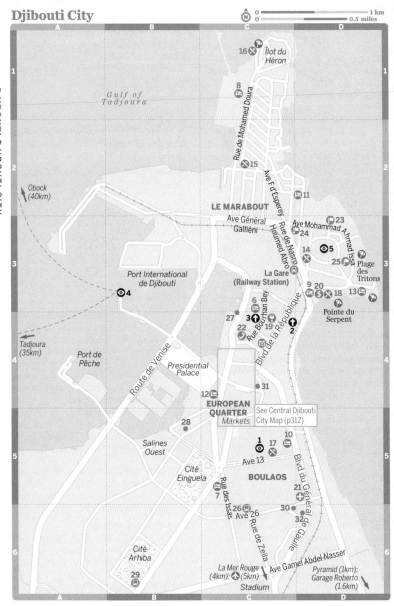

0 — 1 km
0 — 0.5 miles

Îlot du Héron

Gulf of Tadjoura

Obock (40km)

LE MARABOUT

Ave Général Galliéni

Port International de Djibouti

Tadjoura (35km)

Port de Pêche

Route de Venise

Presidential Palace

EUROPEAN QUARTER

Markets

Salines Ouest

Cité Einguela

BOULAOS

Ave 13

Cité Arhiba

La Mer Rouge (4km);
Stadium

Ave Gamel Abdel Nasser

Pyramid (1km);
Garage Roberto (1.6km)

See Central Djibouti City Map (p312)

La Gare (Railway Station)

Plage des Tritons

Pointe du Serpent

Ave Mohammad A.hmad Issa

Rue de Nasro
Houmed Abro

Blvd de la République

Rue Bourhan Bey

Blvd du Général de Gaulle

Rue des Issas

Ave 26

Rue de Zeila

DJIBOUTI DJIBOUTI CITY

This activity has exploded in recent years and plenty of unprofessional operators arrange trips. It's better to stick to established outfits that are ecologically sensitive and follow protocols. Give the sharks a berth of at least 4m; touching is an absolute no-no.

Siyyan Travel & Leisure   DIVING, WHALE-SHARK WATCHING
(☏ 77103674; www.dive-lucy.com) This reliable operator runs excellent live-aboard dive trips around the Gulf of Tadjoura and Les Sept Frères archipelago. The 33m M/Y *Lucy*

Djibouti City

DJIBOUTI DJIBOUTI CITY

is a highly comfortable yacht with private facilities. The usual trip length is six nights. In season, it also organises whale-shark spotting trips. See the website for schedules and contact the operator for a quote.

Youssouf Travel   WHALE-SHARK WATCHING
(☏ 77828166; ⊙ by reservation) Between November and January, Youssouf runs whale-shark spotting trips around the Gulf of Tadjoura. It costs DFr50,000 for the full boat (18 people). If you're travelling solo, contact Youssouf in advance and he'll help you find a group you can join.

⌒ Tours

★ Agence Safar   TOURS
(☏ 77814115; safar.djibouti@gmail.com) Friendly and competent, this operator is easily the most professional tour company in the country and is the one that virtually every overseas tour company offering trips to Sudan uses for on-ground organisation.

It can arrange all kinds of customised tours throughout the country, including multiday guided treks in the Goda Mountains and the Allols as well as excursions to Lac Abbé and Lac Assal. It can also make bookings in the *campements touristiques*

(tourist camps) and supply cars and drivers. The owner, Houmed Ali, knows everything about the Afar culture.

Agence Le Goubet   TOURS
(☏ 21354520; valerie@riesgroup.dj; Rue Clochette; ⊙ 7.30am-12.30pm & 4-6pm Sat-Thu) Can make bookings to Plage des Sables Blancs and in the *campements touristiques*. Also sells flight tickets. Ask for Valerie, who can get by in English.

⊟ Sleeping

The choice of budget accommodation is limited and most hotels tend to be dull multi-storey blocks.

Dar Es Salam   HOTEL $
(☏ 21353334; off Rue des Issas; s DFr6000, d DFr7000-8400; ❀ ⌂) Right in the African Quarter, the Dar Es Salam is a dependable budget choice if you're strapped for cash. Rooms are presentable but vary in size, light and noisiness so ask to see a couple before you settle on one. Facilities include a small restaurant and an internet café. Overall, not a bad deal provided you keep your expectations in check.

Hôtel Horseed
HOTEL $

(📞77017804, 21352316; horseedhotel@gmail.com; Blvd du Général de Gaulle; dm DFr2000, d DFr7500-9000, with shared bathroom DFr6500-8000, s with shared bathroom DFr5000-6500; ❄️🛜) The Horseed is a reliable choice for unfussy budgeteers, with bare but serviceable rooms and a couple of dorms with mattresses (and air-con) at the back. It all feels very compact, but it's well managed and the shared bathrooms are well scrubbed. The owner, Kadar Ismael, lived in Canada for 10 years and speaks excellent English; he's a mine of local information.

Precious perks include an onsite restaurant serving Djiboutian, Yemeni and Ethiopian dishes as well as a cosy lounge where you can linger over a *sheesha* (water pipe).

Auberge Sable Blanc
HOTEL $

(📞21351163; off Rue Bourhan Bey; d DFr7700; ❄️🛜) Tucked away on a quiet street running parallel to Blvd de la République, this little modern construction is a discreet place with eight clean, if rather unloved, rooms and salubrious bathrooms. Note that the air-con is on from 7pm to noon only and there's a mosque nearby – earplug alert!

★ Le Héron Auberge
HOTEL $$

(📞21324343; www.aubergeleheron.net; Rue de l'Imam Hassan Abdallah Mohamed; s/d incl breakfast DFr13,000/15,800; ❄️🛜) An attractive, secure compound in a residential area, Le Héron is one of Djibouti City's best value hotels, with 29 rooms that are well appointed and clean as a whistle. The slightly off-the-beaten-path location on a peaceful street means you can actually get a good night's sleep here. Credit cards (Visa) are accepted but there's a 3% commission. Book ahead.

Nice extra: a shuttle service is available to drive you to the centre (by reservation). Avoid rooms which have only interior windows.

Résidence de l'Europe
HOTEL $$

(📞21355060; Pl du 27 Juin 1977; s/d incl breakfast DFr18,500/20,500; ❄️🛜) Right on the main square, this venture gets by on its tip-top location, a waddle away from the restaurants, bars and clubs. There's no great luxury involved and some of the furnishings have seen better days, but the 24 rooms are spacious and kept in reasonable nick. Credit cards (Visa only) are accepted but there's a commission.

Central Djibouti City

Hotel Alia
HOTEL $$

(📞21358222; Rue Mohamed Dileita Chehem; s/d incl breakfast DFr17,000/19,000; ❄️🛜) The Alia is a solid middle-of-the-road option with its efficient yet down-to-earth staff and good facilities. Rooms are practical with no flouncy embellishments – just good lighting, strong air-con, back-friendly mattresses and salubrious bathrooms. Some rooms upstairs come with partial sea views. It's within walking distance of Place du 27 Juin 1977, and there's an excellent Yemeni restaurant next door.

Menelik Hotel
HOTEL $$

(📞21351177; Pl du 27 Juin 1977; s incl breakfast DFr16,000-18,000; d incl breakfast DFr20,500; ❄️🛜) It's hard to top the Menelik's location, smack-dab in the centre. The rooms, some with good views of the main square, have started to show their age but provide good levels of comfort and hygiene, and there's an onsite restaurant. Cash only.

Central Djibouti City

Sights
1 European Quarter A3
2 Hamoudi Mosque A4
3 Les Caisses Market B4

Activities, Courses & Tours
4 Agence Le Goubet A1

Sleeping
5 Atlantic Hotel B2
6 Menelik Hotel B3
7 Résidence de l'Europe B3

Eating
8 Bunna House A3
9 Casino B2
10 Couleur Café A3
11 La Chaumière B2
12 La Terrasse A4
13 Le Pizzaiolo B2
14 L'Etoile de Kokeb A2
15 Mukbassa Central – Chez Youssouf B4
16 Nil Bleu A4
17 Restaurant L'Historil A2
18 Restaurant Vietnam A4
19 Time Out A3

Drinking & Nightlife
Bar Menelik – VIP (see 6)
20 Club Hermes A3
21 Jus de Fruits Chez Mahad B4
22 Le Palmier en Zinc A3
23 Le Scotch B2
L'Historil (see 17)

Information
24 Amal Express B3
25 ATTA/Globe Travel A2
26 Bank of Africa B2
27 BCIMR B2
28 CAC International Bank B2
29 Canadian Consulate B2
Dilip Corporation (see 31)
30 East Africa Bank A3
31 Mehta B3
32 Pôle Médical A2

Transport
33 City Minibuses Central Hub A4
34 Daallo B4
35 Ethiopian Airlines A2
FlyDubai (see 25)
36 Jubba Airways A3

★ **Atlantic Hotel** HOTEL $$$
(☎21331100; www.atlantichoteldjibouti.com; Rue de Rome; s/d incl breakfast DFr26,000/30,000; P ❄ 📶) Opened in 2016, the professionally run Atlantic is a great place to drop anchor in the centre. Expect efficient service, spacious rooms with balcony, excellent bedding, sparkling bathrooms and a good Italian restaurant beside the reception. Its central location is ideal if you want to immerse yourself in Djibouti City. Rooms 401, 403, 405, 407, 409 and 411 are blessed with sea views.

Credit cards (Visa only) are accepted but there's a 3% commission.

★ **Royal Plaza Hotel** HOTEL $$$
(☎21358001; Blvd Bonhoure; s/d incl breakfast DFr21,000/26,500; P ❄ 📶) This discreet number near the presidential palace is a solid choice, with enticing rooms with all mod-cons and squeaky-clean bathrooms. There are only 12 rooms, which ensures intimacy. Oh, and you can eat well here at the cafeteria.

Djibouti Palace Kempinski RESORT $$$
(☎21325555; www.kempinski.com/djibouti; Îlot du Héron; d incl breakfast from DFr61,000; P ❄ @ 📶 🏊) Well-heeled Arabian and Chinese businessmen, Western military officers and soldiers, tourists and African bigwigs – they all end up here. You know exactly what you'll be getting at the sprawling Kempinski: impersonal yet shiny-clean rooms and a host of top-notch facilities, including three restaurants, two swimming pools, a business centre, a lovely cafe, an ATM, a gift shop, a spa and a gym.

Sheraton Djibouti Hotel RESORT $$$
(☎21328000; www.sheraton.com/djibouti; Plateau du Serpent; s incl breakfast DFr46,000-61,000, d incl breakfast DFr53,000-70,000; P ❄ @ 📶 🏊) Sure, this muscular hotel looks like a common apartment block, the communal parts show signs of wear and tear and service is lackadaisical, but it scores high on its prolific facilities, including two restaurants, a bar, a pool, a gift shop, a fitness centre, a casino, an ATM and a business centre. Be sure to book a room with a sea view.

Eating

For sheer choice and quality of food, Djibouti City ranks among the best places in Africa This is your chance to relish French specialities, scoff absolutely fresh local seafood, savour tasty meat dishes, devour delicious pizzas and treat yourself to exquisite fruit juices or pastries. No alcohol is served in cheaper places.

Bunna House
CAFETERIA $

(Rue d'Ethiopie; mains DFr400-800; ⊘7am-10.30pm Sat-Thu, 8am-2pm & 4-9pm Fri) Located right in the centre, this trendy cafeteria-cum-fast-food outlet is a handy spot for a cheap, uncomplicated, walk-in bite. Tuck into well-made sandwiches, paninis or burgers. The concise menu also includes pastries and pancakes.

Nil Bleu
FAST FOOD $

(Rue d'Ethiopie; mains DFr500-1200; ⊘11am-2pm & 6-10pm Sat-Thu) A great place to quieten a growling stomach without breaking the bank, this busy Djiboutian serves simple fish dishes, salads, rice and spags. It serves great *shwarmas* (kebablike dishes) in the evening, too.

Casino
SUPERMARKET $

(Rue Clochette; ⊘7.30am-1pm & 4-8pm Sat-Thu) This well-stocked supermarket has a good selection of wines and beers.

★Time Out
ITALIAN $$

(✆77889926; Pl du 27 Juin 1977; mains DFr1600-3000; ⊘8am-11.30pm Sat-Thu, 4-11.30pm Fri) You wouldn't know it from the street, but Time Out is one of the most enticing places in town for tasty Italian and Ethiopian food (the owner is Ethiopian-Italian). Savour palate-pleasing pizzas, pastas, steaks or *shiro* (beans served with *injera*) – all fresh and homemade. Something sweet to finish? Try

---

DAILY COSTS

Budget: Less than €80

➡ Budget hotel room: €40–60

➡ Sandwich: €5

➡ Bus ticket: €5

Midrange: €80–300

➡ Double room in a midrange hotel: €60–100

➡ Lunch in a midrange restaurant: €20

➡ Whale-shark-spotting excursion: €60

Top end: More than €300

➡ Luxury hotel room: €150-300

➡ Dinner in top-end restaurant: €40

➡ Car hire per day: from €100

---

the luscious tiramisu or chocolate mousse. The upstairs lounge feels super cosy.

Time Out is also one of the few spots in Djibouti City where you can get served an off-hour meal at say, 4pm.

★Mukbassa Central – Chez Youssouf
YEMENI $$

(✆21351899; off Ave 1; fish menu DFr3000; ⊘11am-2pm Sat-Thu, 6-10pm daily) In business for ages, this Djibouti City icon is famous for one thing and one thing only: *poisson yemenite* (oven-baked fish). It's served with a chapati-like bread and a devilish *mokbasa* (purée of honey and either dates or banana). The colourful, wooden building feels a bit ramshackle, but that's part of the experience. Dessert (pancakes) is extra (DFr400). No alcohol is served.

★La Terrasse
ETHIOPIAN $$

(✆21350227; Rue d'Ethiopie; mains DFr900-1600; ⊘6.30-10.30pm Sat-Thu) Bargain! This place has plenty of character and serves up good Ethiopian food as well as pasta and sandwiches at puny prices. It occupies a rooftop, with a moodily lit dining area and an open kitchen – not to mention the heady scents of incense. If only it was licensed!

For lunch, you can head to the less atmospheric Restaurant La Fontaine, on the 1st floor (same management).

L'Etoile de Kokeb
ETHIOPIAN $$

(✆21350410; Rue de Marseille; mains DFr1500-4200; ⊘noon-2pm & 6-10pm) This Ethiopian restaurant is a good initiation to the cuisine of neighbouring Ethiopia, with all the classics, including vegetarian dishes. European dishes, including beef fillet, also feature prominently. Exotic decor and a dance show add to the pleasure of dining here.

Couleur Café
CAFETERIA $$

(✆21342426; off Pl du 27 Juin 1977; mains DFr600-2500; ⊘7am-11pm Sat-Thu, 5-11pm Fri) Unusually for Djibouti City, this cafeteria comes with a touch of character, created by its snug interior. It's a good place for a light meal any time of the day, with an eclectic menu featuring burgers, salads, chicken dishes and pancakes.

Restaurant Vietnam
VIETNAMESE $$

(✆21351708; Rue Soleillet; mains DFr1100-2000; ⊘5.30-10pm Mon, 11.30am-2pm & 5-10.30pm Tue-Sun) This well-established restaurant serves an exquisite selection of authentic Vietnamese and Chinese dishes – those in the know

WORTH A TRIP

DECAN

Weary of the hustle and bustle of Djibouti City? Have a soft spot for endangered species? The well-organised wildlife refuge **Decan** (☑77609746, 21344977; www.decandjibouti.org; Douda; DFr1500-2000; ☺3.30-7.30pm Mon & Thu-Sat Oct-May, 4.30-7.30pm Mon & Thu-Sat Jun-Sep) is about 10km south of Djibouti City (in Douda, on the road to Somaliland), an easy two- to three-hour excursion from the capital. It's not a zoo, but a small nature reserve, with its own ecosystem. You'll see eight endlessly appealing cheetahs, four lions, as well as ostriches, turtles, Somali donkeys, caracals, squirrels, antelope, kudus, zebras and porcupines.

Run by a French vet, Decan was set up as a rehabilitation centre for various species that have been orphaned or illegally caged for trafficking purposes. There are plans to extend it from 12 hectares to 240 hectares, down to the coastline, which would encompass a mangrove area. Birders, rejoice: a dedicated birdwatching area was under construction at the time of writing – expect to see flamingos, ibises, herons and spoonbills. Decan also runs education programs for customs officers, the police and school kids. Watching the big cats being fed (usually around 5pm) is just one of the many exhilarating moments at Decan. Volunteers are welcome. The only practical option for getting here from Djibouti City is by taxi (DFr3000, including waiting time).

claim that the pork chop suey is among the very best this side of the Rift Valley.

Restaurant National – Chez Hamdani
YEMENI **$$**
(☑21351588; Ave 13; menu DFr2000-3000; ☺11am-2.30pm & 6-9.30pm Sat-Thu) This perennial favourite specialises in *poisson yemenite* (oven-baked fish). There are no menus; just choose your glistening beastie (usually sea bream, grouper or barracuda) in the fridge and it's barbecued *á la Yemeni*: the whole thing is sliced in half, smacked against the walls of a fire pit and baked to a black crisp.

It's sprinkled with hot pepper and served with a chapati (flatbread) and a belt-bustingly good *mokbasa* (purée of honey and either dates or banana). Enjoy it in the colourful dining room. No alcohol is served. It's south of the centre – take a taxi.

La Chaumière
FRENCH, CHINESE **$$**
(☑21357002; Pl du 27 Juin 1977; mains DFr1300-3200; ☺8am-11.30pm) This popular joint overlooking the main square serves well-prepared French favourites as well as a good selection of sandwiches and Chinese dishes. The decor is easy on the eye, with a thoughtful blend of rustic and modern touches. You can also dine alfresco on the agreeable terrace. Oh, and it's open for lunch on Friday (an exception in Djibouti City).

Restaurant L'Historil
FRENCH **$$**
(☑21341364; Pl du 27 Juin 1977; mains DFr2200-3500; ☺noon-2.30pm & 7-10.30pm Sat-Thu) Subdued lighting, cosy surrounds, a soothing blue colour scheme and an ample selection of taste-bud-titillating specialities have made this restaurant one of the most popular in town for a fancy meal. Among the many winners are the rib of beef, steak tartare, fillet of grouper and grilled kingfish. Tempting desserts, too.

Melting Pot
JAPANESE **$$**
(☑21350399; www.meltingpotdj.com; Îlot du Héron; mains DFr1900-3500; ☺11am-2.30pm & 6-10.30pm; ☜) If you have a sashimi or yakitori craving that must be met while in Djibouti, head to cute and cosy Melting Pot for authentic Japanese food. The menu also features French classics, burgers and camel steak (yes!). Another draw is the setting, with a wonderfully overgrown garden. It's tucked away on a little side street in Îlot du Héron.

Le Pizzaiolo
ITALIAN **$$**
(☑21354439; Rue d'Ethiopie; mains DFr1300-3000; ☺11am-2.30pm & 5-11pm) Feast on palate-blowing Italian specialities in this zingy trattorialike venue. The menu roves from faultlessly cooked pizzas to pasta and from salads to meat dishes. A homemade pie or a chocolate mousse will finish you off sweetly. It also does takeaway, and there's a bar section. And yes, it's open on Friday – a rarity in Djibouti City.

Restaurant Saba
SEAFOOD $$

(☑21354244; Rue Mohamed Dileita Chehem; mains DFr1200-2500; ⊙7.30am-2.30pm & 6-10.30pm Sat-Thu, 6-10.30pm Fri) This Yemeni-run institution serves well-prepared fish and meat dishes without fuss. Some reliable choices are skewered fish, fillet of barracuda, camel steak and *poisson yemenite*. There are some good pastas and salads (from DFr800), which will gladden vegetarian hearts, as well as superb fruit juices (from DFr250). Also does takeaway.

★ Café de la Gare
FRENCH $$$

(☑21351530; Rue de Nasro Houmed Abro; mains DFr3200-6000; ⊙noon-2.30pm & 6.30-10pm Sat-Thu) Dining at this upscale gourmet restaurant is a treat. The elegant dining room is decorated with earthy tones and classy furniture, and Café de la Gare is justly revered for its refined French-inspired cuisine with a bow to local ingredients. Highlights include *magret aux girolles* (duck with mushrooms), beefsteak and king prawns. Another draw is the cosy cocktail bar upstairs.

La Mer Rouge
SEAFOOD $$$

(☑21340005; www.lamerrougedj.com; Rte Nelson Mandela, Ambouli; mains DFr2500-5800; ⊙11am-2.30pm & 6-10pm; ☎) Seafood, seafood and seafood – that's all that matters at La Mer Rouge, Djibouti City's premier address for crustaceans and fish. The menu revolves around whatever happens to flop onto the quayside. If they're on offer, plump for the *gambas feta* (king prawns with feta cheese) or splash out on a supersized seafood platter. It's near the airport.

CHAT, ANYONE?

Around 1pm, don't miss the arrival of *chat* – a fascinating slice of local life. Suddenly a cacophony of car horns and shouting breaks out, heralding the marvellous news: *chat*, the nation's daily 'hit', has arrived fresh from Ethiopia. Afterwards a heavy torpor descends on the town and all activity ceases for the afternoon.

During your stay in Djibouti, you might be invited to 'graze'. Don't expect to be stoned, however, and take antidiarrheal tablets, just in case.

Le Mosaic
INTERNATIONAL $$$

(☑21328620; Sheraton Djibouti Hotel, Plateau du Serpent; mains DFr2200-4000, buffet DFr6500-8500; ⊙noon-2.30pm & 6-10.30pm; ☎) Inside the Sheraton Djibouti Hotel, you'll find a casually elegant restaurant that is noted for its lavish dinner buffets – don't miss the seafood buffet on Thursday and the oriental buffet on Tuesday. Lunch is a more relaxed affair, with a menu featuring salads, sandwiches and fish dishes. Prices include access to the swimming pool.

Tentazioni
ITALIAN $$$

(☑21325555; Djibouti Palace Kempinski, Îlot du Héron; mains DFr2500-5000; ⊙12.30-11pm) If pastas, pizzas or creamy risotto make your stomach quiver with excitement, slide into this great Italian restaurant inside the Djibouti Palace Kempinski. It's also known for its great 'business lunch' buffet (DFr6800), which features a tempting selection of antipasti and desserts.

Restaurant Lac Assal
BUFFET $$$

(Djibouti Palace Kempinski, Îlot du Héron; buffet DFr6900-9900; ⊙12.30-3pm & 7-10.30pm) Part of Djibouti Palace Kempinski hotel, this restaurant is renowned for its themed buffet meals. The Friday brunch is popular.

Le Bankoualé
INTERNATIONAL $$$

(Djibouti Palace Kempinski, Îlot du Héron; mains DFr2500-4000; ⊙6-10pm) Part of the Kempinski complex, Le Bankoualé overlooks the beach and is great for a candlelit dinner.

♟ Drinking & Nightlife

There's no shortage of watering holes in Djibouti City, especially around Pl du 27 Juin 1977. Plenty of teahouses are also scattered around the centre.

Most clubs are on or around Rue d'Ethiopie, in the European Quarter. They are at their liveliest on Thursday and Friday nights. Entrance is free, but a beer costs upwards of DFr1000.

★ Jus de Fruits Chez Mahad
JUICE BAR

(☑77866305; Rue Ali Coubèche; juices DFr400-800; ⊙7am-noon & 4-8pm Sat-Thu, 4-8pm Fri) Ah, Mahad and its oh-so-smooth, oh-so-thick fruity concoctions (over 45 varieties)! Grab a seat outside and watch the world go by. Also serves tea, coffee and pastries.

Le Palmier en Zinc PUB
(Pl du 27 Juin 1977; ⊘8am-10pm Sat-Thu, 7-10pm Fri) This smart-looking pub has a respectably long list of beers and cocktails, including excellent mojitos (DFr1500), served with popcorn and veggie dips. It also offers karaoke on selected evenings.

Le Scotch CLUB
(Rue Clochette; ⊘8pm-2am) One of Djibouti City's hot spots. Cosy seats, red lights and the odd full-length mirror surround the dance floor.

Association de la Communauté Ethiopienne de Djibouti BAR
(Club Éthiopien; off Rue Bourhan Bey; ⊘5-10pm) This down-to-earth bar, with its large outdoor courtyard, is a pleasant place to enjoy a very cheap beer – a bottle of St George costs only DFr350. Also known as 'Club Éthiopien', this simple establishment also serves good Ethiopian fare at economical prices.

L'Historil BAR
(Pl du 27 Juin 1977; ⊘7am-midnight) Popularly considered to be Djibouti City's most esteemed bar, L'Historil has an appealing terrace that offers excellent people-watching opportunities. A beer costs DFr1200.

Bar Menelik – VIP CLUB
(Pl du 27 Juin 1977; ⊘8pm-2am) In the basement of Menelik Hotel, this is Djibouti City's 'most happening' (meaning 'least sleazy') place.

Club Hermes CLUB
(Rue de Genève; ⊘8pm-2am) If there's a constant here, it's the promise that the music, whatever the style, will get you groovin'.

❶ Information

INTERNET ACCESS
Most lodging options offer free wi-fi access.

MEDICAL SERVICES
You'll find several well-stocked pharmacies in the centre.

CHA Bouffard (☑21351351; Blvd du Général de Gaulle) The best equipped hospital, south of the city.

Pôle Médical (☑21352724; off Pl du 27 Juin 1977; ⊘8am-noon & 4-7pm Sat-Thu) A small clinic. It's off Pl du 27 Juin 1977.

MONEY
There are banks and bureaux de change in the centre, as well as several Visa-friendly ATMs (but only three ATMs accept MasterCard). Both the Djibouti Palace Kempinski and Sheraton Djibouti Hotel have an ATM.

Amal Express (Ave Mohamed Farah Dirir; ⊘7am-noon & 4-9pm Sat-Thu) Bureau de change.

Bank of Africa (Pl Lagarde; ⊘7.30am-noon & 4.15-6pm Sun & Wed, 7.30am-noon Mon, Tue & Fri) Changes cash and has two ATMs.

BCIMR (Pl Lagarde; ⊘7.30-11.45am Sun-Thu) Changes cash and has ATMs. The branch at **Plateau du Serpent** (Rue Mohamed Dileita Chehem) has an ATM (Visa only).

CAC International Bank (Rue de Marseille; ⊘7.30-11.45am & 4-6pm Sun-Thu) Changes cash and has two ATMs (Visa and MasterCard).

Dilip Corporation (Pl du 27 Juin 1977; ⊘8am-noon & 4-7.30pm Sat-Thu) Bureau de change.

East Africa Bank (Pl du 27 Juin 1977; ⊘7.30am-12.30pm & 4.30-6pm Sun-Wed, 7.30am-noon Thu & Sat) Changes cash and has an ATM (Visa and MasterCard).

Mehta (☑21353719; Pl du 27 Juin 1977; ⊘7.30am-noon & 4-7.30pm Sun-Thu) Bureau de change.

POST
Main Post Office (Blvd de la République; ⊘7am-1pm & 4-9pm Sat-Thu) North of the centre.

TELEPHONE
The most convenient places to make international or local calls are the various telephone outlets scattered around the city centre.

Djibouti Telecom (www.adjib.dj; Rue Bourhan Bey; ⊘7.30am-noon & 5-7pm Sat-Thu) Sells prepaid SIM cards (DFr1000).

TOURIST INFORMATION
Tourist Office (☑21352800; www.visitdjibouti.dj; Rue de Foucauld; ⊘7am-1.30pm Sat-Thu, plus 4-6pm Sat, Mon & Wed) Mildly helpful. Sells a map of the city (DFr1000 to DFr1500). For details on tours, you're better off at a travel agency. On the southeastern side of Pl du 27 Juin 1977.

❶ Getting There & Away

AIR
Djibouti-Ambouli airport (p328) is 5km south of town. **ATTA/Globe Travel** (☑21250297; atta@intnet.dj; west of Pl du 27 Juin 1977) and **Agence Le Goubet** (p311) represent most international and regional airlines. There is no domestic service.

WORTH A TRIP

GRAND BARRA & PETIT BARRA

Grand Barra This spectacular plain of dried and cracked white clay, 27km long and 12km wide, was once an ancient lake. You can't miss it if you're heading to Lac Abbé from Djibouti City – the road skirts it all the way.

Petit Barra The road from Djibouti City to Lac Abbé crosses this desert plain, which was once an ancient lake.

BOAT

A **ferry** (L'Escale) plies the Djibouti–Tadjoura and Djibouti–Obock routes two to three times a week (DFr700 one way, about three hours for either journey). It doesn't operate from mid-June to mid-September. Boats leave from L'Escale.

BUS

Minibuses leave from various departure points south of town, including **Cité Arhiba**. They connect Djibouti City to Tadjoura, Galafi (at the Ethiopian border) and Obock. Minibuses to Tadjoura cost DFr1500 (three hours). Minibuses to Obock cost DFr2000 (about 4½ hours). For Galafi (and Yoboki), you'll pay DFr900 (three hours). Most minibuses leave early in the morning and only when they are full.

CAR

For 4WD rental (from DFr25,000 per day, with driver), contact the following outfits.
Garage Roberto (☑ 21352029; robertosanges@yahoo.fr; Route de Boulaos)
Europcar Djibouti (Marill; ☑ 21329425; www.europcar-djibouti.com; Route de l'Aéroport)
Pyramid (☑ 21358203; www.pyramidrental.com; Route de Boulaos)

❶ Getting Around

The central hub for **city minibuses** (Pl Mahmoud Harbi) (all tickets DFr50) is on Pl Mahmoud Harbi. A taxi ride within the centre costs about DFr600 (DFr1200 to or from the airport).

AROUND DJIBOUTI

Lac Assal

Just over 100km west of the capital lies one of the most spectacular natural phenomena in Africa: Lac Assal. Situated 155m below sea level, this crater lake is encircled by dark, dormant volcanoes. The vast depression, which represents the lowest point on the continent, is an impressive sight. The aquamarine water is ringed by a huge salt field, 60m in depth. The banks of salt and gypsum surround the lake for more than 10km, and the blinding white constrasts starkly with the black lava fields around it. The water is totally saturated with salt, so there's not much chance of a swim.

❶ Getting There & Away

Lying 107km west of the capital and connected by a decent sealed road, Lac Assal is within easy reach of Djibouti City. That said, there's no public transport – most visitors come with tours out of the capital.

Lac Abbé

You'll never forget your first glimpse of Lac Abbé. The scenery is sensational: the plain is dotted with hundreds of limestone chimneys, some standing as high as 50m, belching out puffs of steam. Located 140km southwest of Djibouti City, it is often described as 'a slice of moon on the crust of earth'.

Though desolate, it is not uninhabited. Numerous mineral-rich hot springs feed the farms of local nomads who graze their camels and goats here. Flamingos also gather on the banks of the lake at dawn.

The best time to visit the lake is in the early morning, when the chimneys appear to emit smoke in the cool morning air. An even better plan is to arrive in the late afternoon, stay the night, and leave after sunrise the following morning. In the evening, when the sun sets behind the chimneys, the landscape can look almost magical.

☞ Tours

A guide to Lac Abbé is essential. Not just to get here, but also to steer you clear of the quicksand and pits said to riddle certain areas of the banks. Guides can also give you a proper tour of the site, which should include the chimneys, the boiling, sulphurous-smelling springs and the flamingos. Some of the chimneys can be climbed, if you fancy it. There's a great view of the lake and surrounding plain from La Grande Cheminée (The Big Chimney), but you should take care, as the shifting shale can make it a bit treacherous underfoot. Don't forget sunscreen and lots of water.

Houmed Loita TOURS

(📞21357244, 77822291; houmed_asboley@hotmail.fr) Friendly Houmed Loita runs the Campement Touristique d'Asboley and can organise all kinds of cultural trips and excursions in the area.

🛏 Sleeping & Eating

There's only one option for accommodation or eating.

★Campement Touristique d'Asboley HUT $$

(📞77822291; houmed_asboley@hotmail.fr; Lac Abbé; huts with full board & transfers per person DFr21,500; 🅿) This *campement touristique* (traditional Afar huts with shared showers and toilets) is set in the most surreal landscape you've ever imagined. It lies on a plateau that proffers stupendous views of the big chimneys – whatever the time of the day, you're guaranteed to be hypnotised by the scenery. The ablution block is rudimentary but OK. Prices include a guided walk to the chimneys. Meals come in for warm praise – hmmm, stuffed kid.

ℹ Getting There & Away

The only way of getting here is by hiring a 4WD with driver or by taking a tour. If you are (or can find) a party of four, the *campement touristique* can arrange all-inclusive packages for about DFr24,000 per person per day – prices include transfers from Djibouti City, accommodation, meals and guided walks.

Goda Mountains

Northwest of the Gulf of Tadjoura, the Goda Mountains rise to a height of 1750m and are a strange natural oddity. This area shelters one of the rare speckles of green on Djibouti's parched map, like a giant oasis – a real relief after the scorched desert landscapes. A few Afar villages are scattered around and merit at least a couple of days of your time to soak up their charm. It won't be long before you're smitten by the region's mellow tranquillity and laid-back lifestyle. For outdoorsy types, this area offers ample hiking opportunities.

Various Afar entrepreneurs have set up ecofriendly campements touristiques in the villages of Bankoualé, Dittilou and Day. They feature daboyta (traditional huts), with communal showers and toilets.

Bankoualé

If you want to get away from it all, look no further. The green and fertile oasis of Bankoualé boasts one of the most spectacular settings in Djibouti, with staggering mountain scenery, impressive canyons, terraced gardens and a few scenic waterfalls.

◉ Sights & Activities

On the way to Bankoualé – just 2km down the dirt road – you'll pass the little village of **Ardo**, which has a small **craft centre** run by Afar women. It's a great opportunity to see the well-known and highly accomplished Afar basketware. Any purchase you make will directly benefit the community.

A variety of walks will take you up to the waterfalls, streams, fruit trees and little gardens around Bankoualé. Don't miss the walk to the **Grotte de la Chauve-Souris** (Bat's Cave; four hours return). It's also possible to walk to Dittilou (four hours one way) and Forêt du Day (4½ hours one way).

A guide is essential because trails are not marked and it's easy to get lost. You can organise a guide through the Campement Touristique de Bankoualé. Costs vary according to the duration of the walk.

🛏 Sleeping

Campement Touristique de Bankoualé HUT $$

(📞77814115; Bankoualé; full board per person DFr8000; 🅿) This ecofriendly camp (electricity is solar powered) in a scenic location – it's

---

HIKING IN DJIBOUTI

Hiking is popular in the Goda Mountains. From canyons and valleys to waterfalls and peaks, the mountainscape is fantastic and you'll be rewarded with lovely vistas. Most *campements touristiques* can organise guided nature walks, from one-hour jaunts to more challenging day hikes.

Various treks led by Afar nomads can also be arranged along ancient salt routes in western Djibouti. It's the best way to immerse yourself in traditional nomadic culture. Duration varies from two-day hikes near Lac Assal or Les Allols to 10-day expeditions as far as Ethiopia. Contact tour operators in Djibouti City.

WORTH A TRIP

LES ALLOLS

It doesn't get the hype of the iconic Lac Assal and Lac Abbé, but **Les Allols** depression is one the most spectacular natural sites in the Horn. The landscape is an extraordinary geological showcase of faults, folds, ancient lava, salt fields and igneous black rocks. It's possible to drive down to a large inhabited oasis at the entrance to Les Allols but the best way to explore this geological wonder is to hike across the depression. **Agence Safar** (p311) can arrange logistics. Trips vary from two to four days and can be combined with Lac Assal.

perched on a hillside and overlooks a deep valley – is a lovely place to spend a couple of days, particularly if you're keen on hiking. Huts are equipped with traditional Afar beds made of wood, and the views of the valley are sensational.

ℹ Getting There & Away

The road to Bankoualé is a very bumpy track, and there's no public transport to Bankoualé from either Djibouti City or Tadjoura. You'll need to rent a 4WD with driver or take a tour from the capital to get there. Access is from the main Djibouti City–Tadjoura road.

Dittilou

A visit to Dittilou, at the edge of vegetation around the Forêt du Day, should not be missed. Set 700m above sea level on the flank of Mt Goda, it features an enchanted landscape of dripping forest and viewpoints swirling in mist. This explosion of green amid a desert land is extraordinary. You'll find it hard to believe that Dittilou belongs to the same country as the one you left on the burning coastal road just one hour before.

Dittilou is a good base for **hiking**. The owners of Campement Touristique de Dittilou will be happy to suggest guided walks suited to your level of ability. Don't miss the waterfall of Toha (a four-hour loop); another lovely walk goes to a plane wreck (a six-hour loop). You can also walk to Bankoualé (four to five hours one way).

On the way to Dittilou you'll pass the little village of **Dogum**, which has an excellent craft centre. It sells elaborate Afar basketware as well as goat cheese (yes, cheese!).

🛏 Sleeping & Eating

Campement Touristique de Dittilou   HUT $
(☑21354520, 77810488; Dittilou; full board per person DFr8000; ℗) This *campement* has helpful and friendly management offering a series of well-designed *daboytas* (traditional huts) brimful of rustic charm. They are set against a spectacular and peaceful landscape. The laid-back restaurant is chilled and the food is great. The gang of green monkeys that roam around the place are either a nuisance or an attraction, depending on your perspective.

ℹ Getting There & Away

The road to Dittilou is little more than a very bumpy track, and there are no minibuses to Dittilou from either Djibouti City or Tadjoura. You'll need to rent a 4WD with driver or take a tour from the capital to get there. Access is from the main Djibouti City–Tadjoura road.

Forêt du Day

Situated at 1500m above sea level, this tiny pocket of vegetation benefits from its proximity to Mt Goda. As rain clouds and mist from the mountain drift into the forest, considerable condensation forms. The soil, as wet as after a storm, releases humidity, which allows the plants and trees to flourish despite the infrequent rains. From December to March, the temperature at night can drop sometimes to just above freezing.

The forest is home to the country's only endemic bird species, the Djibouti francolin. Common sightings include various species of monkey and deer and several birds of prey, including Bonelli's eagles. Unfortunately, because of overgrazing and drought, this forest is under threat.

Guides from the Campement Touristique de la Forêt du Day can take you on beautiful **walks** in the forest and the surrounding mountains (about two hours return). You can also walk to Bankoualé or Dittilou (four hours one way).

🛏 Sleeping & Eating

This remote corner of Djibouti has only one lodging option.

★ **Campement Touristique**
de la Forêt du Day HUT $

(☑ 77728544, 77829774; Day; full board per person DFr8000) If you like peace, quiet and sigh-inducing views, you'll have few quibbles with this atmospheric *campement* in the village of Day, at an altitude of 1500m, close to the Forêt du Day. The traditional huts are welcoming and the toilet blocks are kept clean. Other draws include the host of walking options available and the healthy food, including delicious *kemir* (pancakes) for breakfast.

❶ Getting There & Away

You'll need to rent a 4WD with driver or take a tour from the capital to get there. Access is from the main Djibouti City–Tadjoura road.

Plage des Sables Blancs

Plage des Sables Blancs, 7km east of Tadjoura, is tranquillity incarnate and a lovely place to sun yourself, with a good string of white sand and excellent facilities. Small wonder that it's hugely popular with weekending expats. Your biggest quandary here: snorkelling, kayaking or a snooze.

▦ Sleeping

★ **Hôtel Village Vacances**
Les Sables Blancs RESORT $$

(☑ 77073377, 77182822; www.sablesblancs.com; Plage des Sables Blancs; beds with full board DFr12,000, d/q incl breakfast DFr 25,000/35,000; P ❋ 🛜) Right on the beach, this is a lovely place to chill out for a couple of days. Accommodation is simple (huts with beds and mattresses only) or you can opt for a spacious room with all mod cons in the small hotel at the western tip of the beach. All rooms face the sea. The on-site restaurant (set menus DFr4000) serves up toothsome local dishes.

Kayaks and snorkelling gear are available for hire. One grumble: although it has only 10 rooms, the hotel – a concrete block – feels a bit incongruous in such a scenic setting. Hasna, the manager, speaks very good English.

Tadjoura

POP 26,000

Nestled in the shadow of the green Goda Mountains with the bright-blue sea lapping at its doorstep, Tadjoura is a picturesque little place. With its palm trees, whitewashed houses and numerous mosques, it has an Arabian feel to it. There's little to do here besides stroll around and soak up the atmosphere, but it's a great place to spend a few hours before heading to Plage des Sables Blancs or Obock.

▦ Sleeping & Eating

There aren't any lodging options in the town itself but you'll find two well-equipped hotels about 1.5km west of the centre.

Apart from a couple of basic cafeterias, there aren't any eateries in the town itself. Your best bet is to to head to one of the two hotels. Both have good restaurants overlooking the Gulf of Tadjoura

Hôtel-Restaurant Le Golfe HOTEL $$

(☑ 77846598, 77839533; http://hotel-restaurant-le-golfe-djibouti-tadjourah.e-monsite.com; d/q incl breakfast DFr11,000/15,000; bungalow P ❋ 🛜) Under French-Ethiopian management, this low-key but well-kept resort with a family atmosphere is situated in a relaxing waterfront setting, about 1.5km from the town centre. The 28 units, 10 of which come with sea views, are not fancy but are functional, and there's an excellent on-site restaurant (mains DFr1500 to Dfr2600) with a terrace facing the Gulf of Tadjoura.

The menu concentrates on well-prepared seafood, French specialities and voluminous sandwiches. There's no beach to speak of but the owners can organise transfers to Plage des Sables Blancs (DFr7000 for four people).

Le Corto Maltese HOTEL $$

(☑ 77859574; d incl breakfast DFr12,000; P ❋ 🛜) Le Corto Maltese is right on the seashore, about 1.5km west of the town centre, but there's no real beach. The adjoining 18 rooms are well organised, with good bedding and large bathrooms, and we hear good things about the on-site restaurant (mains DFr1200 to DFr2600). It feels a tad imper-

ABOURMA ROCK ART SITE

This superb **Abourma Rock Art Site** features well-preserved rock engravings dating back to Neolithic times, which are striking both for their rich complexity and their incredible variety. Many of the engravings depict animals that are no longer found in the area – giraffes, cows, antelopes, kudus, oryxes and ostriches. Human figures are also represented. The rock art works were uncovered by a team of French archaeologists in 2008. Some 30km northeast of Randa, the site is only accessible on foot.

The usual starting point for the hike is the tiny Afar settlement of Giba Gebiley, about 22km north of Randa. You'll need a rented 4WD with driver to get here. From Giba Gebiley, allow eight hours there and back. Following the completion in 2014 of a dirt road from Giba Gebiley, it's now possible to drive nearer to the site (provided the dirt road is well maintained) and reduce the duration of the walk to a much more manageable two hours return. You'll be rewarded with spectacular landscapes consisting of undulating rocky hills, small gorges, barren ridges and vast expanses of chaotic boulders.

A knowledgeable guide (usually somebody from Randa who has worked with the archaeologists) is mandatory and can be arranged through Agence Safar (p311) in Djibouti City for around DFr5000.

There are no facilities at all and no shade, so bring several litres of water, as well as a hat and plenty of sunscreen.

---

sonal, though. Transfers to Plage des Sables Blancs can be arranged.

ℹ Getting There & Away

Regular morning buses ply the route between Cité Arhiba in Djibouti City and Tadjoura (DFr1500, three hours). A passenger ferry runs two to three times weekly between L'Escale in Djibouti City and Tadjoura (DFr700 one way, about three hours).

Obock

POP 45,000

Obock exudes a kind of 'last frontier' feel, light years away from the hullabaloo of Djibouti City. This little town is something of a backwater, and survives primarily from its small fishing industry. For the visitor, Obock is a good place to get away from it all. Its greatest attractions are the golden beaches and coral reefs, which are the best in the country.

◉ Sights

Cimetière Marin CEMETERY
The eerily quiet Cimetière Marin (Marine Cemetery), on the western outskirts of town, contains the graves of French soldiers who died from fever on their way to Indochina between 1885 and 1889.

Ras Bir Lighthouse LIGHTHOUSE
About 6km east of the centre, this well-kept lighthouse is worth a gander. It's completely isolated and there's an eerie atmosphere.

Governor's House HISTORIC BUILDING
Obock is where French colonialism all began. In 1862, the Afar sultans of Obock sold their land to the French, and construction of the town began. But it was soon eclipsed by Djibouti City. All that remains of its past glory as the capital is this stately house (the first official building erected on the site).

⬛ Sleeping & Eating

Apart from a simple *campement touristique* and a low-key resort-like establishment, there's not much in the way of accommodation in Obock.

Both sleeping options provide meals. In the centre of town, you'll find a smattering of very basic cafes serving up cheap fare.

Village Mer Rouge BUNGALOW **$$**
(d incl breakfast DFr10,000-12,000; ☺ Oct-Apr; P ❄) This welcoming establishment about 2km west of the centre features five rustically cosy bungalows on the beach as well as 10 'hill bungalows' with air-con and private facilities, six of which come with breathtaking sea views. Expect some water shortages, though. The open-air restaurant serves up toothsome local dishes with an emphasis on seafood (menus DFr3000).

Campement Oubouky   HUT **$$**
(☑ 77816034; full board per person DFr8000-
10,000; ℗) Facilities are fairly rundown at
this rustic *campement* (huts with shared
showers and toilets) about 5km west of the
centre, but the location is ace – it's right on
a blissfully quiet beach with excellent swim-
ming and snorkelling – and the welcome
is friendly. Lovers of seafood will enjoy the
cooking here. Electricity is available in the
evening. Fishing trips can be organised.

❶ Getting There & Away

A couple of morning minibuses operate between
Cité Arhiba in Djibouti City and Obock (DFr2000,
about 4½ hours). There's a twice-weekly pas-
senger ferry service between L'Escale in Djibouti
City and Obock (DFr700 one way, about three
hours).

UNDERSTAND DJIBOUTI

Djibouti Today

Djibouti's stability and neutrality, combined
with its strategic position, have brought lots
of benefits, especially in terms of foreign
assistance, economic growth and employ-
ment – Djibouti is not dubbed 'the Dubai of
the Horn' for nothing. In an effort to com-
bat piracy off the Somali coast and counter
terrorism in the region, the Americans have
reinforced their military presence here. As
if this wasn't enough, the Japanese set up
a huge military base near the internation-
al airport in 2011. Germany and Spain also
maintain a significant military presence.
The total number of foreign soldiers on the
Djiboutian territory is estimated at 7000,
which contributes directly or indirectly to
the country's income.

Djibouti City's strategic value as a port is
today as important as ever. As a key trade
hub to Asia, Europe and the rest of Africa,
it provides the biggest source of income in
a country devoid of natural resources. The
port handles most of Ethiopia's imports and
exports, which brings lots of fees and transit
taxes. A second port is being built in Tad-
joura and should be ready by 2020, and a
second international road to Ethiopia – via
Randa and the north – is also under con-
struction.

Foreign investors from Asia and the Gulf
are increasingly active in Djibouti, and there
are building projects springing up all over
the capital. There are also plans to upgrade
the road system throughout the country.
Last but not least, the 750km railway line,
which links Addis Ababa and Djibouti City,
was inaugurated in late 2016. Built by two
Chinese companies, it will transport cargo
and passengers between the two cities in
less than 10 hours.

History

The powerful Ethiopian kingdom of Aksum,
which lasted until around AD 700, encom-
passed present-day Djibouti. Then came
Islam and the Arab traders. The opening
of the Suez Canal in 1869 let loose a stam-
pede of Europeans into East Africa, and
the French took control of Djibouti. In 1977,
the country gained its independence. Since
then, it has tried to present a neutral politi-
cal face in the Horn of Africa.

From Aksum to Islam

Around the 1st century AD, Djibouti made
up part of the powerful Ethiopian kingdom
of Aksum, which included modern-day Eri-
trea and even stretched across the Red Sea
to parts of southern Arabia. It was during
the Aksumite era, in the 4th century AD,
that Christianity first appeared in the region.

As the empire of Aksum gradually fell
into decline, a new influence arose that
would forever supersede the Christian reli-
gion in Djibouti: Islam. It was introduced to
the region around AD 825 by Arab traders
from Southern Arabia.

European Ambitions

In the second half of the 19th century, Euro-
pean powers competed to grab new colonies
in Africa. The French, seeking to counter
the British presence in Yemen on the oth-
er side of the Bab al-Mandab Strait, made
agreements with the Afar sultans of Obock
and Tadjoura that gave them the right to
settle. In 1888, construction of Djibouti City
began on the southern shore of the Gulf of
Tadjoura. French Somaliland (present-day
Djibouti) began to take shape.

France and the emperor of Ethiopia then
signed a pact designating Djibouti as the

'official outlet of Ethiopian commerce'. This led to the construction of the Addis Ababa–Djibouti City railway, which was of vital commercial importance until recently.

Throwing Off the French Yoke

As early as 1949 there were a number of anticolonial demonstrations that were led by the Issa Somalis, who were in favour of the reunification of the territories of Italian, British and French Somaliland. Meanwhile, the Afars were in favour of continued French rule.

Major riots ensued, especially after the 1967 referendum, which produced a vote in favour of continued French rule – a vote achieved partly as a result of the arrest of opposition leaders and the massive expulsion of ethnic Somalis. After the referendum, the colony's name was changed from French Somaliland to the French Territory of the Afars and Issas.

In June 1977 the colony finally won its sovereignty from France. The country became the Republic of Djibouti.

Small Country, Adroit Leaders

Despite continuous clan rivalries between the two main ethnic groups, Afars and Issas, who have been jostling for power since the 1970s, Djibouti has learnt to exploit its strategic position.

When the Gulf War broke out in 1990, the country's president, Hassan Gouled Aptidon, while appearing to oppose the military build-up in the Gulf, simultaneously allowed France to increase its military presence in the country, as well as granting the Americans and Italians access to the naval port. And he skilfully managed to retain t he support of Saudi Arabia and Kuwait for the modernisation of Djibouti port. During the war between Eritrea and Ethiopia in the 1990s, Djibouti port proved to be strategic when Ethiopia diverted its foreign trade through it (which it still does).

During the Second Gulf War in 2003, Djibouti continued to play an ambivalent role, allowing a US presence in the country – to the great displeasure of France.

In 2006 the first phase of the Doraleh Project, which consists of a large-capacity oil terminal about 8km east of the current seaport, was completed. Thanks to this mega-project, partly financed by Dubai Port International, Djibouti aims to be the 'Dubai of East Africa'.

Djibouti maintains good relations with Ethiopia and Somaliland, which are considered 'partners'. However, it clashed with Eritrea, its northern neighbour, in June 2008. Since then, the borders between the two countries have remained closed.

The Culture

Djiboutians are charming, respectful and very hospitable people. This has its origins in the traditionally nomadic culture of the two main ethnic groups, the Afars and Issas. Despite an increasing tendency towards a more sedentary lifestyle, most Djiboutians living in towns retain strong links with their nomadic past.

One of the most striking features in Djibouti is the overwhelming presence of *chat* (leaf chewed as a stimulant). The life of most Djiboutian males seems to revolve entirely around the consumption of this mild narcotic. Every day, *chat* consumers meet their circle of friends in the *mabraz* (*chat* den) to *brouter* (graze). Only 10% of women are thought to consume the plant regularly.

Of Djibouti's estimated 920,000 inhabitants, about 35% are Afars and 60% are Issas. Both groups are Muslim. The rest of the population is divided between Arabs and Europeans. The south is predominantly Issa, while the north is mostly Afar. Ethnic tensions between Afars and Issas have always dogged Djibouti. These tensions came to a head in 1991, when Afar rebels launched a civil war in the north. A peace accord was brokered in 1994, but ethnic hostility has not completely waned.

Arts & Crafts

Dance is arguably the highest form of culture in Djibouti, along with oral literature and poetry. Some dances celebrate major life events, such as birth, marriage or circumcision. If you are looking for handicrafts, the traditional Afar and Somali knives and the very attractive Afar woven straw mats (known in Afar as *fiddima*) are among the finest products.

Environment

Djibouti's 23,000 sq km can be divided into three geographic regions: the coastal plains which feature white, sandy beaches; the volcanic plateaus in the southern and central parts of the country; and the mountain ranges in the north, where the altitude reaches over 2000m above sea level. Essentially the country is a vast wasteland, with the exception of pockets of forest and dense vegetation to the north.

The country forms part of the Afar Triangle: a triangular depression that makes up part of the East African Rift Valley. This landscape is characterised by a series of volcanic plateaus, sunken plains and salt lakes.

Djibouti's arid land is among the least productive in Africa. Agricultural production is very limited. Livestock rearing is the most important type of farming. As demand for scarce grazing land mounts, the forests of the north are increasingly coming under threat, including the fragile Forêt du Day.

Food & Drink

Djibouti City is endowed with a plethora of tasty restaurants that will please most palates – a testimony to the French presence. You'll find excellent seafood, rice, pasta, local meat dishes, such as stuffed kid or lamb, and other treats imported from France. In the countryside, choice is obviously more limited, with goat meat and rice the main staples. There are also superb Yemeni-influenced dishes.

Although alcohol is frowned upon by Islam, alcohol consumption is freely tolerated in Djibouti. Beer is widely available, as are wines, spirits and liqueurs (many of them French imports). All alcohol is relatively expensive; the cheapest place to buy it is in the local supermarkets.

Bottled water is widely available in shops, restaurants and hotels. International soft drinks are also on offer; both coffee and tea are widely available and are well prepared.

EATING PRICE RANGES

The following price ranges refer to a main course.

$ less than DFr1000

$$ DFr1000-2500

$$$ more than DFr2500

SLEEPING PRICE RANGES

The following price ranges refer to a double room with bathroom.

$ less than DFr10,000

$$ DFr10,000 to DFr25,000

$$$ more than DFr25,000

SURVIVAL GUIDE

ℹ Directory A-Z

ACCOMMODATION

Most hotels are in the capital, with few options outside. Hotel categories are limited in range; most of them fit into the upper echelon and are expensive. At the lower end, the few budget hotels that exist tend to be pretty basic. There's a limited choice in between.

A rather popular sleeping option that is developing around the major attractions in the hinterland is the *campements touristiques*. These are traditional huts with shared showers and toilets. These quaint, low-key establishments are great places to meet locals and get an authentic cultural experience. They're family-run, which ensures your money goes straight into local pockets. They're also good budget options, although there's no public transport to get there..

CHILDREN

➡ Many important facilities for children, such as cots in hotels, safety seats in 4WDs and highchairs in restaurants, are almost totally lacking.

➡ Items such as nappies, baby food and mineral water are easily available in the well-stocked Western supermarkets (but are between two to three times their normal price) in Djibouti City.

➡ For youngsters, snorkelling with whale sharks (between November and January) is a sure-fire hit. For kids, visiting the Decan (p315), a small wildlife refuge, can be fun. Near Tadjourah, Plage des Sables Blancs (p321) is also a great place for families.

CUSTOMS REGULATIONS

There is no restriction on bringing in currency. Visitors may bring in the following amounts of duty-free items:

➡ up to 200 cigarettes or 250g of tobacco

➡ one bottle of alcohol

➡ one flask of perfume

ELECTRICITY

Djibouti uses 220V, 60Hz AC; plugs in general have two-round-pin plugs.

EMBASSIES & CONSULATES

The following is a list of nations with diplomatic representation in Djibouti City.

Canadian Consulate (☎ 21355950; Pl Lagarde; ⊙ 8am-noon Sun-Thu)

Ethiopian Embassy (☎ 21350718; Blvd Idriss Omar Guelleh; ⊙ 8am-2pm Sun-Thu, to noon Sat)

French Embassy (☎ 21350963; www.amba-france-dj.org; Ave Mohammad Ahmad Issa; ⊙ 7am-1.30pm & 3-6pm Mon & Wed, 7am-1.30pm Sun, Tue & Thu)

Somaliland Bureau de Liaison (Somaliland Liaison Office; ☎ 21358758; Ave Mohammad Ahmad Issa; ⊙ 8am-2pm Sat-Thu)

US Embassy (☎ 21453000; djibouti.usembassy.gov; Lotissement Haramous; ⊙ by appointment)

INSURANCE

A travel-insurance policy to cover theft, loss and medical problems is a good idea. Some policies specifically exclude dangerous activities, which can include scuba diving, motorcycling and even hiking. Always check the small print and make sure that the policy covers ambulances or an emergency flight home. If you plan on diving, we strongly recommend purchasing dive-specific insurance with DAN (www.diversalertnetwork. org). Worldwide travel insurance is available at www.lonelyplanet.com/travel-insurance. You can buy, extend and claim online anytime – even if you're already on the road.

INTERNET ACCESS

➡ There are a couple of internet cafes in Djibouti City. Outside the capital, internet cafés are virtually nonexistent.

➡ Wireless is widespread and free in most hotels in Djibouti City.

PRACTICALITIES

Newspapers The most widely read newspaper is *La Nation* (www.lanation. dj), published weekly in French.

TV Radiodiffusion Télévision de Djibouti (RTD) broadcasts news and sports. Programs are in Somali, Afar, Arab and French. Most top-end hotels also offer satellite TV.

Weights & Measures The metric system is used.

➡ Connection is fairly good by Western standards.

LEGAL MATTERS

Possession and use of drugs – with the exception of *chat* – is strictly illegal and penalties are severe. So don't think about bringing anything over the borders or buying it while you're here.

Djibouti's security services are sensitive and active. There is no reason why travellers should attract the attention of the police, but if it happens, it's usually pretty harmless information gathering. Police, military and immigration officials are generally courteous and calm. In your dealings with officialdom, you should always make every effort to be patient and polite in return.

If you find yourself in a sticky legal predicament, contact your embassy.

LGBTI TRAVELLERS

Although homosexuality is not illegal per se in Djibouti, it's severely condemned by both traditional and religious cultures, and remains a topic of absolute taboo. Although gay locals obviously exist, they behave with extreme discretion and caution. Gay and lesbian travellers are advised to do likewise.

MAPS

The best map is the 1:200,000 *Djibouti* map published in 2004 by the IGN (French Institut Géographique National; www.ign.fr).

MONEY

➡ The unit of currency is the Djibouti franc (DFr). Coins are in denominations of DFr1, 2, 5, 10, 20, 50, 100 and 500. Notes are available in DFr1000, 2000, 5000 and 10,000.

➡ All the ATMs in Djibouti City accept Visa. ATMs accepting MasterCard are harder to find.

➡ Visa credit cards are accepted at some upmarket hotels and shops, and at some larger travel agencies and airline offices. Some places levy a commission of about 5% for credit-card payment.

➡ There are many banks and a couple of authorised bureaux de change in the capital. Outside the capital, banking facilities are almost nonexistent.

➡ The euro and the US dollar are the favoured hard currencies; euros and dollars in cash and an ATM card – preferably Visa – are the way to go.

➡ Service charges are generally included in the bill and tipping is not normally expected.

OPENING HOURS

The following are common business hours in Djibouti. Friday is the weekly holiday for offices and most shops.

Banks 7.30am-12.30pm and 4-6pm Sun-Thur

Government offices 8am-12.30pm and 4-6pm Sat-Thur

Restaurants Breakfast 6.30am-8am, lunch 11.30am-2.30pm, dinner 6.30-10pm

Shops and businesses Typically 7.30am-1.30pm and 4-6.30pm Sat-Thur

POST

The cost for a letter is DFr170 to Europe and DFr190 to North America or Australia.

PUBLIC HOLIDAYS

As well as Islamic holidays, which change dates every year, these are the principal public holidays in Djibouti:

New Year's Day 1 January

LabourDay 1 May

Independence Day 27 June

Christmas Day 25 December

SAFE TRAVEL

Djibouti is one of the safest destinations in Africa, partly because of the large Western military presence.

➡ Serious crime or hostility aimed specifically at travellers is very rare, and there's no more to worry about here than in most other countries.

➡ In Djibouti City, take care in crowded areas and markets, as pickpockets may operate, and avoid walking on your own in the Quartier 1, immediately south of Les Caisses market.

➡ The risk of theft and pickpocketing diminishes considerably outside the capital.

➡ Note that Djibouti's security services are sensitive and active. Remain polite and calm if questioned by police officers.

Government Travel Advice

The following government websites offer travel advisories and information for travellers.

Australian Department of Foreign Affairs & Trade www.smartraveller.gov.au

Canadian Department of Foreign Affairs & International Trade www.voyage.gc.ca

French Ministère des Affaires Étrangères et Européennes www.diplomatie.gouv.fr/fr/conseils-aux-voyageurs/

New Zealand Ministry of Foreign Affairs & Trade www.safetravel.govt.nz

UK Foreign & Commonwealth Office www.gov.uk/foreign-travel-advice

US Department of State www.travel.state.gov

TELEPHONE

➡ When phoning Djibouti from abroad, you'll need to dial the international code for Djibouti (☑ 253), followed by the 10-digit local number. There are no area codes.

➡ Mobile numbers start with 77; landline numbers start with 21 or 27.

➡ International and local calls are best made from the post office or from one of the numerous phone shops (look for the *cabine telephonique* signs).

Mobile Phones

➡ Mobile phone coverage is pretty good across Djibouti.

➡ Depending on which mobile network you use at home, your phone may or may not work while in Djibouti – ask your mobile network provider.

➡ If you have a GSM phone and it has been 'unlocked', you can use a local SIM card (DFr1000) purchased from **Djibouti Telecom** (p317).

➡ You can buy credit at some shops in the form of scratch cards (DFr500 to DFr5000).

TIME

Djibouti is on GMT plus three hours. When it's noon in Djibouti City, it's 9am in London, 10am in Paris, 4am in New York and 8pm in Sydney. Djibouti does not operate a system of daylight saving; being close to the equator, its sunset and sunrise times vary only slightly throughout the year.

TOILETS

➡ There are two main types of toilet: Western sit-down, with a bowl and a seat; and African squat, with a hole in the ground. Standards vary tremendously.

➡ There are no public toilet facilities, but you can use the toilets in hotels or restaurants.

TOURIST INFORMATION

The Office National du Tourisme de Djibouti (ONTD; www.visitdjibouti.dj) is the only tourist information body in Djibouti. It has one tourist office (p317) in the capital. Tour agencies are also reliable sources of travel information.

Information for travellers is hard to come by outside the country. In Europe, contact **Association Djibouti Environnement Nomade** (ADEN; ☑ 01 48 51 71 56; domglobetrotter@gmail.com; 64 rue des Meuniers, 93100 Montreuil-sous-Bois, France), which functions as a kind of tourist office abroad. Run by Dominique Lommatzsch, a French national, it promotes sustainable tourism and can help with bookings in the *campements touristiques*.

TRAVELLERS WITH DISABILITIES

People with limited mobility will have a difficult time travelling around Djibouti, as there are very few facilities here and much of the country can be an obstacle course. Along streets and footpaths, kerbs and uneven surfaces will often present problems for wheelchair users, and only a handful of upmarket hotels and restaurants have installed ramps and railings. Also, getting to and around any of the *campements touristiques* will be extremely difficult given their remote and wild locations.

It is also worth bearing in mind that almost any destination in Djibouti will require a long trip in a 4WD.

VISAS

Tourist visas cost from US$50 to US$80 depending on where you apply, and are valid for one month. Visas can be obtained at the nearest Djibouti embassy (including Addis Ababa if you're in the Horn). Some embassies are easier to deal with than others.

Travellers from most Western countries can also obtain a single-entry tourist visa on arrival at the airport, but you'll need a letter of invitation from a sponsor – a local tour operator or a hotel. Be sure to arrange it a few days prior to arrival. If you're travelling with a tour company they will take care of this for you. The visa costs €55 for three days and €80 for one month. Payment can also be made in US dollars.

You must have a valid visa to enter overland as none are available at borders. That said, travellers coming from Somaliland have reported having been allowed to purchase their visa at the Loyaada border for €80 or the equivalent in US dollars.

Visas for Onward Travel

Ethiopia A one-month, single-entry visa costs DFr7200 (DFr12,600 for US nationals). You need to supply two photos. It takes 24 hours to process. Visas are also easily obtained at Bole International Airport in Addis Ababa.

Somaliland A one-month, single-entry visa costs DFr5600. You need to supply one photo and it's issued within 24 hours.

VOLUNTEERING

Outside the odd humanitarian program, there is little volunteer work available in Djibouti. One option is **Decan** (p315), an animal-rescue centre south of Djibouti City.

WORK

There are very few work opportunities in Djibouti for travellers. Possible exceptions include jobs in the hotel industry (mostly at management level) and jobs for experienced divers at the country's only dive centre.

If you are looking for work, you will need to contact prospective employers directly and they should be able to advise on the necessary visa requirements.

ⓘ Getting There & Away

Most visitors arrive by air. A few come overland from Ethiopia or Somaliland.

ENTERING DJIBOUTI

Entering Djibouti is usually straightforward for visitors carrying a valid passport. Visas are available on arrival for most nationalities provided visitors have a letter of invitation from a local tour operator or a hotel.

Passport

You'll need a valid passport and a visa to enter Djibouti. Disembarkation at the airport is usually simple. You'll be asked for a letter of invitation from a travel agent or a hotel in the country. Crossing at land borders is relatively easy, too, but be sure to have your passport stamped with an entry/exit stamp if you enter/leave the country.

AIR

Airports & Airlines

Djibouti has one international gateway for arrival by air, **Djibouti-** (☑21341646; www.aeroport-jib.com)**Ambouli Airport** (☑21341646; www.aeroport-jib.com), about 5km south of Djibouti City. Djibouti does not have a national airline.

Air Djibouti (☑21343737; www.air-djibouti.com; Ave Georges Pompidou; ☺7.30am-2.30pm & 4.30-6pm Sat-Thu) Two flights a week to/from Addis Ababa and three flights a week to/from Hargeisa (Somaliland). Also flies to Dire Dawa and Dubai, and has plans to fly to Paris and London.

Air France (☑21351010; www.airfrance.com; Salines Ouest; ☺8am-12.15pm & 4-6.30pm Sat-Wed, 8am-12.15pm Thu) One weekly flight to/from Paris.

Daallo (☑21353401; www.daallo.com; Rue de Verdun, cnr Rue de Verdun & Rue de Paris; ☺7.30am-12.30pm & 4-6.30pm Sat-Thu) Two flights a week to/from Hargeisa and on to Dubai. Also flies once weekly to/from Mogadishu and to/from Jeddah.

Ethiopian Airlines (☑21351007; www.flyethiopian.com; Pl du 27 Juin 1977; ☺7.30am-12.30pm & 4-6.30pm Sat-Thu) Two daily flights to/from Addis Ababa (one via Dire Dawa).

FlyDubai (☑21350964; www.flydubai.com; west of Pl du 27 Juin 1977; ☺7.30am-12.30pm & 4-6.30pm Sat-Thu) Operates three flights a week to/from Dubai.

Jubba Airways (☑21356264; www.jubbaairways.com; Rue de Bir Hakeim; ☺7.30am-12.30pm & 4-6pm Sat-Wed, to 5pm Thu) Two flights a week to/from Hargeisa and on to Dubai. Also flies once weekly to/from Mogadishu and to/from Jeddah.

Kenya Airways (☑21353036; www.kenya-airways.com; Rue de Bruxelles; ☺8am-12.15pm & 4-6.30pm Sat-Wed, 8am-12.15pm Thu) Six flights a week to/from Nairobi.

Qatar Airways (☑21346123; www.qatarairways.com; Djibouti Palace Kempinski, Îlot du

Héron; ☺8.30am-5.15pm Sun-Thu, 9am-noon Sat) Flies six times a week between Djibouti and Doha.

Turkish Airlines (☑21340110; www.turkishair-lines.com; Djibouti Palace Kempinski, Îlot du Héron; ☺8.30am-5pm Sun-Thu) Daily flights to/from Istanbul.

Tickets

If you're coming from Europe or North America, your best bet is to fly to Dubai, Doha, Addis Ababa, Istanbul or Nairobi and find an onward connection to Djibouti. You can also fly direct from Paris.

From Australasia, fly to Dubai or Doha and find an onward connection to Djibouti.

LAND
Border Crossings

Eritrea The border with Eritrea is closed.

Ethiopia The two crossings from Ethiopia are Gelille and Galafi.

Somaliland The border crossing is at Loyaada. All borders are open daily. Border posts are generally open at least between 8am to 5pm.

Bus & 4WD

There are services to/from Ethiopia and to/from Somaliland.

Ethiopia

There is a daily bus service between Djibouti City and Dire Dawa – a strenuous 10- to 12-hour ride on a gravel road (which is being upgraded and asphalted). Take your first bus to the border town of Gelille (DFr1500), then another bus to Dire Dawa (Birr185). Bring plenty of water.

From Djibouti City, buses leave around 7.30pm from a bus station located on the southern outskirts of the city, in an area called Balbala. The company is called Assajog (p291). Buy your ticket at least a day in advance to be sure of getting a seat.

Somaliland

From Ave 26, **4WDs** (Ave 26) depart daily to Hargeisa and Borama (Somaliland). They usually leave around 3pm (it's wise to buy your ticket in the morning). It costs US$40 (front seat). Be warned: it's a taxing journey of about eight to nine hours. Bring plenty of water.

Hitching

Hitching is never entirely safe in any country, and we don't recommend it. Travellers who hitch should understand that they are taking a small but potentially serious risk. Still, if you want to enter Djibouti from Ethiopia via the border town of Galafi, you can hitch a lift (front seats only) with one of the legions of trucks that ply the route between Addis Ababa and Djibouti City via

Awash, Gewane, Logiya and Dikhil. This option is best avoided by women.

Train

Launched in 2017, a Chinese-built railway line links Djibouti City to Addis Ababa in Ethiopia. It should carry passengers.

Sea

There are no passenger services from Djibouti to other countries.

Getting Around

AIR

There are no domestic services in Djibouti.

BICYCLE

Unless you're an experienced cyclist and equipped for extreme conditions, abandon any ideas you may have about a Djiboutian bicycle adventure – Djibouti's climate, terrain and rough roads are not suited to cycling.

BOAT

A reliable passenger boat operates twice weekly between Djibouti City and Tadjoura and between Djibouti City and Obock, north of the Gulf of Tadjoura.

BUS

Public transport is available between Djibouti City and major towns, including Dikhil, Tadjoura, Obock and Galafi. It's a cheap way to get around but services are infrequent in remote areas.

CAR & MOTORCYCLE

The Route de l'Unité, a good sealed road, covers the 240km from the capital around the Gulf de Tadjoura, as far as Obock.

Off-road excursions into the interior are usually off limits to anything other than a 4WD.

Most rental agencies make hiring a driver compulsory with their vehicles.

There are several car-hire agencies in Djibouti City, but the prices really don't vary much. For a 4WD with driver expect to pay around DFr25,000 a day. Fuel is generally extra, although not always.

HITCHING

With trucks and private 4WD vehicles providing the only transport along many roads in Djibouti, hitching is a tempting option for travellers on a restricted budget. Hundreds of trucks make the long, hot journey from Djibouti to Addis Ababa in Ethiopia each day. If you're determined to hitch, you could try hanging around outside Djibouti's port in the early morning, or at one of the main petrol stations in or just out of town. Remember that hitching is always a risky option and best avoided by women.

HEAT EXHAUSTION

One of the biggest hazards in Djibouti, and the one taken least seriously by travellers, is the sun. Heat exhaustion occurs following heavy sweating and excessive fluid loss with inadequate replacement of fluids and salt, and is particularly common in hot climates when taking unaccustomed exercise before full acclimatisation. Symptoms include headache, dizziness and tiredness. Dehydration is already happening by the time you feel thirsty – aim to drink sufficient water (never drink untreated tap water) to produce pale, diluted urine. Self-treatment is by fluid replacement with water and/or fruit juice, and cooling by cold water and fans. The treatment of the salt-loss component consists of consuming salty fluids such as soup, and adding a little more table salt to foods than usual.

Heat exhaustion is a precursor to the much more serious condition of heatstroke. In this case there is damage to the sweating mechanism, with an excessive rise in body temperature; irrational and hyperactive behaviour; and eventually loss of consciousness and death. Rapid cooling by spraying the body with water and fanning is ideal. Emergency fluid and electrolyte replacement is usually also required by intravenous drip.

TOURS

Djibouti is not properly geared up for DIY tourism. The only way of getting to some of the country's principal attractions is by joining an excursion. Tours are expensive (from DFr20,000 per person), but the price includes food and accommodation. Try to be part of an existing group – the more people, the less you pay. Your chances of joining an existing tour group are decidedly greater at weekends.

TRAIN

Launched in 2017, the train linking Djibouti City to Addis Ababa in Ethiopia does not make stops any other in Djibouti.

🛈 Health

Health care in Djibouti is varied: Djibouti City has good facilities with well-trained doctors and nurses, but outside the capital, health care is patchy at best. Medicine and even sterile dressings and intravenous fluids might need to be purchased from a local pharmacy by patients or their relatives. For more information see the Health chapter on p302.

Language

Amharic is Ethiopia's national language. It belongs to the Semitic language group of the Afro-Asiatic language family, along with Arabic, Hebrew and Assyrian.

While regional languages such as Oromo, Somali and Tigrinya are also important, Amharic is the most widely used and understood language throughout the country. It is the mother tongue of the 12 million or so Amhara people in the country's central and north-western regions, and a second language for about one third of the total population.

If you read our pronunciation guides as if they were English, you'll be understood. The apostrophe (') before a vowel indicates a glottal stop, which sounds like the pause in the middle of 'uh-oh'. Amharic's 'glottalised' consonants (ch', k', p', s' and t' in our pronunciation guides), are pronounced by tightening and releasing the vocal cords, a bit like combining the sound with the glottal stop. Note also that ai is pronounced as in 'aisle', ee as in 'see', ow as in 'now', uh as the 'a' in 'ago', ny as in 'canoyn', sh as in 'shot', zh as the 's' in 'pleasure', and that r is trilled.

Amharic word endings vary according to the gender and number of people you're speaking to. Gender is indicated in this chapter where relevant by the abbreviations 'm' (for speaking to a male) and 'f' (for addressing a female).

BASICS

Hello.	ሰላም	suh·lam
Goodbye.	ደህና ሁን	duh·na hun (m)
	ደህና ሁኚ	duh·na hun·yee (f)
Yes.	አዎ	'a·wo
No.	አይደለም.	'ai·duh·luhm
Please.	እባክህ	'i·ba·kih (m)
	እባክሽ	'i·ba·kish (f)
Thank you.	አመሰግናለሁ	'a·muh·suh·gi·na·luh·hu
Sorry.	ይቅር	yi·k'ir·ta

How are you?

እንዴት ነህ? 'in·det nuh·hi (m)

እንዴት ነሽ? 'in·det nuhsh (f)

Fine, and you?

ይመስጣሉው yi·muhs·guh·nuhw

አንተስ/አንቺስ? 'an·tuhs/'an·chees (m/f)

What's your name?

ማን ትባላለህ? man ti·ba·la·luh (m)

ማን ትባያለሽ? man ti·ba·ya·luhsh (f)

My name's ...

... ነኝ ... nuhny

Do you speak English?

እንግሊዘኛ 'in·glee·zuh·nya

ትችላለህ/ ti·chi·la·luh·hi/

ትችያለሽ? ti·chia·luhsh (m/f)

I don't understand.

አልገባኝም 'al·guh·bany·mi

Can I take a photo (of you)?

ፎቶ ላነሳ(ህ)/ fo·to la·nuh·sa(h)/

ላነሳ(ሽ) la·nuh·sa(sh)

እችላለሁ? 'i·chi·la·luh·hu (m/f)

ACCOMMODATION

Can you recommend somewhere (cheap/good)?

(ርካሽ/ጥሩ) ቦታ	(ri·kash/t'i·ru) bo·ta
ልትጠቁመኝ	li·ti·t'uh·k'u·muhny
ትችላለህ/	ti·chi·la·luh·hi/
ትችያለሽ?	ti·chi·ya·luhsh (m/f)

Where's a ...? ... የት ነው? ... yuht nuhw

campsite	የድንኳኑ	yuh·din·ku·wa·nu
	ቦታ	bo·ta
guesthouse	የእንግዳ	yuh·'in·gi·da
	ማረፊያ	ma·ruh·fee·ya
hotel	ሆቴሉ	ho·te·lu
youth hostel	ሆስቴሉ.	hos·te·lu

Do you have ... ክፍል ... ki·fil
a ... room? አላችሁ? 'a·la·chi·hu

single	እንድ	and
double	ሁለት	hu·luht
twin	ሁለት አልጋ	hu·luht 'al·ga
	ያለው	ya·luhw

How much is it per night/person?

| በቀን/በሰው ዋጋው | buh·k'uhn/buh·suhw |
| ስንት ነው? | wa·gow sint nuhw |

DIRECTIONS

Where's the (ቅርብ) ያለ (k'irb) ya·luh
(nearest) ...? ... የት ነው? ... yuht nuhw

internet	ኢንተርኔት	'een·tuhr·net
cafe	ካፌ	ka·fe
market	ገበያ	guh·buh·ya

Is this the road to (the museum)?

| ይህ መንገድ ወደ | yih muhn·guhd wuh·duh |
| (ሙዚየም) ይወስዳል? | (mu·zee·yuhm) yi·wuhs·dal |

Can you show me (on the map)?

(ካርታ ላይ)	(kar·ta lai)
ልታሳየኝ ትችላለህ/	li·ta·sa·yuhny ti·chi·la·luh/
ትችያለሽ?	ti·chi·ya·luhsh (m/f)

What's the address?

| አድራሻው የት ነው? | 'ad·ra·show yuht nuhw |

How far is it?

| ምን ያህል ይርቃል? | min yahl yir·k'al |

NUMBERS

Although there are Amharic script numerals, Arabic numerals (ie those used in English) are now commonly used in writing throughout Ethiopia. Amharic words are used to refer to numbers in speech.

1	አንድ	and
2	ሁለት	hu·luht
3	ሶስት	sost
4	አራት	'ar·at
5	አምስት	'am·mist
6	ስድስት	si·dist
7	ሰባት	suh·bat
8	ስምንት	si·mint
9	ዘጠኝ	zuh·t'uhny
10	አስር	a·sir
20	ሃይ	ha·ya
30	ሰላሳ	suh·la·sa
40	አርባ	'ar·ba
50	ሃምሳ	ham·sa
60	ስልሳ	sil·sa
70	ሰባ	suh·ba
80	ሰማንያ	suh·ma·nia
90	ዘጠና	zuh·t'uh·na
100	መቶ	muh·to
1000	ሺ.	shee

How do I get there?

| እዚያ እንዴት | 'i·zee·ya 'in·det |
| መሄድ ይቻላል? | muh·hed yi·cha·lal |

Turn left/right.

| ወደ ግራ/ቀኝ | wuh·duh gi·ra/k'uhny |
| ታጠፍ | ta·t'uhf |

It's ... ... ነው ... nuhw

behind ...	... ከኋርባ	... kuh·juhr·ba
in front of ...	... ፊት	... feet
	ለፊት	luh·feet
near ...	... እጠገብ	... 'a·t'uh·guhb
next to ...	... ቀጥሎ	... k'uh·t'i·lo
on the	መታጠፊያው	muh·ta·t'uh·
corner	ላይ	fee·yow lai

QUESTION WORDS

when	መቼ	muh·che
where	የት	yuht
who	ማን	man
why	ለምን	luh·min

opposite ...	... ትይዩ	... ti·yi·yu
straight ahead	ቀጥታ	k'uh·t'i·ta
there	እዚያ	'i·zee·ya

EATING & DRINKING

Can you recommend a ...?	ጥሩ ... ልትጠቁመኝ ትችላለህ?	t'i·ru ... li·ti·t'uh·k'u·muhny ti·chi·la·luh
bar	ቡና ቤት	bu·na bet
dish	ምግብ	mi·gib
place to eat	ምግብ ቤት	mi·gib bet

Do you have vegetarian food?

| የጾም ምግብ አላችሁ? | yuh·s'om mi·gib 'a·la·chi·hu |

Could you prepare a meal without (eggs)?

| ምግብ ያለ (እንቁላል) ልታዘጋጂልኝ ትችያለሽ? | mi·gib ya·luh ('in·k'u·lal) li·ta·zuh·ga·jee·lin ti·chi·ya·luhsh (f) |
| ምግብ ያለ (እንቁላል) ልታዘጋጅልኝ ትችላለህ? | mi·gib ya·luh ('in·k'u·lal) li·ta·zuh·gaj·lin ti·chi·la·luh·hi (m) |

I'd like ..., please.	እባክህ/ እባክሽ ... እፈልጋለሁ	'i·ba·kih/ 'i·ba·kish ... 'i·fuh·li·ga·luh·hu (m/f)
a table for (two)	ጠረጴዛ (ለሁለት) ሰው	t'uh·ruh·p'e·za (luh·hu·luht) suhw
that dish	ያንን ምግብ	ya·nin mi·gib
the bill	ቢል	beel
the menu	ሜኑ	me·nu

coffee ...	ቡና ...	bu·na ...
tea ...	ሻይ ...	shai ...
with milk	በወተት	buh·wuh·tuht

| without sugar | ያለ ስኩዋር | ya·luh si·ku·war |

beer	ቢራ	bee·ra
bottle	ጠርሙስ	t'uhr·mus
breakfast	ቁርስ	k'urs
cold	ጉንፋን	gun·fan
dairy products	የወተት ተዋጽኦ	yuh·wuh·tuht tuh·wa·s'i·'o
dinner	እራት	i·rat
drink	መጠጥ	muh·t'uht'
fish	አሳ	'a·sa
food	ምግብ	mi·gib
fork	ሹካ	shu·ka
fruit	ፍራፍሬ	fi·ra·fi·re
glass	ብርጭቆ	bir·ch'i·k'o
gluten	አንጸባራቂ	'an·s'uh·ba·ra·k'ee
hot	ሙቅ	muk'
knife	ቢላዋ	bee·la·wa
lunch	ምሳ	mi·sa
meat	ስጋ	si·ga
nuts	አቾሎኒ	'o·cho·lo·nee
plate	ሳህን	sa·hin
restaurant	ሬስቶራንት	res·to·rant
seafood	የባህር ምግቦች	yuh·ba·hir mi·gib·och
spoon	ማንኪያ	man·kee·ya
vegetable	አትክልት	'at·kilt
waiter	አስተናጋጅ	as·tuh·na·gaj
(boiled) water	(የፈላ) ውሃ	(yuh·fuh·la) wi·ha
wine	ወይን	wuh·yin
with	ጋር	gar
without	ያለ	ya·luh

EMERGENCIES

Help!

| እርዳታ እርዳታ! | 'ir·da·ta 'ir·da·ta |

I'm lost.

| ጠፋብኝ | t'uh·fa·biny |

Where are the toilets?

| ሽንት ቤት የት ነው? | shint bet yuht nuhw |

Call ...!	... ጥራልኝ	... t'i·ra·liny (m)
	... ጥሪልኝ	... t'i·ree·liny (f)
a doctor	ዶክተር	dok·tuhr
an ambulance	አምቡላንስ	'am·bu·lans
the police	ፖሊስ	po·lees
My ... was/	የኔ ...	yuh·ne ...
were stolen.	ተሰረቀ	tuh·suh·ruh·k'uh
bags	ሻንጣ	shan·t'a
credit card	ክሬዲት	ki·re·deet
	ካርድ	kard
handbag	የጅ ቦርሳ	yuhj bor·sa
money	ገንዘብ	guhn·zuhb
passport	ፓስፖርት	pas·port
wallet	የኪስ ቦርሳ	yuh·kees bor·sa

It hurts here.

| እዚህ ጋ ያመኛል | 'i·zeeh ga ya·muhn·yal |

I'm allergic to (penicillin).

| ለ(ፔኒሲሊን) | luh·(pe·nee·see·leen) |
| አለርጂ ነኝ | 'a·luhr·jee nuhny |

asthma	አስም	as·m
constipation	ድርቀት	dir·k'uht
diarrhoea	ተቅማጥ	tuh·k'i·mat'
fever	ትኩሳት	ti·ku·sat
headache	ራስ ምታት	ras mi·tat
heart condition	የልብ ሁኔታ	yuh·lib hu·na·te
nausea	ማጥወልወል	mat'·wuhl·wuhl
pain	ህመም	hi·muhm
pregnant	እርጉዝ	'ir·guz
sore throat	የቆሰለ	yuh·k'o·suh·luh
	ጉሮሮ	gu·ro·ro
toothache	የጥርስ	yuh·t'irs
	ህመም	hi·muhm

SHOPPING & SERVICES

I'm looking for ...

| ... እፈልጋለሁ | ... 'i·fuh·li·ga·luh·hu |

How much is it?

| ዋጋው ስንት ነው? | wa·gow sint nuhw |

Can you write down the price?

| ዋጋውን ልትጥፍልኝ | wa·gown li·ti·s'if·liny |
| ትችላለህ? | ti·chi·la·luh |

What's your lowest price?

| መጨረሻውን | muh·ch'uh·ruh·sha·win |
| ስንት ትለዋለህ? | sint ti·luh·wa·luh·hi |

I'll give you (five) birr.

| (አምስት) ብር | ('am·mist) bir |
| እከፍላለሁ | 'i·kuhf·la·luh·hu |

Do you accept credit cards?

| ክሬዲት ካርድ | ki·re·deet kard |
| ትቀበላላችሁ? | ti·k'uh·buh·la·la·chi·hu |

There's a mistake in the bill.

| ቢሉ ላይ | bee·lu lai |
| ስህተት አለ | sih·tuht 'a·luh |

I'd like a receipt/refund, please.

እባክህ/እባክሽ	i·ba·kih/'i·ba·kish
ደረሰኝ/ገንዘቤ	duh·ruh·suhny/guhn·zuh·be
እንዲመለስልኝ	'in·dee·muh·luhs·liny
እፈልጋለሁ	'i·fuh·li·ga·luh·hu (m/f)

Can I have my ... repaired?

| ... ማስጠገን | ... mas·t'uh·guhn |
| እችላለሁ? | 'i·chi·la·luh·hu |

When will it be ready?

| መቼ ይደርሳል? | muh·che yi·duhr·sal |

closed	ዝግ	zig
currency	የውጭ	yuh·wich'
exchange	ምንዛሪ	mi·ni·za·ree
email	ኢሜይል	'ee·me·yil
exchange	የውጭ	yuh·wich'
rate	ምንዛሪ ዋጋ	min·za·ree wa·ga
open	ክፍት	kift
post office	ፖስታ ቤት	pos·ta bet
shop	ሱቅ	suk'
telephone	ስልክ	silk
travel agency	የጉዞ	yuh·gu·zo
	ወኪል	wuh·keel

TIME & DATES

What time is it?

| ስንት ሰአት ነው? | sint suh·'at nuhw |

It's (two) o'clock.

| (ስምንት) ሰአት ነው | (si·mint) suh·'at nuhw |

Quarter past (one).

| (ሰባት) ከሩብ ነው | (suh·bat) kuh·rub nuhw |

LANGUAGE OF DJIBOUTI

Djibouti's languages are Afar, Somali, Arabic and French. In Djibouti town you should also get by with English, and some French basics (included below) might prove helpful too during your visit to this country.

Hello.	Bonjour.	bon·zhoor
Goodbye.	Au revoir.	o·rer·vwa
Excuse me.	Excusez-moi.	ek·skew·zay·mwa
Sorry.	Pardon.	par·don
Yes./No.	Oui./Non.	wee/non
Please.	S'il vous plaît.	seel voo play
Thank you.	Merci.	mair·see

Where's ...?
Où est ...?   oo ay ...

What's the address?
Quelle est l'adresse?   kel ay la·dres

Can you show me (on the map)?
Pouvez-vous   poo·vay·voo
m'indiquer   mun·dee·kay
(sur la carte)?   (sewr la kart)

Help!
Au secours!   o skoor

I'm lost.
Je suis perdu/   zhe swee·
perdue.   pair·dew (m/f)

Call a doctor.
Appelez un médecin.   a·play un mayd·sun

Call the police.
Appelez la police.   a·play la po·lees

Where are the toilets?
Où sont les toilettes?   oo son lay twa·let

Can I see the menu, please?
Est-ce que je peux voir   es·ker zher per vwar
la carte, s'il vous plaît?   la kart seel voo play

What would you recommend?
Qu'est-ce que vous   kes·ker voo
conseillez?   kon·say·yay

I don't eat ...
Je ne mange pas ...   zher ner monzh pa ...

Please bring the bill.
Apportez-moi   a·por·tay·mwa
l'addition,   la·dee·syon
s'il vous plaît.   seel voo play

Cheers!	Santé!	son·tay
eat/drink	manger/boire	mon·zhay/bwar
local speciality	spécialité locale	spay·sya·lee·tay lo·kal
market	marché	mar·shay

I'd like to buy ...
Je voudrais acheter ...   zher voo·dray ash·tay ...

How much is it?
C'est combien?   say kom·byun

It's too expensive.
C'est trop cher.   say tro shair

post office	bureau de poste	bew·ro der post
tourist office	office de tourisme	o·fees der too·rees·mer

morning	matin	ma·tun
afternoon	après-midi	a·pray·mee·dee
evening	soir	swar
yesterday	hier	yair
today	aujourd'hui	o·zhoor·dwee
tomorrow	demain	der·mun

1	un	un
2	deux	der
3	trois	trwa
4	quatre	ka·trer
5	cinq	sungk
6	six	sees
7	sept	set
8	huit	weet
9	neuf	nerf
10	dix	dees

boat	bateau	ba·to
bus	bus	bews
plane	avion	a·vyon
train	train	trun

Does it stop at ...?
Est-ce qu'il s'arrête à ...?   es·kil sa·ret a ...

At what time does it leave/arrive?
À quelle heure est-ce   a kel er es
qu'il part/arrive?   kil par/a·reev

Can you tell me when we get to ...?
Pouvez-vous me dire   poo·vay·voo mer deer
quand nous arrivons à ...?   kon noo za·ree·von a ...

I want to get off here.
Je veux descendre   zher ver day·son·drer
ici.   ee·see

Half past (one).

(ሰዓት) ተኩል ነው		(suh·bat) tuh·kul nuhw

Quarter to (eight).

ለ(ሁለት) ሩብ		luh·(hu·luht) rub
ጉዳይ ነው		gu·dai nuhw

At what time ...?

በስንት ሰአት...?		buh·sint suh·'at ...

At ...

በ ...		buh ...
morning	ጠዋት	t'uh·wat
night	ምሽት	mi·shit
today	ዛሬ	za·re
tomorrow	ነገ	nuh·guh
tonight	ዛሬ ማታ	za·re ma·ta
yesterday	ትላንትና	ti·lan·ti·na

Monday	ሰኞ	suh·nyo
Tuesday	ማክሰኞ	mak·suh·nyo
Wednesday	ሮብ	rob
Thursday	ሃሙስ	ha·mus
Friday	አርብ	'a·rib
Saturday	ቅዳሜ	k'i·da·me
Sunday	እሁድ	'i·hud

TOURS & SIGHTSEEING

When's the next ...?	የሚቀጥለው ... መቼ ነው?	yuh·mee·k'uh· t'i·luhw ... muh·che nuhw
day trip	ውሎ ገባ ጉዞ	wi·lo guh·ba gu·zo
tour	ሽርሽር	shi·ri·shir
Is (the) ... included?	... ይጨምራል?	... yi·ch'uh·mi·ral
admission charge	የአገልግሎት ዋጋን	yuh·'a·guhl· gi·lot wa·gan
food	ምግብን	mi·gib·n
transport	ትራንስፖርትን	ti·rans·por·tin

How long is the tour?

ሽርሽሩ ምን ያህል		shi·ri·shi·ru min ya·hil
ጊዜ ይፈጃል?		gee·ze yi·fuh·jal

What time should we be back?

በስንት ሰአት		buh·sint suh·'at
እንመለሳለን?		'in·muh·luh·sa·luhn

game park	ፓርክ	park
guide	መሪ	muh·ree
museum	ሙዚየም	mu·zee·yuhm
national park	ብሄራዊ ፓርክ	bi·he·ra·wee park
palace	ቤተ መንግስት	be·tuh muhn·gist

TRANSPORT

A ... ticket (to Bahir Dar), please.	አንድ ... ትኬት (ወደባህር ዳር) እባክህ/ እባክሽ?	and ... ti·ket (wuh·duh ba·hir dar) 'i·ba·kih/ 'i·ba·kish (m/f)
one-way (going)	የአንድ ጉዞ (መሄጃ) ብቻ	yuh·and gu·zo (muh·he·ja) bi·cha
one-way (returning)	የአንድ ጉዞ (መመለሻ) ብቻ	yuh·and gu·zo (muh·muh· luh·sha) bi·cha
return	ደርሶ መልስ	duhr·so muh·lis

airport	አይሮፕላን ማረፊያ	ai·rop·lan ma·ruh·fee·ya
bus stop	ፌርማታ	fer·ma·ta
first class	አንደኛ ማእረግ	'an·duh·nya ma·'i·ruhg
train station	ጣቢያ	t'a·bee·ya

Is this the ... to (Dire Dawa)?	ይህ ... ወደ (ድሬዳዋ) የሚሄደው ነው?	yih ... wuh·duh (di·re da·wa) yuh·mee·he· duhw nuhw
boat	ጀልባ	juhl·ba
bus	አውቶቢስ	'ow·to·bees

| plane | አውሮፕላን | ow·rop·lan |
| train | ባቡር | ba·bur |

I'd like a smoking/nonsmoking seat, please.

መቀመጫ	muh·k'uh·muh·ch'a
የሚጨስበት/	yuh·mee·ch'uhs·buht/
የማያጨስበት	yuh·mai·ch'uhs·buht
ቦታ ጋ እፈልጋለሁ	bo·ta ga 'i·fuh·li·ga·luh·hu

How long does the trip take?

| ጉዞው ምን ያህል | gu·zo·wi min ya·hil |
| ይፈጃል? | yi·fuh·jal |

Is it a direct route?

| ይሄ ዋናው | yi·he wa·now |
| መንገድ ነው? | muhn·guhd nuhw |

How long will it be delayed?

| ምን ያህል ይዘገያል? | min ya·hil yi·zuh·guh·yal |

How much is it to ...?

| ወደ ... ለመሄድ | wuh·duh ... luh·muh·hed |
| ዋጋው ስንት ነው? | wa·gow sint nuhw |

Please take me to (the museum).

እባክህ/እባክሽ	'i·ba·kih/'i·ba·kish
ወደ (ሙዚየም)	wuh·duh (mu·zee·yuhm)
ውሰደኝ/	wi·suh·duhny/
ውሰጂኝ	wi·suh·jeeny (m/f)

I'd like to hire a car.

እባክህ/እባክሽ	'i·ba·kih/'i·ba·kish
መኪና መከራየት	muh·kee·na muh·kuh·ra·yuht
እፈልጋለሁ?	'i·fuh·li·ga·luh·hu (m/f)

bicycle	ብስክሌት	bisk·let
brakes (car)	ፍሬን	fi·ren
oil (engine)	የሞተር	yuh·mo·tuhr
	ዘይት	zuh·yit
park (car)	ማቆም	ma·k'om
petrol	ቤንዚን	ben·zeen
road	መንገድ	muhn·guhd
tyre	ጎማ	go·ma

GLOSSARY

Ethiopian culinary terms are found in the Ethiopian Cuisine chapter on p264.

abba – a prefix used by a priest before his name; means 'father'

abuna – archbishop of the Ethiopian Orthodox church, from the *Ge'ez* word meaning 'our father'

agelgil – round, leather-bound lunch boxes carried by locals

amba (also *emba*) – flat-topped mountain

azmari – itinerant minstrel (Ethiopia)

asmat secret name of God; if invoked it provides protection from illness and misfortune

bajaj –auto-rickshaw

bet – Amharic word meaning 'place' that is attached to the end of other words, eg *azmari bet* (Ethiopia)

buna – coffee (Ethiopia)

campement touristique – traditional huts with shared showers and toilets (Djibouti)

chat – mildly intoxicating leaf that's consumed primarily in eastern Ethiopia and Djibouti

cheka – home-brewed sorghum beer

contract taxi – private, or nonshared, taxi

Derg – Socialist military junta that governed Ethiopia from 1974 to 1991; derived from the *Ge'ez* word for 'committee'

dula – wooden staff carried by many Ethiopian highlanders

emba – see *amba*

enset – false-banana tree found in much of southern Ethiopia, used to produce a breadlike staple also known as *enset*

EPLF – Eritrean People's Liberation Front; victorious guerrilla army in the 'Struggle for Independence'

etan – incense used in coffee ceremonies

Falasha – Ethiopian Jew

faranji – foreigner, especially Western ones (Ethiopia)

gada – age system of male hierarchy among the Oromo

gari – horse-drawn cart used for transporting passengers and goods in the towns

Ge'ez – a forerunner of modern Amharic

gegar – a rectangular, two-storey structure with a flat roof

genna – a game like hockey, without boundaries

gommista – tyre-repair shop (Italian)

habesha – Ethiopian

injera – an Ethiopian pancake upon which sits anything from spicy meat stews to colourful dollops of boiled veg and cubes of raw beef

jile – the curved knife that is carried by Afar nomads

katickala – a distilled alcohol

Kiddus – Saint, eg Kiddus Mikael translates to St Michael

maqdas – inner sanctuary of a church (holy of holies)

mesob – hourglass-shaped woven table from which traditional food is served (Ethiopia)

qat – see *chat*

ras – title (usually of nobility but given to any outstanding male) similar to duke or prince

shamma – a white, light cotton toga

shifta – traditionally a rebel or outlaw; today a bandit or roadside robber

tabot – replica of the Ark of the Covenant, kept in the *maqdas* of every Orthodox church

tankwa – traditional papyrus boat used on Lake Tana and elsewhere (Ethiopia)

tef – an indigenous grass cultivated as a cereal grain; the key ingredient of injera

tej – wine made from honey, popular in Ethiopia

tella – home-brewed beer made from finger millet, maize or barley, popular in Ethiopia

tilapia freshwater fish

tukul – traditional cone-shaped hut with thatched roof; like South Africa's rondavel

wadi – a river that is usually dry except in the rainy season

waga – carved wooden sculptures raised in honour of Konso warriors after their death

Behind the Scenes

SEND US YOUR FEEDBACK

We love to hear from travellers – your comments keep us on our toes and help make our books better. Our well-travelled team reads every word on what you loved or loathed about this book. Although we cannot reply individually to your submissions, we always guarantee that your feedback goes straight to the appropriate authors, in time for the next edition. Each person who sends us information is thanked in the next edition – the most useful submissions are rewarded with a selection of digital PDF chapters.

Visit **lonelyplanet.com/contact** to submit your updates and suggestions or to ask for help. Our award-winning website also features inspirational travel stories, news and discussions.

Note: We may edit, reproduce and incorporate your comments in Lonely Planet products such as guidebooks, websites and digital products, so let us know if you don't want your comments reproduced or your name acknowledged. For a copy of our privacy policy visit lonelyplanet.com/privacy.

OUR READERS

Many thanks to the travellers who used the last edition and wrote to us with helpful hints, useful advice and interesting anecdotes:

Alex Sternick, Amira Elwakil, Ankerstjerne Rønneberg, Arie van Oosterwijk, Barney Smith, Basia Jozwiak, Bettina Voss, David French, Denise Hunter , Elizabeth Greive, Fabrice Cairaschi, Gregory Kipling, Helen Boxwill, Ido Gottlieb, Jan van Berkel, Jean Bayle, Laurence West, Lucy Moodie, Magda Bulska, Maria Junyent, Matthew Taylor, Nona Caulkins, Peter McFadden, Polly Compston, Raphael Hernandez, Roy Sells, Rupert Wilkinson, Simone Fischer, Stefan Kühne, Tajan Tober, Tesfa Gebreab, Timophey Chichkan, Wolfgang Gehring.

WRITER THANKS

Jean-Bernard Carillet

A huge thanks to everyone who helped out and made this trip an enlightenment, including Wegene, Tania, Houmed, Dominique, Osman, Olivier, Sonja and all the people I met on the road. At LP I'm grateful to Matt for his trust and support, and to the hard-working editors. It has been a huge pleasure to work with co-author Anthony, who shares the same passion for Africa. At home, a gros bisou to Eva and lots of love to Morgane, whose support was essential.

Anthony Ham

Special thanks to so many people in Ethiopia –Tania, Cheru, Fre, Ingeda, Luigi, Françoise, Shif, Julia, Nick, Melako, Mohamed, Mulugeta and others. Wegene Temesgen was a wonderful driver, guide and travel companion. Matt Phillips continues to be a firm friend and fine editor and a man whose passion for Africa rivals my own. Huge thanks also to Jean-Bernard, another Africa friend and expert of long standing. And as always to my family who wait patiently at home for me to return – *gracias amores*.

ACKNOWLEDGEMENTS

Climate map data adapted from Peel MC, Finlayson BL & McMahon TA (2007) 'Updated World Map of the Köppen-Geiger Climate Classification', Hydrology and *Earth System Sciences*, 11, 1633–44.

Cover photograph: Hamar woman with copper bracelets, David Schweitzer/Getty Images

THIS BOOK

This 6th edition of Lonely Planet's *Ethiopia & Djibouti* guidebook was researched and written by Jean-Bernard Carillet and Anthony Ham. The previous edition was written by Jean-Bernard Carillet, Tim Bewer and Stuart Butler. This guide-book was produced by the following:

Destination Editor Matt Phillips

Product Editor Paul Harding

Senior Cartographer Diana Von Holdt

Book Designer Jessica Rose

Assisting Editors Andrew Bain, Judith Bamber, Imogen Bannister, Nigel Chin, Melanie Dankel, Jodie Martire, Jenna Myers, Monique Perrin

Cartographer Hunor Csutoros

Assisting Book Designer Michael Buick

Cover Researcher Naomi Parker

Thanks to Kate Chapman, Catherine Naghten, Tania O'Connor

Index

NOTES -

Map Legend

Sights

- Beach
- Bird Sanctuary
- Buddhist
- Castle/Palace
- Christian
- Confucian
- Hindu
- Islamic
- Jain
- Jewish
- Monument
- Museum/Gallery/Historic Building
- Ruin
- Shinto
- Sikh
- Taoist
- Winery/Vineyard
- Zoo/Wildlife Sanctuary
- Other Sight

Activities, Courses & Tours

- Bodysurfing
- Diving
- Canoeing/Kayaking
- Course/Tour
- Sento Hot Baths/Onsen
- Skiing
- Snorkelling
- Surfing
- Swimming/Pool
- Walking
- Windsurfing
- Other Activity

Sleeping

- Sleeping
- Camping

Eating

- Eating

Drinking & Nightlife

- Drinking & Nightlife
- Cafe

Entertainment

- Entertainment

Shopping

- Shopping

Information

- Bank
- Embassy/Consulate
- Hospital/Medical
- Internet
- Police
- Post Office
- Telephone
- Toilet
- Tourist Information
- Other Information

Geographic

- Beach
- Gate
- Hut/Shelter
- Lighthouse
- Lookout
- Mountain/Volcano
- Oasis
- Park
- Pass
- Picnic Area
- Waterfall

Population

- Capital (National)
- Capital (State/Province)
- City/Large Town
- Town/Village

Transport

- Airport
- Border crossing
- Bus
- Cable car/Funicular
- Cycling
- Ferry
- Metro station
- Monorail
- Parking
- Petrol station
- Subway station
- Taxi
- Train station/Railway
- Tram
- Underground station
- Other Transport

Note: Not all symbols displayed above appear on the maps in this book

Routes

- Tollway
- Freeway
- Primary
- Secondary
- Tertiary
- Lane
- Unsealed road
- Road under construction
- Plaza/Mall
- Steps
- Tunnel
- Pedestrian overpass
- Walking Tour
- Walking Tour detour
- Path/Walking Trail

Boundaries

- International
- State/Province
- Disputed
- Regional/Suburb
- Marine Park
- Cliff
- Wall

Hydrography

- River, Creek
- Intermittent River
- Canal
- Water
- Dry/Salt/Intermittent Lake
- Reef

Areas

- Airport/Runway
- Beach/Desert
- Cemetery (Christian)
- Cemetery (Other)
- Glacier
- Mudflat
- Park/Forest
- Sight (Building)
- Sportsground
- Swamp/Mangrove

OUR STORY

A beat-up old car, a few dollars in the pocket and a sense of adventure. In 1972 that's all Tony and Maureen Wheeler needed for the trip of a lifetime – across Europe and Asia overland to Australia. It took several months, and at the end – broke but inspired – they sat at their kitchen table writing and stapling together their first travel guide, *Across Asia on the Cheap*. Within a week they'd sold 1500 copies. Lonely Planet was born.

Today, Lonely Planet has offices in Franklin, London, Melbourne, Oakland, Dublin, Beijing and Delhi, with more than 600 staff and writers. We share Tony's belief that 'a great guidebook should do three things: inform, educate and amuse'.

OUR WRITERS

Jean-Bernard Carillet
Southern Ethiopia, Eastern Ethiopia, Djibouti

Jean-Bernard is a Paris-based freelance writer and photographer who specialises in Africa, France, Turkey, the Indian Ocean, the Caribbean and the Pacific. He loves adventure, remote places, islands, outdoors, archaeological sites and food. His insatiable wanderlust has taken him to 114 countries across six continents, and it shows no sign of waning. It has inspired lots of articles and photos for travel magazines and some 70 Lonely Planet guidebooks, both in English and in French. One of his favourite continents is Africa, which he has travelled the length and breadth of for more two decades and been thoroughly enlightened by 24 of its amazing countries. Jean-Bernard also researched the Understand Ethiopia section.

Anthony Ham
Addis Ababa, Northern Ethiopia, Western Ethiopia

Anthony is a freelance writer and photographer who specialises in Spain, East and Southern Africa, the Arctic and the Middle East. When he's not writing for Lonely Planet, Anthony writes about and photographs Spain, Africa and the Middle East for newspapers and magazines in Australia, the UK and US. In 2001, after years of wandering the world, Anthony finally found his spiritual home when he fell irretrievably in love with Madrid on his first visit to the city. Less than a year later, he arrived there on a one-way ticket, with not a word of Spanish and not knowing a single person in the city. When he finally left Madrid 10 years later, Anthony spoke Spanish with a Madrid accent, was married to a local and Madrid had become his second home. Now back in Australia, he continues to travel the world in search of stories. Anthony also researched the Plan Your Trip, Survival Guide and Health sections.

Published by Lonely Planet Global Limited
CRN 554153
6th edition – Sep 2017
ISBN 978 1 78657 040 6
© Lonely Planet 2017   Photographs © as indicated 2017
10 9 8 7 6 5 4 3 2 1
Printed in China